What Every Great Teacher Knows

Practical Principles for Effective Teaching

Richard A. Gibboney
With Clark D. Webb

What Every Great Teacher Knows

Practical Principles for Effective Teaching

Richard A. Gibboney
With Clark D. Webb

Holistic Education Press
Brandon, VT 05733-0328

1-800-639-4122

http://www.sover.net/~holistic
holistic@sover.net

ACKNOWLEDGEMENTS

The authors gratefully acknowledge the many educators who have contributed their stories to this book. They are all Great Teachers in every sense of the phrase.

They also thank *The Active Learner: A Foxfire Journal for Teachers* for its permission to reprint "Offering Challenges..." (p. 33) and "Seven Years in a Foxfire Classroom..." (p. 93).

WHAT EVERY GREAT TEACHER KNOWS

ISBN: 0-9627232-8-2

Copyright © 1998

Holistic Education Press

P.O. Box 328, Brandon, VT 05733-0328

Table of Contents

Part One

Introduction

Part Two

Eighteen Teaching Principles
With Illustrative Stories

Thinking and Experience

038283|

Teaching Objectives

Subject Matter

Teaching Methods

To my granddaughter
Megan Elizabeth Carr
Whose eagerness to learn
Reminds me daily of
What many of us
Have lost.

— R. G.
Birchrunville, PA
April 1998

Part One

Introduction

Introduction

It is essential that you read Part 1; Part 1 tells why *What Every Great Teacher Knows* was written and how you and your colleagues might use the powerful ideas in the 18 principles. The principles provide a framework of ideas which gives the wonderful stories told by teachers intellectual power. The "teacher knowledge" in the stories is a beautiful and too often overlooked complement to academic knowledge. Each kind of knowing is necessary and enriched by the other.

We know that you are busy and more than a little tired. Good teachers often feel this way. We also know that you are "fed up to here" with schemes marketed as "quick fixes" for whatever ails you educationally — schemes that promote the "easy implementation" of supposedly failure-proof programs more than the imaginative efforts of intelligent teachers.

We share these concerns. We believe deeply in the role that teachers play in our society. We believe that teachers and principals have had too little opportunity to share ideas about issues affecting the quality of learning with others at the school level. Too often talk about learning and teaching is lost in the welter of routine meetings; predictable, narrowly-focused staff development sessions; outside speakers with jokes; and the near-frantic worry about test scores — all of which de-emphasize the importance of learning and teaching and informed conversation with colleagues.

WHY THIS BOOK WAS WRITTEN

What Every Great Teacher Knows was written to help preservice and inservice teachers in two ways.

1. To provide a framework of ideas and values within which teachers could think about and discuss the ambiguities, problems, and satisfactions in teaching. We wanted to write a book about teaching that avoided

the shallow how-to technique trap that degrades the office of teacher (see Barth 1990; Gibboney 1994; Goodlad 1984; and Little 1982).

We wanted to write a book that assumed the intelligence of preservice and inservice teachers. We wanted to write a book structured by ideas (the principles) whose content (the teachers' stories) might encourage teachers to talk among themselves about the ideas and practices in their school. *What Every Great Teacher Knows*, in short, is to be used as an open-ended discussion guide in which teachers, through conversation, bring their knowledge and experience to bear on the fundamental issues raised in this book. Through these conversations, teachers may, in a true sense, talk and think their way to their own "book" on teaching.

This book is an invitation to think and talk about ways for teachers and students to create a school that honors one's mind — a place that asks the "why" questions, that engages teachers in critical conversation, and that seeks out and argues the merits of various teaching practices.

2. *What Every Great Teacher Knows* was written — we shall be blunt — to provide an antidote to the intellectual vacuity of most methods books on teaching and the offensive recipes for teaching offered in almost all inservice programs (Campbell 1989, pp. 114-117). We also want to avoid the academic posturing of books that claim to make teaching a "science" based on the nonscientific findings of research on teaching.[1]

Until the education of teachers moves toward its intellectual and artistic base, teaching will be lost in the sinister alleys of technique isolated from thought. Thought and practice — doing teaching — are not fierce competitors for your attention; each needs the other, each enriches the other. So long as teachers themselves pine for the easy fix of technique cut off from ideas, there will be no end of entertaining charlatans willing to provide a fix — for a high fee. Our obsession with techniques raises doubts when we rightfully claim that teaching is a profession.

The import of these two purposes is to make *What Every Great Teacher Knows* a different kind of book; it is not a methods book although it deals with teaching; it is not an academic book *about* teaching, or the present state of teaching in America, because we want you to use the ideas and stories in *What Every Great Teacher Knows* to explore your own teaching. This journey may lead to other books and experiences that will further deepen your appreciation of the teacher's art. There are many technocrats in business and the information technologies who can't wait to displace your humanness with one of their computers and an interactive video.

Teachers now and in the future will have to be able to give *reasoned* explanations why certain ways of teaching are better than other ways. To speak of informed conversation as an important way to improve the quality of schools and teacher education sounds terribly old-fashioned in this day of high-tech buzz words and slick commercial programs. Talk — sustained, informed talk about learning and teaching — is a rare visitor to faculty meetings or to staff development programs. This assertion is validated both by many teachers' experience as well as by the research of such investigators as John Goodlad (1984). In *A Place Called School*, Goodlad reports that he and his colleagues rarely found school faculties giving *sustained* attention to *significant* school-wide problems of learning and teaching, despite his finding that overconcern with facts and routine textbook learning deadened the intellectual quality of what was learned and taught. Other educators speak to this unfortunate condition and provide some evidence of the benefits of serious dialogue (see Barth 1990; Brown 1991; Gibboney 1994; Little 1986; Webb et al. 1996).

A Teacher Says "Enough is Enough"

Patrick Welsh is a high school English teacher in Alexandria, Virginia, who has spoken out against the corruption of teaching and the harassment of teachers when school boards and administrators go all out for the easy fixes promised by slickly packaged techniques. Welsh (1986) cites incident after incident in his book, *Tales Out of School*, where teachers have been forced to ignore their own intelligence and instincts for a "new" way of teaching by administrators (who, themselves, too often avoid the messiness of thinking deeply about teaching by adopting a "program" they picked up in a two-day smoothly presented workshop 500 miles from their schools).

Welsh tells how a teacher evaluation plan adopted by the Alexandria schools in 1984 demoralized good teachers. Teachers, for example, had to have a "sponge activity"[2] (giving kids a short assignment to keep them from talking with each other when they entered a classroom) and a "closure activity" that neatly summed up a 50-minute lesson. Welsh protested. "Why," he asked, "should I be forced to go through a set of prescribed mechanistic procedures" merely to show the public that the school system was trying to improve teaching? The attitude of the principal, when confronted with this and other teachers' objections, seemed to be "I've got the latest secret about teaching — you don't" (Welsh 1986, pp. 168-169).

Welsh distrusted the assumption that "desirable teaching procedures … could be boiled down to a single Xeroxed page [by which to evaluate a teacher]" (p. 170).

Another teacher wrote in protest that "the evaluation process is like writing a review of a play [after seeing] one or two acts. There is no awareness of [the teacher's] long-term goals.…" (Welsh, p. 170).

The technique package Welsh is criticizing swept the country in the 1980s (and continues to have an influence) as "Elements of Effective Instruction" or simply as Madeline Hunter's model. The tragedy is that relatively few teachers and principals had any *idea* that this plan was an educational fraud on students and teachers if the cultivation of the mind is the primary aim of education, as John Dewey (and common sense) states.

Teachers eager for mechanistic techniques to use on their students will surely suffer when their "superiors" use mechanistic techniques on them. Both teachers and administrators who cry only for the "practical" (technique) in easy-to-swallow two-day inservice packages, are the ones who avoid serious informed discussion of *fundamental* issues in learning, teaching, and teacher evaluation. "Too boring," they say. "Let's get practical!" is the cry. We've heard it often in dialogues with teachers and their principal. This cry is the death blow to informed conversation. It makes a joke of teaching as an intellectual activity.

Dewey's Theory

The eighteen principles in this book are fundamental ideas about teaching. They are rooted in John Dewey's theory of education and our own humbling experience over decades in which we used Dewey's theory as a compass in our public school and university teaching, in formal teacher education programs, and, richest of all, when we "left" the low oxygen altitudes of the university to work as peers with hundreds of teachers and their principals on *their* turf to help them make their schools more intellectually stimulating places.

Why Dewey's theory and not someone else's? "Surely there are other theories comparable to his" is a common response to our belief that Dewey's *educational* theory is superior to all others. Consider the theories we are rejecting. Plato is the first to go (philosopher-kings do not fit well with the U.S. Constitution). Theories based on any sectarian religion fail to meet our democratic criterion. Out go the mechanistic conditioning learning theories of E. L. Thorndike and B. F. Skinner and a legion of followers. Robert Hutchins and the Great Books, solid as they are, do not meet our criterion of comprehensiveness. What about Piaget, or Abraham Maslow and the humanistic psychologists, or Karl Marx or Michel Foucault? Why not Howard Gardner and multiple intelligences or Leslie Hart's theory based on brain research or — the favorite of many educational psychologists and educational researchers — collections of empirical research studies such as those on "effective teaching" that Barak Rosenshine and Madeline Hunter accept? Sorry, but none of these even come close to being an acceptable theory of *education* in a democratic society.

We accept Dewey's theory because it is the only one that meets the following three major criteria of usefulness.

1. A useful theory of education must be comprehensive rather than partial (one that deals with only *some* of the elements that should be treated in a comprehensive theory). Piaget, for example, deals with the intellectual development of mathematical concepts among others, but he is silent about the nature of the society in which the learning child lives. Thus, his theory is limited; nor does he think of himself primarily as an educator (Elkind 1970, p. 81). (Since "comprehensiveness" is a critically important criterion, we illustrate more completely in the next section what comprehensiveness means in Dewey's theory when he puts the theoretical light on thinking.)

2. A useful theory must commit its adherents to the intellectual growth of teachers *and* students; further, the theory must reasonably suggest how and why this growth ought to occur and what it looks like in the real world of day-to-day living.

3. A useful theory of education must be consistent with democratic values and show how education in a democratic society may help students and teachers to become both critics and intelligent shapers of their society, the outcome of which is surely unknowable and the success of which is ever in doubt. One is always running with uncertainty in a democratic state (which is one practical reason why teachers and principals need to encourage student initiative and responsibility and not be "spooked" into rigidity by ambiguity and the shades of gray that exist in any subject matter honestly pursued. Year after year of tight and tidy lesson plans, such as those based on the weak research on effective teaching, stunt the mind and sterilize the democratic spirit).

In short, if the complexities of education are thought of as a novel, Dewey's novel has a complex cast of believable characters, a good plot, and, best of all, there are no essential chapters missing. Dewey does not retreat before the *complexity* of the problems he chooses to address, as do weaker theorists and most empirical researchers in learning, teaching, or school reform policy. The empirical research approach to "theory" has given us hurtful "theories" such as Direct Teaching, Madeline Hunter, and the "thinking skills" embarrassment. All of these prescriptions de-skill teaching and routinize learning. Dewey wisely avoids the empirical research trap in his theorizing.

A Short Illustration of Dewey's "Comprehensiveness" in Thinking

Dewey's theory directs the compass of ideas in *What Every Great Teacher Knows* because Dewey's is the only comprehensive theory of education we have that is hospitable to two important values — the cultivation of teachers' and students' intelligence *and* democratic values. These two values are linked with each other; they are not separate fragments as in lesser, partial theories. Without the ability to consider social problems such as poverty, for example, or the decline of well-paying jobs for our youth in whatever "track" their high school might have put them, the quality of democratic life is reduced or threatened. To solve a significant problem that is important to society and which helps the problem solver to grow is one facet of thinking in Deweyan terms.

A good comprehensive theory makes larger and clearer *patterns* from the scattered pieces of experience; bad theories take legitimate pieces of education such as cooperation, discipline, motivation, multiculturalism, or even thinking and break them into even smaller pieces called skills. Thus, we have kits that purport to teach the skills of reading; to teach the skills of cooperative learning (which is primarily a means and not a major educational end in itself); to teach the skills of classroom management; to teach the skills of teaching and so on, world without end. In a comprehensive theory such as Dewey's, skills are there, of course, information and facts are there (one cannot think without content, i.e., something to think *with*), *but ideas are there too.*

Dewey's "theory of thinking," which is a major element in his larger theory, is indeed comprehensive. Dewey first places thinking in a social context: democratic society. Thinking, then, is an individual act that relates to and affects others. Most psychological theories of thinking, in contrast, view thinking as an individual act rather than an act that is both an individual and a social phenomenon. It is easy to see why Dewey opposed IQ testing in the 1920s in *The New Republic,* when many of his peers were mesmerized by this latest "scientific wonder" from psychology. Intelligence testing, Dewey feared, would limit individual growth and serve undemocratic elite interests. History has confirmed his judgment.

Dewey makes other connections with what otherwise would be unrelated pieces in weak theories:

- Thinking is in one's ordinary life experience and requires action, a trying out of possible solutions to a problem.

- The intellectual value of an experience or learning is in the cumulative increase in wider relationships and meaning one perceives.

- In education words often obscure ideas because there is no action by the learner — a trying out — that might make the consequences of an idea known.

- Thinking begins with an uncertain, problematic situation, something incomplete and unfulfilled.

- Thinking implies some emotional concern with an issue or a problem.

- Acquiring knowledge and skills is always secondary to the act of inquiring, i.e., problem solving.

- All thinking results in knowledge, but the ultimate value of knowledge is that it aids thinking because the world is an unsettled place.

Dewey states that in education the primary goal of teaching is thinking: "… all [that] the school can or need do for pupils, so far as their *minds* are concerned … is to develop the ability to think" (Dewey 1916, p. 152, emphasis in original). Dewey put thinking first in 1916, but this profundity seems to have passed over us in the ensuing eight decades.

The quality of the problem generated is the most important thing one can ask of an educational experience, Dewey states. No amount of improved teacher technique will compensate for a poor classroom environment in which there is little stuff (Dewey's word) to stimulate thought; stuff like workbenches and wood, laboratory equipment, things and social situations that cause one to think in ways that are more like ordinary life outside school. The material of thinking is not thoughts, "but actions, facts, events, and the relations of things" (p. 156). Facts, data, and knowledge lead to conjectured meanings, tentative explanations, possible relationships of piece A to piece F and piece X — in short, ideas, according to Dewey.

Another example of comprehensiveness is a favorite of both students and teachers in the field: "No thought, no idea, can possibly be conveyed as an idea from one person to another. When it is told, it is, to the one to whom it is told, [just] another given fact, not an idea" (p. 159). Try to find something that profound in your thinking skills kit! This quotation itself is well worth discussion in several class sessions because it says that *ideas* cannot be given from teacher to student merely through teacher talk.

One last quotation from *Democracy and Education*, also a favorite: Dewey first says that facts and information alone merely locate the problem and help to clarify it. Data may stimulate possible solutions. Data — bits of information — represent what is settled and known about the problem. Dewey then makes a further point that is of fundamental importance to our fact-bound, information-overloaded schools: Inferences drawn from data suggest possible results or things to do, not facts that are already known. "Inference is always an invasion of the unknown, a leap from the known" (p. 158). Is it not understandable why teachers and principals in our democratic and commercially restricted culture might tread lightly on the cultivation of thought? How many teachers (or lawyers or craftsmen or professors) dare too often to think and mount "an invasion of the unknown"? To think may endanger one's career.

Go back over the example. How many otherwise loose educational "colors" such as data, action, and inference, to cite only three, does Dewey tie together to make a larger, more colorful quilt of thinking? This is what comprehensiveness means. Good theories try for an elegant simplicity. Physicists dream of one final theory that will explain the physical universe. Good theories go for unified wholes, not tortuously patched together, incoherent pieces of wholes.

How to Use This Guide

In the preceding section we argued briefly that the primary goal of Dewey's theory is to encourage thought among teachers, principals, and students. If teachers or principals are unthinking and too routinized in their work, it is unlikely that the students they teach will make conjectures or critically review data in a subject field, and so forth. Thinking adults within a school environment give the cultivation of intelligence a big assist, although this "teaching resource" is shamefully neglected in most preservice and in virtually all inservice education. Thinking teachers are worth more than the most expensive computers in a school (and teachers are not sent to the scrap heap as quickly).

Since thinking permeates Dewey's theory, we intend each of the 18 principles to throw some light on one or more aspects of thought. So our first suggestion on how to use this guide is that *all* of the principles speak to some aspect of thinking as worked out in Dewey's theory. If you are interested in improving the quality of your teaching with respect to thinking, you might scan the informal wording of each principle listed in the Table of Contents. Your eye might fall on Principle 2, which speaks of encouraging students to ask questions rather than only the teacher asking "pat" questions of students. The second tale under Principle 2 is an interview with Alfie Kohn, who tells of his struggles as a teacher to give students more *real* choices in school as one way of developing student initiative and responsibility. His account tells how he dealt with a "bad" English class and the "solid wall of hostility [he] met in that classroom." Classroom management techniques were not helpful, but a change to a "curriculum worth learning" did help. There is much to think about in this teacher's story.

Principles 13 and 14 state that the total classroom environment educates and that if teachers teach too directly for results — memorization and drill for a test — they short-circuit thought. The tales show how one group of elementary teachers in a school-based dialogue created a better learning environment by reorganizing their curriculum around unifying themes that permitted some correlation of content among several subjects. The second tale tells how Susan Moon, a veteran Foxfire teacher in rural Georgia, has made the transition from traditional teaching to Foxfire's more holistic approach. Ms. Moon captures the spirit of her teaching when she shows how she brings in interesting real-life experiences — such as mentoring projects with elementary students — to create a total classroom environment that encourages student initiative, writing, and thinking.

We have found that sometimes it is one line in a tale, the comments that precede the tale, or an experience or idea recalled by a teacher in a dialogue group, that sparks an insight related to the thrust of the principle itself. One should read the comments and stories in this book in a relaxed, creative attitude. You will not always find a neat, one-to-one correspondence between the content of the tales, the comments, and the principle; but if you approach them imaginatively and broadly as you read and discuss them, you will always find something in the story or in the principle that should spark a fruitful conversation. In this way teachers using this guide to more thoughtful teaching can "write" their own version as they read and discuss the principles in their education courses or in school-based inservice sessions.

The principles truly contain profound, although out-of-fashion, ideas for academia and for schools. As Dewey says, we cannot "give you" a complex idea by words alone; to you it is only one more burdensome, isolated fact — it becomes merely another entry in your education encyclopedia. More academic exposition here will only obscure the ideas and keep you from your initial engagement with them. *So you (as will your own students) sneak up on these elusive tigers in the conceptual jungle the only way you can: you read, you discuss, you debate various meanings and applications, you try some out until — slowly — over time these ideas slip into your mind and grow as your own experience becomes richer and as you construct ever better conceptual nets to snare the always elusive tiger.*

A Little More Help to Get Started

Since *What Every Great Teacher Knows* is a book to stimulate thought and discussion among preservice and inservice teachers — an intellectual element which John Goodlad has found is pushed aside for ever more technique — it need not be read "front to back" as other books usually are. The lean format and content of this book are intentional. We want to make it more likely that a *theory-centered* book might take its complementary place among other more traditional methods texts. Teaching and public education desperately need to mend their intellectual fences — and more professors of education need to be in the front ranks of this reform, along with teachers themselves and those principals and superintendents who can manage, yes, but who are educators enough to know that the end of management is not managemen itself. (See Raymond Callahan's 1962 *Education and the Cult of Efficiency* for a classic exposition of how American schools were modeled on factories to increase schools' efficiency and productivity.)

To make it easier for you to get into this book and to see what light *What Every Great Teacher Knows* may cast on a concern you have, or to get another slant on a topic of interest such as school structure or small group work, we offer below an illustrative index to some of the important topics treated. Pick a topic, jump in, read a few of the principles and tales that relate to it and see what you think. Remember that this book is a *guide* to thinking about better teaching through seminal *ideas* invigorated through discussion with your peers and tested for usefulness by you in your own classroom. This is not another book *about* education; this is a book that *does* education.

"Fishing around" in the topic-principle index is the best way to begin using *What Every Great Teacher Knows*. "Fishing around" in the index, choosing the principles and tales you may want to scan, requires an action on your part — which is what Deweyan theory holds is true for learning at any level or any age. The learner (with some assistance from a teacher or, in this case, a book) must *himself* forge some *imaginative link* with the lesson or the book's contents; that is, he approaches the content with a question in mind; e.g., "Yeah. I hear a lot about 'motivation.' We had a workshop on it last year. What do these guys have to say about it? Will it help me?" A preservice teacher might muse as she picks up this book, "We heard in another course that teachers talk too much — about 70% of the time. But what's the corrective? Maybe if we encouraged more student responsibility and initiative over the six years of elementary school, there would be less need for teachers to talk too much. I think I'll take a look at that topic."

None of this is dazzling, but it *is* fundamental. Making American schools as good as they can be requires initiative from more teachers and principals. This book is lean in words and simple in format to encourage you to be more active — to exercise initiative — because this is a quality good teachers have. We want you to engage this book actively in the same way that whole language teaching theory encourages your students to be active rather than passive readers.

GETTING STARTED:
AN ILLUSTRATIVE INDEX OF TOPICS AND
RELATED PRINCIPLES AND STORIES

Topic	Principles
Testing; Assessing Learning	1. The Cultivation of Thinking 3. Never Underestimate What is Involved in Knowing Something Well 6. Objectives Suggest the Learning Environment 7. The What and How of Learning 13. Good Methods Shape the Whole School Environment 14. Real Learning Cannot Be Hurried
Learning	1. The Cultivation of Thinking 5. The Connection Between Thinking and Doing 6. Objectives Suggest the Learning Environment 7. The What and How of Learning 10. Essential Content is Knowledge of General Social Significance 11. Your Community is an Essential Content Source 13. Good Methods Shape the Whole School Environment
Motivation	1. The Cultivation of Thinking 5. The Connection Between Thinking and Doing 8. Objectives Must be Tied to Larger Aims 9. Teaching Objectives Need to Make Sense to the Learner 18. Teachers Guide Students Towards Larger Perspectives
School Structure	4. The Importance of Foresight, Purpose, and Reflection 10. Essential Content is Knowledge of General Social Significance 11. Your Community is an Essential Content Source 12. The Purpose of Education is Not Fact-Gathering but Inquiry and Meaning-Making
Small Group Work	6. Objectives Suggest the Learning Environment 7. The What and How of Learning 9. Teaching Objectives Need to Make Sense to the Learner 13. Good Methods Shape the Whole School Environment 14. Real Learning Cannot Be Hurried 17. The Contribution of the Individual to the Group — and the Group to the Individual

Topic	Principles
Relating Content to Students' Lives	2. The Value of Questions 3. Never Underestimate What Is Involved in Knowing Something Well 4. The Importance of Foresight, Purpose, and Reflection 5. The Connection Between Thinking and Doing 15. Real Learning Starts With Ordinary Problems
Democratic Values	2. The Value of Questions 8. Objectives Must be Tied to Larger Aims 10. Essential Content is Knowledge of General Social Significance 11. Your Community is an Essential Content Source 13. Good Methods Shape the Whole School Environment 14. Real Learning Cannot be Hurried
Organizing the Curriculum	7. The What and How of Learning 8. Objectives Must be Tied to Larger Aims 9. Teaching Objectives Need to Make Sense to the Learner 10. Essential Content is Knowledge of General Social Significance 11. Your Community is an Essential Content Source 13. Good Methods Shape the Whole School Environment 14. Real Learning Cannot Be Hurried
Student Responsibility and Initiative	2. The Value of Questions 3. Never Underestimate What is Involved in Knowing Something Well 6. Objectives Suggest the Learning Environment 10. Essential Content is Knowledge of General Social Significance 11. Your Community is an Essential Content Source 16. Abstract Ideas Need to be Applied in Practical Contexts
Teacher/Student Planning	2. The Value of Questions 3. Never Underestimate What Is Involved in Knowing Something Well 13. Good Methods Shape the Whole School Environment 14. Real Learning Cannot Be Hurried 15. Real Learning Starts With Ordinary Problems

Four Arbitrary Categories of Teaching

For convenience and simplicity, we have organized the principles, comments, and tales into four functional categories. In real teaching and in Deweyan theory, of course, all of the four categories interact and simultaneously influence each other as a learning experience unfolds. With this caution in mind, the four categories may lend a legitimate simplicity to the complex social interaction we call teaching. Thinking and Experience contains five principles; Teaching Objectives, four; Subject Matter, three; and Teaching Methods, six.

A Practical Application: Principle 7

Principle 7 states, *"The [teaching] objectives value both what is to be learned and how it is to be learned. [Objectives reflect the understanding that] the quality of learning is critically dependent on how the objective is achieved."*

The unwarranted separation of the "what" and "how" in learning and teaching is a feature of many reforms advanced by legislatures, reform commissions, and university researchers to the perceived problem that students are not achieving well in school.[3] A clear example of the separation of the "what" from the "how" is illustrated by the "thinking skills" movement, an expert-driven effort that separates thinking from content. For example, two widely-known "thinking skills" programs, CoRT and Instrumental Enrichment, define thinking as skills, i.e., what one does when one thinks. The presumed skills of thinking (CoRT defines 60) are taught as separate subjects in both programs; that is, the skills taught become a new subject with unique content that is *added* to the curriculum (Thrush 1987, pp. 133-170).

The companion phenomenon of "critical thinking" may suffer from the same limitation: Many supporters of critical thinking treat its subject matter as an add-on to the regular curriculum (see, for example, Paul 1992), similar to CoRT and Instrumental Enrichment. Critical thinking is considered to be new knowledge, requiring the mastery of logical rules as well as numerous "strategies." Later, its proponents say, critical thinking will be brought to bear on other school subjects (as well as on life's problems). One more "extra" for busy teachers to worry about.

The aim of programs such as these is worthy; however, a problem arises when thinking — even critical thinking — is defined in terms of *arbitrary "skills" separated from opportunities to think that arise in learning the content in the school's regular curriculum.* This separation violates

Principle 7 that hinges on the subtle *quality* relationship between *how* we learn something and the *thing* learned — the learning outcome. Principle 7 suggests that educators use care both in selecting *what* is to be learned and deciding *how* it is to be taught. The isolation of thinking from the content of the curriculum is undesirable.[4]

Further, CoRT and Instrumental Enrichment do not agree, even broadly, on what the skills of thinking are.[5] Finally, they are taught in a drill-like fashion that markedly reduces flexibility for the teacher and the student. We believe that the application of Principle 7 to the teaching of thinking leads to the conclusion that a faulty definition of "what" is to be taught — skills — isolates thinking from the curriculum, which leads to the mechanical teaching of fragmented bits of (supposedly) "skilled" knowledge. These programs permit little flexibility in the ways the skills are to be learned (the "how" of learning). The two programs, in sum, define thinking as a skill that creates a falsely efficient learning process.

The ideas expressed in Principle 7 (and in all the other principles) are useful. They can serve our practical interest by helping us avoid the pitfalls of the thinking skills and critical thinking fads.

WHY DO TEACHERS TALK TOO MUCH?

A final illustration follows to show how teachers' comments that arise in discussion are relevant to the principles we have proposed. This example comes from a verbatim excerpt from a dialogue session in the Lower Merion School District, Lower Merion, Pennsylvania. We eavesdropped here on 20 high school teachers and their principal and vice principal who are using dialogue as a fundamental reform process (Bolton 1994, pp. 390-415; Gibboney 1994, pp. 205-207). The question that had arisen from a discussion of *Horace's Compromise* is, why do teachers talk about 70% of the time when they are "teaching"? (Lower Merion is one of the wealthiest school districts in Pennsylvania. We note this fact to suggest that money alone does not wash away the need to confront basic issues arising in learning and teaching in any school that hopes to become a more thoughtful place.)

> *Teacher:* The readings say that changing the structure of a school means more staff involvement. Now one thing that hit me in the readings is that teachers need more involvement, interaction with their students. So conceptually we are talking about the same idea for kids that we are talking about

for teachers. The same idea works both ways, it seems to me.

Teacher: But when we are dealing with teachers and administrators we are dealing with adults about professional things. Dealing with kids is different.

Teacher: I disagree. We stand up front and lecture. We do "top down." But I know why. It's what we are supposed to do — it's what teaching is to the students. They want me to learn it for them.

[The discussion continued with neither teachers nor administrators willing to make an educated guess on the amount of teacher talk in the school.]

Moderator: Let's take humanities — your fields. How much do teachers talk in your subjects?

Teacher: Well, it depends again. In honors sections, there is more discussion. The regular sections need more direction because of the materials and the students.

Moderator: But those are choices teachers make. There are other choices. Don't you have a gut feeling on teacher talk? Let's walk around 10 minutes on each floor and I'd bet we would know.

Teacher: Okay. There are times when we all talk too much. But I find that to get students to talk takes more time, it's more work with all the other things. When I have more student talk, I run short on time. It is much easier to just tell the kids what's what. Days I talk too much, I feel bad about it.

Moderator: There are lots of influences on teacher talk.

Teacher: That's what everybody ignores in these books and articles. The articles imply that teachers do it on purpose because they don't know better.

Teacher: Isn't it because we want to be in control? There's lots of stuff wrapped up in this one....

This excerpt shows how we let ourselves *unthinkingly* be pushed by time, or by our implicit "theories" about what and how "nonhonors students" can best learn, among other influences. This interior "push" from our unexamined theories most often results in too much teacher talk and a dash for the content-to-be-covered-by-June goal line. Nothing drains the intellectual content from a subject worth learning more than rapid, drill-like coverage. If you want to do only one thing to make your elementary or secondary school more intellectual and democratic (more time for students to talk and explore ideas, for example), SLOW DOWN. You will find, too, that slowing down generates student interest and reduces behavior problems. Slowing down increases your job satisfaction because educationally unproductive pressures to "cover and test" are rechanneled into a more coherent focus on student learning (rather than on teacher teaching). Democracy is served when teachers cultivate responsible independence in students. Excessive teacher talk is one way teachers exert control even when such a high level of control is unnecessary. The Lower Merion teachers were discovering this condition for themselves as they talked.

This dialogue excerpt shows how one tale may suggest many topics worth exploring: the negative power of unexamined "theories"; how reading a serious book informed the teachers' professional intelligence (and serious reading is nonexistent in inservice programs and one has good reason to doubt its presence in many education courses); how community norms influence how teachers teach; changing school structure; the initial reluctance of the teachers and administrators to admit the extent of excessive teacher talk; and the invidious distinction in methods between smart students (they get the more Deweyan method) and the less bright students (they get the good old Thorndike-Skinner-work-book-memorize-and-drill routine — just the ticket for boring them and turning them off to reading and discussion and other intellectual pursuits).

The challenge to reading *What Every Great Teacher Knows* and its practical payoff lies in your (imaginative) ability to make connections such as these with its content — connections that might not be obvious at first glance. And "making connections" is one aspect of thinking that Dewey develops in his theory.

What Every Great Teacher Knows speaks to ideas such as these. They may sound a little strange at first because we are more accustomed to buying ready-made *programs* to solve the practical problems of teaching than we are to weighing *ideas* about teaching. In spite of the uncertainty you may first experience in thinking about these principles, you will be able to construct a thoughtful perspective on teaching. *What Every Great*

Teacher Knows does not oversimplify the complexities of learning and teaching as does much of the research on teacher or school effectiveness. "Rules" based on this research lead to stiff and mechanical actions that will not meet the intellectual and democratic aims that a sound theory of education must endorse.

We hope you will read, discuss, and apply the principles in *What Every Great Teacher Knows* to important problems of learning and teaching in your classroom and school. The book should be used as a "starter kit" to provoke thoughtful talk among teachers and among preservice teachers and professors about learning and about teaching. The talk should be serious and unhurried. Do not rush through the principles in a session or two in a too-quick search for "solutions." Give the ideas time to grow — in your mind and in the minds of colleagues. Remember, learning — your own or your students' — cannot be rushed without a big drop in quality.

Schools are lonely places for too many of us. This need not be so. When teachers and principals come together to engage their minds about the problems we know exist in our schools, our decades-long experience in schools says that not only do they face the intellectual elements in learning, but improvement in teacher and administrator morale results. Teachers and administrators feel less isolated from each other once the conversation is underway, according to our research data (Gibboney 1994, chapters 5 and 6). The consequent enthusiasm, hard won, is beautiful to see but impossible to convey to anyone who has not felt it first-hand. Perhaps this finding confirms part of our conviction that any intellectual effort is accompanied by emotional effects. We hope you'll try serious conversation and see if it works for you.

Part Two

Eighteen Teaching Principles
With Illustrative Stories

Thinking and Experience

Dewey (1944/1916) may have said it best: "Thinking is the intentional endeavor to discover specific connections between something which we do and the consequences which result, so that the two become continuous" (p. 145). In other words, thinking is what connects "cause and effect, activity and consequences." Its purpose is control — to increase the degree of an individual's mastery over his or her own destiny. Thinking multiplies our alternatives. Thinking expands insight; expanded insight makes foresight — the agent of control — "more accurate and comprehensive" (p. 145). Thinking and ordinary experience are inextricably connected.

PRINCIPLE 1

EVERY GREAT TEACHER
MAKES THE CULTIVATION OF THINKING
IN A DECENT AND HUMANE ENVIRONMENT
THE PRIMARY GOAL OF TEACHING.

All of the principles in *What Every Great Teacher Knows* speak to elements related to thinking (and to the feelings that always go along with thinking). Because all of the ideas we discuss bear on the intellectual quality of what the teacher does, as well as the quality of the students' thinking and feeling, we will not try to wrap up "thinking" in several easy-to-read pages. Thought is too subtle to treat as a single variable removed from other things that go on in the classroom.

To expand on a topic discussed earlier, when we say "thinking skills," typically lurking in the back of our mind is the idea of discrete, identifiable, and universal actions; behavioral performances at which one is adroit. The lingering learning from our psychology courses reminds us that skill means a smooth and integrated performance of a learned motor activity.[6] The assumption is that such skills exist more or less independently of whether our thinking is about writing a composition, choosing a mate, or understanding a theory in physics or linguistics.

The belief that thinking can be reduced to skills promotes a pedagogy that yields mechanical performances, linear sequences of actions that are assumed to add up to "reading," "critical analysis," or "thinking." But thinking, when we consider it in light of our own experience, is more like creative exploration than something that follows a step-wise sequence.

Perhaps skill is to thinking as the ability to use a dictionary is to an excellent essay. Spelling correctly and hyphenating consistently make the essay better, but alone they contribute little to the ideas, images, and nuances that make the essay worth reading in the first place. If thinking is more than a skill, what might it look like when teachers and students engage in activities that are truly intellectual or thoughtful?

We tell two teachers' tales that bring teaching thinking into the classroom. One teacher's story shows how a change in a science test encouraged thinking; the second story is based on an observer's account of a mathematics teacher, Hal Honig, who creates a "total math environment" in his class that leads students to think — and to enjoy the experience.

The way we test students may encourage or hinder their willingness to think. The following account, reported by Mr. William Rohrer, then Assistant Principal, Penn Manor High School, Millersville, Pennsylvania, makes the point that testing is teaching too.

A Science Test

It is an educational cliché to say that what we test is what we really value. When students ask "What is going to be on the test?" they are really making a statement like this: "What is tested is what is important for me to learn." The content of a test is a mirror that reflects the content that we truly value.

Our ninth-grade Earth Science course was planned so that half of the class time was spent in experiments and demonstrations that made more concrete such ecological forces as acid rain or the influence of the land's physical features on the economic life of the people. These experiments were to be hands-on, synthesizing activities that were made intellectual by using scientific concepts to understand real-life phenomena.

The problem was that the teacher-made tests did not test for this more complex activity. There were no questions, for example, that related the physical properties of acid rain to the social effects of water pollution, to fish kills, or to the stunting of the growth of trees in forest lands. The tests asked for fact recall and ignored the more conceptual and integrative laboratory work that dealt with *science.*

The testing/learning problem was rather easily resolved once it was defined as a problem. The faculty decided to test for two class periods. The first period test was primarily short-answer type questions with some application-of-content questions. The second period test required the student to solve problems. This test was "open book." Students were permitted to bring any material to the test that they thought might be helpful.

While getting the correct solution was important, the students knew that the quality of the solution process used was also to be evaluated. This feature of the test reduced the tendency of students to go only for the correct answer, and to see the answer as something isolated from a process of reasoning, by selecting content appropriate to the problem, or using concepts to simplify and make sensible the countless "facts" associated with something as complex as air or water pollution. Half of the student's grade was based on the problem-solving test.

I know that this example is not glamorous or exciting. It cost little in time or money. But it paid a dividend in higher student interest, and in making our testing procedure support the thinking processes that we were spending half of our class time teaching.

How we test is one important element that influences the quality of a classroom or school. Two other elements more directly related to quality are what and how one teaches. Given a limited amount of reform energy and money, if forced to choose, first, we would put our energy into the quality of the educational water entering the upstream end of the pipe, improving the quality of the learning and teaching in a school; second, we would devote our remaining energy to devising ways to assess learning that supported and extended a more intellectual and democratic way of teaching. The following account by a mathematics teacher reflects a mix of thoughtful teaching and, possibly, more conventional testing. After you have read the account, you might ask yourself, and discuss with others, whether Hal Honig is a good "progressive" teacher, a good "traditional" teacher, or some mix of both. (Or maybe even a not-so-good teacher, if you wish.) This account was written by Ms. Johanna Rebarchak, Great Valley High School, Pennsylvania, a colleague of Mr. Honig, who observed the class over several months as a hands-on project for a supervision course.

An Uncommon Classroom

Sunrise at Great Valley High School, Great Valley, Pennsylvania, is an experience. As one looks across the fields from the front door, one feels as if there are no boundaries to the world; everything is open. The trees, hills, and sky are not marred by man-made distractions. It is a picture of beauty and freedom. Sometimes when I arrive in the early morning, I take a moment to stop, turn around, breathe deeply, and capture nature at her best. I feel unlimited possibilities for the day ahead. This sense of beauty, joy, freedom, and growth are feelings that children should have when they enter a school building; these should not be benefits that come only from the outdoors.

As visitors enter, they are greeted with a surprise. The beauty of nature has not been closed off to those within. Inside the front door and ahead is the Senior Court where the sun cascades through glass walls that enclose an outdoor courtyard complete with trees, plants, flowers, and benches. Great Valley High School was built in the 1960s and true to the spirit of the time, combines a mixture of glass and open spaces uncommon to the 1990s-style building. Winding through the maze-like hallways, visitors sense the influence students have at GVHS as evidenced by the displays of their work throughout the building. But we have a destination; let's continue on to Room 104. From the outside it looks like any other classroom, but the similarity ends as one crosses the threshold.

The horizon of the outdoors is captured within the four walls of the classroom. Room 104 holds many possibilities for growth and intellectual stretching; but it is not the physical layout of the room that interests me, but the individual there who guides his students in learning. Hal Honig, an exceptional math teacher by many people's standards, focuses the minds in Room 104 not on "right answers," but on experiencing the complexity and challenge of math.

The room itself is a math teacher's room. The order of the classroom makes me very comfortable. I could learn here. On the solid inside wall above the blackboard there are student-made posters. Opposite is a glass wall with a blackboard running through the middle; in the front of the room is an overhead projector with a screen that always seems to be pulled down. There is Hal's desk, a bookcase with math books, and the students' desks. They are usually facing front for the beginning of the lesson but do not stay that way for long.

The crispness of the winter day hints at a fresh beginning. It is the first class after the midterm exam and the students filter into the room in small groups. "How did you graph number 15?" "Were you able to do the last problem?" "I had a hard time with the graph for that last problem." The bell sounds. The conversation continues as before only with Hal Honig directing its path. "Any questions?" Hal asks. This will become a familiar phrase over the next several weeks. The students respond immediately. It seems that the students are not quite ready to put the past semester in for its winter's nap. Some unfinished business must be settled before they begin the second semester. There is a great deal of interest in reviewing some of the midterm problems. Since GVHS does not return exams to students, they rely on their memories for the problems. In this task they are as crisp as the day. They focus on the content of the exam rather than on their grades.

Hal uses the overhead projector to illustrate, requesting that student talk guide the process. There is a quiet bantering back and forth of ideas between Hal and the students and among the students. Thoughts swirl like the dry, brown leaves outside, blown by the wind. Brad moves quietly to the blackboard to work out a problem: "... $y = x2$ and $y = 4x2$ — here the integral is between 4 and 0. The graph is a parabola...." Hal fields questions about the exam until everyone is satisfied. "Most of you did very well on the exam. Remember our long-term goal is the AP test. We have sixteen sections to cover before the end of the year. We have three months to get it done, so we won't have to fly. Everyone will do okay; don't worry."

The winds of change are sweeping across Room 104; the old is laid to rest, and it is time for the new. The class moves quickly from the past to the present. "Our goal is to identify the Mean Value Theorem for Integrals." Hal spends the next several minutes demonstrating how to derive the formula; the students take notes, commenting casually to one another as the lesson proceeds. "Brad, are you getting this?" Brad may be getting it, but it's Greek to me. Hal assigns a problem, "Do the problem; when you have the answer, raise your hand." Hal quietly canvasses the room, checking individuals for understanding. The students welcome Hal's intrusion into their space. Mark raises his hand then moves quickly to the board. Chantel changes her seat to have a better vantage point from which to see. "The problem is to graph $y = 2x^2 - 2$. The figure is a parabola with the limits of integration of 1/2 and 0," Mark explains. "How many see that?" inquires Hal. As Mark solves the problem, another student who has the answer to Part B puts this section on the blackboard and waits to demonstrate his procedure. Time passes quickly. A homework assignment is given. Hal details what they will be working on the next day, and the bell sounds the end of this class.

A curious occurrence led me to select Mr. Honig as the teacher I would like to observe for my supervision project. As

Resource Room teacher, I have heard just about every negative comment that can be imagined about teachers. Typically, when students are frustrated, unsuccessful, and uninterested, they shift the blame for their failure to the teacher. However, this is not the case with Mr. Honig's students. For example, I have several senior students who are taking Algebra II and experiencing great difficulty. It is necessary for them to pass the course to graduate. This places an inordinate amount of stress on them. Each student displays the effects of stress in a unique way, but one thing is true about all of them — they never blame Mr. Honig for their lack of success. "Mr. Honig cares that I learn, but I can't seem to understand." "He explains it and I ask questions, but I just can't get it." "I just can't see it." Their perception of the problem is self-related. They don't report, "He can't teach," or "He won't let me ask questions," or "He moves too fast." Hearing Mr. Honig's students' comments over several weeks raised this question: What is happening in his classroom that is not happening in other rooms?

On A Clear Day (You Can See Forever)

Calculus is a lot like a winter day — brisk, clear, and predictable. You know the answers by graphing the lines, angles, and curves, using the formulas to solve the problems. Today, there are twenty students in the class — an even mixture of boys and girls. Outside, the chill of winter's breath is in the air; inside, the satisfaction of problems being solved warms the air. Math class, while it does not exude the excitement of a football game, possesses a good feeling of quiet persistence until the goal is reached; this quality generates its own excitement. Entering through the door, Kevin says, "Got that problem!" with a sense of achievement. Several other students gather around him and an animated conversation ensues. The starting bell rings. "How many were successful with those two problems last night?" Hal queries. A show of hands indicates success. "Who has the answer to the first one, $y = x^2$, $y = 4x^2$?" Mark responds in the affirmative and moves to put it on the board. "And the second one?" Laurel goes to the board. Solution procedures are demonstrated by the volunteers with both students and Hal focused on the presenters. Next, Hal moves to the overhead and teacher and students discuss alternative strategies for solving the problems. Hal raises a new problem: "Take this rotten thing [the problem] and solve it in terms of x.... Let's do it." The students put their heads together in quiet conversation to arrive at a solution. Hal randomly moves from group to group commenting here and there, "Yeah" or "Good," sometimes just watching and nodding in assent. "How many are sitting there with the right answer?" Hal asks. A number of students nod in the affirmative.

An unintentional loudspeaker announcement disrupts the moment. The students laugh and there are several moments of chatter. Hal checks the time and draws the students quickly back into focus with a new problem on the overhead. "When you have the integral, let me know." Calculus is back on the agenda. "You can work in groups or on your own. Check page 358 in your text for some other problems.... We won't get through all these today. Ask yourself some questions [as you are going along]." The students spend about fifteen minutes working independently. Periodically, questions are raised; there is a shared sense of ownership of these problems; a quiet "uh-huh" (if I may borrow a phrase from Ray Charles) arises when a solution is reached. Hal calls the group back together. "We will spend Monday, and Tuesday on this." Kevin says, "No homework for the weekend, right?" Hal: "Please attempt every problem — the more you do, the more you get out of it [homework]."

The closing bell sounds. The students are looking forward to seeing lines, angles, and curves all right, but not those of the math problems; rather, they see those of the barren trees and the streets outside as they make their way home for a weekend break. Friday is here — one period down and six more to go.

There is a nice comfort level in this classroom. A rapport exists between the teacher and the students and among the students themselves. It shows itself in a number of ways. There is little standing on ceremony here. Students question the teacher and each other frequently, persisting when they do not understand. The method is more important than the answer; this is obvious to me. A sense of cooperation and sharing prevails. There is no copying of answers here. Let me explain. I am a realist. Some students copy answers when they have not done their homework. This does not seem to be the case in Hal's class. Upon entering the classroom (before the bell) students are already talking easily about the problems they did for homework. They are not saying, "Let me see your answers"; they are saying, "How did you do number 3?" Did you try number 5?" "I had a hard time with number 10." When Mr. Honig asks if anyone has figured out how to do a problem and someone responds positively, the person immediately goes up and puts the problem on the board. Every student who puts a problem on the board explains the thought processes he or she has gone through to solve the problem. Students do not seem to be intimidated by talking in front of their peers. I never heard any snide, critical remarks about anyone, whether the problem was done correctly or not.

What do you think? Does Mr. Honig teach "thinking" in a humane environment?

PRINCIPLE 2

EVERY GREAT TEACHER VALUES AND ENCOURAGES STUDENT QUESTIONING BECAUSE QUESTIONS ENCOURAGE STUDENT AND TEACHER THOUGHT.

If teachers do not help students to inquire on their own, at least to some level, they sever learning from life. This is true because we grow toward intellectual maturity through recognizing, and working to satisfy, our perplexities. J. T. Dillon (1988) points out that perplexity is a "precondition of questioning and thus the *prerequisite* for learning" (p. 18, emphasis added). Without some sense of discrepancy between old and new learning, neither students nor teachers will be provoked to question, much less examine, ideas. This is Dewey's point in *Democracy and Education*: "Where there is reflection there is suspense"; that is, thinking occurs precisely "when things are uncertain or doubtful or problematic" (p. 148). And it is not enough that the *teacher* frame questions by the dozen, because those questions may not be the *learner's* questions. Unless the learner herself raises questions, no meaningful learning can occur. Answers are not enough, either: You cannot give an answer to someone who has not asked the question. The idea that school teaching and learning are best conceived as a perplexity-free and learner-inquiry-free effort has resulted in the "trivialization of valuable knowledge, habits of mind, and skills" (Lanier and Sedlak 1989, p. 119).

The following two tales illustrate important facets of Principle 2. The first shows what an eight-year-old student has learned about asking questions in school. The second illustration suggests the importance of greater student initiatives in learning, which includes the opportunity for students to pose questions about what they might learn and why it would be worthwhile to learn it. The interview with Alfie Kohn is about student choice in learning. This interview was conducted by Sara Day Hatton, editor of Foxfire's excellent magazine, *The Active Learner: A Foxfire Journal for Teachers*. This interview was published in the March 1997 issue of *The Active Learner*.

Mrs. Lillian Zarndt, a mother and the owner of a primary school in Springville, Utah, offers the following conversation with her eight-year-old daughter. The story demonstrates how easy it is for hard-working teachers to neglect the cultivation of thinking in their classes.

"Mom, You Don't Get It"

Elizabeth: Mom, do numbers ever end?

Mom: Wow! That's a really neat question. Even people who have studied math all their life wonder about a question like that ... (we go into a long discussion about the pro's and con's of this idea). Did you have math today?

Elizabeth: Um-hm.

Mom: What wonderful questions did you ask in school today?

Elizabeth: I didn't.

Mom: Why not?

Elizabeth: M-o-m (she rolls her eyes in exasperation), you just don't get it. School isn't the place to ask questions.

Teachers "teach" students not to ask questions by indirectly — and unknowingly — discouraging them. This action alone markedly lowers the quality of the classroom environment. But the lowered "thinking quality" of the environment does not stop here. Since twenty students are not asking questions in a class, there are fewer ways for the teacher to get clues firsthand that reveal student interests or their understanding of what is being taught. Even more damaging in this question-free environment is that students have fewer opportunities to explore alternative ways of doing things, or to creatively "play" with an idea or a problem. And, too, the students' use of oral language is reduced when it need not be. The language loss further reduces the intellectual quality of whatever a teacher might teach.

If, on the other hand, one teaches in a Deweyan-progressive way — that is, thoughtfully — giving due regard to the students' interests and needs but not to the exclusion of intellectual growth and teacher guidance, an attitude of questioning often prevails. Alfie Kohn gives some practical advice in the interview that follows on how teachers might make their teaching more thoughtful and thus encourage a higher and more satisfying intellectual exchange in their classrooms.

Offering Challenges, Creating Cognitive Dissonance: An Interview with Alfie Kohn

by Sara Day Hatton
(Editor of *The Active Learner:*
A Foxfire Journal for Teachers)
Introduction by Julia Osteen

Squirming in my seat, I turned the pages of the article very slowly, one by one, until I had read the entire contents. I immediately proceeded to read it again. I experienced feelings which ranged from outrage to embarrassment to disbelief. The article was "Choices for Children: Why and How to Let Students Decide." The experience was my first contact with the beliefs of Alfie Kohn. The problem with the article was that it was all too true. He made me look at situations that occurred in the classroom in a much different light.

Punished by Rewards was my next encounter with his beliefs. Again, he made me think about my interactions with children in a way that was different. Since then I no longer use an individual reward/behavior management system in my classroom. My students and I conference weekly regarding behavior. These conferences are individual and a documentation of the conference goes home to the parent on a form which contains our class agreements. When children ask me "Did I do a good job?" (like little kids will often do), I ask them "What do you think?" I am nowhere near the ideal that Kohn espouses; however, I am closer than before.

In the following interview, he challenges all teachers to examine their beliefs and practices. He provides food for thought and not just oatmeal but steak! It takes a lot of chewing before you can swallow. Enjoy!

Q: At Foxfire, student choice is extremely important in all we do. When did you become aware of the need for student choice, and what are some of the ways you involved your students in your classes?

A: I became aware of most of what students need after I taught, I'm sorry to report. I did several things that in retrospect gave me some source of satisfaction or pride but a lot more that make me wince when I look back on how little I knew about what teachers ought to do. I brought students in, for the most part, in a peripheral way in deciding how they would respond to an essay question or to pick from a range of questions when it was time for assessment, because that was all I knew; it was all that I had experienced from elementary school to graduate school. I missed the point about how important it is for kids to have substantial amounts of discretion in figuring out what they are going to learn and how and why. I came to that belatedly from watching teachers who were much better than I was, reading research and other people's views from Dewey to the present day, and thinking about it a lot. Were I to go back in the classroom today, I would certainly do things differently.

Q: In witnessing other teachers, did you observe obstacles they encountered and can you tell us how they dealt with them?

A: One major impediment to giving students choice is the teacher's own reservations about it. There's no magic solution for someone who isn't sure this is going to work except to be in a community of adults who can talk together at regular intervals about what they are doing and to complain and to search for solutions together and to visit each other's classrooms. I think some of the best teachers are those who are lucky enough to be in the best schools and are able to do that. Another obstacle is that the students themselves are unaccustomed to freedom and react at least at first by engaging in more kinds of behavior, good and bad, than ever before because the controls have finally been loosened. They're able to exercise their autonomy for the first time and that's messy and noisy and aggravating. The teachers I've talked to always suggest patience and also bringing the students in on this very problem. Then if, for example, students make ridiculous choices or sit there paralyzed, unable to do anything except to say "You're the teacher; this is your job," the great teachers are able to react without resentment and too much confusion. They say, "What a great topic for discussion! What's my job? How do you feel when someone tells you what to do all day? Will you say you're too young to make decisions?" Or if students are sitting there impassive during class, that opens all kinds of possibilities, providing the teacher can figure out why this is happening. Is it because they don't feel safe in this classroom? If so, how can we — underline we — change this situation so that nobody is afraid of being left out? If students are sitting there quietly because they have nothing to say at the moment, then forcing them to speak up is worse than doing nothing. If they're merely shy by temperament, that leads you to react in a very different way than if they don't feel their comments are going to be taken seriously.

I think most teachers who have tried to give students choices have realized that the worst of all possible courses is to ask their opinion and then dismiss it. For example, by saying they haven't made a responsible choice, which means they haven't done what the teacher wanted and that therefore their decision doesn't count, they feel used and therefore are unlikely to make that mistake again.

There are educators, William Glasser among them, who talk about the importance of class meetings and inspire teachers to try it out. Often they don't realize just how difficult that transition can be, especially when students are accustomed to being rewarded and punished into compliance and simply told what to do all their lives. You can't go from 0 to 60 overnight, and I always advise teachers to start out easily with a decision or a question that is circumscribed and the results of which they can live with until they are able to fashion with the students a classroom that's more democratic.

I made a few efforts along those lines when I was teaching. I gave them the chance to write in journals back before that was fashionable. I'm not sure if it was the dimension of choice to make the decision about what to write, or what made that such a good decision. It opened up a new world to me of the students' inner lives. I went from looking at the surface of the ocean to becoming Jacques Cousteau, explorer of the deep, where even students who had never come up to talk to me and who would not feel safe talking in front of their peers about the things that gripped their inner lives were opening up to me. If only because it created a kind of relationship under the surface or alongside our public life in the classroom, it was a valuable decision, and the only restraint I put on the journals was that they be something more than a dry chronicle of events. They had to talk about how they thought or felt about what was going on and, of course, I promised them confidentiality, and that stuff was far richer and more meaningful to them than almost anything I was doing in the regular curriculum.

Q: Did you encounter obstacles?

A: With the journals, no, primarily not. But I wish I had done more along those lines so that I could have had to work through obstacles I know good teachers do every day. It took me some years to figure this out but I had the idea when I was teaching high school that a course was something a teacher developed on his or her own, built in the garage and polished like an automobile and took pride in as I did in one course that I taught for many years on existentialism. I honed that reading list, I carefully constructed the balance of activities in the class, and the papers to assign and the reading. Then I took it out of the garage when it was time to teach and brought it out to the students. It took me many years to figure out that as good a course as that was or as exciting a reading list that it had, I didn't understand the first thing about teaching, because it made approximately as much sense to think of a course that way as it would for a single person to say that "I have this great marriage waiting — I can't wait to meet somebody to be my husband or wife and take part in it with me."

It was based on a fallacious view of learning. There is no course until the students and you create it together and I didn't see that when I was teaching. When you get right down to it, either you believe the course is fully formed and delivered to the students or you realize there is nothing but a framework and hunches and first starts and the course itself is created together. I think I see it now but I didn't then. It's not just a matter of how much choice about what books they're going to read; it is a matter of a philosophy of teaching. So a lot of the bumps and barriers and obstacles that great teachers encounter, I, like the great majority of teachers, never had to contend with because I was not teaching authentically to begin with. That's a hard thing for me to admit, and I can only say I wish I had seen it sooner.

Q: Many of our readers are trying to implement learner-centered classrooms such as you describe in your writing. However, they tell us they feel isolated in teaching environments that are not supportive. In your own work, have there been times when you felt this isolation and lack of support and can you give us specific examples?

A: I taught one year at a small independent school in rural Pennsylvania where, even despite all my failings I described, I was the only person even doing rudimentary progressive things; and I had no support whatsoever for that. This was a girl's school and I was the closest thing to a feminist on campus. I think it was the social and political challenge I posed that isolated me more than my pedagogical practice, in part because of how reactionary and cloistered a community it was.

Q: How did you get through that?

A: By keeping my own journal and talking to myself because there was no one to talk to. I wrote letters to my friends and read voraciously but my frustration was poured out into the pages of what turned out to be a book-length manuscript about what I was facing. I draw material from that year that I still remember and that has informed my thinking since then.

I'll give you one example which I have thought about often. I had one class that year where the kids gave me a terrible time. They, as I see it, must have stayed up nights trying to figure out how to make my life a living hell because they couldn't have been that good at it spontaneously. And I'm able to laugh about it now but I was reduced almost to tears sometimes because of the solid wall of hostility I met in that classroom. I thought I was doing things right, you know. I didn't just give them Wordsworth to read, I would give them Joni Mitchell, and I might as well have given them Hegel in the original German. At one point, I said, "Fine, you find me the song lyrics and you can teach them."

But that didn't change the atmosphere in the classroom — it came no closer to creating a situation where we were on a mission of learning together. If you had asked me then what I needed, I would have replied in an instant that I needed a classroom management system, a way to discipline these kids who were obstreperous and noncompliant. What I realize now is I really needed a curriculum worth learning. For the most part, I was using Warriner's, which is essentially "Our Friend, the Adverb" stuff that few members of our species would find intrinsically motivating. And I resorted, to my later shame, to the Grade Book, that combination of bribes and threats to make them learn this material. What I realized much later was that I needed for them to have more choices; I needed a more accurate view of how learning happens and the respects in which students have to construct meaning for themselves instead of swallowing whole the ideas and skills offered to them by a teacher. So that one experience has colored my view of classroom management and the respects in which it is inextricable from and largely a function of the academic learning that is going on in a classroom.

Q: As teachers we really struggle with how we can help students learn to make good choices. Have you struggled with that, and what is your thinking on it?

A: Well, the first step in making a good choice is to have a choice rather than being told what to do most of the time. Kids learn to make good decisions by making decisions, not by following directions. If we want our kids to take responsibility for their behavior, then we have to give them responsibilities along with guidance and support and love.

But they also have to be making decisions that matter. I often hear teachers talk about how they give kids the chance to choose when the teachers don't really care about the outcome and, of course, that's nothing close to a democratic classroom. The kids have to be able to make decisions when it matters very much to the teacher because that's authentic choice.

There are examples all over the place of what I call pseudo-choice where they have to make the so-called right decision or it doesn't count or it's these awful attempts to coerce kids that are wrapped in the language of choice, such as "Would you like to finish your homework now or do it after school?" This is not a choice at all, of course. It's saying to the kid, "Do what I tell you or I'll punish you," and this is a staple of many disciplinary programs. We help kids make good choices by making sure they are informed about the options they have and also that the options are appealing. A kid who gets to choose between two workbooks or silly essay questions or the time of day in which to memorize math facts is not being offered real choice. Somewhere Shakespeare says there is little choice in rotten apples.

Q: When teachers tell you they are offering choice in the classroom, do you find what some of them describe is superficial choice rather than real choice?

A: Many times, yes. Many times. In fact, even the major vehicle by which students can choose together, the class meeting, turns out to be a charade in many classes. First of all, it is often not used at all in secondary schools. Give elementary teachers credit for at least trying this kind of thing. Everybody gets to get in a circle on a regular basis, to reflect and plan and decide; but in many classes where the teachers are proud of themselves for doing this, they are running the whole show. They are asking or answering every question and driving the agenda and rarely trying to bring the students in on what they had already decided has to happen and that's hardly worthy of the name "choice."

I witnessed one class meeting where — I still shudder thinking about it — where every child in the room was to say something good and bad that had happened that week, and most of the bad stories had to do with one little boy named Charles. It became in effect an Orwellian hate session focused on this boy, and instead of intervening, the teacher underlined each comment by adding her own criticism addressed to the boy who had this eerie, blank expression the whole time.

Had you asked the teacher, she would have said, "Yes, we do class meetings, or we work on community in our classroom." But there was nothing worthy of the term *community-building* in what she modeled to the other kids, much less what she did to that one little boy.

Q: Have you talked to teachers who are struggling with this with positive results?

A: Yes, absolutely. That's where I've learned most of what's going on in my thinking. It's the practical realities in classrooms around the country that I've witnessed that animate my work and inform it. When I walk into a second-grade classroom in St. Louis and watch the kids running their own class meetings to solve problems that have come up, where one child is the facilitator and another is the recorder, thus teaching language skills, and the teacher is just sprawled out on the floor with the rest of them as they maintain a discipline, a patience, and a respect that would have blown me away if they were 17 but they were in fact seven years old. Or the story of a teacher in California who came back from her break to find the kids already huddled together excitedly talking about something, even though recess wasn't over, and when she asked what was going on was told a problem had happened during recess and they were holding a meeting to fix it by themselves. The kids didn't get there right away. In both those examples and many others I could share, what I'm really looking at is the hard work of the teacher in helping them to become empowered, to take responsibility not only for their own behavior but for the actions and values and feelings of everyone else as well as learning the skills of how to make decisions together.

For heaven's sake, most books and classes to which teachers are exposed take it for granted that the teacher must be in control of the classroom; and the only question is how you get and keep that control most effectively. What I want to call into question is the idea that the teacher ought to be in unilateral control of what's going on. I didn't question that premise when I was teaching. I never saw a classroom where a group of learners democratically figured out what the course ought to be, what to learn, how to learn, why to learn, how to treat each other, how they wanted to solve problems. I'd never read about or seen it, so my classrooms reflected my own experience. I imagine that's true for millions of teachers around the country. It's all the more remarkable, then, when you come across an example of somebody who miraculously has figured out that kids have to be active learners and that the best teaching is not where the teacher is most firmly in charge.

One caution must be mentioned — a perplexity with Deweyan-progressive teaching methods that goes back to many "progressive" schools of the 1920s and 1930s. This misunderstanding hinges on a reluctance — a guilty feeling even — to give necessary direction to what the students do when direction is needed. As one teacher wrote, "I felt [that] ... it is okay to slip in a few ideas of your own and lead the kids a little to get a good project going." Of course it is! Students at almost any level (including graduate school) need teacher guidance and suggestions at times when they are learning to learn in a more independent and responsible way that is at variance with their previous school experience.

The teacher must always be the one who is responsible for the educational worth of a thematic unit or any other experience in the classroom. She knows more; she is mature; she is the one who, as Dewey writes, can see where the students' partial and less formed present knowledge might be directed (see Principle 18). The students can do most or some of this, but the teacher should have no hesitation to offer ideas, direction, and structure to make a faltering activity more educationally worthy. Students are learners who may be becoming more self-reliant and socially responsible, but when they need help, give it! That is what the office of teacher requires. If you are teaching thoughtfully, you need not worry that you will consistently over-direct or control as too many teachers do who subscribe to a more traditional teaching theory.

Dewey says, for example, in *Experience and Education* (1938), that "guidance given by the teacher to the exercise of the pupils' intelligence is an aid to freedom, not a restriction upon it" (pp. 84-85). This slim volume is well worth reading and discussing if a group of teachers is beginning to explore the educational moors where challenging progressive practice and seminal ideas push and shape each other.

PRINCIPLE 3

EVERY GREAT TEACHER
UNDERSTANDS THAT HE/SHE CANNOT
AFFORD TO UNDERESTIMATE WHAT IS
INVOLVED IN "KNOWING SOMETHING" WELL.

What does it mean to know history, or to be able to read? It must mean more than a grade or a standardized test score — yet, this is often the working definition schools give to these complex and potentially rich experiences. To "know" means active *thinking* in the sense that *more is learned than taught*. It means going beyond what is given. (See Dewey 1944, chaps. 11 and 12; Gardner 1991; Mitchell 1987; Newmann 1990a, 1990b; Perkins 1992).

Certainly knowing of some kind occurs at the level of factual recall or routine operations; however, if the teacher wishes to release potential in students, to promote individual growth, recall is not enough. Until learners are challenged to elaborate on what the world presents to them through their senses, they perpetuate an inadequate understanding of their own capabilities, contenting themselves with the naming, only, of what is presented. A hundred years ago William James wrote about the "going beyond": "But when we know about [something], we do more than merely have it; we seem, as we think over its relations, to subject it to a sort of treatment and to operate upon it with our thought" (1992/1890, p. 144). And if we who teach do not enable the elaborating, the going beyond what is given, we assume some of the guilt for the resulting inadequate self-understanding in students.

We can convey the spirit of what is involved in knowing by citing Jerome Bruner's (1966, 103-104) recollection of a notable event in his student days:

> We have all discovered [the active enterprise of reading], with delight, on our own. As a student, I took a course with I.A. Richards, a beautiful man and a great necromancer. It began with that extraordinary teacher turning his back to the class and writing on the blackboard in his sharply angular hand the lines [from Goethe's *Faust*]: "Gray is all theory; Green grows the golden tree of life."

For three weeks we stayed with the lines, with the imagery of the Classic and Romantic views, with the critics who had sought to explore the two ways of life; we became involved in reading a related but bad play of Goethe's, *Torquato Tasso*, always in a state of dialogue though Richards alone spoke. The reading time for eleven words was three weeks. It was the antithesis of just "reading," and the reward in the end was that I owned outright, free and clear, eleven words. A good bargain. Never before had I read with such a lively sense of conjecture, like a speaker and not a listener, or like a writer and not a reader.

One practical way for teachers to not underestimate what is involved in knowing a thing, is to observe and talk with their students as much as possible. In the example that follows, Ms. Shelly Salaman, Warminster, Pennsylvania, reveals Howard's process of thinking as he writes an essay on a topic he has chosen. This example leaves no doubt about many details involved in Howard's "knowing a thing": writing an essay on living in the country. Howard's story reveals, too, how thinking and feelings occur simultaneously in thought. Notice, for example, the strong feelings Howard has toward owning the future house he is writing about.

This interview between Howard and his teacher was tape recorded. Howard has some difficulty with learning and wisely (we think) refused placement in a special education class. Instead he was placed in classes of average ability with on-demand help as needed.

My House in the Country

Teacher: Is there anything you'd particularly like to write about, Howard? I'd like you to pick the topic.

Howard *[After a short pause]*: Living out in the country.

Teacher: Fine. Now, what I'd like you to do is just tell me aloud whatever goes through your mind as you work on this assignment.

Howard: [*Immediately*] Future — where I want to live — who with — married or something — I am going to build my own house — environment — surrounded by trees, all in backyard, mountains, lake — then I wake up.

Teacher: You mean you come back to reality? [*laughter*]

Howard: Dune buggy, horse, animals, pets — what type of people? — transportation — I said that already — schools — what do you call it, shopping centers — how is the community about you? That's about it. [*Pause of about one minute*]

Teacher: It seems to me that what you've done is to freely associate ideas which are connected to the topic you chose. Is this the way you usually begin a writing assignment?

Howard: Yes, I get it all together.

Teacher: What is your next step?

Howard: I write it.

Teacher: Well, go to it. [*Howard writes for three minutes steadily; then he seemed to be reading his writing back to himself*] What are you doing now?

Howard: Reading it back, making sure I put down every word I said, checking for spelling, thinking what is next.

[*He went on reading another minute but made no changes. Next he wrote for about two more minutes; reread for about one minute and made a change on the seventh line of the rough draft*]

Teacher: Why did you make that change?

Howard: I wrote it backwards. I change something because I can add words and make a different meaning — spelling, if I can see it; my spelling is so bad. For example, I want to build my house and I added "own" [*said with great forcefulness*] because it's mine and means a lot to me.

Teacher: Yes, I can tell you feel strongly about the house. I bet you'll get it one day. [*Howard went on writing for about two minutes.*]

Howard: I'm reading the last sentence and maybe this is the ending. Or should I just leave it? [*Rereads, "mouthing" to self for about five minutes; he puts a period in.*] I don't know if I should write more or stop. I think I'm out of thoughts. [*Adds final words, "and then I woke up."*] I had a thought.

Teacher: Let me look at it.

Howard: [*Anxiously*] I'd normally write a rough copy and then reword it, change sentences around, add words, take them out — like right here: "I would like to live out in the country where the air is fresh ... ," I would change it and write "because" in there.

Teacher: Well, do that.

Howard: I'll probably add stuff.

Teacher: Great!

Interview held one day after the original writing session

Teacher: Howard, I was very pleased with the results of your writing, because I think it is the best writing you've ever done for me. Why do you think it was so good — so much better than other things you've done?

Howard: It was the topic. I've thought about it a lot, and I had a lot to say on it.

Teacher: I especially liked your first draft. Do you remember what you did or thought about as you changed your rough draft?

Howard: I reread it, adding words, changing words and sentences around to say what I wanted. Normally when I write, I leave out words — endings — my tutor told me that — same as when I read — I go back and try to put them in. That's why I do better orally in tests. In junior high a few of my teachers let me take tests orally.

Teacher: Do you still do that?

Howard: No, I don't need to do that now. I'm doing O.K. in my courses.

Teacher: How do you see yourself as a student?

Howard: I do well — I get mostly "B's" and some "C's" — but I know I need help with my writing and spelling.

Teacher: How do you feel about yourself as a writer?

Howard: The way I feel about writing is not too good because I can't write all the words I say and feel.

Teacher: Do you think you have any strengths and weaknesses?

Howard: My strong parts are that I can think of a lot to write about, but I can't write it down. My weakness is spelling.

Teacher: How do your teachers make you feel about your writing? Do they help you or make you feel worse?

Howard: I have five teachers. Four out of the five help me because I can always ask them questions about what's going on. I like all my teachers and most of them know I have a problem in reading and spelling.

Teacher: Was there anything any teacher has done that's been particularly helpful with your writing?

Howard: Yes, in 6th grade a teacher helped me. I stayed after school one day and she told me to use these questions — Who, What, When, Where, Why, and How, and they really help.

Teacher: Did that help you yesterday?

Howard: Yes, it told me how — how I wanted to live — and that's what I wrote about; and where, and when, in the future, and why.

Teacher: Let's talk specifically about your writing now. How do you go about writing?

Howard: First, I think of what I'm going to write and I say to myself, What am I going to say? [*pause*]

Teacher: Yes, I could see you doing that yesterday. It seemed to me that you followed a process of free association where you just let ideas happen, one triggering the next one.

Howard: Yes, I guess that's it.

Teacher: Look, let me show you the tape transcript. [*Shows him the transcript.*] See where you went from the word "future" to "where I want to live," to "who with" and so on, then to "dune buggy," "horse," "animals," "pets." That's a good process, Howard, to just let your thoughts flow.

Howard: Well, good.

Teacher: What do you do next, after the thinking?

Howard: Next, I write it. I'll write what I thought and reread it, and then go on — rereading helps me to figure out what to say, and I keep doing that — rereading to decide what to say — to put in words I missed....

Teacher: You know, Howard, one of the reasons I was so excited with yesterday's results is that you followed the same process that authors on writing recommend as being helpful.

Howard: Oh?

Teacher: Yes. There was planning or thinking like we just talked about, and then the writing of a rough draft with lots of rereading backwards for checking and more planning and thinking, and then there was final revision stage....

Howard: But what about my spelling?

Teacher: I have a book for that. I'll show it to you. [*Gives Howard a book for remedial students based on linguistic patterns.*] Let's get back to the writing process. Do you follow the same process I saw yesterday in your writing-up of class assignments?

Howard: No, I don't have time, and I'm not always as interested in the topic as yesterday.

Teacher: Well, I agree that interest is important. I couldn't agree more; but you can't always pick the topic in school. Still, there is something else you can do: Try to get to know as much about the topic as possible.

Howard: Thanks.

Teacher: Now, what I have to offer you in the way of help is this. If you really want to improve your writing, I'm going to demand from now on that at least one part of each of your papers for me be written with your best efforts, and I think following the right process, the one you followed yesterday, will make a big difference. I think I've been too easy on you in the past, but I'm going to demand more now.

Howard: [*Laughing*] Thanks a lot!

Schools are such busy places that "doing" teaching or administering become ends in themselves. We rarely stop the clock, step back, and try to see what we as teachers or administrators are doing. Only a few of us can observe our "Howards" carefully to see what they may be thinking or feeling.

Since we do not try to look critically at ourselves or our students too often, learning/teaching routines become part of the school's woodwork, where they lurk unseen to work their "will" for good or mediocre ends.

Fred Newmann's (1990a, 1990b) extensive work in high school social studies classes on "going beyond what is given" is a good empirical statement of what this criterion can mean. Newmann maintains that the "defining feature of higher order thinking … is tasks or questions that pose cognitive challenge and require students to go beyond the information given" (1990b, p. 256). In his studies, six minimal criteria assumed to constitute "thoughtfulness" were developed from extensive classroom observation: (1) "Sustained examination of a few topics rather than superficial coverage of many"; (2) "Substantive coherence and continuity"; (3) "Students were given an appropriate amount of time to think and to respond"; (4) "The teacher asked challenging questions or structured challenging tasks"; (5) "The teacher was a model of thoughtfulness"; (6) "Students offered explanations and reasons for their conclusions" (1990b, p. 257).

Teachers who attend to these features of classroom interaction will increase their chances of not underestimating what is involved in "knowing something" well.

PRINCIPLE 4

EVERY GREAT TEACHER REALIZES THAT
PRODUCTIVE EXPERIENCE RESULTS FROM
DOING SOMETHING WITH FORESIGHT,
WITH PURPOSE IN MIND,
THEN REFLECTING ON THE CONSEQUENCES.

This principle captures the essence of thinking in real life. We are faced with a problem whose solution is unclear, for example, or we are engaged in a routine activity such as driving, when new elements enter the routine situation and confound it. Most of us use foresight when we drive and do think of the possible consequences of our actions. (If we did not do this, many of us would have long ago passed on!)

Teacher Estelle is driving home from school. But there is more to the driving situation than "driving home." Estelle is to pick up her daughter downtown. Estelle is a few minutes late. She drives faster. Her worry grows. She is further delayed by road construction. She is now fifteen minutes late. The psychological pressure mounts. Estelle is behind a slow-moving car as they approach a long curve. She cannot see far enough down the road to be certain that she can safely pass the car; on the other hand, she probably could make it. Feelings fight with judgment. Anxiety about her child says, "Pass. Take a chance." Because Estelle is a thoughtful person, she resists the pressure of her emotions and foresees the consequences of a risky driving decision: a possible head-on accident, injury, even death. This thinking process somehow relaxes Estelle. Being late to pick up her daughter has fewer bad consequences (although there are some) than the closer and more likely consequences of a risky driving decision that may save only a minute but take a life.

This illustration is unremarkable in itself, even obvious. "Obviousness" is one characteristic of doing some things with foresight. We do it routinely in many situations and are, therefore, oblivious to the thinking process involved. But there is an elusive quality in doing something with foresight, and in evaluating the goodness or badness of the consequences that follow the action. The elusiveness of foresight is dominant in too much teaching. Teacher Estelle, in other words, may be a thinking wizard behind the wheel of her Ford Escort, but in class she may see few consequences to children of her actions; she lacks foresight because she does not link her actions with their consequences — what her actions "bring out" in the complexity of a classroom. Sometimes whole school faculties are blind to the consequences of their actions to themselves and students as the following anecdote makes clear.

How Two Elementary Schools Became Entangled in a Web of Unforeseen Consequences

The principal author is in the third year of a five- to eight-year reform effort with seven schools in a middle-class school district enrolling 3,500 students. All of the administrators and about 60 percent of the teachers are engaged in a dialogue process in which the participants bring their practical knowledge to bear on some classical readings in history and educational theory. Presently (1994) each of the school dialogue groups is moving to practical action in reform through the development of school "action plans" while direct attention to the readings and their discussion is reduced. The school action plans, in short, reflect whatever influence the readings and discussion have had on the teachers' and principals' real-life theory of education. The action plans are always tentative.

So much for background. We share now the revealing events in two elementary schools that show the blindness of the collective faculty to the consequences of its actions until conversation in the dialogue yanked off the cover under which those consequences had been hiding for years.

The topic for the session was the practical implications, if any, of Lawrence Cremin's history, *The Transformation of the School*, for them as teachers and for their action plan. Cremin's book tells about the people, ideas, and events that shaped the progressive education movement. Someone mentioned Francis Parker's work in the 1870s that anticipated the whole language movement (Parker's students wrote much of the material they read) and today's "outcome-based" education movement. This led to a discussion of thematic units and the integration of subject matter around rich themes or topics. One subject that fits nicely into most thematic units is art. The art teacher saw a problem with that and said to the moderator something like, "You said an art teacher could spend two hours over several days or more working with teachers and their classes. I can't do that. I have to give every teacher in this building one-half hour or so on a regular schedule. I have to see everyone. I can't miss anyone." When asked why she thought this was true, she replied that the union contract demanded it. Hold this situation in your mind while we visit another elementary school one week later whose teachers were discussing Cremin's book in relation to their action plans.

In the second elementary school the teachers talked about thematic units, portfolios, and authentic assessment, among other topics. The question of time for teachers to plan came up as it had before. This led to a discussion of how often teachers in self-contained classrooms were disturbed by kids being pulled out of class for such things as speech correction, remedial work, gifted work, music, guidance. The teachers' comments made it clear that the self-contained classroom was in shreds. The moderator asked one teacher who was known to be a superb teacher how many hours each week she had her class intact. "Oh! About one hour," she calmly replied. No teacher seriously differed with her statement.

What do these abbreviated vignettes have to do with foresight and consequences of which Principle 4 speaks? Over a period of at least ten years, actions had been taken by the central administration (which preceded the current one) to add specialized programs from self-esteem lessons to speech to art to Chapter 1 classes in a helter-skelter manner unguided by an explicit, coherent theory of education. The principals never questioned this because, for example, lessons in self-esteem seemed like a good idea, and they, too, had no clear philosophy to guide them. The teachers, likewise, went along with each little added piece that did not seem to be bad in itself until today, years later, the teachers have lost much control over how time is used in their supposedly self-contained classrooms!

Elementary schools willy-nilly shaped themselves on the worst features of most middle and high schools. Art teachers are not certain that they can work in thematic units, and the classroom teachers are beginning to realize that they have lost one of their most valuable educational assets: virtually a whole day every day with the same group of kids. What harmful consequences of mindless acts!

Today these elementary schools are relatively time- and schedule-bound to the detriment of students and teachers alike. Teaching and learning has been made more difficult than need be. The future will tell whether or not these teachers and their principals can reform their shredded day into a more coherent whole.

What could be further from cultivating thinking in the minds of many of us than the *educational connections* that might be made between five seemingly unrelated elements: school buses, discipline problems on the buses, conversation, homerooms and the bus drivers themselves? Ms. Sybil Gilmar, then a vice principal at the Welsh Valley Middle School, Lower Merion, Pennsylvania, gives us a shining example of thinking within one's ordinary experience.

Thinking and the School Bus Problem

I found myself wasting a lot of time on student misconduct on the bus. The misconduct reports dealt with such things as noise level, disobeying the driver, and squabbles over who sat where. Do you know that each hat tossed out a school bus window costs about three hours in administrator and secretarial time? This is the kind of thing that I didn't want to dedicate my life to, although the safety implications of some of this behavior were potentially serious.

What to do about these endless reports? How could I avoid wasting time on educationally trivial matters, and still deal with the problem?

I decided to put the social responsibility idea of Dewey's to work. I created a dialogue among students, staff, and bus drivers. I began by asking students to respond to a survey that asked four open-ended questions about riding on the school bus.

1. The thing I dislike most about riding the school bus is…

2. The thing I like best about riding the school bus is…

3. Students can help to make a ride safe and pleasant by…

4. Bus drivers can help to make a ride safe and pleasant by...

Before these questions were given to the students, I discussed concerns about the buses with the teachers, and asked if they would run the survey in homerooms or in other classrooms. Mr. Brubaker, our principal, met three times with the bus drivers to discuss the survey results.

The survey summary is given below. Two of the results that later events proved to be important were the students' feeling that they liked bus drivers who were firm and friendly; the major concern of bus drivers was that they were often treated with disrespect by the students.

1. Major complaints were overcrowding, saving seats, picking on younger and smaller students, and the noise level.

2. One of the things students like about the bus is meeting their friends and socializing. A large number of students also appreciate getting a ride to school.

3. Most students understand what constitutes a safe and pleasant ride. They also understand the rules: (a) stay seated; (b) use a quiet voice; (c) line up without butting and pushing.

4. Students respected bus drivers who were firm but fair; that is, who did not allow "mayhem" and were also friendly to the students. Bus drivers, in turn, would like respect from the students. Some feel that they have a job that is not appreciated by the community.

5. Since school started in September, there have been 47 detentions for bus misconducts, one student has been denied bus privileges for a week, and one student was suspended from school for two days for inappropriate behavior on the bus.

The questions for discussion in the 26 homerooms are given below:

1. What's the best way to avoid being picked on?

2. What do you see as your role if you see someone being picked on?

3. What's the best way to get a seat if someone is "hogging" and even intimidating students?

4. How can the noise level be reduced, especially in light of the fact that students want to talk and see friends?

5. How can we raise the level of respect for bus drivers?

Although the survey aroused some interest, my main idea was that the dialogue in 26 homerooms, built around the discussion questions, might be the thing I wanted to raise the students' consciousness of the problem. The student/teacher dialogue was held during the guidance period.

The teachers reported the major feelings and ideas expressed by students in their homeroom discussions during a faculty meeting. All students saw the film, "And Then It Happened," the point of which is that misconduct can lead to a bus accident.

One of the major outcomes of the dialogue was that kids want bus drivers to be friendly — to say "Hello" and to know the children's names. This is one aspect of the respect desired by the drivers. Both the students and the drivers were aware of the suggestions and concerns of the other group.

The results of our talking were beyond anything we had hoped for. *Four months after our exchange of views, bus misconduct reports had dropped over 50 percent,* slightly higher than the drop that occurred immediately following the student-teacher-bus driver dialogue.

Dewey's idea that learning is problem-solving in which individual experiences are shared with others through the give-and-take of thoughtful talk worked well on the mundane problem of bus discipline. Both the students and the bus drivers "re-connected" in a socially positive way.

More rules and more detentions pushed from my office would only have increased the trivial element in my work. It is doubtful that such actions would have brought results comparable to that achieved by open conversations.

Ms. Gilmar's story not only shows how smart teachers can use in-school social situations as powerful civic content, but demonstrates as well Dewey's dictum that the worth of an idea acted upon can best be determined from the consequences that flow from that act. The 50 percent drop in bus misconduct reports is one indication that the homeroom dialogues (an action) by Ms. Gilmar led to desirable consequences.

PRINCIPLE 5

EVERY GREAT TEACHER RECOGNIZES
THAT THINKING IS NOT SEPARATED FROM
DOING SOMETHING WITH A PURPOSE IN MIND;
THAT MIND IS IN THE DOING,
NOT OUTSIDE IT.

In schools we find from time to time a needless division of experience into two worlds — ideas and practical affairs. That separation impoverishes both ideas and practice since ideas have meaning only within the continuous experience, that is, the practical life, of the individual or the larger social group (classroom, school, school district, state, nation, and beyond); and, conversely, practical life is meaningless unless informed by ideas. It is as if we have not learned to trust ourselves or our students to *think*.

The truth is, thinking comes dressed in the most ordinary of clothes, the clothes of day-to-day life experience. It is uncomfortable with the dress schools often drape on its figure, a fashion that often mimics a scarecrow. Thinking is not in tests; thinking is not in grades; thinking surely is not in dry, *Reader's Digest*-like textbooks that give a black-and-white sketch of history or literature, yet pretend to present the subject in living color.

Thinking is common, yet elusive. The teacher in the example of Principle 3 who carefully studied Howard's way of writing was thinking and not merely "assessing for a grade"; the elementary teachers who seem to have lost control over their self-contained classrooms discussed in Principle 4 are beginning to think after a decade-long "blackout" in which the cumulative consequences of many isolated actions in adding programs to the schools seems to have lowered, not raised, the quality of the schools for students.

This principle places thinking in *activity,* trying to do something the outcome of which is in doubt, uncertain, problematic. Reread the principle. It implies that inquiring is primary; acquiring is secondary. The short first phrase means that the process of trying to solve some problem, or doing something socially complex like raising a child, or restoring a car — the *activity* itself that requires *thinking* (i.e., inquiry) — is the essential thing. The second phrase means that in a true activity of thinking, one "picks up" (i.e., acquires) facts and values that, combined with thoughtful doing, enable one to construct personal and social knowledge. This is precisely what Frank Smith means when he notes that "knowledge is a byproduct of experience, and experience is what thinking makes possible" (1990, p. 12).

In thoughtful *doing* one learns persistence, discipline; in thoughtful doing one learns to appreciate the materials and people one works with in the activity, to appreciate the complexity and the quiet joy of doing something well, and depending on the range of activities over several years, a whole book of powerful learning could be compiled. If one thinks, according to Deweyan theory and to writers such as Smith, an almost unlimited range of learning occurs, much of which cannot be predicted beforehand by the teacher. Learning falls from thought as surely as the rain from clouds.

Greg Wegner (1990) of the University of Wisconsin at LaCrosse tells how family photographs can be used to encourage kids to "think history." The following is an excerpt from his article, "What is History?" (from the Spring 1990 issue of *Democracy & Education)* that views students as imaginative *makers* of history.

What is History?
Time, Imagination, and Creative Thinking
for Students as Makers of History

History is inherently controversial. What we think we know about history is rooted in conflicting interpretations about reality and the meaning of the past. The power to interpret, which speaks directly to the process dimension of history ... [encourages students] to build upon and go beyond memory-based learning into a higher level of thinking.

One of the legacies left to education by Mark Twain is the understanding that the young, through their innate creativity and imagination, have a natural affinity toward learning about the historical process through the all important lens of interpretation. Developing the power of interpreting the past demands the kind of classroom environment where students can discover, in various ways, that they are active agents in the historical process and that their own generation occupies a time frame in history. Each human being is thereby seen as a maker of history rather than a passive observer....

Photographs and Social History

One of the catalysts for attempting the difficult challenge of seeking some kind of union between content and process in the classroom came through a box of old family photographs at an estate auction that no one wanted.... The images subsequently found a special home in the classroom where they became the centerpiece for a lesson associating creative writing and thinking with the study of history.

What follows are a number of ideas on how photographic imagery, in this case family pictures, can be introduced into the history curriculum as a way of advancing the content and process dimensions of history....

The photographs could be introduced as part of a unit on "What is History?" during the first day or week of a history curriculum. One essential learning goal growing out of the activity is engaging students in the challenging prospect that the meaning of history cannot possibly be encompassed within the pages of a textbook. An understanding of history also involves a certain command of one's mother tongue. The written record of the past requires that people attach meaning or *interpretation* to historical evidence. It is at this point in the classroom that historical information becomes knowledge.

With unnamed and undated photographs in hand, students are asked to surmise the date the picture was taken and to provide clues from the photograph that might aid them as historians in this decision. The possibilities, depending on the collection, might range from clothing and hair styles to jewelry and the technology of the period necessary to produce the picture. The role of the students as "history detectives" might also extend to a discussion on why these people bothered to have these family portraits taken in the first place. It should be added that for most of us and our forebears, the only public documents marking the passing of a human life are found in family photographs, the obituary column of a newspaper, a death certificate, and a tombstone. The family pictures therefore represent part of the grist or raw material of social history.

To accentuate the importance of time frames and generations, students can focus on one historical personality in the photograph. After giving a first and last name to that individual, the class can then make a judgment on the year the person was born as well as the possible date of death. Such an activity will reinforce the fact that the person pictured occupied a time frame in history and was an active participant in the historical process. One related exercise that could be introduced at this point is the discussion of possible changes in American or world history which took place during or since the lifetime of the person in the picture. By not giving the actual date of the photograph at the outset, even if it is available, students can actively use their historical imaginations and knowledge about history.

As a corollary to Twain's insistence that children make their own historical pictures, it is suggested here that students *write* their own historical interpretation as a way of attaching meaning to the historical lives of people in the old photographs. Taking an example out of E. L. Masters' *Spoon River Anthology*, students can write an essay from their own historical imaginations about the daily life experienced by the subject of the picture. An exchange of student essays the following day might serve as the basis for a discussion of the similarities and contrasts of the life experiences of the personalities in the picture.

The importance of perception and its relationship to conflicting interpretations in the history among the young writers in the class is illustrated with even greater force if every student has been given a copy of the *same photograph* as a preliminary to this writing exercise. The clash of interpretations stemming from something as profound as what we actually "see" in the photograph can be related to the serious difficulty of interpreting the meaning of past personalities, developments, and events among historians. By exploring these considerations, students of history may come to the healthy notion that historical knowledge is not something that is poured from one standing brain to another in the form of dates and names stripped of historical context. On the contrary, the box of old photographs should leave investigators of the past with the conclusion that historical facts devoid of context and the acceptance of a consensus view of the meaning of the past do not mean "history" at all.

Extending Time and Imagination

Using the process orientation of history and the foundation created through the box of old family photographs, a number of other classroom activities can serve as additional points of departure.

Assume that the old box of family photographs included pictures of only white families. How might the essays written on "A Day in the Life of ..." be different if the people in the pictures were Black? Hispanic? Asian Americans? After conducting a search of photographs from their own family histories, students could take time to consider the conclusions they, as social historians a century from now, might draw concerning American culture using the pictures as evidence.

As a way of bringing the concepts of time, history, and imagination into sharper focus, one could consider the following problem: Is there anything from present-day American culture worthwhile enough to save for generations of human beings 3,000 years from now? What historical artifacts from American culture should be included in a time capsule which could give historians from that era an accurate picture about the society in which we live? What values should be represented? What artifacts, including photographs, in such a time capsule would symbolize those values? The preparations for the time capsule could include student essays describing American culture for future historians. Some of the topics can range from school culture to music, art, sports, death customs, and the influence of computers as well as other technological changes. Additional essays might advance a set of predictions describing the condition of human culture in the world at some time in the future.

The study of history can contribute to the mental health of young people. It has this potential when it advances critical thinking about the nature of what it means to be a mortal human being and an active member of the body politic. This contribution is further reinforced when members of the younger generation in classrooms are given the challenge to think about the profound notion that they occupy their own time frame in history and are in their own right active participants in the historical process. Time and imagination, concepts central to the legacy left by Mark Twain and Edgar Lee Masters, are critical for this kind of history teaching.

Mr. Wegner has shown us one practical way to encourage students and teachers to "think history."

Teaching Objectives

The spirit of this principle is most directly illustrated by reflecting on two alternative objectives, both of which many teachers would endorse. One objective might be stated this way: "Sixth-grade students are expected to score at or above grade level in social studies on the 'Bull's Eye' standardized test." The second objective is stated as follows: "Sixth-grade students are expected to learn social studies and literature content in small groups by the beginning of the spring semester."

To simplify this explanation, assume two conditions to be true: (1) that the teachers will act on one or the other of these objectives in class — the objectives are not window dressing; and (2) that one of these objectives is the only one that the sixth-grade classes in an imaginary school will try to meet this year.

The objective related to the Bull's Eye standardized test scores might reasonably suggest a classroom and school environment marked by the following qualities:

- Textbooks and workbooks will be the primary materials for learning because they are readily available, they cover the content to be tested, and they are judged to be efficient.

- Facts in social studies will be emphasized over concepts because the test involves fact recall.

- Social studies content that differs from that on the test may not be taught if time pressures are great or if the school is publicly ranked with other schools on the basis of standardized test scores.

- Instruction will be didactic: pupils will read the book, listen to the teacher's elaboration of the text, and take the chapter quizzes.

Allowing for the possibility of many other (perhaps better, perhaps worse) responses to this objective, the learning/teaching environment suggested by these qualities might well have these characteristics:

- The teacher is active, the students more passive.

- The teacher/student talk in the classroom is dominated by the teacher 70% or more of the time (Goodlad 1984; Hillocks 1989). Most student talk will be in the form of short-answer responses to the teacher. This limits the amount of student talk which directly lowers the intellectual quality of the learning. Most talk will take place within the total class group.

- Trade books, such as biographies or historically-based fictional accounts of life in the colonial period, for example, are less likely to be used to supplement the text material.

- Writing experiences for the pupils may not be perceived as relevant to the test or to learning the content. Responses in workbooks or on dittoed sheets take precedence.

- Art or music activities are not thought to be substantively or motivationally related to social studies because they take time away from the "content" to be covered and tested.

So we see how an objective with certain characteristics limits the quality of the learning environment, depending on the individual and collective response of teachers. The environment developed here in response to a standardized test objective responds to the limited objective, which shows how poor objectives can drain the intellectual and social vitality from a classroom or school.

The idea connoted by Principle 6 is not to hold ourselves to a too-demanding standard that practical circumstances might well proscribe, but rather to squeeze the best learning environment possible from whatever real constraints exist. We *are* accountable for thinking and for trying things out. We *are not* responsible for achieving perfection removed from the conditions of practice.

The second objective for the imaginary 6th-grade class, to work constructively in small groups, suggests such qualities as the following:

- School is a place in which both individual and cooperative work is valued.

- Student learning activities do not have to be continuously directed nor controlled by the teacher. A social situation itself, properly set up over time, can exert a disciplinary influence.

- Group work can allow students of differing talents and abilities to succeed. This opportunity offers an alternative to dependence on total class instruction. It also opens up new avenues for student success, provides a task-oriented situation for useful talk and activity, and provides students with a chance to plan, to talk, to write, to read and discuss, or to construct something that has purpose and intellectual value.

- Students can be taught gradually to work under general teacher supervision if learning to work in groups is perceived as a complex activity in which certain skills and attitudes necessary for its success are taught.

- Students can help each other to learn by sharing responsibilities to achieve a common goal.

It is reasonable to assume that the classroom environment suggested by this objective would help to develop capacities in pupils to become more independent in their learning; to share work and responsibility among peers; to plan, organize, and execute some program or event; and to learn the persuasive, social, and political skills needed to accomplish a purpose requiring mutual sustained thought and effort. The open quality of the second objective is its strength — in the hands of good teachers; in the hands of poor teachers, its openness becomes a weakness.

The two objectives that illustrate Principle 6 suggest two very different learning environments. Each environment values certain things to be learned, and each will lead to different teacher and student behaviors and learning outcomes. Those who say that an objective is merely a clear target and all that counts is hitting it forget that to "hit it" certain *means* must be chosen. The means alter elements of the classroom environment and exert an educational influence in their own right. The quality of the *means* chosen to reach an objective may be educationally more important than the objective itself, once the latter has been chosen and judged to be desirable. This idea leads us to the next principle.

PRINCIPLE 7

EVERY GREAT TEACHER KNOWS THAT THE OBJECTIVES VALUE BOTH WHAT IS TO BE LEARNED AND HOW IT IS TO BE LEARNED. THE QUALITY OF LEARNING IS CRITICALLY DEPENDENT ON HOW THE OBJECTIVE IS ACHIEVED.

One learns both from the end achieved — the skill of adding, for example — and the process of learning itself. What one learns from the process of learning is usually implicit, subtle, below the level of conscious analysis. Processes used, however, strongly influence attitudes toward the subject, teacher, and school; they may help or hinder learner motivation. In fact, the learning processes typically used are the *primary* determinant of the *quality of the learning* (and consequently of the quality of any classroom, school, or school system).

The single most important source for improving the quality of education lies in the processes (means) used by the students, teachers, and administrators while they are learning, teaching, and leading. Any *single* "product" measure, such as standardized tests, behavioral objectives, or criterion-referenced tests, undervalues those processes. Tests alone are an insufficient base to answer questions like those posed by state legislatures and boards of education: How good are our schools? What are we getting for the millions of dollars we are spending?

One should not be intimidated by foolish talk about the measurability (often couched in the language of accountability) of school outcomes — as in "if it can't be measured, we can't know if anything good is occurring." Friendship cannot be quantitatively assessed; nor can loyalty, or love, or self-discipline, or ethical behavior, or initiative. Most of us, however, would call them "significant outcomes." Similarly, there are centrally important school goals that do not easily lend themselves to numerical ranking.

The essence of the idea behind the fundamental relationship between process and product is simple: The quality, good or poor, of any learning result (reading, say) lies in the quality of the processes used to reach it — "learning to read." As conceived by "practical" educators, objectives are qualitatively neutral, i.e., "This class will be on, or six months above, grade level by May 15." Once this objective, however limited, has been set, the only *proper* and *practical educational* concern should be a rigorous comparison and selection of the best qualitative means to get there.

Once the goals are established, the emphasis shifts to the processes used to reach them. Everything lines up behind the goals: the kinds of instructional materials used; the things kids, teachers, and principals do in school; the explicit and subtle qualities of classroom and school environment (its socio-psychological "feel"; its ethos); the kinds of student, teacher, principal, and school evaluation procedures that are used, and so on. The "lining-up" cannot be done rapidly — not even in a one-week "inservice" program! Under good conditions, coherence between means and ends is likely to be achieved slowly over years, not weeks or months.

Let's take an example at the senior high school level.

Processes Used to Achieve the Goal of Being Able to Write Standard English in Reports	
E. L. Thorndike School	Francis Parker School
Formal grammar is taught in a programmed text format.	Writing is integrated within a core block of English-Social Studies that meets eight hours per week.
Skill exercises in elements of writing (topic sentence, transitions, etc.) are completed.	Half of the work is built around periods of American history in which themes (child labor, unions, industrialization) are approached from the perspectives of literature and history.
Twice a month short papers are graded by the teacher and discussed in the total class setting.	Written work grows out of the theme work and involves experiences in peer group criticism and discussion of substantive English-Social Studies content.

Processes Used to Achieve the Goal of Being Able to Write Standard English in Reports	
E. L. Thorndike School	Francis Parker School
Grammar is taught separately from writing.	The teacher evaluates written work and shares the evaluation with the student. Occasional total class sessions on grammar are held as dictated by the written work; otherwise, grammar is taught as needed based on what a student writes.
Evaluation consists of completion of programmed text exercises, and changes in writing achievement are plotted on standardized tests required by the state.	Qualitative evaluation of the year's papers is done by each student and by small task groups; the teacher and students evaluate class processes; and standardized tests required by the state are administered.

Although the processes used by the Thorndike and the Parker schools are somewhat stereotypical, they will serve our purpose: to make more concrete the fundamental idea that educational *quality* is "built-in" by the processes used over weeks and months, and is not assessed simply by standardized test scores.

In general, Thorndike uses a more direct, "practical" approach: Grammar is taught as a separate skill indirectly related to writing; the subject is arranged in a logical, linear sequence by the programmed text; the process generally ignores factors such as integrating writing within larger "wholes" of experience; and writing is seen more as an end in itself rather than as a means to larger ends, such as creating and then sharing meaning. Parker, on the other hand, uses a meaningful process that embeds the writing in a larger "unit" and makes writing more functional and presumably more interesting. Small groups are used for peer teaching for both substantive content and writing process; they also provide a group context for oral and written communication.

This progressive and thoughtful process, in sum, provides a richer experience for all of the learner's work in English-Social Studies which should add depth to the learning. The process makes the learning more functional without detracting from its academic quality.

The evaluation of outcomes in the Parker school includes both product and process. The evaluation of the course process by both teachers and students reinforces the importance of the learning/teaching processes used and provides a valid data source from which to improve the course — at little or no cost. The qualitative assessment of written work by the teacher *asserts* the necessity for subjective, professional effort in evaluation, and recognizes that writing assessment is *inherently* subjective because of its complexity. Finally, as Calfee (1988) and Wiggins (1993) recommend, the locus of the evaluation is with those closest to the students, not in a test-construction factory miles away.

It would be reasonable to assume that although both schools teach to the target writing objective, the learning by students in the Parker school would be qualitatively superior because the means chosen to reach the objective are in themselves qualitatively superior to those of the Thorndike school.

Similarly, the teaching of science offers another way of viewing this dichotomy. Laboratory work may be used to explore questions so that the student will arrive at a solution through his or her inquiry. One school might provide laboratory work as a *verification* of what was learned in class and from the textbook. Another school might *open* the issue under investigation to a wide range of experiments. In the latter school, the solutions are unknown at the beginning of the experiment, and the student subsequently checks his or her conclusions against the established body of knowledge. Here again the two processes are qualitatively different and thereby have a different impact on the outcome.

Lynn Romney, a biology teacher at Vernal Jr. High (Utah), has a simple way to improve the "how" of learning for some students, according to Katherine Smith, a fellow teacher.

> Lynn carefully matches up students as lab and study partners. She makes sure that every student who is struggling has a partner capable of explaining labs and concepts, and then encourages cooperation. At the same time, she makes sure that the students have had a chance to learn every important concept through a variety of ways, and that students have an opportunity to pursue each topic in greater depth, according to interests and abilities.

In stark contrast to this approach, a biology department at a large high school in Salt Lake City is run in a unique fashion. Sharyle Karren, an intern in the principal's office at the time, tells the tale.

Kids in a Test Tube

The four biology teachers have their course pre-designed for them. Each teacher is expected to give the same lesson on the same day. The materials, worksheets, and guides are prepared ahead of time. When it is time for an examination, the department chair runs off the test and hands it out to the teachers on the very morning it is to be given so that the material does not get into "forbidden hands."

Each teacher complies with the pre-arranged curricular schedule and there are never any exceptions. As a consequence of the rigid sequencing of concepts, students are, in effect, "traded" back and forth among the teachers, according to who owes whom a favor and which teacher is tired of handling certain students in his or her class.

All students taking biology are expected to master the material at the same rate and under the same teaching style. As one could imagine, grading is an unpleasant reality: I know of a class in which 60% of the students received a "D" or an "F," one student received an "A," no student received a "B" and the rest received a "C"!

The pedagogical discrepancy between these two schools is staggering; yet, it is "biology" that is taught in both. Would anyone deny the validity of our claim that good objectives "reflect the understanding that the quality of learning is critically dependent on how that learning is achieved"? An interesting question that you may want to consider is, What realities might have led the high school department to adopt the sterile learning processes Karren describes above?

Finally, a mother, Lillian Zarndt, tells a poignant story of ends and means in an elementary art unit through a dialogue with her daughter.

Garbage Can Art

Elizabeth: Wow, Mom, look at those trees! They have eyes in them! (We are reading a book about a Caribbean legend, called *The Nutmeg Princess*. Elizabeth is in her pajamas; it's our good-night story.)

Mom: Yeah, I really love the artist's ideas. Look at this!

Elizabeth: It's a good thing my art teacher, Mrs. — , isn't seeing this! She'd make her throw it in the garbage and make her start over.

Mom: What do you mean? I don't understand.

Elizabeth: Well, when our pictures aren't what Mrs. ____ wants, we have to throw them in the garbage and start over. You know, the garbage can by the door. And besides, we get about three minutes to draw, and the rest of the time we're always cleaning up.

Mom: Really?

Elizabeth: Yup! And guess what. I was drawing this picture of white horses with golden hooves and the teacher said the hooves were too big and she made me throw it in the garbage and start all over again and it was just two minutes before the bell rang and then I couldn't finish my second picture and she always puts them away and then the next time I can't finish because I don't know where to find it. I think she has a closet somewhere.

Mom: Did you like your horse picture?

Elizabeth: It was sooo neat, Mom! I made the hooves really shiny and big because this was a magic horse that can fly and the hooves helped him fly and I could travel with him to places nobody knows about, just me.

Mom: Why did the teacher think the hooves were too big?

Elizabeth: Well I had to make them big because they were so important. How could the horse take off from the ground without big strong hoofs, huh?

Mom: I would love to see your white horse with golden hooves. Would you like to draw another one at home?

Elizabeth: Not really, Mom.

This story might help us understand that the quality of learning is determined by the quality of the processes used in the learning as Principle 7 suggests. It is sad when a student's best efforts end up as "garbage can art."

PRINCIPLE 8

EVERY GREAT TEACHER KNOWS THAT THE
IMMEDIATE CLASSROOM OBJECTIVES ARE
MADE WITH LARGER, OVERARCHING AIMS IN
MIND; THAT THEY FREE THE STUDENT
TO ATTAIN THE LARGER AIMS.

We teach reading in a limited setting so that students may read beyond those limits. This is obvious when stated in isolation from the flux of day-to-day school life; in practice, however, the point isn't all that clear. Consider that it was not until the 1970s that most Pennsylvania elementary schools had library collections of 8,000-10,000 books. Prior to that, it was apparent that teaching reading was implicitly viewed (insofar as the school was concerned) as an end in itself rather than as a means to wider learning.

Keeping one eye on this principle helps us to be less "teacherish," less myopic, less locked into immediate ends while forgetting ends beyond our classrooms. For example, the true end of teacher education is not ten semester credits at X university, but "good" teaching in Y town. The principle suggests that when we teach literature, for example, we ask, Does our teaching go *beyond* the teaching of literature? What proportion of our high school (or college) graduates voluntarily read literary works after graduation? If we knew the proportion, at what point would we become concerned that the objectives and processes of teaching literature may have become self-limiting, not "going beyond themselves"? Can our teaching be said to provide initiating experiences, or terminal experiences? If a high school or college graduate reads only *Time, People Magazine,* and *Cosmopolitan,* his or her whole education was indeed terminal in all senses of this scary word.

Literature is an area rich in possibilities for attending to this principle. If high school students study Camus' *The Stranger,* objectives beyond analysis and comprehension of the piece include interest in issues that emerge from it and extend beyond the school experience. For example, Is the death penalty an appropriate punishment for murder? This question itself is a stimulating source for an inquiry into the sensitive issue of how society protects itself from delinquent behavior. Other examples found in Camus' work are questions of personal integrity and the implications of compromising one's values.

Where Principle 8 speaks of "overarching aims" giving life to short-term objectives, instead of this more academic term we might have said, "a generous and humane vision." It is as true as it is unremarked by most educators that one's sense of life — how one sees its meaning and purpose — takes the clay of our intentions and makes something real of them. We ultimately teach what we are; we cannot escape the light and darkness in ourselves; it all comes out in the act of teaching or leading.

We share below the generous and humane vision of Terrance Furin, who, as superintendent of schools in the Owen J. Roberts School District, Pottstown, Pennsylvania, is bringing a moribund system to educational life. We can attest that the spirit of this lovely essay guides what Furin does when he works with groups of new teachers, with his board members, with teachers and principals in dialogue-based school reform, and with the "shop kids" who are too often written off by many of us who value a restricted view of the intellect much too highly. This piece first appeared in the Pottstown, PA, *Mercury* on September 23, 1992 (p. A8).

The Cathedral Within

Over the course of his career, Norman Cousins, editor of *The Saturday Review*, interviewed most of the world's influential people. In the course of these interviews, he usually asked the same question — "What is the most important thing you have learned in your lifetime?" The most moving response he received was from 1952 Nobel Peace Prize recipient Albert Schweitzer.

Schweitzer was a famous writer, musician, doctor, and missionary. Cousins went deep into what was then known as French Equatorial Africa to find Schweitzer, who was sharing his gifts of medicine with the native population. Over a meal one evening, Cousins asked his question. Schweitzer said that he would have to think about it and give his response at a later time. The next day Cousins awoke to find that Schweitzer had gone into a neighboring village to deliver a baby. After his return much later in the day, Schweitzer said that the most important thing he had learned in his lifetime was that each person contains a "cathedral within."

I was very moved when I heard Cousins tell his story at an educational convention several years ago. It has remained with me because the imagery of a "cathedral within" is so strong. It carries powerful implications for educational systems which are dominated by factory models of mass-production that have existed since the early 1900s.

Cathedrals are vast, complex, towering monuments to mankind's deepest yearnings and noblest aspirations. They are filled with intricate workmanship of awesome beauty containing masterworks of art and music. They are dedicated to celebrating the spiritual core of every being. Although containing many similarities, each cathedral is unique — as unique as each individual whose own cathedral embodies the unlimited grace of intelligence.

"Learning as the cultivation of intelligence" is the first of four design principles [that form] the basis of discussions for restructuring in the Owen J. Roberts School District. These discussions with teachers, administrators, students, parents, and citizens will take place over the next few years. They will sharpen the vision of the future, manifest the district's philosophy, and guide the growth of our schools. The cathedral of every person's special intelligence needs to be seen as something incredibly vast, complex, and spiritual. Such a conceptualization moves us beyond the behaviorist psychology common in the educational assembly-line emphasis on sameness — a sameness marked by uncritical memorization of encyclopedic facts.

Factory models of learning rely upon the teacher to provide "correct" information as a stimulus and the students to provide "uniform" responses. These models often break knowledge into small segments called behavioral objectives which are learned through repetitive drills. Learning seldom concentrates on higher thinking processes. Assessment is usually done through simple, machine-gradable, true-false or multiple-choice tests. Examples of sophisticated educational programs built upon these principles include Individually Prescribed Instruction (IPI), Individually Guided Education (IGE), and Mastery Learning. Other examples include reading systems which emphasize memorization of isolated rules and symbols outside of the texture and meaning of language, such as the Initial Teaching Alphabet (ITA) or a total phonics system. A basic assumption in these factory models is that general intelligence can be measured by mass tests based solely upon linguistic abilities. A different view of intelligence — and of education — is needed if American public schools are to progress beyond the factory model and prepare students for the different world of the 21st century.

Intelligence and learning need to be viewed in all of these vast complexities. Current psychologists, such as Howard Gardner, propose that the human mind is not one general intelligence but rather multiple intelligences. In his 1985 book, *Frames of Mind: A Theory of Multiple Intelligences,* Gardner develops the idea that there are essentially seven major intelligences: logical-mathematical, linguistic, musical, spatial, bodily-kinesthetic, interpersonal, intrapersonal. Schools need to recognize and develop each of these. This requires rich settings that provide for multiple differences. Intelligence has many faces, and the rote reciting of facts removed from ideas is not one of them.

One example of such a setting might be a study of the American Revolution which involves more than a memorization of chronological facts and examines alternative causes and effects based upon a hands-on study of actual historical documents. Such a study would emphasize economic, political, and social analyses and synthesize differing interpretations into a new evaluation developed by the student. Another example could be an integration of elementary art, music, and physical movement into a curriculum organized around various elements such as harmony, texture, color, and repetition.

Advocates of gifted education are well aware of the powerful possibilities which these and other examples hold for learning. What is true and good for gifted students is true and good for all students. Over the past two years, a group of students from Owen J. Roberts High School who were, for the most part, "turned off" to traditional schooling, has been involved in reading Nobel Prize authors, learning the history of Philadelphia through field experiences, and studying the ancient history of the Sumerians and Egyptians. On a recent visit to the University of Pennsylvania's Museum of Archaeology and Anthropology, one student said to another, "We're actually learning something today!" Amen.

If we are to take seriously the challenges facing our public school systems and if we hope to prepare our students for participation in the world of the next century, then we need to recognize that both intelligence and learning are extremely complex. We need to progress beyond the behaviorists' stimulus-response approaches and recognize that each person does contain a "cathedral within." Most of all, we need to help all students realize the beauty of each cathedral and act with reverence for the riches it contains.

PRINCIPLE 9

EVERY GREAT TEACHER KNOWS THAT MOST
TEACHING OBJECTIVES OUGHT TO MAKE
SENSE TO THE LEARNER AT THE TIME OF
LEARNING AND THAT FUTURE LEARNING IS
BUILT BEST ON WHAT THE STUDENT
HAS ALREADY LEARNED.

Our theory permits no gaps in one's experience. Your life experience from birth to today looks like this:

Fig. 1. "Ups" and "downs," yes; but no gaps.
There was never a day in which you did not experience something.

Your life experience does not look like the sketch in Figure 2.

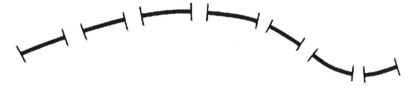

Fig. 2. Our life experiences are not disconnected from each other.

When you try to "teach" a student something, the new experience has to fit into that continuous life flow. Deficiencies in experience or knowledge cannot be filled by the teacher proposing something verbally, no matter how great the lesson plan. The lesson plan, in practical terms, can only enter at the "end" of the learner's "experience line" which occurs the moment before you teach. One's experience is continuous throughout life — not discontinuous. Life experience is like a wide river that a teacher must enter cautiously from the banks. Slowly a river will change over time, but it takes something as potent as the Army Corps of Engineers to make major changes in the river in a short time, often at great environmental cost. As a teacher you cannot, as can the engineers, change the student's "river of experience" quickly. You must know its flow and gently enter its water.

A recent Hebrew school class illustrates the point.

> The aim was to learn the Ten Commandments. It was obvious to the teacher that the Commandments, as they appear in the Bible, did not mean much to the students. Hence, the teacher undertook to view the intended learning from various perspectives which were significant to the students. The students worked in small groups on the following assignments provided to them by several teachers: give examples of each Commandment to explain its meaning; arrange them in priority according to our current social and religious values; according to your own beliefs, compare the Ten Commandments to the United States Constitution; and write your own ten commandments. The students compared their group activities and reflected upon the experience in discussion and drama.
>
> Although the students did not suggest this approach, it was of great interest to them because it fulfilled their needs. Their study was not of an isolated chapter in history, literature, or religion. Rather, it became meaningful through its relevance to current prevailing social and religious values. The ideas suggested by the teacher were stimulating; students contributed to group learning by sharing their or their families' experience in problems concerning the Ten Commandments. In this sense, the work was related to each student's continuous experience. Peer teaching, social interaction, mixing attitudes with skills and knowledge (not separating them), and showing (not telling) the significance of the subject matter to the child are all means a teacher can use to help pupils connect their present life with "today's" classroom goals.

This story suggests that even abstract content such as the Ten Commandments can sometimes be embraced by the students' previous experience if the teacher is imaginative enough to build a variety of "learning roads" that link the students' *past* experience to the *present* learning experience.

Subject Matter

PRINCIPLE 10

EVERY GREAT TEACHER KNOWS THAT ESSENTIAL CONTENT IS KNOWLEDGE OF GENERAL SOCIAL SIGNIFICANCE THAT IS RELEVANT TO ALL STUDENTS, WHATEVER THEIR ABILITIES OR INTERESTS.

PRINCIPLE 11

EVERY GREAT TEACHER KNOWS THAT CONTENT MUST BE RELATED TO THE NEEDS OF THE LOCAL AND REGIONAL COMMUNITY. IT IS INTENDED TO IMPROVE THE QUALITY OF FUTURE LIVING FOR BOTH THE COMMUNITY AND THE INDIVIDUAL. CONTENT MUST ILLUMINATE SIGNIFICANT SOCIAL ISSUES.

PRINCIPLE 12

EVERY GREAT TEACHER KNOWS THAT CONTENT DOES NOT CONSIST EXCLUSIVELY IN INFORMATION OR DATA READILY AVAILABLE IN BOOKS, COMPUTERS, OR OTHER MEDIA. RATHER, GOOD CONTENT IS SUBJECT MATTER THAT ASSISTS LEARNERS IN THEIR INQUIRY AND THEIR ATTEMPT TO CREATE MEANING.

These three propositions reinforce and build on each other in their focus on the content of subject matter. If subject matter is taught primarily as a study for specialists (as many courses from high school to college do), its significance for the broader social life is ignored. Science, for example, is typically treated in school from a technical perspective — as if science existed for its own sake. Where are the science courses that treat science as a liberal study, i.e., courses that consider what values underlie science, whether it is morally neutral, what its socially integrative and disintegrative influences are, and how it is related to technology?

Given undisputed facts about pollution of ground water in thousands of locations throughout the United States, for example, can we claim that chemistry is not also a *social* study? Given the problems of space exploration, can we say that physics, aeronautics, and space research are not also connected to social issues? We know, for example, something about earthly environmental pollution. What does that knowledge suggest about the possible pollution of space? Are we comfortable with cost estimates for space stations and military spy satellites that run to the scores of *billions* of dollars while lamenting the lack of human services for children or the homeless? And can we as a society fully confront such questions until we feel comfortable with our ability to understand them, instead of relegating them to the deliberations of biochemists, geneticists, and astrophysicists who alone, supposedly, are able to deal with such erudite topics?

In fact, the experts in too many cases have proven to be more of a bane than a boon to society. One commentator (Saul 1992) has depicted vividly the anti-social effects of technology run amok. He notes that "the experts are [not] held responsible for their own actions in any sensible manner because the fracturing of memory and understanding [in society generally] has created a profound chaos in the individual's sense of what responsibility is" (p. 17). School teachers and principals are in an enviable position to help society think sanely about the relationship between the technological and the social.

While it is true that as students mature, their ability to handle abstractions increases, teachers should not make the error of teaching as if content could be meaningfully divorced from present concerns and interests — something Principle 11 seeks to avoid. This idea suggests the importance of seeing uses for what is learned, and to be aware of how specific content relates to other pieces of content. John Holt (1964) observes: "A field of knowledge, whether it be math, English, history, science, music or whatever, is territory, and knowing it is not just a matter of knowing all the items in the territory, but of knowing how they relate to, compare with, and fit in with each other.... It is the difference between knowing the names of all the streets in a city and being able to get from any place, by any desired route, to any other place" (p. 106).

The subjects taught in schools, viewed from this larger perspective, would not primarily be seen as ends in themselves, or as something merely to be "learned" in the protective environment of the school removed from the larger social life.

With increasing amounts of information in all subject matters, you may feel a need to teach faster in order to "cover" as much material as you can, hoping that the information pumped into the learner's head will turn out somehow to be useful. Unfortunately, students cannot realistically use information that constitutes a basket of facts instead of coherent, meaningful knowledge.

In this connection, we should consider media and instructional aids provided by recent technology. Their apparent, even seductive, usefulness may lead us to provide them as a surrogate for teaching, rather than as an adjunct to it. They are so appealing and visually (or auditorily) dramatic that, without reflection, we may believe them capable of solving much of the problem of the information explosion. But, as Neil Postman (1992) points out in *Technopoly,* the attempt to relay information at greater and greater speeds and with greater and greater efficiency contributes to the *problem,* not to the solution. The problem is the *integration* and *coherence* of information, not its lack. Thus, subjecting the learner to multiple information transmitters does not necessarily serve as a base for understanding, applying, generalizing, analyzing, synthesizing — in other words, for creating personal meaning.

Rather than boring students with too many facts about World War II — the location of the Maginot Line, for example — one might instead focus on a "world-sized" idea, say the Holocaust, and have the students learn it by discovery. Probably every history book on the war mentions the terrible plight of the Jews. This string of words, likely emotion-free for many high school students today, can be given significant meaning as they start to inquire about the general issue of genocide (Indians in the United States in the 18th and 19th centuries, Armenians at the hands of the Turks in World War I, Kurds by the Iraqis in the 1960s and 1980s, and the Rwandan and the Serbian-Bosnian-Moslem horrors of the 1990s).

One could deal with the Holocaust from the standpoint of children and adolescents, using, for example, *Friedrich and I Was There* by Haris Peter Richter, *Night* by Elie Weisel, *I Never Saw A Butterfly* by H. Valavkova, and drawings and poetry by children in the Terezin concentration camp. Students could look for materials on the Holocaust with a focus on one aspect of the ordeal. They could be helped to express their knowledge, feelings, and impressions in writing, painting, discussion, or any other form.

Media (films, records, newspapers) *can* supplement classroom activities or initiate discussion of the topic, but they should not be allowed to take the place of inquiry. Basic problems, typically in the form of questions, must be explored: Why the Jews? What are sources of anti-Semitism? Why the Germans? Should the Jews have resisted more extensively? *Could* they have resisted more extensively? How is anti-Semitism connected to racism and prejudice in our society?

Have the students deal with real-world daily situations while they pursue their work: What happens if you disobey your parents or the law? If a person were being attacked physically, would you walk away, watch, call for help, or take steps to stop the fight?

Drama can play an important role in understanding the attitudes and behavior of the Germans, Jews, and other contemporaries. One could use literature about the Holocaust written by survivors (*Escape from Freedom* by Erich Fromm, *Man's Search for Meaning* by Viktor Frankl), literature about Nazi Germany (*The Tin Drum* by Gunter Grass, *Propaganda: The Art of Persuasion, WW II* by Anthony Rhodes), art created during the war, and contemporary documents to stimulate thinking, draw conclusions, and generalize ideas. Reflection on the Holocaust from the perspective of the present can be convincingly shown to be important inasmuch as neo-Fascist groups and racism are currently in the news. A visit to the Holocaust Museum in Washington, D.C., cannot but give one an almost life-like feel for this chapter in history.

When learning goes beyond registering collections of information, when it engages the learner's mind and feelings, allowing that mind to take the grasp of itself, the power and the joy of teaching and learning are realized.

Dewey believed that any normal student has the potential to share in activities that are intellectual or aesthetic — things we vaguely associate with a snobbish, museum-like idea of "culture." The typical idea of culture or of the humane studies is that they are mere ornaments —

something with which we paint the grim face of real living to impress others or to cover over what truly matters or is too painful to think about. In the democratic vein of Dewey, Richard Mitchell (1987) has made an eloquent case for the thinking ability of students. In *The Gift of Fire* he writes that the great human possibility is that the mind "can take the grasp of itself and its works" (p. 22). While this power is, he acknowledges, "probably unavailable to infants and lunatics, *in the absence of some such special impediment, who can be without it?*" (p. 22, emphasis added).

Let us back up a bit here. These propositions are demanding. No school on earth can meet the spirit of these propositions every day with every student or every teacher. Public schools typically are not organized to give everyone "broad and liberal studies," i.e., studies worthy of a free individual in a democratic society (including, yes, the "vo-tech kids," and the kids in the "low reading group"). Nor are schools typically eager to relate learning to the people, activities, and institutions in the local community as Principle 11 emphasizes. Nor are schools "big" on using subject matter to further inquiry, the thoughtful consideration of ideas, by students or teachers as Principle 12 requires. Yet, since schools do not typically do these things, all the more reason to do them as often and as well as we can. Leavening the boredom and rigidity of schooling in itself is a good thing. By doing so, we give our students and ourselves a hint of what learning and teaching could be. Teacher and students improve their intellectual and social growth in these ways. Why not cultivate ourselves for a more rich and generous life as we cultivate our gardens in the warming sun of summer?

Before we give some positive examples that relate the spirit of these principles to real-life teachers and students, let us insert a brief story about the potential problems flowing from the impersonal nature of technology, an implication of Principle 12. This is from Forrest Williams, then a high school English teacher in Provo, Utah.

Ask the Computer!

Recently, I read a piece by Vito Perrone (1989) in *A Letter to Teachers* in which he was concerned about the learner's inability to assess his or her own performance in a social studies class. My concern went even deeper, however. In Perrone's example, the student responded to the question, "How are you doing in social studies?" with the admission, "I don't know, you'll have to ask my teacher." Yet, the very day I read this I was asked by one of my students, "Mr. Williams, how am I doing in English?" to which I responded, "I don't know; I'll have to check the computer. That's the only way I can be sure how you are doing."

Even as the event unfolded I was shocked! There was I — in my own mind a fine, progressive teacher — a living example, right out in public, of the very problem that Perrone was writing about: *Students* aren't expected to know how they're doing — *teachers* are; or in my case, the *computer* was the source of knowledge!

Now, to some vignettes illustrating the difficulty in bringing about the changes prefigured by the three subject matter principles. That difficulty is suggested in the examples from the Owen J. Roberts School District, Pottstown, Pennsylvania, in which one of the authors is working with teachers and principals in a dialogue-based reform effort. At the time of this writing (early 1994), most of the progressive examples of learning and teaching in this district are add-ons to standard curriculum, teaching, and testing practices, such as those John Goodlad (1984) describes so well in *A Place Called School*. But these add-ons to a standard curriculum demonstrate some feeling by teachers that improvement is needed.

The first example shows how housing for poor families, landscape architecture, and historical preservation link in a volunteer-community project by high school students in the district. The story was printed in the Owen J. Roberts School District bulletin, *The Advocate*, published in December, 1993.

Building Houses and Restoring a Meadow

"Not expecting to be paid for their work [repairing a floor for a needy family] was a new concept for them," said Ms. Tinder. "They learned how important it is to extend a hand and help people out. I think the kids felt good about a hard day of physical work, learning something new and helping a needy family."

The outing was also an opportunity to extend the classroom beyond its walls at the high school, and give the students a chance to put theory into practice, she said. And there are plans for more such expeditions in the future.

In another project the students and their talents in landscaping have caught the eye of Robert W. Montgomery, owner of the region's award-winning nursery and landscape design firm in Chester Springs. The result is a collaboration with Historic Yellow Springs where efforts are underway to recreate the natural ambience that surrounded the historic buildings in the 1920s when the Pennsylvania Academy of Fine Arts conducted their landscaping school there.

One of the major projects at Yellow Springs has been the restoration of a meadow that reflects a turn-of-the-century design with ponds, a stream, spring houses, appropriate planting, and a pathway that winds through it all. This fall the OJR students planted bulbs as part of that project, and next spring they will plant a butterfly garden there.

Mr. Montgomery, said Ms. Tinder, has been a terrific resource for the program. He donated the materials for last year's open house, he conducted the class with the Yellow Springs project, and he hires the students to work in his business.

These experiences lead the students in new directions, and help them solidify choices about their futures, observed Ms. Tinder. They also enhance the reputation of OJR and its students in the community.

The next example from an elementary school in the district extends the idea of community to the rain forests of South America (Principle 11), involves all students in the unit regardless of their ability (Principle 10), and surely helps these third and fourth graders to create "personal meaning," a goal some critics might reject as being too soft, too unmeasurable for a rigorous education (Principle 12). The principal and teachers involved are the source of this narrative.

Tropical Rain Forest Thrives

When the Vincent Elementary PTO invited rain forest expert Bruce Segal for a school-wide assembly about this threatened ecosystem, little did anyone realize what doors this single event would open. In preparation for Segal's visit, third- and fourth-grade teachers decided to incorporate the rain forest into their lessons. And like a wild vine, the rain forest become an integral part of not just science class, but wrapped around reading, writing, art, and social studies, too.

Eventually, the entire student body hopped on the wave of enthusiasm, and what finally emerged in a formerly empty room was a true model of the rain forest in all its splendor.

There is the floor of the forest, the understory, the canopy and the emergent layer. And there are the creatures that call the rain forest home — delightfully colorful and whimsical paper renditions of monkeys, anteaters, toucans and other birds, three-toed sloths, frogs and butterflies. To complete the scene a tape of rain forest sounds plays softly in the background.

This magical room is a vivid example of what can happen when creativity and flexibility merge into an explosion of learning.

"It was total integration — total submersion into the subject," said fourth-grade teacher Nancy Swart. "It engaged every child, it gave a reason for learning, it was totally motivating. However bright they are, they were challenged to the limits."

For example, in language arts class the students read a book about the rain forest and the efforts being made to save it from destruction. They wrote a play based on the book, made their own masks for different roles in the play, and video-taped the production for other classes to use.

They learned about the impact of deforestation on the ecosystem and what its loss means to them. And they learned about the lives of people who live there.

Instead of some far-off remote place where Tarzan swings on the vines, the rain forest became something real and vital in the students' lives, said Swart.

By setting aside the artificial boundaries of time, and integrating the basics into a smooth unit of study that encompassed the 3 R's and much more, simple words on a page were transformed into an exciting chance to learn.

One of the writers of this book had an opportunity to visit this colorful, papier-mâchè rain forest with its butterflies, anteaters, flowers, vines, and trees. To the taped sounds of jungle birds and animals in the background, Angelika, my fourth-grade guide, took me on a tour. Angelika seemed knowledgeable. Explanations and sentences flowed easily: "A lot of animals climb trees to the upper canopy of the rain forest." Pause. She adds thoughtfully, "But not if they don't fly!" As we climbed through vines and stepped across a small stream, she said, "Iguanas run on the top of water. Like on water skis, sort of." We pause to look at a land crab and her babies in the water. "Mike and Josh made those," Angelika notes; her voice suggests pleasure at their accomplishment.

At the end of the tour, Angelika agreed to do a short interview.

Interviewer: Did you like the project?

Angelika: Lots. Kids see their work when they go on tour in the forest. If one kid did it, it would not be as neat.

Interviewer: What did you enjoy most?

Angelika: Writing reports on the forest and papier-mâché. I'm a very organized person. I like to write anything.

Interviewer: What did you learn?

Angelika: Need to protect the rain forest in other countries. They give us oxygen and animals. There are five layers in the rain forest. I will remember some of this when I grow up. Then I want to explore it with my own eyes … see the real thing. This is just a paper rain forest here.

Interviewer: What did your parents think about this unit?

Angelika: They like it a lot. They think it's "extra," though. I think it's part of what we study. All schools should do school-wide projects [this statement refers to rain forest visits by children in other grades]. We did all the work, and we like to show it to people.

Interviewer: Would you like to tell me anything else?

Angelika: The whole thing makes me feel good. I like to answer questions. Feel proud. All of us put a lot of work into it. We shared. Everyone got to have some fun in making things to be part of the rain forest. There is lots to see in here. Someone showed me a sock animal. I didn't see it before. Lots of things you don't notice the first time.

There is no doubt that Angelika is a good student (the teachers were taking no chances with my guide!). Nonetheless, I am certain that if I interviewed every student in the grades who worked on the unit, their responses would show the same joy, personal meaning, and knowledge of something beyond their direct personal experience as Angelika displayed. An activity like this rain forest unit is "all" (to oversimplify in the interests of clarity) that the principles we write about require to make learning and teaching more thoughtful and more personally and socially useful. Try something like this unit with some of your colleagues. It's work, but it's usually work with additional satisfaction.

Teaching Methods

PRINCIPLE 13

EVERY GREAT TEACHER RECOGNIZES THAT
GOOD METHODS MEAN THE CREATION OF A
TOTAL SCHOOL/CLASSROOM ENVIRONMENT FOR
LEARNING THAT CULTIVATES THE
INTELLIGENCE AND SENSITIVITIES OF
LEARNERS, TEACHERS, AND ADMINISTRATORS.

PRINCIPLE 14

EVERY GREAT TEACHER UNDERSTANDS THAT
DIRECT ATTENTION TO RESULTS FOR THEIR
OWN SAKE THROUGH ROTE LEARNING
SHORT-CIRCUITS MEANINGFUL EXPERIENCE
AND CLOSES DOWN THE GROWTH OF
INTELLIGENCE. NEITHER ENDS NOR MEANS
CAN BE HURRIED IF ONE WISHES TO
PROVOKE THOUGHTFUL LEARNING.

A good school creates learning environments. Although a good school has a general plan for curriculum and may use textbooks (but not to the exclusion of real books from the library), and the teachers in a good school do plan lessons, all of these elements are directed and unified by a few big ideas that help shape a better classroom and school learning environment. Every classroom and school in this country has a learning environment whether the teachers and principals ever think or talk about it or not. The environment is simply there because it is precipitated by what the principal, the teachers, the students, and the community think is important in life and by what all of these actors on the school stage do.

The Owen J. Roberts School District, Pottstown, Pennsylvania, uses four big ideas to guide its reform effort. These design principles arose from discussions with teachers and principals and from a survey and discussion with several hundred parents and citizens in the community. The school board adopted the four principles which we elaborate below.

Four Principles on Which to Build a Better School Environment

- The primary purpose of learning is to cultivate the intelligence and sensitivities of students and teachers.
- Learning is an active process.
- The interaction of students and teachers should be dynamic, inquiring, and vigorous so that increasingly more *independent learning* is desired by students and teachers.
- Flexible patterns of organizing time, subjects, and teachers with students need to be used to support the first three principles.

These principles and a dialogue-based inservice program in which teachers and principals read serious books on learning, educational history, and theory (such as John Dewey's), are beginning to show some concrete results. The account below shows how three teachers who are in the dialogue group at the Warwick School, Owen J. Roberts School District, took action that reflects the spirit of Principles 13 and 14. This account is taken from *The Advocate*, November, 1993, a school district newspaper that goes to people in the community.

Children Make the Connections

During this past summer three fourth-grade teachers at Warwick — Fern Gleason, Darlene Hofmeister, and Nick Zurga — took a hard look at the curriculum and realized that, based on their classroom experiences, there was a better way of teaching it.

So, with a little tinkering here and there, they have modified the current curriculum and turned it into a lively, dynamic learning experience for their students. They accomplished this by rearranging the old lessons into a group of ten unifying themes — themes that serve to tie all the lessons from science, social studies, language arts, and math together into integrated units.

The result is a much more natural learning style, say the teachers, one that is more "hands on" for the students and one that is more flexible for the teachers, freeing them from the constraints of the clock. One lesson flows into the next keeping students' interest at a peak and reinforcing previous lessons.

"The children are making connections," said Ms. Hofmeister. "This makes learning more valuable because it makes more sense. It gives classes more of a focus."

At the beginning of each thematic unit, basic questions about that theme are posed and, by the end of the unit, the students are expected to answer them.

"Systems" was the first theme of this year, and the questions asked required the students to identify the reasons systems are important in everyday life, and what can be learned from them. Their interest was piqued by an introductory brainstorming session in which students identified systems in their lives — everything from stereo systems to septic systems.

Then they got to work. In social studies they learned as part of geography the systems used to design maps and how to read them, and that process carried over into current events. Science focused on weather systems, including air currents, air pressure, moisture in the air, and the water cycle.

Under the language arts banner, their writing skills — another system — were developed. They designed graphic organizers, and read books that enhanced their study of weather systems such as *Night of the Twisters*. In math they learned about temperature, weight, and how to use systems to solve problems.

The knowledge gained from this theme was demonstrated when the children were asked to design a system and then explain through writing and demonstration how it worked — a form of testing known as performance assessment.

Theme units for the rest of the year include challenges, structure and function, balance, diversity, patterns, cycles, changes, interactions, and time and progress. The amount of time spent on each theme varies between two and five weeks, depending on the complexity of the material studied.

Parents are excited by the concept, asking that they be informed of the theme in advance so they can follow through at home. The integrative model can also be adapted by other grades and curricula throughout the district.

Since most of us are traditional teachers trying to make the transition as educational pilots to the more exotic and satisfying "progressive" type of airplane, it is worthwhile to hear the story of Susan Moon, a veteran high school teacher in rural Georgia. Ms. Moon has made the transition from more traditional teaching to Foxfire's holistic approach. Moon's story is in the same vein as that of the three Warwick teachers who are experimenting with larger themes and frameworks to make the content they teach more coherent. Foxfire's eleven core practices[7] provide the framework for Ms. Moon's teaching.

Foxfire's core practices help insure that a supportive classroom and school environment are being created within which the teachers and students do their learning. This meets the criteria of Principle 13. As you read Ms. Moon's story, it becomes clear that this is no drill-for-skill classroom in which subject matter is cut off from students' meaningful experience, as Principle 14 suggests ought not be done. "I like being a facilitator," Ms. Moon writes. "It is pretty exciting when my students become articulate...enough to...be successful in ways that I could not have planned or even imagined." Our experience suggests that if more classrooms offered the rich environment that Susan Moon offers, the number of kids "diagnosed" as learning disabled and ADD (Attention Deficit Disorder) would drop markedly. Ms. Moon's story appeared in the December 1996 issue of *The Active Learner: A Foxfire Journal for Teachers*.

Ms. Moon's English-journalism class is made up of students in grades 9 through 12. This Foxfire class does more than publish a good newspaper — important as that is — but it also is filled with real-life experiences that make a class hum: folklore, oral histories, and mentoring.

Seven Years in a Foxfire Classroom
"Itching" to Re-examine the Core Practices

As I enter my seventh year of implementing the Foxfire approach, I am reminded of the title of a Marilyn Monroe movie, *The Seven Year Itch*. I am "itching" to re-examine the Core Practices as I use them in my classroom.

Please pardon me while I scratch....

Core Practice #1: All the work teachers and students do together must flow from student desire, student concerns.

M-m-m-m! This one feels good!

I can definitely attest to the fact that work in my Back Roads class is infused from the beginning with student choice, design, revision, execution, etc. In fact, the whole first two weeks of each term is spent brainstorming what this year's group wants our class to be.

Even when I tell them that Back Roads does not have to include a product, each class since the first one in the fall of 1990 has chosen to focus on newspaper and magazine production. Storytelling, oral histories, folklore, sharing family traditions, and mentoring projects with the primary and elementary schools are other aspects of the class that have continued to crop up in our brainstorming sessions.

How can I be sure that students' ideas are not overly influenced by me? It helps that during those brainstorming sessions, I am walking around the room with mirrored shades covering my eyes and a wide piece of masking tape covering my mouth, so that I can't influence the students' brainstorming with wide or rolling eyes, excited gasps, or dejected moans.

I have not always agreed with the projects they have come up with, but I have learned from experience to let them work through the projects themselves. Sometimes, I've been pleasantly surprised that a project I felt was completely undoable turned out to be not only doable but profitable as well. One example was our Back Roads Rock-a-Thon, an all-night outside affair that debuted on the coldest night in November, with twenty-odd students rocking in rocking chairs to collect pledge money.

Now the Rock-a-Thon is an annual tradition with former students returning to rock along with us. And you ought to see all the kinds of writing that goes into that project: advertisements, brochures, pledge letters, and much, much more.

Core Practice #2: Therefore, the role of the teacher must be that of collaborator, team leader, and guide rather than boss.

Oooh, yeah! This one's feelin' good, too.

I like being a facilitator, though it isn't always easy. I can see concrete examples of the effects that turning responsibility for learning back on students has on their lives. It is pretty exciting when my students become articulate and powerful enough to take on and be successful in ways that I could not have planned or even imagined.

Still, I admit that it is a struggle each year to get my new students to adjust to my role as a facilitator. Some students who haven't developed the self-discipline required to guide their own learning keep waiting for me to stand over them with a yardstick every minute saying, "Do this! Do that! Not that way! This way!" Sometimes, these students catch fire and become the most active and assertive learners of all. More often than I would like (which is never!) they struggle the entire semester and make a quick exit at the end of the term. It kills me because it doesn't hit every student, and I wish I knew why.

It amazes me that in 1996, there are still students who just can't handle being in a classroom where the teacher asks — yes, even expects — them to take responsibility for their own learning. In the words of several former Back Roads students, "Back Roads is what you make it: It works if you work!"

Core Practice #3: The academic integrity of the work must be absolutely clear.

That's it! Keep scratchin', baby!

I believe this question is answered in my school system every year when my Back Roads juniors' scores are consistently among the highest in our school on the Georgia High School Graduation Test in Writing. Now, I do not take full credit for those scores — they are the sum total of our work together and the good teaching that came before. However, the fact that all my students have scored consistently higher, and that none of them has ever failed the test the first time, does speak pretty loudly.

But then we take our skills seriously. The second week of school, my Back Roads students are introduced to the State Language Arts and Composition objectives. They are also informed that whatever projects and activities they choose must — no excuses accepted — ensure that they meet these objectives. I find that as the year progresses, the objectives are met time and again — and then some.

Core Practice #4: The work is characterized by student action rather than passive receipt of processed information.

Core Practice #5: A constant feature of the process is its emphasis on peer teaching, small group work, and teamwork.

Core Practice #7: There must be an audience beyond the teacher for student work.

and ...

Core Practice #8: As the year progresses, new activities should gracefully spiral out of the old, incorporating lessons learned from past experiences, building on skills and understandings that can now be amplified.

My Back Roads students do not use a textbook to learn about magazine and newspaper production. They learn from studying other newspapers and magazines, and they learn through experience — their own and that of previous students who teach them how to avoid making the same mistakes. Each experienced student has to train another student to take his place.

Taking ownership of the newspaper and magazine also teaches students how to think for themselves. The key word in that last sentence is *think*. The Foxfire approach encourages students to think, to act for themselves, and to accept the responsibility for their thoughts and the consequences of their actions. Sometimes when my students try a new idea for the newspaper or magazine, it bombs! In other words, they fail, but in failing they learn that falling flat on your face means you're still heading forward, and that's what counts. The only true failure in my class is failing to try.

Another case emphasizing just how well these four Core Practices have been "scratched" is my Spanish I class. They asked one day, "Why can't we do something fun like Back Roads is always doing?" This led to a brainstorming session about how they could prove to me that they had learned the language. Several students piped up with, "Why can't we go teach what we learn each week to some students in the primary school?" Thus another project was born — with three groups of Spanish I students traveling across the street to visit three primary school classes (K-2) every other week. There, they taught the little ones what they themselves had learned the previous week.

My students made lesson plans, activities, and evaluation instruments geared to the young learner. Their own evaluation instrument invited the primary school teachers to evaluate their success in implementing the Spanish language with that teacher's class.

What happened as a result of this approach to Spanish? When these same students took Spanish II with me the next year, they wanted to pursue the project again. This time so many primary and elementary teachers had heard of their success, we had twelve partnered groups of students traveling weekly to the primary and elementary classes, serving more than twenty-four teachers in kindergarten through fifth grade.

Now, that's some spiraling, folks!

May I insert an interesting tidbit here? Because my students were doing all this teamwork and peer teaching at the primary and elementary school, we were unable to cover as many chapters in the Spanish text as had the students across the hall. Was I worried? You bet! Would my students be able to compete at the end of the year? Happily, I can answer this with a resounding YES! My students placed second in State Spanish I competition and first in State Spanish II competition.

What does this prove? In my opinion, it proves that living the language, experiencing it, and becoming actively engaged in it provided my students with a learning experience unequaled by a mere textbook approach. Applying the Foxfire approach to Spanish I and II gave my students ownership in the language. I'll never be able to go back to the old way.

Core Practice #6: Connections between the classroom work and surrounding communities and the real world outside the classroom are clear.

and …

Core Practice #9: As teachers, we must acknowledge the worth of aesthetic experience, model that attitude in our interactions with students, and resist the momentum of policies and practices that deprive students of the chance to use their imaginations.

OooEeee! That scratch feels S-O-O-O-O GOOD!

Students in my American Lit, Spanish I and II, and Back Roads classrooms make dozens of connections between the classroom work, their own communities and the world beyond. This happens when students:

- gather and publish "Eldertales"
- travel to the home of Mrs. Bertha Bankston, whose grandmother was a slave in Pike County, in order to capture her essence on paper

- interview local artisan and potter, Jim Webber, to learn about an ancient art form and his link to "brothers in clay"
- strengthen their interviewing skills by inviting speakers to class from the surrounding communities

While watching a potter spin his wheel may be an aesthetic experience all its own, the personal aesthetic experience is best summed up by former student Ryan Wisler, an editorial cartoonist who ended up expressing himself through his artwork. As a newcomer from Oregon, he was thrown into Back Roads because of scheduling problems and wondered what he was doing in a writing class when he "couldn't write." Ryan won the Back Roads award his junior year because, as he realized, "This is the only class I've ever had which played on my strengths and not my weaknesses."

Students who are willing to look can find their own niches in Foxfire classrooms across the nation because Foxfire lends itself to individual aesthetic experiences.

Core Practice #10: Reflection — some conscious, thoughtful time to stand apart from the work itself — is an essential activity that must take place at key points throughout the work.

Core Practice #11: The work must include unstintingly honest, ongoing evaluation for skills and content, and changes in student attitude.

I think that the real itch is over here and that by scratchin' it I've died and gone to heaven!

These two practices have become such an important component of my own classroom that it is hard for me to believe I ever existed without them. On any given day, you might walk into my classroom and find a class meeting in progress. It has usually been called by a student to iron out some problem, discuss a change of plans or simply to get feedback from the rest of the class on an idea she/he has had.

Journals are a weekly part of this class and students don't get any more honest than in their journal entries. They tell me the good, the bad and the ugly about the class, which helps me assess the climate of the classroom.

The finished products — the newspaper, the literary magazine — allow us to stand back and take a good long look at what we have accomplished. Is it all we had imagined or hoped it would be? Better? Worse? How can we make it better? It is during these periods of reflection and ongoing evaluation that the beauty of the Foxfire teaching approach shines through for me. During those class meetings, reflective brainstorming sessions, and journal reading, I can see wheels of thought turning, ideas forming and problem-solving taking place. It is then that I catch a glimpse of my future, which is in good hands if run by students like these, who have learned to think for themselves and work together to reach a democratic solution to that which ails us.

I guess you could say I'm a Foxfire-convinced teacher. But you need to know, folks, Foxfire is not a panacea or miracle cure for all that ails education and schools today. It does encourage students to take an active role in the learning process by including them in decisions about how — not whether — they learn. And when they catch the fire, they really excel.

Yep, I'd say that my seven-year itch has just been scratched. These eleven Core Practices are not only viable in my classroom, they have become a part of me.

Having had that itch scratched so well, I will lay me down to rest.

What idea (or ideas) — basic principles of learning and teaching — did Susan Moon try to follow in constructing her learning environment? Do you think Ms. Moon needs to buy and use a commercial communications package to raise her students' self-esteem, or use other popular packaged topics, such as "conflict resolution," "thinking skills," "cooperative learning," or "classroom management"? Perhaps she should avail herself of the very latest hot inservice topic — "social skills training" — that invokes rat-maze psychology (Behaviorism) to make kids unthinkingly conform to unnecessarily restrictive school rules, the kinds of rules that support the boring teaching John Goodlad describes so well in *A Place Called School*.

Other principles in *What Every Great Teacher Knows* suggest some of the elements in learning and teaching that must be modified to avoid too direct attention to results. See, for example, Principle 4 on the learner's foresight of ends, and Principle 10 that says broad, general knowledge of social significance should be taught (particularly in the unspecialized world of K to 12 public education).

We make our schools what they are for good or ill by the things we *do*. Our actions, not our words or good intentions, reveal our implicit, generally unexamined *theories* of learning and teaching. "Simple" actions shape the social and intellectual environment — and the emotional environment — in our classrooms. Patti Mortensen, then a third-grade teacher in Provo, Utah, recounts an anecdote about a teacher who probably thought she was doing fine teaching. From this one incident, assuming that this event is true of the teacher's larger pattern of teaching, can you infer some of her deepest beliefs about children, motivation, and learning?

"Losers" Are Made, Not Born

I once substitute-taught for a third-grade teacher. After each and every assignment that was completed, the children would pass their paper to the person behind them for correcting. After the correcting was completed a percentage grade was assigned to each paper and returned to its owner. At this point, the children were then called upon to call out their scores to the teacher for entry into the grade book. I was astonished at the thoughtless disregard for the children's feelings. One student consistently received the lowest score on every assignment and each time he called out his score he was labeled by himself and other students as a "loser."

It is painful to think that there is even one teacher whose *theory* of teaching could lead her to this kind of unnecessary hurtfulness.

PRINCIPLE 15

EVERY GREAT TEACHER SELECTS PROBLEMS FOR THOUGHTFUL AND MEANINGFUL ANALYSIS THAT ARE WITHIN THE EXPERIENCE OF THE LEARNER AT THE START OF THE LEARNING, RELATED TO THE PROBLEMS OF ORDINARY LIFE, AND REQUIRE THOUGHT OR REFLECTION ABOUT THE CONSEQUENCES OF ACTIONS TAKEN TO SOLVE THE PROBLEM.

Learning begins with a problem of concern to the learner. He or she tries to do something, the content of which is within his or her present experience (read a book, solve x + 2 = -3, understand a word, sing a piece of music, sketch a boulder, pass a football, approach the problems of how we can change what we do in this school to cultivate more effectively intelligent actions by teachers, students, and administrators).

If a school faculty (or a subgroup of the faculty) asked itself how their school might be made more thoughtful, Principle 15 would apply explicitly. The question calls for action that is within the present experience of the faculty, that relates to the concerns of their everyday life, and that requires thought.

Educators cannot forget or ignore the following fundamental principle, laid down not only by Dewey, but by other educators: Learning, i.e., growth, cannot "skip over" essential experiences that connect the past to the present. There should be an overlap between the student's previous experience (past learning) and the new experience (present learning or what-is-to-be-learned). Figure 3 presents these ideas visually. Sometimes the "linking experiences" can be adequately supplied by vivid vicarious experience such as a film, field trip, or even a discussion.

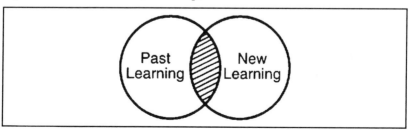

Figure 3. Desirable Education. The shaded area represents past learning (all of one's experiences) overlapping with new learning (what one has not experienced).

The overlap of past and new experiences increases the likelihood that the new learning will "take root" because the new learning is linked to, and becomes an outgrowth of, one's past learning. You as a teacher or principal constantly invoke this principle when it comes to *your own learning*. If we said to you, for example, that we would read and discuss selected chapters from Lawrence Cremin's classic history of education, *The Transformation of the School,* your first comment would be: "Why read *that*? What good will it do [me]? All I want is something concrete to make this curriculum better." If we were moderating your staff development dialogue, the question of "connection" to your past learning should be addressed up front; however, the worth of Cremin's book can only be assessed during and after you encounter it because as you read and discuss it in the dialogue, many of you will make connections that cannot be foreseen prior to the experience with the book.

Learning at any present moment is fed and nurtured by all of one's past learning. New learning enters the mind through the door of memory, past learning. What we have experienced in life — what we have truly learned — influences what we choose to learn in any present time, how deeply we learn it, and how much we like learning what is new. Sometimes when we are pursuing an interest on our own, or working through some complex issue whose core solution seems to lie within shields of granite, we feel as if our mind, feelings, and body have pushed out a bit and led us to occupy a richer life space. Our satisfaction is deep, the air intoxicating. These rare moments of deep intrinsic learning must be an organic development beyond all the learning that preceded them: beyond, yes, but rooted in and growing from all that one had previously learned. This is the psychological continuity of which Dewey speaks and toward which mere "curriculum continuity" — often helpful but still more paper intentions than anything psychologically real — points us. Our teacherly work can only come to life in the theatre of the mind, a theatre of "simultaneous possibilities," as William James said.

We know that teachers and principals invoke this principle often *when their own learning is at issue*. If we said to you, for example, in the first two years of a teacher/principal dialogue that we ought to read the piece from which James's quotation is taken, would we not get many comments like these: "Why read that? What good will I get from it? Why not something practical and contemporary that speaks to my problems of classroom management?" One thing these not-so-hypothetical comments say is this: *"Given all that I have learned to this moment, William James and that stuff doesn't seem to 'fit.' And because it doesn't 'fit' with my past experience, I cannot ingest it and I must, therefore, reject it."*

Your students are very much like you. They try to fit what you are trying to teach them into their past experience. Even rejection speaks to this connection between past and new learning. Although you as a teacher cannot make a tight connection with your students' past learning, even three days a month with 25 or 120 kids, you can try. You can try to build bridges (however small their timbers) that might invite more of your students to surmount the void between what they now know and what they do not know — the new content you are about to teach. The right kind of discussion about how new content might inform some issue of importance (such as the apparent decline in relatively secure, well-paying jobs for white- and blue-collar, middle-class workers) might help forge that essential connection between what you are teaching and the students' past experience. The job future is not very bright for the students in your classes, far less bright than it was, say, for youth beginning work before 1980.

Or you might provide a "linking bridge" between what they know and what you want them to know through a field trip, a speaker, a good film, or maybe even a keen and well-prepared lecture-pep talk — by you. Or you might jump right in and build your linking bridges later. In an English class, for example, the novel to be studied is *Huckleberry Finn*. Although you do the usual things to orient students to the novel and to arouse interest, you might also say, "We are going to spend the first third of our time on this story by addressing this question: How does it help you to see some of your concerns as a teenager in new ways? Is there any connection between Huck's and Jim's concerns and yours? Of course, you might not see any connection between your life and the novel. We'll air these ideas, too." The point here is not the novel as a thing to be learned, but the novel as a vehicle to begin a consideration of their life experience in the context of formal school subject matter.

The arrows in Figure 4 below represent the "experience gap" between what the student knows — his past experience — the minute before you launch your "hot" lesson — his new learning; the new learning has not yet entered his experience stream.

In this diagram, because the new learning does not overlap with past learning, the continuity of experience is broken. Both the student and the teacher may then be forced into the expedients of rote "learning" and

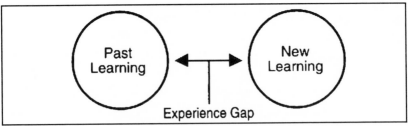

Figure 4. Undesirable Education

drill on unrelated parts of the content such as formulas in mathematics, dates in history, or the textbook definition of inertia in physics.

Two mistakes are to be avoided as we try to apply this principle to our work as teachers. First, we must not expect complete success immediately. "Success" in teaching, as in learning, comes slowly over long periods of time (perhaps two to three years, in the case of complex ideas; perhaps even a lifetime). Learning to meet the spirit of Principle 15 is more difficult, for example, than learning to write the crisp, clear (and often trivial) behavioral objectives advocated by supporters of mastery learning or other ways of teaching that are rooted in a mechanical theory of learning and teaching.

Second, we must not in the early stages of application feel an obligation to try out this principle simultaneously in most of the subjects we teach. Instead, we should try it out in the areas with which we are most comfortable. We should be sensitive, change, adapt, and respect criticism, but not give up with a feeling of failure. The secret consists in steady, persistent efforts to achieve an *environment* where teacher and student will want to participate, communicate, and experience learning. The answer is not a revolution of current practice but rather a gradual evolution and expansion of improved practice.

John Dewey (1944/1916) posed the challenge clearly:

> No one has ever explained why children are so full of questions outside of school ... and the conspicuous absence of display of curiosity about the subject matter of school lessons. Reflection on this striking contrast will throw light upon the question of how far customary school conditions supply a context of experience in which problems naturally suggest themselves. No amount of improvement in personal technique of the instructor will wholly remedy this state of things. There must be more actual material, more stuff, more appliances, and more opportunities for doing things, before the gap can be overcome [p. 155].

We never educate directly, but indirectly by means of the environment [p. 19] ... [in] setting up conditions which stimulate certain
visible and tangible ways of acting [p. 34]. In such shared activity,
the teacher is a learner, and the learner is, without knowing it, a
teacher — and upon the whole, the less consciousness there is, on
either side, of either giving or receiving instruction, the better [p.
160].

Some aspects of Piagetian theory support parts of Principle 15, although Piaget was less interested in the "problems of ordinary life" than
he was in reasoning in science and mathematics.

- For Piaget and his followers, intelligence is the most necessary
  instrument of learning; hence, learning of facts and skills is
  subordinate in importance and emphasis to the thinking aspect,
  the primary reason for all activities (Furth and Wachs 1974).

- It is not how *fast*, but how *far* we can facilitate the growth of
  intelligence that is significant (Duckworth 1979).

How does the learner "move" to a higher level of understanding?
What Piaget found significant is that understanding *results from a conflict
arising in the child's own mind*. It is the child's own *effort* to resolve a conflict
that takes him or her to another level (Duckworth 1979; see Principle 2).
It occurs when "truth is not given ready-made in the world, nor is an
absolute norm imposed on the child" (Furth & Wachs 1974, p. 19).

- Commenting on the use of outside stimuli in learning
  acceleration experiments, Piaget questioned whether new ideas
  introduced in this way might not create learner dependency on
  such outside "pushes" to learn, rather than developing the
  learner's own initiative in pursuing relationships among ideas
  (Duckworth 1979). The motivation for learning is intrinsic when
  children move into situations they find rewarding (Furth and
  Wachs 1974).

- New knowledge is always based on previous knowledge; new
  knowledge is a result of the refinement and reintegration of the
  knowledge one already has (Duckworth 1979).

We argue, with respect to these principles, that Piaget's ideas require
an intelligent (less hurried and more democratic) adaptation of many
present practices in school administration, curriculum, and teaching.

Take, for example, typical "practical" school procedures. A good case (not an absolute one) can be made that present types of school organization, as well as curriculum and instruction practices, either (1) do not "work" for many kids (be they "bright" or average), or (2) work less well if *educational* criteria are used, rather than the more circular *schooling* criteria: student passivity, facts and skills isolated from problem solving, excessive teacher talk and direction, and little chance for students to generate problems of academic and democratic significance. Educational criteria relate learning to life outside the school and are not limited to tiny, fragmented steps of lessons, or even one-year courses or grades; they contemplate learning that results in understanding something; learning that enhances one's capacity and confidence; learning that is thinking.

It is time that teachers and administrators speak up for the conditions required for better learning. No other source is so powerful and so close to the action. Reflect on one very practical problem — that of trying to teach a great deal of content in an effort to accelerate learning. If we selected learning experiences in a manner consistent with the spirit of Principle 15, think of the changes that might result in the never-ending "content" of social studies, sciences, and English/Language Arts. Adoption of the following provocative idea from Grant Wiggins and exploration of the practices that flow from it would foster intelligent curriculum development: The right curriculum, Wiggins asserts, is the one that "develops in students the habits of mind required for a lifetime of recognizing and exploring one's ignorance" (1989, p. 57).

If social studies is, for example, among the subjects least liked by secondary students, and if the content is not learned, even measured by its own limited criteria, what do we have to lose by more intelligently redefining it?

Our reform agenda for better civic preparation might come from a small-as-yet, but growing, number of educators who propose a *thoughtful* social studies curriculum radically at variance with the "skill and drill" technology so much in evidence these days. For example, Fred Newmann and associates conducted a large-scale examination of classroom discourse in high school social studies classes (1990a, 1990b, 1991). While not disparaging the acquisition of skills (by which Newmann means the "tools for manipulating knowledge" [1990a p. 47]), the researchers note that without a *disposition* to act thoughtfully, learners will tend toward both rote learning and rote application of knowledge. The investigators propose six "dimensions" of teaching and learning to define the thoughtful classroom (adapted from 1992, pp. 68-69):

- A few topics received sustained examination rather than many topics being covered superficially.

- The lesson displayed substantive coherence and continuity.

- Students were given an appropriate amount of time to think, that is, to prepare responses to questions.

- The teacher asked challenging questions and/or structured challenging tasks (given the ability level and preparation of the students).

- The teacher was a model of thoughtfulness.

- Students offered explanations and reasons for their conclusions.

For other examples of both philosophy and curricula of "thoughtful" schools, see Brown 1991; Webb et al. 1996; Wiggins 1989.

Marilyn Prettyman, principal at Longview Elementary School in Murray, Utah, reports a school experience that we would wish for all secondary learners.

Out of the Cocoon

In my senior year at the Idaho Falls High School I spent nine wonderful months with a master teacher. It was as though I had existed the previous eleven years in a cocoon and emerged from her room with the freedom of a butterfly. She took us from the dry farms of Idaho on a marvelous trip around the world and back through time. We debated with the citizens of Athens and Sparta as to the merits of their communities, ruled with Charlemagne, discussed revolution with the Russians and the French, painted with Monet and Picasso, heard music with Beethoven and Mozart, and learned about the dark side of man in World War II. I don't know how she had the time to correct all the reports, maps, and essay tests or the hours it took to plan each lesson for us. I only know that my life was never the same after Miss Neuber's class. Some of the greatest joys of my life come in those moments when my mind reaches and stretches; a feeling I had not known until that year.

We catch the excitement and poetry in Ms. Prettyman's account of her trip around an intellectual world. Notice her images — she emerged from her school cocoon as a butterfly; her "debate with the citizens of Athens and Sparta; she painted with Monet. Surely Ms. Prettyman's vital experience meets the substance of Principle 15. How could something so educationally good be without thought, be beyond her experience? Need we doubt that this class, and Miss Neuber, have become part of the writer's "ordinary experience"?

In *Teacher Efficacy and Quality Schooling*, Lanier and Sedlak offer a precise, strongly-worded critique of teaching and "learning" that does not provide what Principle 15 suggests: "School learning is severed from learning and living outside of school.... The trivialization of valuable knowledge, habits of mind, and skills into school learning has been one of the greatest failures of our efforts to educate effectively" (1989, p. 119).

PRINCIPLE 16

EVERY GREAT TEACHER ALLOWS STUDENTS
TO TRY OUT IDEAS FROM THE CURRICULUM IN
THEIR PRESENT EXPERIENCE BECAUSE,
WITHOUT THIS "TRYING OUT," IDEAS DO NOT
MOVE FROM THE REALM OF THE ABSTRACT OR
"SCHOOL" TO THE STUDENTS'
PERSONAL AND COMMUNITY LIFE.

PRINCIPLE 17

EVERY GREAT TEACHER KNOWS THAT
INDIVIDUALS MUST HAVE AN OPPORTUNITY TO
CONSIDER AND SHAPE GROUP ENDS.
LEARNING ACTIVITIES SHOULD SUPPORT
EDUCATIVE GROUP WORK, SHARED
EXPERIENCE, CONVERSATION, AND
INDIVIDUAL WORK.

One of the best kept secrets in education is the learning power generated when small groups of students discuss and defend ideas, suggest and defend alternatives to solve a problem, or share information and tentative understandings about something worth talking about. Yet teachers rarely use small groups to energize intellectual, social, and moral learning. As studies repeatedly show, most classrooms are taught as a total group with teacher talk dominating 70 percent of the talking time (Cuban 1984; Goodlad 1984). And most of this talk deals with low-level fact recall that demands only short, phrase-like answers. Rarely do students use oral language to "compose" sentences and paragraphs. This avoidance of self-constructed learning fails to arouse interest and inhibits the development of the power to think, analyze, defend, or explain. Principles 16 and 17 offer an antidote to the anti-social work environment of most schools. Small group work within a thematic unit or a project is a practical way for students to set some goals of their own, which should increase student interest and sense of personal responsibility for their actions.

Group work, while it does not automatically do so, can lead to the formation of learning communities — groups of individuals bound by mutual ties of inquiry. Powerful learning forces are generated in such groups. As Piaget (1932) notes, one does not "get" or "receive" an idea or a moral value from the outside. Such things do not come in packages to be given by teachers to their students. Ideas and values can only be *constructed* from *within* the learner. In this construction (note its active rather than passive quality) the learner tries to form relationships with and connections to what he or she already knows.

Social interactions — such as talking in small groups — are essential for this cognitive construction to take place: Exchanges of points of view lead to intellectual, moral, and social learning. Cooperation — individuals operating together to frame and to solve a problem, mutually supportive, yet without losing their individuality — is necessary for intellectual development. Talking about ideas or other sensible things leads to criticism of ideas by others. This suppresses a thoughtless "I am right" attitude because the students have a chance to introduce other content, to counter ideas and questions, to request justifications, and to evaluate the logic of what others say.

Finally, the power of learning in small groups leads to the optimistic view that

> schools remain one of the few institutions that have potential for strengthening America's sense of community [because] they encourage and reward the involvement of both children and adults in matters of mutual interest, in the identification and solution of vital community problems: isolation, poverty, physical deterioration. (Lanier & Sedlak 1989, p. 130)

Thus, something very ordinary like "discussion" turns out to be a worthy intellectual process because it is reflective and interactive. It is not something nicely sequenced in advance, with students routinely jumping the hurdles of textbook questions or workbook exercises. The conversation is more truly intellectual because of the give-and-take of serious talk.

Dewey's contribution to this idea is the notion that all learning is social (learning requires people to interact within a culture and to talk — use language — in social interaction); that learning is active, not passive; that present learning is built on past learning; and that the essence of intellectual activity is the solving of problems of social and personal importance.

Notice that these ideas do not talk alone of "skills," of test scores, of more time in school, of self-esteem or cooperative learning that come in a kit, of time-on-task, of remedial instruction, nor of a dozen other things that occupy the attention of "practical" educators in staff meetings, school board meetings, and quick-fix inservice programs, world without end, as the preacher says.

Constance Kamii has given illustrations of teacher questions that focus small group student talk: What do you think of…? Does everybody agree with…? How many different interpretations of the poem did we have in this group? She also reports (1984) a study by Perret-Clermont that draws this conclusion: When children confront the ideas of other children for as brief a time as 10 minutes, higher levels of reasoning often result. Moreover, the children could transfer this level of reasoning to areas not covered in the experiment. This and other related studies support Piaget's and Dewey's belief in the power of social interaction to affect something as seemingly remote as reasoning.

The following vignette is derived from Kamii (1984)

Sentence Diagramming as a Thoughtful Activity

The very idea that thinking — the development of the cranial super-computer that we call "mind" — can be energized by something as ordinary as thoughtful talk sounds so effete that it demands an earthy classroom example. Let's use a grammar lesson. Certainly, if small group effort is effective in a grammar lesson — given that the subject must rank close behind economics and education in God's list of deadly subjects — teachers can have confidence in the application of the method to other, less lethal, subject matter. Remember, too, that small group work in which students *learn* to become more responsible learners, has been part of good progressive schools since the 1920s.

The point of the lesson is this: By embedding the diagramming of a sentence in a dialogue/small group process, the intellectual and interest level of the lesson was raised a metaphorical 5,000 feet in educational altitude.

A class of 30 sixth-grade students was divided into groups of five students. The teacher gave the groups 20 minutes to diagram the same sentence. One student from each group wrote the diagram of the sentence on the board, thus displaying the work of each group for all to see.

Having set the stage, i.e., created a rich environment for some high-level learning, the teacher then said something like this, "O.K. Explain and defend your diagram." From this point on, the teacher moved to the background, intervening only to facilitate the explain-and-defend lesson. The students got into the discussion by giving well-reasoned arguments in favor of each group's version of the correct sentence diagram. Counter-arguments filled the air. Discussion was intense. After a while, only two of the six diagrams survived the give-and-take of criticism. After recess, the teacher asked if the students wanted to know the correct answer. As some said "Yes" and others said "No," no answer was given. Discussion continued. The class finally agreed on the superiority of one sentence. In sum, a sixth-grade class spent an afternoon on a "grammar" lesson; yet the students did not suffer the ignominy of passive "mind-stuffing," but rather produced a high-energy session of personally significant learning.

This lesson is worth thinking about. What reasons can you give, from your own knowledge and what you have picked up so far in *What Every Great Teacher Knows*, to support the contention that this lesson is superior from the perspective of both practice and theory? Or why is it not superior, if you believe that to be true? (You might want to break into small groups to discuss this question!)

Mr. Larry Dean, a high school teacher at Aspen Elementary, Orem, Utah, tells of a personally significant experience illustrative of the kind of action suggested by Principles 16 and 17.

Interest Up, Scores Up in Social Studies

As I studied [books on thinking], I became uncomfortably certain that my teaching approach of many years was wanting, so I decided to make a change. Beginning with a unit on the Civil War, I pretested both my morning and afternoon 10th-grade core classes on the concepts to be covered. Both classes averaged about 39% on the pretest.

Using my conventional classroom approach, I taught the unit to my morning group of students, relaying the information from the text using my all-too-familiar lecturing approach.

With the afternoon core group, I tried other ideas: I tried to create a classroom setting in which thoughtful learning might occur. Dividing the 30 students into two groups of 15, I asked a student teacher to advise one group and I advised the other. We assigned a project leader from each of the sub-groups. We brought in 40 books (for example, *The Blockade: Runners & Raiders; The Confederate High Tide; Sherman's March to the Sea)* and three video tapes about the war. The project leaders divided their groups into three groups of five students each.

To help with the group effort, the individuals were assigned different tasks, e.g., finding out all they could about several of the great battles of the war. Throughout the activity, we advisors offered advice if asked, leaving full autonomy to both of the original sub-groups. (Some examples of the limited advice that was sought: Advanced vocabulary was explained; suggestions for how to motivate less enthusiastic group members was provided.) After just three weeks of this arrangement, I simply was not prepared for what followed: I have never seen my students so energized and full of enthusiasm. They devoured the information in the books as if they were starving for knowledge nourishment. At the same time, of course, my morning group, learning about the same unit, was acting lethargic as usual.

To satisfy my old habits, we administered the same end-of-unit test to both groups. The morning group scored a class average of 68%. The afternoon group scored a class average of 90%.

It was a bitter pill to swallow: In the guise of efficiency, but in reality for the sake of class control, I had been boring my students to tears for some 12 years.

Mr. Vernon Dunn, a teacher at Bingham High School, near Salt Lake City, tells of his experience in allowing students to take a hand in the conduct of their class as suggested by Principle 17.

Students as Co-Conspirators in Learning

At the beginning of this school year, our high school adopted a new attendance policy. We have implemented a new one about every three years for a long time. I was not really happy with the new one, but did very little about it to start with.

In January I picked up a tape recording of a book on leadership. I wasn't initially thinking of the attendance policy as I listened to the tape, but in the middle of the tape, as he was explaining how employees perform better when they sense ownership in the business and its products, I began to wonder if that might also be true of students in the classroom. I decided to find out. I thought I would begin the third quarter with a new attendance policy that had been devised by the students in class.

As I read and prepared to begin this experiment, I began to feel that if I were to let the students have a say in the attendance, I would be hypocritical if I didn't allow them to voice their concerns about other classroom issues, too. I ended up giving them the assignment to devise an attendance policy, a grading policy and scale, and a curriculum for the remainder of the year.

I told them that I knew that this was a high-risk approach, and that if it were to work, they would have to take it seriously. In order to give them some direction, I explained some principles to them and shared with them the mission statements of the school and the English Department. I also explained to them that their class and individual mission statements had to be in alignment with the departmental and school mission statements if they were to be acceptable and successful.

To get each student involved in the decision-making process, I split each class into groups of four or five students with the assignment to generate written solutions for curriculum, attendance, and grading. After each group had completed its proposals, I put them on the board and moderated the class discussion before conducting a class vote on each proposal.

In each area I provided them with three or four alternatives that I had found could at least serve as springboards for their group discussions. In the area of curriculum, I gave them 12 or 13 books and topics that I was or could be prepared to study with them. They were to pick three or four that could be covered by the end of the year.

The attendance policies (each class devised its own) they established contained two or three key ingredients. First, they felt that any policy that did not reward them for promptness and regular attendance would not motivate them very much. Second, they included methods to recover lost attendance points that were fair to both the teacher and the student. Third, while they steadfastly maintained that attaching any penalty to the grade was unfair, eventually they concluded that nothing else would motivate a student to attend class.

In both 11th-grade college preparation English classes, the grade scale they settled on was the same one that I had been using before — even though five or six other scales had been proposed. In the regular 11th-grade English class the students chose to lower the grade scale 10% from 60% to 50% for a passing grade. True, one scale was proposed by one group that 10% would be a passing grade, but the rest of the class immediately emphasized in loud terms that such a scale would not be in alignment with the established mission statement of the school and the department. I didn't have to say anything.

The long-term effects are not yet evident, but so far attendance in my regular English class has risen about 10 to 15%. While attendance is seldom a problem in the college preparation classes, four or five habitually tardy students have made a concerted effort not only to be on time, but to be the first students in the room, as they remind me almost daily. It is still too early to determine the effect of the overall class grades, but more students are approaching me with genuine concern over what they will miss when they need to be gone for athletic and other school activities.

One thing that might be perceived as a drawback is that it took three to four weeks of class discussion and presentation to arrive at the policies in each class. While that seems to be a lengthy process and much time away from "English" studies,

I was prepared to spend that much time because I knew that this is one process that cannot be rushed. I anticipated that it would not be easy for students who had never before had the opportunity to make democratic decisions for themselves. After going through the process, I do not consider the time wasted in any way. Much more was learned by each member of the class than I had hoped for. One student commented that she had no idea how hard it would be to get 30 people to agree on anything.

A second drawback, and this is a real one, is that now instead of two preparations for three English classes, I must prepare for three that have different curricula, different attendance policies, and different goals as independent classes. I am convinced, however, that all the extra work is more than worth the results gained from giving the students ownership in their classes.

There are several other concerns that keep occurring that tell me that I have not come to the end of the process, nor have I solved all the problems that are attached to this approach, but I am still convinced that this is the right direction to go.

Mrs. Beverly Adair, who then taught at Monticello Elementary School in southeast Utah, tried to involve second graders in real-world problem-solving.

But What Does the Principal Do?

During the 1988–1989, school year my class of second graders held a class meeting each week during which time students identified a problem. We discussed it and considered multiple solutions. During the first meetings, the children had difficulty identifying problems and the discussion was more show and tell than problem solving. However, after several discussions some children began to present problems such as tattling, fighting on the playground, or how to be a good friend. They also discussed questions such as, "Is there a Santa Claus?" "Why do we have school?" and "What does the principal do?"

The children did not always come to a conclusion or find a solution, but they did, from time to time, solve some important problems such as identifying the need for more equipment for use during recess. They also had experience in identifying multiple solutions and working together. I was surprised when, at the end of the year, more than half of the students listed class meetings as their favorite activity.

The more "natural" school activities become, the more students will like them — and learn.

PRINCIPLE 18

EVERY GREAT TEACHER UNDERSTANDS WHERE A SERIES OF LESSONS IS HEADING, SEES THE LOGICAL ORDER OF THE CONTENT, AND TRIES TO RELATE THAT CONTENT TO THE LEARNER'S MORE FLUID, PARTIAL VIEW OF IT.

The following two teachers' tales illustrate the importance of direct experience in students' *and* teachers' learning. In the first tale, a teacher tells how a trolley ride helped students see that not all neighborhoods in their city were marked by buildings with boarded-up windows and broken glass on the streets. Ms. Gail Raznov, then Coordinator of the Mission Excellence program for the Philadelphia Schools, tells how she and parents used the trolley ride to link kids' present and partial experience to a social studies-English unit on understanding the place where they lived — a complex entity we call a city.

A Trolley Ride as Social Studies

Ride the #23 trolley from one end of Philadelphia to another and see the world change every mile or so. That's what an entire school of 180 urban black and white youngsters in grades K-7 did as part of their study of cities. Most had never traveled by public transportation outside of their immediate neighborhood.

We rode the bus to Chestnut Hill and boarded the trolley. Chestnut Hill with its stately mansions and manicured lawns led into quaint storefronts, boutiques, fashionable restaurants. Students' eyes bulged. They asked in disbelief, "Is this Philadelphia?" When I replied that it is, some said, "I want to live here someday." "Do you see any black people around here?" snapped one. "I'll live here if I want," asserted another.

Chestnut Hill gave way to Mount Airy. Trees still abounded, but the difference was perceptible to the students. They noticed that the stores weren't as quaint, houses were closer to each other, and there were black people on the street; people wore jeans, not that preppy look of a few miles back. When the evaluations were tallied the next day, this neighborhood — Mount Airy — rated the highest for the type of area students would choose to live in.

Ludlow scored the lowest. Boarded-up windows and doors, graffiti-scarred walls, abandoned and gutted cars, trash and swirling dirt made them wince. The last stop, in South Philadelphia, featured a tour of the Italian Market and lunch in a restaurant where waiters served and cloth napkins were used. Older students, who had been paired with the younger, reminded them of their table manners. "Please" and "Thank you" were used often, and everyone was on his or her best behavior. It was an eye-opening, consciousness-raising experience.

When the students discussed the trip the next day, some decided to write letters to the mayor, others plotted the trip on a city map. Pictures and stories and poems were generated. Older people reported that they tended to look at things they would normally pass by, such as pocket playgrounds, wall murals, brightly colored signs and the street vendors. They reported that they felt, not unpleasantly, like a kid again and could appreciate things they usually took for granted. Youngsters enjoyed the attention and help, especially in writing their reports, that the olders gave them. There was a flood of questions about the Italian Market from kids who were used to the antiseptic flavor of the supermarket. They were curious about the many blocks of the market they had missed and said they wanted to return with their families. The spice and cheese shops, the poultry and rabbit shops with their redolent odors, stuck in students' memories. This shared experience, with the follow-up activities and conversation, provided a rich base for learning and expression of feelings.

Linking the present experience of the learner to the content is central if a teacher wants to avoid the learning-as-trivial-memorization syndrome. Students *learn* to consider school teaching insignificant when it aims at subject matter divorced from their present lives. Dewey (1944/1916) noted the unfortunate consequence of extensive experience in such classrooms: "Unconsciously, but none the less surely, the student comes to believe in certain 'methods' of learning and ... of teaching which are somehow especially appropriate to the school...." and inappropriate to real life.

Principle 18 may sum up John Dewey's view of teaching, learning, teachers, and kids — if indeed one sentence can point to his views on something so devilishly difficult. One way to restate this principle is to say that the teacher's essential purpose is to create bridges and links between a learner's partial view of, say, language or science, and the more logical, organized view of these subjects held by the adult. If a teacher can slip into the "experience stream" of her students, what is learned will be more interesting and meaningful. This challenging principle is as true for a graduate school professor as it is for an elementary school teacher.

Oh, how easily these words roll off the keys and onto the paper. Too easily. The words are true, we do believe, but they miss ... they miss the learner's experience as she tries this idea in real life — the very thing demanded by Principle 18. That is why we shall introduce you to Tracy, a teacher who is struggling in the choppy seas that separate standard teaching from a Deweyan-progressive kind of teaching. Tracy's story is told with empathy and insight by Melanie W. Chadwick, of West Chester, Pennsylvania. Melanie, a graduate student, struggled herself to write this account as part of a hands-on experience in a supervision course that viewed teaching as art and the observer/supervisor as an art critic. The purpose of the teacher observation was to make the art work of teaching more available to the teacher and to others. Tracy's story is much longer than the other stories we have told. We want you to know Tracy, to see her on stage, to meet some of the actors in her drama, not all of whom act with intelligence, thereby increasing the difficulty for this strong teacher as she tries to become a better, more thoughtful one.

Tracy's struggle, the nearly irresistible pull, for example, of nine years of standard teaching in a parochial school, is the struggle each of us has if we are trying to grow, first, as a human being, second, as a teacher. Our past experience holds both the flowers of what we might become as well as the weeds of what we are leaving behind. And, as Tracy's story leads us to believe, schooling, when it operates as a bureaucratic system, cultivates in unequal measure the weeds and the flowers within the school experience. All of this makes learning to teach in better ways insuperably difficult. We are proud to share with you the story of Tracy, a teacher in transition and under pressure.

What particular insights about you and your own school situation are illuminated by Tracy's story?

Tracy: A Teacher in Transition and Under Pressure

A Few Words of Introduction

I know Palace Park Elementary School from the viewpoint of a long-term visitor. I have been assigned to this primary school (kindergarten through second grade, special education, and special-needs kindergarten) for five years. While I teach in Palace Park I teach for the special school for orthopedically handicapped children. The special school occupies five of the 27 classrooms in Palace Park.

During the 25-year-old life of the school, the beige brick, E-shaped structure has remained the same while the suburban neighborhood has evolved from white-collar to blue-collar. Low-income housing has attracted many black families from the nearby city. Teachers, who have been teaching in the building for years, now commute to work from distant, more spacious developments.

Whatever is now occurring in the building is best understood in contrast to what the school was like when I first saw it. Once yellowing plants in the entrance way are fresh with new green growth. Giant papier-mâché spiders and fantastic spider webs replace dusty cobwebs. The glass show cases previously filled with static uniform displays now contain projects and artwork that spill over to the surrounding wall. Missing fluorescent fixtures have returned, lending lightness and brightness. Real children's work has begun to cover the gray tile walls.

While Houghton-Mifflin still dominates, teachers have tentatively begun to explore the unknown Houghton-Mifflin "Whole Language" series. Teachers go forth in a great deal of uncertainty and doubt, hoping to find a well-charted map for a strange new direction. Quick-credit-accumulating teacher center courses still exist, but the inservice program of choice is the University of Pennsylvania Literacy course, sponsored by the new superintendent.

Other changes are filtering into the school. Slowly, teachers are replacing their two-inch heels with sneakers and flats. Suede and wool straight skirts are giving way to loose washable skirts and slacks. Gone are the daily booming five-minute interruptions over the public address system. Much administrivia is now handled daily in written form. Once the school had a principal who enjoyed making a grand entrance in the cafeteria draped in a red cape and crown. He was the king of the palace; the teachers his "girls." Two years ago a new principal arrived in suit and tie whose presence in the cafeteria fosters order and cleanliness. Professionalism reigns.

Tracy

Tracy strides into school wearing a smile. She never seems to take herself too seriously. One of her favorite subjects for humor is herself. As Tracy passes our jovial "queen-sized" librarian, they exchange friendly jabs about each other's hips. Whenever Tracy is in the midst of a group of teachers, laughs are bound to erupt. Tracy's chuckle clearly chimes over the rest.

This is Tracy's second year of teaching at Palace Park, following a seven-year sabbatical from the profession. After teaching for the local Catholic archdiocese for nine years, Tracy left to explore the business world, "travel, have fun and meet some men." Tracy married a man living with his two adolescent children. Two cherubic baby girls later, Tracy was ready to return to the classroom. She wants to "make school more fun and less severe" than her previous school was. "And I did!"

she proudly says to friends. Bringing fun to her classroom is important to Tracy.

From today's reading lesson Tracy leads the children into a spirited discussion of cheerleading. Boys and girls eagerly raise their hands to share what they know. Tracy indicates the next activity is to produce their own cheer. Tracy scans her teacher manual, puts it aside, and enthusiastically declares, "Let's do it in groups. O.K., everybody, line up." The children eagerly scuffle to line up in front of Tracy. On Tracy's request they begin to count off by fours. Tracy stops the group. "Guys, do you think you could do this in groups of three or four that you choose yourself? You've done it before."

"Yeah!"

"Wow!"

"Sure!"

"O.K., O.K., no more than four in a group and remember everyone needs to be a part of a group. You've got ten minutes to write your cheers then share them with the class. Find a place to work and get started."

The class quickly divides itself. Tracy finds a place for a couple of stragglers. The room is buzzing…. The class is ready in record time. Tracy lets the children know she is impressed with their speed.

The children collect around the rug in front of the room. Tracy sits in her rocking chair, asking each group to perform for the others. She has Jennifer work the lights as the dim room signals a curtain between acts. Self-satisfied smiles abound with the pleasure of their work as the children applaud each other's performances.

Tracy always speaks enthusiastically about her job in Pioneer School District. Last summer she was a participant in a two-day "whole language" workshop and was determined to "give it a try." Her arm shot up at the first faculty meeting this year when the principal asked for a volunteer to use the new Houghton-Mifflin series. Tracy has nothing but positive comments about Palace Park. "This place is great! You can learn so much. The public schools provide so many inservice programs. Not like the parochial schools." She shares with me a book the principal had purchased for each second-grade teacher. The book contains activities a teacher might use instead of traditional worksheets. Tracy likes to experiment with the suggestions the book offers.

As openly as Tracy accepted me in her classroom, she shares her concerns and insecurities about teaching science. Yet Tracy is willing to tackle a lesson on magnets and an exploration of circuits. I have visited Tracy's class several afternoons during her scheduled science time. She tells me how she charmed her husband into spending the previous evening explaining the concept of the magnet activity in a science kit.

In her first year at Palace Park, Tracy had been assigned to a special second grade. The children had been together the year before as a first-grade "readiness class." I recall conversations with Tracy last spring in which she had been given the word to "get the children through" certain second-grade basals. The principal didn't care how she did it, even if it was just to teach to the unit tests. She was feeling overwhelmed. The principal was feeling pressure from central administration to decrease the number of retentions in the building while getting the children "ready" to move on to the upper elementary school.

No "readiness" classes exist in the building this year. Tracy has a heterogeneous second-grade class. However, all Chapter I children have been grouped in two other classrooms. The seven second-grade teachers have attempted to eliminate the typical three reading groups in each classroom. The teachers' goal was to reduce the amount of time the children were doing busy work in their seats and increase the time for reading. To accomplish this the second-grade children change classes for a single 75 minutes of reading each day. The reading groups are determined by ability — the grades the children received in first grade. Tracy was thrilled to be a part of such an arrangement and to have a "class of kids that could do something." Tracy told me she has "the A-B kids" — the children who had received A's and B's in reading in first grade. While 75 minutes seems a generous time block, the pressure to "complete" reading in a designated period takes its toll on Tracy and the children.

As I open the door to Tracy's room, two or three children wave tentatively and smile. It is reading time. I tiptoe to my usual seat in the back of the room. A few familiar faces look up at me. Tracy is slowly pacing between the double rows of desks, the Houghton-Mifflin teacher's manual held open in her arms. "My teacher's book says you should be able to read the whole book by yourself by now. But let's read page 79 together." Some read, some drone, some play with their fingers and some let their eyes drift out the window. "O.K. Next paragraph, take turns reading. Girls, then boys. Girls…. " Girls read. Boys read. Girls read. Boys read.

I start to play with my fingers. My eyes drift out the window. A child walking to the bathroom breaks my mental drift. A sign — BATHROOM — dangles from his arm.

"Justin!! Write your name on the board"! I look about. What did I miss? The children are no longer reading from their "anthologies" — collections of stories by well-known authors. "Let's read the next question in your journal together."

I feel confused. I look about. A booklet of activities and questions lies open on each child's desk. This is the Houghton-Mifflin "journal." The children join in choral reading, "How could you earn enough money to buy a guitar?" Tracy repeats the question and a few hands go up. Children respond with short answers. Tracy expands upon each child's ideas. "Now work on this section by yourself. You must make good sense. You are in second grade. Give me grown-up answers that let me know you know the answer." Gazing up at the clock, "You have five, hmmm, seven minutes to do this part."

Below the clock is a sign:

They may forget
what you said
But they will never forget
how you made them feel!

Tracy walks about the room as the children begin to write. She peers over Robby to see his scratched pencil responses. "What's strung from the neck of the guitar?" Robby looks puzzled. "The neck of the guitar?" Tracy's voice rises as she repeats herself. Robby cocks his head and shrugs his shoulders. "I told you to go back to the story." As Tracy points at the page she asks, "Does this tell you what is strung on the neck of the guitar?" She pauses just a second. Again she asks, "What's strung from the neck of the guitar? Just read it again, Hon." Tracy raises her eyebrows and rolls her eyes in frustration as she looks at me and walks toward another child.

Tracy wanders about the room commenting as she stops at different desks. "You could'a' put down more...."

Near the front of the room Tracy again glances at the clock. Confusing, disjointed directions follow. Tracy calls the class to focus on her. "O.K. kids, we've got lots of work to do today. We've got to catch up. We've spent too long on this story. If you haven't finished take it home for homework. Mark the page number with HW [homework]."

On the board in neat, bold primary print are two columns of words labeled Consonant Clusters.

As Tracy talks the task begins to emerge — underline the consonant cluster. Tracy alternately calls on boys and girls. She adds to the task as each of the first three children attempt to follow her changing directions. By the third child the task has expanded to say the word, underline the consonant cluster and say, "The consonant cluster is _____." She prompts the next two children to restate the complete sentence. By the end of the first column of words a child manages to meet all of Tracy's revised expectations without a prompt.

[Lesson continues]

"We have three minutes left. Quick, who can tell me a word beginning with a consonant cluster?" A few hands go up, a few answers are blurted into the air. Tracy writes. Children tell. Tracy tenders, "Good." "That's right." "Great word, Hon."

As children flow out of the room, one small boy in a coat edges his way in. "Where have you been, honey?" Tracy asks.

"The dentist."

With her arm around his shoulder Tracy quips, "Bet you'd rather have been here." Maybe Tracy would rather have spent the morning at the dentist.

The 75-minute reading period is just one piece of evidence that the staff and administration are struggling with the meaning and understanding of "whole language." Tracy also speaks to me in frustration about all the materials she needs to cover before June, especially the English book. She says the second-grade teachers are weighing the pros and cons of grouping the children for intensive reading for 75 minutes a day. The reading series has so many activities there is not enough time to do all of them. While English is taught as a separate subject, Tracy does not believe she has a good sense of the English skills her students are covering in their separate reading groups. During an inservice-day activity, Tracy illustrates her pull between integrated and traditional language arts pedagogy.

A portion of the inservice day in February was devoted to literacy and whole language. The teachers are sharing activities they and their children enjoyed which supported literacy development. Tracy first shares a page of contractions which could be used for varied flashcard and seat-work activities. She expresses her concerns that the children aren't learning some important material. She thinks the new reading materials and Penn Literacy were too "lah-dee-dah" about grammar and English. "That's the advantage of parochial school. The kids had to memorize this stuff and really learn it." She also shares a book about Harriet Tubman which she used in class integrating vocabulary and writing activities with her February social studies unit for Black History Month.

Today, Tracy introduces me to a new boy, Tommy, who has just arrived in her room. She then directs Robert to tell him about tornadoes. As Robert begins his enthusiastic explanation Tracy pipes up, "No, No, silly! Go get the *Weekly Reader* and read the part to him." Robert complies. He walks over to the counter and returns with the *Weekly Reader.* He reads to Tommy in a halting, flat voice. Tommy glances down and around.

The pressure to cover material also short-circuits Tracy's discussions. This pressure makes thinking virtually impossible and reduces students' self-confidence.

Tracy looks at her teacher manual. The children have just finished an autobiographical story by a famous author and illustrator. In preparation for a follow-up activity they are putting crayons on their desk.

"Are you ready? I'll wait 'til you're ready. I have one minute to explain it. You have five minutes to do this part. We've read a story about Tomi dePoala when he was a child. He wanted to be an artist. What is an artist?"

Children call out, "He paints." "A person that draws." "He uses clay."

Quickly, Tracy defines for the children, "An artist is someone who paints or draws. You take it seriously. You are good at it. You spend a lot of your free time doing it."

Tracy directs the children to read the directions in their books in chorale style.

Although Tracy at times seems to be searching for "right answers," she is willing to change things in her room. She also seems very comfortable with student movement while other activities are going on. Student desk arrangements change every other week or so. When I asked Tracy about new arrangements she replied how she likes to rearrange furniture, but her husband doesn't like her to do it at home, so she does it at school.

> Tracy has recently lost her bright smile and positive attitude. The school district may not muster enough support to pass the tax referendum. Tracy, a nontenured teacher, is scheduled to get her pink slip the first week in May.

Tracy has the makings of a risk taker. She feels comfortable with children working in different physical and social arrangements. She is willing to try a new reading series. She is attempting to replace worksheets with activities that are not neat, prescriptive, and boring. Tracy tackles science although she admits that she may not understand the activities herself. She volunteers to join a few teachers using a new whole-language-basal series. She wants the children to have fun in her classroom.

Tracy is trying to learn and grow. She expresses excitement over the inservice opportunities in the district. She is trying to learn alternative approaches to teaching reading.

We believe Tracy is a teacher under pressure to cover material before the year is over. The message she received from her principal last year lingers. The regrouping of children for reading as a 75-minute subject adds to the pressure. This kind of grouping separates reading from the English content that Tracy feels compelled to cover.

Tracy compartmentalizes subject matter. English, reading, and science have their own scheduled blocks of time. When anything else comes up, science is replaced. The reading series dictates themes. Because of scheduling and the push to "cover material," even the prescribed themes from the reading series appear lost as potential units within which to integrate some of the content.

Though Tracy is trying the whole language series and has participated in the first Penn Literacy course and a two-day whole language inservice session, she still believes children need to memorize certain material out of context to "learn it." She is struggling to put theory into practice. Reading, writing, and speaking are seen as separate entities. Because of the uniqueness of the new reading program, Tracy follows the teacher's manual like a recipe book. Tracy has had nine years of teaching experience in a very traditional school.

Tracy's style suggests certain beliefs about learning: teaching is telling and learning is remembering. Tracy dominates the discussions she starts. She tells the children much. We rarely observed her encourage the children to search for deeper meanings, encourage thinking, or try to understand thought processes. Does Tracy believe second-graders don't have the mental ability or that children need to be told the "right" answers, or that time is too "valuable" to try alternative approaches? We sometimes think Tracy believes "right" answers come from the teachers, administrators, and textbook publishers.

Unknowingly, the administration hampers Tracy's development. If the administration doesn't understand how and why whole language, Penn Literacy, thematic units, and interesting activities all fit together, how can the administration support Tracy's mindful growth as a teacher? Tracy feels pressured to cover material in breadth, not depth. As a condition for being a pilot teacher for the new reading series, she was asked to make the series her complete reading program. Using any textbook exclusively contradicts the idea of whole language. By supporting regrouping for reading, the administration implicitly supports discrete subject matter knowledge, something that is played out in Tracy's room. A book of activities becomes simply activities and supports the mindset that "this new stuff," this new way of teaching, is just that — a bunch of activities. "It is not enough just to introduce ... games, handwork.... Everything depends upon the way in which they are employed" (Dewey 1944/1916, p. 196).

Tracy has begun her journey in understanding the relationship between children's learning and a dynamic curriculum. In-depth, child-centered discussions and problem solving need to replace short answer and "right answer" sessions. Who is challenging Tracy's assumptions about teaching or learning, or are these the assumptions of her peers and principal? Where are the support systems to encourage Tracy to reflect and develop activities for thoughtful work for children? To make major changes in her pedagogy and curriculum is an overwhelming experience for any teacher without help. Deborah Meier says that making changes in one's teaching practice is like learning "how to drive while changing not only the tire but also the transmission system" (Meier 1995, p. 601). Tracy has come a long way in the two years she has been at Palace Park. We have great confidence in her desire and ability to keep growing. Keep on truckin', Tracy!

Tracy's story helps us see that content can be "fluid" for a teacher in transition to progressive teaching while, at the same time, the content is "fluid" for the teachers' less mature students. Such is the baffling complexity of our enterprise. Deborah Meier's (1995) practical account of teaching in a progressive high school is important reading for teachers who, like Tracy, are trying to travel beyond standard practices.

A Final Comment

In *What Every Great Teacher Knows* we have provided an opportunity for you — teachers and teachers-to-be — to engage in thoughtful discussions about significant ideas. We see the ideas contained in this book as springboards from which you launch intelligent dialogue, which in turn leads to knowledge, convictions, and practical decisions that affect both adults and pupils in schools. We have tried to be brief in our comments on the principles — provocatively brief, we hope — intending thereby to avoid constraining or coercing your talking and thinking; we have tried to direct your thinking and conversation to humane and intellectual concerns that have always directed intellectual, progressive education.

As we have claimed throughout the book, mind-expanding teaching does not lend itself to prescribing narrow "outcomes" of learning. Rather, it aims at freeing one to sense one's own perplexity and, hence, one's own questions, in order to construct personally and socially significant meaning. Certainly, we do not have in view some precise "learning outcome" that we expect you to "achieve" as a result of working through *What Every Great Teacher Knows*.

On the other hand, our broad aim has been that you would be intellectually and even emotionally engaged with the ideas and stories of *What Every Great Teacher Knows*, and that this, in turn, would lead you to want to talk to colleagues, to engage more formally in a dialogue that requires reading and discussing some classic and contemporary books (Gibboney 1994). The best assurance that a school will become a thoughtful place is that the teachers and principal in the school themselves become more thoughtful.

Notes

[1] Thomas A. Romberg and Thomas P. Carpenter, two top experts in progressive mathematics education, criticize the research on effective teaching by saying this research confuses teaching substance with fancy statistics, that this research is intellectually incoherent, and because this research is guided by no ideas, its empirical findings are circular and not useful. See their article titled "Research on Teaching and Learning Mathematics: Two Disciplines of Scientific Inquiry," in the *Handbook of Research on Teaching, 3rd edition*, Merlin G. Wittrock, ed. (New York: Macmillan, 1986, 865); quoted in Gibboney 1994, pp. 138-140.

[2] The unintended irony in the term "sponge activity" is evidence enough of the plan's machine-like quality.

[3] The report, *A Nation at Risk: The Imperative of Educational Reform* (National Commission on Excellence in Education, 1983), was the first of a series of national reports on education which drew attention to the problem.

[4] The research evidence to show that isolated skills transfer to thinking about the content in the curriculum is not persuasive. A readable argument against this isolation tendency is found in Frank Smith's *to think* [sic] (1990) in which he, echoing Dewey, maintains that thinking is necessarily unitary, not neatly divisible into self-contained compartments, such as remembering, understanding, learning. "Learning is not something that is done separately from thinking.... Inferring, concluding, deciding, and solving problems are inseparable from learning" (p. 42). Smith's point is that the "brain is not doing [a number of] things at once.... It is doing one" (p. 44). All of the categories of thinking are invented by us; they are perspectives on human mental activity, which in fact is a "single, continual, undifferentiated event — the brain at work, going about its own affairs" (p. 44).

[5] Nor do other programs agree with the two under consideration: For example, a video/workbook program from the Association of Supervi-

sion and Curriculum Development (ASCD) proposes that there are precisely 23 "tactics for thinking" (Alexandria, VA: ASCD, n.d.).

[6] Hyde and Bizar (1989) believe that "the reduction of reading, writing, mathematics [and thinking] to overt behaviors that can be considered skills ... [is] a tragically mistaken notion" (p. 7). The idea, they claim, has "resulted in many teachers unwittingly destroying the *meaningfulness* for children performing these activities."

[7] For an updated list of Foxfire's core practices, contact Sara Day Hatton, Communications Manager, Foxfire Fund, P.O. Box 541, Mountain City, GA 30562-0541.

Appendix

Eighteen Principles That Every Great Teacher Knows

THINKING AND EXPERIENCE

The principles in this section are intended to help teachers (and principals) explore the understanding of thinking and experience that underlies thoughtful and democratic teaching.

1. Every great teacher makes the cultivation of thinking in a decent and humane environment the primary goal of teaching. (Page 23)

2. Every great teacher values and encourages student questioning because questions encourage student and teacher thought. (Page 31)

3. Every great teacher understands that he/she cannot afford to underestimate what is involved in "knowing something" well. (Page 43)

4. Every great teacher realizes that productive experience results from doing something with foresight, with a purpose in mind, then reflecting on the consequences. (Page 50)

5. Every great teacher recognizes that thinking is not separated from doing something with a purpose in mind; that mind is *in* the doing, not *outside* it. (Page 56)

Teaching Objectives

The principles below apply to the goals for student learning set by administrators, teachers, and students.

6. Every great teacher knows that the learning objectives suggest the kind of environment needed to increase the capacities of the learner. (Page 63)

7. Every great teacher knows that the objectives value both *what* is to be learned and *how* it is to be learned. The quality of learning is critically dependent on *how* the objective is achieved. (Page 66)

8. Every great teacher knows that the immediate classroom objectives are made with larger, overarching aims in mind, that they free the student to attain the larger aims. (Page 72)

9. Every great teacher knows that most teaching objectives ought to make sense to the learner at the time of learning and that future learning is built best on what the student has already learned. (Page 77)

Subject Matter

The following principles pertain to the content, the subject matter, considered here apart from method for clarity.

10. Every great teacher knows that *essential* content is knowledge of general *social* significance that is relevant to all students whatever their abilities or interests. (Page 79)

11. Every great teacher knows that content must be related to the needs of the local and regional community. It is intended to improve the quality of future living for both the community and the individual. Content must illuminate significant social issues. (Page 79)

12. Every great teacher knows that content does not consist exclusively in information or data readily available in books, computers, or other media. Rather, good content is subject matter that assists learners in their inquiry and their attempt to create meaning. (Page 79)

TEACHING METHODS

The principles in this section encourage teachers and principals to consider some generic indicators of quality for professional and thoughtful teaching.

13. Every great teacher recognizes that good methods mean the creation of a total school/classroom environment for learning that cultivates the intelligence and sensitivities of learners, teachers, and administrators. (Page 89)

14. Every great teacher understands that direct attention to results for their own sake through rote learning short-circuits meaningful experience and closes down the growth of intelligence. Neither ends nor means can be hurried if one wishes to provoke thoughtful learning. (Page 89)

15. Every great teacher selects problems for thoughtful and meaningful analysis that are within the experience of the learner at the start of the learning, related to the problems of ordinary life, and require thought or reflection about the consequences of actions taken to solve the problem. (Page 101)

16. Every great teacher allows students to try out ideas from the curriculum in their present experience because, without this "trying out," ideas do not move from the realm of the abstract or "school" to the students' personal and community life. (Page 109)

17. Every great teacher knows that individuals must have an opportunity to consider and shape group ends. Learning activities should support educative group work, shared experience, conversation, and individual work. (Page 109)

18. Every great teacher understands where a series of lessons is heading, sees the logical order of the content, and tries to relate that content to the learner's more fluid, partial view of it. (Page 117)

References

Barth, K. 1990. *Improving schools from within: Teachers, parents, and principals can make a difference.* San Francisco: Jossey-Bass.

Bolton, D. 1994. *The documentation and critique of the dialogue approach to professional development in two schools.* Doctoral dissertation. Philadelphia: University of Pennsylvania.

Brown, R. 1991. *Schools of thought: How the politics of literacy shape thinking in the classroom.* San Francisco: Jossey-Bass.

Bruner, J. 1966. *Toward a theory of instruction.* Cambridge, MA: Harvard University Press.

Calfee, R. August, 1988. *Indicators of literacy.* Publication JNE-04 of the Rand Corporation and the Center for Policy Research in Education. Santa Monica, CA: Rand Corporation.

Callahan, R. 1962. *Education and the cult of efficiency.* Chicago: University of Chicago Press.

Campbell, G. 1989. *Staff development through dialogue: A case study in educational problem solving.* Doctoral dissertation. Philadelphia: University of Pennsylvania.

Cremin, L. 1961. *The transformation of the school: Progressivism in American education 1876-1957.* New York: Knopf.

Cuban, L. 1984. *How teachers taught: Constancy and change in American classrooms, 1890-1980.* New York: Longman.

Dewey, J. 1944/1916. *Democracy and education.* New York: Free Press.

Dewey, J. 1938. *Experience and education.* New York: Macmillan.

Dillon, J. 1988. *Questioning and teaching: A manual of practice.* New York: Teachers College Press.

Duckworth, E. 1979. Either we are too early and they can't learn it or we are too late and they know it already: The dilemma. *Harvard Education Review* 49: 297-312.

Elkind, D. 1970. *Children and adolescents: Interpretative essays on Jean Piaget.* New York: Oxford University Press.

Furth, H., and H. Wachs. 1974. *Thinking goes to school: Piaget's theory in practice.* New York: Oxford University Press.

Gardner, H. 1985. *Frames of mind: The theory of multiple intelligences.* New York: Basic Books.

Gardner, H. 1991. *The unschooled mind: How children think and how schools should teach.* New York: Basic Books.

Gibboney, R. 1994. *The stone trumpet: A story of practical school reform 1960 –1990.* Albany: State University of New York Press.

Goodlad, J. 1984. *A place called school.* New York: McGraw-Hill.

Hillocks, G. 1989. Literary texts in classrooms. In P. Jackson, ed. *From Socrates to software: The teacher as text and the text as teacher.* 89th yearbook of the National Society for the Study of Education, Part I. Chicago: The Society.

Holt, J. 1964. *How children fail.* New York: Delta.

Hyde, A., and M. Bizar. 1989. *Thinking in context: Teaching cognitive processes across the elementary school curriculum.* New York: Longman.

James, W. 1992/1890. Two kinds of knowledge. In *Principles of psychology.* (*Great Books of the Western World,* vol. 53). Chicago: Encyclopedia Britannica.

Kamii, C. 1984. Autonomy: The aim of education envisioned by Piaget. *Phi Delta Kappan* 65(6).

Lanier, J., and M. Sedlak. 1989. Teacher efficacy & quality schooling. In T. Sergiovanni and J. Moore, eds. *Schooling for tomorrow: Directing reforms to issues that count.* Boston: Allyn and Bacon.

Little, J. 1982. Seductive images and organizational realities in professional development. In *Rethinking school improvement: Research, craft, and concept,* edited by A. Lieberman. New York: Teachers College Press.

Meier, Deborah. 1995. *The power of their ideas : Lessons for America from a small school in Harlem.* Boston : Beacon Press.

Mitchell, R. 1987. *The gift of fire.* New York: Simon & Schuster.

National Center on Effective Secondary Schools. Research/technical report. ERIC Document ED 326 465.

Newmann, F. 1990a. Higher order thinking in teaching social studies: A rationale for the assessment of classroom thoughtfulness. *Journal of Curriculum Studies.* 22(1)

Newmann, F. 1990b. Qualities of thoughtful social studies classes: An empirical profile. *Journal of Curriculum Studies* 22(3).

Newmann, F. 1991. Higher order thinking in the teaching of social studies: Connections between theory and practice. In J. Voss, D. Perkins, and J. Segal, eds., *Informal reasoning and education.* Hillsdale NJ: Erlbaum.

Paul, R. 1992. *Critical thinking: What every person needs to survive in a rapidly changing world* (rev. 2nd ed.). Rohnert Park, CA: Foundation for Critical Thinking.

Perkins, D. 1992. *Smart schools: From training memories to educating minds.* New York: Free Press.

Perrone, V. 1989. *Working papers: Reflections on teachers, schools, communities.* New York: Teachers College Press.

Piaget, J. 1932. *The moral development of the child.* New York: Free Press.

Postman, N. 1992. *Technopoly.* New York: Knopf.

Saul, J. 1992. *Voltaire's bastards: The dictatorship of reason in the west.* New York: Free Press.

Sharan, S. 1980. Cooperative learning in small groups: Recent methods and effects on achievement, attitudes, and ethnic relations. *Review of Educational Research* 50: 241-271.

Sizer, T. 1984. *Horace's Compromise: The dilemma of the American high school.* Boston: Houghton-Mifflin.

Slavin, R., S. Sharan, S. Kagan, R. Hertz-Lazarowitz, C. Webb, and R. Schmuck, R. (eds.). 1985. *Learning to cooperate, cooperating to learn.* New York: Plenum.

Smith, F. 1990. *to think.* New York: Teachers College Press.

Thrush, A. 1987. *A. Deweyan analysis of the CoRT and instrumental enrichment thinking skills programs.* Doctoral dissertation. Philadelphia: University of Pennsylvania.

Webb, C., L. Shumway, and W. Shute. 1996. *Local schools of thought: A search for purpose in rural education.* Charleston, WV: ERIC/CRESS.

Wegner, G. 1990. What is history? *Democracy & Education* 4:3.

Welsh, P. 1986. *Tales out of school.* New York: Penguin.

Wiggins, G. 1989. The futility of trying to teach everything of importance. *Educational Leadership* 47(3): 44-59.

Wiggins, G. 1993. *Assessing student performance: Exploring the purpose and limits of testing.* San Francisco: Jossey-Bass.

À L'ORÉE DES BOIS

UNE ANTHOLOGIE DE L'HISTOIRE DU PEUPLE DE KANEHSATÀ:KE

BRENDA GABRIEL
ARLETTE KAWANATATIE VAN DEN HENDE

PUBLIÉ PAR LE CENTRE CULTUREL ET DE LANGUE TSI RONTERIHWANÓNHNHA NE KANIEN'KÉHA

Auteures : Brenda Gabriel et Arlette Kawanatatie Van den Hende

Recherches principales : Louise Johnston

Publication en anglais : Centre d'éducation de Kanehsatà:ke
Publication en français : Centre culturel et de langue Tsi Ronterihwanónhnha ne Kanien'kéha
    14 A, rue Só:se Onahsakèn:'rat (Joseph Swan)
    Kanehsatà:ke (Québec) J0N 1E0
    Tél. : 450 479-1651
    Courriel : kononkwe@inbox.com
Conception de la page couverture : Ellen Katsi'tsákwas Gabriel
Copyright 2010
Tous droits réservés
Imprimé au Québec
ISBN 978-1-896729-15-2

DÉDICACE

C'est avec grand respect que la communauté Kanien'keha:ka (Mohawk) de Kanehsatà:ke dédie la version française de *At the Woods' Edge: An Anthology of the History of the People of Kanehsatake* à Francine Lemay.

À la suite de son voyage de guérison vers la réconciliation, Francine a bénévolement travaillé sans relâche à la traduction de ce livre qui, nous l'espérons aidera les lecteurs à mieux comprendre l'historique et les défis des peuples autochtones. Ce n'est que par la connaissance et la compréhension que nous pouvons commencer à nous « voir » mutuellement comme des êtres humains.

Merci Francine.

WA'AKHIKWÉNIENHSTE

Ne kwah é:neken tiótte tsi kakwenienhstahtsherá:kon tsi wa'akhihsennakará:tate ne Francine Lemay ne Kanien'kehá:ka iakwanakerahserá:ien ne Kanehsatà:ke, tsi O'seronni'kéha teiakowennaténion ne tsi Iotéhrhate tsi nontaiawenhserón:ne tsi nonkwá ne ontionkwe'ta'ó:kon ne Kanehsatà:ke.

É:so tsi iakotkaronní:'on ne Francine, iako'nikonhratshá:ni tánon tiako'nikonhrahsa'áhton tsi wa'onthonkária'ke, wa'tiewennaté:ni ne Tsi Iotéhrhate, tsi skén:non saión:ton tsi wa'onthahíta ne aonsaiontewihrón:ni tsi iakotkaronní:'on. Iakwahská:neks ne ón:kwe aiako'nikonhraièn:ta'ne nahotén:shon tsi nontaiwenhserón:ne teiako'nikónhrhare ne Onkwehón:we. Ne khok ne karihonniennihtshera tánon ka'nikonhraientáhtshera entkáhawe ne taetewatate'nikonhraièn:ta'ne tsi na'tetewátere tsi tión:kwe.

Niá:wen Francine

RECHERCHE

Louise Johnston, Gordie Oke, Melanie Tiawèn:ta's Gabriel, Brenda Gabriel, Arlette Kawanatatie Van den Hende.

ASSISTANCE TECHNIQUE

Leona Bonspille, Joyce Nelson, Marie Kasennenhá:wi David, Valerie Wahiarónkwas David, Susan Kaniehtenhá:wi Oke.

PHOTOGRAPHIE

Brian Beaver, Valerie Wahiarónkwas David, Marie Kasennenhá:wi David, Susan Kaniehtenhá:wi Oke, William Tiaokàthe Nelson, Gordie Oke, Sheila Watson, Perry Bonspille, Brenda Gabriel, Arlette Kawanatatie Van den Hende.

MISE EN PAGE

Leona Bonspille

TRAVAIL ARTISTIQUE ORIGINAL

Ellen Katsi'tsákwas Gabriel

LECTURE DE LA VERSION ORIGINALE EN ANGLAIS

Linda Simon, Linda Katsitsaha:wi Cree, Hilda Kanerentenhawi Nicholas, Maurice Tehonatonkwa Gabriel, Denis Onerahtó:'a Nicholas; Raymond Kanatase Gabriel.

RÉVISION DE LA VERSION ORIGINALE EN ANGLAIS

Linda Simon, Linda Katsitsaha:wi Cree, Hilda Kanerahtenha:wi Nicholas, Melanie Tiawèn:ta's Gabriel.

CONSULTANTS EN LANGUE KANIEN'KEHA

Skawá:nati Montour, Audrey Kawinónhsen Nelson, Phyllis Konwahawén:se Montour, Hilda Kanerahtenha:wi Nicholas, Alice Karonhianó:ron McDonald.

TRADUCTION DE L'ANGLAIS

Francine Lemay

LECTURE DE LA VERSION FRANÇAISE

Arlette Kawanatatie Van den Hende, Daniel Lacasse, Céline Bastien Genest

RÉVISION DE LA VERSION FRANÇAISE

Pascale Monosiet

REMERCIEMENTS

NIAWENHKÓ:WA À TOUS LES KANEHSATA'KEHRÓ:NON QUI ONT CONTRIBUÉ DE PRÈS OU DE LOIN À CE LIVRE :

Edna Beauvais, Helen Beauvais, Mina Beauvais, Lawrence Beauvais, Brian Beaver, Ada Bonspille, Dorothy Bonspille, Kathleen Bonspille, Leona Bonspille, Maurice Bonspille, Perry Bonspille, Ruby Bonspille, Steven Bonspille, Judy Caldwell, Gary Carbonnell, Ann Cree, Linda Cree, John Cree, Dorothy Currie, Danny David, Walter David, Valerie David, Marie David, Jonas Etienne, Selina Etienne, Melanie Gabriel, Ellen Gabriel, Ronnie Gabriel, Raymond Gabriel, Maurice Gabriel, Richard Gabriel, Samson Gabriel, Ida Gabriel, Paul Gareau, Louise Gaspé, Eunice Laforce, Hazel Laforce, Andrew Martin, Eleanor Montour, Skawá:nati Montour, James Nelson, Minnie Nelson, John Nelson, Diane Nelson, Joyce Nelson, William Nelson, Jessie Nelson, Marianne Nicholas, Hilda Nicholas, Sonia Nicholas, Denis Nicholas, Muriel Nicholas, Velma Nicholas, Gordie Oke, Susan Oke, Lily Oke, Emily Oke, Eddie Oke, Vivian Oke, Roy Rennie, Clarence Simon, Linda Simon, Helen Simon, Norman Tewisha père. Nos remerciements à tous ceux qui restent anonymes et à toutes les personnes de Wahta qui ont aimablement contribué à la recherche.

NOUS REMERCIONS SINCÈREMENT LES PERSONNES ET LES INSTITUTIONS SUIVANTES :

Les Archives nationales du Canada, à Ottawa; la collection nationale des cartes géographiques et la collection de photographies des Archives nationales du Canada; la Bibliothèque nationale du Canada, à Ottawa; Joyce Banks, de la collection des livres rares de la Bibliothèque nationale du Canada; Robert Allen, du Département de recherche historique et des revendications territoriales du département des Affaires indiennes, à Hull; Carole Thibault, du Service du patrimoine, ministère des Affaires culturelles, à Québec; les Archives nationales du Québec, à Montréal; Pierre-Louis Lapointe, aux Archives nationales du Québec, à Québec; les bibliothèques et le bureau des systèmes de l'Université McGill, à Montréal; Richard Virr et le personnel, du Département des livres rares de l'Université McGill; Denis Plante du Fonds Faillon, à l'Université de Montréal; le Département des livres rares de l'Université de Montréal; la Bibliothèque nationale du Québec, à Montréal; les Archives de la Compagnie de la Baie d'Hudson, à Winnipeg; Moira McCaffrey, de la collection d'ethnologie du Musée McCord de l'histoire canadienne, à Montréal; Conrad Graham, du Musée McCord de l'histoire canadienne; Pamela Miller, bibliothécaire au Musée McCord de l'histoire canadienne; la collection Notman du Musée McCord de l'histoire canadienne; le projet Shingwauk de l'université Algoma, à Sault-Sante-Marie; Jacques Cinq-Mars, de l'archéologie du Québec du musée de la civilisation, à Hull; Bernard Assiniwi, à l'ethnologie du musée de la civilisation; David M. du musée Stewart, à Montréal; la collection de photographies du musée Royal Ontario, à Toronto; James Corsaro, Henry Ilnicki et le personnel aux Archives de l'État de New York, à Albany; James Folts de la bibliothèque publique de New York, à Albany; l'évêque Leslie Petersen du diocèse anglican d'Algoma, à Sault-Sainte-Marie; John Bird, adjoint spécial du primat des pensionnats de l'Église anglicane du Canada, à Toronto; Susan Stanley et Mary-Lou Smith, archivistes aux Archives de l'Église Unie, à Montréal; Conférence, Bishop's University, à Lennoxville; John Siebert, de la division des Missions au Canada, de l'Église Unie du Canada, à Toronto; Gerry Kelly du Groupe de travail national catholique sur les pensionnats, à Ottawa; le révérend Raymond Hodgson des ministères de justice de l'Église presbytérienne au Canada, à Don Mills; Roger Marinier pour la collection de photographies de feu René Marinier, p. p. s de Saint-Sulpice, à Saint-Eustache; Gilles Boileau, du Département de géographie de l'Université de Montréal; la Société historique du comté d'Argenteuil, à Carillon; Rod Hodgson, président de la Hudson Historical Society, à Hudson; Sheila Watson de Kanehsatà:ke Alternative School; Steven L. Bonspille, du Centre culturel de Kanehsatà:ke, Kanienkehaka Otiohkwa, de Kahnawake.

Légende des pictos

Hochet-gourde

Panier en frêne blanc

Loup

Ours

Planche-berceau

Sac à tabac en peau de daim

Hochet-tortue

Épi de maïs

Boîte d'écorce de bouleau

Coiffe mohawk Kostowa traditionnelle

Bâton de guerre

Motif de poterie

Fraises sauvages

Motif de broderie Woodland

Vêtement et ceinture de rupture

Feuille d'érable

Ceinture Wampum à deux rangs

Poterie iroquoise

Haricots

Pipe en argile rouge

Mocassin avec motif Woodland

Peigne de condoléances

Hochet d'écorce

Nouveau et ancien bâton de lacrosse

Arbre de paix dont les racines s'étendent dans les quatre directions

Soleil

Lune

Ceinture Wing ou Dust Fan des nations confédérées

Chaîne de l'alliance brisée

Ceinture deux rangées

Ceinture de condoléances

Ceinture d'invitation au gouverneur Denny en 1758

Tortue

Ceinture de la rançon des femmes

Soleil et montagnes

Table des matières

Préface

Les paroles qui viennent en premier[1]

Les paroles qui suivent sont prononcées au début et à la fin de tous les rassemblements du peuple. Il revient à chacun de les connaître.

Le peuple a appris que, lorsqu'il s'assemble pour quelque raison que ce soit, il doit rappeler à chacun les paroles qui lui ont été données. On m'a demandé de les exprimer du mieux que je pouvais pour que nous soyons d'une même pensée. En voici une version.

Nous avons appris que notre première pensée devrait être pour notre mère la terre, parce que c'est d'elle que nous venons et que c'est elle qui nous nourrit et nous soutient tout au cours de notre existence.

Nous unissons maintenant nos esprits pour saluer notre mère la terre et lui exprimer notre gratitude pour le soutien et la subsistance qu'elle continue de nous procurer.

Nous sommes d'une même pensée.

En regardant tout autour de nous, nous voyons la vie végétale : la haute et la basse végétation qui, depuis la création, remplissent leur devoir. En ce moment, nous reconnaissons la basse végétation, dont la première est la fraise, qui a accepté de nous donner la nourriture, les remèdes, ses parfums délectables et sa variété de couleurs. Nous reconnaissons également la haute végétation, dont le premier est l'érable, qui a accepté de nous donner, de temps à autre, quelques membres de sa famille pour que les nôtres aient un abri et soient au chaud ou pour que nous puissions nous déplacer et fabriquer des ustensiles et toutes les autres choses qui contribuent à notre existence.

Nous unissons maintenant nos pensées pour saluer toute la vie végétale et la remercier de continuer à nous soutenir dans cette vie.

Nous sommes d'une même pensée.

Nous portons maintenant notre attention sur nos frères les quadrupèdes dont le premier est le cerf. Depuis la création, les quadrupèdes ont accepté, de temps à autre, de donner des membres de leur famille pour fournir à nos familles la nourriture, le vêtement et d'autres nécessités.

Nous unissons maintenant nos pensées pour saluer nos frères les quadrupèdes et les remercier.

Nous sommes d'une même pensée.

Nous portons maintenant notre attention sur nos frères ailés dont le premier est l'aigle. Depuis la création, eux aussi ont accepté de nous donner, de temps à autre, des membres de leur famille pour nous nourrir. Ils nous ont également donné leurs beaux chants et leurs plumes resplendissantes.

Nous unissons maintenant nos pensées pour saluer nos frères ailés et les remercier.

Nous sommes d'une même pensée.

Nous portons maintenant notre attention sur nos frères qui vivent dans l'eau dont le premier est la truite. Depuis le commencement de cette vie, eux aussi ont accepté de soutenir les diverses formes de vie créées. Ils nous fournissent nourriture et remèdes et nous ont aidés de maintes façons.

Nous unissons maintenant nos pensées pour saluer nos frères qui vivent dans l'eau et les remercier pour qu'ils continuent de suivre leurs directives originales.

Nous sommes d'une même pensée.

Nous nous concentrons maintenant sur les nombreuses eaux qui nous soutiennent. Ce sont les eaux souterraines, les étangs, les lacs, les ruisseaux, les rivières et les fleuves et le grand-père, les eaux salées. Depuis le début de la vie, elles ont fourni la nourriture essentielle au maintien de toute la création.

Nous unissons maintenant nos pensées pour saluer toutes les eaux et les remercier du soutien et de la nourriture qu'elles pourvoient.

Nous sommes d'une même pensée.

En regardant en haut, nous portons d'abord notre attention sur le monde céleste inférieur et sur tous nos parents qui y résident. Nous remercions notre grand-mère la lune, notre frère aîné le soleil et notre grand-père le tonnerre pour leur rôle permanent dans la vie de la création. Notre grand-mère continue son travail auprès de toute la vie femelle de la création. Notre frère aîné nous donne toujours sa lumière et sa chaleur. Nos grands-pères continuent de nous donner les eaux purifiantes et de garder les grands serpents dans les profondeurs de la mère terre.

Nous unissons maintenant nos pensées pour saluer nos parents du monde céleste inférieur et les remercier de leur soutien continu et de leur direction.

Nous sommes d'une même pensée.

Nous nous concentrons maintenant sur le monde céleste supérieur. Nous remercions le chemin céleste que nous empruntons tous pour retourner vers la terre de notre grand-mère. Nous reconnaissons le travail continu des quatre êtres qui veillent sur nous et aident la création en lui apportant direction et protection. Nous remercions tous nos ancêtres qui avant nous ont parcouru le chemin céleste, qui sont maintenant réunis dans la terre de notre grand-mère en attendant que nous ayons fini de le parcourir.

Nous unissons maintenant nos pensées pour saluer tous nos ancêtres et parents du monde céleste supérieur et les remercier.

Nous sommes d'une même pensée.

Nous portons maintenant notre attention vers l'être qui a créé toutes choses. Nous ne comprenons pas sa puissance. Nous ne le désignons ni comme mâle ni comme femelle, mais nous reconnaissons qu'il est la source de tout ce qui existe.

Nous unissons maintenant nos pensées pour saluer et remercier le créateur de toutes choses.

Nous sommes d'une même pensée.

Il est possible que j'aie fait un oubli ou que vous soyez particulièrement reconnaissant pour un bienfait.

C'est maintenant le moment d'offrir vos salutations et de témoigner votre gratitude pour les ajouter à tout ce qui a déjà été dit, alors que nous sommes d'une même pensée.

Nous sommes d'une même pensée.

Nous avons fait ce qu'on nous demandait.

Nous sommes maintenant prêts à commencer ce pourquoi nous nous sommes réunis ici.

THÓ NIKAWÉN:NAKE

---

[1] Allocution d'ouverture et remerciements de Haudenosaunee prononcés à l'ouverture de l'exposition des pièces de musée Kahswenhtah et Kariwatatie, à Kanehsatà:ke, au cours de l'été 1993.

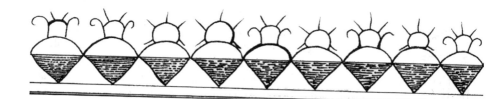

CHAPITRE 1

DEPUIS DES TEMPS IMMÉMORIAUX

TIONONTE'KÓ:WA

 Skén:nen (paix), voilà les paroles qui ont été prononcées. Elles sont les racines du peuple qui vit ici. Les Kanehsata'kehró:non (peuple de Kanehsatà:ke) ont reçu cette ancienne sagesse depuis aussi longtemps qu'ils peuvent s'en souvenir. Ces paroles sont aussi vraies maintenant qu'elles l'ont toujours été. Comme un remède, elles soulagent et enlèvent la douleur.

Aujourd'hui, je suis très étonnée d'entendre votre voix traverser la forêt jusqu'à dans cette clairière. Vous avez franchi tous les obstacles avec un esprit préoccupé. Vous avez vu les lieux où nos aînés avaient l'habitude de se réunir et les empreintes de pas de nos ancêtres. Comment votre esprit peut-il être tranquille, alors que vous pouvez presque apercevoir la fumée où ils avaient l'habitude de fumer ensemble? Pouvez-vous être en paix lorsque vous pleurez en chemin?

Je suis très heureuse parce que vous êtes arrivés sains et saufs. Faisons maintenant brûler du tabac ensemble. Partout aux alentours, il y a des groupes hostiles qui se disent: *Nous allons contrecarrer leur but.* Voici des chemins épineux, des arbres qui tombent et des bêtes sauvages qui attendent en embuscade. Vous auriez pu périr par ces choses, être détruits par des inondations, par la hachette levée contre vous dans l'obscurité à l'extérieur de la maison, ou par une maladie mortelle invisible. Chaque jour, ces choses nous affaiblissent.

Je suis très reconnaissant parce que vous avez traversé la forêt en toute sécurité. Il aurait été regrettable que vous ayez péri en chemin et qu'on nous ait annoncé cette nouvelle saisissante: «Voici le lieu où reposent les corps des hommes et de leurs chefs». Et ils auraient été consternés à la pensée de ce qui serait arrivé.

Nos ancêtres nous ont enseigné: «Ils sont ici pour allumer un feu. À l'orée des bois, ils doivent exprimer leurs sympathies les uns aux autres avec peu de mots». Mais ils sont allés à la maison du Conseil pour terminer toutes les affaires comme il convient, de même que pour offrir leurs condoléances.[1]

Grâce à ces paroles, on peut commencer à comprendre le peuple et son origine. Il a recours à l'ancienne cérémonie des condoléances pour se libérer de sa douleur et de sa peur et pour retrouver de saines pensées. Je suis la montagne, et le peuple m'appelle Tiononte'kó:wa. Laissez-moi vous raconter les choses que j'ai vues.

Ensemble, le peuple a parcouru bien des chemins. La route était parfois difficile: des roches et des arbres tombés nous bloquaient la route. Les Kanehsata'kehró:non s'employaient toujours à la dégager pour faciliter la marche. Souvent, les rivières coulaient doucement et le peuple arrivait en toute sécurité à sa destination. Je le voyais vivre comme le Créateur le voulait. Parfois, il trouvait très difficile d'assumer ses responsabilités, mais il a toujours dit: «Nous sommes issus de cette terre».

Avec le temps, de nombreuses forces ont frappé le peuple et l'ont divisé. De l'autre côté de la grande mer, des étrangers sont arrivés et ont essayé de leur faire abandonner leurs coutumes et leurs terres. Ils ont utilisé tous les moyens possibles pour y arriver. Les Kanehsata'kehró:non ont ouvert les bras aux nouveaux arrivants pour ensuite être trahis par eux. En échange de nourriture, d'abri et de commodités, ceux-ci ont introduit des maladies inconnues chez les Onkwehón:we (le peuple original). Les nouveaux arrivants ont donné au peuple des substances puissantes qui altèrent l'esprit et, plus tard, ils ont pris leurs enfants.

Les Kanehsata'kehró:non ont réagi avec patience et bonté. Par de bonnes paroles et un esprit ouvert, ils ont cherché des moyens pacifiques d'enlever les nouveaux obstacles de leur chemin. Aussitôt le chemin dégagé, d'autres obstacles se dressaient autour d'eux. Pour ce peuple la vie était devenue une lutte pour conserver les choses que le Créateur lui avait données, ainsi qu'un combat pour survivre.

Venez maintenant et assemblons-nous à l'orée des bois.

Unissons nos pensées. Essuyons les larmes de nos yeux et écoutons les paroles qui sont prononcées.

Je suis Tiononte'kó:wa. Le temps est venu de parler.

LE COMMENCEMENT : LES ENSEIGNEMENTS DU PEUPLE[2]

J'ai promis de vous raconter l'histoire du peuple, les Kanehsata'kehró:non. Pour la commencer, nous devons remonter très loin, à l'époque où notre monde n'était rien d'autre qu'un globe d'eau qui tournait comme une énorme goutte de pluie. Laissez-moi vous amener à un endroit qui n'est pas de ce monde. C'est là que notre histoire commence.

Le monde dont je parle s'appelait le monde céleste; il était peuplé par des êtres qui allaient et venaient à peu près comme vous. Il y avait des plantes, des oiseaux et d'autres créatures semblables à ceux qui partagent notre monde actuel. Dans cet endroit, il y avait aussi un arbre très spécial dont les grandes branches portaient toutes sortes de fruits. Cet arbre était connu comme l'arbre de vie ou l'arbre céleste. Grand et magnifique, on pouvait l'apercevoir de très loin.

Cet arbre était une source de puissance et un moyen de subsistance pour les habitants du monde céleste. À ses pieds et sur ses branches poussaient toutes les plantes médicinales dont les gens avaient besoin. À cette époque, dans le monde céleste, il y avait un homme et son épouse qui s'aimaient beaucoup. Leur maison était remplie de paix et d'harmonie. Quand vint le temps pour la femme d'enfanter, le couple était rempli de joie et d'anticipation dans l'attente de cette nouvelle vie. L'homme, qui était un bon mari, se donnait beaucoup de mal pour s'assurer que sa femme ne soit pas irritée, qu'elle ne souffre pas de faim ni ne manque de quoi que ce soit. Avec amour et compassion, il prenait les mesures nécessaires pour que sa femme soit en paix et en joie.

Le jour arriva où la femme fut prise d'un désir étrange et inconnu. L'homme se mit donc à chercher partout la chose qui satisferait ce désir. À maintes reprises, il retourna auprès de sa femme rien que pour être déçu, car il était incapable de combler son besoin. Puis, un jour, il lui apporta une racine de l'arbre céleste; c'était de cela dont elle avait envie. Tout allait bien pour le moment, mais son désir insatiable ne tarda pas à augmenter et à augmenter, si bien qu'elle eut besoin de plus en plus de racines pour le satisfaire. Son mari ne lui en rapportant pas suffisamment, la femme alla elle-même à l'arbre s'en chercher.

Quand la femme arriva à l'arbre céleste, elle remarqua un gros trou noir à l'endroit où son mari avait creusé. Elle s'agenouilla et regarda attentivement dans ce trou, mais n'y vit que noirceur. En se penchant un peu plus dans le trou, elle put voir une boule d'eau. Soudain, elle perdit l'équilibre et tomba. Saisissant le bord du trou, elle tenta de s'y agripper pour se sauver, mais trop tard. Elle tomba dans le trou et traversa le monde céleste. Durant sa chute, la femme céleste tenait dans ses mains une fraise et du tabac.

La chute dura très longtemps et, dans l'obscurité, la femme céleste entendit un bruit de tourbillon et de glissement. En fait, le son qu'elle percevait ressemblait beaucoup au bruit d'un hochet. Au fur et à mesure qu'elle tombait, la boule d'eau grossissait et, en s'en approchant de plus en plus, elle pouvait voir des êtres qui y nageaient. D'autres créatures volaient au-dessus de sa surface. À ce moment, les êtres aquatiques regardèrent en haut et virent quelque chose qui tombait sur eux. Constatant que c'était un être vivant, ils décidèrent rapidement d'envoyer certains des leurs à la rencontre de la femme céleste. Les cygnes, les oies, les canards, les huards et tous les autres oiseaux aquatiques volèrent très haut et se formèrent comme un drap pour amortir sa chute. Ensemble, ils la descendirent lentement et la placèrent doucement sur la carapace de la grosse tortue.

Comme la femme céleste se reposait sur la carapace de la tortue, toutes les créatures aquatiques se réunirent autour d'elle et se mirent à lui parler. Ils lui souhaitèrent la bienvenue dans leur monde et lui demandèrent de quelle manière ils pouvaient lui être utiles. La femme céleste les remercia de leur gentillesse et admit qu'elle se sentait seule et qu'elle s'ennuyait de son chez soi. « Il n'y a pas de terre ici, dit-elle, rien que de l'eau. » Les êtres aquatiques lui dirent qu'il y avait de la terre sous l'eau et décidèrent d'aller lui en chercher. Étant un être brave et vigoureux, le castor fut le premier à essayer. Il plongea dans les profondeurs, mais rapidement vaincu, il ne put atteindre le fond. L'un après l'autre, le huard, le rat musqué, le canard et tous les animaux essayèrent, mais aucun ne réussit à rapporter de la terre. Finalement, la loutre offrit à son tour d'essayer.

Bonne nageuse, la loutre était certaine de pouvoir réussir. Elle plongea donc, de plus en plus profondément, jusqu'à ce qu'elle sente que ses poumons allaient éclater. Puis, soudain, elle vit de la terre devant elle. À l'aide de ses pattes, elle s'empressa d'en ramasser le plus possible et retourna vers la surface. La loutre n'eut malheureusement pas la force d'aller jusqu'au bout. Elle était allée trop loin, pendant trop longtemps. Elle mourut juste avant d'atteindre la surface. Son petit corps remonta et flotta sur les vagues, mais la petite motte de terre resta agrippée à ses pattes.

La femme céleste se pencha, saisit la terre des pattes de la loutre et la plaça sur la carapace de la tortue. Elle prit ensuite la fraise et le tabac qu'elle avait apportés du monde céleste et les planta dans la petite motte de terre qui commença à grossir. La femme céleste se mit alors à marcher en cercle et, ce faisant, la motte devint un grand continent. Des montagnes, des vallées et des canyons se formèrent.

À ce moment-là, de cette petite motte de terre, je me mis moi-même à grandir. C'était la naissance de notre grand continent, l'île de la Tortue. Beaucoup de choses se passèrent par la suite, des choses merveilleuses et, selon certains, des choses incroyables. J'étais là et je les vis toutes. Je regardais quand les forces jumelles de l'ordre et du chaos augmentèrent, puis luttèrent ensemble. Je vis la tête de la grand-mère, la femme céleste, être projetée vers le ciel. Je vis le monde, tel que nous le connaissons aujourd'hui, prendre forme, ainsi que des êtres humains et toutes sortes d'animaux être créés. Je vis ces choses et je peux vous les raconter, mais ce sera pour une autre fois.

La femme céleste qui regarde la terre
de Katsi'tsakwas

L'ARRIVÉE DE L'ARTISAN DE LA PAIX

Permettez-moi maintenant de vous parler des choses dont on discutait autrefois autour de divers feux durant les longues nuits d'hiver. À tour de rôle, les grands-mères et les grands-pères dispensaient leurs instructions aux enfants, mais ne le faisaient que sous forme d'histoires. Bien des choses se transmettaient ainsi.

Vous savez peut-être déjà que les Kanehsata'kehró:non formaient une petite communauté d'une nation appelée Kanien'kehà:ka (le peuple du silex, les Mohawks). Ceux-ci étaient frères de plusieurs peuples et alliés de nombreux autres. Pendant longtemps, la paix régnait sur le territoire. Le peuple de Kanehsatà:ke, comme leurs frères des communautés voisines et éloignées, prospérait et se fortifiait. Les récoltes et le gibier abondaient. Le peuple voyageait partout pour chasser, commercer et se visiter. La vie d'alors était très belle.

Toutefois, le temps vint où le peuple fut déchiré par la guerre. C'était bien avant que les O'serón:ni (les Français, les Européens) n'arrivent ici. La guerre éclata entre les diverses nations, entre les villages, les clans et même les familles. La peur régnait partout. À cause de la colère et de la douleur, les gens avaient perdu la raison et leur capacité de s'aimer. Souffrant et cherchant à se venger, ils avaient mis de côté les instructions que le Créateur leur avait données. On ignore si c'est par oubli ou négligence qu'ils le firent, mais les effets désastreux de leurs actions se faisaient sentir partout.

Le peuple était sur le point de s'autodétruire quand, un jour, un étranger arriva parmi eux, apportant un message de paix. Ce messager rappela aux gens les manières d'après lesquelles ils étaient censés vivre. Il leur offrit ses condoléances et, ce faisant, enleva le fardeau de douleur et de colère qui pesait sur leur cœur et qui embrouillait leur esprit. Il utilisa la peau de biche la plus douce pour essuyer les larmes de leurs yeux, et leur vision fut rétablie. Il prit la plume d'un aigle pour dégager leurs oreilles de ce qui les obstruait, et leur entendement fut rétabli. Il leur donna de l'eau de source pure pour nettoyer la bile de leur gorge, et ils purent alors parler librement. Ils étaient de nouveau sains d'esprit et disposés à accepter le message de la paix.

Cet étranger était l'Artisan de la paix et il aida les gens à être unis en esprit.[3] Ceux-ci formèrent la Grande Ligue de la paix – la Kaianere'kó:wa – et, avec leurs frères des nations O'nientehá:ka (le peuple du rocher debout, les Oneidas), Ononta'kehàka (le peuple de la colline, les Onondagas), Kaionkeháka (le peuple du grand calumet, les Cayugas) et Shenekeháka (le peuple de la grande montagne, les Sénécas) et l'aide de l'Artisan de la paix, ils créèrent un mécanisme pour maintenir la paix. Désormais unies, ces nations devinrent connues sous le nom de Rotinonhseshá:ka ou peuple de la maison longue.

Avant d'entrer dans le premier village des Kanien'kehà:ka pour apporter la bonne nouvelle de la paix, l'Artisan de la paix arriva à une petite cabane faite d'écorce. Cette cabane était située juste à côté d'un sentier que les guerriers empruntaient lors de leurs expéditions de guerre.

Dans cette cabane vivait une femme qui avait décidé de nourrir et de réconforter ces guerriers. Avec grand enthousiasme, elle écoutait leurs histoires de guerre et de destruction. Elle ne refusait de nourriture à personne. En voyant l'Artisan de la paix approcher, elle lui prépara à manger et l'accueillit. L'Artisan de la paix lui partagea sa vision et lui demanda de ne plus encourager ces guerriers. Réfléchissant aux bonnes paroles qu'elle venait d'entendre, cette femme accepta de ne plus nourrir les guerriers. Elle voyait que cette grande paix était une bonne chose.

Elle fut connue sous le nom de Tiekonhsá:se, qui signifie «nouveau visage», parce qu'elle fut la première à accepter le message de l'Artisan de la paix. Le peuple l'appelle «Mère de toutes les nations».

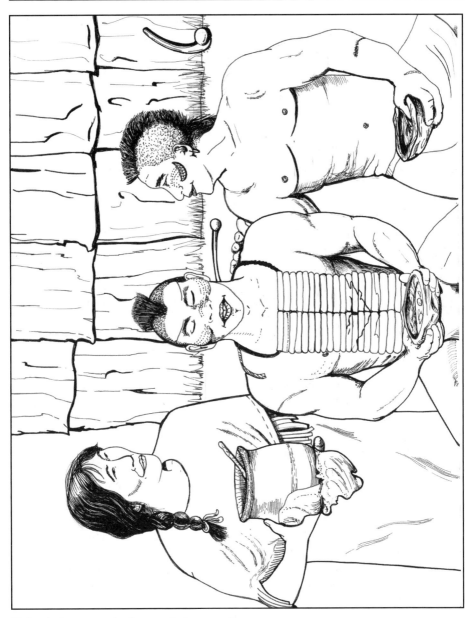

Tiekonhsá:se en train de nourrir les guerriers
de Katsi'tsakwas

La Kaianere'kó:wa rassembla les peuples et leur donna les moyens de maintenir et de promouvoir la paix; et les cérémonies renouvelaient leurs forces spirituelles. En réinstallant et en fortifiant l'ancien système de clans, ils élargirent les liens de parenté au sein de toutes les communautés et nations de la Ligue. Ils se débarrassèrent de leurs armes de guerre et firent le serment de ne plus jamais les utiliser les uns contre les autres. Ils bannirent le meurtre et défendirent de répandre le sang sur leur territoire. Je pouvais les voir commencer à marcher comme s'ils étaient dégagés d'un fardeau insupportable.

Ce lourd fardeau de douleur et de colère avait disparu et fut remplacé par un sentiment d'appartenance et de quiétude.

Les gens avaient accompli une chose vraiment merveilleuse. Ils vécurent ainsi pendant des centaines d'années jusqu'à ce que les premiers arrivants malavisés débarquent sur les rives de l'île de la Tortue.

LA KAIANERE'KÓ:WA :
LE GRAND BIEN, LA GRANDE PAIX, LA GRANDE LOI

L'histoire des Rotinonhseshá:ka (peuple de la maison longue) se transmet oralement de génération en génération sous forme de récits et d'enseignements. Ces enseignements leur servent à se rappeler leurs racines dans cette terre et à se souvenir que le Créateur les y a placés pour jouer un certain rôle et assumer certaines responsabilités. C'est un devoir sacré qu'ils accomplissent, une lourde tâche qu'ils acceptent joyeusement.

De temps à autre, des messagers étaient envoyés pour rappeler au peuple ses responsabilités en tant qu'êtres humains et sa place dans le monde naturel. À ces occasions, quand ils avaient oublié comment vivre en harmonie avec la nature et les autres, un messager venait et leur rappelait les choses qu'ils avaient mises de côté. Grâce à l'aide du messager, le peuple retrouvait des habitudes pacifiques et vivait de nouveau en équilibre. La création d'un nouveau mode de vie permettait au peuple de croître et de prospérer.

À une époque où, sur des continents lointains, d'autres croyaient qu'ils étaient le centre de l'univers et que la terre était plate, les Rotinonhseshá:ka avaient acquis une compréhension profonde de leur monde et du rôle qu'ils y jouaient.

Il y a longtemps, avant l'arrivée des O'serón:ni (les Français) dans cette partie de l'île de la Tortue (Amérique du Nord), les Rotinonhseshá:ka avaient élaboré et établi un système complexe de gouvernement et de diplomatie. Ce système créait un lien étroit entre la spiritualité et leurs politiques. Ils l'appelèrent Kaianere'kó:wa : le Grand Bien, la Grande Paix, la Grande Loi.[4] La reconnaissance et le respect de toutes formes de vie et des droits fondamentaux de chaque personne en font partie intégrante.[5]

La date de la création de la Kaianere'kó:wa est toujours un sujet de débat : certains érudits prétendent qu'elle débuta après l'arrivée des Européens en Amérique du Nord, tandis que d'autres la situent autour de l'an 1300 apr. J.-C.[6] De nombreux Rotinonhseshá:ka croient qu'elle est beaucoup plus vieille, puisque le présent Athotarho est apparemment la 200e personne à occuper ce poste. Le titre d'Athotarho, comme tous les titres des Rotinonhseshá:ka, est transmis de génération en génération, et le poste est généralement occupé toute une vie. Avant la dévastation entraînée par les maladies européennes, dont la varicelle contre laquelle le peuple n'était aucunement immunisé, une longévité de cent ans n'était pas rare. Selon une estimation conservatrice, une personne pouvait garder le titre pendant cinquante ans. Il ne fait aucun doute que beaucoup le conservèrent plus longtemps. Ainsi, la création de la Kaianere'kó:wa pourrait remonter à l'an 1100 apr. J.-C.[7]

Le message de l'Artisan de la paix reposait sur le simple fondement que toute personne capable de raisonner désire naturellement la paix. Même si les gens avaient cette capacité, leur douleur et leur colère les empêchaient d'atteindre ce but.

La première tâche de l'Artisan de la paix consistait à ramener le peuple à la raison en utilisant la douceur et des paroles d'encouragement. Les gens commençaient à apaiser leur douleur et leur colère par des moyens non belliqueux. Ils réapprenaient à s'aimer et à résoudre pacifiquement les questions qui étaient à l'origine d'un conflit. Beaucoup d'obstacles à la paix étaient ainsi surmontés.

Les disputes au sujet des territoires de chasse empêchaient les gens de vivre en paix. Les nations des Rotinonhseshá:ka décidèrent donc de mettre les terres en commun.[8] Tous auraient un droit égal de les utiliser pour la chasse et la culture. Ainsi, personne ne manquerait de nourriture ni d'abri. Le peuple se rendit compte également que la hiérarchie favorisait des abus de pouvoir et se révélait une source importante de conflit. Les Rotinonhseshá:ka décidèrent qu'ils ne devraient pas avoir de relations avec une personne ou un groupe qui en domine un autre. Le Créateur avait mis toutes choses sur cette terre pour que nous assumions certains devoirs et certaines responsabilités. On demanda aux Rotinonhseshá:ka d'honorer et de respecter toute vie. Le Créateur n'avait jamais prévu que les êtres humains se détruisent. Ils acceptèrent donc de ne plus se faire la guerre.

La société des Rotinonhseshá:ka est bâtie sur un fondement de paix, de justice et de respect. Au lieu d'être hiérarchique et coercitive, elle met l'accent sur la justice, l'égalité, la spiritualité et le respect. La justice ne comprenait pas nécessairement des mesures punitives prises contre ceux qui commettent des crimes. Par la médiation et la compensation, elle était plus efficace pour résoudre les disputes à la satisfaction de tous les partis. Parfois, et seulement en dernier recours, les incorrigibles étaient bannis pour préserver le bien-être de toute la communauté.

En instaurant un système de consensus réalisé par une délibération pacifique, les Rotinonhseshá:ka éliminèrent le factionnalisme et la polarisation au sein de leurs communautés. Selon son clan et sa nation, chaque personne était représentée par un des cinquante Rotiiá:nehr (chefs). Ces dirigeants étaient choisis par les femmes de leur clan qui étaient investies des titres héréditaires d'autorité. Le peuple était représenté au conseil de la Ligue par les Ronteriiohserakwe'ní:io (chefs de guerre) qui eux aussi étaient choisis par les femmes du clan.

Les Ronteriiohserakwe'ní:io ne participaient pas aux délibérations entre les Rotiiá:nehr du conseil, mais observaient les procédures et s'assuraient qu'elles soient suivies correctement. Leur devoir consistait à présenter les questions et les préoccupations du peuple devant le conseil, en les soumettant au Well (tribunal). Le Well est l'entité responsable de préparer le programme des conseils, et ce sont les Kanien'kehà:ka (Mohawks) qui occupaient cette position dans le conseil. Les Ronteriiohserakwe'ní:io étaient également responsables de livrer les avertissements des mères de clan aux Rotiiá:nehr. Si un Roiiá:nehr fautif négligeait de considérer les avertissements de sa mère de clan, les Ronteriiohserakwe'ní:io prenaient les mesures nécessaires pour le dépouiller de son titre. En dernier recours, le Roiiá:nehr qui refusait de s'amender était matraqué à mort par les Rotisken'raké:ta (les guerriers).

Les Ronteriiohserakwe'ní:io étaient souvent délégués pour agir en faveur des Rotiiá:nehr durant la négociation d'alliances et la prolifération de la Kaianere'kó:wa. Le but de la Kaianere'kó:wa était la paix dans le monde, et sa nature consistait à la promouvoir. Parfois, les négociations se terminaient par une guerre contre des nations hostiles. Si une nation étrangère s'opposait toujours à la Kaianere'kó:wa, après avoir épuisé tous les moyens pacifiques, les Ronteriiohserakwe'ní:io lui déclaraient la guerre avec la sanction

L'Artisan de la paix
de Katsi'tsakwas

du conseil. La guerre se poursuivait jusqu'à ce que les Rotinonhseshá:ka gagnent, puis la paix était rétablie. Les nations qui acceptaient la paix devenaient des alliés ou membres de la Confédération, mais conservaient toujours leur gouvernement interne et leur culture. Les nations vaincues lors d'une guerre étaient parfois dispersées dans tout le territoire des Rotinonhseshá:ka et réintégrées dans ces communautés par des adoptions à grande échelle.[9] La plupart du temps, reconnaissant les avantages d'une union pacifique, les autres nations s'alliaient de leur propre gré aux Rotinonhseshá:ka.

Pendant qu'ils élaboraient la Kaianere'kó:wa, l'Artisan de la paix et les Rotiiá:nehr des Rotinonhseshá:ka produisaient plusieurs documents sous forme de ceintures de wampum. Ces ceintures déclaraient, confirmaient et ratifiaient les concepts et les politiques exprimés dans la Kaianere'kó:wa. Le wampum en cercle est un registre de la fondation et de l'organisation de la Kaianere'kó:wa. Les deux rangées de wampum blanc qui sont entrelacées pour former un cercle représentent le fait que les aspects spirituels et politiques de la Kaianere'kó:wa sont inséparables. À l'intérieur du cercle, cinquante ficelles de wampum blanc représentent les cinquante titres des Rotiiá:nehr de la Ligue.

Le cercle wampum évoque une croyance des Rotinonhseshá:ka selon laquelle la spiritualité est la forme la plus élevée de conscience politique. La spiritualité devient alors beaucoup plus qu'un rituel. Le cercle révèle les liens invisibles qui existent entre les êtres humains et la vie végétale, les animaux et les oiseaux, les poissons et le monde minéral. Il traduit ces liens en actions, en paroles et en chants. C'est une célébration du lien commun appelé « force de la vie ». Le lien relationnel très fort qui est ainsi nourri favorise, en retour, un respect et un sentiment d'appartenance au grand cercle de la vie.

Les cérémonies rappellent aux Rotinonhseshá:ka l'aspect sacré de l'esprit et les responsabilités que chaque personne doit toujours assumer. Des aînés aux touts petits, chacun porte ce fardeau et cette joie. Tout le monde et toutes choses sont liés et en même temps interdépendants. La dignité et le respect s'étendent à tous. C'est ainsi qu'ils apprennent à voir le monde.

Les Rotinonhseshá:ka adoptaient donc leurs politiques de manière à tenir compte, non seulement du bien-être de leur propre peuple, mais aussi de l'équilibre qui doit être maintenu en chaque personne, entre les gens et dans le monde dont nous faisons partie. Une paix durable ne s'obtient pas seulement par des moyens militaires ou politiques, mais aussi par une prise de conscience plus forte et une meilleure compréhension. Une telle paix ne peut subsister quand les gens vivent dans la peur ou la colère, ni prévaloir quand ils ne reconnaissent pas les autres comme des êtres humains et des frères. Il n'est pas suffisant de simplement tolérer ceux qui sont différents, puisque la tolérance peut facilement se dissiper dans les moments difficiles. Les Rotinonhseshá:ka reconnaissent que toute vie a un but et un sens et qu'elle doit être honorée et respectée.

Le wampum blanc représente la paix et la pureté. Il indique que les hommes qui sont Rotiiá:nehr ne devraient jamais prendre les armes ou aller à la guerre. Étant les dirigeants spirituels et politiques du peuple, les Rotiiá:nehr doivent travailler au maintien et à la promotion de la paix. On dit qu'ils devraient avoir une peau de sept épaisseurs et qu'ils ne devraient pas être influencés par les jalousies et les irritations ou laisser la colère et l'impatience embrouiller leur raisonnement.

Sur le plan matériel, les chefs des Rotinonhseshá:ka sont les plus pauvres du peuple. On s'attend à ce qu'ils partagent leurs biens avec ceux qui sont encore plus pauvres qu'eux. La richesse du peuple est partagée entre tous et n'appartient pas à quelques-uns. Les conflits engendrés par l'avidité associée au matérialisme sont ainsi éliminés. La véritable richesse des Rotinonhseshá:ka se trouve dans la terre, la culture, la langue, le pouvoir des cérémonies et l'esprit du peuple.

La Kaianere'kó:wa, appelée la « Constitution des Iroquois », aborde autant les questions relatives aux rapports entre les nations qu'aux droits des enfants. Dans les clans matrilinéaires, les enfants ont l'assurance d'avoir droit à une famille et d'occuper une place dans la société. Tout enfant né dans l'une des cinq nations reçoit un nom au cours d'un des principaux festivals qui a lieu durant l'année. Cet enfant fait automatiquement partie du clan de sa mère. En cas du décès prématuré de ses parents, l'enfant est élevé par les membres de sa famille maternelle. Toutes les femmes du clan sont pour l'enfant des mères, des grands-mères et des tantes et elles partagent une égale responsabilité de l'élever. Ainsi, aucun enfant n'est privé du bienfait de faire partie d'une famille. Dans tout le territoire des Rotinonhseshá:ka, les personnes d'un même clan se considèrent comme apparentés, et c'est pour cela que les femmes et les hommes d'un même clan ne peuvent se marier entre eux. La politique de se marier en dehors du clan sert à renforcer les liens entre les clans, les villages et les nations. Traditionnellement, un couple marié vit dans la communauté de la femme, même si l'homme ne devient pas membre de son clan.

Les femmes sont investies du droit à la terre et de sa sauvegarde, ainsi que de la culture du peuple. Les Ioti'tarakéhte (mères de clan) ont la responsabilité de choisir les hommes qui recevront les titres de dirigeants, ainsi que les chefs de guerre. Puisqu'elles portent la plus grande part de la responsabilité d'élever les enfants, elles savent quels garçons et quels hommes possèdent les qualités nécessaires pour diriger. Quand un Roiiá:nehr meurt, la Iako'tarakéhte (mère de clan), qui possède le titre du défunt, consulte ses parentes et choisit avec elles un remplaçant. Ce choix doit franchir plusieurs étapes de confirmation unanime avant d'être ratifié par le conseil des Rotiiá:nehr. Un Roiiá:nehr conserve son poste jusqu'à ce qu'il devienne infirme ou qu'il meurt. Il sera parfois démis de son poste – ou «dé-cornu» – s'il néglige de rechercher les intérêts du peuple. Cela n'arrive qu'après avoir reçu un avertissement ou une directive de changer de vie.

L'autorité et la responsabilité de répandre le message de la paix sont représentées dans la ceinture Hiawatha. C'est l'emblème de l'unité des Rotinonhseshá:ka. C'est une grande ceinture mauve ornée d'un dessin fait de wampum blanc qui consiste, de gauche à droite, de deux carrés blancs, d'un arbre ou d'un cœur blanc et de deux autres carrés blancs. Une ligne blanche passe à l'intérieur de chaque extrémité reliant chaque carré au cœur. De gauche à droite, les carrés représentent le peuple, la culture et les territoires des Kanien'kehà:ka, des O'nientehá:ka, des Kaionkeháka et des Shenekeháka. L'arbre ou le cœur blanc représente le peuple, la culture et le territoire des Ononta'keháka. Il symbolise également que les Rotinonhseshá:ka ne forment qu'un même esprit, un même cœur et un même corps, unis dans leur loyauté envers la Kaianere'kó:wa. Tout comme cinq flèches solidement attachées ensemble se brisent moins facilement qu'une seule, un peuple uni est moins facilement vaincu qu'un peuple dont les membres se battent entre eux.

La Kaianere'kó:wa unit les gens spirituellement et politiquement en renforçant les liens déjà existants de parenté et de culture. Elle leur permet de décider collectivement des questions qui touchent tous les Rotinonhseshá:ka, tout en laissant les diverses nations et communautés jouir d'une grande autonomie.

La ligne blanche qui traverse la ceinture Hiawatha symbolise le chemin de la paix que doivent suivre les autres peuples qui cherchent refuge sous l'arbre de la paix. Ils peuvent s'en approcher par la porte orientale – les Kanien'kehà:ka – ou la porte occidentale – les Shenekeháka. Une nation qui ne fait pas partie de la Ligue doit d'abord passer par le Kanien'kehà:ka ou le Shenekeháka pour y être admise. À un moment ou à un autre, au moins trente-neuf nations Onkwehón:we différentes trouvèrent refuge sous l'arbre de paix auprès des Rotinonhseshá:ka. Elles formèrent avec eux une alliance politique et diplomatique et, à l'occasion, cherchèrent protection sur leur territoire. Parfois, des villages entiers s'y réfugièrent pour se protéger et se cacher de l'ennemi.

Toutes les nations furent invitées à se joindre à la Ligue et à résoudre pacifiquement leurs différends. Pour symboliser la Grande Paix, un grand arbre fut planté à Ononta'keháka. Ses racines blanches s'étendent dans les quatre directions pour que toute nation ou toute personne qui désire la paix puisse suivre les racines jusqu'à leur source et s'abriter sous l'arbre. Un aigle placé à la cime de l'arbre avertit les gens d'un danger imminent. L'aigle, qui possède une vision exceptionnellement claire, peut voir à une grande distance. Il est le symbole de la vigilance éternelle nécessaire pour préserver une véritable paix durable. Pour les Rotinonhseshá:ka, la paix n'est pas quelque chose de passif qui n'existe qu'en l'absence de guerre. La paix est une façon de vivre qui doit être activement maintenue et protégée.

Ensemble, les nations unies des Rotinonhseshá:ka forment le fondement d'une maison agrandie, habitée par une très grande famille élargie. Lors des conseils, on fait référence à chaque nation comme à des frères. Ces liens de parenté impliquent des responsabilités et des obligations plutôt qu'un rang ou une autorité. Les Kanien'kehà:ka et les Shenekeháka sont des frères aînés – désignés aussi respectivement par la porte orientale et la porte occidentale. Les O'nientehá:ka et les Kaionkeháka sont des frères cadets. Les Ononta'keháka, gardiens du feu central, sont également désignés comme des frères aînés.

Lorsqu'il faut prendre des décisions, chaque nation joue son rôle dans les délibérations; aucune n'exerce d'autorité sur les autres. On dit que le plancher de cette maison symbolique représente l'étendue et les limites de la terre des Rotinonhseshá:ka et que le plafond rappelle l'étendue du ciel. Les chevrons de la maison évoquent les lois de la Kaianere'kó:wa. Lorsque de nouvelles lois sont créées, on dit qu'on ajoute des poutres. Quand une nouvelle nation se joint à la Ligue, elle est vue comme une poutre qui soutient la maison et la fortifie. Tout comme la maison peut être agrandie pour inclure beaucoup d'autres personnes, la Kaianere'kó:wa peut être élargie et s'adapter pour répondre aux besoins des gens et aux défis auxquels ils font face.

C'est ce qu'on appelle la Kaianere'kó:wa : le Grand Bien, la Grande Paix, la Grande Loi. C'est une tradition ancienne fermement enracinée dans le passé, qui possède également une capacité inhérente de s'adapter aux situations modernes. Ses idéaux, ses philosophies et ses politiques sont toujours pertinents. C'est le moyen par lequel les Rotinonhseshá:ka se dirigeront vers l'avenir. La Kaianere'kó:wa renferme de nombreuses réponses aux questions et aux défis auxquels ils sont confrontés aujourd'hui.

Alors que le peuple retourne s'abriter sous le grand arbre de la paix, beaucoup de gens prennent conscience que de nombreuses vérités leur sont révélées lorsque l'on suit les racines jusqu'à la source.

Ce n'est qu'en connaissant nos origines que nous pourrons comprendre notre situation présente et notre destination.

La clé de l'avenir du peuple se trouve dans le passé.

L'ORIGINE DE KANEHSATÀ:KE

À l'occident, l'ancien descend lentement dans le ciel, au-dessus du lac. Notre frère aîné laisse derrière lui un autre jour et, ce faisant, peint le firmament de pastels chatoyants. Les couleurs éclatantes qui miroitent sur le lac dansent sur les douces vagues perpétuelles. Chaque ondulation, comme un moment dans le temps, rappelle les générations à venir et celles qui les ont précédées.

Je pense aux temps anciens, à l'époque où les premiers êtres humains arrivèrent ici. Il y a fort longtemps que des gens marchent sur cette terre. Pendant de nombreuses années, de grandes étendues d'eau et de glace couvraient la terre.[10] Peu à peu, à mesure que la terre émergeait, je pouvais voir de petits groupes de personnes qui chassaient et pêchaient. On aurait dit qu'ils sortaient de la terre et poussaient. Ils venaient souvent dans les environs ramasser l'argile pour fabriquer leur poterie. Parfois, en route vers un autre lieu, ils ne faisaient que passer. En ce temps-là, le gibier était abondant et les eaux regorgeaient de poissons. Comme une grande partie de la vie végétale et animale, les gens arrivèrent d'abord avec les saisons. Et comme les grands arbres au fil des ans, leurs racines s'étendirent plus profondément dans cette terre. Chaque visite durait plus longtemps que la précédente et, après un certain temps, les gens durent rester. Ils en étaient venus à éprouver un sentiment d'appartenance, une sorte de lien, comme celui d'un enfant dans le sein de sa mère. Ils hésitaient à partir, même pour le plus court des voyages.

Ici même, à côté de moi, ils construisirent leur village qui donna naissance à l'ancienne bourgade du clan de la Tortue, appelée Kanehsatà:ke. Protégeant le petit village et veillant sur lui, je le vis grandir en une communauté de taille considérable. Par la rivière, les gens voyageaient facilement et rapidement vers des territoires de chasse éloignés, des routes commerciales et d'autres communautés où ils avaient de la parenté.

Quand le peuple recevait le don du maïs, des haricots et de la courge, il remerciait le Créateur pour la nourriture qui améliorait sa vie.[11] Il avait reçu tout ce dont il avait besoin. Les hommes aidaient à préparer la terre, tandis que les femmes l'ensemençaient et la cultivaient. Le peuple ne faisait pas de coupes à blanc dans les forêts comme les O'serón:ni (les Français) allaient plus tard le faire, mais il cultivait dans les forêts, gardant à l'esprit l'équilibre naturel qui existait.

Je vous ai parlé du respect du peuple pour toute forme de vie; il ne prenait donc que ce dont il avait besoin. Il ramassait du bois mort pour ses feux et ne coupait des arbres vivants qu'en cas de besoin absolu. Il était entendu que chacun avait ses responsabilités dans les cycles du monde naturel. De temps à autre, le cerf et les autres animaux donnaient leur vie pour servir de nourriture et de vêtement pour le peuple. En retour, le peuple prenait soin de la terre pour que les animaux aient plus à manger. Quand il tuait un cerf, il honorait l'animal en se servant de toutes ses parties sans rien en perdre. Il remerciait tous les cerfs d'avoir offert l'un des leurs.

Quant aux femmes, elles passaient leurs journées à s'occuper des récoltes, à préparer et à entreposer la nourriture, à fabriquer et à raccommoder les vêtements et à élever les enfants. À Kanehsatà:ke, on peut trouver de la bonne argile à de nombreux endroits. Les femmes et les enfants la ramassaient pour en fabriquer de la poterie qu'ils utilisaient pour cuisiner et entreposer les aliments.

Les hommes du village s'occupaient du tabac et procuraient de la viande et du poisson au peuple. Ils partaient souvent pour des expéditions de chasse et de commerce, pendant lesquelles ils parcouraient de grandes distances pour échanger avec des peuples vivant très loin. Durant les mois d'hiver, ils partaient chasser pendant de longues périodes, laissant les femmes, les enfants et les aînés dans le village.[12]

De temps à autre, le peuple déplaçait le village quand le bois de chauffage devenait rare ou que le sol avait besoin de repos. Le nom du village ne changeait jamais, et le peuple revenait toujours à cet endroit. Kanehsatà:ke était devenu leur foyer. Leur vie remplie et saine serait restée la même si ce n'avait été des problèmes grandissant parmi les Rotinonhseshá:ka (peuple de la maison longue).

De nombreuses hostilités avaient pénétré le cœur du peuple, ce qui le rendait assoiffé de vengeance et de sang. La colère avait remplacé le bon sens. Les yeux du peuple ne pouvaient plus voir la bonté ni leurs oreilles entendre la vérité. Voyant des ennemis partout, il fortifia le village avec des palissades de bois et se réfugia à l'intérieur pour se protéger. Les hommes voyageaient loin à cause de la guerre. Quand l'Artisan de la paix passa par chez eux avec le message de paix et de bonne nouvelle, le peuple exprima un grand désir de l'accepter. Il s'était battu trop longtemps et avait perdu trop d'hommes. Il était fatigué de la guerre. Kanehsatà:ke fut l'un des premiers villages Kanien'kehà:ka à embrasser la paix, et cela est encore mentionné dans les anciennes cérémonies de condoléances des Rotinonhseshá:ka.

Après la Kaianere'kó:wa, le peuple retourna à une vie normale. Il était de nouveau libre de voyager et de visiter la parenté éloignée. Pendant très longtemps, il vécut en paix et en harmonie avec son monde. Bien des années s'étaient écoulées quand pour la première fois le peuple entendit parler d'étrangers dans leur région. Ils venaient de l'autre côté de la grande eau et visitaient les autres villages du bas du fleuve.

Peu après, le peuple fut attaqué au nord et à l'est par des nations Onkwehón:we qui étaient en guerre contre les Rotinonhseshá:ka.[13] Une fois de plus, il fortifia le village et se prépara pour la guerre. Quand les villages du bas du fleuve furent attaqués, les femmes et les enfants se réfugièrent dans le cœur de Kanién:keh (territoire Mohawk) où ils demeurèrent pendant plusieurs années.

Après beaucoup de luttes, les nations en guerre demandèrent la paix aux Rotinonhseshá:ka. Tous purent alors retourner chez eux en toute sécurité. Les Kanehsata'kehró:non s'établirent d'abord sur la grande île, près du fleuve, la même île qui, avant la guerre, avait été le site d'un grand village Kanien'kehà:ka.[14] Il semble que le peuple n'était pas heureux à cet endroit qui avait déjà été un village prospère, mais qui portait désormais le souvenir de ceux qui l'avaient quitté. Beaucoup de ces membres voulaient retourner à Kanehsatà:ke, tandis que d'autres voulaient rester. Ce débat créa de la dissension parmi le peuple et, finalement, un grand groupe retourna à Kanehsatà:ke. Ceux qui restèrent sur l'île rencontrèrent plus tard les O'serón:ni qui revenaient de l'autre côté de l'océan. Les O'serón:ni appelèrent cet endroit Ville-Marie, mais pour les Kanien'kehà:ka, c'était Tiohtià:ke, ce qui signifie «l'endroit où le groupe se sépare».[15] C'est encore ainsi qu'on l'appelle aujourd'hui.

Lorsqu'il retourna à Kanehsatà:ke, le peuple n'avait aucune idée que, des années plus tard, avec l'arrivée des Roti'kharahón:tsi, il serait de nouveau réuni à ses frères. À ce moment-là, beaucoup de choses avaient changé, et c'était avec des sentiments partagés que les Kanehsata'kehró:non permirent aux autres de revenir.

La vraie histoire de l'été indien

Quand les aînés de Kanehsatà:ke racontaient des histoires, ils parlaient de la manière dont ils vivaient dans leur jeunesse. À cette époque, les Onkwehón:we avaient l'habitude de s'entraider à décortiquer le maïs à l'automne. Ils se racontaient alors toutes sortes d'histoires, et c'est ainsi que les jeunes les apprenaient. Un des hommes très âgés raconta l'histoire qui suit.

Les Onkwehón:we avaient l'habitude de venir du sud et de suivre la migration des outardes. Quand ils les voyaient voler du sud, ils savaient qu'il était temps d'aller vers le nord. C'était il y a environ 500 ans. À l'automne, quand les outardes retournaient vers le sud, le peuple savait que c'était le temps de déménager de nouveau. Et chaque année, c'est ce qu'ils faisaient.

En cette période, il y a du givre, les feuilles deviennent rouges, jaunes et de différentes couleurs et les jours sont beaux. Je crois que c'est vers la fin septembre début octobre. On voit également les collines changer au rouge et les oiseaux voler haut dans le ciel en direction du sud. À l'aide de ces signes, les Onkwehón:we savaient que l'hiver arrivait. C'était le temps de se préparer à suivre les oiseaux vers le sud.

À cette époque, la région était le territoire de chasse des Kanien'kehà:ka de la Confédération des Iroquois.

C'est ainsi que le vieux Onkwehón:we racontait l'origine de l'été indien. Ce n'est pas au début de novembre comme les Blancs le disent.

Le murmure du vent

Comme un murmure, une douce brise souffle, bruisse dans les arbres et au-dessus de l'herbe. J'entends les voix des anciens, le rire des enfants et les conversations tranquilles des femmes. Cette histoire est écrite sur la terre avec le sang du peuple. Elle est transportée par le vent comme le son d'un tambour lointain. Elle vit dans le cœur du peuple.

J'ai connu les espoirs et les craintes des Kanehsata'kehró:non, et j'ai vu la fumée monter pour porter leurs prières au Créateur.

J'ai été témoin du courage de ceux qui portent le fardeau de la paix lorsqu'ils combattaient pour protéger la terre, le peuple et les intérêts de ceux qui n'étaient pas encore nés. Venez et je vous raconterai les autres choses que j'ai vues. Beaucoup de changements sont sur le point de se produire, et le peuple a peur, car peu de ces changements sont bons.

[1] Ces paroles de condoléances tirées de l'histoire traditionnelle de la Confédération des Six Nations ont été préparées par un comité des chefs. Elles ont été lues le 16 mai 1911.

[2] L'histoire de la création fait partie de la tradition orale des Rotinonhseshá:ka. Même si, d'une communauté à une autre et d'une nation à une autre, des détails peuvent varier, le contenu principal de l'histoire reste le même. Pour d'autres exemples de l'histoire de la création, voir *Traditional Teachings*, North American Indian Travelling College, rr 3, Cornwall Island, Ontario, K6H 5R7, et *Legends of Our Nations*, North American Indian Travelling College, *Legends of the Longhouse*, J. J. Cornplanter.

[3] Pour annoncer son message, l'Artisan de la paix fut aidé par Aionwatha. Parce qu'il avait perdu toute sa famille, Aionwatha était rempli de douleur quand l'Artisan de la paix le vit près d'un ruisseau. Par hasard, Aionwatha avait trouvé des coquillages avec lesquels il avait fabriqué un wampum. Il en fit trois cordelettes qu'il suspendit à un poteau et dit : « Si je vois quelqu'un qui souffre beaucoup, je prendrai ces cordelettes et je le consolerai. Elles deviendront des paroles qui enlèveront l'obscurité qui le couvre. C'est ce que je ferai sûrement. » Voilà d'où vient la cérémonie des condoléances des Rotinonhseshá:ka.

[4] Pour une discussion sur la Grande Loi, voir *A Basic Call to Consciousness: The Haudenosaunee Address to the Western World*, Genève, Suisse, automne 1977, anon. Les érudits autochtones de la Grande Loi comprennent Jacob Thomas : *The Great Law Takes a Long Time to Understand* dans Indian Roots of American Democracy.

[5] Notamment, les civilisations européennes n'ont pas pleinement reconnu ou compris ce concept avant un moment beaucoup plus tardif dans leur évolution. Elles ne reconnaissent ni ne comprennent exactement encore le lien entre les êtres humains et toutes les autres formes de vie, ainsi que l'équilibre délicat qui doit être maintenu pour assurer la survie de toute vie sur cette planète. Ce n'est qu'en 1948, avec la Déclaration universelle des droits de la personne adoptée par l'assemblée générale des Nations Unies, que les Européens ont officiellement reconnu et fait la promotion des droits fondamentaux de chaque personne.

[6] Ronald Wright dans *Stolen Continents: The New World Through Indians Eyes* date la Confédération vers 1000 apr. J.-C., quand l'agriculture a été introduite aux diverses nations qui ont formé la Ligue, p. 115. Dans *Canada's First Nations*, Olive Patricia Dickason date l'adoption de l'agriculture vers 800 apr. J.-C., p. 69, et la création de la Confédération vers 1451, p. 71. William N. Fenton dans *Structure, Continuity and Change in the Process of Iroquois Treaty Making, The History and Culture of Iroquois Diplomacy* écrit : « Cependant, il est certain que la Ligue a été fondée avant la colonisation européenne, probablement vers 1500 apr. J.-C., plus ou moins vingt-cinq ans, même si des exemples pour des dates antérieures ou postérieures abondent. » p. 16. Pour une discussion de ces exemples, voir *The League of the Iroquois, Its History, Politics and Ritual* d'Elisabeth Tooker, dans Bruce C. Trigger, vol. 15 du Handbook of North American Indians, p. 418-422.

[7] Depuis l'arrivée des Européens, les Rotinonhseshá:ka et tous les peuples autochtones d'Amérique du Nord ont connu un déclin de leur qualité de vie, résultat de siècles d'oppression, ainsi que de la perte de terres cultivables et de leur système économique traditionnel. Tout cela, jumelé à l'attaque constante de maladies et à une alimentation insuffisante, a réduit la longévité des peuples autochtones à un nombre inférieur que celui de leurs voisins Blancs. « En 1961, la longévité des non-autochtones était de dix ans supérieure à celle des autochtones. En 1981, l'écart était toujours de dix ans. L'Autochtone canadien moyen peut aujourd'hui s'attendre à vivre jusqu'à 66 ans, tandis que la longévité moyenne des Canadiens non autochtones est de 76 ans. » Geoffry York, *The Dispossessed: Life and Death in Native Canada*, Vintage U. K. Copyright Geoffry York, 1990.

[8] Sha'teionkwá:wen : les terres que nous partageons. Le peuple n'avait aucun concept de la propriété. On croyait, et beaucoup le croient toujours aujourd'hui, que le peuple appartenait à la terre, en faisait partie et en était responsable.

[9] Chez les Rotinonhseshá:ka, les femmes possédaient le droit et l'autorité d'adopter des prisonniers de guerre. Cette autorité est représentée dans la ceinture de rachat. « La ceinture enlevait la nuée de deuil de la femme et lui redonnait un fils par l'adoption d'un prisonnier. »

[10] Des archéologues croient qu'il y a 11 000 ans, cette région était submergée par un vaste plan d'eau qu'ils ont nommé la mer Champlain. Il y a entre 9000 et 5000 ans, le niveau de la mer Champlain ayant baissé, des gens ont commencé à habiter la région. Pour plus d'information, voir *Quebec Prehistory* de J. V. Wright, Van Nostrand Rienhold Ltd., 1979.

[11] Les gens vivant dans la région de l'État de New York pratiquaient la culture du maïs dès 800 apr. J.-C. Elle a été introduite dans cette région vers l'an 1000 apr. J.-C., voir *Quebec Prehistory* de J. V. Wright. Dans la tradition les Rotinonhsesha:ka, le maïs, les haricots et la courge étaient connus comme les trois sœurs et auraient poussé du cœur de la mère Terre après avoir succombé à la naissance de jumeaux. « La nourriture du sein des mères continue donc d'alimenter ses enfants », voir *Creation Story, Legends of Our Nations, North American Indian Travelling College*, Cornwall Island Ontario, ainsi que *Indian Corn of the Americas, Gift to the World, NorthEast Indian Quarterly*, printemps-été, 1987.

[12] Voir *Maisons longues et palissades* pour une description des premiers villages iroquoiens.

[13] Les Rotinonhseshá:ka étaient en guerre avec une alliance de peuples Huron, Montagnais et Algonquin.

[14] Hochelaga.

[15] Tiohtià:ke, « L'endroit où le groupe se sépare » connu aussi sous les noms d'Hochelaga, Ville-Marie et Montréal. Hochelaga est un mot que des gens vivant à Stadacona (où se situe la ville de Québec) ont dit à Jacques Cartier pour désigner l'établissement en amont du fleuve où se trouve maintenant Montréal. Ce n'est pas nécessairement le mot que le peuple d'« Hochelaga » utilisait pour se désigner ou désigner leur maison.

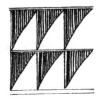 

CHAPITRE 2

LES ROTI'KHARAHÓN:TSI : LES ROBES NOIRES

UN ACTE DU CŒUR

Alors que les grands froids d'hiver s'abattaient sur le village et que les Kanehsata'kehró:non se préparaient pour la fête du milieu de l'hiver, ils furent surpris d'entendre des cris retentir dans l'air vif et de voir apparaître des coureurs. De mon sommet couvert de neige, je regardais pendant que les Kanehsata'kehró:non accueillaient les visiteurs et leur permettaient de rester avec eux. Pour la plupart, ces nouveaux venus, qui parlaient Kanien'kéha, furent reçus comme de la parenté par leur clan.

Ils amenaient avec eux leur Ro'khakòn:tsi (robe noire ou prêtre). Combien il ne semblait pas à sa place, ce petit homme maigre et nerveux, en robe noire, qui sautillait et essayait d'être partout à la fois!

J'entendis le Ro'khakòn:tsi faire référence à ses disciples comme à son « troupeau », et c'était vrai parce qu'il essayait toujours de rassembler les gens qui s'étaient dispersés partout, riant, parlant et sortant avec leur parenté. Ce Ro'kharahòn:tsi paraissait perdu, il tournait en rond, cherchant de tous côtés ses brebis perdues.

Après que les visiteurs furent installés, je regardai de nouveau Kanehsatà:ke et je vis le petit homme vêtu de noir, le Ro'kharahòn:tsi. Il semblait si modeste, mais je le voyais commander tout le monde. Plus étrange encore est le fait que ceux à qui il commandait écoutaient et obéissaient à ses ordres. J'ignore si ces gens se pliaient simplement à ses désirs ou s'ils se sentaient obligés d'écouter chacune de ses paroles parce qu'ils le croyaient important. Je me suis demandé s'il était sage de faire l'un ou l'autre. Les Rotinonhseshá:ka n'ont pas l'habitude d'obéir aveuglément. Espérons qu'en recevant ces visiteurs, les Kanehsata'kehró:non auront la prévoyance de dissiper tout problème avant qu'il ne survienne.

Si les Kanehsata'kehró:non acceptèrent d'accueillir leurs visiteurs en cette froide journée d'hiver, c'est parce qu'ils s'étaient laissés guider par leur cœur.

LA RÉALITÉ SUR LES ORIGINES DE KANEHSATÀ:KE ET LE MYTHE DE 1721

Selon le dictionnaire, un mythe est un point de vue qui repose davantage sur ce qui nous convient que sur un fait. Même si un mythe renferme un peu de vérité, il n'est souvent constitué que de demi-vérités. Il donne vie à des émotions profondes communément ressenties qui découlent de connaissances communément acceptées. Par exemple, quand Christophe Colomb traversa l'Atlantique en 1492, il était généralement accepté que la terre était plate, et la plupart des gens croyaient que son bateau tomberait au bout de la terre. Cette croyance reposait sur une connaissance obtenue par l'interprétation d'information incomplète ou insuffisante. Les mythes ont un pouvoir : ils revêtent une vie bien à eux et, avec le temps, ils font partie de l'idéologie d'une société. L'histoire et la manière dont les gens la perçoivent donnent naissance à des mythes. Le peuple de Kanehsatà:ke voit l'histoire d'une manière, et la société eurocanadienne, qui la voit autrement, a pu la façonner à sa guise. Ainsi, l'histoire de Kanehsatà:ke, comme le public la connaît – selon laquelle la communauté prit naissance lorsque le séminaire de Saint-Sulpice établit une mission en 1721 –, reflète les émotions généralement ressenties et les connaissances communément acceptées par les

Eurocanadiens. Les connaissances et la tradition orale du peuple de Kanehsatà:ke sont complètement absentes de cette histoire. N'étant constituée que de demi-vérités, elle n'est donc pas beaucoup plus qu'un mythe.

Indiens de la mission arrivant à Kanehsatà:ke
de Katsi'tsakwas

En 1721, alors que les vents glaciaux de février balayaient la terre que les Européens appelaient la Nouvelle-France, l'histoire, devenue un mythe, raconte qu'un groupe d'Onkwehón:we accompagné d'un prêtre du séminaire de Saint-Sulpice quitta la mission des Sulpiciens, situé à Sault-aux-Récollets sur la rive nord de l'île de Montréal, et se dirigea vers l'Ouest en passant par les eaux gelées de la rivière des Prairies. Ils marchaient en raquettes ou se déplaçaient en traîneaux. Puis, à l'endroit où la rivière des Prairies joint le fleuve Saint-Laurent et la rivière des Outaouais, les voyageurs montèrent vers le nord et entrèrent dans le Lac des Deux-Montagnes. Lentement, ils traversèrent le lac et atteignirent finalement leur destination, la seigneurie du Lac des Deux-Montagnes sur la rive nord-ouest. Dans ce lieu inhabité et désert, le prêtre et le groupe d'Onkwehón:we entreprirent une nouvelle vie ensemble. C'est là que le séminaire de Saint-Sulpice établit une mission indienne, c'est là que les Indiens s'installèrent, et c'est là que vivent, jusqu'à ce jour, leurs descendants.

Ce récit poignant et romantique sur la fondation de Kanehsatà:ke vient d'un mythe encore plus grand et plus puissant : celui de l'héroïsme européen. Ce deuxième mythe évoque des images d'une époque héroïque au cours de laquelle les Français arrivèrent sur une terre rude et sauvage pour offrir les grandes traditions religieuses de l'Europe au peuple « sauvage » du Nouveau Monde. Les Jésuites arrivèrent les premiers, suivis par les Sulpiciens, puis, par d'autres ordres religieux français. Des nouvelles occasionnelles de l'Ancien Monde soutenaient ces hommes et ces femmes dans leur travail. En même temps, leurs écrits et leurs visites en France servaient à nourrir la croyance européenne selon laquelle le monde entier progressait lorsqu'ils apportaient leur civilisation avancée aux autres.

Alors, quelle est la nature du mythe de 1721 ? Quelle image évoque-t-il ? À maintes reprises, il a été raconté par des historiens et par beaucoup d'autres qui, pour différentes raisons, se sont intéressés à la communauté. En fait, cette version des origines de Kanehsatà:ke a été si souvent répétée qu'elle est devenue une croyance populaire dans la plupart des milieux. L'histoire qui tire son origine du séminaire de Saint-Sulpice, à qui le roi de France avait accordé le territoire de Kanehsatà:ke, est maintenant acceptée comme le seul rapport authentique des débuts de la communauté. Ce récit est si puissant et frappant qu'il a atteint des proportions mythiques, et qu'il a enseveli toute autre preuve de l'histoire de Kanehsatà:ke avant l'arrivée des Sulpiciens.

Depuis 1721, cette version des origines de la communauté a été utilisée de bien des manières pour convaincre les puissantes forces de la loi et le gouvernement que les Kanehsata'kehró:non n'ont aucun droit légitime au territoire. En même temps, elle a servi à plusieurs occasions à renforcer la revendication du séminaire de Saint-Sulpice au territoire et, finalement, à se transformer en loi.[1]

Le manque de curiosité des historiens et des gouvernements pour examiner, révéler, puis rechercher plus de renseignements sur l'histoire primitive de Kanehsatà:ke est étonnant en soi, et cette lacune fait en sorte que la perspective du séminaire domine presque entièrement la littérature actuelle.[2] Sa version de l'histoire contient la croyance étendue du *Terra Nullius*, telle que Boyce Richardson en parle et la définit dans son livre. « *Terra Nullius*, écrit Richardson, est une terre inhabitée. C'est un concept juridique que les Européens utilisèrent à leur arrivée en Amérique du Nord. Ils voulaient justifier leur revendication de posséder tout le territoire, prétendant que personne d'autre ne l'avait habité. »[3]

Il ne fait aucun doute que vers 1721, un groupe d'Onkwehón:we accompagné d'un prêtre du séminaire de Saint-Sulpice s'établit à Kanehsatà:ke. Et il ne fait aucun doute que les Sulpiciens fondèrent une mission et que les descendants de ce groupe d'Onkwehón:we vivent maintenant à Kanehsatà:ke.[4] Ces faits sont bien documentés, mais au-delà de ce simple récit, il existe une grande richesse d'histoires orales, d'autres preuves documentées et quelques découvertes archéologiques qui, tout au moins, montrent que le territoire était habité longtemps avant l'arrivée du séminaire. Même un examen superficiel des divers registres de la colonie prouve l'existence d'un village avant l'arrivée des Sulpiciens. Il est donc clair qu'il faut accorder plus de poids aux renseignements fournis par d'autres sources que celles du séminaire de Saint-Sulpice. Ce n'est qu'en explorant diverses preuves et différents points de vue qu'une nouvelle lumière peut être jetée sur le passé.

DES ENSEIGNEMENTS TRADITIONNELS AUX PREUVES DOCUMENTÉES

Selon les enseignements traditionnels des Rotinonhseshá:ka, l'Artisan de la paix voyagea partout pour livrer son message et parler au peuple de « Ka-ne-sa-da-ke – sur le flanc de la colline », un endroit qui, avec d'autres villages des Rotinonhseshá:ka, faisait partie « des clans de la Tortue ».[5] Depuis le commencement, ce clan existait à Kanehsatà:ke et il existe toujours aujourd'hui avec ceux du Loup et de l'Ours.[6] Le nom Kanehsatà:ke est cité dans la cérémonie des condoléances, même si son emplacement n'est pas mentionné. Cela indique que Kanehsatà:ke, en tant que lieu et concept, existait et faisait partie des Rotinonhseshá:ka bien avant la venue des nouveaux arrivants.

En 1613, quand les Hollandais et les Rotinonhseshá:ka (peuple de la maison longue) conclurent un traité, les « Caghneghsattakegy » présents participèrent à la création de la désormais célèbre ceinture Wampum à deux rangées (Two Row Wampum).[7] Aucune autre explication n'est donnée sur la manière dont les Kanehsata'kehró:non furent représentés lors de la signature de ce traité. Le fond de la ceinture est blanc et deux rangées parallèles de wampums mauves la traversent. Les lignes mauves représentent deux embarcations – l'une transportant les Rotinonhseshá:ka et l'autre, les Européens – qui sillonnent une rivière suffisamment large pour permettre aux deux embarcations d'avancer séparément sur une voie parallèle, sans jamais se rencontrer.

Cette ceinture établit les règles d'une coexistence pacifique entre les Européens et les Rotinonhseshá:ka. « Ce sera la responsabilité des gens dans chaque embarcation de la diriger en ligne droite. Ni les Européens ni les Rotinonhseshá:ka ne se croiseront ou n'interféreront dans la vie des autres. Aucun des deux ne tentera d'imposer ses lois, ses traditions, ses coutumes, sa langue ou sa spiritualité sur les gens de l'autre embarcation.[8] La majorité des Européens voulaient que les gens se donnent la main, mais les Rotinonhseshá:ka insistèrent pour fabriquer une chaîne à laquelle les deux partis s'accrocheraient. Ainsi, ils pouvaient la lâcher s'ils le devaient. La chaîne était composée de trois maillons représentant la paix, l'amitié et le respect – les trois principes qui devaient régir les relations entre les deux nations. La chaîne devait être d'argent pour rappeler aux deux partis l'importance d'entretenir de bonnes relations. L'argent se ternit rapidement et doit être souvent poli pour garder son lustre. Il rappelle aux deux partis la nécessité de poser des gestes positifs pour maintenir et promouvoir la paix.

Quand les Européens et les Rotinonhseshá:ka conclurent ce traité, le mot Kanehsatà:ke, ainsi que le concept auquel il se rattache, faisaient partie de la liste des peuples de la Confédération qui participèrent au traité.

À partir du moment où les Français commencèrent à explorer le cours de la rivière des Outaouais en 1613, un climat de méfiance et d'hostilité existait entre les Rotinonhseshá:ka et les Français. Samuel de Champlain avait rencontré des « Iroquois » en 1612, à l'entrée du lac des Deux-Montagnes.[9] En 1660, il était « connu que de nombreux guerriers iroquois avaient passé l'hiver dans les forêts [de la rivière] des Outaouais », et c'est cette même année qu'eut lieu le désormais célèbre affrontement entre Dollard des Ormeaux et les « Iroquois » aux rapides du Long-Sault, à Carillon.[10]

Deux autres affrontements entre les Français et ceux qui sont décrits comme l'« ennemi iroquois » se produisirent sur le lac des Deux-Montagnes en 1689 et en 1690. En 1689, Montréal fut attaqué par « l'ennemi » et, en octobre la même année, 150 « Iroquois » descendirent dans l'île. Les Français « détachèrent un groupe de 170 Indiens au lac des Deux-Montagnes pour tenter d'empêcher la retraite de l'ennemi ». En 1690, un deuxième affrontement entre Daniel Greysolon (Sieur Dulhut) et les « Iroquois » eut lieu au lac des Deux-Montagnes. Dulhut tua 18 hommes. Un s'échappa et trois autres, faits prisonniers, furent amenés à Montréal où on les brûla sur un bûcher.[11]

Un autre récit d'un affrontement entre les Français et les Rotinonhseshá:ka en 1694 prouve davantage l'existence d'une communauté Kanien'kehà:ka avant l'arrivée du séminaire. Voici la description de cet incident.

[…] en passant au dernier endroit (Trois-Rivières), il [Sieur Levasseur] apprit que l'ennemi avait récemment frappé au lac des Deux-Montagnes, près de la pointe de l'île de Montréal. Ce qui suit est un bref récit de toute l'affaire.

Sieur Charleville, ayant aperçu du fort une fumée dense, eut la curiosité […] d'aller sur place pour voir si elle provenait d'hommes (au travail) ou de l'ennemi. Il s'embarqua avec sept Indiens et, ayant découvert devant lui un canot avec quinze Iroquois, il l'attaqua vigoureusement. Le combat se termina rapidement, mais Charleville, qui reçut deux balles et une flèche, mourut. Ne pouvant plus offrir de résistance, nos Indiens […] battirent en retraite […].

Cette attaque obligea M. de Callière à envoyer immédiatement quarante Algonquins et plusieurs autres Indiens, y compris des Népissingues et ceux qui appartiennent au Sault [et] à la montagne, à la recherche de l'ennemi […] Après avoir atteint la pointe de l'île [de Montréal], ils partirent dans différentes directions à la recherche des Iroquois, mais en vain.[12]

Ces soi-disant « ennemis iroquois » étaient-ils les Kanehsata'keró:non? Où sont-ils allés? Un récit oral des années 1960 soutient le point de vue selon lequel un village existait à Kanehsatà:ke avant même que les Français commencent à contrôler les eaux de la rivière des Outaouais. Selon ce rapport, ces gens étaient des Kanien'kehà:ka.

Les deux chefs, Angus (85 ans) et James Montour, me dirent qu'après 1608, quand les Iroquois subirent une terrible défaite aux mains des Français sur l'île de Montréal, ceux-ci s'établirent sur les rives du lac des Deux-Montagnes. Cet endroit était sûrement bien connu des Mohawks et peut avoir été un lieu de chasse et de pêche de prédilection.[13]

Et qu'en est-il de l'usage du mot Kanehsatà:ke? Il est utilisé par le peuple de la communauté depuis le début de son existence. De nombreux registres témoignent de la véracité de la nomenclature. Dans les *New York Colonial Documents*, par exemple, le nom Kanehsatà:ke est souvent employé par les archivistes des assemblées où on échangeait des ceintures wampum. Même si l'épellation varie – Canessadage, Canasadaga et Ganagsadaga –, la prononciation reste la même dans tous les cas.[14]

Toujours selon ces mêmes documents, le village de Kanehsatà:ke était situé près de l'île de Montréal.[15] L'usage archivé le plus ancien du nom Kanehsatà:ke, qui apparaît dans une collection de plusieurs volumes, remonte à 1694 quand, à un endroit non précisé, le gouverneur du Canada adressa un message aux Cinq Nations.[16] À cette époque, Kanehsatà:ke était appelé un « fort » ou un « château », et ce terme descriptif dénote un village de taille considérable qui était probablement fortifié par une palissade de bois.[17]

En règle générale, les Britanniques étaient plus disposés que les Français à utiliser le mot Kanehsatà:ke. À la fin des années 1600, quand les Britanniques entraient en contact avec le peuple de Kanehsatà:ke lors d'assemblées tenues à Albanie ou ailleurs, ils parlaient des « Canassadagas » comme d'un groupe distinct; ils utilisaient probablement le terme pour essayer d'établir des liens étroits avec le peuple. Les Canassadagas qui vivaient sur les terres revendiquées par les Français et aux environs étaient communément décrits comme les « Indiens prieurs » en raison de leur association avec les Français.[18]

Les Britanniques déduisirent avec justesse que rencontrer le peuple selon ses conditions était le meilleur moyen d'assurer des alliances, et que l'appeler par le nom qu'il se donnait y contribuait. Même après que le séminaire de Saint-Sulpice eut établi la mission à Kanehsatà:ke, les Anglais continuèrent à faire référence aux « Canassadagas », sans doute très conscients qu'ils devaient maintenir les liens établis antérieurement. De nombreux rapports d'assemblées avec les Six Nations et beaucoup de lettres contenues dans *The Papers of Sir William Johnson* reflètent cette façon de penser : le peuple y est presque toujours désigné comme les « Canasadagas » ou les « Caneghsadageys » et ainsi de suite.[19]

En effet, pendant la période précédant la conquête de la Nouvelle-France, les Britanniques recherchèrent activement à conclure des alliances avec les Rotinonhseshá:ka. Toutefois, durant la période post-conquête, alors que la paix et la stabilité s'installaient sur le territoire, l'usage du mot Kanehsatà:ke par les Britanniques disparut graduellement. En 1840, quand le gouvernement britannique émit une ordonnance confirmant le titre de propriété du territoire du Lac des Deux-Montagnes au Séminaire de Saint-Sulpice, le mot Kanehsatà:ke avait complètement disparu de la discussion et, avec lui, la grande estime jadis accordée au peuple.

Les Français utilisaient le plus souvent le terme générique « Iroquois » pour désigner le peuple, même si, à l'occasion, quand des fonctionnaires cherchaient un appui ou demandaient la loyauté du peuple, ils utilisaient le mot « Ganughsadages ».[20] Les Français donnèrent à Kanehsatà:ke le nom de Lac des Deux-Montagnes, et les Sulpiciens désignaient régulièrement le village par ce nom. La préférence des Français d'utiliser le terme « Lac des Deux-Montagnes » ou « mission du lac des Deux-Montagnes » plutôt que celui de Kanehsatà:ke comme lieu-dit indique qu'ils ne reconnaissaient pas le peuple de cet endroit.

Le nom « mission du lac des Deux-Montagnes » fut donc peu à peu inséré dans les langues française et anglaise, et le nom Kanehsatà:ke disparut de la littérature et des documents du gouvernement.

Quand le temps vint, en 1868, de changer le nom du lieu pour quelque chose de plus facile et de plus moderne, les Sulpiciens choisirent « Oka ».[21] On dit que ce mot vient de l'algonquin et qu'il signifie « laquaiche aux yeux d'or », un poisson qui vivait probablement dans les eaux du lac des Deux-Montagnes.[22] Les habitants de Kanehsatà:ke devinrent connus sous le nom d'« Indiens d'Oka ». ou simplement les « Okas ».

Le nom d'origine algonquine fut donné à tous les Onkwehón:we qui vivaient dans la communauté et servait à désigner les Kanehsatakehró:non en particulier, même s'ils étaient Kanien'keha. Ironiquement, le nom Oka apparut après que la plupart des Algonquins de la communauté eurent déménagé sur des terres à Maniwaki, au nord d'Ottawa.[23]

Le nom « Oka » fut alors graduellement inséré dans les langues française et anglaise, et le concept des Kanehsata'keró:non comme groupe distinct de personnes disparut de la littérature, à mesure que leur influence politique et leur utilité militaire diminuaient.

Alors que l'influence européenne, puis canadienne commençait à dominer la vie des Kanehsata'kehró:non, ces derniers durent aussi utiliser les termes « lac des Deux-Montagnes », « Lake of the Two Mountains » et « Oka » pour communiquer avec les Blancs. Et comme les Kanehsata'kehró:non envoyaient de plus en plus de pétitions au gouvernement, ils durent rechercher des Anglais ou des Français lettrés pour écrire pour eux. Au début de la colonisation, ils étaient instruits uniquement dans leur propre langue. Les quelques-uns qui savaient lire et écrire ne pouvaient le faire qu'en Kanien'kehà:ka. Dorénavant, s'ils voulaient que leurs pétitions soient comprises, ils devaient les écrire en français ou en anglais. Les pétitions et les lettres écrites dans ces deux langues faisaient toujours référence au village en le désignant par le nom Oka ou lac des Deux-Montagnes. Quand on trouve de la correspondance écrite en Kanien'kehà:ka, on peut remarquer que le peuple continuait de désigner leur village par le nom Kanehsatà:ke. Il est évident que ceux qui traduisaient la correspondance en français et en anglais laissaient tomber le mot Kanehsatà:ke et le remplaçaient par les termes « Oka » et « Lac des Deux-Montagnes ».

En remplaçant graduellement le mot Kanehsatà:ke par les termes Lac des Deux-Montagnes, Lake of Two Mountains et Oka, la société euro-canadienne essayait de nier l'existence même des Kanehsata'kehró:non. De plus, en utilisant ces termes, elle tentait de dépouiller le peuple de Kanehsatà:ke de son identité. Cette tentative délibérée ne réussit pas complètement. Même si certains Kanehsata'kehró:non soutinrent et appliquèrent activement les politiques d'assimilation du gouvernement et des Églises, dans l'ensemble, le peuple ne perdit jamais le sentiment d'être enraciné dans cette terre et d'y appartenir.

Sur l'archéologie et les enseignements traditionnels

 Des recherches archéologiques dans la région de Kanehsatà:ke pourraient mener à une meilleure compréhension de l'histoire plus ancienne de la communauté, mais un tel travail est presque complètement absent. Dans les milieux archéologiques du Québec, Kanehsatà:ke est reconnu comme l'un parmi un tout petit nombre de sites de la période du Middle-Woodland (sylvicole moyen) et peut-être des sites de la Point Peninsula, mais aucune excavation approfondie n'y fut jamais réalisée.[24] Deux ou trois fouilles superficielles furent entreprises dans la région de la plage du parc d'Oka, mais selon les archéologues qui effectuèrent le travail, une érosion considérable avait détruit le site.[25] Cela laisse toutefois le peuple de Kanehsatà:ke se demander pourquoi, si le site est détruit, des gens continuent de trouver des tessons de poterie et d'autres artefacts. Dans son rapport de 1988, Claude Chapdelaine fait remarquer que, même avec les trouvailles limitées à la plage, la région reste un lieu archéologique important. Selon lui, la découverte et l'excavation d'autres sites autour de la communauté montreraient comment le territoire était occupé durant la période du Middle-Woodland.

Le peu de fonds mis à la disposition de la communauté archéologique est la raison majeure pour laquelle aucun travail approfondi ne fut réalisé. Beaucoup de temps, d'énergie et d'argent sont investis dans le travail à Pointe-du-Buisson, à l'ouest de Kahnawà:ke, et ce site se révèle très fructueux.[26] Un travail intensif de cette sorte à Kanehsatà:ke révélerait, selon toute probabilité, une histoire ancienne riche et fascinante. Les archéologues conviennent qu'il faudrait effectuer plus de fouilles. Cependant, il n'était pas politiquement opportun pour les gouvernements d'appuyer un tel projet, parce qu'il était prévu que la région serve à un développement important et que les Kanehsata'kehró:non pourraient utiliser des découvertes archéologiques pour appuyer légalement leurs revendications territoriales. Il est remarquable qu'aucun peuple autochtone ne réclame le territoire à Pointe-du-Buisson où d'importants travaux sont exécutés.

Dans presque chaque maison à Kanehsatà:ke, il y a des trésors du passé. Le peuple a extrait du sol des fragments de poterie, des têtes de flèches et des outils. Le musée McCord d'histoire canadienne à Montréal et le ministère des Affaires culturelles à Québec possèdent chacun de petites, mais intéressantes, collections de tels artefacts. Des gens continuent de trouver des morceaux de poterie et d'autres artefacts qui reposent sur le sol.[27]

La théorie des Iroquois du Saint-Laurent est un autre aspect de l'archéologie souvent discuté au sein du peuple de Kanehsatà:ke. Les partisans de cette théorie affirment que les Iroquois du Saint-Laurent n'étaient pas apparentés aux Kanien'kehà:ka et qu'à un moment donné, avant l'an 1600, le groupe du Saint-Laurent disparut.[28] Cette théorie est mise en doute par les Kanien'kehà:ka vivant au Québec qui croient que les Iroquois du Saint-Laurent non seulement leur étaient étroitement apparentés, mais qu'ils faisaient partie de leur peuple. Ils disent que les archéologues établirent une fausse distinction entre les deux groupes. Pour les archéologues, la preuve la plus évidente qui distingue les Iroquois du Saint-Laurent des Kanien'kehà:ka est la différence dans les styles et la décoration de la poterie. Les Kanien'kehà:ka, pour leur part, croient que davantage de recherche des aspects sociaux des Rotinonhseshá:ka contribuerait à jeter plus de lumière sur les similitudes, plutôt que sur les différences, entre les Iroquois du Saint-Laurent et les Kanien'kehà:ka.

Un aspect de la structure sociale que les archéologues n'ont pas examiné est le système de clans qui faisait partie intégrante du message de la Kaianere'kó:wa et du mode de vie des Kanien'kehà:ka. En fait, le système de clans peut avoir précédé l'Artisan de la paix. Des preuves physiques des symboles particuliers à chacun des clans – Tortue, Ours et Loup, par exemple – ne survécurent probablement pas aux ravages du temps, puisque les matériaux organiques de ce genre se seraient depuis longtemps détériorés. De toute façon, les Onkwehón:we du Rotinonhseshá:ka n'auraient pas tué des animaux pour obtenir les symboles du clan. D'autres preuves du système de clans peuvent exister dans les registres anciens. De plus, les décorations de poterie et les symboles sur des pipes d'argile peuvent, en réalité, être des symboles de clans; ils indiqueraient alors l'existence des clans longtemps avant la création de la Confédération. Nous ne pouvons pas présumer qu'il existait des règles strictes pour la décoration de la poterie. Les autochtones utilisaient les outils qu'ils avaient sous la main, et ces outils auraient influencé la manière dont ils concevaient leurs dessins.

L'examen des origines des clans et des règles sur les mariages créées par le système de clans pourrait offrir de nouvelles possibilités aux recherches archéologiques. Un tel examen pourrait, en revanche, mener à une plus grande compréhension des origines des clans et de son système, des déplacements du peuple, de l'évolution des langues, des pratiques et des cérémonies spirituelles et, finalement, de la relation entre les Iroquois du Saint-Laurent et les Rotinonhseshá:ka.

LE PEUPLE MARCHE À LA LUMIÈRE DU SOLEIL

Le peuple est patient et persévérant; la nature l'a bien instruit. Cette patience lui sera grandement nécessaire dans les jours à venir, et il aura besoin d'être très clairvoyant et d'user de paroles des plus convaincantes pour traiter avec les nouveaux arrivants.

Il y a tant de choses au sujet du peuple que les O'serón:ni choisissent de ne pas comprendre. Il leur est difficile d'accepter que les autres soient différents d'eux. Les O'serón:ni essaient de changer trop de coutumes des Onkwehón:we. Ils sont agités et trouvent toujours quelque chose qu'ils n'aiment pas. Leur visage est toujours obscur, comme si une brume l'entourait; il n'est jamais clair.

Pour moi, le peuple marche à la lumière du soleil, et son ombre le suit. Je ne vois aucun secret dans leurs yeux. Quand ils viennent sur mon sommet, leurs enfants les accompagnent toujours. Tandis qu'ils enseignent aux plus vieux ce qui a trait aux remèdes ou à la cueillette des racines et des baies, les petits dorment, leur berceau se balançant doucement au gré de la brise. Qu'ils soient une feuille, une branche, un tronc ou une racine, ensemble ils font tous partie du même arbre.

C'est pourquoi je dis que le peuple aura besoin de toute la patience et de toute la persévérance qu'il possède. Il devra essayer de ramener les O'serón:ni vers la sagesse qu'ils ont perdue il y a longtemps. Les Kanehsata'kehró:non devront faire attention à ne pas s'égarer durant ce voyage difficile.

À NOUS POUR TOUJOURS

En 1787, le chef Aghneetha de Kanehsatà:ke rencontra Sir John Johnson lors d'un conseil. Il lui expliqua les circonstances qui occasionnèrent le déplacement du peuple de Sault-aux-Récollets à Kanehsatà:ke.

Avant la construction du mur autour de cette ville, nous demeurions au pied de la montagne [à Montréal], près de l'endroit où les prêtres du séminaire ont leur résidence. Nous vivions dans la tranquillité depuis longtemps quand le prêtre installé parmi nous et l'autre clergé de l'île nous ont présenté lors d'un conseil les inconvénients que notre présence si près d'une ville occasionnait aux Blancs [...]. Ils nous ont exhortés fermement à déménager loin de la ville [...] en nous désignant Sault-aux-Récollets comme lieu de résidence, près des moulins des prêtres. Nous nous sommes donc pliés à leurs demandes, nous avons quitté nos habitations et déménagé avec nos femmes et nos enfants au lieu qui nous était réservé. Nous y vivions depuis 23 ou 24 ans quand, une fois de plus, notre prêtre [...] nous a dit que nous devions redéménager avec nos familles parce qu'il n'était plus approprié qu'un Indien vive sur l'île. Si nous consentions à aller nous établir au Lac des Deux-Montagnes, nous aurions un grand territoire pour lequel le roi de France nous accorderait un acte de propriété, et qui nous appartiendrait pour toujours, à nous et à nos héritiers, et nous ne serions plus importunés dans nos habitations.

Même si cela nous dérangeait beaucoup de quitter nos maisons et nos petites clairières, le désir de posséder une propriété fixe nous a cependant incités à nous soumettre. Nous sommes donc partis et avons pris possession de la terre qui nous était assignée [...][29]

Dans ce discours, le chef Aghneetha déclare que le peuple fut forcé de quitter l'île de Montréal parce qu'il était considéré comme un obstacle à la colonie des Blancs. Pour s'assurer de ne plus jamais être contraint de redéménager, il accepta l'entente selon laquelle le territoire lui appartiendrait pour toujours. Même si la couronne de France avait peut-être une autre intention en créant la seigneurie du Lac des Deux-Montagnes, le chef Aghneetha crut que le roi avait essayé d'enchâsser les droits de propriété sous forme de concession.

Un document – un acte de propriété – était la manière européenne de réglementer les questions de propriété. Pour leur part, les Rotinonhseshá:ka devaient aussi entrer dans cette entente selon leurs propres conditions et, conformément à leur tradition, ils fabriquèrent une ceinture wampum qu'ils échangèrent avec les Français au moment du déménagement. Alors, comme égaux, les deux partis en étaient venus à une entente amicale et durable. Cette ceinture s'appelle «Two Dog Wampum».

Bon nombre d'années plus tard, le séminaire de Saint-Sulpice nia avoir connaissance de la ceinture en question, déclarant qu'elle n'était qu'un faux-semblant.[30]

ALLÉGER LE FARDEAU

Les Kanien'kehà:ka étaient des cultivateurs très productifs depuis plus de mille ans. Leurs produits et ceux d'autres Onkwehón:we étaient si différents et délicieux que les Européens les adoptèrent et les intégrèrent dans leur cuisine et leurs habitudes alimentaires. Les Onkwehón:we révolutionnèrent l'alimentation européenne, mais cette grande contribution aux délices culinaires occidentaux est rarement reconnue.[31]

Gédéon de Catalogne, ingénieur français, avait nettement une admiration pour les réalisations agricoles des Kanien'kehà:ka. En 1712, il décrivit les récoltes des Onkwehón:we à Sault-aux-Récollets.

Même si elle est rocailleuse, la terre [à Sault-aux-Récollets] est très bonne et produit une quantité considérable de maïs indien, de fèves, de haricots, de citrouilles, de melons et de tournesols, qui constitue les récoltes habituelles de ce peuple. Les forêts contiennent toutes sortes d'arbres. Comme il y a un très grand nombre d'érables, ils font beaucoup de sucre qu'ils apportent à la ville et qu'ils vendent. Au cours de l'été, ils apportent des adiantes (genre de fougère) qu'ils vendent également. Les femmes font presque tout le commerce parce que les hommes sont occupés à chasser, à pêcher ou à faire la guerre.[32]

Malheureusement, les chroniqueurs français ne firent pas d'observations détaillées sur les activités agricoles dans les autres villages des Onkwehón:we. Toutefois, nous savons qu'à l'automne 1722, un an seulement après le déménagement dans la communauté des Sulpiciens et des Onkwehón:we de Sault-aux-Récollets, «les Indiens du Lac des Deux-Montagnes avaient cultivé plus de terre que ceux de Sault-aux-Récollets».[33] En 1716, cinq ans avant le déménagement, le peuple de Sault-aux-Récollets avait défriché environ 400 arpents de terre.[34] Il y vivait depuis environ vingt ans, puis, en quelques mois seulement, il avait défriché plus de terre que durant toutes les années précédentes. C'est un accomplissement extraordinaire, considérant le fait que le peuple de Sault-aux-Récollets avait déménagé à Kanehsatà:ke au milieu de l'hiver de 1721. Il occupa ses premiers mois au Lac des Deux-Montagnes à construire des abris, à chasser pour se nourrir et à défricher peu à peu la terre. Il n'eut pas beaucoup de temps entre la fonte de la neige et l'ensemencement pour défricher la terre. Le fait qu'il ait défriché et cultivé en si peu de temps plus de terre que les Onkwehón:we de Sault-aux-Récollets indique la présence d'une communauté déjà existante au Lac des Deux-Montagnes. On ne peut expliquer cette réalisation que par le fait qu'il y avait déjà des terres cultivées à Kanehsatà:ke quand le peuple de Sault-aux-Récollets y arriva.

En 1748, quelques jours seulement après avoir visité Kanehsatà:ke, le scientifique et voyageur suédois Peter Kalm fit une description formidable de la nourriture cultivée et mangée par les Indiens. L'activité agricole à Kanehsatà:ke dut l'avoir inspiré à écrire ce qui suit:

> Des légumes qu'ils plantent, il y a le maïs, les haricots rouges de toutes sortes, divers types de citrouilles, les courges, un genre de gourde, les pastèques et les cantaloups. Les Indiens cultivaient toutes ces plantes longtemps avant l'arrivée des Européens. Ils mangeaient aussi divers fruits qui poussent dans leurs forêts. Le poisson et la viande constituent une grande partie de leur alimentation, et ils aiment notamment la viande de bovidés sauvages, de chevreuil, de cerf, d'ours, de castor et de quelques autres quadrupèdes. Parmi leurs plats préférés, ils apprécient l'ivraie que les Français appellent «riz sauvage», et qui pousse en abondance dans leurs lacs, dans des eaux stagnantes, et parfois dans des rivières à faible débit. Ils récoltent leurs céréales en octobre et les préparent de différentes façons, surtout comme le gruau d'avoine qui a presque aussi bon goût que le riz. Ils préparent aussi beaucoup de mets délicieux à partir de nombreuses sortes de noix, de châtaignes, de mûriers, d'acimine, de chinquapins, de noisettes, de pêches, de prunes sauvages, de raisins, de baies de toutes sortes, de divers néfliers, de mûres et d'autres fruits et racines. Mais les espèces de céréales si courantes dans ce qui est appelé l'Ancien Monde étaient totalement inconnues ici avant l'arrivée des Européens, et même aujourd'hui, les Indiens n'essaient jamais de les cultiver.[35]

Le fait que les Kanehsata'kehró:non aient résisté à cultiver les céréales des Européens est facilement explicable. Comme tout ce qui vit fut créé pour assumer certains devoirs et responsabilités, toutes les formes de vie, y compris les êtres humains, ont aussi leurs propres aliments à manger. Les Rotinonhseshá:ka avaient reçu certains produits à manger et la connaissance pour les cultiver. Ces produits étaient destinés à les rendre forts et en santé, tel que prévu par le Créateur. Les aliments conçus pour les autres ne donnent pas la force au peuple et peuvent, en réalité, le rendre malade.

Le séminaire de Saint-Sulpice sollicita d'abord le territoire du Lac des Deux-Montagnes en 1712 et en fit la demande officielle en 1714.[36] Malheureusement, nous ignorons la nature exacte de cette demande puisque le document disparut.[37] Un document de 1724 qui avait subsisté explique clairement les démarches du séminaire pour obtenir le territoire de Kanehsatà:ke.[38] Selon les Sulpiciens, le Lac des Deux-Montagnes offrait de meilleures possibilités de chasse et de pêche aux Onkwehón:we. Les tentations de l'alcool qui, au dire des Sulpiciens, infestaient les deux missions à Montréal, seraient moindres à la nouvelle mission, étant donné la grande distance qui les séparait de la colonie de Montréal.

Cependant, la raison principale invoquée par les Français pour déplacer la mission au Lac des Deux-Montagnes était de protéger le flanc nord-ouest de la colonie des incursions de l'«ennemi iroquois». Les partis en guerre passaient souvent par la rive nord du lac des Deux-Montagnes pour attaquer Montréal. Dans le passé, les tentatives des Français pour prévenir ces incursions avaient misérablement échoué. Avec les «Indiens de la mission» à Kanehsatà:ke, les Français essayaient de séparer les Kanehsata'kehró:non du reste des Rotinonhseshá:ka. Le séminaire de Saint-Sulpice fournirait les commodités et développerait des forces militaires en cas de besoin.

Les Sulpiciens avaient une bonne raison d'être fiers d'avoir obtenu cette concession pour «les Indiens sous leur protection».[39] Entre 1711 et 1732, la couronne de France imposa un moratoire sur toutes les concessions seigneuriales au Québec.[40] Deux seules exceptions furent faites à la loi, dont une en 1718 pour accorder la concession de la seigneurie du Lac des Deux-Montagnes au séminaire de Saint-Sulpice.[41]

Le 17 octobre 1717, la couronne de France concéda au séminaire de Saint-Sulpice un territoire à Kanehsatà:ke et, le 27 avril 1718, la concession fut ratifiée. Cette concession fut accordée sur la base de deux pétitions que le séminaire avait adressées au roi. Le contenu exact de ces pétitions est inconnu et, comme la demande originale du territoire, elles ont disparu.[42] La concession de 1717 explique les obligations du séminaire de Saint-Sulpice. Le territoire du Lac des Deux-Montagnes fut accordé, stipule la concession, « à la condition qu'ils [les Sulpiciens] couvrent toutes les dépenses nécessaires au déplacement de la dite mission et y construisent également à leurs frais une église et un fort en pierre pour la sécurité des Indiens [...] »[43]

En conséquence, le supérieur du séminaire, M. de Belmont, dessina un plan qui se rendit finalement au bureau de Chassegros de Lery, ingénieur du roi, pour subir une inspection. M. de Lery le rejeta catégoriquement. Le plan de M. de Belmont comprenait une église et un mur en pierre, tel que stipulé, mais les maisons du peuple de Kanehsatà:ke se trouvaient à l'extérieur du mur. Dans le plan, 72 maisons longues complètes avec cheminées pour la fumée étaient dessinées en six rangées distinctes, douze par rangée.

M. de Lery était sans équivoque, il rejeta complètement le plan. Il écrivit : «Le plan ne sert pas de refuge aux Indiens en cas de guerre et n'est pas non plus suffisant pour abriter une garnison». Selon lui, le plan n'était «utile que pour les missionnaires». M. de Lery dessina lui-même le plan officiel qui, comme la concession le spécifiait, assurait «la sécurité des Indiens».[44] Ce plan comprenait un mur de grandes proportions, complet avec des redoutes, à l'intérieur duquel il plaça 72 maisons longues. À côté du village de maisons longues, il dessina le fort, avec plus de redoutes, pour abriter les missionnaires et une garnison.

Le fort de M. de Lery ne fut jamais construit. En fait, aucun fort d'une quelconque importance ne fut jamais érigé. Les Sulpiciens bâtirent seulement une église et un presbytère. Une palissade de bois fut plus tard construite, mais les maisons du peuple se trouvaient à l'extérieur de l'enceinte de bois. Dans ses mémoires, Roy Franquet, ingénieur de la colonie, remarqua que l'église et le presbytère fortifiés pouvaient servir comme dernier recours en cas d'attaque. Toutefois, si les Kanehsata'kehró:non décidaient de participer à l'attaque, ils pourraient, avec l'ennemi, être pris à l'extérieur.[45]

Si le peuple de Kanehsatà:ke était des «Indiens de la mission», comme le séminaire s'en vantait, pourquoi alors était-il exclu de la protection de l'église et du presbytère? Le séminaire et les autorités françaises ne faisaient-ils pas confiance à leurs «alliés indiens»? Ou était-ce la présence des Kanehsata'kehró:non outre les «Indiens de la mission» qui les rendaient nerveux?

Les Sulpiciens protestèrent auprès du gouvernement colonial; ils affirmèrent que les conditions de la concession de 1718 étaient trop lourdes. Les coûts liés au déplacement de la mission de Sault-aux-Récollets au Lac des Deux-Montagnes dépassaient ce qui avait été prévu, et les coûts potentiels de la construction du plan des fortifications de M. de Lery étaient trop élevés. Une deuxième, puis une troisième fois, le séminaire de Saint-Sulpice fit une demande pour acquérir davantage de terres adjacentes à la seigneurie originale.

Le 26 septembre 1733, dans son palais de Versailles, le roi Louis XIV de France prit sa plume et signa un acte de concession pour un terrain triangulaire contigu au sud de la seigneurie. Le 1er mars 1735, il ratifia cette concession, ainsi qu'une autre encore plus grande derrière la seigneurie originale. Dans un geste magnanime, il dispensa les ecclésiastiques de Saint-Sulpice de l'obligation de construire un fort en pierre. L'église, le presbytère et la palissade de bois « leur ont occasionné [aux ecclésiastiques] des dépenses qui excédaient de loin la valeur des terres leur étant concédées par le présent acte de propriété et, à partir de 1718, il leur sera impossible de construire un fort en pierre […], et du reste, le fort en pierre serait maintenant inutile, puisque la terre à la pointe du pays est occupée par la veuve du Sieur d'Argenteuil […].[46]

Le roi accorda aux Sulpiciens «le droit de juridiction supérieure, moyenne et inférieure, ainsi que celui de chasser, de pêcher et de commercer avec les Indiens dans les limites de ladite seigneurie […]»[47] Les Sulpiciens récoltèrent donc les bénéfices de leurs démarches auprès de la Couronne.

Au cours des années qui suivirent la dispensation de 1735 de construire un fort, le séminaire reçut une subvention annuelle de 2000 livres de la Couronne.[48] Une partie de cet argent servit probablement à acheter trois canons, mais il existe peu de preuves pour montrer que les fortifications furent élargies au-delà de la structure de base construite dans les années 1740.[49]

STRATÉGIE MILITAIRE

Par la pétition qui nous a été présentée par Messieurs les ecclésiastiques du séminaire de Saint-Sulpice établis à Montréal, ceux-ci déclarent qu'il serait avantageux pour la mission des Indiens de Sault-aux-Récollets située sur l'île de Montréal qui est sous leur protection, qu'elle soit immédiatement transférée au-delà de ladite île et établie sur les terres situées sur la rive nord-ouest du lac des Deux-Montagnes. Cette mission serait avantageuse non seulement pour la conversion des Indiens […], mais aussi pour la colonie [de Montréal] qui serait ainsi protégée contre les incursions des Iroquois en temps de guerre […][50]

Protection contre les incursions des Iroquois... conversion des Indiens... L'union de ces deux idées arriva à un moment où les Français craignaient des attaques sur Montréal, comme celle où la colonie fut incendiée par le fameux ennemi iroquois en 1660. En 1700, les Français et les Cinq Nations avaient signé un traité de paix, mais Vaudreuil et le séminaire de Saint-Sulpice avaient peur que les Iroquois attaquent de nouveau. Leurs craintes étaient évidemment injustifiées étant donné qu'avec la paix de 1700, la possibilité d'invasion était «largement diminuée [...] [et] la question disparut de la correspondance officielle».[51] En effet, après 1700, il n'y eut aucune menace pour la colonie, même venant de la région de la rivière des Outaouais et de ses affluents qui menaient au cœur des Cinq Nations. Néanmoins, Vaudreuil, Bégon et le séminaire purent présenter des preuves convaincantes au roi de France, et l'idée que la mission fournisse une protection à la colonie devint la raison principale évoquée pour déplacer la mission de Sault-aux-Récollets à Kanehsatà:ke.

Considérant Kanehsatà:ke comme un secteur militaire stratégiquement important, les Français espéraient que «les Indiens de la mission avec les Kanehsata'kehró:non se montreraient loyaux et seraient des alliés efficaces». Même s'il y a amplement de preuves d'une alliance militaire entre les Kanehsata'kehró:non et les Français, il est clair que le peuple de Kanehsatà:ke ne favorisait ni les Britanniques ni les Français, mais s'associait avec celui qui lui offrait le meilleur avantage. La volonté des Kanehsata'kehró:non de commercer avec les Britanniques et de participer à des assemblées avec eux était une source constance d'inquiétude pour les Français.

Personne ne peut craindre d'affirmer que les sauvages, à quelques exceptions près, n'affectionnent ni les Français ni les Anglais, car ils savent que les deux ont besoin d'eux [...]

[...] ils croient que nous ne cherchons qu'à commercer; c'est pourquoi nous devons pouvoir les attirer avec certitude par ce moyen. Mais puisque les Anglais agissent de la même manière avec eux et nous surpassent en présents et en attentions, il est à craindre que ces sauvages se détachent complètement de nous.[52]

Craignant également l'association que les Kanehsata'kehró:non entretenaient avec le reste des Rotinonhseshá:ka, les Français faisaient consciencieusement campagne pour les séparer les uns des autres. Ils croyaient avoir plus ou moins réussi, mais ils avaient tort. Les Kanehsata'kehró:non n'étaient pas disposés à faire la guerre aux Rotinonhseshá:ka.

En effet, la loyauté des Iroquois canadiens n'était jamais complètement au-dessus de tout soupçon. Même si les guerriers mohawks d'Oka et de Caughnawaga avaient participé à des raids aux côtés des Français contre les colonies anglaises et le territoire de la Ligue, et même si les Iroquois canadiens étaient eux-mêmes l'objet d'attaques par des partis de la Confédération en guerre, les Français ont remarqué que les Iroquois canadiens hésitaient à faire la guerre contre leurs frères iroquois. Ils étaient également conscients qu'ils s'efforçaient de rester neutres quand cela était possible.[53]

En 1721, quand le séminaire de Saint-Sulpice établit finalement sa mission à Kanehsatà:ke, la paix régnait au sud de la rivière des Outaouais. Pendant ce temps, les Rotinonhseshá:ka ne lancèrent aucune attaque contre la colonie française, et il n'y eut aucune menace immédiate de guerre contre les Britanniques. Cependant, le manque d'hostilité ne satisfaisait pas les Français, et chaque occasion était bonne pour continuer à éloigner les Kanehsata'kehró:non des Rotinonhseshá:ka.

Pour sa part, le séminaire était très heureux de garder les Kanehsata'kehró:non prêts pour la guerre. Il désapprouvait leur commerce puisqu'il impliquait souvent un partenariat avec les Rotinonhseshá:ka et leurs alliés, les Britanniques. En 1732, lorsque le commerce avec les Britanniques augmenta à un rythme alarmant, l'intendant de la colonie en fut très affligé. À la suite d'une visite à Kanehsatà:ke :

> [...] il fut fâché de voir presque tous les sauvages porter des vêtements de tissu britannique et de laine rouge. Les missionnaires lui dirent que, jusqu'à présent, il avait été impossible de les arrêter, que ces sauvages croyaient toujours avoir la liberté de commercer avec qui ils voulaient [...] mais qu'ils avaient donné leur parole de ne pas servir d'intermédiaires dans le commerce frauduleux des Français avec les Britanniques.[54]

Les Français cherchèrent des moyens de mettre fin au commerce, mais en vain. Finalement, il fut décidé que, s'ils ne pouvaient empêcher les Kanehsata'kehró:non de commercer avec qui ceux-ci voulaient, ils détermineraient qui pouvait et ne pouvait pas commercer avec eux. Par la concession de 1735, le séminaire gagna le contrôle complet du commerce des fourrures au Lac des Deux-Montagnes.

Vers 1740, alors que la lutte politique et militaire avec les Britanniques se dessinait à l'horizon, les missionnaires sulpiciens se mirent à préparer les guerriers de Kanehsatà:ke pour la bataille. En 1743, François Picquet, jeune abbé de 35 ans, poursuivait la mission sulpicienne, à savoir défendre la colonie quand, en 1745 et en 1746, il réussit à rassembler les Kanehsata'kehró:non pour se battre contre les Britanniques au fort Edward à la frontière de New York.[55]

L'abbé Picquet quitta Kanehsatà:ke en 1749 pour se rendre à Oswegatchie où il fonda une autre mission sulpicienne appelée La Présentation.[56] Il revint brièvement en 1758 et, avec Montcalm, le général français, il persuada les Kanehsata'kehró:non de se battre encore.[57] Cet homme était, et est toujours, chéri et respecté par son ordre.[58] Le séminaire de Saint-Sulpice exalta ses accomplissements malgré ses méthodes douteuses et son caractère équivoque. On nous dit que :

> Picquet était un petit homme étrange qui brûlait de fanatisme pour essayer de convertir les sauvages aux préceptes du catholicisme, tout en ne tenant presque aucun compte des commandements les plus fondamentaux du christianisme et en enseignant les concepts de la religion d'une manière qui peut seulement être décrite comme pervertie.

> Pour lui, il justifiait ses interprétations en invoquant qu'elles étaient beaucoup plus faciles à saisir pour les sauvages. Cependant, en même temps, il pensait qu'il n'était pas mal de faire tout en son pouvoir pour que les Indiens se soulèvent d'une manière tout à fait inattendue et massacrent les colons et les commerçants anglais partout où ils les trouvaient.

> Homme extrêmement égoïste, le père Picquet considérait que ses efforts personnels à combattre la menace anglaise étaient de loin incomparables à ceux du gouvernement français, sur les plans politique et militaire, et n'hésitait pas à le dire dans ses lettres.[59]

L'abbé Picquet programma ses alliés de la mission à faire la guerre lorsqu'ils traversaient les stations de la croix situées sur le Calvaire. À cet endroit, les symboles du christianisme se juxtaposent à la nature. Le Calvaire se trouve sur le sommet d'une montagne. « Le choix de ce lieu est révélateur [...] Il est situé dans un environnement naturel [...] dans une forêt superbe [...] où les Indiens ne pouvaient pas mieux se sentir [...] ».[60] Le chemin de la croix visait à remplacer les cérémonies traditionnelles que les Sulpiciens considéraient comme des «danses nocturnes» et de la «sorcellerie».[61] Dans les chapelles, les Kanehsata'kehró:non étaient exposés aux images de Christ sur la croix.

En choisissant les épisodes de la passion de Christ, les Sulpiciens avaient considéré attentivement l'attitude des Indiens. Chaque image, qui était facilement comprise, illustrait la violence et la souffrance infligées à Christ. La violence et la souffrance étaient familières aux Indiens engagés dans des guerres tribales et mêlés aux conflits entre les Français et les Anglais. Ils ne pouvaient pas être indifférents au réalisme des peintures […] Les Sulpiciens leur faisaient revivre la passion de Christ à l'aide d'images où les principaux acteurs du drame étaient représentés presque en grandeur nature.[62]

Pour les Kanehsata'kehró:non, la guerre était une chose sérieuse. Ils la faisaient en vue d'établir la paix, l'harmonie et l'honneur chez le peuple. Ils s'aperçurent vite des contradictions inhérentes de la religion des nouveaux arrivants, mais beaucoup n'en tenaient pas compte. Dans la tradition des Rotinonhseshá:ka, la guerre était parfois un moyen nécessaire pour apporter ou établir la paix. La religion des nouveaux arrivants était un moyen, une arme pour créer la guerre. Avec l'arrivée des Ratihnarà:ken (les Blancs), la guerre sur le territoire changea de signification et de but. Pour une multitude de raisons, bon nombre choisirent de s'engager dans les conflits des nouveaux arrivants. Même si, à maintes occasions, les Kanehsata'kehró:non choisirent de rester neutres, beaucoup d'autres fois, ils firent la guerre aux Britanniques. L'abbé Picquet peut s'être félicité d'avoir réussi à motiver les Kanehsata'kehró:non à se battre pour sa cause. En réalité, il se donna beaucoup trop de mérite, car le peuple ne se battait que lorsqu'il croyait que cela servait ses intérêts.

En ce temps-là, les Kanehsata'kehró:non prirent des décisions pour les générations futures en fonction de la connaissance et de l'information qu'ils possédaient. S'ils avaient su, comme nous le savons aujourd'hui, que ni les Français ni les Britanniques ne respectaient leurs ententes, leurs décisions auraient certainement été différentes.

LEÇON DE PAIX

De temps à autre, le peuple a besoin de se faire rappeler ses responsabilités. Le Créateur de toutes choses choisit la meilleure façon possible de lui faire reprendre le fardeau dont il s'est déchargé. Ainsi, les événements se déroulent et indiquent la direction qu'il doit prendre pour marcher sur le chemin que le Créateur lui a préparé.

Vous connaissez tous l'Artisan de la paix et son message, mais même avant lui il y eut quelqu'un qui parla de déposer les bâtons de guerre et les lances. Son histoire est si ancienne qu'elle est presque oubliée. Ce personnage se trouve dans le passé lointain, non seulement des Kanien'kehà:ka, mais aussi des Rotinonhseshá:ka et d'autres Onkwehón:we. Le messager est parfois un homme, parfois une femme. Les Kanehsata'kehró:non l'appellent l'homme en robe blanche.

Au fil des saisons je reste une montagne, il en est de même du message, peu importe celui qui le communique, il demeure.

Quand une personne veut vraiment écouter le message, les paroles remplissent son cœur de bonté.

L'HOMME EN ROBE BLANCHE

Voici une légende très ancienne qui nous vient des aînés de Kanehsatà:ke. Il y a environ 1900 ans, un clan d'Onkwehón:we établi quelque part sur le territoire vivait de la chasse. À cette époque, plusieurs nations indiennes se battaient entre elles.

Nomades, ces Onkwehón:we voyageaient un peu partout pour chasser et vivre de la terre. Soudain, un homme leur apparut. Vêtu d'une robe blanche, il leur dit qu'il était mal que les Indiens se battent, que des frères se disputent. Très fâchés, pointant leurs lances et leurs flèches vers l'homme qui leur était apparu, les Indiens étaient prêts à le tuer. Mais ils n'en firent rien.

L'homme leur dit qu'il partait, qu'il traverserait les grandes eaux et qu'il reviendrait dans trois jours. Au bout de trois jours, il leur apparut de nouveau. Voyant qu'ils vaquaient à leurs occupations quotidiennes et que rien d'inhabituel ne se passait, il les rejoignit. Il portait la même robe blanche que la première fois où il leur était apparu.

Il leur dit : « Vous, le clan d'Indiens qui vivez ici, ce n'est pas vous qui m'avez tué. Où je suis allé par-delà les grandes eaux, c'est là qu'ils m'ont tué. » Les Indiens étaient très effrayés. L'homme leur montra ses blessures. Sa main droite et sa main gauche étaient percées, et il avait aussi une plaie à la poitrine. Les Indiens étaient vraiment stupéfaits qu'un homme puisse être vivant après avoir subi de si graves blessures.

Les Onkwehón:we crurent qu'il était mal de se battre les uns contre les autres. L'homme leur dit qu'il n'aimait pas qu'ils mettent leur peinture de guerre et s'entretuent parce qu'ils étaient frères. Il fit ensuite un mouvement étendu de la main droite et, devant les Indiens, apparut un ruisseau clair. Il leur ordonna d'enlever la peinture de guerre de leur visage. Ils lui obéirent et chacun se nettoya le visage. Après s'être lavés, ils furent étonnés de voir que le ruisseau, dont l'eau était très claire auparavant, était devenu de la couleur du sang.

Cet homme annonça aux Indiens qu'il partait pour aller visiter d'autres tribus. Et c'est ce qui se passa. Il était là, puis il disparut comme il leur était apparu en premier lieu.

UNE OMBRE SUR LE TERRITOIRE

Quand les Kanehsata'kehró:non accueillirent leur parenté et leurs Roti'kharahón:tsi il y a quelque temps, il était convenu que personne ne se mêlerait de la vie des autres. Pendant une courte période, c'est exactement ce qui se passa, mais les choses ne sont jamais aussi simples qu'elles ne le paraissent.

En peu de temps, tous les habitants de Kanehsatà:ke étaient devenus des « Indiens de la mission », même les Kanehsata'kehró:non. Les noms des deux communautés s'entremêlèrent et, puisqu'un seul nom était de plus en plus utilisé, les deux groupes distincts se confondirent.

Bien sûr, les O'serón:ni favorisaient les disciples des Roti'kharahón:tsi parce qu'ils pouvaient gagner les autres Onkwehón:we à la cause des O'serón:ni.

Il faut se rappeler que de tous les Onkwehón:we qui étaient venus à Kanehsatà:ke avec les Roti'kharahón:tsi en passant par la rivière gelée beaucoup avaient antérieurement été des Rotinonhseshá:ka. C'est pourquoi les O'serón:ni dirigeaient leurs affaires avec le peuple d'après les conseils des Rotinonhseshá:ka.

Peu à peu, les Ratihnarà:ken (hommes Blancs) changèrent le sens des enseignements des Rotinonhseshá:ka pour n'en laisser qu'un squelette. Ainsi, ne pouvant plus être nourri par ses enseignements, le peuple devint faible et conciliant. Il était de plus en plus difficile pour ceux qui tenaient ferme à la Kaianere'kó:wa de se faire entendre. En regardant un conseil qui se tenait à Kanehsatà:ke, je vis le O'serón:ni, que le peuple appelle «Onnontio», établir des chefs. Il dit ensuite au peuple que ses chefs auraient le même pouvoir que les chefs de chaque clan. Bon nombre les refusèrent et partirent, mais beaucoup d'autres les acceptèrent.

Tout ce que le peuple avait mis en place disparaissait comme de la poussière. Nombreux étaient ceux qui échangeaient leur canot d'écorce contre le bateau des O'serón:ni. Ne craignaient-ils pas la confusion que cela pouvait engendrer? Réalisaient-ils ce qu'ils établissaient pour les sept générations suivantes? Faisaient-ils un choix éclairé? Le doute peut beaucoup influencer l'esprit d'une personne; il peut ronger ses valeurs tout comme la négligence ronge une habitation abandonnée.

Les femmes aussi avaient changé. Même si certaines s'accrochaient à leurs responsabilités comme la mousse s'accroche aux roches, d'autres adoptaient les coutumes des Ratihnarà:ken et étouffaient leur voix sur les questions de la nation. La vie des Kanehsata'kehró:non avait pour toujours changé et, même moi, je ne pouvais pas prévoir l'étendue que cette ombre jetterait sur le territoire.

PLAN POUR DIVISER LE PEUPLE

 Dans les premiers temps, quand les pays d'Europe se mirent à réclamer le «Nouveau Monde» et à coloniser ses habitants, ils accordaient une grande importance à la nécessité d'apprendre et de comprendre les cultures et les traditions des peuples qu'ils espéraient coloniser. Les Français réussissaient particulièrement dans ce domaine grâce aux efforts de leurs missionnaires. En essayant de convertir les «sauvages» au christianisme, les prêtres apprirent beaucoup sur les coutumes et les pratiques des Onkwehón:we. Les Français et les Britanniques eurent souvent recours à ces renseignements pour inciter le peuple à prendre des décisions qui étaient rarement dans son intérêt. Les Français comprenaient si bien l'organisation spirituelle et politique des Rotinonhseshá:ka qu'ils pouvaient manipuler le symbolisme familier et les métaphores du peuple en déformant leur signification pour arriver à leurs fins.

Mes enfants,

Anciens, hommes, femmes et enfants. Écoutez ma voix aussi longtemps que vous êtes ici; considérez attentivement mes paroles.

Mes enfants,

Je ne pouvais pas oublier les paroles que vous m'avez adressées quand votre village était au début établi à la montagne [de Montréal], quand vous m'avez dit que vous vous mettiez sous mon aile et que vous avez ajouté que ceux qui me mordraient vous mordraient aussi.

Vous m'avez redit que vous seriez, en un instant, ma main droite pour frapper mes ennemis. J'ai toujours devant mes yeux la ceinture que vous m'avez donnée à cette occasion, m'assurant de votre promesse et de votre fidélité.

Mes enfants,

Vous avez toujours gardé cette promesse, et vous m'avez donné, à moi et à mes pré-décesseurs, une preuve de votre grand attachement à moi. En retour, je désire vous transmettre des marques raisonnables de mon amitié et vous unir à moi par une chaîne que rien ne peut jamais briser […]

Voici la ceinture avec laquelle j'allume le feu de votre grand conseil, autour duquel vous pourrez vous réunir en paix, vous entretenir de mes affaires et des vôtres avec les diverses nations de ce pays. Ce sera alors l'endroit où mon feu brûlera vraiment, puisque c'est le premier que j'ai allumé dans cette colonie […].

Le présent message vous communiquera aussi que vous devez vous attacher au grand Maître de la vie; écoutez avec soumission et respect vos pères les missionnaires et obéissez-leur en toutes choses qu'ils vous recommanderont de faire pour le bien de vos âmes […].

Mes enfants,

Chaque fois que vous regardez cette ceinture, elle vous dira que je suis votre père et grand chef et donc, à la tête de toutes vos affaires […]

Ceinture lancée dans le feu

Mes enfants,

C'est la ceinture avec laquelle j'allume le feu de votre assemblée. Considérez-la très attentivement pour ne jamais l'oublier.

Plantation de l'arbre du village par une ceinture

Mes enfants,

Écoutez-moi bien. Par cette ceinture, je demande que, de la terre que vous habitez, pousse un grand arbre qui me représente. Sous son ombre, toutes les nations qui sont mes enfants peuvent venir et se reposer en paix.[63]

Ainsi commençait un message du marquis de Beauharnois aux « Indiens du Lac des Deux-Montagnes ». En fait, il fut adressé par M. Claude de Ramezay, l'homme qui avait commandé la milice lors de la guerre du comte de Frontenac contre les Iroquois en 1696. Cette missive fut remise le 12 août 1741, à un lieu non indiqué.

Beauharnois parle de la ceinture qu'il est sur le point de lancer, ceinture faite à l'époque où la mission de la montagne sur le Mont-Royal fut fondée en 1660. Il pouvait très bien avoir décrit la ceinture Two Dog Wampum. Malheureusement, Beauharnois ne décrivit pas complètement la ceinture de 1660 qu'il lança en 1741. En 1781, les Kanehsata'kehró:non la décrivirent ainsi :

Selon nos coutumes anciennes, vous voyez notre engagement : vous voyez cette ligne blanche qui montre la longueur de notre terre. Les personnages aux mains jointes qui touchent la croix représentent la loyauté que nous avons à notre foi. Le corps représente le feu du conseil de notre village. Les deux chiens à l'extérieur sont cen-sés garder les frontières de notre territoire, et si quelqu'un essaie de prendre notre possession, il est de leur devoir de nous en avertir en aboyant […][64]

Certains disent que la ceinture Two Dog Wampum signifiait que les Kanehsata'kehró:non étaient devenus chrétiens puisqu'une croix y occupe une place importante. Ils affirment qu'en faisant la ceinture, le peuple de Kanehsatà:ke exprimait sa loyauté à la foi chré-tienne.[65] Cela n'est pas nécessairement vrai. Plutôt qu'une expression de foi chrétienne, la croix au centre de la ceinture dépeint les Français. Pour eux, la croix était un symbole facilement reconnaissable en raison de leur pratique d'en planter partout où ils allaient pour réclamer le territoire au nom du roi. De plus, utiliser la croix pour représenter les Français ne voulait pas nécessairement dire que les Kanehsata'kehró:non exprimaient leur loyauté envers eux (les Français). Ils disaient clairement qu'ils faisaient alliance avec les Français pour vivre paisiblement sur ce territoire.

Pour sa part, le marquis de Beauharnois affirme que la ceinture signifiait que le peuple s'était lié aux Français en 1660. En 1741, il essaya de renouveler ce lien et, ce faisant, il crut que le peuple se soumettait aux Français. Une telle interprétation n'était pas inhabituelle, car les Français considéraient souvent la bonne volonté des Onkwehón:we de faire des alliances comme un signe de faiblesse.

Il n'est pas étonnant que Beauharnois ait demandé que les Kanehsata'kehró:non se soumettent aux missionnaires et leur obéissent sous peine de pécher contre le grand Maître de la vie et donc d'être punis. Beauharnois est venu dangereusement près de se faire lui-même le grand maître de la vie. Il essaya de manipuler et de tordre le symbolisme de la Kaianere'kó:wa afin d'être le seul à guider les gens dans les questions de guerre, de paix et de toutes autres affaires.

De façon arrogante, il tenta de se mettre à la place du grand arbre de la paix, suggérant que les gens «viennent et se reposent en paix» sous lui. Ce faisant, Beauharnois essayait de transférer l'allégeance des Kanehsata'kehró:non des Rotinonhseshá:ka (peuple de la maison longue) aux Français et, plus particulièrement, à la mission des Sulpiciens au Lac des Deux-Montagnes. Le marquis de Beauharnois poursuit ainsi son message.

Par une ceinture aux guerriers [iroquois]

Mes enfants,

Vous tous qui êtes dans le village du Lac des Deux-Montagnes pour défendre mes intérêts dans les différentes guerres que je dois mener dans ce pays. Par cette ceinture, je vous lie à Garontouanen et je vous exhorte à ne pas faire ou à entreprendre quoi que ce soit dans une guerre quelconque sans sa participation. Je n'ai plus d'autres ordres à vous donner. Les chefs de guerre de chaque tribu doivent être nommés. J'espère le faire à la prochaine occasion et je compte sur votre soumission et votre fidélité, comme vous pouvez dépendre de ma bonté et de ma bienveillance.

Par une ceinture aux Algonquins et aux Népissingues

Par cette ceinture, je renouvelle cette alliance qui, je l'espère, durera aussi longtemps que durera cette terre. En même temps, je vous lie d'une manière inséparable à vos frères iroquois du Lac des Deux-Montagnes, dont je désire allumer le feu. Je ne vous exhorterai pas à répondre à mes intentions puisque je connais votre fidélité et votre soumission [...][66]

Reconnaissant l'importance de l'appui des Kanien'kehà:ka de Kanehsatà:ke, Beauharnois recherchait leur loyauté et leur soumission. En allumant un feu et en croyant nommer des chefs, il essayait de gagner la faveur des Kanehsata'kehró:non en prétendant les honorer. De toute évidence, certains se firent jouer par ce stratagème, tandis que d'autres perçurent son arrogance et sa prétention. En se mêlant des affaires internes de la communauté, Beauharnois perpétuait un plan destiné à diviser le peuple. Beauharnois et les Français apprirent à utiliser cette division à leur avantage. Il était utile non seulement que les Kanehsata'kehró:non se disputent entre eux, mais aussi qu'ils aient des conflits avec d'autres nations. La difficulté pour Beauharnois était de maintenir entre les partis un niveau d'animosité suffisant pour empêcher la proximité, sans toutefois provoquer une bataille. En octobre 1740, Beauharnois écrivit une lettre codée au comte de Maurepas.

Je compte, mon seigneur, sur six cents réguliers. Il peut y avoir entre douze et quinze mille miliciens qui serviraient bien quand l'occasion le nécessite, mais sur qui je ne peux absolument pas compter comme sur des troupes disciplinées, puisque la longue continuité de paix a calmé l'ardeur des Canadiens : quatre cents Iroquois de Sault-Saint-Louis et du Lac des Deux-Montagnes, deux cents Algonquins et Népissingues et plus de sept cents Abénaquis de l'Acadie et de ce lieu. En ce qui concerne ces nations, vous connaissez, mon seigneur, leur inconstance. À l'aide de quelques cordes de Wampum, j'ai pris la précaution de faire savoir à nos Indiens domiciliés de ne pas s'éloigner de chez eux, au cas où on aurait besoin d'eux.[67]

De toute évidence, Beauharnois trouvait difficile de garder les Onkwehón:we dans un état d'alerte, prêts pour la guerre. Il peut avoir été pratique de fomenter des incompréhensions entre divers groupes pour maintenir un certain niveau de frustration et d'agressivité. Ce qui se passa exactement entre le moment où Beauharnois écrivit la lettre en 1740 et celui où il envoya un message aux Kanehsata'kehró:non en 1741 n'est pas clair. Mais il avait une situation explosive sur les bras : le peuple de Kanehsatà:ke et celui de Kahnawà:ke étaient sur le point de se battre à propos de la tournure très déplaisante que prenait leur relation commerciale.[68] Beauharnois s'inquiétait que les deux villages ne se massacrent à cause de la jalousie qui régnait entre eux.[69] La situation était si tendue que le peuple de Kahnawà:ke refusa de rencontrer le messager de Kanehsatà:ke.[70]

Atinon, chef des Népissingues à Kanehsatà:ke, était déconcerté par l'altercation. Il était « étonné que ceux du Sault-des-Récollets refusent de recevoir leurs frères du Lac des Deux-Montagnes, qui étaient de la même nation, et que lui-même ne s'était jamais aperçu de leurs différends. Il ajouta en confidence à quelques personnes qui me l'ont répété [Beauharnois] que cette affaire ne passerait pas sans coups des deux côtés ».[71]

Pour cet état des affaires dangereux, Beauharnois mit le blâme directement sur les épaules des missionnaires Jésuites à Kahnawà:ke et sur les « demoiselles Desauniers » qui toutes deux commerçaient avec les Britanniques à New York. Il ne voyait qu'une façon de régler le problème : « Il est vrai, mon seigneur, qu'étant parfaitement au courant de ces abus, je pourrais y remédier en enlevant ces missionnaires et leurs associés. » Le comte de Maurepas n'allait pas le lui permettre.[72]

Puisque Beauharnois ne pouvait pas contrôler la situation à Kahnawà:ke, il se tourna vers ses amis les Sulpiciens à Kanehsatà:ke. À sa satisfaction, il put rapporter qu'il avait « la soumission de ces Indiens [Lac des Deux-Montagnes] à [sa] volonté », et qu'il était donc « libre de disposer d'eux, et de profiter de cette occasion pour les assujettir complètement à sa Majesté ».[73] Beauharnois se donna beaucoup trop de mérite et se dupa lui-même concernant la loyauté des Kanehsata'kehró:non. En réalité, à mesure que les événements se déroulaient, il devint évident que les Kanehsata'kehró:non continuaient de prendre des décisions dans l'intérêt du peuple. Le problème est que le peuple ne pouvait plus s'entendre sur ce qui était dans son intérêt.

En 1743, le marquis de Beauharnois échafauda un autre plan pour diviser le peuple. Il décrit son grand accomplissement dans une lettre adressée au comte de Maurepas.

Quand l'expédition organisée par les Iroquois du Lac des Deux-Montagnes contre les Têtes-Plates [probablement les Catawbas de Détroit][74] est revenue avec un ou deux scalps de ces derniers, l'idée m'est venue de leur proposer un plan. Je m'attendais, en effet, à ce qu'il ne remporte pas un grand succès, puisque les partis de ce genre limitent ordinairement leurs conquêtes à des affaires très banales, mais j'ai considéré que le meilleur moyen de saboter les négociations des Têtes-Plates avec les Chaouanons et les Iroquois était qu'ils soient harcelés par les nations avec lesquelles ils s'attendaient à pouvoir conclure un traité de paix. Sieur de Joncaire m'écrit que les Sénécas ont soulevé divers partis contre eux, que certains sont revenus avec des scalps et que d'autres sont immédiatement partis en quête de plus de scalps. Il ajoute que ces Indiens sont plus enthousiastes que jamais dans cette guerre et il voit qu'ils ne sont pas disposés à accepter toute proposition de paix que les Têtes-Plates pourraient leur offrir. Je recommande à cet officier de les garder dans ces sentiments et je les encouragerai davantage à cet égard au cours de la visite qu'ils me rendront l'été prochain. Ils m'ont en effet envoyé un mot disant qu'ils ne pouvaient pas venir cette année parce qu'ils étaient occupés à armer divers partis contre les Têtes-Plates.

Je continuerai, mon seigneur, à créer une diversion dans ce groupe contre les Chicachas jusqu'à ce que M. de Vaudreuil m'informe de la nécessité de les arrêter.[75]

Beauharnois avait consciemment et inconsciemment commis l'acte de manipulation ultime. Détenant un pouvoir considérable, il l'utilisait à des fins à la fois personnelles et politiques. Non seulement il n'avait aucun scrupule d'avoir agi ainsi, mais il y prenait même plaisir. La violence manifestée contre les Kanehsata'kehró:non augmenta rapidement.

Picquet, prêtre sulpicien à la mission, put au moins à deux occasions persuader les Kanehsata'kehró:non de se battre dans la guerre du roi George (1744-1748).[76] Comme Beauharnois, il travaillait aussi à les diviser en envoyant de leurs guerriers dans une mission d'espionnage contre leurs frères des Cinq Nations.[77]

Une paix relative s'installa de 1748 à 1754, mais cette brève période de grâce avant la bataille finale entre les Français et les Britanniques pour la conquête de l'Amérique du Nord fut difficile pour les Kanehsata'kehró:non en raison de la première d'une série d'épidémies de varicelle. Comme tous les Onkwehón:we, le peuple de Kanehsatà:ke n'avait aucune résistance contre cette maladie. L'épidémie qui frappa à la fin des années 1740 décima la communauté.[78] Les missionnaires regardèrent les Kanehsata'kehró:non succomber à la maladie qu'ils avaient contribué à introduire. Se tournant vers la vierge Marie, le séminaire apporta à l'église missionnaire une statue d'argent fabriquée en France.[79] Cela ne fit rien pour empêcher l'épidémie de se propager.

En 1754, la guerre de Sept Ans commença et, en 1755, une deuxième épidémie de varicelle frappa. En août 1756, plus d'une centaine de personnes périrent dans le sillage d'une troisième épidémie de varicelle.[80]

En 1757, l'abbé Picquet retourna brièvement à Kanehsatà:ke où il joignit le général des troupes françaises, le marquis de Montcalm.[81] Des guerriers de Kanehsatà:ke partirent apparemment pour Oswegatchie où ils firent au moins un prisonnier britannique[82] et, en juillet 1758, ils accompagnèrent Montcalm au fort Carillon (Ticonderoga). Après une bataille intense entre les Français et les Britanniques qu'il avait gagnée, Montcalm tourna le dos aux guerriers de Kanehsatà:ke qu'il ridiculisa pour ne pas avoir apparemment exécuté leur devoir aussi bien qu'il le désirait.[83] Les guerriers retournèrent chez eux et, à la fin de juillet, ils rencontrèrent le gouverneur de la Nouvelle-France, le marquis de Vaudreuil. Ils s'adressèrent ainsi à lui :

Père [marquis de Vaudreuil],

Nous venons vous exprimer la douleur profonde que nous ressentons concernant la manière dont M. de Montcalm nous a reçus à Carillon [fort Ticonderoga]. Nous lui avons déjà communiqué que nous étions grandement humiliés de ne pas avoir pris part à sa victoire. Il nous a sèchement répondu : « Vous arrivez au moment où je n'ai plus besoin de vous. Êtes-vous venus seulement pour voir des cadavres? Allez derrière le fort, vous en trouverez quelques-uns. Je n'ai pas besoin de vous pour tuer des Anglais. » Nous nous sommes retirés dans ses quartiers pour nous consulter.

Le lendemain matin, nous sommes allés le saluer et lui avons demandé la permission de partir sur le chemin de Lydius. Il a frappé la table en disant : « Morbleu! Vous ne vous en irez pas. Allez au diable si vous n'êtes pas satisfaits! »

Père,

Nous n'avons pas eu besoin d'un interprète pour comprendre ces paroles. Nous lui avons immédiatement répondu que nous étions étonnés qu'il se soit mis en colère sans que nous l'ayons provoqué. Le conseil n'a pas duré; nous sommes tous retournés chez nous.[84]

Les hommes décidèrent de ne plus se battre; ils n'allaient plus jamais tenir compte des ordres de Montcalm. Les Français avaient poussé les Kanehsata'kehró:non à bout. Le peuple avait entendu les paroles de Montcalm et les avait très bien comprises. Ils commencèrent à prendre leurs distances de la cause perdue d'avance des Français. Il leur était devenu impossible de continuer de se battre à leurs côtés.

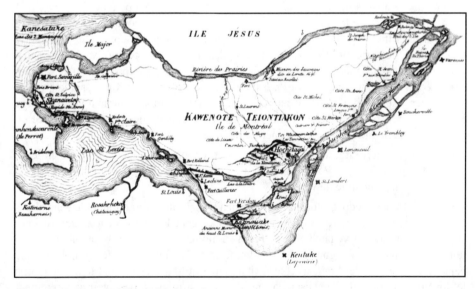

Carte historique de l'île de Montréal
Gracieuseté du musée David M. Stewart

UN MOMENT DIFFICILE POUR ÉCOUTER

J'entends les paroles du peuple lorsqu'il passe du temps près de moi à ramasser des racines, des herbes médicinales et des baies sauvages qui poussent un peu partout. Même s'il est confus par les manières des nouveaux arrivants et s'inquiète que leurs requêtes deviennent de plus en plus exigeantes, il prend toujours le temps de rire et de jouir de la vie. Les mères font toujours pour leurs filles des poupées avec des feuilles de maïs, et les fils pratiquent leurs habiletés de chasse en attrapant des lapins et des perdrix.

Les hommes sont occupés à chasser le gros gibier, à participer aux conseils et à enseigner souvent aux nouveaux arrivants à bien se comporter quand ils s'adressent à d'autres nations.

Il semble que ces O'serón:ni aient des problèmes à écouter. Il leur est très difficile de s'asseoir tranquille pendant un certain temps sans bouger. Le peuple se dit que les petits dans leur berceau savent mieux se comporter que ces hommes adultes.

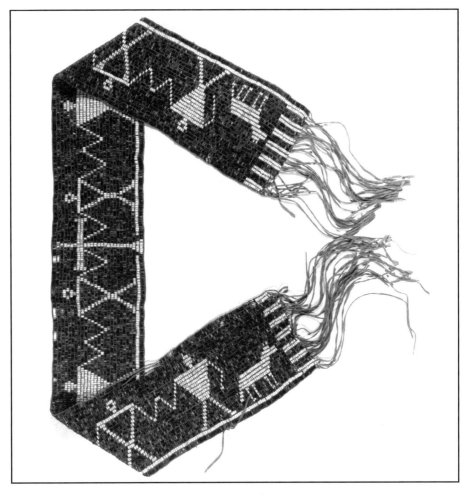

Ceinture Two Dog Wampum
Gracieuseté du musée McCord

[1] Cette vision de l'histoire a été utilisée aussi récemment qu'en 1990, durant la soi-disant crise des Mohawks, quand le ministère des Affaires indiennes a publié un communiqué de presse sur la «question d'Oka». Il y explique le rejet du gouvernement du Canada de la revendication territoriale des Kanehsata'kehró:non de 1975 selon les conditions de 1721. *An Overview of the Oka Issue*, Affaires indiennes et du nord Canada, juillet 1990. *Comprehensive Land Claims of the Kanesatake Indians*, Affaires indiennes et du Nord Canada, juillet 1990. Une revendication territoriale détaillée faite en 1975 par le peuple de Kanehsatà:ke (avec Kahnawà:ke et Akwesasne) a été rejetée puisque les «Mohawks présents dans la région ne s'y trouvaient pas avant l'arrivée des Européens, mais qu'ils sont venus s'établir à Oka seulement après que la Mission fusse établie en 1721», et que «les Mohawks ne pouvaient pas réclamer un titre de propriété puisqu'ils n'ont pas gardé possession de la terre depuis des temps immémoriaux. La terre a été alternativement et concurrentiellement occupée par les Népissingues, les Algonquins et les Iroquois».

[2] Voir par exemple, *Travels in North America*, Peter Kalm, 1749, *Travels in the Americas; History of the Catholic Missions Among the Indian Tribes of the United States, 1529-1854*, John Gilmary Shea, 1899; *Les premières réserves indiennes au Canada*, Revue d'histoire de l'Amérique française, vol. 4, n° 2, septembre 1950 et W. N. Fenton et Elisabeth Tooker, dans *Northeast*, p. 472. Certains historiens ont suggéré une présence des Cinq Nations dans la région. Par exemple, dans son ouvrage de plusieurs volumes sur la France et l'Angleterre en Amérique du Nord, 1893, Francis Parkman discute assez longuement de la présence de l'«ennemi iroquois» aux alentours du cours inférieur de la rivière des Outaouais en 1660. Dans *Le Dictionnaire historique et géographique des paroisses, missions et municipalités de la province de Québec* de Hormisdas Magnan, 1925, l'auteur remarque qu'«avant 1700, la paroisse [de L'Annonciation] était composée de sauvages iroquois et algonquins.» Dans sa thèse, *La politique missionnaire des Sulpiciens aux XVIIᵉ et XVIIIᵉ siècles, 1668-1735*, Louise Tremblay fait mention d'une présence Mohawk au Lac des Deux-Montagnes avant l'arrivée des Sulpiciens. Selon Mᵐᵉ Tremblay, les Mohawks se sont installés au Lac des Deux-Montagnes après le déclin des Cinq Nations. De plus, l'histoire orale de Kanehsatà:ke est remplie de preuves d'un village de Kanien'kehà:ka connu sous le nom de Kanehsatà:ke avant 1721, situé au Lac des Deux-Montagnes.

[3] *People of Terra Nullius: Betrayal and Rebirth in Aboriginal Canada*, Boyce Richardson, Douglas & McIntyre, Vancouver/ Toronto, 1993, p. vii.

[4] *Oka, les Vicissitudes d'une mission sauvage*, revue trimestrielle canadienne, XVI, juin 1930, p. 121-149 et *Histoire d'Oka, la mission du Lac des Deux-Montagnes, fondée en 1721*, René Marinier, p. s. s. Cahier du Lac des Deux-Montagnes.

[5] *Traditional History of the Confederacy of the Six Nations*, préparée par un comité des chefs, présentée par Duncan C. Scott, F. R. S. C., lue le 16 mai 1911, transactions du R. S. C., section II, 1911, p. 238.

[6] Il sont aussi membres du clan bécassine à Kanehsatà:ke, bien que ce ne soit pas à l'origine un clan Kanien'kehà:ka.

[7] *Oral Memory of the Haudenosaunee: Views of the Two Row Wampum*, Richard Hill dans Indian Roots of American Democracy, Jose Barreiro, ed., Akwe:kon Press, Ithaca, 1988, p. 151.

[8] Tiré du texte de l'exposition Kahswenhtha, produit par le Centre culturel de Kahnawà:ke.

[9] The Works of Samuel de Champlain, volume II, p. 74-204 passim, publications de The Champlain Society, Toronto

[10] *The Old Regime in Canada*, Francis Parkman, 1893, p. 128.

[11] W. S. Eccles, Frontenac the Courtier Governor, McClelland and Stewart Ltd., copyright 1959, p. 195.

[12] New York Colonial Documents, vol. IX, New York Colonial Manuscripts, p. 602.

[13] *Roving writer visits Oka reserve, pow-wows with Mohawk chiefs*, The Lachute Watchman, 20 décembre 1961.

[14] Le nom Kanehsatà:ke est écrit de 23 façons différentes dans The Papers of Sir William Johnson, et de 22 façons différentes dans The New York Colonial Documents.

[15] Un autre village avec une nomenclature semblable «Conesedago» a déjà existé près du lac Sénéca dans les parties ouest des terres de la confédération des Cinq Nations.

[16] New York Colonial Documents, vol. IV, New York Colonial Manuscripts, p. 120.

[17] *Longhouse and Palisade: Northeastern Iroquoian Villages in the Seventeenth Century*, Thomas S. Abler, Ontario History, vol. 62, 1970, p. 17-40 et *A Journey into Mohawk/Oneida Country*, 1634-1635, journal de Harmen Meyndertsz van den Bogaert, Syracuse University Press, 1988.

[18] Les mots «Indiens prieurs» ou «Indiens de la mission» étaient librement utilisés pour faire référence aux Onkwehón:we qui vivaient dans et aux alentours des diverses missions romaines catholiques au Québec. De quelle manière ces Onkwehón:we étaient «chrétiens» est décrit ci-dessous. Par exemple, des représentants français utilisaient souvent les symboles des Kanien'kehà:ka et des Cinq Nations dans leurs conseils avec le peuple. À l'époque qui suivit la conquête, des militaires britanniques ont, à maintes occasions, observé des cérémonies de condoléances pour des chefs décédés. De plus, au 19ᵉ siècle, le peuple faisait souvent référence à ses clans quand il écrivait des lettres et des pétitions. Dans sa biographie *The life of Amand Parent*, 1880, Parent, un missionnaire méthodiste basé à Kanehsatà:ke, fait plusieurs références à ce qu'il décrit comme des «idoles» et de la «sorcellerie».

[19] The Papers of Sir William Johnson, vol. I-XIII.

[20] *Réponses des Iroquois, Algonquins et Népissingues du Lac des Deux-Montagnes aux paroles de M. le Marquis de Beauharnois, gouverneur général de la Nouvelle-France, le 12 août 1741*, Bulletin des recherches historiques, juillet 1930, p. 396-399.

[21] Voir le chapitre 5 pour l'histoire de l'«Origine du nom du village d'Oka».

[22] Voir Elisabeth Tooker, *Northeast, Handbook of North American Indians*, vol. 5, p. 479.

[23] En 1853, le gouvernement britannique réserva des terres au Québec pour l'usage «des tribus indiennes du Bas-Canada». En 1858, ces terres sont devenues des réserves. La réserve à Maniwaki a été créée pour les Algonquins et les Népissingues du Lac des Deux-Montagnes et pour tous les autres «Indiens dispersés».

[24] Au Québec, la période woodland a commencé environ 1000 ans av. J.-C.

[25] L'information sur les fouilles archéologiques qui ont été effectuées est contenu dans *An Archaeological Reconnaissance of the Eastern Portion of the Triangle of Land between the Ottawa & St-Lawrence Rivers in 1965*, de James Pendergast, 1965; *Évaluation archéologique sur le site préhistorique BiFm-1, parc Paul Sauvé, Oka*, de Claude Chapdelaine, 1988b; *Reconnaissance et fouille archéologique à Kanasatake* de Lorraine Létourneau Parent, 1971; *Kanasatake-Oka Tetenre-Hier* de Lorraine Létourneau-Sicotte dans *Cahier d'histoire de Deux-Montagnes*, vol. 1, n° 2, juin 1978; *Poterie, ethnicité et Laurentie iroquoienne* de Claude Chapdelaine, dans *Recherches Amérindiennes au Québec*, vol. XXI, n°s 1-2, p. 44-52. Dans son rapport de 1965, James Pendergast remarque que l'érosion a détruit deux sites sur la plage.

[26] Pour une discussion sur les trouvailles à Pointe-du-Buisson, voir Norman Clermont et Claude Chapdelaine, *Pointe-du-Buisson 4 : quarante siècles d'archives oubliées*, Recherches amérindiennes au Québec, 1982.

[27] À St-Andrews East, une cache d'artefacts a été découverte dans les années 1950 durant la construction d'un terrain de golf, mais la plupart de ces trésors ont disparu. Un article sur cette trouvaille a paru dans une publication de courte durée, St-Andrews East News, vol. 1, n° 10, novembre 1956, édité par Sally Hungerbuhler.

[28] Pour une discussion sur la théorie des Iroquois du Saint-Laurent, voir James F. Pendergast, *The St-Lawrence Iroquoians: Their Past, Present, and Immediate Future*, bulletin de l'association archéologique de l'État de New York, printemps 1991, n° 102, p. 47-74 et *Essays in St-Lawrence Iroquoian Archaeology*, James F. Pendergast et Claude Chapdelaine, éditeurs, *Essays in St-Lawrence Iroquoian Archaeology*.

[29] Discours d'Aghneetha, chef principal du village du Lac des Deux-Montagnes, adressé à Sir John Johnson, Baronet, le 8 février 1787.

[30] Dans la liste n° 48, *Réponses pour les messieurs ecclésiastiques de Montréal*, qui a été déposée à la cour supérieure de justice à Montréal comme faisant partie de la cause Angus Corinthe contre les ecclésiastiques du séminaire de Saint-Sulpice au sujet de la Commune, les Sulpiciens ont dit ceci : « Enfin que la harangue des Sauvages n'a pour base que des fables de leur génie, et un prétendu collier qu'ils avouent avoir fait eux-mêmes » p. 104.

[31] Peter Kalm faisait partie des quelques voyageurs européens qui ont exprimé un intérêt dans les aliments cultivés par les Onkwehón:we et les Kanien'kehà:ka.

[32] Gédéon de Catalogne, *Mémoire sur Canada*, 7 novembre 1712, dans William B. Monro, documents relatifs au régime de tenure seigneuriale au Canada, Toronto, 1908, p. 94-151.

[33] *Les premières « réserves » indiennes au Canada*, revue d'histoire de l'Amérique française, vol. 4, n° 2, septembre 1950, p. 207. Selon Gédéon de Catalogne, les Indiens de Sault-aux-Récollets avaient, en 1712, plus de 400 arpents cultivés.

[34] Procès-verbal du conseil de Marine, 31 mars 1716, à la cour supérieure de justice, Angus Corinthe et al. contre le séminaire de Saint-Sulpice, registre des procédures, vol. 1, Centre national des arts, RG 13, vol. 2432, dossier A 500.

[35] *Peter Kalm's Travels in North America*, 1749, p. 511.

[36] Mémoires des différentes choses qui concernent l'administration des seigneuries du séminaire de Montréal sur lesquelles on souhaite d'être instruit en ce pays. Avec réponses données par le séminaire de Paris en 1713, Tremblay, p. 118 et 120.

[37] Rowell, Reid, Wood & Wright, Barristers à E. L. Newcombe, ministère de la Justice, 20 avril 1912, département de la Justice, A-500.

[38] Lettre de M. Magnien à M. Chaumaux, 22 mai 1724, Tremblay, p. 142.

[39] Consulter la concession de 1717.

[40] Richard Colebrook Harris, *The Seigneurial System in Early Canada: A Geographical Study*, p. 35.

[41] Ibid. La seule autre seigneurie concédée durant cette période l'a été au marquis de Beauharnois. Toutes les autres requêtes ont été refusées. La concession à Beauharnois a été faite en 1729.

[42] Rowell à Newcombe.

[43] Concession originale de 1717.

[44] Extrait du procès verbal du conseil de Marie, MM. de Vaudreuil et Bégon, à Québec, le 14 février 1719, registre des procédures, vol. P.52 A500.

[45] Guillaume Dunn, *Les Forts de l'Outaouais*, citant l'ingénieur pour la colonie, Roy Franquet, p. 39.

[46] Concession de 1735.

[47] Ibid.

[48] Extrait d'une lettre du comte de Maurepas à M. le marquis de Beauharnois, le 20 avril 1742, registre des procédures, vol. 1, p. 80

[49] Le seul rapport sur un fort devant être construit l'a été par Roy Franquet. Peter Kalm, dans son journal en 1747, ne fait aucune référence à un village hautement fortifié tel que suggéré par Franquet.

[50] Concession de 1717.

[51] Richard Colebrook Harris, *The Seigneurial System in Early Canada: A Geographical Study*, Philippe de Rigaud, marquis de Vaudreuil et Michel Begon, 1717, p. 173.

[52] Mémoires de M. Hoquart, intendant de la Nouvelle-France, 1736, registre des procédures, vol.1, doc. n° 45, p. 83, Centre national des arts, RG 13, vol. 2432, dossier A500.

[53] Robert J. Surtees, *The Iroquois in Canada, in The History and Culture of Iroquois Diplomacy*, p. 69. « En 1731, les représentants français persuadèrent les Hurons de Detroit de faire la guerre aux Outagamies. Ceux-ci envoyèrent des messagers aux Iroquois convertis de la mission de Deux-Montagnes et les invitèrent à se joindre à eux pour en finir avec les Outagamies. » Francis Parkman, *A Half Century of Conflict*, vol. 1, p. 341.

[54] Extrait du rapport de M. Hoquart, 10 novembre 1732, registre des procédures, vol. 1, n° 34, p. 78, R113, vol. 2342, A500.

[55] E. B. O'Callaghan, M. D., *The Documentary History of the State of New York*, vol. 1, p. 428, 429.

[56] Urgel Lafontaine, un missionnaire sulpicien à la mission du Lac des Deux-Montagnes a beaucoup écrit dans son journal sur l'abbé Picquet. Pour Lafontaine, l'époque Picquet en a été une de grande gloire pour la mission, cahier 15.

[57] *The Documentary History of the State of New York*, vol. 1, Weed, Parsons & Co., Public Printers, Albany, 1849, p. 429-431.

[58] Pour une biographie récente et brève de l'abbé Picquet, voir *Les prêtres de Saint-Sulpice au Canada* avec une préface de Raymond Denville, 1992, p.181-184.

[59] Allan W. Eckert, *Wilderness Empire, A Narrative*, Little Brown & Company, p. 160.

[60] Pour une biographie récente et brève de l'abbé Picquet, voir *Les prêtres de Saint-Sulpice au Canada* avec une préface de Raymond Denville, 1992, p.181-184.

[61] Ibid.

[62] Porter et Trudel, *The Calvary at Oka*, p. 43.

[63] Message du marquis de Beauharnois, gouverneur de la Nouvelle-France, aux Indiens du Lac des Deux-Montagnes, livré par M. de Ramezay qui est envoyé pour rallumer le feu qui avait déjà été ravivé par les Hurons de Lorrette et pour replanter l'arbre qui était tombé à cause desdits Hurons qui avaient emporté quelques ceintures. Le 12 août 1741, New York Colonial Documents, vol. IX, New York Colonial Manuscripts, p. 1076-1081.

[64] Paul William, *Reading Wampum Belts as Living Symbols*, Northeast Indian Quarterly, vol. VII, n° 1, été 1990, p. 31-35.

[65] Message du marquis de Beauharnois, gouverneur de la Nouvelle-France, 12 août 1741, New York Colonial Documents, vol. IX, New York Colonial Manuscripts, p. 1076-1081.

[66] M. de Beauharnois au comte de Maurepas, 31 octobre 1740, New York Colonial Documents, vol. IX, New York Colonial Manuscripts, p. 1168-1175.

[67] Ibid.

[68] Ibid.

[69] M. de Beauharnois au comte de Maurepas, 31 octobre 1740, New York Colonial Documents, vol. IX, New York Colonial Manuscripts, p. 1168-1175.

[70] Ibid.

[71] Ibid.

[72] Ibid.

[73] Selon Richard White, *dans Middle Ground*, p.193, le terme Têtes-Plates (Flat Heads) était un « terme générique pour désigner les Indiens du sud, mais qui dans ce cas fait probablement référence aux Catawbas » qui vivaient près de Détroit. Le terme n'était pas utilisé pour décrire les Flat Heads qui vivent sur la côte ouest canadienne et américaine.

[74] M. de Beauharnois au comte de Maurepas, 13 octobre 1743, New York Colonial Documents, vol. IX, Documents de Paris : VIII, p. 1095-1099.

[75] *The Documentary History of the State of New York*, vol. 1, p. 428, 429.

[76] E. B. O'Callaghan, M. D., *The Documentary History of the State of New York*, p. 428.

[77] Maurault, *Les vicissitudes d'une mission sauvage*, Olivier Maurault, *Les vicissitudes d'une mission sauvage*, revue trimestrielle canadienne, Montréal, 1930, p. 138.

[78] Ibid.

[79] John Gilmary Shea, *History of the French Catholic Missions Among the Indians of the United States : 1529-1854*, Excelsior Catholic Publishing House, 1899, p. 339.

[80] Papers of Sir William Johnson, *The Documentary History of the State of New York;* arrangé sous la direction de l'Honorable Christopher Morgan, secrétaire d'État. Par E. B. O'Callaghan, M. D. vol. 1, p. 438, 439, Albany, Weed, Parsons & Co. Public Printers, 1849.

[81] Journal de l'expédition contre le fort William Henry, du 12 juillet au 16 août 1757, documents de Paris: XIII. p. 599, 607, New York, DC, vol. X, New York Colonial Manuscripts.

[82] Papers of Sir William Johnson, vol. 3, *7 Years War*, p. 241.

[83] Discours des Iroquois, des Népissingues, des Algonquins, des Abénakis et des Mississagues, 30 juillet 1758 à New York. D. C., vol. X, Documents de Paris : XIV, p. 805.

[84] Ibid.

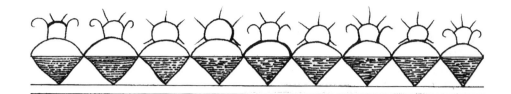

CHAPITRE 3

GUERRE ET PAIX

TRANSMISSION DES TRADITIONS

Les Kanien'kehà:ka installés autour de moi vivaient vraiment en des temps étranges. Comment est-ce que je le sais? Eh bien, une montagne ressent des choses et, seulement par la façon dont j'ai ressenti leurs pas résonner sur le sol, je pouvais voir ce qui se passait.

Certains étaient inquiets, confus, pourrait-on dire. Ils avaient vu tellement de choses en si peu de temps. Il était devenu difficile de savoir quoi garder, quoi rejeter et comment assembler tout cela.

Les Roti'kharahón:tsi (robes noires) prétendaient que les anciennes traditions n'étaient pas bonnes et qu'eux seuls détenaient la vérité. Haut et fort, ils disaient beaucoup de belles paroles. Ils grondaient et retentissaient comme les ratiwè:ras (tonnerres) mais, contrairement au rawè:ras (tonnerre), ils ne produisaient aucune pluie pour aider la création.

Les paroles des Roti'kharahón:tsi se faisaient l'écho de la vérité, mais leurs actions démontraient autre chose. Ils donnaient peu et prenaient beaucoup. Ils parlaient de paix, puis disaient aux Kanehsata'kehró:non d'aller en guerre pour eux. Ils se disaient honorables, mais prenaient la nourriture des enfants affamés. Les Roti'kharahón:tsi cherchaient à tout changer, mais aux yeux du peuple, ce changement semblait les désavantager.

Certains prirent conscience que cette confusion contribuait à ce que plusieurs des leurs adoptent les coutumes des Ratihnarà:ken (les Blancs). Se demandant ce qui devait et pouvait être fait, ils allèrent vers les animaux pour trouver une réponse. Comme l'écureuil, ils cachaient leurs traditions et, comme le renard, ils se déplaçaient rapidement et doucement. C'est ainsi qu'ils transmettaient beaucoup de choses. C'était une réaction dissimulée, mais nécessaire, pour s'assurer que les enseignements ne disparaissent pas. Il fallait mettre en place un moyen pour s'assurer que ceux qui cherchent des conseils puissent se tourner vers leurs propres enseignements. Les Kanehsata'kehró:non allaient traverser cette période difficile grâce à la prévoyance de ceux qui s'assuraient d'assumer leurs responsabilités.

LE RENOUVELLEMENT DE LA CHAÎNE D'ALLIANCE
ET DE LA CEINTURE DE DEUX RANGÉES

Avant et après la défaite des Français sur les plaines d'Abraham, les Britanniques travaillèrent à régler tout différend qui subsistait entre eux et les Onkwehón:we qui résidaient dans les missions françaises au Québec. Les Kanehsata'kehró:non furent les premiers à tendre la main d'amitié par des paroles de condoléances et leur message universel.

Malgré quelque vingt années de guerre, de maladie et de pertes de vies humaines aux mains des Européens, le peuple de Kanehsatà:ke réussissait encore à surmonter sa douleur et sa souffrance afin de trouver la bonne volonté qu'il fallait pour écarter tout obstacle à une paix durable.

En août 1760, comme les forces britanniques avançaient, Sir William Johnson offrit protection aux Onkwehón:we du Canada. Les chefs de Kanehsatà:ke se rendirent à Oswegatchie (Ogdensburg, dans l'État de New York) pour rencontrer Sir William qui leur remit la ceinture Two Dog Wampum.[1] Le 8 septembre 1760, le marquis de Vaudreuil capitulait à Montréal. Quelques jours plus tard, les Rotinonhseshá:ka tinrent à Montréal un important conseil avec les Britanniques,[2] et les Kanehsata'kehró:non y étaient présents. Le 20 septembre 1760, des bateaux britanniques vinrent à Kanehsatà:ke pour récupérer les prisonniers qui étaient toujours détenus dans la communauté.[3] Sans hésitation, les guerriers de Kanehsatà:ke les leur rendirent tous indemnes. Les Britanniques les remercièrent en échangeant avec eux une ceinture de wampum qui ratifiait une entente entre eux. Les deux parties rétablirent ce qui avait été perdu durant la longue période de guerre : la paix, la fraternité et le respect mutuel.

Sir William Johnson semblait désirer que les Onkwehón:we soient justement traités. Au nom des Britanniques, il s'engagea personnellement à protéger les terres, les droits et la liberté du peuple.[4] Cette promesse prit plus de force lorsqu'elle fut inscrite comme l'Article 49 dans l'Acte de capitulation. La bataille des plaines d'Abraham eut lieu le 13 septembre 1759 et Québec capitula cinq jours plus tard. Au début de 1760, quand la guerre entre les Français et les Anglais reprit, des guerriers de Kanehsatà:ke se rendirent au fort Johnson, à New York, pour discuter de paix et remettre quelques prisonniers britanniques. Le 16 février, les Kanehsata'kehró:non échangèrent des ceintures avec les Britanniques.[5]

En août 1760, à Oswagatchie, Sir William remit la ceinture Two Dog Wampum au peuple. En 1787, quand la vie des Kanehsata'kehró:non commença à se dégrader, le chef Aghneetha tint un conseil avec les Britanniques et livra un discours à Sir John Johnson, le fils de Sir William. Dans ce fameux discours, Aghneetha raconte les événements de 1760.

Peu de temps après avoir reçu, à notre village, un autre message de Sir William Johnson, qui était alors à Oswegatchie, ayant le même but que celui que nous nous étions proposé […], nous avons immédiatement convoqué un conseil et décidé d'accepter la protection que vous nous avez offerte. Par conséquent, les chefs de notre village, ainsi que ceux d'autres villages, ont accompagné Sir William Johnson à Oswegatchie, où il a reçu les soumissions de tous les représentants du Canada. Là, dans un grand conseil, il nous a accordé sa protection au nom du roi et nous a consenti nos terres, telles que concédées par le roi de France. Il nous a donné le libre exercice de notre religion, […] en confirmation de laquelle il nous a remis la ceinture que nous déposons maintenant à vos pieds. Si nous avions quelque doute concernant la tenure selon laquelle nous possédons nos terres, nous demanderions qu'un nouveau titre de propriété porté à Sir William nous soit administré […] puis remet une grande ceinture de vingt-sept rangées confectionnée à l'occasion de la première colonie du lac des Deux-Montagnes.[6]

Par cet échange de ceinture wampum, Sir William Johnson reconnaissait et confirmait le droit des Kanehsata'kehró:non à leurs terres. En redonnant la ceinture wampum, il acceptait de protéger ces terres des empiétements des colons blancs. En échange, les Kanehsata'kehró:non acceptèrent de rester neutres dans leur conflit avec les Français.

Un an plus tard, une délégation de Kanehsatà:ke se rendit à Albany pour renouveler et confirmer cette entente. Comme c'était la coutume à la suite d'ententes importantes de cette nature, ils se rencontrèrent pour polir la chaîne d'alliance en argent. La rencontre était un rappel à chaque partie de la nature et du contenu de leur entente et constituait un renouvellement de leur engagement à assumer les responsabilités et les obligations qui s'y rapportaient.

M. Croghan accueillit d'abord les [représentants de Coghnawagas, de Cannassadagas et d'autres nations indiennes] selon les cérémonies habituelles, puis leur transmit ses condoléances pour la perte du Sachem, décédé le printemps précédent à Conassadaga. Ensuite, après avoir procédé à la même cérémonie, les Indiens dirent ce qui suit :

Frère Warraghiyagey,

Quand vous avez parlé à nos nations au Canada, vous avez dissipé toute mésentente entre nous, enterré tout ce qui était mauvais, vous vouliez que nous oubliions ce qui a précédé cette guerre. Frère, nous vous assurons maintenant que nous sommes sincères et que nous avons agi selon votre désir. Nous espérons que vous nous dirigerez toujours à promouvoir l'amitié qui subsiste entre nous.

Une ceinture de 8 rangées

Frère,

Depuis le début de la présente guerre, nous avons perdu un grand nombre de nos frères et amis par l'instigation du mauvais esprit et, avec cette ceinture, nous recueillons les ossements des deux côtés et les enterrons pour que ce qui est arrivé puisse être oublié.

Une ceinture de 11 rangées

Frère,

Par cette ceinture, nous désirons au nom de toutes les nations que vous nous aidiez à fortifier la paix si heureusement établie entre nous à l'automne dernier, grâce à vous. Vous avez le pouvoir de la faire durer.

Une ceinture de 11 rangées

Frère,

Cette ceinture vient de nos guerriers qui ont accepté avec nous de contribuer à fortifier la paix et l'amitié, et nous espérons que vos guerriers feront de même.

Une ceinture de 8 rangées

Frère,

Par cette ceinture, je vous assure que nos guerriers ont pris les résolutions les plus absolues de se comporter de manière qui soit agréable à nos frères et de faire en sorte que cette paix dure.

Une ceinture de 9 rangées

Frère,

Je vous ai parlé des résolutions de nos guerriers de fortifier la paix. Au cas où quelque chose de mauvais demeurerait dans le cœur de l'un d'eux, nous leur donnerons une Dose, ce qui les obligera à se débarrasser de leurs mauvaises pensées et à nettoyer leur cœur.

Une ceinture noire de 5 rangées

Frère,

Depuis un certain temps déjà, des ténèbres couvrent ce territoire, et nous dispersons donc maintenant tout nuage noir qui flotte au-dessus de nos têtes pour que nous et nos enfants à naître puissions voir le soleil briller dès leur naissance.

Une ceinture de 9 rangées[7]

Les Kanehsata'kehró:non déclarèrent et confirmèrent leurs obligations et réitérèrent leur intention de maintenir une paix durable. Ils parlaient de rassembler les ossements, ce qui veut dire qu'ils mettaient derrière eux tous les événements du passé. Ils enterraient toute rancœur. Ils parlaient de dissiper toute mésentente entre eux et les Britanniques. C'était leur engagement à garder les voies de communication ouvertes pour préserver la paix. Même s'il n'était pas présent à la réunion à Albany, Sir William Johnson prépara néanmoins la réponse suivante qu'il envoya par le capitaine Claus, qui se rendait à Montréal.

Frères de Caghnawaga, de Ganaghsadaga et tous nos autres amis au Canada,

L'an dernier, j'ai été empêché de vous rencontrer à Albany parce que je me préparais à aller à Détroit, mais M. Croghan, qui s'est entretenu avec vous, m'a transmis votre discours. Je profite maintenant du retour de mon député au Canada, le capitaine Claus, pour vous répondre, vous ayant avisé, il y a quelque temps, du succès de mes négociations et de la condition amicale dans laquelle j'ai quitté Détroit l'an dernier.

Frères,

J'ai appris par le capitaine Claus que, depuis mon départ du Canada, vous aviez perdu beaucoup de vos frères par la maladie et j'en suis désolé.[8] Par son entremise, je profite maintenant de l'occasion pour vous transmettre mes condoléances et essuyer vos larmes afin que vous puissiez vous tourner vers l'être divin et implorer sa bénédiction pour qu'il accorde une bonne santé aux survivants et vous permette de considérer joyeusement vos frères, les Anglais, et de constater ce qu'ils ont fait et continuent de faire pour vous.

3 cordons très longs [...]

Frères,

Puisque vous formez désormais un seul peuple avec nous, j'accepte joyeusement de fortifier et de polir la chaîne d'alliance de paix et d'amitié. Vous pouvez être assuré que rien sur terre ne peut la briser, aussi longtemps que vous y restez tous strictement attachés. Et comme vous n'avez pas l'avantage des registres comme nous, je vous recommande de souvent répéter à vos jeunes gens ce qu'elle signifie, ainsi que tous nos engagements mutuels afin qu'ils ne soient jamais oubliés.

Une ceinture d'engagement de 8 rangées

Frères,

Je suis heureux de voir que vos guerriers sont très sensibles aux leurs et aux intérêts de votre peuple et qu'ils se joignent à nous pour fortifier et maintenir la paix et l'amitié établie récemment entre nous. Soyez assurés que nos guerriers sont également disposés à faire de même.

Une ceinture de 7 rangées....

Frères,

Je suis désolé d'apprendre que vous ayez rencontré tant de souches çà et là sur la route. Étant donné qu'elle a été récemment réparée, vous devez considérer qu'elle ne peut pas être aussi unie que lorsqu'elle sera un peu plus utilisée. Je vous aiderai à la rendre à niveau, unie et large pour que vous et nous puissions l'emprunter en toute sécurité et satisfaction, le jour comme la nuit, en route vers nos villes.

Une ceinture de 9 rangées ayant un chemin noir au centre[9]

La paix et l'amitié furent rétablies, et les Britanniques exprimèrent la marque de respect que les Kanehsata'kehró:non méritaient en s'adressant à eux comme à des « frères », et non comme à des « enfants ».[10] Cependant, ils affirment que les Kanehsata'kehró:non forment un seul peuple avec eux. Les Kanehsata'kehró:non, ayant conclu une entente avec les Britanniques, puis s'étant rendus à Albany pour renouveler et confirmer cette entente, et ayant reçu l'engagement de Sir William Johnson de « participer joyeusement à fortifier et à améliorer la chaîne d'alliance de paix et d'amitié », crurent qu'ils seraient sains et saufs sur leurs terres. Ils ne pouvaient aucunement savoir que Sir William Johnson et les Britanniques changeraient d'attitude envers leurs alliés, une fois les hostilités avec les Français terminées. Quant à lui, Sir William adopta une attitude résolument arrogante envers ses alliés Rotinonhsehá:ka après la chute de Québec.

APRÈS LA CAPITULATION

Si les chanoines, les prêtres, les missionnaires, les prêtres de la communauté des missions étrangères et de Saint-Sulpice, ainsi que les Jésuites et les Récollets, veulent aller en France, il leur sera accordé passage dans les navires de Sa Majesté Britannique et ils auront toute liberté de vendre, en tout ou en partie, les biens et meubles qu'ils possèdent dans les colonies, soit aux Français ou aux Anglais, sans le moindre empêchement ou obstacle de la part du gouvernement britannique.

Ils peuvent emporter avec eux, ou envoyer en France, le produit de quelque nature des dits biens vendus, en payant le transport, tel que mentionné dans l'Article 26. Et lesdits prêtres qui choisissent de partir cette année seront nourris durant le voyage aux frais de Sa Majesté britannique et prendront leurs bagages avec eux.

Ils pourront disposer de leurs propriétés et en envoyer le produit en France, être maître de leur personne et de tout ce qui leur appartient.[11]

Si la défaite des Français au Canada marquait la promesse d'un avenir meilleur pour les Kanehsata'kehró:non, elle était accueillie avec appréhension par le séminaire de Saint-Sulpice. Selon l'Article 35 de l'Acte de capitulation, le séminaire devait abandonner toutes ses possessions au Canada, puisque ses membres étaient obligés de quitter le pays. L'autorité de l'Église catholique romaine au Québec serait affaiblie – son existence était même menacée. Le séminaire de Saint-Sulpice attendait nerveusement pendant que les gouvernements des deux majestés entamaient une longue série de négociations qui se terminèrent par la conclusion du traité de Paris de 1763.

En 1761, un événement à Kahnawà:ke envenima encore plus les relations entre l'Église catholique romaine au Québec et les Britanniques. Au cours de cette année, une dispute s'éleva entre les Jésuites qui dirigeaient la mission à Sault-Saint-Louis et les Kahnawa'kehró:non, concernant la vente de terrains par cet ordre religieux aux colons. Les Kahnawa'kehró:non présentèrent la question à l'armée britannique, et le général Thomas Gage trancha en leur faveur. Puisque le territoire était soumis à la juridiction de la couronne britannique, les Jésuites devaient partir. L'avocat qui défendait la cause du peuple de Kahnawà:ke était Daniel Claus, militaire britannique responsable des Affaires indiennes pour le Québec et gendre de Sir William Johnson.[12] Pendant qu'il travaillait à corriger la situation à Kahnawà:ke, Claus fit plusieurs visites à Kanehsatake.[13] Son service envers les Kahnawa'kehró:non lui mérita apparemment leur respect et leur amitié. Les Kanehsata'kehró:non étaient également impressionnés par le sens d'équité et de justice de Claus. Dans des lettres écrites à Sir William, Claus souligne avoir été accueilli chaleureusement à Kanehsatà:ke. À l'occasion d'une de ses visites, on l'avait salué en tirant des coups de canon dans le village.[14]

Avec le jugement de Thomas Gage contre les Jésuites, la possibilité que le séminaire de Saint-Sulpice soit forcé d'abandonner ses terres au Québec devint une véritable menace. Les Sulpiciens étaient tellement inquiets par cette décision que la peur les poussa, lors d'un conseil convoqué par le séminaire, à essayer d'inciter les Kanehsata'kehró:non et d'autres Rotinonhseshá:ka qui étaient dans la communauté à se révolter contre les Britanniques. Le séminaire devait être au courant de l'impossibilité de remporter une telle bataille et l'improbabilité que les Kanehsata'kehró:non puissent chasser les Britanniques du Bas-Canada. L'intervention des Sulpiciens dans cette question était probablement motivée par un désir d'éloigner les Kanehsata'kehró:non des Britanniques, réduisant ainsi leur influence et la volonté britannique de s'associer aux Kanehsata'kehró:non contre eux, comme ce fut le cas à Kahnawà:ke avec les Jésuites. Cependant, le peuple de Kanehsatà:ke ne voulut aucunement prendre part au complot, et les Britanniques condamnèrent sans équivoque le séminaire. Un militaire britannique décrivit la situation en détail :

[…] On m'a parlé d'une ceinture envoyée de Montréal à tous les Indiens du nord les invitant à s'assembler à Canasadaga au début du printemps pour entamer des hostilités […] que le prêtre [Picquet] des Indiens d'Oswegatchie, en présence du grand vicaire [le supérieur du séminaire] et le reste du clergé à Montréal, a remis trois ceintures à deux des chefs de cette nation, après que le grand vicaire leur en eut donné la signification, que ces ceintures étaient envoyées aux Cinq Nations et, de là, à tous les Indiens du nord […][15]

L'incident était «entièrement dû à l'influence que les prêtres et les Jésuites exerçaient sur eux […] Je pense qu'il est de mon devoir, écrit l'officier britannique, de vous envoyer ces renseignements, parce que suis absolument persuadé, d'après ces circonstances et d'autres, que les prêtres et les Jésuites soudoient les Indiens, ce qui peut engendrer de graves conséquences à un moment ou à un autre».[16] Une confrontation potentiellement désastreuse entre les Britanniques et les Français fut empêchée, mais Thomas Gage avait apparemment impliqué les Kanehsata'kehró:non dans l'incident, accordant ainsi une certaine mesure de réussite au complot du séminaire. Lors d'un conseil, le peuple de Kanehsatà:ke fit connaître à Daniel Claus son désir de vivre en paix :

Les chefs de Canasadaga, au sujet des questions déjà mentionnées, ainsi que d'autres qui leur ont été présentées, s'inquiétant que le général Gage les soupçonne de mauvais desseins, ont supplié le capitaine Claus d'assurer son Excellence, d'une manière des plus solennelles, de leur sincérité et de leur amitié pour les Anglais. Ils espéraient donc que se dissiperait toute méfiance à l'effet qu'ils seraient trop sensibles aux bénédictions de paix et à un gouvernement tranquille après avoir éprouvé les misères d'une guerre difficile encore récente dans leur mémoire, et qu'ils promeuvent ou s'engagent dans d'autres hostilités qui engendreraient probablement leur destruction.[17]

Ayant conclu un traité avec les Britanniques et accepté de maintenir la paix, les Kanehsata'kehró:non étaient déterminés à honorer leur promesse dans l'espoir que les Britanniques honoreraient la leur. En 1761, à cette époque terrible, après avoir perdu tant des leurs à cause de la guerre et de la maladie, les Kanehsata'kehró:non savaient qu'ils étaient loin d'être forts ni en position de s'éloigner des Britanniques. Au début de la guerre, les Britanniques les avaient menacés de prendre leurs terres et de détruire leur village s'ils ne combattaient pas à leurs côtés. Ne voulant pas se battre contre les Français avec qui ils étaient devenus amis, les Kanehsata'kehró:non promirent plutôt de rester neutres.

Le peuple de Kanehsatà:ke était déterminé à survivre, et le séminaire de Saint-Sulpice l'était tout autant. Le séminaire était « le type du catholicisme, de ce qui est français et de l'ancien régime [...] ». L'autorité britannique était cependant « loin d'être désastreuse : ni une pénurie ni une véritable restriction de pouvoir ne suivirent le drapeau britannique ». La couronne d'Angleterre avait l'intention d'utiliser les églises établies pour assimiler graduellement les Canadiens français. « Les prêtres prépareraient le chemin à l'Église d'Angleterre en maintenant l'ordre et la vertu pendant que la papauté était ébranlée. »[18] « Durant les 85 années qui suivirent 1760, le séminaire continua d'exercer son pouvoir seigneurial; il collectait de plus en plus de revenus et conservait son rôle social. »[19] En 1763, après le traité de Paris, parut la Proclamation royale. « Selon les conditions de paix [...] les sujets français avaient dix-huit mois pour liquider leurs possessions canadiennes et retourner en France. Aucun Sulpicien n'accepta l'offre et chaque membre de la compagnie [le séminaire] jura allégeance à l'Angleterre. »[20]

Qui étaient ces Sulpiciens? « Fondé pour former une prêtrise réformée, le séminaire de Saint-Sulpice était une communauté religieuse d'élite qui soulignait son indépendance de la juridiction du diocèse et du soutien financier des paroissiens. »[21] Contrairement à d'autres ordres religieux, les « Sulpiciens ne faisaient pas de vœux de pauvreté ». Ils restaient propriétaires de leurs biens personnels et en disposaient librement au moyen de testaments. Les Sulpiciens n'étaient pas non plus liés à la communauté puisqu'ils n'avaient pas fait de vœux de perpétuité. Jusque dans les années 1790, tous les membres du séminaire à Montréal étaient Français et « fils de juges, d'officiers, de médecins et de petits propriétaires [...] »[22]

En prêtant serment d'allégeance à la couronne britannique, le séminaire lui prouvait sa loyauté. Cependant, se sentant toujours vulnérables, les Sulpiciens préparèrent un plan qui, ils l'espéraient, réglerait le problème. En avril de cette année-là, le séminaire de Saint-Sulpice à Paris, et à qui le roi de France avait concédé des terres en Nouvelle-France, transféra toutes ses propriétés au séminaire de Saint-Sulpice à Montréal. Les Britanniques approuvèrent silencieusement « par crainte que la communauté religieuse canadienne soit dirigée par la France [...] ».[23] Le séminaire de Saint-Sulpice avait donc la permission de garder ses propriétés, mais à la condition « qu'il reste complètement indépendant [de Paris] et n'admette aucun nouveau membre français ».[24] Les Sulpiciens avaient alors trouvé une solution à la menace de perdre leurs propriétés. Ce transfert allait plus tard être examiné par les meilleurs législateurs de la province, mais à ce moment-là, il s'effectua sans qu'aucune question ne soit soulevée concernant sa légalité.[25] Cependant, en 1773, alors qu'on rédigeait l'Acte de Québec, Sir James Mariott, avocat et adjoint du procureur général pour le Québec, remettait en question la légalité du transfert. En 1804, dans un avis juridique, Jonathan Sewell, ministre de la Justice, mit en doute le transfert et l'existence permanente du séminaire de Saint-Sulpice à Montréal. En 1828, James Stuart, avocat général, déclara dans un avis juridique que le transfert de 1764 était illégal et que la couronne d'Angleterre avait tous les droits de prendre possession des propriétés du séminaire. Il semble que l'idée répugnait aux Britanniques puisque ces recommandations ne furent jamais suivies.

Les mésententes entre Français et Britanniques au sujet des terres et de la guerre n'empêchèrent pas le peuple de Kanehsatà:ke de répondre à des demandes d'aide aux gens dans le besoin quand un feu dévastateur à Montréal détruisit plus de cent maisons, laissant la ville remplie de sans-abri. Le «zèle et la charité des Indiens […] ne diminuèrent pas, nous dit-on. Quand la conflagration de 1765 dévasta Montréal et laissa des centaines de démunis, les Indiens de Caughnawaga et de Cannassadage vinrent à leur secours en vendant leurs ornements d'argent, leurs wampums, des paniers, des couteaux garnis de riches crosses et autres articles, afin de collecter des fonds pour aider les pauvres».[26] En septembre de la même année, le peuple de Kanehsatà:ke fut lui-même dans une situation désespérée: la varicelle avait de nouveau frappé la communauté.[27]

En 1767, un autre genre de calamité s'abattit sur Kanehsatà:ke: le commerce du brandy. Puisque le séminaire de Saint-Sulpice ne voulait pas arrêter ce trafic, les Kanehsata'kehró:non allèrent vers les Britanniques pour obtenir de l'aide. «C'est suite aux prières répétées et aux requêtes urgentes de ces Indiens, écrivait le gouverneur Guy Carleton à Daniel Claus, que ce groupe [de soldats] a été envoyé […] [pour arrêter] les revendeurs de spiritueux […].»[28] Dans une seconde lettre, Guy Carleton décrivit la situation à Kanehsatà:ke de façon plus détaillé:

Les Indiens du Lac des Deux-Montagnes m'ont fait de nombreuses représentations selon lesquelles plusieurs personnes sont coupables de vendre de l'alcool à leurs jeunes hommes. Les conséquences pernicieuses de cette vente sont que pas moins de cinq meurtres, dus aux effets lamentables et infaillibles de ces boissons enivrantes sur ces créatures malheureuses, ont dernièrement été commis parmi eux. Malgré qu'on ait vivement conseillé à la magistrature civile de ce district d'exercer son autorité en la matière, son interposition s'est d'une manière ou d'une autre montrée inefficace jusqu'à présent. J'ai donc décidé d'envoyer un officier, que j'ai investi de la Commission de la paix, vivre dans leur village dans l'espoir que cette mesure produise l'effet désiré.[29]

Daniel Claus fut si préoccupé par la situation qu'il se rendit à «Caneghssadagay» pour voir ce qui pouvait être fait. De petits commerçants infestaient la communauté et, selon Claus, le commerce du brandy était potentiellement désastreux parce qu'«aucun poste dans cette province n'est plus nécessaire que celui-là […]; il est le seul passage vers le nord et le nord-ouest […]». Le commerce diminua, mais seulement pour une brève période. En 1772, Claus fut de nouveau forcé d'écrire à ce sujet:

Les [Indiens du Lac ou de Candghsadagey] se sont appliqués pendant plusieurs années à empêcher les commerçants de venir parmi eux sur leur territoire de chasse du Long-Sault ou chute des Outaouais ou Grande rivière, le lac Népissingue qu'ils ont toujours occupé et réclamé, où aucun commerçant ne s'était jamais rendu à l'époque des Français. Comme ils voyaient leur ruine approcher et qu'il n'y avait aucune perspective de redressement, les trois nations acceptèrent lors d'un conseil d'envoyer trois canots armés de 25 hommes et de ramener deux ou trois de ces commerçants avec leur marchandise […] La raison pour laquelle les Indiens n'apprécient pas que ces commerçants soient sur leur territoire de chasse est que ceux-ci apportent de l'alcool avec eux, ce qui empêche les Indiens de poursuivre leur chasse. En effet, sachant que toutes les fois où ils ont une peau de castor, etc. ils peuvent obtenir de l'alcool si près que les (jeunes) gens vont boire. Par conséquent, leurs familles sont dépourvues des nécessités pendant toute l'année […].[30]

En septembre 1769, alors que les Kanehsata'kehró:non pleuraient la perte d'un chef algonquin, Daniel Claus alla leur rendre visite à leur demande. Il écrivit un récit de son séjour :

> Je suis allé à Caneghsadagey. Les trois nations m'attendaient impatiemment et, à mon arrivée, ils m'ont manifesté plus de respect que jamais auparavant en me saluant par la décharge de trois canons et de trois rafales de petites armes. Leurs jeunes hommes très bien vêtus se sont approchés de moi, alignés en deux rangées, pour m'accueillir […] un messager est entré, envoyé par le chef Arundax [Algonquin] […] qui, m'a-t-on dit, était sur son lit de mort depuis une quinzaine de jours […] Je l'ai trouvé gravement atteint de tuberculose, dans un état squelettique […] Je l'ai ensuite quitté et il a expiré quelques heures plus tard. On l'a enterré décemment, et un chef de Caghnawagy qui était avec moi a procédé à la cérémonie des condoléances.[31]

Claus remarqua également que «plusieurs pauvres étaient morts de faim» à cause de la famine de l'automne précédent. La récolte de 1769 fut cependant excellente et Claus rapporta que le peuple de Kanehsatà:ke «jouissait maintenant d'une période d'abondance après une récolte riche de toutes sortes de céréales».[32]

Au printemps 1770, le peuple pleura la perte d'un autre chef, «le vieux Jacques», décédé à l'âge de 100 ans. Le 12 septembre, Claus revint dans la communauté et participa à une cérémonie de condoléances pour le chef et les autres disparus.[33] Cette même année, onze Kanehsata'kehró:non se rendirent à une importante conférence de paix à German Flatts. Ils faisaient partie des quelque 2300 personnes des Six Nations qui y prirent part.[34] En 1771, d'autres cérémonies de condoléances pour deux autres chefs eurent lieu.[35]

«NOUS VOUS AVONS OUVERT NOTRE CŒUR»

En 1781, à cause de problèmes qui surgirent à Kanehsatà:ke entre le peuple et les prêtres, les chefs se rendirent à Montréal pour rencontrer le colonel Campbell.

Nous vous informons de ce qui se passe dans notre village. Nous avons toujours cru que nous étions sur nos propres terres, d'après les déclarations de nos ancêtres, mais aujourd'hui, on nous affirme le contraire […]

Nous vous avons dit que notre père [M. Legarde, prêtre de Saint-Sulpice] s'est mis en colère. Après avoir usé de dures paroles à notre endroit, les jeunes gens présents ont été irrités et lui ont répondu : «Dans ce cas, père, nous avons dû tuer et être tués durant la guerre pour protéger notre propriété, et maintenant c'est à vous! À l'avenir, vous irez faire la guerre et nous resterons au village.» Il nous a répondu qu'il ne nous avait jamais forcés (à faire la guerre) et que c'était notre désir de nous y engager. Agacés, les jeunes gens sont sortis sans dire un mot, suivis par la majorité des chefs. Seuls le défunt chef Entaritta et quelques autres sont restés au conseil. Ce chef a poursuivi la conversation en disant : «Père, je suis étonné qu'un homme de votre caractère se fâche si facilement contre nous. Je n'ai jamais entendu de telles paroles sortir de la bouche d'un prêtre. Vous nous dites que nous n'avons aucun droit à ces terres. Aucun de vos prédécesseurs ne nous a jamais parlé de cela. En voici une preuve. Quand le général Carleton est venu à Chaudières, il a traversé ce village, et notre défunt M. Terlay m'a choisi pour l'accompagner et m'a avisé que, si le général Carleton me posait une question pour savoir à qui appartenaient ces terres cultivées sur la rive nord, je devrais lui répondre qu'elles appartenaient aux Indiens du lac. C'est ce qui est arrivé, et le général a semblé satisfait de la réponse.»

[…] Nous avons essayé de vivre unis, mais nous n'y sommes pas arrivés. Notre seul recours est auprès de vous, père, puisque nous sommes vos enfants fidèles et que notre travail ne peut produire que de bons résultats. Examinez notre situation lamentable. Vous entendez nos gémissements, non seulement les nôtres, mais aussi ceux de nos femmes et de nos enfants. Même nos troupeaux ressentent notre malheur, puisque nous n'avons que les roches comme ressources, et si nous ou notre bétail voulons dépasser les limites, on nous oblige à reculer […].[36]

En 1781, au moment où les chefs de Kanehsatà:ke adressèrent ce discours au colonel Campbell, quelques nouveaux développements surprenants avaient lieu. En 1780, le séminaire «jugea prudent de faire arpenter la seigneurie du Lac», écrivait Olivier Maurault.[37] En 1781, les Sulpiciens purent régler une dispute de longue date au sujet des limites avec la seigneurie voisine d'Argenteuil quand ils arrivèrent à un arrangement avec le nouveau seigneur, Pierre-Louis Panet.[38] La même année, «les revendications particulières du séminaire à ses seigneuries semblaient progresser […] quand on permit aux Sulpiciens de jurer fidélité et hommage à la couronne britannique».[39] Jusque là, ils avaient été réticents à revendiquer le territoire, sachant que leur position était délicate et sujette à la bonne volonté de la Couronne. Maintenant qu'ils lui avaient juré fidélité et rendu hommage, les Sulpiciens interprétaient l'acceptation de ce serment comme une reconnaissance de leurs droits et titres de propriété par la Couronne. Dès 1789, cette interprétation de l'effet du serment suscita des doutes quand des représentants de la Couronne présentèrent un tout autre avis juridique au gouverneur du Canada, affirmant que le séminaire n'avait aucun titre de propriété valide du territoire et que ce titre appartenait à la Couronne.[40]

Aussitôt que le territoire fut arpenté et subdivisé, la colonisation à très grande échelle de la seigneurie du Lac des Deux-Montagnes débuta. En 1780, le séminaire accorda 66 concessions à des colons. En 1781, il en accorda 21 autres et 54 de plus en 1783.[41] La colonie de la seigneurie s'étendait alors jusqu'à la côte Saint-Joachim. En 1787, elle atteignait la Belle Rivière. En 1796, un record de 102 concessions fut atteint en une seule année. En 1801, vingt ans après le relevé topographique, en tout 732 lots avaient été concédés aux colons. En 1835, le nombre total des concessions atteignait 1307. Dans les années 1830, tout le territoire qui comprenait l'arrière et les parties sud de la seigneurie était occupé par des colons,[42] et des commerçants étaient déjà bien établis le long de la rivière des Outaouais. À Kanehsatà:ke même, des colons commençaient à aménager et à travailler la terre. Les chefs terminèrent leur discours en remettant la ceinture Two Dog Wampum au colonel Campbell en lui demandant de désigner les terres des Kanehsata'kehró:non du bout de son doigt. Il semble que le colonel Campbell n'acquiesça pas à la requête des chefs. Pour sa part, le séminaire de Saint-Sulpice proposa une autre solution. «Toujours et en vue de satisfaire les Indiens, écrivait Olivier Maurault, nous leur avons offert un grand territoire adjacent à la seigneurie des Iroquois à Saint-Régis.» Maurault nota que l'offre fut «refusée avec mépris».[43]

Conseil avec le colonel Campbell

En 1787, le peuple de Kanehsatà:ke fit une nouvelle demande d'aide aux Britanniques. Dans un discours adressé à Sir John Johnson, le fils de Sir William Johnson, le chef Aghneetha lui rappela la promesse de son père d'accorder sa protection aux Onkwehón:we, de reconnaître et de confirmer leurs droits au territoire qu'ils occupaient. Aghneetha termina avec la supplication suivante :

Nous vous avons ouvert notre cœur et fait connaître nos craintes, et nous croyons que vous êtes sensible au fait que nous portons un lourd fardeau pour lequel nous vous prions de faire tout votre possible afin de nous soulager et de témoigner votre intérêt auprès du gouverneur, Lord Dorchester [Sir Guy Carleton], pour qu'un nouvel acte de propriété pour les terres sur lesquelles nous vivons nous soit accordé et pour que nous puissions les posséder au même titre que les Mohawks à Grand River et à la baie de Quinte détiennent les leurs.[44]

Aghneehta remit la ceinture Two Dog Wampum et demanda que sa requête soit envoyée au gouverneur, Sir Guy Carleton. À son tour, ce dernier la présenta devant un comité du conseil britannique qui refusa la requête d'un nouveau titre de propriété. Dans leur rapport, les membres déclarèrent que «[…] le comité n'a reçu aucune preuve satisfaisante qu'un titre de propriété a été accordé aux Indiens du village en question, soit par la couronne de France, soit par une quelconque concession de cette Couronne». On n'accorda aucune considération aux droits territoriaux des Kanehsata'kehró:non, droits acquis en vertu de l'avoir occupé et utilisé depuis des temps immémoriaux. Une telle considération aurait d'abord mis en doute la souveraineté de la couronne de France sur ce territoire, puis celle de l'Angleterre. Les membres du comité poursuivirent en disant que la question de titre de propriété était une décision qui relevait des tribunaux.[45] Une telle poursuite ne fut jamais entreprise.

Sir Guy Carleton, l'homme qui quelques années auparavant avait accepté la parole du peuple comme «une preuve satisfaisante» lorsqu'il avait fait une demande spécifique pour connaître le propriétaire du territoire de Kanehsatà:ke, appuyait maintenant la décision d'un comité du conseil britannique qui statua contre les Kanehsata'kehró:non au sujet de la même question.

La relation politique qui existait originalement entre les Britanniques et les Kanehsata'kehró:non était alors remplacée par une association juridique. La manière dont la loi était interprétée reflétait les limites du système judiciaire et imposait donc des limites à la recherche d'une solution juste.

En 1787, la décision prise par le comité du conseil britannique de renvoyer aux tribunaux la question de régime foncier à Kanehsatà:ke permit aux Britanniques d'éviter de traiter la question de façon juste et équitable.

Quand le conseil britannique refusa le nouveau titre tel que demandé par le chef Aghneetha, les Kanehsata'kehró:non surent à ce moment-là que les Britanniques abandonnaient les conventions que la ceinture Two Row Wampum et la Chaîne d'alliance représentaient. Les Britanniques n'honoreraient même pas les lois qu'ils avaient eux-mêmes créées ni leur engagement à protéger les Onkwehón:we sur leurs terres. Les concepts de justice et d'équité représentés dans les ceintures wampum n'avaient rien à voir avec les nouvelles lois que les Britanniques instauraient et appliquaient.

En exigeant un titre de propriété pour le territoire de Kanehsatà:ke, le chef Aghneetha et le peuple de Kanehsatà:ke demandaient aux Britanniques d'honorer leur promesse de protéger le territoire contre la colonisation par les Blancs. Détenir un titre de propriété était un moyen prévu par la loi britannique d'assurer des droits territoriaux exclusifs au peuple de Kanehsatà:ke et d'empêcher l'empiétement des colons blancs. En refusant d'accorder un nouveau titre de propriété, les Britanniques refusaient de reconnaître l'engagement qu'ils avaient pris en 1760 selon lequel ils devaient protéger le territoire à Kanehsatà:ke. «Vous n'avez pas l'avantage des registres comme nous», avait dit Sir William Johnson au peuple en 1762. Il n'avait que partiellement raison : les Kanehsata'kehró:non n'avaient pas de registres écrits, mais ils avaient d'autres sortes de registres : des traditions orales et les ceintures wampum. En 1787, les Britanniques écartaient les registres des Onkwehón:we, car ils se fiaient plutôt à leurs propres registres : des documents écrits en français et en anglais. Même s'ils avaient l'avantage des registres des traités et des ententes qu'ils avaient conclus, les Britanniques choisissaient très souvent de ne pas en tenir compte. L'esprit et le but des traités étaient abandonnés en faveur d'interprétations littérales.

CHANT DE LA FORÊT

Pendant longtemps, les Kanehsata'kehró:non essayèrent de rester neutres et de garder la paix. Ils essayèrent de se conduire honorablement et s'efforcèrent de toujours garder l'ordre dans leur maison.

Tandis qu'ils respectaient du mieux possible les enseignements de l'Artisan de la paix, un jour, l'aigle leur lança des avertissements. Sachant que le Créateur leur avait donné l'aigle pour faire le guet, ils cherchèrent à calmer leurs craintes en rappelant aux O'serón:ni leur engagement de laisser le territoire tranquille aux Onkwehón:we à en être les gardiens.

Les O'serón:ni sont comme le temps qu'il fait au début du printemps; celui-ci peut changer à tout moment, de sorte que le matin, le soleil brille, et le soir, la neige tombe si fort que toute trace de pas disparaît rapidement.

C'est ainsi que les O'serón:ni nièrent l'existence de toute entente entre les deux parties.

J'ai vu le peuple envoyer leurs meilleurs orateurs et leurs dirigeants les plus honorables pour essayer d'aplanir le sentier entre les nouveaux arrivants et les Onkwehón:we. Je les ai aussi vus revenir, et il semblait qu'ils portaient un lourd fardeau sur leurs épaules.

«Nous allons attendre, les ai-je entendus chuchoter. Sûrement que les choses s'amélioreront quand les nouveaux arrivants réfléchiront à nos paroles.»

Tout ce que je sais est que le peuple s'enracinait toujours davantage et portait le chant de la forêt dans son cœur.

DEVONS-NOUS ÊTRE PAUVRES TOUTE NOTRE VIE?

Quand la situation empira à Kanehsatà:ke, le peuple demanda encore une fois l'aide des Britanniques. Cette fois-ci, il envoya un message à Lord Dorchester en passant par Joseph Chew. Il donna aux Britanniques une autre chance de respecter leur engagement.

Cela fait maintenant quinze ans que les chefs entendent dire que le territoire ne leur appartient pas.

À la dernière guerre, on nous a dit: «Mes enfants, combattez pour votre territoire et quand la guerre sera terminée vous le posséderez», mais nous n'avons toujours aucune assurance de cela. On nous dit que le roi aime le village du lac des Deux-Montagnes. Mais qu'est-ce que cela veut dire? N'avons-nous aucune terre qui nous appartienne, et devons-nous être pauvres toute notre vie? […]

Nous disons maintenant que ce Château est composé de trois nations unies: les Iroquois, les Algonquins et les Népissingues – à la demande de la paroisse, les Népissingues vivaient sur Pidgeon Island[46] parce qu'ils étaient méchants. Quand ils se comporteront mieux, ils pourront redéménager et s'installer entre les Iroquois et les Algonquins.

Nous, les chefs des trois nations du lac des Deux-Montagnes, désirons que vous transmettiez à notre père Lord Dorchester, gouverneur général à Québec, la situation réelle concernant nos terres et qu'il nous réponde aussitôt que possible.[47]

La réponse tarda à venir et n'était pas celle que les Kanehsata'kehró:non espéraient.

Mes enfants,

Lors d'un conseil tenu le 7 novembre dernier, vous m'avez demandé beaucoup de choses que j'ai transmises fidèlement au gouverneur, votre père.

C'est le désir du gouverneur de vous faire justice en tout temps, et c'est également la volonté de notre père.

Le gouverneur était heureux de me convoquer pour me consulter en ce qui concerne vos revendications et les moyens de satisfaire vos demandes. Écoutez ses paroles.

Vous, mes enfants établis au Lac des Deux-Montagnes, avez affirmé que les prêtres de Saint-Sulpice réclament la seigneurie de ce lac. Ils la réclament parce que le roi de France, en l'an [...] [1717] la leur a accordée. Cela s'est passé il y a plusieurs années, avant que les sujets du roi, votre père, arrivent au Canada. Voici une copie du titre de propriété par lequel la seigneurie a été donnée et que le gouverneur vous envoie pour vous satisfaire. Il est désolé que vous ayez été trompé, mais vous devez vous rappeler que cela a été décidé par les Français, et non par les Anglais [...]

Mes enfants,

Retournez dans vos villages. Soyez heureux, satisfaits, loyaux et attachés au roi votre père, comme vous l'avez toujours été, et soyez assurés que c'est son désir, le désir de votre père le gouverneur, mon désir également comme votre père et celui de tous les sujets du roi dans cette province de vous faire tout le bien en notre pouvoir.[48]

Par ces quelques paroles, les Britanniques se libéraient de l'obligation qu'ils savaient avoir envers le peuple de Kanehsatà:ke. Ils n'assumaient pas du tout les responsabilités que leur conféraient les ententes qu'ils avaient conclues avec les Kanehsata'kehró:non. Ils minimisaient le problème, affirmant que ce n'était pas leur faute, et suggéraient que les Kanehsata'kehró:non retournent chez eux et attendent qu'on leur fasse la charité.

La réticence des Britanniques à prendre la défense des Kanehsata'kehró:non ou à honorer leurs ententes donnait pleine liberté au séminaire de coloniser le territoire à très grande échelle. Les territoires de chasse étaient grugés par les colons et la menace de conflit augmentait chaque jour. Les conditions de vie des Kanehsata'kehró:non se détérioraient rapidement sous le regard indifférent des Britanniques.

Leur situation devient toutefois alarmante à cause de la colonisation rapide des terres situées sur les rives de la rivière des Outaouais, où ils avaient été placés par le gouvernement en 1763, qu'ils considéraient naturellement comme leurs [...] Ce n'est pas à moi de décider de la politique visant à satisfaire ces désirs, mais le résultat de l'état présent est évident. Il est si grave qu'il peut presque, avec le temps, être accompagné par le sang et le meurtre, car privés de leurs ressources, ils pénétreront illégalement sur les territoires des autres tribus, qui sont autant jalouses de l'intrusion de leurs frères rouges que de celle des Blancs. Les plaintes de cette nature augmentent quotidiennement [...][49]

Feux ravageurs
de Katsi'tsakwas

En considérant les événements, les Britanniques remarquèrent que les conditions empiraient. Cependant, aucune action ne fut prise pour améliorer la situation.

Les Indiens du Lac des Deux-Montagnes ne sont pas du tout sur le même pied d'égalité que ceux des villages de Saint-Régis, de Sault-Saint-Louis et de Saint-Francis – qui possèdent chacun une seigneurie qui leur accorde un certain revenu annuel. Les pauvres Indiens du lac n'ont aucune terre qu'ils peuvent considérer comme leur. Ils sont totalement dépendants des missionnaires qui leur permettent de cultiver, çà et là, à quelque distance du village, de petits lots et terrains qui sont vraiment insuffisants pour subvenir à leurs besoins si les récoltes ne sont pas assez abondantes […] Anciennement, ils tuaient suffisamment d'animaux pour se vêtir très confortablement, et les cerfs étaient assez nombreux pour assurer leur subsistance. Mais maintenant ils sont privés de leurs meilleurs territoires de chasse (ils ont été accordés aux émigrants qui y vivent). Ces pauvres Indiens sont maintenant réduits à la misère et à la pauvreté. Le colon qui défriche le territoire sur les lots avant le fait par le feu – qui se propage souvent à une grande distance dans les colonies arrière – ou par la coupe de bois – qui détruit toutes les espèces d'animaux à fourrure et fait fuir les cerfs –, et les pauvres Indiens n'ont que la famine devant eux.[50]

Dans ces passages, le général de division Darling et James Hughes décrivent l'effet très grave de la colonisation à grande échelle sur les Kanehsata'kehró:non. James Hughes semble particulièrement étonné par le brasier déchaîné auquel le peuple semble quotidiennement confronté. Il savait que les Britanniques avaient laissé la situation du peuple devenir terrible, mais il ne pouvait pas parler contre son propre gouvernement. Il rendrait seulement aussi explicite que possible son récit sur «la misère et la pauvreté» qui se déployaient devant lui. Parce qu'ils avaient choisi de laisser le séminaire violer les droits des Kanehsata'kehró:non, les Britanniques devaient fournir au peuple de plus en plus de nourriture, de vêtements et d'autres fournitures. Ce faisant, ils augmentaient la dépendance dans laquelle ils l'avaient placé.

Les terres que le roi de France avait réservées comme territoire de chasse et de pêche pour les Kanehsata'kehró:non leur furent enlevées. Comme le roi l'avait remarqué en 1735, ces gens en avaient besoin parce qu'«ils étaient habitués à changer souvent de domicile [...]».[51]

Au cours des années 1790, le nombre de terres concédées aux colons augmenta régulièrement. En trois ans, de 1793 à 1795, on accorda 121 concessions. En 1794, le séminaire régla une autre dispute sur les limites territoriales avec la seigneurie voisine des Mille-Îles.[52] La colonisation poursuivait son expansion.

NE LUI FAIS RIEN MALGRÉ CE QU'IL T'A FAIT

Rononhkwíhseres (cheveux longs) était un bon guérisseur. On ignore s'il venait de Kanehsatà:ke, de Oswego ou de Kahnawà:ke, mais il vivait ici. Nous étions un même peuple, les Kanien'kehà:ka, ou le peuple du silex.

Il habitait ici, et le peuple dépendait de sa connaissance de la médecine.

À cette époque, les Indiens étaient des chasseurs saisonniers. À l'automne, durant l'été indien, ils partaient et s'enfonçaient dans la forêt vers le nord où la chasse était bonne. Ils y restaient tout l'hiver. Ils s'installaient partout dans les bois. Certains y construisaient leur maison de billots, d'autres vivaient sous des tentes de peaux, et d'autres encore se faisaient des abris de branches de pin. Chaque année, ils y retournaient.

Il y eut un homme qui partit d'ici pour aller chasser. On dit qu'il vivait quelque part près de la route d'Ahsenenhson (du Milieu) et qu'il s'appelait Sha'tewa'skó:wa (même grande taille). Il partit d'ici et emmena sa famille chasser avec lui.

Son voisin resta ici et n'alla pas chasser. Il était probablement fermier. On disait que ce voisin pratiquait la sorcellerie. Cet homme utilisa donc ses pouvoirs pour empêcher Sha'tewa'skó:wa de tuer du gibier durant l'hiver pendant qu'il partait à la chasse.

Sa famille commença alors à avoir faim. Sha'tewa'skó:wa ne voyait aucun cerf ni aucun lapin à tuer pour se nourrir. Rononhkwíhseres, le bon guérisseur, savait que quelque chose allait très mal pour cette famille indienne qui se trouvait au cœur de la forêt. Il savait qu'elle avait faim. Rononhkwíhseres vivait ici, à Kanehsatà:ke, avec sa femme et ses petits-enfants. Ces derniers le regardaient faire cuire de la viande de cerf ou de bœuf, peu importe, il cuisinait.

Les enfants se demandaient pourquoi il faisait cuire tant de viande. Alors, l'un d'eux lui demanda : « Grand-père, pourquoi fais-tu cuire beaucoup de viande? » Rononhkwíhseres lui répondit : « Nos frères qui sont au cœur de la forêt sont affamés, ils sont presque morts de faim. J'irai leur porter à manger. » Quand la nourriture fut prête, il la mit dans deux seaux, semblables à des seaux d'eau. La nuit commençait à tomber quand il termina la cuisson et tous les préparatifs. Il dit : « Je dois maintenant partir et aller aider notre frère et ses enfants qui sont affamés. »

Il avait une grange située au bord de la forêt. Il en fit le tour et chaussa ses raquettes. Il tenait aussi les deux seaux de nourriture, un de chaque côté.

Les enfants allèrent voir où leur grand-père était parti. Tout ce qu'ils virent fut les dernières empreintes de raquettes, car Rononhkwíhseres s'était envolé, il en avait le pouvoir.

Puis, quand Rononhkwíhseres arriva, nos frères avaient vraiment faim. Ils étaient étendus sur le sol. C'était la coutume il y a longtemps.

Les enfants, le père et la mère étaient mourants tellement ils étaient affamés. Alors, Rononhkwíhseres commença à les nourrir en ne leur donnant que le bouillon de la viande. On ne peut pas donner de la nourriture solide à une personne affamée, car cela la tuerait. Il leur donna ce bouillon. Tard dans la soirée, ils revinrent à eux et commencèrent à mieux se sentir parce que leur corps avait été nourri. Le jour suivant, ils purent manger et furent tous rétablis. Personne ne mourut. Le surlendemain, ils mangèrent davantage.

Rononhkwíhseres demanda au chef de la famille : « Que s'est-il passé? Pourquoi mourrez-vous de faim? » Il répondit : « Je n'ai vu aucun animal à chasser, aucun cerf ni aucun lapin que nous pouvions manger. C'est ce qui est arrivé et nous sommes à plusieurs jours de route de notre maison. Il y a tant de neige et il fait si froid. » Cet homme pensait qu'il allait bientôt voir un animal qu'il pouvait tuer.

Rononhkwíhseres répondit : « Quelqu'un essaie de vous faire du mal en vous empêchant de voir du gibier. » Les méchants sorciers avaient l'habitude d'utiliser leur pouvoir pour empêcher un homme d'attraper du gibier.

Il ajouta : « J'arrangerai ton fusil. » Il utilisa son pouvoir de guérison sur le fusil, puis dit : « Tu verras de nouveau des animaux que tu pourras tuer pour te nourrir. Nous découvrirons également qui t'a fait cela. » Il utilisa son pouvoir et l'image du sorcier apparut.

Rononhkwíhseres demanda s'il connaissait l'homme. Notre frère regarda et dit : « Je connais cet homme, il vit à côté de chez nous. » Le nom de l'homme était Mikah. C'était lui qui empêchait le gibier de venir vers notre frère.

Rononhkwíhseres dit alors : « Si c'est ton désir, nous lui percerons les yeux pour qu'il ne puisse plus chasser et lui aussi souffrira de la faim. »

Cet homme qui était au cœur de la forêt dit : « Non, ce n'est pas la bonne chose à faire, peu importe […] Tu as arrangé mon fusil et permis que je voie le gibier. Je pourrai de nouveau chasser et ma famille n'aura plus faim. »

Rononhkwíhseres lui dit que personne ne pourra plus jamais éloigner le gibier de lui. Notre frère répondit : « C'est tout ce qui m'intéresse, même s'il m'a fait du tort. »

Rononhkwíhseres essayait seulement de voir si cet homme était bon ou non. Il lui dit : «C'est bien que tu aies une telle attitude. Ne lui fais rien, malgré ce qu'il t'a fait.»

Puis, notre frère continua de chasser et Rononhkwíhseres retourna chez lui. Il raconta à ses petits-enfants comment nos frères mouraient de faim dans la forêt et comment il les avait aidés.

LA MISSION

 En 1789, la situation faisait en sorte que le séminaire n'allait pas abandonner le territoire de Kanehsatà:ke. En réponse au discours du chef Aghneetha, les Sulpiciens justifièrent leur droit au territoire en affirmant qu'ils en étaient les véritables propriétaires, puisqu'ils y vivaient depuis soixante-dix ans et qu'ils avaient juré fidélité et hommage à la couronne britannique. Ils ne s'intéressaient pas aux droits des Kanehsata'kehró:non ni au bien-être de la mission. En réalité, les Sulpiciens de Montréal étaient très préoccupés par les événements qui se déroulaient dans leur mère patrie. La France était au bord de la révolution, et les propriétaires, la noblesse et l'Église étaient menacées de perdre leurs terres, leurs richesses et leur position sociale.

Pour les Sulpiciens de Montréal, la lutte outremer n'était pas seulement une quelconque lutte lointaine. L'avenir de l'ordre – le séminaire de Saint-Sulpice à Paris – était remis en cause. C'est pourquoi le groupe de Montréal travaillait d'arrache-pied pour maintenir la continuité et le calme dans leur propre maison. En outre, l'avenir de l'ordre des Sulpiciens à Montréal était tout autant remis en cause, car, selon les conditions du Traité de Paris, le séminaire n'avait pas le droit de recevoir de nouveaux membres de la France. En 1755, le séminaire comptait quarante-cinq membres, mais en 1789, «la compagnie était réduite à dix membres».[53] Cette diminution était due au refus des Sulpiciens d'accepter que des prêtres nés au Canada fassent partie de l'ordre.[54] À ce point, cherchant son intérêt personnel, le séminaire avait déjà oublié la raison pour laquelle, au départ, on lui avait accordé le territoire de Kanehsatà:ke.

Le discours d'inauguration de la concession du Lac des Deux-Montagnes de 1717 disait que le territoire avait été accordé au séminaire de Saint-Sulpice pour les «sauvages» qui étaient «sous leur protection» à Sault-aux-Récollets. Les Français voyaient les Onkwehón:we comme des citoyens français potentiels. La conversion des Onkwehón:we au christianisme était un moyen d'atteindre cette fin qui, en retour, était le moyen par lequel la couronne de France pouvait réclamer la souveraineté sur ces terres. Convertir les Onkwehón:we de Sault-aux-Récollets au christianisme était difficile en raison de la présence des commerçants d'alcool. Les Sulpiciens, comme la couronne de France, reconnaissaient le grand obstacle au bien-être du peuple sous leur protection que représentait l'alcool. Cependant, ni les prêtres ni la couronne de France n'étaient disposés à faire quoi que ce soit pour y remédier. Dans une lettre à M. de Belmont, prêtre de Saint-Sulpice à la mission de Montréal, Louis Tronson, supérieur du séminaire à Paris, écrivit :

> Ils (la cour française) sont suffisamment convaincus que l'ivresse causée par le trafic du brandy engendre de graves désordres au Canada, mais ils sont à la fois persuadés qu'il est nécessaire pour le commerce […] Les exemples de ces désordres, au sujet desquels vous m'avez écrit, sont terribles, mais ils ne changeront pas d'avis. Selon eux, la colonie périrait sans ce commerce.[55]

Les Canadiens français de Lachine s'enivraient également et causaient du grabuge à la mission.[56] Réinstaller la mission à un endroit «plus éloigné de la ville» où les Onkwehón:we «n'auraient pas la possibilité de s'enivrer» protégerait le peuple des ravages de l'alcool et des désordres causés par les colons ivres. Cela libérerait aussi les grandes étendues de terrains déjà défrichés et cultivés par les Onkwehón:we pour les colons français.

Qu'est-ce que «sous leur protection» suggère? Dans cet exemple, considérant le commerce galopant du brandy à Sault-aux-Récollets, «sous leur protection» aurait dû signifier défendre le peuple de l'agression, de la méchanceté et de la cupidité des vendeurs d'alcool. Cela aurait dû aussi vouloir dire aider les Kanehsata'kehró:non à s'adapter à un environnement qui se transformait rapidement et assurer la disponibilité des ressources nécessaires à leur santé et à leur bien-être. Le désir d'assurer le bien-être des Onkwehón:we à la mission de Sault-aux-Récollets était la raison que le séminaire avait donnée pour justifier sa demande du territoire de Kanehsatà:ke – les Sulpiciens l'avaient eux-mêmes clairement déclaré –, et c'est pour cette raison que le roi de France leur a accordé la concession. Cependant, les Sulpiciens ne firent rien pour empêcher les marchands de brandy de suivre la mission jusqu'au Lac des Deux-Montagnes. Comme nous l'avons vu, seuls les Britanniques prirent des mesures pour interrompre efficacement le commerce du brandy, et ce, seulement après que le commerce des fourrures fut presque terminé. Le territoire du Lac fut, par ailleurs, concédé pour que les Onkwehón:we sous la protection de la mission aient des territoires de chasse, puisque ceux de Sault-aux-Récollets avaient été envahis par les colons. Les Sulpiciens se préoccupaient tellement de leurs protégés qu'ils encourageaient la colonisation rapide dans presque toutes les parties de la seigneurie, ce qui engendra la quasi-destruction des territoires de chasse des Kanehsata'kehró:non.

Puisque protéger le peuple était une obligation, le séminaire fit de grands efforts pour paraître la remplir. Depuis les débuts, les Sulpiciens étaient parfaitement conscients de devoir paraître prendre soin du peuple et remplir les obligations de la mission. En juin 1677, Tronson, le supérieur à Paris, écrivit :

Il (de Bretonvilliers) nous a accordé 1000 écus. Mais ils ont ordonné que cet argent serve aux enfants des autochtones. Cette clause me rend perplexe, car il semble que nous n'avons pas de tels enfants et nous ne pouvons en avoir sans augmenter les dépenses. Cela ne nous est pas commode. Comment pensez-vous que quelqu'un puisse faire quelque chose pour arranger tout cela [...] Il est possible que, parmi les autochtones que nous aidons, il y ait des enfants qui pourraient prendre la place de ceux que nous aimerions instruire et aux besoins desquels nous affirmons contribuer.[57]

La première concession que le roi de France accorda aux Sulpiciens en 1666 leur donna la permission de s'établir en Nouvelle-France et de fonder des missions pour convertir les Onkwehón:we au christianisme.[58] À cette époque, le commerce du brandy n'était pas une menace sérieuse, mais en 1717, il l'était. Cependant, ni les Sulpiciens ni la Couronne n'étaient disposés à prendre les mesures extrêmes nécessaires pour mettre fin au commerce, préférant sacrifier le bien-être des Onkwehón:we pour le bien de la jeune et vulnérable colonie. De plus, les problèmes engendrés par l'alcoolisme augmentaient la dépendance des Onkwehón:we aux missionnaires et facilitaient le processus de contrôle français sur le territoire des Onkwehón:we.

La concession de 1717 pour le territoire de Kanehsatà:ke servit de compromis entre les désirs contradictoires de la couronne de France. D'une part, il y avait le commerce

« La Mer Du Nord »
Musée David M. Stewart, Matthieu Albert, cartographe CA 1778

qui était nécessaire pour la croissance et la survie de la colonie et, d'autre part, il y avait le désir de convertir les autochtones au christianisme. Déplacer le peuple dans un endroit éloigné visait plusieurs buts utiles. D'abord, cela séparait, du moins temporairement, le peuple des commerçants d'alcool. Ensuite, cela servait à améliorer la sécurité de la colonie en établissant une présence française à la tête du pays et permettait la colonisation des terres abandonnées par le peuple de Sault-aux-Récollets. Et finalement, et non par ordre d'importance, les Sulpiciens pouvaient augmenter le nombre de personnes au sein de leur mission en la déplaçant vers un lieu où un village Kanien'kehà:ka existait déjà.

La protection du peuple, qui était le principe directeur de la concession de 1717, fut complètement ignorée. En réalité, ce principe avait très peu à voir avec la manière dont le séminaire traitait le peuple. Les Sulpiciens utilisaient le principe pour justifier les concessions qu'ils avaient reçues. Une fois qu'ils devinrent sûrs de leur position, ils abandonnèrent entièrement le prétexte invoqué pour l'avoir. Leur manque total de respect envers le peuple fut manifesté en 1781 quand les colons commencèrent à aménager et à brûler les terres, et encore, en 1789, quand les Sulpiciens firent passer leur propre survie avant le bien-être de ceux qui leur avaient été confiés. Une soif insatiable de pouvoir et de contrôle obligea les Sulpiciens à avoir recours à de plus en plus de nouveaux moyens, y compris la loi, pour justifier leur droit à la seigneurie du Lac des Deux-Montagnes.

Durant cet hiver froid de février 1721, les Kanehsata'kehró:non avaient accueilli les prêtres de Saint-Sulpice. Ils l'avaient fait sans grand enthousiasme et contre leur bon sens. Sous certaines conditions, ils avaient néanmoins accepté de partager leurs terres et leurs ressources, mais le séminaire était de moins en moins disposé à les partager. Comme le serpent à deux têtes (voir chapitre 4), il commençait à dévorer ceux-là mêmes qui lui avaient manifesté bonté et générosité.

La tendance du séminaire à pousser à l'avant-plan la question de titre de propriété avait d'abord tout simplement déconcerté les Kanehsata'kehró:non. Les Sulpiciens n'avaient pas besoin du territoire pour survivre – ils le savaient bien – mais, en 1789, ces hommes étaient tellement désespérés qu'ils revendiquèrent d'une manière des plus brusques et insensibles ce qu'ils croyaient être leurs droits. Les Kanehsata'kehró:non, habitués à discuter des questions importantes d'une manière calme et délibérée pour en venir à un consensus, furent grandement offensés par la réponse du séminaire à la demande de protection du chef Aghneetha. En 1792, la couronne britannique permit à onze prêtres du séminaire de Paris, qui avaient fui la Révolution française, de s'installer à Montréal. Plus tôt, en 1783, un groupe de Sulpiciens arrivant de France, fut obligé, par ordre de Frederick Haldimand, d'y retourner.[59] Un supérieur sulpicien décrivit l'arrivée des onze hommes comme celle des «sauveurs du séminaire».[60] La situation du peuple empira immédiatement avec l'arrivée des prêtres émigrants.

C'est par pure détermination que les Sulpiciens maintinrent leur emprise sur le territoire. Puisqu'il était clair qu'ils ne partiraient pas volontairement ou calmement, les Britanniques, réticents à les chasser par la force, leur permirent de rester. Quand le chef Aghneetha demanda qu'un titre de propriété soit accordé aux Kanehsata'kehró:non pour qu'ils puissent posséder leurs terres «au même titre que les Mohawks de Grand River et de la baie de Quinte»[61], il demandait que le territoire soit protégé pour que le peuple mène une vie indépendante et autosuffisante. Cependant, cela n'était pas sur le point de se produire.

Depuis 1764, les Britanniques et le séminaire utilisaient, de façon interchangeable, les lois française et britannique pour priver les Kanehsata'kehró:non de leurs terres. La Proclamation royale de 1763 et l'article 49 de l'Acte de capitation étaient censés protéger les Onkwehón:we pour qu'ils ne soient pas dépossédés de leurs terres et que personne ne les empiète. Cependant, ils ne furent jamais appliqués pour la protection des Kanehsata'kehró:non sur leurs terres. À chaque occasion, Kanehsatà:ke fut l'exception à la règle. La question est pourquoi? Il n'y a qu'une seule réponse. Le séminaire de Saint-Sulpice était beaucoup trop puissant et influent et beaucoup trop important dans les plans de colonisation des Britanniques. Ce ne fut jamais une question de justice, mais une question d'opportunisme.

Un tourbillon de changements

 Même si vous pouvez penser que pour une montagne le temps avance lentement et que le changement n'est apparent qu'au fil des saisons, ce n'était pas le cas pour le peuple. Pour lui, le changement était comme un tourbillon, un ouragan qui, en créant son propre sentier, le saisissait et le projetait çà et là, insouciant des conséquences et inconscient du ravage qu'il laissait derrière.

Même le territoire avait changé. En le regardant, je ne voyais plus les grands champs de maïs cultivés par le peuple. Cette relation d'échange qui constituait le lien du peuple avec la terre avait disparu; elle n'était plus possible. D'autres s'en étaient emparé, et des feux faisaient rage partout, détruisant arbres et animaux.

Les Roti'kharahón:tsi y avaient introduit des leurs et forcé les Kanehsata'kehró:non à déménager de plus en plus loin du territoire. Comme pour les éprouver davantage, la maladie venait souvent réclamer plus d'enfants, plus de pères et plus de mères. La tristesse n'épargnait aucune famille.

Malgré tout, les Kanehsata'kehró:non observaient leurs instructions originales et, même si plusieurs d'entre eux suivaient les Roti'kharahón:tsi, les cérémonies étaient maintenues et la fumée du Oien'kwa'on:we (tabac) continuait à transmettre les paroles du peuple au Créateur.

Le peuple ne pensait pas seulement aux tâches à accomplir pour subvenir aux besoins quotidiens, mais participait également aux feux des conseils au sud et à l'est. Il travaillait d'arrache-pied pour faire entendre sa voix. Il croyait fortement que ses actions enseigneraient à ses enfants et à ses petits-enfants à ne pas désespérer, mais à chercher de la bonne façon des solutions à leurs problèmes.

Je continue de regarder le peuple pendant qu'il travaille, lutte et vient à moi pour être consolé et fortifié et repartir le cœur de nouveau rempli de paix.

[1] Discours du chef Aghneetha.

[2] William N. Fenton, *The History and Culture of Iroquois Diplomacy, An Interdisciplinary Guide to the Treaties of The Six Nations and Their League*, Syracuse, Syracuse University Press, 1985, p. 192.

[3] Papers of Sir William Johnson, division des archives et de l'histoire, Milton W. Hamilton (historien), vol. XIV, Albany, Université de l'État de New York, 1965, p. 187, 188.

[4] Même si William Johnson avait l'autorité de conclure des ententes avec les Onkwehón:we pour les Britanniques, il n'avait pas le pouvoir de contraindre sa propre nation à s'y conformer. En conséquence, toutes les ententes conclues entre William Johnson, pour les Britanniques, et les Onkwehón:we furent subséquemment violées par les colons. Ces violations engendrèrent des conflits nécessitant la conclusion de nouvelles ententes qui furent aussi violées subséquemment. Les ententes ou les traités avec les Britanniques revenaient à des promesses vides et résultaient toujours en la perte des terres des Onkwehón:we et non en leur protection.

[5] Papers of Sir William Johnson, Fort Johnson, 13 et 14 février 1760, p. 188.

[6] Discours adressé par Aghneetha, chef principal du Lac des Deux-Montagnes, 8 février 1787.

[7] Procédures lors d'un conseil tenu à Albany, le 28 juin 1761, par George Croghan Esq. député, agent des Affaires indiennes auprès des représentants de Coghnawagas, de Canassadagas et d'autres nations indiennes, par ordre de Sir William Johnson Esq. Papers of Sir William Johnson, vol. X, *The Seven Years War*, p. 302-305.

[8] Durant l'hiver 1760-1761, la varicelle ravagea encore la communauté. Papers of Sir William Johnson, vol. III, p. 393-396.

[9] Discours adressé par Daniel Claus, le 6 mai 1762, Papers of Sir William Johnson, vol. X, *The Seven Years War*, p. 445-449.

[10] En 1688, Edmund Andros, le gouverneur du dominion de la Nouvelle-Angleterre, qui traita avec les Cinq Nations à Albany, s'adressa au peuple en disant «Mes enfants». Un an plus tard, lors d'un autre conseil des Cinq Nations qui se tint aussi à Albany, le peuple insista pour que le mot «frères» soit utilisé. *Iroquois Diplomacy*, p. 161, 162.

[11] Beta, *To a proper understanding of the Oka question, and a help to its equitable and speedy settlement*, Montréal, 1878, Article 35 de l'Acte de capitulation.

[12] David Blanchard, *Seven Generations: A History of the Kanien'kehà:ka*, p. 249.

[13] Papers of Sir William Johnson, vol. III, *The Seven Years War*.

[14] Ibid., vol. VII, Post War, 1763-1774, p. 129.

[15] Papers of Sir William Johnson, vol. X, *Seven Years War*, p. 380-381. Lettres d'Henry Gladwin à Jeffrey Amherst, 4 février 1762.

[16] Ibid.

[17] Ibid., p. 399. Daniel Claus en conférence avec les Indiens de Canasadaga, 15 mai 1762.

[18] *Rebellion The Rising in French Canada 1837*, Joseph Schull, Macmillan of Canada, Toronto, 1971, p. 3.

[19] Brian Young, *In Its Corporate Capacity: The Seminary Of Montreal as a Business Institution*, p. 39.

[20] Ibid.

[21] Ibid., p. 6

[22] Ibid.

[23] Ibid.

[24] Ibid.

[25] Pour une discussion complète de cette question et pour le texte intégral du rapport Stuart, voir Robert Christie, *A History of the Lake Province of Lower Canada*, vol. VI, p. 424-434.

[26] John Gilmary Shea, *History of the Catholic Missions among the Indian Tribes of the United States*, 1529-1854, p. 341

[27] Papers of Sir William Johnson, vol. IV, p. 849.

[28] Lettre de Guy Carleton à Daniel Claus, 3 septembre 1767, Papers of Sir William Johnson, vol. V, p. 650.

[29] Lettre de Guy Carleton à Sir William Johnson, Papers of Sir William Johnson, vol. XII, p. 347.

[30] Lettre de Guy Carleton à Sir William Johnson, Papers of Sir William Johnson, vol. XII, p. 971, 972.

[31] Lettre de Daniel Claus à Sir William Johnson, 25 août 1769, Papers of Sir William Johnson, vol. VII, p. 129, 130.

[32] Ibid.

[33] Journal de Daniel Claus, Papers of Sir William Johnson, vol. VII, p. 948.

[34] William Fenton, *The History and Culture of Iroquois Diplomacy*, p. 197.

[35] Papers of Sir William Johnson, vol. XIII, p. 710.

[36] Discours de plusieurs chefs du Lac des Deux-Montagnes au Colonel Campbell lors d'un conseil à Montréal, le 7 février 1781. Interprété par Chevalier de Lorimier du registre des procédures, à la cour supérieure de justice, les ecclésiastiques du séminaire de Saint-Sulpice de Montréal contre Angus Corinthe, vol. 1, p. 93-96, département de la justice, A-500.

[37] Olivier Maurault, *Les vicissitudes d'une mission sauvage*, p. 130.

[38] Germain Lalande p. s. s., *Une histoire de bornage qui dure depuis près d'un siècle*, Cahier d'histoire Deux-Montagnes, vol. 3, n° 4, p. 8.

[39] Brian Young, p. 40.

[40] *A History of Lower Canada*, vol. 6, Robert Christie, Richard Worthington publisher, 1866, *Memorial of the Law Officers of the Crown*, p. 227-230.

[41] Christian Dessureault, *La Seigneurie du Lac des Deux-Montagnes, de 1780 à 1825*, thèse de maîtrise, Université de Montréal, septembre 1979, p. 177.

[42] Ibid.

[43] Olivier Maurault, p. 131.

[44] Discours du chef Aghneetha.

[45] Rapport d'un comité de tout le conseil concernant les Sulpiciens et la revendication des Indiens, dans le registre des procédures, vol 1, Centre national des arts, RG 13, vol. 2432, dossier A500, p. 96.

[46] C'est-à-dire l'Île-aux-Tourtes

[47] Essentiel d'une lettre reçue par Joseph Chew, surintendant des Affaires indiennes, 7 août 1795, de la part des nations indiennes algonquine, iroquoise et népissingue du Lac des Deux-Montagnes. Du registre des procédures, p. 132-134.

[48] Extrait d'un conseil tenu à Québec, le 5 juin 1797. Correspondance de Sir John Johnson, RG 10, vol. 10, p. 9236-9240.

[49] Extrait du rapport de H. C. Darling, surintendant des Affaires indiennes à son excellence le comte de Dalhousie, le 24 juillet 1828, RG 10, vol. 2029, dossier 8946.

[50] Extrait d'un rapport de James Hughes, surintendant du département des Affaires indiennes pour le district de Montréal au lieutenant-colonel Napier, surintendant des Affaires indiennes pour Québec, le 15 février 1834, RG10, vol. 2029, dossier 8946.

[51] Concession de 1735.

[52] Gilles Boileau, *Les silences des Messieurs*, p. 140, 141.

[53] Brian Young, p. 7.

[54] Ibid.

[55] Les lettres de Louis Tronson, partie 1, 1677-1691, Centre national des arts, F397, parag. 320

[56] Ibid.

[57] Tronson à Lefèvre, le 6 juin 1677, Centre national des arts, F397, p. 106.

[58] Contrat de donation au dit séminaire, en date du 9 mars 1663, registre des procédures, Centre national des arts, RG 13, vol. 2432, dossier A500, p. 251-256.

[59] André Cuoq, p. s. s., *Histoire de la mission indienne du Lac des Deux-Montagnes*, 1848-1859, cahier 29, A. S. S. S., Université de Montréal.

[60] Brian Young, p. 40

[61] Discours adressé par Aghneetha.

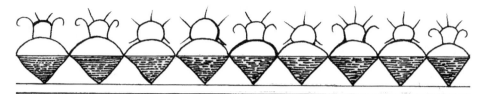

CHAPITRE 4

LE CALME AVANT LA TEMPÊTE

LE CALME AVANT LA TEMPÊTE

 Le vent d'automne souffle doucement, en murmurant et en nous caressant. À l'ouest, j'entends le Ratiwè:ras (tonnerre) qui ronfle et gronde. Une tempête se prépare à l'horizon. Un calme soudain s'installe et tout devient tranquille en attendant la tempête. Dernièrement, le peuple est silencieux parce qu'il a faim. Il semble avoir peu de temps pour rire ou pour jouer. Même les enfants se taisent à cause des gargouillements de leur estomac.

Depuis de nombreuses saisons, le peuple s'emploie à défricher plus de terrain. C'est ce que les Roti'karahòn:tsi (robes noires) leur ont dit de faire. Au début, ils ne savaient pas pourquoi. Leurs petits champs de maïs, de courge, de fèves et de pommes de terre leur avaient toujours suffi. Maintenant, les O'serón:ni (Français) sont arrivés comme un essaim de sauterelles pour les déloger de leur territoire. Ils détruisent les forêts et font fuir les animaux et les oiseaux qui y vivent.

Les Kanehsata'kehró:non doivent maintenant aller plus loin pour trouver du gibier, mais où qu'ils aillent, c'est la même chose. Le peuple est fier, mais les enfants meurent de faim parce que la récolte de maïs n'a pas été bonne. Il s'adresse aux Roti'karahòn:tsi et leur demande de l'aider, mais ces prêtres n'ont pas d'affection pour les Kanehsata'kehró:non; ils n'en ont que pour les objets brillants que les O'serón:ni leur ont donné.

Pendant ce temps, les O'serón:ni continuent d'arriver et de prendre plus de terres. Je peux voir les Roti'karahòn:tsi s'assembler et se cacher avec leurs mains pour murmurer. Ils ne veulent pas être entendus. Ils préparent quelque chose. Je vois alors le peuple sous le choc garder le silence. Pour l'instant, il se sent vaincu, mais leur silence, je le sais, n'est que le calme avant la tempête.

P. M. O'Leary, 1853
Gracieuseté des Archives nationales du Canada, C12290

À L'AUBE D'UN NOUVEAU SIÈCLE

L'aube du 19ᵉ siècle amena, encore une fois, la guerre quand les Américains envahirent le Canada. Ce fut le dernier combat sur le continent au cours duquel les Kanehsata'kehró:non combattirent aux côtés des Britanniques, et la dernière fois qu'ils furent appréciés comme guerriers. Avec la fin de la guerre arriva un changement d'attitude qui allait modifier le statut du peuple : de guerriers et alliés, ils deviendront enfants et prisonniers. Au moment où la guerre fut déclarée, environ 150 guerriers Kanehsata'kehró:non étaient prêts pour le combat, en plus de 100 Algonquins et Népissingues de Kanehsatà:ke.[1]

Des guerriers de Kanehsatà:ke combattirent à Châteauguay, à Beaver Dam et peut-être aussi à Fort George. Le 26 mai 1813, quelque 120 guerriers de la communauté accompagnèrent Dominique Ducharme à Beaver Dam.[2]

Le nombre de morts est inconnu, mais au moins deux hommes, Abaaghninkissorn et Louis Tekanitontus, furent tués et cinq autres blessés. Un guerrier de Kanehsatà:ke reçut une compensation pour ses blessures subies à Fort George.[3]

Une fois de plus, les hommes de Kanehsatà:ke s'étaient bien battus et, à ce moment, leur aide fut probablement très nécessaire et grandement appréciée. Après la guerre de 1812, il fut vite évident que les Britanniques en Amérique du Nord ne connurent aucune autre menace de guerre. Ils n'avaient plus besoin de leurs alliés indiens et les laissèrent tomber brusquement. « L'objet, le principe fondamental de la politique indienne britannique au cours de la guerre de 1812, était de courtiser les Indiens et de maintenir leur affection pour qu'ils fournissent une aide militaire continue […] »[4] « Mais au milieu de l'année 1814, l'utilité des alliés indiens dans le Haut-Canada avait tellement diminué qu'ils étaient plutôt considérés comme un handicap ».[5] Pour la plupart, les Onkwehón:we s'étaient battus non seulement pour protéger les intérêts britanniques au Canada, mais aussi pour empêcher les Américains de prendre possession de leur territoire. Après le conflit, les Britanniques choisirent de remettre aux Américains de grandes étendues de territoire au lieu de les accorder à leurs alliés Onkwehón:we qui avaient combattu à leurs côtés pour les défendre. Dans une certaine mesure, cette trahison se fit ressentir partout. À Kanesatà:ke, elle prit la forme d'une plus grande réticence de la part des Britanniques à prendre des mesures pour protéger les droits du peuple. Non seulement ils négligèrent de faire respecter ces droits, mais ils cherchèrent activement à les réduire à néant.

Dès les années 1820, le peuple de Kanesatà:ke était déjà soumis à de lourdes restrictions imposées par le séminaire. « Tout Indien qui récoltait plus que pour les besoins de sa famille ne pouvait pas utiliser son profit pour acheter davantage de terre. »[6] En outre, « tout Indien qui quittait la mission pour vivre à tout autre poste où il n'y avait aucun missionnaire perdait tout droit à ses terres et à ses prés s'il ne revenait pas à la troisième année au temps des semences ».[7]

Les Sulpiciens essayèrent aussi de dicter au peuple de Kanehsatà:ke ce qu'il pouvait et ne pouvait pas lire. À l'hiver 1826, ils réussirent à capturer un guide algonquin du Lac des Deux-Montagnes qui avait obtenu de la littérature que les Sulpiciens jugeaient offensante. Il était à des centaines de kilomètres, dans la région du fort Coulonge, avec John McLean de la Compagnie de la Baie d'Hudson. McLean décrivit ainsi l'incident :

> Deux missionnaires itinérants sont arrivés au Lac des Deux-Montagnes et ont distribué un certain nombre de tracts religieux parmi les autochtones, en plus de quelques exemplaires de l'Évangile de Jean, dans la langue indienne. Il s'est trouvé que mon

interprète algonquin, qui en avait obtenu un exemplaire, prenait plaisir à le lire. Vers la fin de la saison, j'ai reçu un colis de mon supérieur du Lac [des Deux-Montagnes] et, à ma surprise, j'y ai trouvé une lettre portant le sceau de l'Église et adressée à mon interprète, que je lui ai remise. Je le regardais la parcourir très attentivement, puis me tirant à l'écart, il m'a dit que la lettre du prêtre lui transmettait l'ordre tranchant de détruire le mauvais livre qu'il avait en sa possession, sans quoi on refuserait les rituels de la sépulture chrétienne pour son enfant qui était mort à l'automne [...] Je lui ai demandé s'il avait l'intention d'obéir aux ordres de son père spirituel. « Pas exactement, m'a-t-il répondu; je lui enverrai le livre et le laisserai faire ce qu'il en veut; [...] pourquoi la "robe noire" le qualifie de mauvais est un mystère pour moi. »[8]

De plus, le séminaire essaya de limiter les mariages à la mission. En 1826, M. Roupe, supérieur de la mission du Lac des Deux-Montagnes, interdit les mariages entre Kanehsata'kehró:non et Canadiens. Les mariages entre Kanehsata'kehró:non et d'autres Onkwehón:we, même les Kanien'kehà:ka de Kanahwà:ke ou d'Akwesasne, étaient également interdits.[9] En 1823, il n'y avait plus que 283 âmes dans le village des Iroquois, et il fut plus tard remarqué qu'à cause de l'interdiction de M. Roupe, le peuple avait de la difficulté à trouver un conjoint, puisque la plupart des gens du village étaient apparentés.[10] Lord Dalhousie se rendit à Kanehsatà:ke pour entendre les raisons de cette position prise contre de tels mariages qui « ne contrevenaient à aucune loi divine ni humaine ».[11] Roupe lui expliqua que, si de tels mariages arrivaient trop souvent, « la mission serait ruinée ».[12] Il ajouta :

Depuis que je suis ici, il peut y avoir eu quelques [mariages mixtes], mais je m'y suis toujours opposé et, avec l'aide de Dieu, aucun n'a été célébré. C'est pour éviter ces alliances qu'il est interdit aux Blancs de vivre sous le même toit qu'eux. C'est aussi la raison pour laquelle nous nous opposons absolument à ce qu'ils adoptent des enfants canadiens, et c'est seulement avec regret que nous avons toléré que quelques enfants dans le besoin leur soient confiés. Cela nous préoccupe grandement qu'ils soient élevés comme des sauvages.[13]

Selon leur loi, les Kanehsata'kehró:non ne pouvaient pas se marier avec quelqu'un de leur propre famille. À cause de l'interdiction de Roupe, ils ne pouvaient épouser ni Canadiens, ni Onkwehón:we, ni même des personnes de leur propre peuple d'autres villages. Qui alors étaient-ils censés épouser? Ils n'avaient pas non plus le droit d'adopter des enfants. Alors comment étaient-ils censés avoir des enfants s'ils ne pouvaient ni en adopter ni trouver de conjoint? Cette interdiction demeura en vigueur jusqu'en 1867 quand un nouveau directeur prit d'autres arrangements.

En 1823, une autre épidémie de varicelle frappa Kanehsatà:ke. Le secrétaire militaire n'était pas impressionné par le traitement accordé aux gens qui souffraient de cette maladie. Dans une lettre à Sir John Johnson, il le lui fit savoir clairement :

[...] il y a plusieurs Indiens qui sont malades et qui ne reçoivent aucune aide médicale; et je profite de l'occasion pour vous informer que le commandant de l'armée désire que vous considériez comme une partie essentielle de votre devoir de vous assurer que des arrangements soient faits pour [...] [aider] ces pauvres créatures et soulager avec attention leurs souffrances.[14]

En 1824, des colons et des commerçants chassaient les Algonquins et les Népissingues de Kanehsatà:ke de leurs territoires de chasse traditionnels, le long des régions supérieures de la rivière des Outaouais. Leur situation était devenue sérieuse. Le 29 juillet, dans une pétition adressée à Sir John Johnson, les Indiens expliquèrent le problème, et Sir John parut sympathique à leur situation. Dans une note datée du 5 novembre 1824 et adressée aux forces militaires britanniques, il souligna :

> [les] [...] Indiens algonquins et népissingues, contrairement aux autres tribus dans le Bas-Canada, ne possèdent aucun territoire dont ils peuvent tirer un revenu. Ils doivent donc dépendre de la chasse pour vivre. Et même s'ils ont assurément perçu la progression de la colonisation sur leur territoire de chasse comme une violation de la proclamation de Sa Majesté, ils se sont abstenus, pendant plusieurs années, de faire toute représentation à ce sujet [...][15]

Sir John décrivit que l'invasion des territoires de chasse semblait être « faite au hasard et peu judicieuse [...] » À titre d'information, Sir John Johnson, alors propriétaire de la seigneurie d'Argenteuil, était en train de la développer et de la coloniser.

En 1823, on comptait 26 familles canadiennes-françaises au Lac des Deux-Montagnes. En 1847, quand la concession des terres à la seigneurie du Lac des Deux-Montagnes fut terminée, plus de 600 familles de colons avaient emménagé sur le territoire. De ce nombre, 500 étaient fermiers.[16] Le territoire avait été divisé en douze paroisses. Dans onze de ces paroisses, toutes les terres avaient été concédées. La seule partie de la seigneurie qui ne fut pas concédée était la « réserve » : une partie de territoire triangulaire de Pointe-aux-Anglais à Pointe-Calumet et au nord à l'intersection de la petite rivière du Chêne et du rang Saint-Joseph. Même à l'intérieur de la réserve, des empiétements se produisaient.

Les conditions de vie des Algonquins et des Népissingues empiraient régulièrement. En 1839, James Hughes remarqua qu'il avait « souvent déposé des plaintes contre des individus qui empiétaient sur leurs territoires de chasse et les détérioraient. Ces territoires comprenaient les îles situées dans la rivière des Outaouais, aussi bien que la vaste étendue de terres de chaque côté de cette rivière et de la petite rivière, de Pointe-à-l'Orignal jusqu'au lac Népissingue [...] ».[17] Aucune mesure ne fut prise pour trouver une solution aux difficultés auxquelles les Algonquins et les Népissingues faisent face avant 1853, quand la Couronne leur réserva des terres à Maniwaki.

En 1834, alors que le peuple de Kanehsatà:ke, confronté à la famine, voyait son territoire disparaître, le choléra ravagea la communauté. L'épidémie décima la population. M. Cuoq décrivit dans son journal l'étendue de la dévastation : « Presque tous les habitants du village, Canadiens ou sauvages, ont été plus ou moins affligés et, pendant un certain temps, il a été difficile de trouver des hommes pour transporter les morts au cimetière. »[18] Il continua ainsi :

> Cette période a été marquée par la conversion de quelques-uns des pires pécheurs, notamment ce fameux Karihwí:io. Comme beaucoup d'autres Iroquois à cette époque, il n'avait même pas fait sa première communion, et il était âgé de plus de 73 ans quand il est mort du choléra en 1834. Avant de mourir, on lui a administré les derniers sacrements, et ainsi celui qui avait été la terreur du village durant son adolescence, et qui avait vécu d'une manière abominable, a reçu la prière des fidèles dont il s'était moqué dans sa jeunesse.[19]

Même si l'épidémie fut très désastreuse pour les Kanehsata'kehró:non, grâce à elle, les Sulpiciens purent trouver consolation dans le fait que beaucoup plus d'Indiens acceptèrent de se convertir. Dans son rapport, en 1834, James Hughes souligna que, lorsqu'il s'agissait d'instruction religieuse, les missionnaires « assujettissaient grandement » le peuple. Il fit également la remarque suivante : « Il n'y a aucune école dans le village et il n'y en a jamais eu d'établie. Les Indiens aimeraient bien en avoir une, mais ils craignent beaucoup que si le maître d'école est d'une confession autre que catholique romaine, les missionnaires s'y opposent.[20] Le peuple, dit-il, est généralement autodidacte.»[21]

LE SERPENT À DEUX TÊTES

 Voici une histoire qui nous fut d'abord racontée par nos ancêtres, puis transmise de génération en génération. Elle était, il y a longtemps, un avertissement des choses qui se produiraient. Elle parle de ce qui est arrivé, de ce qui arrive et de ce qui arrivera. C'est la prophétie du serpent à deux têtes ou du grand serpent blanc.

Jadis, avant que l'homme blanc arrive sur ce continent, il y avait un jeune garçon qui vivait dans un village des Rotinonhseshá:ka. Un jour, alors qu'il chassait, ce garçon aperçut un très petit serpent d'apparence chétive. C'était une créature très étrange qui avait deux têtes : une en argent et l'autre en or. Le jeune garçon eut pitié de la créature parce qu'elle était malade et agonisante. Elle ignorait comment trouver de la nourriture et un abri et prendre soin d'elle-même. Parce qu'il avait deux têtes, le serpent ne savait jamais dans quelle direction aller. Le garçon prit donc le serpent et l'apporta au village. Il décida d'en prendre soin pour qu'il devienne fort et en santé.

Quand le jeune garçon montra le serpent aux habitants de son village, ceux-ci ne réagirent pas comme il s'y attendait. On lui dit que ce serpent venait de loin, de l'autre côté d'un grand océan. Il n'était pas naturel et il les détruirait s'ils l'aidaient. Ils décidèrent qu'on devait ramener le serpent où il avait été trouvé et l'abandonner à son sort. Étant en désaccord avec cette décision, le jeune garçon, au lieu de laisser le serpent mourir, l'apporta dans un lieu secret loin du village, où il en prit soin et lui donna des herbes médicinales pour le guérir.

Au fil des jours, le serpent grandissait et se fortifiait, son appétit augmentait aussi. Il devint plus difficile pour le garçon de chasser suffisamment de gibier pour le nourrir. Il craignait que le serpent s'en aille et que quelqu'un du village le voie. Il lui construisit donc une cage, mais elle devint vite trop petite pour l'animal. Ne pouvant plus lui trouver assez de nourriture, le garçon décida qu'il était temps d'avouer sa désobéissance aux gens du village.

Devant l'énormité de l'animal, les gens du village furent très effrayés; ils construisirent donc une grande clôture pour le contenir. Comme l'appétit du serpent augmentait, tous les chasseurs du village furent forcés de le nourrir. Beaucoup de gens souffraient de la faim, mais ils craignaient ce qui pourrait arriver s'il ne mangeait pas.

Puis un jour, le serpent avait tellement grossi qu'il brisa sa clôture. Il alla au village et commença à dévorer les gens, y compris le garçon qui avait pris soin de lui. À mesure qu'il avançait, il continuait à grossir. Après avoir tué et mangé la plupart des gens du village, le serpent se dirigea à l'ouest vers d'autres nations. Étant devenu énorme, il tua et détruisit tout sur son passage, il dévora toutes les personnes qu'il trouvait.

Les sages de plusieurs nations se réunirent pour décider comment ils pourraient arrêter la créature, mais ils ne trouvèrent aucune solution. Et le serpent continua sa course, laissant mort et destruction sur son sillage.

Il existe diverses versions de la fin de cette histoire. Certains disent que le grand serpent blanc disparut un jour après avoir tout détruit, tandis que d'autres croient que le Peuple du tonnerre réussit à vaincre le serpent et à le forcer à rentrer dans la terre. D'autres encore affirment qu'à mesure que le serpent avançait, détruisant et dévorant tout sur son passage, les deux têtes se mirent à se battre parce qu'elles ne s'entendaient pas entre elles. Il s'ensuivit un combat terrible qui fut ressenti partout dans le monde. Finalement, les deux têtes s'entretuèrent.

C'est la prophétie du serpent à deux têtes qui prédit la venue de l'homme blanc. Comme l'homme blanc, le serpent était faible et chétif quand il arriva ici. Le peuple en prit soin et, à mesure qu'il grossissait, comme l'homme blanc, le serpent commença à dévorer les gens qui lui avaient manifesté de la bonté. Aujourd'hui, en regardant notre monde, nous constatons que la plupart de la prophétie s'est réalisée, que les rivières et les ruisseaux sont pollués, que l'air que nous respirons nous rend malades et que beaucoup des animaux ont disparu. Partout sur la terre, les peuples autochtones ont été réduits et, dans certains cas, anéantis par les armes, les maladies et l'avidité insatiable du serpent. Mais il est encore temps de changer la fin de l'histoire, et c'est pourquoi cette prophétie est racontée.

Une récompense pour faveurs rendues

En 1837, une rébellion éclata dans le Haut et le Bas-Canada. Pour la plupart, c'était une rébellion contre le système féodal de classes des Britanniques, de même qu'une rébellion contre le système de tenure seigneuriale. Le peuple de Kanehsatà:ke vivait une situation bien pire que celle de leurs voisins canadiens-français, puisqu'il ne jouissait pas des droits et des privilèges des colons. Une fois de plus, il était confronté à la perspective d'une guerre qu'il n'avait pas initiée. Il décida de rester neutre et refusa de combattre avec l'un ou l'autre parti. En novembre 1837, les Kanehsata'kehró:non déclinèrent une demande des Patriotes de leur remettre les canons qu'ils avaient en leur possession. Un chef de Kanehsatà:ke répondit ainsi à la demande des Patriotes :

> Frères, je n'interviendrai pas dans cette dispute entre vous et votre père. Défendez vos droits et quand j'entendrai le tonnerre de vos armes, je me demanderai si je dois vous aider. Si vous avez agi en homme sage et avez semé du bon maïs dans le jardin de votre frère, vous mangerez de son pain avec lui.[22]

Pendant que les Kanehsata'kehró:non demeurèrent résolument neutres dans le conflit, les Sulpiciens gardèrent leurs intentions dans le plus grand secret. Le séminaire resta officiellement loyal envers les Britanniques, tandis que des membres de l'ordre s'agitèrent ouvertement contre ceux-ci et suscitèrent la rébellion. L'abbé Étienne Chartier, curé de Saint-Benoît, en est un exemple. « Depuis 1835, à son arrivée à Saint-Benoît, par sa voix débitant de la chaire et dominant les assemblées publiques, il avait d'abord recruté des patriotes, puis appelé aux armes. »[23] C'était dans les intérêts du séminaire de rester loyal envers les Britanniques, puisque ces derniers avaient jusqu'à ce moment toléré les activités du séminaire, malgré le fait que de nombreuses questions avaient été soulevées concernant leurs droits. « Au cours de la décennie instable précédant 1837, les relations du séminaire avec les autorités britanniques étaient essentielles. En s'associant socialement avec la plupart des gouverneurs britanniques, le séminaire travaillait à s'intégrer en tant qu'institution de l'ancien régime, lequel était utile pour perpétuer les valeurs paternalistes et féodales.»[24] Inutile de dire que cette politique du séminaire n'était pas très appréciée des classes les plus pauvres. Les domaines contrôlés par le séminaire furent les plus touchés par le désordre, alors que les gens protestaient et se rebellaient contre lui. Les Patriotes étaient de toute évidence une menace pour lui. Cependant, le gain qu'il recherchait en permettant à certains de ses membres d'inciter ces hommes à la rébellion n'est pas clair.

Au temps de la rébellion, cherchant de nouvelles façons de gagner sa vie, le peuple de Kanehsatà:ke commença à couper et à vendre du bois. Les Sulpiciens agirent sur-le-champ pour stopper cette activité. En juin 1839, James Hughes rencontra les Sulpiciens et exigea d'eux qu'ils promettent de laisser le peuple couper et vendre du bois. Il s'avéra que la promesse fut de courte durée. Les Britanniques avaient une dette envers le séminaire. En 1838, au summum de la rébellion, les prêtres gagnèrent la faveur des Britanniques en montrant à Sir John Colborne une carte géographique de la région. Ils «lui ont indiqué la route à emprunter pour se rendre à Saint-Eustache sans entrave; ainsi, en ne prenant pas le chemin direct qui traversait les bois et d'autres obstacles, il a pu déjouer tous les plans des rebelles».[25] À l'aide d'information fournie par le séminaire, les Britanniques réussirent à écraser la rébellion à Saint-Eustache et à Saint-Benoit. «Après avoir fait pleuvoir un barrage d'artillerie sur l'église, les forces britanniques y mirent le feu et tuèrent sans merci les Patriotes, alors qu'ils sautaient par les fenêtres pour échapper aux flammes.»[26]

Sydney Bellingham, magistrat britannique qui plus tard devint député d'Argenteuil, rappelle les actions du séminaire durant la rébellion. «Les services du clergé ont été inestimables pour le gouvernement britannique [...] et [ils] ont été récompensés par une loi confirmant leur titre de propriété de leurs seigneuries.»[27] Bellingham faisait référence à l'ordonnance de 1840 qui avait été rédigée par Sir John Colborne, l'homme qui avait plus tôt appuyé les efforts du peuple de Kanehsatà:ke pour gagner sa subsistance de la vente de bois. Après des mois de «négociations de haut niveau et souvent secrètes», l'ordonnance fut facilement votée par un conseil extraordinaire attitré. Ce conseil remplaça l'assemblée représentative qui avait été suspendue après la rébellion. Seuls deux membres du conseil, John Molson et George Moffat, votèrent contre l'ordonnance.[28] C'était l'une des 67 ordonnances votées par l'assemblée extraordinaire durant ses deux premiers mois d'existence.[29] Grâce à la rébellion et à ses retombées, le séminaire ne connut que très peu d'opposition à son désir de s'établir légalement comme corporation dans ses seigneuries. De nombreux opposants sincères furent «réduits au silence, emprisonnés, [ou] exilés»[30] à cause de leur implication dans la rébellion. «Dans ces conditions, le séminaire put dans le secret négocier avec assurance et légaliser son problème de société et de seigneurie grâce à une ordonnance exécutive et à un statut impérial.»[31]

La décision du séminaire d'appuyer les Britanniques durant la rébellion n'était pas suscitée par un quelconque amour envers eux. De 1800 à 1837, les activités des Sulpiciens furent constamment examinées par les législateurs du Bas-Canada. Dans un rapport transmis en 1804, le juge Jonathan Sewell, alors ministre de la Justice pour le Bas-Canada, confirma le point de vue de Sir James Marriot, à l'effet que le séminaire de Paris n'avait aucun droit de transférer le territoire au séminaire de Montréal. Pour sa part, Sewell déclara que le séminaire de Montréal, en tant qu'entité juridique, «était depuis longtemps dissous par la mort naturelle de ses membres [...]».[32] Les possessions du séminaire devaient donc être remises à la Couronne. Seuls les prêtres français émigrés avaient sauvé d'extinction le séminaire de Montréal. Selon Sewell, ces prêtres ne pouvaient pas «[...] soit comme individus, soit comme membres d'une société, détenir des biens immobiliers dans la colonie».[33] À la lumière de ces faits, Sewell dit qu'une poursuite civile devait être lancée contre plusieurs Sulpiciens qui détiennent des terres en tant qu'individus. Il ajouta que les prêtres devaient « être incités à se retirer (surtout les étrangers nés en France) [...] ».[34]

En 1819, les droits et les titres de propriété du séminaire furent de nouveau remis en question. À la troisième lecture du projet de loi du canal de Lachine, une motion fut votée pour éliminer une clause réservant certains droits au séminaire de Saint-Sulpice. Elle se lisait comme suit :

> Parce que nous n'avons aucune preuve de l'existence légale d'une société appelée le séminaire de Saint-Sulpice de Montréal, possédant le droit de propriété à [...] Parce que les Sulpiciens, qui sont restés au Canada après la conquête de la province par les armes de Sa Majesté, n'avaient pas un titre de propriété valide pour les terres qui leur ont été transférées par la communauté de Paris, il est indispensable que le parti qui accepte un tel transfert ait un pouvoir juridique de posséder des terres. Il semble n'y avoir aucun fondement pour dire que les membres de la société de Saint-Sulpice demeurant au Canada avaient un tel pouvoir, distinct de l'organisation de Paris (qui a depuis été dissoute) ou que la licence requise par la Couronne, qui aurait été requise sous la loi française et exigée par Sa Majesté britannique, leur ait déjà été accordée.[35]

En 1828, James Stuart, ministre de la Justice, remit un autre avis juridique contre le séminaire. Il était d'accord avec le point de vue de Sewell à l'effet que, sans l'émigration des prêtres de Paris, le séminaire de Montréal aurait disparu en 1795 ou 1796, quand le dernier survivant de la période précédant la conquête est décédé. Il contesta le transfert des biens immobiliers de 1764, affirmant qu'il était illégal. « Je suis d'avis, écrivit Stuart, que le séminaire de Montréal n'a jamais eu d'existence juridique distincte du séminaire de Saint-Sulpice à Paris. »[36] Remarquant de plus que le territoire avait été accordé au séminaire pour la protection spirituelle des Onkwehón:we, Stuart émit très clairement son point de vue sur cette question : « Ni le travail ni les revenus du séminaire de Montréal n'ont été, et ne seront probablement jamais, investis pour "la conversion des Indiens". »[37]

Les avis juridiques n'étaient pas les seuls problèmes à troubler le séminaire. Dans les années précédant 1840, « il y avait une résistance massive dans les trois seigneuries [des Sulpiciens] concernant l'encaissement des lods et ventes (taxes seigneuriales) ».[38] Les Sulpiciens étaient si méprisés qu'ils n'osaient pas essayer de collecter les arrérages des colons.

> Des mois avant l'éruption de la rébellion, en octobre 1837, il y a eu des émeutes et des tirs à la seigneurie des Deux-Montagnes; en juillet, la grange du prêtre de Saint-Benoît a été incendiée [...] L'agent de police local a procédé à des arrestations, mais il a refusé de garder des prisonniers dans la région puisqu'il « était certain qu'un sauvetage aurait réussi ».[39]

Les Sulpiciens faisaient face à une révolte ouverte sur les seigneuries. À Montréal, des anticléricaux comme Louis Joseph Papineau, un des dirigeants de la rébellion, étaient également hostiles au séminaire. En 1838, Papineau revendiqua l'abolition catégorique du système seigneurial et l'annulation de toutes les dettes seigneuriales. Le séminaire craignait tellement une « invasion patriote » durant les années de la rébellion qu'il brûla une grande partie de ce qu'ils considéraient des « documents compromettants ».[40]

L'ordonnance de 1840 changea la nature de la tenure seigneuriale, mais les Sulpiciens s'assurèrent que celle-ci ne fut pas abolie. Durant la rébellion, ils avaient entamé une série de négociations hautement secrètes avec les Britanniques. Comme l'évêque Exeter de la

Chambre des lords britannique le nota, une entente fut conclue. En 1841, malgré les objections de l'évêque Exeter et d'autres, le parlement britannique donna aux Sulpiciens un titre de propriété sur leurs seigneuries, y compris celle du Lac des Deux-Montagnes. Avant l'ordonnance de 1840, le séminaire « achetait des terres au nom de certains Sulpiciens » que ces derniers transféraient ensuite à l'ordre. Ces transferts ne furent effectués qu'après la confirmation des pouvoirs de corporation du séminaire en 1840.[41] Ce fait jette la lumière sur la confiance du séminaire en la légalité de ses revendications aux droits absolus sur les seigneuries.

Dorénavant, les Sulpiciens pouvaient légalement collecter des arrérages avec intérêts aux colons. Jusqu'à ce moment, à cause de son « insécurité politique et de son état juridique [...], le séminaire était incapable d'imposer ses prérogatives dans ses trois seigneuries ».[42] De plus belle, ils se mirent immédiatement à collecter ces arrérages. « Au printemps 1842, des débiteurs résidant dans la seigneurie des Deux-Montagnes ont livré du blé, de l'argent et même de l'ancienne monnaie française à deux notaires et au meunier du séminaire [...] »[43] Vers la fin de la décennie, de l'agitation parmi des colons à la seigneurie du Lac des Deux-Montagnes éclata en émeutes. « Durant l'année violente de 1849, les Sulpiciens disaient être assis sur un volcan fumant et être contraints de protéger durant tout l'été leurs propriétés des pyromanes. Dans les années 1850, les émeutes et des incendies n'étaient pas rares, alors que la protestation rurale contre la taxation municipale et scolaire augmentait. »[44] En 1852, le séminaire avait collecté des milliers de dollars en arrérages à la seigneurie.

D'après les termes de l'ordonnance, le séminaire devait, sur demande, transférer en pleine propriété[45] les terres occupées par les colons. À la seigneurie du Lac des Deux-Montagnes, un nombre infime, seulement neuf concessions sur 1260, fut transféré en pleine propriété.[46] Les colons étaient devenus si endettés envers le séminaire qu'ils ne pouvaient plus acheter les droits de pleine propriété.

Si les colons français établis sur la seigneurie avaient de graves problèmes avec le séminaire de Saint-Sulpice, les Kanehsata'kehró:non, eux, faisaient face à la misère. Un rapport de 1842 l'explique en détail. De leurs 97 hectares de terres en culture, ils récoltèrent 750 boisseaux de maïs, 750 d'avoine, 200 de pois et de fèves et 460 de pommes de terre. « Quelques Iroquois trouvent du travail durant l'été, comme conducteurs et flotteurs sur les radeaux transportés d'Ottawa à Montréal. Cependant, leur condition est loin d'être prospère, et puisque l'agriculture est leur seule ressource, de mauvaises récoltes les réduisent à un état de misère absolue ».[47]

En 1843, James Hughes rapporta encore une fois la condition des Indiens de Kanehsatà:ke : « [...] leurs vêtements sont des loques, ils souffrent très souvent de la faim à cause de la trop grande présence de Blancs parmi eux. »[48] L'effet d'une malnutrition prolongée commençait à se manifester sous de nouvelles formes. La tuberculose était maintenant la maladie la plus répandue parmi le peuple. La mortalité infantile était en hausse. Les enfants mouraient de la varicelle, de la tuberculose et de la rougeole. Hughes dit aussi que les jeunes étaient indisciplinés et représentaient un problème pour la communauté. Il suggéra qu'on établisse une ou deux écoles « à une certaine distance de leurs parents et amis, et même de toutes tribus indiennes ». Il dit que « le meilleur endroit serait dans les Cantons de l'Est, étant donné que trop d'Indiens vivent sur les rives de la rivière des Outaouais ».[49]

LES GUERRES SONT DÉSORMAIS TERMINÉES

J'ai vu les O'serón:ni chercher à avoir les Kanehsata'kehró:non comme alliés. Au lieu de la gloire de la victoire qu'ils leur avait promise, ils leur donnèrent des babioles et des couvertures minces pour leur engagement. Les Tio'rhen'shá:ka (les Anglais) avaient aussi besoin du peuple. Leurs couvertures étaient plus épaisses, mais leurs paroles reflétaient celles des O'serón:ni.

J'ai vu les hommes partir pour combattre dans les guerres des Ratihnarà:ken (les Blancs). «Qu'un côté ou l'autre ait gagné, le peuple était toujours perdant.»

Les guerres sont désormais terminées. Les nouveaux arrivants n'ont plus besoin des habiletés de combattant des Kanehsata'kehró:non. Ils ont oublié que des alliés sont égaux. Ils considéraient maintenant le peuple comme des enfants indisciplinés et exigeants. Les babioles sont maintenant perdues ou brisées, les couvertures effilochées et rongées par les mites. Le peuple, jadis un allié important, est abandonné à lui-même sur un territoire qui, dit-on, ne leur a jamais appartenu.

EXCLUSION ET COERCITION

Dans les années 1840, alors que la politique coloniale passait en haute vitesse, la vie du peuple de Kanehsatà:ke atteignait son niveau le plus bas. Voyant et enregistrant la situation qui régnait à Kanehsatà:ke, les Britanniques exprimèrent leurs préoccupations, déplorèrent la conduite de colons indisciplinés et critiquèrent parfois le séminaire de Saint-Sulpice. Toutefois, ils n'essayaient pas vraiment de résoudre les problèmes de pauvreté et de famine. En fait, les Britanniques subissaient peu de pression pour remédier à la situation, car personne, à part le peuple qui y vivait, ne s'intéressait à Kanehsatà:ke.

La relation entre les Britanniques et le séminaire de Saint-Sulpice durant la période précédant l'ordonnance de 1840 fut tenue secrète. Ce qui s'était véritablement passé fut plus tard vivement débattu, mais les critiques restèrent sans effet. La guerre des mots et des points de vue focalisait sur la possession la plus précieuse du séminaire : l'île de Montréal. On ne discutait des Kanehsata'kehró:non qu'en termes généraux et, malgré les observations des Britanniques, on ne faisait aucun lien direct entre la misère du peuple et les actions du séminaire. Ce débat n'allait commencer que dans les années 1870, lorsque les problèmes des Kanehsata'kehró:non devinrent finalement un sujet de discussion publique. Pendant ce temps, les Britanniques s'occupaient du problème au sein du Département indien et de manière galante avec le séminaire de Saint-Sulpice.

Dans leurs négociations avec le peuple de Kanehsatà:ke, les Britanniques, ne tinrent pas la promesse faite par Sir William Johnson, à l'effet que les Onkwehón:we ne devaient être malmenés d'aucune manière et qu'ils pouvaient rester sur les terres qu'ils occupaient au moment de la conquête britannique. Le peuple de Kanehsatà:ke crut certainement qu'il était inclus dans le traité de Sir William, mais les Britanniques soutinrent le séminaire à maintes reprises. Plus important encore est le fait qu'ils n'exercèrent pratiquement aucun contrôle sur la manière dont les Sulpiciens traitaient avec les Kanehsata'kehró:non. Par exemple, les deux concessions seigneuriales de 1733 et de 1735 montrent clairement que le territoire fut concédé aux Onkwehón:we afin qu'ils aient suffisamment d'espace pour chasser et pêcher. Toutefois, quand le séminaire commença à subdiviser et à concéder ce territoire aux colons, les Britanniques n'intervinrent aucunement dans l'exécution, n'offrirent pas de compensation immédiate au peuple, ne lui procurèrent pas d'autres terres sur-le-champ et ne s'assurèrent pas qu'il ait d'autres moyens de subsistance. Ce n'est qu'en 1912 que le gouvernement canadien reconnut que les Sulpiciens avaient reçu trop de liberté pour poursuivre leurs propres intérêts, et ce, même dans le contexte de l'Ordonnance de 1840.

De toutes les manières possibles, les Kanehsata'kehró:non demandèrent à la couronne britannique de leur rendre justice. Le langage de leurs discours était direct, mais toujours courtois. Ils expliquaient les problèmes le plus simplement possible, mais le message était toujours clair. Le territoire du Lac des Deux-Montagnes appartenaient aux Kanehsata'kehró:non par le droit d'occupation depuis des temps immémoriaux, par le traité Two Dog Wampum et par l'engagement de Sir William Johnson. Les Kanehsata'kehró:non (ou tout autre Onkwehón:we) ne furent jamais invités à participer aux comités qui discutaient de leurs demandes et qui décidaient de la question du titre de propriété à Kanehsatà:ke. Même s'ils y participèrent par des conseils et des pétitions adressées au gouvernement, leur opinion n'était jamais prise au sérieux.

Avant la conquête du Québec, les Kanehsata'kehró:non avaient été traités avec un certain respect par les Européens, seulement parce qu'ils étaient grandement estimés comme guerriers. L'époque où les Français et les Britanniques les recherchaient en qualité d'alliés, de guerriers et de diplomates était depuis longtemps révolue. La condescendance avait remplacé le respect, et on ne considérait plus les Onkwehón:we comme des «nations». Les Britanniques réduisirent leur statut à celui d'«enfants» ou de «mineurs» et s'attendaient à ce qu'ils acquiescent et soient satisfaits, alors qu'on leur refusait toute demande de justice. Quant aux Sulpiciens, des gens orientés vers les affaires et qui cherchaient à augmenter les revenus de la seigneurie du Lac des Deux-Montagnes, ils considéraient les Kanehsata'kehró:non comme un obstacle au progrès, puisque ces Indiens n'avaient pas grand-chose à offrir. Durant les beaux jours de la traite des fourrures, le peuple avait été une source importante de revenu pour le séminaire, mais vers 1840, la traite était terminée. La majeure partie de la seigneurie était occupée par des colons qui payaient des taxes au séminaire, mais comme les Sulpiciens le constatèrent, les Kanehsata'kehró:non occupaient toujours une partie considérable du précieux territoire dont ils ne pouvaient tirer profit. S'ils ne pouvaient pas légalement exiger de taxes seigneuriales des Kanehsata'kehró:non, ils allaient essayer de les contrôler par d'autres moyens.

Le séminaire élabora des lois et des règles que les «sauvages» devaient suivre. Le peuple ne pouvait pas occuper les terres à moins de les cultiver, ni construire de maisons ou de granges sans la permission du séminaire. Les Sulpiciens commencèrent à imposer ces restrictions dans les années 1830 et au cours des années qui suivirent, ils essayèrent à maintes reprises de les faire respecter. Ils faisaient signer au peuple des «permis d'occupation» qui expliquaient en détail les conditions relatives à l'usage de la terre. Dans la plupart des cas, on demandait aux Kanehsata'kehró:non de défricher leur ferme en cinq ans. Ils ne pouvaient engager personne pour les aider, surtout pas des Blancs, et pendant ce temps, ils ne réussissaient pas à subvenir à leurs besoins en vendant du bois de leur ferme.[50] En général, les conditions des ententes étaient impossibles à remplir. Par conséquent, le séminaire, déclarant ces ententes nulles et non avenues pour non-conformité, justifiait la reprise de possession de la terre pour y installer des Canadiens français. À une époque où peu de Kanehsata'kehró:non pouvaient lire et écrire, même dans leur propre langue, ces «permis d'occupation» étaient rédigés en français, puis interprétés par les Sulpiciens ou leurs agents. On ne sait pas si les signataires des ententes comprenaient la véritable nature des conditions qu'ils acceptaient.

Les Britanniques étaient parfaitement conscients de l'état désespéré des affaires à Kanehsatà:ke, mais ils ne faisaient pas grand-chose pour corriger la situation. À l'époque, ils étaient en train d'élaborer une politique indienne qui était, en fait, la genèse de la Loi sur les Indiens de 1876. Le territoire de Kanehsatà:ke, il faut bien le remarquer, n'était pas (et ne l'est toujours pas) soumis à la Loi sur les Indiens, puisqu'il n'est pas officiellement reconnu comme une réserve. Cependant, la Loi sur les Indiens fut systématiquement appliquée à Kanehsatà:ke, comme si le territoire l'était véritablement, sauf quand c'est dans l'intérêt du peuple. Le plus souvent, cela fut fait pour exclure les Kanehsata'kehró:non ou pour user de coercition envers eux.[51] Les missions catholiques du Québec faisaient partie intégrante de la création de l'ancêtre direct de la Loi sur les Indiens, le système de lois coloniales développé par les Britanniques sur 100 ans.

Les Britanniques voyaient les Indiens «nomades» comme l'un des obstacles majeurs à la colonisation.[52] Par ailleurs, ils considéraient comme idéales les communautés autochtones où il y avait des missions catholiques. Un critique de la politique coloniale britannique décrit les buts des législateurs.

Pour les hommes publics du dix-neuvième siècle, les Indiens idéaux étaient ceux des réserves du Québec, établis depuis longtemps dans des villages sous l'autorité des prêtres […] Ces gens étaient louangés dans les récits officiels, en raison de leurs nombreux mariages avec des Blancs, de leurs familles nombreuses, de leur participation régulière aux cultes de l'église, de leur réussite en agriculture et de l'abandon de leurs cérémonies et de leurs croyances «païennes» […] Un des buts principaux des gouvernements coloniaux était d'étendre ce modèle des villages indiens du Québec aux nombreux Indiens sauvages et nomades de l'Ontario.[53]

Les Britanniques reprirent le modèle missionnaire français et l'appliquèrent. Ainsi commença le système des réserves, de même que la politique qui consistait à réglementer, à christianiser et, en fin de compte, à assimiler les Onkwehón:we. La Loi canadienne sur les Indiens est notoire pour son invasion dans la vie privée des Onkwehón:we. Le fondement de cette invasion fut posé dans les années 1840. Un rapport d'une Commission sur les affaires indiennes du Canada, de 1847, menée par le gouverneur général, montre à quel point les Britanniques voulaient connaître les occupations, l'éducation, les habitudes personnelles et les caractéristiques des Onkwehón:we.[54] En 1843, James Hughes, commissaire aux Affaires indiennes du district de Montréal, comparut devant la Commission pour répondre à 53 questions concernant la vie dans les missions. Une comparaison entre les manières de vivre des Onkwehón:we et les normes des Blancs infiltrait les questions. «Prennent-ils leurs repas à des heures régulières comme c'est la coutume chez les Blancs?» La réponse était «non». «Les Indiens n'ont généralement aucun moment déterminé pour prendre leurs repas, sauf le déjeuner.»[55] «Dans les cas où il y a eu des mariages avec des Blancs, considérez-vous que la condition de l'Indien s'est améliorée?» La réponse était «non». Dans les cas où des femmes ou des hommes blancs s'étaient mariés avec des Onkwehón:we, ils adoptaient les coutumes des Onkwehón:we. En ce qui concerne le contact entre Blancs et autochtones, Hughes fit l'observation suivante: Les Népissingues et les Algonquins «qui, dix mois par année, sont enfoncés dans leurs vastes forêts, très loin du monde civilisé, sont en général beaucoup plus intelligents et civilisés que ceux qui restent dans les environs de nos grandes villes».[56] Selon Hughes, les Onkwehón:we n'avaient aucun problème aussi longtemps qu'ils vivaient loin des villages des Blancs.[57] En outre, quand on lui demanda si les Onkwehón:we vivant près des Blancs, ou en contact avec eux, étaient «sensibles à l'amélioration de leur condition», Hughes répondit : «Loin d'être convaincus ou sensibles à toute amélioration de leur situation, ils disent qu'ils étaient beaucoup plus heureux il y a quarante ans qu'ils le sont maintenant».[58] Hughes témoigna aussi :

> S'ils [les Indiens de la mission] restaient dans la situation où ils sont maintenant, ils n'atteindraient jamais un parfait état de civilisation; et aussi longtemps que les missionnaires insistent pour qu'ils assistent aux cultes de l'église, comme des Indiens, enveloppés dans leurs couvertures, et célèbrent le culte divin dans les langues indiennes, ils resteront toujours dans le même état, c'est-à-dire une bande de pauvres êtres ignorants et superstitieux.[59]

Les contradictions dans le témoignage de Hughes sont frappantes, cependant, ni lui ni les commissaires n'en furent troublés. D'une part, ces Onkwehón:we, qui étaient en contact constant avec la société blanche, n'en tiraient aucun ou peu d'avantages, tout en devant en subir des effets nuisibles dont l'alcoolisme et la maladie. D'autre part, ceux qui étaient séparés de la société blanche étaient heureux, autosuffisants et généralement en meilleure santé. Malgré ces faits, le gouvernement décida qu'il était préférable que tous les Onkwehón:we soient sous l'influence des églises et de la société blanche. Le seul moyen d'y parvenir consistait à isoler le peuple dans de petites réserves loin des villages blancs, afin de les protéger des influences négatives de ceux-ci, sauf celle de l'Église. Il serait alors nécessaire de retirer les enfants des familles et des communautés pour qu'ils soient éduqués dans des pensionnats à vocation industrielle et agricole.

Les Britanniques étaient eux-mêmes déterminés à transformer tous les Onkwehón:we en des agriculteurs modèles. Toute une série de questions de la Commission ciblait les pratiques agricoles des Kanehsata'kehró:non et d'autres Onkwehón:we résidant dans les missions. Quel genre de machinerie utilisent-ils? Que font-ils pousser et en quelle quantité? Combien d'animaux de ferme possèdent-ils? Réussissent-ils à subvenir à leurs besoins? Sont-ils experts en agriculture?[60]

Le motif de toutes ces questions devint clair lorsque Hughes parla d'éducation : «Les enfants indiens, dit-il, devraient être rassssemblés dans des pensionnats où ils apprendraient entre autres choses «à aider le fermier dans les domaines les plus laborieux du travail, comme labourer, herser, creuser des fossés, installer des clôtures, couper et traîner le bois de chauffage, etc.»[61]

Le témoignage de Hughes à l'audience de la Commission se termina sur une note curieuse. Les commissaires semblaient sonder le terrain pour savoir comment les Onkwehón:we considéraient leur situation par rapport à la société blanche et au système judiciaire. «Les Indiens jouissent-ils d'une partie ou de tous les droits civils et politiques, à part ceux des enfants des hommes blancs instruits, mariés à des femmes indiennes?» Hughes répondit alors : «Je ne connais aucun homme blanc instruit qui soit marié à une femme indienne dans ce district [de Montréal]; les Indiens sous ma surveillance ne jouissent d'aucun des droits civils ou politiques qu'ont les autres sujets de Sa Majesté.»[62] Il conclut en disant que si le peuple indien possédait des droits, comme ceux dont jouissent les Blancs, il serait parfaitement capable de les exercer.

Promesses brisées

Si les Indiens sont pauvres, écrivit le supérieur du séminaire en 1848, c'est parce qu'ils sont «fainéants et naturellement paresseux».[63] Pour les Kanehsata'kehró:non, une telle idée était absurde. Dans les années 1830, après avoir perdu leurs territoires de chasse et de pêche, ils s'étaient tournés vers la coupe et la vente de bois pour se procurer un revenu dont ils avaient grandement besoin. Presque immédiatement, le séminaire essaya d'y mettre fin. Les Kanehsata'kehró:non réagirent et, en 1839, ils exigèrent une promesse verbale du séminaire de Saint-Sulpice à l'effet qu'ils pouvaient couper et vendre du bois de chauffage «sur les terres qu'ils occupaient, ou pourraient dans l'avenir désirer occuper [...]» dans la seigneurie des Deux-Montagnes. Selon l'entente, ils «comprenaient bien qu'ils devaient donner la préférence de ladite vente de bois à leur missionnaire [...] si celui-ci jugeait bon de l'acheter».[64] James Hughes fut témoin de cette promesse et en fit un compte rendu écrit qu'il remit à Ononhkwatkó:wa (Ononk8otkoso) [Ocite], un des chefs présents au conseil.[65] Les Kanehsata'kehró:non vendaient la plupart de leur bois à Vaudreuil et à Como (Hudson), de l'autre côté de la rivière.[66]

En moins de neuf ans, les Sulpiciens avaient contrevenu à leur propre entente. En mars 1848, alors qu'ils coupaient et vendaient du bois, des Kanehsata'kehró:non furent arrêtés et emprisonnés à Montréal durant huit jours. Selon Ononhkwatkó:wa, «douze fiers-à-bras canadiens» vinrent au village pour procéder à des arrestations et menacèrent de tuer les hommes s'ils résistaient.[67] L'inculpation? Avoir coupé du bois sans la permission du séminaire. Ononhkwatkó:wa présenta le problème à la plus haute autorité britannique au Canada, le général Lord Elgin et, avec dix autres chefs et 42 Kanehsata'kehró:non, il signa une pétition dans laquelle il décrivit l'arrestation.[68] Pour défendre leur geste, les Sulpiciens répliquèrent promptement en écrivant trois lettres à Lord Elgin dans lesquelles ils disaient que le bois de la seigneurie était la propriété du séminaire.

Les arguments du séminaire eurent apparemment plus de poids auprès de Lord Elgin que la pétition des Kanehsata'kehró:non. Après avoir examiné l'allégation, il conclut «que les Indiens n'avaient aucune raison justifiée de se plaindre de leurs missionnaires». De plus, Elgin était d'accord avec les Sulpiciens pour dire que le «bois sur la Seigneurie est la propriété du séminaire de Saint-Sulpice et que les Indiens n'ont aucun droit de le couper et d'en vendre sans le consentement des missionnaires [...]».[69] Ce message fut transmis aux Kanehsata'kehró:non, mais ceux-ci ne lâchèrent pas prise. L'entente originale ne stipulait nullement qu'ils avaient besoin du consentement du séminaire pour couper du bois et ils ne voyaient aucune raison de céder à cette demande. En juillet, le colonel D. C. Napier fut envoyé à Kanehsatà:ke pour livrer, en personne, un autre message de la part de Lord Elgin. Il devait informer «les chefs et les guerriers qui pouvaient être impliqués dans ces actes d'outrage [qu'ils] seraient, à l'avenir, privés de la prime annuelle de Sa Majesté et qu'ils subiraient les conséquences de leurs poursuites illégales».[70]

Une promesse était une promesse, et les Kanehsata'kehró:non conclurent qu'ils ne laisseraient pas le séminaire la trahir. S'il leur fallait une permission pour couper du bois, alors Lord Elgin devait la demander au séminaire pour eux. De plus, ils voulaient une garantie: pouvoir vendre du bois à qui ils veulent, ou le vendre au séminaire à un prix équitable.[71]

L'arrestation de 1848 pour la coupe du bois était sûrement la première, mais nullement la dernière. Le gouverneur général avait clairement fait connaître sa position : la Couronne n'interviendrait pas. Le peuple de Kanehsatà:ke savait qu'il devait se débrouiller seul quand il était question de défendre ses droits et il savait que ce ne serait pas facile. Il avait besoin de membres de la communauté qui pouvaient voir clair dans les propos ambigus et la rhétorique du gouvernement. Plus d'instruction était donc la solution. Les Algonquins et les Népissingues de Kanehsatà:ke pensaient comme les Kanehsata'kehró:non et, en février 1851, ils demandèrent au gouverneur général de nommer un agent indien pour les aider dans les domaines de l'agriculture et de l'éducation.[72] En avril, les Kanehsata'kehró:non envoyèrent leur propre demande et expliquèrent sans mâcher leurs mots les raisons pour lesquelles la communauté avait besoin d'un agent indien :

> Qu'ils ont depuis longtemps subi divers torts, injustices et oppressions trop tristes pour ennuyer votre Excellence avec les douloureux détails actuels.

> Que leur situation malheureuse provient principalement de la mesure malavisée de les avoir remis sous la direction et le pouvoir incontrôlés de leurs prêtres en ce qui a trait aux questions temporelles et spirituelles.[73]

Les 14 chefs qui signèrent la pétition mentionnèrent que l'éducation qu'ils avaient reçue les rendait « inégaux pour affronter efficacement les agressions continuelles d'une société en place aussi puissante ».[74] Un agent indien, F. B. Pillet de Sainte-Geneviève, fut dûment attitré pour s'occuper des protestations des Sulpiciens.[75]

Le vocabulaire employé dans la pétition révolta les Sulpiciens qui le considéraient blasphématoire. Une poursuite devait être intentée contre ceux qui l'avaient signée et, en avril 1852, après une requête du supérieur du séminaire, l'évêque de Montréal imposa le châtiment le plus sévère de l'Église catholique romaine.[76] Quinze chefs Kanehsata'kehró:non et algonquins furent excommuniés : Joseph Ononhkwatkó:wa, Joseph Teha8eiakenrat, Paul Sakoianisaka, Pierre Otiokoir, Charles Teshok8en, Leon Nikahian, Nicholas Tekanatoken, J. B. Tedasontionini, Paul Tehanekorens, Etienne Te8enssiseroken, Thomas Oniatariio, François Papino, Paul Chimaganish, Vincent O. Kapeia et J. B. Kikous.[77] La pression exercée sur eux pour se rétracter dût avoir été énorme car, plusieurs mois plus tard, les chefs signèrent une rétraction publique pour avoir utilisé un « langage inadéquat et offensant ». En septembre 1852, l'excommunication fut levée.[78]

En 1851, un autre événement irrita encore plus les Sulpiciens. Peter Jones, pasteur ojibwa, visita Kanehsatà:ke à la demande de l'Église méthodiste. Venu dans le but de convertir les Kanehsata'kehró:non au protestantisme, il passa plusieurs jours au sein de la communauté. Il n'eut aucun succès, mais les Sulpiciens virent cette visite d'un mauvais œil et dirent qu'il était « un individu intéressé à fomenter des troubles […] »[79]

Pendant ce temps, tout progrès en vue d'obtenir un quelconque programme scolaire pour le peuple de Kanehsatà:ke tardait à venir malgré le désir ardent qu'avait exprimé la communauté à cet égard. En 1858, le rapport d'une Commission pour les affaires indiennes suggéra que seule une formation en agriculture soit offerte aux garçons.[80] Aucune école pour filles ne fut mentionnée, bien que certaines filles fréquentaient probablement une petite école dirigée par la communauté religieuse des Sœurs de la Congrégation de Notre-Dame. Le révérend Dufresne, missionnaire sulpicien, qui avait travaillé au Lac des Deux-Montagnes pendant plusieurs années, tenait en haute estime l'école d'agriculture dirigée par le séminaire. Son point de vue sur les avantages de l'enseignement agricole pour les Indiens était identique à celui que les Britanniques exprimaient depuis longtemps. « Le meilleur moyen, selon moi, d'établir des écoles industrielles est d'adopter le plan suivi par les messieurs du séminaire de Montréal qui, pendant quelques années depuis [1851] ont établi dans cette mission une ferme modèle pour l'instruction des jeunes Indiens [...]»[81]

Collection de René Marinier

Il s'avéra que l'école d'agriculture n'avait presque aucun attrait auprès des Kanehsata'kehró:non. En 1859, seulement un an après le rapport de Dufresne sur la réussite de l'école, elle ferma ses portes faute d'inscriptions.[82] Plusieurs années plus tard, un autre prêtre sulpicien, Olivier Maurault, remarqua que le séminaire avait dû fermer l'école parce que les Iroquois étaient «obstinés» et qu'ils ne voulaient plus y envoyer leurs enfants. À cela il ajouta: «Les Sauvages désiraient-ils vivre à ne rien faire?»[83] En plus de les avoir insultés, Maurault n'y comprenait rien. On enseignait aux Kanehsata'kehró:non à devenir laboureurs ou ouvriers dans les fermes des autres, mais pour beaucoup d'entre eux de tels emplois n'étaient pas disponibles, surtout pour ceux qui tenaient tête au séminaire. De plus, les Sulpiciens contrecarraient les tentatives de ceux qui essayaient de gérer leur propre ferme. En raison des restrictions du séminaire, les Kanehsata'kehró:non ne pouvaient pas cultiver suffisamment de terrain pour rendre l'exploitation agricole profitable. Dans de nombreux cas, ils ne pouvaient pas produire assez de nourriture pour suffire à leurs besoins. Souvent, lorsqu'un fermier de Kanehsatà:ke produisait au-delà du nécessaire pour pourvoir aux besoins de sa famille, le séminaire saisissait ses produits. Dans le meilleur des cas, il était difficile pour le peuple de survivre en cultivant la terre. Un rapport de 1843 souligna la situation: «Puisqu'ils n'ont aucune terre qui leur appartienne et que l'espace qui leur est réservé par les prêtres est très limité, les Iroquois de ce village ne font que peu de progrès en agriculture.»[84] En 1858, les commissaires spéciaux firent la même remarque quand ils dirent que les terres que le peuple cultivait n'étaient pas «favorables aux efforts agricoles, étant pour la plupart stériles et pierreuses».[85] La famine amplifia le problème. En 1853, la récolte de maïs fut absolument piteuse, ce qui laissa les gens sans nourriture suffisante et sans grains à semer l'année suivante. Le peuple de Kanehsatà:ke fut obligé de demander l'aide du gouvernement.[86] Si on lui avait permis de cultiver à sa façon sans l'interférence du séminaire, il n'y aurait probablement pas eu de famine.

« Pour les tribus indiennes du Bas-Canada »

En 1851, le parlement britannique vota deux lois accordant 93 000 hectares de terre à l'usage des tribus indiennes du Québec[87] et, deux ans plus tard, en 1853, il vota un décret pour la distribution de ces terres.[88] Près de 18 620 hectares furent réservés à Maniwaki, au nord d'Ottawa, pour les Algonquins et les Népissingues de Kanehsatà:ke, et 6500 hectares à Doncaster pour les Kanehsata'kehró:non et les Kahnawà:kehró:non.[89]

Les terres réservées à Maniwaki pour les Algonquins et les Népissingues le furent en réponse à leurs nombreuses demandes d'indemnisation pour la perte de leur territoire de chasse en bordure de la rivière des Outaouais en amont de l'Original.[90] En 1858, quelques familles algonquines avaient déménagé à Maniwaki.[91] Après de longues discussions et de nombreuses pétitions, la majorité des Algonquins quittèrent Kanehsatà:ke à la fin de 1869. Cependant, un certain nombre resta, y compris des membres des familles Vincent, Merry (Murray), Mingahi, Cemukons, Kapeia et Wabiship.[92] Les Algonquins n'étaient peut-être pas heureux de leur déménagement, mais ils semblaient satisfaits de l'entente en vertu de laquelle ils iraient à Maniwaki. Ils avaient demandé une concession de terre et ils l'avaient obtenue.

Pour leur part, les Kanehsata'kehró:non n'étaient pas sur le point de déménager en masse à Doncaster. Ils n'avaient jamais demandé de concession de terre dans ce but ni demandé d'être déplacés. On décida de leur réserver un territoire à Doncaster à leur insu; ils n'eurent aucun mot à dire sur la question. Doncaster pouvait offrir au peuple un territoire de chasse et de pêche, mais il était inutile sur le plan agricole. À plusieurs occasions, les Kanehsata'kehró:non s'étaient rendus à Doncaster pour voir si un déménagement valait la peine. Ils étaient sceptiques, et avec raison. Un rapport du département des Affaires indiennes de 1903 décrit le terrain :

> […] le terrain, ainsi que les communes avoisinantes, consiste en des collines escarpées et rocheuses, pratiquement sans plaines entre elles. Le sol […] est sans exception une marne sableuse de qualité moyenne, et personne, sauf ceux qui acceptent de travailler très dur et de vivre sobrement, ne peut gagner sa vie dans cette région sablonneuse […]
>
> Il est évident qu'aucun Indien et très peu d'hommes blancs ne peuvent être persuadés de vivre sur ce territoire […] Je ne comprends pas pourquoi il a été choisi [en 1853] comme réserve indienne, puisqu'il n'a aucun attrait pour le recommander à cet effet.[93]

Vu sa disposition, pourquoi le territoire à Doncaster a-t-il été réservé pour les Kanehsata'kehró:non? Le décret impliquait que l'endroit devait être utilisé comme territoire de chasse et de pêche, mais la possibilité de déplacer le peuple à Doncaster ne fut jamais écartée.

Si Doncaster contribuait d'une certaine manière à compenser les Kanehsata'kehró:non pour la perte de leur territoire de chasse et de pêche au Lac des Deux-Montagnes, ils subissaient toujours le problème des fermes et des pâturages amenuisés, en particulier sur la Commune. Avec les années, les Sulpiciens avaient donné une grande partie de la Commune à des colons qui avaient bien servi le séminaire.[94] Les pâturages disponibles devenaient de plus en plus petits.

Le décret mettant de côté Maniwaki et Doncaster fut voté en 1853. Un an plus tard, le gouvernement prit une autre décision qui eut de profondes répercussions sur le peuple de

Kanehsatà:ke : en 1854, la loi seigneuriale fut abolie.[95] L'abolition de la tenure seigneu-riale au Lac des Deux-Montagnes prit effet en 1858 et, cette même année, le séminaire de Saint-Sulpice reçu toutes les terres non concédées de la seigneurie.[96] Les Sulpiciens devinrent propriétaires de milliers d'hectares de terre, y compris la Commune, le domaine, le village, le territoire où les Kanehsata'kehró:non vivaient et cultivaient, ainsi que toutes les autres terres. En même temps, les colons qui s'étaient installés à la seigneurie reçurent l'option de réclamer pleine propriété de la terre sur laquelle ils vivaient. Pas un mètre carré n'alla aux Kanehsata'kehró:non, aucun ne fut acheté par la Couronne en leur faveur.

Les Sulpiciens formulèrent alors de nouvelles règles pour les Kanehsata'kehró:non. Un des articles stipulait que le séminaire avait le droit d'agrandir ses fermes en y annexant les terres de la Commune.[97] Aussitôt que les règles furent écrites, le séminaire exerça ce soi-disant droit. En 1865, il utilisa une partie de la Commune pour agrandir la ferme de Saint-Vincent-de-Paul[98] et, plus tard, il en prit une autre partie quand les fermes de Saint-Isidore, de Saint-Vincent-de-Paul et du Calvaire se fusionnèrent pour former la ferme de Saint-Sulpice.[99] Selon le commentaire d'un chroniqueur, les Sulpiciens n'avaient pas vraiment besoin des terres qu'ils prenaient : « En agrandissant les fermes du séminaire, [les missionnaires] exécutaient des "actes de propriétaires" au nom du séminaire, affirmant ainsi le droit du séminaire sur la Commune et le domaine de la mission [...] ».[100] Encore plus de territoire non concédé devenait inaccessible aux Kanehsata'kehró:non. En 1877, au moins 809 hectares avaient été vendus à des particuliers.[101]

Le peuple de Kanehsatà:ke protesta contre le changement de la loi seigneuriale aussi-tôt qu'elle eut des répercussions sur le territoire du Lac des Deux-Montagnes, mais en vain. Le séminaire regarda superficiellement cette protestation en disant que les Indiens n'avaient qu'eux-mêmes à blâmer. Selon les Sulpiciens, le séminaire avait publié des annonces invitant tous les partis intéressés à présenter une demande de terrain au Lac des Deux-Montagnes. Aucun Kanehsata'kehró:non ne présenta une telle demande.[102] Pourquoi ? Aucune explication ne fut donnée. Cependant, il est probable que, si des annonces furent publiées, les gens de Kanehsatà:ke n'avaient pas pu les lire. De plus, s'ils avaient pu les lire, ils n'auraient pas eu les moyens de payer la terre ni consenti à payer pour un bien qui leur appartenait déjà. En tout cas, selon la formulation de ces annonces, les Kanehsata'kehró:non auraient été facilement disqualifiés : « Pour les besoins de cette loi, toute personne occupant ou possédant une terre sur la seigneurie, avec la permission du seigneur ou de la personne chargée de percevoir la redevance foncière ou d'autres taxes seigneuriales, en sera tenu propriétaire, en conséquence censitaire ».[103] N'étant pas cen-sitaires, les Kanehsata'kehró:non ne pouvaient donc pas adresser de demande en ce sens. Les colons qui avaient un « permis d'occupation » depuis 1830 vivaient sur le territoire avec la permission du séminaire, mais celle-ci pouvait leur être retirée sous le moindre prétexte. En tout cas, la plupart des Kanehsata'kehró:non n'avaient pas signé de permis d'occupation. S'ils avaient réellement présenté une demande de terrain, elle aurait été rejetée catégoriquement puisque, comme un ministre de la Justice du Canada l'écrivit plus tard, « il est incontestable qu'ils n'ont aucun droit au territoire. Ils n'ont jamais eu aucun droit avant l'abolition de la tenure seigneuriale, et ils n'en ont certainement pas acquis depuis ».[104] Les Kanehsata'kehró:non et leurs ancêtres vivaient sur le territoire avant l'arrivée du séminaire en 1721 et ne l'avaient jamais quitté, et pourtant, ils n'avaient aucun droit de présenter une réclamation ? Par ailleurs, les colons arrivés à la seigneurie dans les années 1820, 1830 et 1840 en avaient pleinement le droit ?

M3534, détail, carte géographique de la Province du Haut-Canada, 1836
Gracieuseté du musée McCord de l'histoire canadienne, Montréal

De tous les Onkwehón:we du Québec, le peuple de Kanehsatà:ke fut le seul touché par l'abolition de la loi seigneuriale. Le territoire sur lequel il avait vécu depuis des temps immémoriaux lui était interdit. Un ensemble déconcertant d'arguments juridiques et techniques avait été utilisé pour le déposséder de certains, sinon de tous droits, au territoire. Dans les années à venir, les Kanehsata'kehró:non allaient être assujettis à un nombre infini de lois et de règles formulées arbitrairement par le séminaire. Les Sulpiciens ne laissaient rien passer et leur firent constamment obstacle.

IL N'EST PLUS LE BIENVENU

Je peux voir le peuple commencer à émerger lentement. Il sort de son silence pour protester. En grande partie, le territoire a été englouti comme par un serpent gourmand qui laisse ses petits derrière lui pour répandre la misère et la famine parmi le peuple.

Les Kanehsata'kehró:non sont entassés sur des lots de terre toujours plus petits desquels ils ne tirent qu'une maigre récolte. Les nouveaux venus les menacent et les harcellent souvent. Ce n'est pas difficile, car il y a maintenant plus d'O'serón:ni à Kanehsatà:ke que de Kanehsata'kehró:non. Même dans la Commune, où le peuple fait paître son bétail, les prêtres se sont emparés de grandes parties de leurs terres.

Le peuple a remarqué un changement chez le Ro'kharahòn:tsi. Celui-ci ne partage ni sa faim ni sa misère, mais se pavane comme un paon engraissé, résolument satisfait de lui-même. Agressif comme le blaireau, il attaque le peuple sans qu'il l'ait provoqué. Il a abandonné tout faux-semblant et a révélé sa véritable identité.

Les Kanehsata'kehró:non sont affaiblis par la faim et épuisés par les luttes constantes, mais maintenant c'est la colère qui les mène. Un par un, ils tournent le dos au Ro'kharahòn:tsi. Ils lui disent de partir et évitent tout contact avec lui. Il n'est plus le bienvenu sur leur territoire.

[1] Bureau du commissaire général, correspondance 1806-1812, Centre national des arts, RG 10, vol. 11, p. 9622-10222.

[2] *The Valley of the Six Nations*, édité avec une introduction de Charles M. Johnston, The Champlain Society pour le gouvernement de l'Ontario, Presse de l'université de Toronto, 1964, p. 201.

[3] Bureau du commissaire général, correspondance 1813-1816, Centre national des arts, RG 10, vol. 12, p. 10 223-10 931

[4] Robert S. Allen, *His Majesty's Indian Allies,* British Indian Policy in The Defence of Canada, 1774-1815, Dundern Press, Toronto et Oxford, 1992, p. 140.

[5] Ibid., p. 148.

[6] Ibid., p. 140.

[7] Ibid.

[8] La publication de The Champlain Society, notes de 25 ans de service sur le territoire de la Baie d'Hudson de John McLean, Toronto, The Champlain Society, p. 22.

[9] André Cuoq p. s. s., *Histoire de la mission indienne du Lac des Deux-Montagnes*, cahier 29, A. S. S. S., Université de Montréal, 1948-1995.

[10] Ibid.

[11] Ibid.

[12] Ibid.

[13] Ibid.

[14] Secrétaire militaire C. Darling à Sir John Hohnson, 22 septembre 1823, Centre national des arts, RG 10, vol. 15, p. 11 829-12 447.

[15] Note : Les anciens territoires de chasse des Indiens algonquins et népissingues, comprenant les points tournants des rivières des Outaouais et de Mamawaska, département des traités historiques et de recherche DIAND, document n° 1-11, p. 8

[16] Germaine Lalande, *Une histoire de Bronage qui dure près d'un siècle*, vol. 3, n° 4, août 1980, cahier d'histoire de Deux-Montagnes, p. 11.

[17] Note : anciens territoires de chasse des Indiens algonquins et népissingues.

[18] André Cuoq, p. s. s., A. S. S. S., Université de Montréal.

[19] Ibid.

[20] Relevé des statistiques des Indiens du Lac des Deux-Montagnes, James Hughes, 15 février 1834, Centre national des arts, RG 10, vol. 2029, dossier 8946.

[21] Relevé des statistiques, 15 février 1834, Centre national des arts, RG 10, vol. 2029, dossier 8946.

[22] Journal gardé par le regretté Amury Girod, traduit de l'allemand et de l'italien, jeudi 30 novembre 1837, The Durham Papers, vol. I, Sessional Papers n° 23, p. 375-378.

[23] *Rebellion, The Rising in Lower Canada*, Joseph Schull, Macmillan of Canada, Toronto, 1971, p. 104.

[24] Brian Young, *In Its Corporate Capacity, The Seminary of Montreal as a Business Institution, 1816-1876*, McGill-Queen's University Press, Kingston et Montréal, 1986, p. 50.

[25] *Crisis in the Canadas:1838-1839*, The Grey Journals and Letters, édité par William Ormsby, MacMillan of Canada, Toronto, 1964, p. 20.

[26] Herbert Bauch, *Quebec's Memory*, The Montreal Gazette, 25 mars 1995, p. B2.

[27] The Papers of Sydney Bellingham, Centre national des arts, MG24B25, vol. 2, p. 150.

[28] Brian Young, *In Its Corporate Capacity*.

[29] Robert Christie, *A History of the Late Province of Lower Canada*, éditeur Richard Worthington, Montréal, 1866, vol. 5, p. 300. Les membres de l'assemblée extraordinaire étaient : C. E. C. deLery, John Nielson, William Walker, Amable Dionne, Charles Casgrain, M. P. De Sales La Terrierre, T. Pothier, P. McGill, P. deRocheblave, Samuel Gérard, Jules Quesnel, Wm. P. Christie, Turton Penn, John Molson, J. Cuthburt, B. Joliette, Joseph E. Faribault, Paul H. Knowlton, Ichabod Smith, Joseph Dionne, Étienne Mayrand.

[30] Brian Young, p. 57.

[31] Ibid., p. 57.

[32] Robert Christie, *A History of the Late Province of Lower Canada,* vol. 6, p. 241.

[33] Ibid., p. 242.

[34] Ibid., p. 243.

[35] Ibid., p. 389.

[36] Ibid., p. 431.

[37] Ibid., p. 433.

[38] Brian Young, p. 169.

[39] Ibid.

[40] Ibid., p. 49.

[41] Ibid., p. 15.

[42] Ibid., p. 20.

[43] Ibid., p. 79.

[44] Ibid., p. 169.

[45] Pleine propriété : une forme de tenure par laquelle un bien immobilier est tenu en fief simple.

[46] Brian Young, *In Its Corporate Capacity,* p. 101.

[47] Rapport sur les affaires des Indiens au Canada, déposé devant l'assemblée législative, le 20 mars 1845, Centre national des arts, département des Affaires indiennes, p. 76.

[48] Ibid., p. 77.

[49] Ibid.

[50] Permis d'occupation, Centre national des arts, RG 10, vol. 2029, dossier 8946.

[51] Par exemple, dans les années 1880 et 1890, les Kanehsata'kehró:non furent privés de secours et des services d'un agent indien pour les contraindre à aller s'installer à Gibson. On leur disait que s'ils désiraient jouir des droits des Indiens et de la protection de la Loi sur les Indiens, ils devaient déménager à Gibson où ils auraient une réserve.

[52] Boyce Richardson, *The People of Terra Nullius; Betrayal and Rebirth in Aboriginal Canada,* Douglas et MacIntyre, Vancouver, Toronto, 1993, p. 54.

[53] Ibid.

[54] Rapport sur les affaires des Indiens du Canada, soumis à l'honorable assemblée législative pour son information, section 3, imprimé par Rollo Campbell, place d'Armes Hill, Montréal, 1847.

[55] Ibid., p. 75.

[56] Ibid., p. 77.

[57] Ibid.

[58] Ibid., p. 76.

[59] Ibid., p. 77.

[60] Ibid., p. 75.

[61] Ibid., p. 77.

[62] Ibid.

[63] Claude Pariseau, *Les Troubles de 1860-1880; Choc des deux cultures,* thèse présentée au département d'histoire de l'Université McGill, mai 1974, p. 57.

[64] Sessional Papers, volume 6, troisième session du premier parlement du Dominion du Canada, session 1870, n° 55, document 3, p. 10.

[65] Ibid.

[66] Urgel Lafontaine p. s. s., A. S. S. S., Université de Montréal, cahier 19, La Commune d'Oka.

[67] Pétition des chefs d'Oka au gouverneur général du Canada, 21 mars 1848, A. S. S. S., Université de Montréal, n° 73.

[68] Ibid.

[69] F. E. Campbell au lieutenant-colonel Napier, 1er mai 1848, Centre national des arts, RG 10, vol. 2029, dossier 8946.

[70] F. E. Campbell à D. C. Napier, 14 juillet 1848, Centre national des arts, RG 10, vol. 2029, dossier 8946.

[71] Lac des Deux-Montagnes, sgd. D. C. Napier, 20 juillet 1848, Centre national des arts, RG 10, vol. 2029, dossier 8946.

[72] Claude Pariseau, p. 58.

[73] Pétition à Lord Elgin, 23 avril 1851, A. S. S. S., Université de Montréal, classeur 41, dossier n° 79.

[74] Ibid.

[75] Claude Pariseau, p. 58.

[76] Ibid., p. 60.

[77] Urgel Lafontaine p. s. s., A. S. S. S. Université de Montréal, cahier 10, Les droits du séminaire.

[78] Claude Pariseau, p. 60.

[79] Olivier Maurault, *Les vicissitudes d'une mission sauvage*, revue trimestrielle canadienne, Montréal, juin 1930.

[80] Rapport des commissaires spéciaux attitrés le 8 septembre 1856 pour examiner les affaires indiennes au Canada, Toronto, imprimé par Stewart Derbishire et George Desbarats, 1858, département des Affaires indiennes des archives de la bibliothèque.

[81] Ibid., p. 43.

[82] Claude Pariseau, p. 23.

[83] Olivier Maurault, *Les vicissitudes d'une mission sauvage*, revue trimestrielle canadienne, Montréal 1930, p. 141.

[84] Rapport sur les affaires des Indiens au Canada, 1847, p. 88.

[85] Rapport des commissaires spéciaux, 1858, p. 24.

[86] Au colonel Napier des chefs Iroquois du Lac des Deux-Montagnes, 1er mai 1854, A. S. S. S., classeur 41, dossier n° 87.

[87] 1851, 14 et 15 Victoriae, cap. 106, une loi pour autoriser la mise à part de terres pour l'usage de certaines tribus indiennes du Bas-Canada. Onze réserves furent mises à part par cette loi, y compris Doncaster pour les Iroquois de Kahnawà:ke et de Kanehsatà:ke et Maniwaki pour les Algonquins.

[88] Copie d'un rapport sur la pétition des Indiens algonquins du Lac des Deux-Montagnes, sgd. Hector Langevin, Centre national des arts, RG 10, vol. 2029, dossier 8946.

[89] Extrait du programme montrant la distribution du territoire mis à part et approprié en vertu des lois 14 et 15 Vict., c. 106, pour le bénéfice des tribus indiennes du Bas-Canada, Centre national des arts, RG 10, vol. 2029, dossier 8946.

[90] Rapport des commissaires spéciaux, 1858, p. 25.

[91] Ibid.

[92] Claude Pariseau, p. 84.

[93] Mémorandum de S. Bray, 15 mai 1901, Centre national des arts, RG 10, vol. 2163, dossier 34 070.

[94] Les Sulpiciens offrirent en cadeau à Ignace Rising (Raizenne) et à sa femme, Elizabeth Nims, 65 hectares pour la loyauté de la famille envers l'Église catholique romaine. Quatre de leurs filles mariées à Jean-Baptiste Séguin, Louis Séguin, Joseph Chevrier et Pierre Castonguay reçurent des parties de la Commune pour leur fidélité à l'Église. Marie-Louise Lecomte, mère d'un missionnaire, reçut des privilèges sur la Commune, dont sa fille, Marie-Louise Spénard, hérita.

[95] 1854, une loi pour l'abolition de la tenure seigneuriale, amendée en 1855 dans la 8e section de la loi, chap. 41 de *Consolidated Statutes of Lower Canada*, An Act For the General Abolition of Feudal Rights and Dues.

[96] Ibid.

[97] Urgel Lafontaine, A. S. S. S., Université de Montréal, cahier 19.

[98] Ibid.

[99] Ibid.

[100] Ibid.

[101] Ibid.

[102] Ibid.

[103] 1855, chap. 41, *Consolidated Statutes of Lower Canada*, An Act For the General Abolition of Feudal Rights and Dues.

[104] Avis juridique de R. Laflamme, ministre de la Justice: Le séminaire de Montréal, leurs droits et leurs titres de propriété, Saint-Hyacinthe, Courrier de Saint-Hyacinthe, Power Presses, 1880, p. 120.

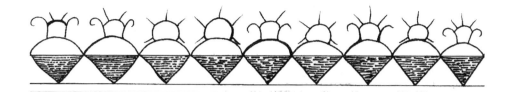

CHAPITRE 5

LE FEU ET L'EAU

PLUS QUE DES HISTOIRES ET DES LÉGENDES

Le jour vient de se lever et je peux déjà voir les Roti'kharahón:tsi (robes noires) parcourir le territoire. J'ai remarqué que cela n'est jamais de bon augure. Leurs pas sont lourds et indifférents; ils ne ressentent pas la terre, et leurs yeux ne peuvent pas voir la vie en elle.

Doucement, mais régulièrement, ils ont introduit leurs fermiers sur le territoire pour en prendre possession. Leur présence ici, ce matin, ne peut vouloir dire qu'une chose : les champs de maïs cultivés par les Kanehsata'kehró:non seront encore une fois rapetissés. Déjà, les plus grands champs ont tous disparu.

Comment le peuple peut-il nourrir la communauté quand on les oblige à vivre sur de petits terrains? Ces Roti'kharahón:tsi veulent continuer à morceler le territoire, ainsi que le peuple, jusqu'à ce qu'il ne reste que de tout petits morceaux que le vent pourra facilement éparpiller.

Les Roti'kharahón:tsi croient que de cette manière les Onkwehón:we n'existeront que dans les histoires et les légendes, et que le peuple deviendra semblable à une ombre qu'on peut parfois entrevoir du coin de l'œil. Combien facilement les Roti'kharahón:tsi oublient ma loi, la loi de la nature!

Même les cendres, qui paraissent sans vie, peuvent guérir et nourrir la terre. Ce qui semble mort se repose et attend. Quand ils croiront le peuple complètement disparu, une nouvelle génération se lèvera aussi sûrement que la sève monte dans les arbres et que le maïs verdit et mûrit au soleil.

RESSERRER LE NŒUD COULANT

Alors qu'ils s'emparaient d'autres terrains sur la Commune, les Sulpiciens restreignaient presque tout ce que les Kanehsata'kehró:non faisaient pour gagner leur vie. Vers la fin des années 1860, ils appliquaient avec vigueur la règle selon laquelle on pouvait agir « seulement avec la permission du séminaire ». Ils se plaignaient que les Kanehsata'kehró:non étaient indolents et naturellement paresseux, mais quand ceux-ci essayaient de gagner leur vie, le séminaire « se précipitait comme un faucon sur sa proie » et saisissait leurs produits et leurs profits.[1] Un incident entre le séminaire et Jean-Baptiste Lacoppre constitue un excellent exemple du mal que le séminaire se donnait pour contrôler les Kanehsata'kehró:non. Un jour, Lacoppre construisit un canot et le vendit. À la « honte » et à la « plus grande confusion » du vendeur, le missionnaire sulpicien saisit promptement le canot de son nouveau propriétaire. Selon le séminaire, les Indiens avaient le droit de fabriquer des canots, mais non de les vendre sans la permission des Sulpiciens.[2]

L'incident du canot visait à montrer aux Kanehsata'kehró:non que le séminaire ne les laisserait pas vendre des biens. Pour empêcher le peuple d'acquérir d'abord la matière première, les Sulpiciens commencèrent à imposer, encore une fois, des restrictions sur la coupe du bois « sans quoi la forêt aurait depuis longtemps été détruite ».[3] Les Kanehsata'kehró:non n'avaient pas le droit de couper ni de vendre du bois sans permission mais, dans la seule année 1868, le séminaire vendit plus de 1000 cordes de bois pour la construction d'une route. Il coupa aussi d'autre bois sur une superficie de douze hectares à La Grande Baie et le vendit.[4] Pour protester contre cette double norme, les Kanehsata'kehró:non coupèrent par défi des arbres sur des terres revendiquées par le séminaire, sans leur en demander la permission. Le séminaire fit donc arrêter six hommes, qui furent trouvés coupables d'avoir coupé du bois illégalement et condamnés à payer une amende ou à purger une peine d'emprisonnement de quatre mois.[5] En fin de compte, les Sulpiciens gardèrent le bois, puis expliquèrent ainsi leurs actions :

> Selon l'entente conclue avec le gouvernement en 1859, à la suite de l'abolition des droits seigneuriaux, le domaine du Lac, qui n'a pas été concédé, est notre propriété en franc-alleu roturier. Il est assez naturel que, pour compenser les grands sacrifices que nous avons consentis, nous devions tirer le maximum de nos nobles forêts. Puisque beaucoup de paroisses dans notre seigneurie sont sans bois de chauffage, les habitants de Saint-Benoît, de Saint-Placide et de Saint-Joseph, attenants à notre domaine, nous ont demandé de leur vendre des terres boisées. Nous en avons déjà vendu quelques-unes et nous sommes disposés à en vendre encore beaucoup plus. Aux Iroquois et aux Algonquins qui se comportent bien, nous laisserons suffisamment de terres pour cultiver et suffisamment de bois pour subvenir à leurs besoins, mais nous voulons être maîtres de notre domaine et couper la quantité de bois que nous jugerons convenable.

> Le jour où les Indiens se sentiront limités sur une étendue trop étroite au Lac, ils pourront alors vivre sur les terres que le gouvernement a mises à leur disposition.[6]

Cette explication est claire, premièrement, le séminaire n'avait pas le désir de préserver la forêt, mais celui de se réserver les profits qui en découlent. Deuxièmement, il prévoyait que même les « Indiens qui se comportent bien » seraient un jour forcés de quitter Kanehsatà:ke. Nous comprenons que ces derniers sont les catholiques soumis au séminaire. Les Kanehsata'kehró:non avaient de bonnes raisons de se croire forcés de quitter leur maison, et le pasteur John Borland, entre autres, ne pouvait pas être en désaccord avec eux.

> Les Indiens croient maintenant que les prêtres sont déterminés à les chasser de la seigneurie et, selon toute apparence, on ne peut vraiment pas dire que leur conclusion est fausse. On amène des Canadiens vivre parmi eux et, de bien des manières, on encourage ceux-ci à réduire les moyens que les Indiens ont toujours utilisés pour subvenir à leurs besoins [...] Par ailleurs, de nombreuses personnes sont embauchées durant l'hiver pour couper énormément de bois de chauffage dans le voisinage. C'est une politique contraire à celle qui a été suivie jusqu'à très récemment et qui n'a qu'une explication : la volonté d'enlever aux Indiens les moyens dont ils dépendent pour se chauffer et travailler, et à les obliger à quitter les lieux.[7]

Borland parla d'un changement de politique relative à la coupe du bois qu'il ne fut pas le seul à remarquer. John McGirr, l'agent indien, observa également qu'auparavant :

> « le Monsieur du séminaire engageait des gardes forestiers dans le seul but de protéger la forêt d'être détruite et laissée en ruine par les Canadiens Français [...] et ils ont à maintes reprises poursuivi en justice ces Canadiens au nom des Indiens pour empiétement et vol de bois ».[8]

Les gardes forestiers servaient plutôt à harceler et à poursuivre en justice les Kanehsata'kehró:non pendant que les Canadiens français dépouillaient de vastes étendues de forêt.

Le village d'Oka tel qu'il était de O. Dicker
Gracieuseté du musée McCord de l'histoire canadienne, Montréal

Le séminaire décida également de réduire à néant toute tentative d'entreprenariat des Kanehsata'kehró:non. Une femme, la veuve Petit'Cri, mère de quatre enfants, décida de louer une partie de sa terre à un fermier contre la moitié de sa récolte. Les Sulpiciens rejetèrent simplement l'arrangement, louèrent la terre à quelqu'un d'autre et donnèrent à « cette veuve autant qu'elle pouvait raisonnablement s'y attendre ».[9] L'homme à qui la femme avait loué la terre était un « Canadien » qui ne pouvait pas, selon le séminaire, « s'établir parmi les Indiens sans notre permission ».[10] En même temps, les Sulpiciens avaient embauché d'autres « Canadiens » pour travailler dans les 22 fermes que le séminaire exploitait.[11] Quand les Kanehsata'kehró:non protestèrent contre l'action du séminaire à l'endroit de la veuve, les Sulpiciens répliquèrent que c'était une « allégation odieuse ».[12]

O'NAHSAKÈN:RAT

Les restrictions que le séminaire imposait aux Kanehsata'kehró:non étaient impossibles à supporter, mais en 1868, ils sentirent l'espoir renaître. Celui qui les aiderait à former une résistance organisée et à affronter de nouveau le système judiciaire canadien était un jeune homme de 22 ans, nommé Joseph O'nahsakèn:rat Swan. Il devint chef en juillet 1868.[13] Peu de temps après, il adressa une pétition au gouvernement canadien, tout en résistant activement au séminaire.

Né le 4 septembre 1845, O'nahsakèn:rat fut éduqué par les Sulpiciens à Kanehsatà:ke et à Montréal. À 15 ans, il fréquenta le séminaire de Montréal. Il fut le premier Kanehsata'kehró:non à être instruit par les Sulpiciens. Au dire de tous, il était un étudiant appliqué et un brillant érudit.[14] Il parlait couramment le Kanien'keha et le français et, plus tard, il apprit l'anglais. À 18 ans, il retourna à Kanehsatà:ke et travailla dans les bureaux du séminaire comme secrétaire. Les Sulpiciens virent qu'il était un bon catholique et crurent qu'il serait un « futur dirigeant sympathique à leur cause [...] ».[15]

Joseph O'nahsakèn'rat Swan
Collection de photos d'Helen Simon

En 1868, O'nahsakèn:rat devint dirigeant, mais pas celui que les Sulpiciens espéraient. Il avait été instruit par le séminaire, mais formé selon les coutumes de son peuple, et quand les Sulpiciens refusèrent aux Kanehsata'kehró:non la vie décente qu'ils méritaient, il aida à diriger la contestation du peuple. Les Sulpiciens n'essayèrent pas de cacher leur mépris à l'égard d'O'nahsakèn:rat qui, à titre de secrétaire, avait fait une découverte dont le peuple de Kanehsatà:ke parle encore aujourd'hui. En effet, dans les dossiers, il trouva un document qui déclarait que les Kanehsata'kehró:non étaient les véritables propriétaires de la seigneurie,[16] document qu'ils ne revirent jamais depuis. Le 25 juillet, ils le choisirent comme chef et, ce même mois, un autre diplômé du séminaire de Montréal et ancien camarade de classe d'O'nahsakèn:rat fut choisi pour diriger son peuple. Cet homme était Louis Riel. Il allait diriger la contestation pour la reconnaissance des droits territoriaux des Métis au village de la rivière Rouge, en Saskatchewan, tandis qu'O'nahsakèn:rat allait diriger celle des Kanehsata'kehró:non au Québec.[17] Les deux hommes moururent dans la fleur de l'âge, l'un pendu et l'autre, dans des circonstances douteuses.

Le courage d'O'nahsakèn:rat lui gagna le respect de nombreuses personnes, et sa mort soudaine le 7 février 1881, à 35 ans, fit les manchettes. À sa mort, il était en santé. La cause officielle de sa mort prématurée ne fut jamais donnée. Jusqu'à ce jour, le peuple de Kanehsatà:ke se demande comment un jeune homme, qui n'était atteint d'aucune maladie, est mort si subitement.[18]

Seulement deux semaines après avoir été nommé chef, O'nahsakèn:rat et deux autres hommes choisis par le peuple, Kanerahtakén:iate (Louis Sanation) et Ohsennakén:rat (John Tewisha), commencèrent la lutte pour récupérer le territoire des Kanehsata'kehró:non. Ils adressèrent une pétition notariée au gouverneur général, le vicomte Charles Stanley Monck, mettant en doute la légitimité de la présence du séminaire au Lac des Deux-Montagnes. Selon O'nahsakèn:rat et le peuple de Kanehsatà:ke, le territoire en question était protégé par la promesse de Sir William Johnson et par les termes de la proclamation de 1763. Les chefs citèrent le chapitre et le verset de la proclamation royale, y compris la clause qui stipule que « toute personne s'étant volontairement ou par inadvertance établie sur le territoire désigné […] pour lesdits Indiens […] doit quitter ce territoire sur-le-champ ».[19]

Les chefs continuèrent alors à expliquer les actions du séminaire contre leur peuple, y compris l'incident du canot de Jean-Baptiste Lacoppre, l'entente de location brisée de la veuve Petit'Cri et l'interdiction de couper du bois promulguée par le séminaire. Les Sulpiciens imposaient également des taxes au peuple « sans qu'ils en aient le droit » et exigeaient qu'il paie pour les baptêmes, les mariages et les enterrements. Selon les chefs, quiconque montrait « le moindre signe d'insatisfaction » à ce sujet était menacé « d'excommunication et de condamnation éternelle […] ». Un problème très important était en tête de liste : le séminaire refusait d'accorder au peuple « des concessions de terre pour les cultiver dans les limites de leur propre demeure, selon les lois, les usages et les coutumes dans le Bas-Canada ». En tout, 119 personnes signèrent le document.

La pétition eut l'effet désiré : les Kanehsata'kehró:non avaient finalement capté l'attention des représentants de haut niveau du gouvernement. Une abondante correspondance commença à affluer entre Ottawa et ses environs et Kanehsatà:ke. Hector Langevin, secrétaire d'État et surintendant général des Affaires indiennes, voulait régler la question territoriale aussi vite que possible afin d'éviter toute confrontation entre le séminaire et les Kanehsata'kehró:non. Il écrivit une lettre confidentielle au supérieur, J. A. Baile, lui suggérant que les Indiens soient déplacés vers un territoire vacant à Kahnawà:ke. Le gouvernement serait ainsi « responsable des sauvages », ajouta Langevin.[20] Pas le moindrement impressionné, Baile répliqua qu'il était « heureux de les garder [...] ».[21] Langevin semble avoir poussé la question un peu plus loin avec Baile. En réponse, Baile se permit de « rappeler » à Langevin que le séminaire détenait des titres de propriété. « En conséquence, dit-il, les terres en culture et les terres occupées par les Indiens nous appartiennent ». Selon Baile « des personnes mal intentionnées » encourageaient « les prétentions des Indiens de notre mission [...] ».[22] Ces personnes étaient le clergé de l'Église méthodiste.

Pendant que le séminaire et le gouvernement discutaient des moindres détails concernant ceux qui étaient les responsables des Indiens, en octobre 1868, Ononhkwatkó:wa conduisit un groupe de Kanehsata'kehró:non à la Commune, planta des pieux sur le terrain et en donna une section à chaque personne. Il autorisa ensuite le peuple « à prendre immédiatement possession du terrain [...] ».[23] Ononhkwatkó:wa agissait avec l'appui d'un représentant du département des Affraires indiennnes. Celui-ci, William Spragge, lui avait dit que « les Indiens avaient parfaitement le droit de prendre possession » du territoire à Kanehsatà:ke puisque les Sulpiciens « n'étaient que les administrateurs de ces terres au profit des Indiens [...] ».[24]

Le séminaire réagit sur-le-champ à la revendication territoriale d'Ononhkwatkó:wa. Un supérieur en colère écrivit à Hector Langevin : « Ce qui était vrai quand notre domaine était seigneurial est encore plus incontestable maintenant, puisque de par nos ententes avec le gouvernement en 1859, le domaine nous appartient en franc-alleu roturier. »[25] En même temps, le juge de paix Charles J. Coursol, accompagné par six agents de police, se trouvait à Kanehsatà:ke pour procéder à une arrestation relativement à une autre affaire. Plusieurs personnes, y compris Michel Shakowenté:tha, furent accusées d'empiétement pour avoir soulevé une contestation au presbytère de l'église. Quatre hommes furent arrêtés et emprisonnés. À la lumière de l'incident dans la Commune avec Ononhkwatkó:wa, Coursol décida, à la demande des Sulpiciens, de laisser les agents de police dans le village pour protéger le séminaire et ses propriétés.[26]

Nullement troublé par l'opinion de William Spragge, selon laquelle les Sulpiciens n'étaient que les administrateurs du territoire, Hector Langevin mit rapidement les choses au clair avec les Kanehsata'kehró:non. Le 20 octobre, il envoya une lettre à Ononhkwatkó:wa, aux soins du séminaire, l'invitant, lui et un autre chef, à se rendre à Ottawa, pour leur « expliquer la position exacte de la concession faite par la couronne de France aux Messieurs du séminaire de Saint-Sulpice, afin d'éviter toute difficulté et toute confusion futures ».[27] Pendant ce temps, le séminaire reçut une copie de la pétition de 119 signatures du mois d'août. Le supérieur envoya une lettre à Langevin pour se défendre.[28] Les Sulpiciens firent très bien connaître leur point de vue, puisque Langevin fut convaincu qu'eux et qu'eux seuls étaient les véritables propriétaires du territoire. Il écrivit donc aux Kanehsata'kehró:non : « les Indiens n'ont aucun droit de propriété dans la seigneurie ». Langevin suggéra que, s'ils n'étaient pas satisfaits de la situation au Lac des Deux-Montagnes, ils pouvaient déménager à Doncaster.[29]

Trois chefs, Kanerahtakén:iate, O'nahsakèn:rat et Ohsennakén:rat
Collection de photos d'Helen Simon

Les Kanehsata'kehró:non furent peut-être frustrés et insultés par les remarques de Langevin, mais ils ne le montrèrent pas. Ils présentèrent plutôt leur cause à Sir John A. Macdonald, ministre de la Justice. Si le secrétaire d'État pour les Affaires indiennes n'écoutait pas, pensa O'nahsakèn:rat, l'autorité judiciaire la plus élevée agirait sûrement en faveur des Kanehsata'kehró:non. Dans un « humble mémorial », ils demandèrent avec respect à Macdonald de reconnaître leurs droits territoriaux, leur liberté de religion et d'éducation, et de leur accorder les mêmes privilèges qu'aux autres fermiers, ainsi que le droit de couper et de vendre du bois de chauffage pour « leur propre profit et avantage […] ». Selon les chefs, le séminaire essayait de faire taire les Kanehsata'kehró:non par « des menaces d'emprisonnement et d'expatriement au-delà des mers par le gouvernement britannique ».[30] Des affidavits accompagnaient la pétition, mais il semble que Macdonald n'y répondit pas.

Au cours des deux mois suivants, durant l'hiver 1868-1869, les Kanehsata'kehró:non désillusionnés examinèrent les options qui s'offraient à eux. Un nouveau gouverneur général, Sir John Young, avait récemment été nommé, et les chefs lui envoyèrent de l'information sur la situation. Ils inclurent une lettre d'accompagnement et le « supplièrent respectueusement d'ordonner au séminaire de Saint-Sulpice de se retirer et de réparer leurs torts ».[31] Aucune réponse immédiate n'arriva, mais, le 18 février, les chefs agirent. Défiant ouvertement les Sulpiciens, O'nahsakèn:rat coupa un orme sans la permission du séminaire.[32] Une semaine plus tard, le 26 février, accompagné de 40 Kanehsata'kehró:non, il avisa les Sulpiciens de quitter la seigneurie et de ne plus jamais y revenir. À cet effet, il envoya une lettre au gouverneur général :

> Qu'il plaise à votre Excellence que vos mémorialistes de la nation ou de la tribu iroquoise ont, par le biais de leurs chefs, avisé les prêtres missionnaires de partir et de ne plus revenir ici, cela étant le désir et le sentiment unanimes de ladite nation. À défaut que justice nous soit rendue, les chefs de la nation utiliseront des moyens pour assurer le déplacement de ces prêtres prétendus successeurs de Saint-Pierre, puisque les Kanehsata'kehró:non ne peuvent plus tolérer leur conduite envers eux.[33]

Un supérieur du séminaire outragé, J. A. Baile, dépêcha une lettre à Isidore Tallet, le missionnaire au Lac. Il ordonna à Tallet d'observer discrètement les sauvages et de ne rien faire ni rien dire pour les forcer à quitter le Lac. Par ailleurs, Tallet ne devait d'aucune manière fournir de l'argent aux Kanehsata'kehró:non ni les aider. Il ne devait leur donner aucun travail jusqu'à ce qu'ils l'en supplient. Baile ordonna à Tallet de ne tolérer aucun acte de « violence » contre le peuple, les maisons ou les arbres.[34]

Baile obtint ensuite un mandat d'arrêt contre les chefs, affirmant qu'« ils étaient venus vers lui [Tallet] agités et armés, à tel point qu'il croyait sa vie en péril ».[35] Curieusement, dans son rapport à Baile concernant l'incident, M. Tallet, directeur de la mission, ne fit aucune mention de menaces. Il décrit plutôt ce qui s'est passé comme un échange délibéré et calme entre lui et les chefs.[36] Le 5 mars, O'nahsakén:rat, Kanerahtakén:iate et Ohsennakén:rat furent arrêtés et envoyés à la prison de Saint-Scholastique. Un quatrième homme, Amable Roussin, fut arrêté « pour avoir trop parlé […] ».[37] Les arrestations furent exécutées en pleine nuit, à 3 h du matin, par la police de Vaudreuil. On émit contre eux huit accusations pour agression et empiétement, deux accusations contre chaque homme. La caution fut établie à 100 $ par accusation.[38] Un groupe de sympathisants montréalais offrirent de les cautionner, et huit Kanehsata'kehró:non signèrent des papiers de libération, mais les prisonniers ne furent pas immédiatement libérés.[39]

Quelles qu'aient été les accusations précises, M. Gaspard T. Delaronde, notaire de St-Andrew, était convaincu que les hommes étaient persécutés « à cause de leur abjuration [renonciation] à l'Église de Rome ».[40] Il rédigea un rapport dans lequel il affirmait qu'une caution de 800 $ était « excessive ». Le rapport se retrouva finalement à la tête du Conseil privé, mais rien ne fut fait concernant la demande d'aide de Delaronde. Pendant qu'O'nahsakén:rat et les autres attendaient en prison, une lettre arriva plutôt du bureau

La première église méthodiste d'Oka qui a été démolie par le séminaire
Gracieuseté du musée McCord de l'histoire canadienne, Montréal

du Secrétaire d'État disant qu'ils « doivent respecter la loi et les droits de propriété des Messieurs de Saint-Sulpice ».[41] La lettre se lisait comme suit :

> Vous devez comprendre qu'agir autrement serait contraire à la loi, et que le meilleur moyen pour vous d'obtenir les faveurs du gouvernement ou des Messieurs de Saint-Sulpice est de vous soumettre sans réserve à la loi, et cela sans défiance.

> Le gouvernement, qui a votre bien-être à cœur, espère que vous écouterez le bon conseil qui vous est donné et que vous rejetterez les mauvais conseils que des étrangers à votre nation peuvent vous offrir, et qui ne vous causeront que du malheur à tous.[42]

Des déclarations comme celle de Delaronde embrouillaient continuellement la question des droits territoriaux. Les Sulpiciens considérèrent vaguement la décision de Delaronde d'aider les hommes. Au grand dam du séminaire, Delaronde s'était apparemment offert comme caution pour le groupe, mais le geste fut refusé.[43] « Que Dieu nous vienne en aide, écrivit Tallet, s'ils sont libérés. Deux chefs intérimaires ont été nommés : Nicolas Tekanató:ken et Thomas Sakokenn, mais ils sont à peine meilleurs que leurs prédécesseurs ».[44] Les quatre prisonniers furent finalement libérés le 22 mars et acquittés de l'accusation de tentative d'agression, et l'accusation d'empiétement fut abandonnée.[45]

Les actions du séminaire obligèrent les Kanehsata'kehró:non à réexaminer promptement leur position envers l'Église catholique romaine. Il semblait qu'aussi longtemps qu'ils étaient sous la domination de l'Église catholique, ils seraient assujettis à l'autorité d'un corps politique et religieux puissant. Dans ces circonstances, la conversion avait moins à voir avec la foi qu'avec la politique. Le peuple prit une décision purement politique visant à briser la servitude que lui imposait le séminaire. Le 31 mars 1869, au cours d'un conseil tenu dans le village, 58 Kanehsata'kehró:non et deux Algonquins se convertirent à l'Église méthodiste.[46] O'nahsakèn:rat, Kanehrakén:iate et Louis Beauvais demandèrent à tous les hommes, aux femmes et aux enfants dans la communauté de cesser de fréquenter l'Église catholique romaine.[47] Isidore Tallet, le missionnaire des Sulpiciens à Kanehsatà:ke, était prêt à se laver les mains du sort des Kanehsata'kehró:non. Dans une lettre au supérieur Baile, Tallet écrivit : « Je crois [...] qu'il est temps d'en finir avec les sauvages. »[48] Selon Tallet, le moment était venu d'exercer des pressions sur les Kanehsata'kehró:non afin de les faire revenir à l'Église catholique romaine en retenant, en totalité ou en partie, l'aide destinée à ceux qui avaient défié ouvertement le séminaire. Le peuple était privé d'emplois et d'aide en raison de ce que le séminaire qualifiait de « mauvaise disposition ».[49] « Aucune aide ne sera accordée à ceux qui se sont révoltés contre nous. Mais pour ceux qui nous sont restés loyaux, ou ceux qui sembleraient dis-posés à le devenir, qu'ils soient Algonquins ou Iroquois, je crois que nous pourrions les aider à peu près de la même manière que dans le passé. »[50]

Au bout de quelques semaines de conversions en masse à l'Église méthodiste, les Kanehsata'kehró:non décidèrent de construire une chapelle. Le nouveau bâtiment servi-rait de lieu d'adoration et d'école. Environ 60 hommes coupèrent des arbres sur la terre de Só:se Tiaokàthe pour la construction, sans la permission du séminaire. Isidore Tallet reçut donc immédiatement des mandats d'arrêt pour six des hommes.[51] Le chef de police Brazeau effectua les arrestations le 16 mai, le lendemain de l'arrivée du nouveau pasteur, François-Xavier Rivet, chargé d'établir la mission méthodiste. Le séminaire saisit alors le bois et le fit livrer à l'Église catholique romaine. Les six hommes, Ononhkwatkó:wa, Louis Kanenrakén:iate, Baptiste le Chantre, le Petit'Cri, Thomas Kastho'serí:io et Louis Tarrenta furent reconnus coupables et condamnés à une amende totale de 125 $ ou à quatre mois de prison.[52] Quelques jours après ces condamnations, un événement inquiétant survint. Il semble que plusieurs jeunes hommes, y compris O'nahsakèn:rat, aient tenté de se suicider. O'nahsakèn:rat fut sauvé de la noyade dans le lac, mais au moins un des autres mourut.[53] La situation devenait insupportable même pour les jeunes et les forts, et les Kanehsata'kehró:non étaient de plus en plus conscients qu'ils avaient peu d'alliés et nulle part où aller.

Rassemblant leur courage, les Kanehsata'kehró:non décidèrent d'essayer de nouveau. Ils écrivirent donc une autre lettre au gouverneur général, cette fois-ci pour demander la permission de couper des arbres destinés à la construction de la nouvelle chapelle. Il ne répondit pas, une courte note d'Hector Langevin arriva plutôt. Le gouvernement disait ne pas pouvoir intervenir dans cette affaire et recommandait au peuple de parler aux Sulpiciens.[54] Pendant ce temps, le séminaire était sur le point de créer une autre règle pour les Kanehsata'kehró:non. Baile envoya à Tallet un ordre interdisant à tout Blanc d'entrer dans les maisons des Kanehsata'kehró:non. Le but était d'empêcher les méthodistes de leur rendre visite, mais Baile dit : « ne parlez jamais du pasteur comme tel [...] ». Baile avisa Tallet de ne pas perdre de vue les « délinquants » et de faire respecter la loi.[55]

Couper du bois sans la permission du séminaire conduisait à l'arrestation de Kanehsata'kehró:non mais, pour eux, une question importante était en jeu : celle de la propriété du territoire. Des hommes furent aussi arrêtés pour violation à la propriété privée et opposition à la présence du séminaire. Ils nièrent être obligés de demander la permission pour couper du bois. Ils affirmèrent plutôt que les restrictions du sémi-naire n'existaient que depuis l'adoption de la loi en 1840 et que ce n'est qu'après leur conversion au protestantisme qu'on leur interdit de couper du bois.[56] Selon eux, après l'adoption de la loi de 1840, le séminaire tint une assemblée publique « à laquelle ont assisté de nombreux Indiens. Les Messieurs du séminaire leur ont déclaré qu'ils [les Kanehsata'kehró:non] avaient déjà été les véritables propriétaires de cette seigneurie, mais que maintenant c'était eux [le séminaire] qui en étaient les propriétaires ».[57] Dès lors, sa situation assurée, le séminaire ne voyait plus le besoin de garder les Kanehsata'kehró:non à la mission. Ces derniers furent persécutés pour avoir revendiqué leurs droits. Un autre type de confrontation, qui survint en 1869 entre une femme enceinte et le missionnaire sulpicien, eut un effet de vague dans toute la communauté. Cet incident a fait l'objet des annales de l'histoire de Kanehsatà:ke, car c'est l'un des plus infâmes qui soient arrivés entre le peuple et le séminaire. Il existe deux versions différentes de la confrontation : celle des Kanehsata'kehró:non et celle du séminaire.

Selon le séminaire, à la fin du mois d'août 1869, Isidore Tallet a rendu visite aux Kanehsata'kehró:non dans l'intention de voir leurs champs et de leur offrir de bons vœux. Il transportait avec lui des images et des médailles pour les enfants. Les fils de Michel Teharihó:ren et de Pierre Karihwí:io l'insultèrent, selon une lettre de Tallet. À un autre moment durant sa visite, il se rendit à la maison de Gabriel Karenhatá:se, mais celui-ci ordonna au prêtre de quitter sa propriété. Selon Tallet, Karenhatá:se était « furieux et vomissait des injures ». Résolu, Tallet essaya d'entrer dans la maison pour parler à la femme de Karenhatá:se, car il la considérait plus souple que son mari.[58] C'est là que la controverse commence. Tallet affirma que Karenhatá:se avait dit à sa femme de frapper le prêtre avec un balai, et que c'est exactement ce qu'elle fit en le frappant à la tête et aux épaules. Son mari prit ensuite le balai et, en essayant de frapper le prêtre, il frappa sa femme sur la tête.

La version des Kanehsata'kehró:non est bien différente. Selon eux, c'est le prêtre qui frappa la femme, et non l'inverse.

La femme balayait sa maison quand M. Tallet est arrivé. Il voulait entrer, mais elle le lui a défendu. Voyant qu'il persistait, elle a mis son balai au travers de la porte et lui a dit qu'il ne devait pas entrer. Il a alors saisi le balai, et durant l'altercation qui s'en est suivie, la femme a été projetée hors de la maison et elle est tombée sur une grosse pierre devant la maison. Dans sa chute, elle a été gravement blessée sur le côté. Comme elle se relevait péniblement à cause de la blessure, très agité et muni du balai, M. Tallet l'a frappée deux fois avec le balai. Un des coups l'a blessée derrière la tête et lui a laissé une marque qui a été visible plusieurs heures […] Même si la femme était très malade à ce moment-là, accompagnée de son mari, elle s'est rendue jusqu'à St-Andrews afin de porter plainte au juge de paix contre M. Tallet pour agression et coups. Après son arrivée à St-Andrews, pendant un certain temps, elle a été trop malade pour poursuivre son chemin jusque chez le juge de paix afin d'y déposer sa plainte. Lorsque tout a été enfin terminé, elle est retournée chez elle et est devenue si malade qu'on craignait pour sa vie. Le huitième jour après l'incident, elle a accouché prématurément […][59]

L'affaire alla devant les tribunaux. Karenhatá:se se rendit au procès, mais sa femme était trop malade pour faire le voyage. Deux des juges, Duncan Dewar, juge de paix, et Charles Wales, également juge de paix, trouvèrent Tallet coupable d'agression et de voie de fait. Ils lui imposèrent une amende en conséquence, ainsi que les frais de cour. Quatre autres juges, qui étaient présents à la demande de Tallet, « rejetèrent la condamnation et les frais ».[60] L'issue de l'affaire suscita un critique à faire le commentaire suivant : « La justice pour l'Indien contre les Messieurs du séminaire est une denrée rare [...] ».[61] Pour leur part, les Sulpiciens avaient une version différente de la décision de la cour. Ils déclarèrent que les accusations contre Isidore Tallet furent abandonnées et que Karenhatá:se fut contraint de payer les frais de cour.[62]

De toutes les confrontations entre le séminaire de Saint-Sulpice et les Kanehsata'kehró:non, l'histoire du missionnaire et de la femme de Karenhatá:se est transmise de génération en génération; de nombreux membres de la communauté la racontent. L'histoire varie légèrement d'une famille à une autre, mais l'essence reste la même.

Peu scrupuleux, Tallet ne voyait aucune raison pour que les Sulpiciens adoucissent leurs façons d'agir envers les Kanehsata'kehró:non. Dans une longue lettre à un sénateur canadien sympathique, il expliqua comment le séminaire dirigeait la mission. Nous permettons « à un certain nombre [d'Indiens] de prendre quelques parcelles [de terrain] et d'en garder le produit, écrivit Tallet. Cette permission leur est donnée sous certaines conditions [...] Le séminaire choisit l'endroit où les maisons et les autres bâtiments des Sauvages sont construits sur leurs terres, et ils ne le sont qu'avec leur permission. Par ailleurs, le séminaire interdit toujours la vente de matériaux de construction pour leurs maisons [...] ». Tallet posa la question suivante : « Après cela, le séminaire est-il censé abandonner tous ses droits, tout son contrôle [...] ? »[63]

Tandis que la communauté devait composer avec la brutalité du séminaire envers la femme de Karenhatá:se, Hector Langevin émettait une proposition pour régler le conflit. Il exposa son idée au juge Charles Coursol dans une lettre confidentielle.[64] Il lui suggéra que le séminaire effectue un règlement financier aux Kanehsata'kehró:non en vue d'atteindre « le but en question » : un déplacement. Le séminaire pourrait verser aux Kanehsata'kehró:non entre 3000 £ et 3500 £.[65] Langevin expliqua que le montant suggéré pour le déplacement « équivalait au montant qu'il leur faudrait pour rénover leurs propriétés existantes au Lac des Deux-Montagnes ». Coursol reçut des instructions de discuter de l'idée avec les chefs, ce qu'il fit, bien qu'aucun montant d'argent ne semble avoir été mentionné. Des réunions se sont tenues pour discuter de la question, et les Kanehsata'kehró:non donnèrent leur réponse : ils ne déménageraient pas.[66] Coursol la cita mot pour mot :

[...] après une longue discussion sur la question et sur tous les points, ils ont unanimement déclaré qu'ils n'avaient pas l'intention de partir; qu'ils étaient trop attachés à leur lieu de naissance, qui leur rappelle constamment les œuvres glorieuses de leurs ancêtres, pour consentir à partir [...].[67]

En février 1870, le gouvernement avait nommé un nouveau secrétaire d'État pour les Affaires indiennes : Joseph Howe. Les chefs lui envoyèrent une pétition lui demandant de « contraindre le séminaire de Saint-Sulpice à mettre fin » aux persécutions.[68] Ils ne reçurent, semble-t-il, aucune réponse. Le 7 février 1870, les Kanehsata'kehró:non, les chefs algonquins, ainsi que 59 autres chefs, signèrent une pétition demandant au gouverneur général que tout le territoire du Lac des Deux-Montagnes soit rendu au peuple de Kanehsatà:ke.[69] Il semble qu'on ne répondit pas non plus à cette pétition.

Une nouvelle lueur d'espoir jaillit le 16 février 1870 quand un député présenta une pétition des Kanehsata'kehró:non à la Chambre des communes.[70] La question fut soulevée quelques jours plus tard pour être débattue. Selon le Hansard (compte rendu des débats), un membre de l'opposition présenta une motion pour avoir des copies de la correspondance déposée devant le parlement afin que la Chambre puisse « donner aux Indiens leurs justes droits ».[71] Ayant appris par le biais des documents publics que la Chambre des communes devait discuter d'une pétition des Iroquois, le séminaire contacta Joseph Howe et George-Étienne Cartier afin d'empêcher toute discussion sur le sujet. J. A. Baile écrivit à Cartier et à Howe pour leur rappeler les titres de propriété du séminaire.[72] Il ajouta :

Il me semble que tous les problèmes ont été suffisamment, et plus que suffisamment, examinés, discutés, jugés et bien jugés. J'ai donc l'assurance que le Conseil des ministres, le Sénat et la Chambre des communes seront unanimes pour rejeter et considérer comme non avenue toutes les nouvelles pétitions dont il s'agit.[73]

Baile semblait certain que les ministres Howe et Cartier appuieraient les requêtes du séminaire, car il offrit généreusement de leur envoyer tout document relatif au titre de propriété du séminaire pour qu'ils les examinent. Baile contacta aussi Hector Langevin pour lui exprimer le désir du séminaire : que les dernières pétitions des Indiens ne soient pas présentées à la Chambre des communes.[74] Quelques semaines plus tard, le séminaire reçut un avis du sénateur D. L. Dumouchel selon lequel la question ne serait pas débattue au Sénat.[75] Même si le séminaire réussit à bloquer la présentation de la pétition, il ne réussit pas à empêcher toute discussion de la question à la Chambre des communes. Hector Langevin, alors ministre des Travaux publics, répondit pour le gouvernement. Les Indiens, dit-il « n'ont aucun droit de propriété sur la seigneurie, mais le séminaire a toujours permis aux Indiens d'utiliser une certaine partie du territoire dans le village de Deux-Montagnes ».[76] Langevin conclut en disant qu'il avait offert de déplacer les Indiens ailleurs, et ajouta « qu'ils voulaient rester là ».[77]

La correspondance fut dûment publiée en 1870 dans les Sessional Papers, n° 55 de la troisième session de premier parlement du Dominion du Canada. En tout, 43 documents en font partie, y compris des pétitions des Kanehsata'kehró:non et des Algonquins et de nombreuses lettres adressées aux représentants du gouvernement fédéral ou envoyées par eux. Cependant, on y omit certains renseignements importants : par exemple, il n'est pas fait mention des arrestations d'O'nahsakèn:rat et d'autres chefs effectuées de nuit, le 5 mars 1869, ni des arrestations de six hommes pour avoir coupé des arbres destinés à la construction de la chapelle méthodiste. La lettre confidentielle de Langevin au juge Charles Coursol n'y est pas incluse, même si une autre lettre écrite le même jour, échangée entre les deux hommes, en fait partie. Les lettres du séminaire à certains ministres du gouvernement n'y sont pas incluses et, tel que demandé par le séminaire, la pétition du 31 décembre 1869 adressée au gouverneur général de la part des Kanehsata'kehró:non fut omise.[78]

ÉTAT DE SIÈGE

En moins de deux ans, de la mi-1868 jusqu'à la fin de 1869, les Kanehsata'kehró:non dépensèrent de l'énergie à essayer de regagner le contrôle de leur vie, de leur communauté et de leur territoire. Les restrictions que leur imposait le séminaire étaient répressives, mais les arrestations, les emprisonnements et les amendes ne pouvaient pas les dissuader de poursuivre la lutte. Leurs ancêtres et les anciens étaient restés fidèles à la terre et au peuple, et la génération des années 1860 devait les imiter et elle le ferait.

Jusqu'en 1870, les Kanehsata'kehró:non avaient combattu pour regagner leur territoire sans beaucoup d'aide. Après, un nouveau groupe, composé de pasteurs et de missionnaires méthodistes, prit leur cause à cœur. Deux hommes, les pasteurs John Borland et Amand Parent, la défendirent vigoureusement. Borland luttait contre le gouvernement fédéral et le séminaire de Saint-Sulpice, tandis que Parent faisait de son mieux pour aider les Kanehsata'kehró:non dans leur communauté. Les deux hommes étaient farouchement anti-catholiques et n'essayaient aucunement de cacher leurs sentiments. Un autre membre du groupe, Beta, était aussi énergique et anti-catholique.[79] Plus d'une douzaine d'autres personnes, tous des membres influents de la communauté professionnelle et religieuse anglophone de Montréal, se joignirent plus tard au groupe.[80] Ensemble, ils formèrent la Protestant Defense Alliance et, plus tard, la Civil Rights Alliance.

Au début de 1870, le pasteur John Borland aborda la question de Kanehsatà:ke dans une vague de correspondance avec les représentants du gouvernement canadien, où il leur demandait justice pour les Kanehsata'kehró:non. Au cours des dix années suivantes, il écrivit des centaines de lettres et publia au moins deux condamnations mordantes du séminaire de Saint-Sulpice. Pasteur méthodiste, Borland travailla comme surintendant des missions méthodistes françaises et indiennes et occupa également, pour un certain temps, le poste de directeur du district du Québec de l'Église méthodiste wesleyenne. Il fut posté brièvement à la fois à Sherbrooke et à Saint-Jean, au Québec.

La relation de Borland avec les représentants du gouvernement commença plutôt mal. En février 1870, il envoya à Joseph Howe une demande de remboursement pour une caution que plusieurs Montréalais avaient versée pour les Kanehsata'kehró:non.[81] Howe refusa la requête disant qu'il fallait d'abord demander la permission pour effectuer de telles dépenses.[82] Dans tous les cas, Howe répondit que la condamnation des chefs prouvait qu'« ils avaient enfreint la loi ».[83] La réponse de Borland au commentaire d'Howe fut immédiate. Dans une deuxième lettre, il écrivit que les hommes avaient été acquittés ou que les accusations avaient été abandonnées.[84] Howe ne crut pas l'argument. Le Conseil privé, tout comme le département de la Justice, avait confirmé que le séminaire était propriétaire du territoire, expliqua Howe : « Je ne peux ni changer la loi ni déposséder les propriétaires, et il ne serait pas approprié pour moi d'en encourager d'autres à contester des droits ainsi reconnus [...] ».[85]

Après quelque hésitation à savoir si les Kanehsata'kehró:non devaient ou non déménager à Doncaster, Borland écrivit au gouvernement pour demander « une juste compensation » pour le peuple. « Le gouvernement, dit Borland, devrait obtenir du séminaire le territoire que les Indiens requièrent pour s'établir de façon convenable et permanente ». Il suggéra que des lots « d'un arpent de façade sur quarante arpents de profondeurs », la même superficie accordée aux colons blancs, devraient convenir.[86] Le gouvernement ne répondit pas à la requête.

Les Sulpiciens avaient leurs propres idées sur la manière dont les Kanehsata'kehró:non occuperaient le territoire. Ils mirent à jour leur ancien « permis d'occupation » et y ajoutèrent quelques nouvelles conditions.

1. L'occupant doit vivre avec sa famille sur ledit lot et y cultiver du foin. Il ne doit ni vendre ni donner le bois qui peut s'y trouver sans la permission expresse du séminaire.

2. L'occupant doit clôturer ledit lot, creuser des fossés et bâtir des ponts au-dessus des cours d'eau selon la loi, de même que payer toutes les taxes municipales auxquelles le lot est assujetti.

3. L'occupant doit payer en loyer aux dits ecclésiastiques, le premier mai de chaque année, la somme de 25 centimes pour l'usage et l'occupation dudit lot.

4. Finalement, le présent permis d'occupation sera en vigueur aussi longtemps qu'il en plaira aux Messieurs les ecclésiastiques du séminaire de Saint-Sulpice de Montréal. Il peut être annulé à volonté et quand ils le jugeront approprié sans aucune formalité ni poursuites judiciaires, et ledit [Indien] se conformera aux lois et quittera les lieux.[87]

Au cours des années 1830, le séminaire essaya de placer les Kanehsata'kehró:non sous la loi seigneuriale lorsqu'il rédigea le permis d'occupation original. La nouvelle version montre que les Sulpiciens essayaient d'assujettir le peuple au Code civil du Québec. Le nombre de fois qu'ils tentèrent d'imposer ces conditions n'est pas précis mais, à plusieurs occasions, en 1875, en 1876 et encore en 1879, ils chassèrent sans explication des Kanehsata'kehró:non de leur terre ou s'en emparèrent simplement.

En plus de rédiger la liste des conditions, le séminaire commença à poser des pancartes sur la Commune, avertissant que toute personne qui coupait du bois pour se chauffer, pour en fabriquer des cerceaux de barils ou pour toute autre raison, verrait le bois confisqué et serait sujette à des poursuites judiciaires. L'ordonnance du séminaire était presque une déclaration de guerre contre le peuple de Kanehsatà:ke; de 1871 à 1877, on procéda à des arrestations de Kanehsata'kehró:non à un rythme étourdissant. En 1871, une arrestation parut particulièrement bizarre à John Borland. Les cerceaux de barils étaient, semble-t-il, très en demande, et les Kanehsata'kehró:non les fabriquaient pour les vendre à Montréal, ce qui leur fournissait un revenu supplémentaire. Ils utilisaient souvent de jeunes arbres parce que le bois était flexible et facile à travailler. Fidèle à sa parole, le séminaire essaya de faire respecter la loi d'« interdiction de coupe de bois ». Quand cela ne réussit pas, le séminaire fit apparemment couper et enlever les jeunes arbres, et quand cette mesure échoua elle aussi, le séminaire ordonna à la compagnie de navigation de la rivière des Outaouais qui dirigeait les bateaux à vapeur, de cesser de transporter la marchandise. Un Kanehsata'kehró:non déterminé à envoyer ses cerceaux au marché se fit un radeau, puis descendit la rivière avec ses cerceaux et le reste de ses effets. Le séminaire lança un mandat, et Borland raconta ce qui arriva par la suite :

> Dès son arrivée à Montréal, il fut arrêté et mis en prison. Après qu'il y eut passé trois jours, on a demandé à un avocat de la ville d'examiner l'affaire. Ce faisant, il a constaté que M. Villeneuve, directeur des affaires du séminaire, était assisté [...] dans cette cause par un fonctionnaire non moindre que le ministre de la Justice de la province. Celui-ci devait se pencher sur une grosse affaire, celle d'une poursuite en justice contre un pauvre Indien qui a présumément commis l'énorme offense d'apporter quelques faisceaux de cerceaux au marché [...].[88]

Vers la même époque, O'nahsakèn:rat fut arrêté pour une troisième fois. Borland raconta aussi cet incident :

> Le chef « Jose », comme il était appelé, a pensé agrandir le petit jardin, d'environ un dixième d'hectare, adjacent à sa maison. Il l'a fait en y ajoutant du terrain inculte et inoccupé [...]. Il l'a clôturé et ne craignait aucun mal, puisqu'il n'était pas conscient d'en avoir commis. Mais un Monsieur du séminaire [...] l'a fait arrêter et amener devant un juge [...] *qui l'a fait emprisonner pendant un mois!* Ce n'est pas tout : puisqu'il n'a pas réussi à persuader aucun des Indiens – même ceux qui adhéraient toujours à l'Église du séminaire – à démolir et à enlever la clôture, on a engagé

des Canadiens avec leurs équipes pour le faire. Puis, une facture de 39 dollars a été déposée contre le chef [...] pour ce travail et son emprisonnement.[89]

En 1872, Gabriel Karenhatà:se fut arrêté pour avoir coupé du bois dans le but de construire une étable. Le séminaire envoya promptement ses hommes pour confisquer le bois, malgré le fait que Karenhatà:se avait conclu une entente avec le séminaire lui permettant de couper du bois à des fins de construction. Karenhatà:se poursuivit en justice le séminaire pour intrusion sur sa terre sans permission, mais il perdit la cause.[90] Plus tard, en 1873, il fut de nouveau arrêté pour avoir coupé des bûches destinées à la fabrication de bardeaux. Il fut condamné à payer une amende de 83,25 $ ou à passer trois mois en prison. Abraham Sickles, pasteur méthodiste d'Oneida, écrivit à William Spragge pour lui demander son aide. Karenhatà:se n'avait pas d'argent pour payer l'amende et devait purger la peine de prison.[91] Selon Sickles, les prêtres étaient très furieux contre Karenhatà:se parce qu'il avait quitté l'Église catholique, et « c'est la raison de son arrestation », écrivit-il.[92] Un autre Kanehsata'kehró:non, qui prit du bois sur la terre qu'il occupait pour construire un petit bâtiment, fut, selon Borland, informé par le séminaire qu'il pouvait continuer seulement s'il revenait à l'Église catholique romaine.[93]

En 1872, un Borland outragé dénonça publiquement ces incidents et d'autres sujets dans une série de quatre lettres à Joseph Howe. Il « examina et réfuta, exposa et dénonça les présomptions du séminaire de Saint-Supice selon lesquelles il serait le propriétaire de la seigneurie du Lac des Deux-Montagnes ». La Gazette Printing House plublia les lettres pour qu'elles soient distribuées.

Pendant que John Borland lançait son attaque contre le séminaire, François-Xavier Rivet, missionnaire méthodiste à Kanehsatà:ke, tentait de démarrer la construction de la nouvelle chapelle. Ce dernier était arrivé à Kanehsatà:ke au printemps 1869 avec l'intention de la construire immédiatement. Il obtint 1200 $ pour acheter le terrain et construire une église. Des gens « de l'autre côté du lac », probablement d'Hudson, donnèrent une cloche d'une valeur de 150 $ pour la nouvelle église.[94] Ses efforts de construction furent déjoués après l'arrestation des six hommes accusés d'avoir illégalement coupé du bois. En 1870, le pasteur Amand Parent fut envoyé à la mission. Il partit en 1872 et fut remplacé par le pasteur Abraham Sickles. Ce dernier essaya plusieurs fois de faire construire une chapelle, mais le projet fut suspendu quand Karenhatà:se fut arrêté pour avoir continué de travailler après que le séminaire l'eut sommé de cesser. Pendant ce temps, les réunions d'église et la toute nouvelle école anglaise se tenaient dans une maison privée.

D'autres arrestations furent effectuées en 1873, 1874 et 1875. En décembre 1873, Joseph Tiaokàthe fut condamné à une amende de 23 $ et à un terme d'un mois d'emprisonnement pour avoir coupé « un grand nombre d'arbres, y compris des érables ».[95] En février 1874, plusieurs Kanehsata'kehró:non furent arrêtés pour avoir essayé de reprendre le bois de Lazarre O'nahsakèn:rat que le séminaire avait confisqué parce qu'il l'avait coupé sans permission.[96] En mars 1875, Vincent Kapeia fut arrêté et condamné à une amende de 2 $ et à huit jours de prison pour avoir coupé du bois.[97] Moses Wiskin fut arrêté le même jour et condamné à une amende de 1 $ et à un mois de travaux forcés pour avoir coupé du bois sans la permission du séminaire.[98] En mai 1875, Moses Wiskin reçut une injonction du séminaire lui ordonnant de quitter la terre où il vivait ou de payer une amende de 1000 $.[99] En juin, Ignace Beauvais était condamné à une amende de 17 $ et à deux mois de prison pour avoir coupé du bois.[100] En septembre 1875, Karenhatà:se mourut et, ce même mois, sa veuve, la même femme qui avait confronté Isidore Tallet en

1869, fut condamnée à une amende de 500 $ pour occupation illégale de terrain.[101] Au cours de l'automne, Pierre Beauvais, Ignace Beauvais et Pierre Catherine furent arrêtés et condamnés à des peines d'emprisonnement.[102]

Les arrestations étaient généralement exécutées sans mandat et, à une occasion, les Kanehsata'kehró:non portèrent plainte contre la police et le séminaire. Un journaliste fit un récit frappant de l'incident.[103] Certains hommes Kanehsata'kehró:non avaient coupé du bois de chauffage que le séminaire saisit promptement. Quand les hommes essayèrent de reprendre le bois, ils furent accusés de vol. L'agent Brazeau et quelques autres policiers arrivèrent à Kanehsatà:ke à 4 h du matin pour procéder aux arrestations. Brazeau ne réussit pas, et les Kanehsata'kehró:non obtinrent alors un mandat d'arrestation contre lui. La cause fut portée devant les tribunaux et, après avoir entendu les témoignages, les deux juges de paix, Duncan Dewar et Charles Wales, condamnèrent Brazeau pour agression et pour « avoir présenté son pistolet » en guise de mandat pour arrêter les hommes. De plus, deux employés du séminaire furent « accusés d'avoir volé du bois d'un Indien […] »[104] Tandis que les Kanehsata'kehró:non témoignaient en cour, le séminaire obtint le mandat d'arrêt approprié contre eux, et les hommes furent incarcérés à leur retour dans la communauté.

Comme la tension montait dans la communauté, William Spragge du département des Affaires indiennes proposa un projet de loi pour régler le problème de titre de propriété. La suggestion résultait de la demande d'un groupe, du comté du Lac des Deux-Montagnes, dirigé par trois juges de paix, John Oswald, M. Inglis et William Morrin, soutenus par 77 autres personnes. Les demandeurs disaient que « le parlement devrait faire voter une loi reconnaissant certains droits de propriété aux Indiens qui avaient été jusqu'à tout récemment, depuis plus d'un siècle, presque les seuls résidents […] ».[105] Il semble que rien ne soit sorti de la requête. La raison est claire : le gouvernement essayait de ne promouvoir que l'idée du déplacement. Accorder aux Kanehsata'kehró:non un titre de propriété pour une quelconque partie du territoire du Lac des Deux-Montagnes était hors de question.

En 1874, la chapelle méthodiste était en pleine activité grâce aux efforts d'Amand Parent qui était retourné à Kanehsatà:ke en octobre 1873. La superficie de la chapelle augmenta du double pour recevoir l'école. Mais aussitôt la construction terminée, le séminaire allégua que le bâtiment était illégal.[106] Le 8 décembre 1875, la chapelle fut démolie; le public en fut atterré. Un débat houleux au sujet des événements qui avaient mené à la démolition du bâtiment faisait rage. John Borland, qui avait encore une fois suggéré que le peuple de Kanehsatà:ke soit déplacé, organisa une campagne massive pour leurs droits au Lac des Deux-Montagnes. D'autres protestants bien connus de Montréal prirent position contre le séminaire. La question de liberté religieuse des Kanehsata'kehró:non fut soulevée et débattue longuement. La Aborigenes' Protection Society, basée à Londres, se jeta dans la mêlée en faveur des Kanehsata'kehró:non. Des dirigeants de l'Église protestante, ainsi que le public en général, envoyèrent au gouvernement des pétitions exigeant justice pour le peuple.[107] On en imprima certaines pour une distribution à grande échelle. Le *Montreal Herald* et le *Montreal Witness* commencèrent à publier des articles sur la situation désespérée des Kanehsata'kehró:non. Le *Huntingdon Gleaner* reprit la cause du peuple et de leur « chef Joseph », O'nahsakèn:rat.[108] La question devint si controversée que le séminaire de Saint-Sulpice fut forcé de présenter publiquement sa défense, ce qu'il avait rarement fait dans le passé.[109] Après la démolition de la chapelle, des représentants du gouvernement se faisaient tout petits et, dans une correspondance avec John Borland, ils vinrent près de le blâmer d'avoir ruiné toute chance de faire réussir un déplacement des Kanehsata'kehró:non.[110] Le *Montreal Herald* avait publié un article citant des déclarations de Borland à l'effet que le gouvernement ne faisait pas tout ce qu'il pouvait pour les Kanehsata'kehró:non.[111]

Aux yeux des ecclésiastiques du séminaire de Saint-Sulpice, la question de la chapelle méthodiste et de sa démolition était « une simple cause de droit de propriété » – la question de liberté religieuse n'entrait pas en ligne compte.[112] Selon eux, la chapelle méthodiste était sur un terrain appartenant au séminaire et, ayant été construite sans leur permission, elle brimait les droits du séminaire. Le fait que l'Église méthodiste avait acheté le terrain d'une femme Kanehsata'kehró:non ne tenait pas debout pour les Sulpiciens puisque, selon eux, la femme n'était pas pleinement propriétaire du terrain. Les Sulpiciens dirent que leurs actes étaient légitimes : ils avaient envoyé une note aux chefs et obtenu une ordonnance du tribunal. De toutes façons, ils se dégageaient de toute responsabilité à cet égard en déclarant que « c'était les autorités policières et non le séminaire qui avaient démoli la chapelle » – « aucun des Messieurs du séminaire n'y avait pris part ni n'était présent ».[113] Les autorités policières ne faisaient que veiller à ce que l'ordonnance du tribunal donnant possession du terrain au séminaire soit exécutée, affirmaient les Sulpiciens.

L'ordonnance du tribunal était-elle légale ? Beta fut l'un de ceux qui soutenaient le contraire. Durant toute l'année 1875, le séminaire et l'avocat des Kanehsata'kehró:non, John J. Maclaren, allèrent plusieurs fois en cour pour une succession d'audiences au sujet de la chapelle méthodiste. La chapelle devint en quelque sorte une cause type pour les Kanehsata'kehró:non. À la fin des audiences, le 13 octobre 1875, le séminaire obtint un « titre de propriété » pour le terrain en question. On ordonna aux Kanehsata'kehró:non d'abandonner le terrain ou d'en payer la valeur, soit 500 $ au séminaire. Puisqu'ils refusèrent les deux options, la chapelle fut détruite.[114] Selon Beta, la signature du greffier sur le document était une contrefaçon.[115] Le séminaire désavoua toute connaissance de l'acte,[116] et le gouvernement ne fit aucun commentaire. Plusieurs années plus tard, la cause fut rouverte après qu'il eut été prouvé que les papiers avaient réellement été falsifiés. Quant à Maclaren, le verdict de la cour n'était pas légal depuis le départ, car il n'avait pas reçu d'avis à ce sujet.

Pendant ce temps, le séminaire avait gagné sa cause. Une nouvelle série d'arrestations et d'ordonnances du tribunal commença. En mars 1876, Peter Beauvais fut condamné à une amende de 18 $ pour avoir coupé des arbres, tandis qu'Ignace Beauvais et Moses Wiskin furent chacun condamnés à une amende de 14,25 $ ou à un mois de travaux forcés pour avoir coupé du bois.[117] En mai, Moses Tharonkiawà:kon fut accusé d'avoir occupé sans permission le terrain du séminaire et fut condamné à une amende de 500 $.[118] Le même jour, on donna 15 jours à O'nahsakèn:rat pour quitter le terrain qu'il possédait sur la Commune et celui qu'il occupait sur la rue Saint-Paul sans quoi il devait payer une amende de 500 $.[119] O'nahsakèn:rat demanda l'aide du gouvernement fédéral, mais celui-ci refusa d'intervenir : l'application de la loi était de juridiction provinciale. Le gouvernement du Dominion ne ferait rien.[120] D'autres ordres d'évacuation de terrain suivirent. En juillet, Antoine Aronhiaké:te reçut une citation à comparaître en justice pour le terrain qu'il occupait sans le permis requis.[121] En août, le pasteur Amand Parent reçut l'ordre de quitter la maison qu'il habitait.[122] En octobre, Thomas Kó:wa fut condamné à une amende de 42 $ ou à deux mois de prison pour avoir coupé du bois.[123] En novembre, Nicolas Kaièn:kwire et J. B. Catherine reçurent une citation à comparaître en justice parce qu'ils vivaient sur le territoire du séminaire.[124]

De nombreux autres ordres d'évacuation suivirent. Selon Beta, trois filles furent arrêtées pour ce qu'il décrivit comme une « offense banale, une offense pour laquelle tout homme de bon sens aurait souri […] ». Trois jours plus tard, en rendant visite aux filles, dit Beta, les chefs virent qu'elles avaient subi « un traitement très grossier et brutal : on leur avait presque arraché leurs vêtements, et leur corps portait des marques de meurtrissure et de contusion à plusieurs endroits ».[125] Trois ans plus tard, O'nahsakèn:rat témoigna en cour qu'au moins 100 arrestations avaient eu lieu.[126] Chacune d'elles affligeait des individus et leur famille, et l'effet des arrestations successives détruisait la communauté. Le pasteur Amand Parent voyait que le peuple s'enfonçait de plus en plus dans la pauvreté et la destitution.

Les Indiens coupaient du bois pour fabriquer des crosses (pour le jeu de lacrosse), des raquettes et des paniers, tous destinés à la vente. On les arrêtait et on les traînait 32 kilomètres pour les traduire en justice. Là, quelqu'un payait leur caution. Quelques mois plus tard, la cour les entendait. Le jury avait une opinion divergente sur un verdict ou les acquittait. Ils n'étaient pas sitôt arrivés chez eux qu'une autre arrestation avait lieu, et la ronde reprenait une fois de plus. Ces arrestations les empêchaient de gagner leur vie, puisque en hiver leur seul moyen de subsistance était les profits que rapportaient les produits faits principalement de bois.[127]

Parent remarqua aussi qu'« il y avait beaucoup de décès prématurés parmi les Indiens. Le taux de mortalité était élevé, surtout parmi les femmes de la tribu ».[128]

L'intérêt et la sympathie du public pour les Kanehsata'kehró:non augmentaient avec chaque arrestation. Des dons de nourriture et de vêtements arrivaient de différents endroits dans la province.[129] En 1877, tous ceux qui avaient défendu les Kanehsata'kehró:non en cour et dans la presse décidèrent qu'il était temps de créer une organisation officielle. Le 27 mars, ils fondèrent la Civil Rights Alliance dont l'un des buts principaux était de recueillir de l'argent pour le Oka Defense Fund qu'elle administrait. John Borland et John Maclaren furent parmi les membres fondateurs. Au moins 11 ecclésiastiques, y compris Dean Bond, l'évêque anglican de Montréal, ainsi que des enseignants de l'université McGill et un conseiller municipal, grossirent ses rangs. Un jeune dentiste au franc-parler, W. George Beers, également amateur de lacrosse, était l'un des organisateurs.[130] Les fondateurs de l'Alliance jurèrent de travailler pour « la résistance constitutionnelle contre toute organisation qui tente de violer les principes de la liberté civile ».[131] Le groupe espérait créer des services dans tout le pays mais, après quelques années, l'Alliance était en ruine. W. George Beers, ainsi qu'un autre membre fondateur, N. O. Greene, faisaient des pressions sur les Kanehsata'kehró:non pour qu'ils déménagent. Mais en 1877, les membres de l'Alliance étaient enthousiastes et leurs demandes de justice non équivoques.

Une publicité considérable sur des événements survenus à Kanehsatà:ke et la fondation de la Civil Rights Alliance avaient peut-être calmé les ardeurs du séminaire, puisque les arrestations semblaient avoir diminué durant les premiers mois de 1877. Cette période tranquille fut, comme il s'avéra, le proverbial calme avant la tempête. Le 25 mai, les Sulpiciens obtinrent le mandat le plus considérable jamais émis. Il accusait 46 hommes d'avoir coupé des arbres sur le territoire du séminaire et exigeait leur arrestation. La police attendit presque trois semaines avant d'exécuter l'ordre. Finalement, le 14 juin, aux petites heures du matin pendant que le village était endormi, le colonel Amyot et 15 agents de la police de Montréal y firent leur entrée et arrêtèrent huit hommes. Selon Beta, « aucune loi ni aucune règle ne furent observées, et des actes de grande brutalité se produisirent ».[132]

Le 27 juin, quand la cause fut présentée devant le juge de Saint-Scholastique, celui-ci inculpa les hommes de révolte. J. J. Maclaren, avocat des Kanehsata'kehró:non, soutint que la cause devait être présentée devant un jury, puisqu'elle n'était pas sous la juridiction du juge.[133] Le 2 juillet, la cause fut entendue devant un grand jury. L'accusation de révolte ne fut pas retenue, et la cause fut rejetée par la cour.[134]

Jusqu'au 15 juin 1877, le peuple de Kanehsatà:ke n'avait pas résisté aux arrestations quand la police présentait le mandat nécessaire, et il avait rarement résisté même quand aucun mandat n'avait été émis. Témoignant sous serment, O'nahsakèn:rat expliqua plus tard la situation à un juge et à un jury :

> Depuis les sept ou huit dernières années, la police a l'habitude de venir en groupe de 40 ou plus pour arrêter des gens au milieu de la nuit. Ils brisent les portes, tirent des coups de feu et amènent des gens sans mandat. Quand ceux-ci comparaissent devant le juge, les causes sont rejetées parce que la police n'avait aucun mandat d'arrêt ni aucune accusation valable.[135]

Après l'arrestation de nuit et sans mandat de huit hommes, les Kanehsata'kehró:non jurèrent que ce serait la dernière. Des rumeurs couraient à l'effet que d'autres arrestations suivraient bientôt.[136] À l'aube du 14 juin, ils se réunirent à l'école « pour monter la garde et empêcher d'autres arrestations », raconta O'nahsakèn:rat.[137] Ils « décidèrent que, si la police venait de façon légale pour procéder à des arrestations, ils s'y soumettraient, mais s'ils venaient comme dans la nuit précédente, ils lui résisteraient, même jusqu'à la mort ».[138] Les hommes firent le guet toute la journée à l'école, ainsi que toute la nuit jusqu'au matin du 15 juin. Ils discutèrent longuement et sérieusement de l'état de siège dans lequel ils vivaient. Avec réalisme, ils considérèrent les options qui s'offrent à eux et décidèrent qu'ils ne se soumettraient pas à de fausses arrestations ni ne déménageraient sur de nouvelles terres. « Il fut décidé qu'après huit années de persécution, il vaudrait mieux mourir que d'être envoyés à la baie d'Hudson », témoigna plus tard, Martin Anonhsawén:rate.[139]

La paix de la nuit fut troublée vers 4 h du matin le 15 juin, quand un coup de canon sonna l'alarme incendie. L'église catholique romaine et le presbytère étaient en flammes.[140] Le séminaire ne fit aucune tentative pour éteindre le feu et les bâtiments furent rapidement détruits.[141] Les Kanehsata'kehró:non avaient sonné l'alarme à coup de canon, mais se tinrent à l'écart d'après le conseil d'O'nahsakèn:rat. Il disait que le feu était un piège pour rassembler les hommes de la communauté afin qu'ils soient tous arrêtés.[142] À 10 h, le colonel Amyot et 15 agents de police étaient de retour à Kanehsatà:ke.[143] Les Kanehsata'kehró:non devinrent alors très inquiets. Puisque dans le passé des gens avaient été arrêtés sous de fausses accusations, à quoi d'autre pouvaient-ils s'attendre à la suite de ce terrible incendie? Les hommes n'avaient d'autre choix que de fuir pour sauver leur vie.[144] En quête de sécurité, ils se rendirent de l'autre côté du lac, à Hudson, où ils se réfugièrent dans une grande maison en pierre mise à leur disposition par un résident du village.[145] À 15 h 30, J. A. Baile, le supérieur du séminaire, envoya un télégramme au ministre de l'Intérieur, disant que le feu était un « acte incendiaire et qu'il craignait d'autre violence ».[146] À midi le jour suivant, le pasteur Amand Parent envoya un télégramme à Ottawa annonçant au ministre de l'Intérieur que les « Indiens fuient parce qu'ils craignent pour leur vie, laissant leur famille sans ressources et dans la misère ». Craignant que le séminaire se venge, Parent demanda « protection pour lui et sa famille ».[147]

Les ruines de l'église d'Oka après 1877 de O. Dickers
Gracieuseté du musée McCord de l'histoire canadienne, Montréal

Pendant ce temps, le colonel Amyot demanda une rencontre avec O'nahsakèn:rat et Akwirén:te et l'obtint. Amyot proposa que la rencontre ait lieu au milieu du lac, et les hommes acceptèrent. À bord de leur canot, O'nahsakèn:rat et Akwirén:te rejoignirent Amyot qui leur dit que la police était venue à Kanehsatà:ke « non pour faire la guerre, mais pour faire la paix ».[148] Les Kanehsata'kehró:non étaient sceptiques. Des avis affichés partout dans le village annonçaient qu'une récompense de 100 $ serait versée pour l'arrestation du ou des incendiaires.[149] En juillet, les pires craintes des Kanehsata'kehró:non se réalisèrent. Un mandat pour incendie criminel fut émis contre 14 hommes qui furent aussitôt arrêtés, soit O'nahsakèn:rat [Onasakenrat], Oheróskon [Oheroskin] (Pierre Dicker), Matthias Thanonhianíhtha [Tanonhianhte], Pierre Ponspiel, Lazarre Akwirén:te [Akwirente], Xavier Dicker, Só:se Tiaokatte [Sose Tiaokatte] (Joseph Denys), Napoleon Commandant Tekanató:ken [Tekanatoken], Louis Larivière, François Anenhrén:te [Anerente], Xavier Karihwí:ios [Kariwis], Matthias Akwirà:'es [Akwirahas] et Antoine Tewíshia [Tiwesha].[150] Amand Parent fut consterné par les arrestations, mais pas du tout étonné. Comme il le dit, « la présomption de culpabilité qui pesait sur eux était forte ».[151] Pendant ce temps, la police s'installa à Kanehsatà:ke pour une longue période; elle y resta du 15 juin jusqu'à la fin août : 76 jours en tout.[152]

Dans les jours qui suivirent l'incendie, avant que les hommes soient arrêtés pour incendie criminel, le gouvernement fédéral entama de sérieuses discussions en vue de déplacer les Kanehsata'kehró:non. A. N. McNeil du département des Affaires indiennes est venu d'Ottawa pour prendre un relevé. Le 24 juin, il envoya un télégramme au ministre de l'Intérieur. « Les Indiens semblent d'accord pour quitter Oka sous certaines conditions – devrais-je tenir une réunion pour déterminer quelles sont les conditions précises ? »[153] Deux jours plus tard, McNeil traversa le lac pour rencontrer O'nahsakèn:rat. Il dit qu'« un grand nombre des hommes de la bande » se réfugiaient toujours à Hudson.[154] Les Kanehsata'kehró:non avaient fortifié la maison en pierre pour empêcher toute arrestation. Le séminaire vit cela comme un signe que les hommes étaient violents, mais ni les habitants d'Hudson ni McNeil ne virent aucune preuve de violence.[155] Au contraire, les hommes se maîtrisaient remarquablement bien.

Après avoir discuté avec ces gens et d'autres personnes de la région, McNeil conclut que le séminaire et les Indiens ne pourraient jamais vivre paisiblement ensemble. « Il semblerait donc nécessaire que les Messieurs du séminaire cèdent tous les intérêts qu'ils peuvent avoir dans le territoire ou que les autorités légales déplacent les Indiens. » McNeil rapporta que le séminaire « ne consentait pas à faire un compromis à ce moment-ci ». Par ailleurs, McNeil dit que les Indiens et leurs sympathisants étaient prêts à déménager.[156]

En janvier 1878, les 14 hommes arrêtés pour incendie criminel comparurent devant les tribunaux à Saint-Scholastique. Vingt-cinq personnes témoignèrent en faveur du séminaire et 23 autres en faveur des 14 hommes.[157] Au cours du procès, le séminaire tenta de le faire transférer à Montréal.[158] L'avocat de la Couronne expliqua dans une lettre au ministre de la Justice du Québec la raison pour laquelle le séminaire insistait sur ce transfert. Le séminaire « est en train de négocier avec le gouvernement fédéral pour régulariser les difficultés à Oka. Un verdict de culpabilité contre un ou deux des principaux incendiaires contribuerait à faciliter le règlement [du problème] et à apporter la paix à Oka ».[159] Le changement de lieu ne se produisit pas. Puisque le jury de Saint-Scholastique ne pouvait s'entendre sur un verdict, les hommes furent relâchés sous caution.[160] Le juge ordonna un deuxième procès qui se tint à Saint-Scholastique en juin 1878. Encore une fois, le jury ne put rendre un verdict unanime, et encore une fois les hommes furent libérés sous caution.[161] Le juge ayant conclu qu'aucun jury de Saint-Scholastique ne pouvait rendre de verdict, le ministre de la Justice du Québec déplaça le procès à Aylmer, au Québec. En février 1880, presque trois ans après l'incendie, un troisième procès eut lieu. Il dura deux semaines. Encore une fois, le jury ne put se mettre d'accord sur un verdict et, encore une fois, les hommes furent relâchés. Selon Amand Parent, le coût des cautions atteignit 28 000 $.[162]

Le 7 février 1881, O'nahsakèn:rat mourut, mais la Couronne ne voulut lui accorder, ainsi qu'aux autres encore vivants, aucun repos. En juin 1881, un quatrième procès fut ordonné. John J. McLaren, avocat des Kanehsata'kehró:non, avait peine à croire que la Couronne faisait des pressions pour obtenir un autre procès. Il écrivit à L. O. Loranger, ministre de la Justice du Québec : « Je n'ai nul besoin de vous souligner la très grande affliction que ces hommes subissent d'avoir ces accusations qui pendent au-dessus de leur tête depuis quatre ans, ainsi que les dépenses élevées que ces procès successifs ont occasionnées à leurs amis, tous les six mois durant la majeure partie de cette période. »[163] Comme McLaren le souligna, le seul verdict rendu fut celui « d'acquittement ». Il ne pouvait qu'en conclure que la Couronne était motivée par « un esprit de vengeance apparent » contre les Indiens. Le quatrième procès, qui se tint également à Aylmer, débuta le 3 juillet 1881 et dura cinq semaines. Le jury délibéra pendant deux nuits et un jour, mais puisqu'il ne pouvait rendre un verdict, l'accusation fut finalement abandonnée.

Tandis que les procès s'éternisaient, le gouvernement fédéral continuait à exercer des pressions sur les Kanehsata'kehró:non pour qu'ils déménagent. En 1878, l'agent indien, John McGirr, travailla avec le pasteur John Borland et des membres de la Civil Rights Alliance pour élaborer des plans précis de déménagement avec le séminaire de Saint-Sulpice.[164] Le gouvernement et le séminaire échangèrent d'innombrables lettres et rédigèrent et présentèrent aux Kanehsata'kehró:non des listes de conditions pour leur déplacement.[165] En janvier 1878, à la demande du Département indien, John McGirr rencontra Baile pour discuter des plans de déménagement. Il lui demanda quel serait le montant maximal que le séminaire serait prêt à payer aux Indiens pour le territoire que ceux-ci revendiquaient et occupaient. Baile répondit qu'il préférait se rendre à Ottawa pour discuter de cette question particulière « car il ne voulait pas le faire par écrit ».[166] Au bout de deux mois, le séminaire avait offert 20 000 $ aux Kanehsata'kehró:non pour abandonner le Lac des Deux-Montagnes et déménager sur l'île Cockburn. Ceux-ci refusèrent l'offre, car « le montant n'était pas suffisant pour les compenser de leurs intérêts dans ces terres ».[167]

Alors que ces négociations avaient lieu, les Kanehsata'kehró:non tentaient de présenter une cause type devant les tribunaux. Leur avocat, J. J. McLaren, avait l'intention d'utiliser la cause de la démolition de l'Église protestante dans ce but, mais il subit de multiples retards, parce que l'avocat du séminaire faisait durer le processus pour empêcher l'audience de toute cause type, et ce même s'il y avait déjà consenti. Dans une lettre à L. Vankoughnet, surintendant général adjoint des Affaires indiennes, McLaren écrivit :

> Cependant, l'avocat du séminaire a maintes fois exprimé son intention d'empêcher qu'une décision sur le bien-fondé de la cause soit prise. Celle-ci a été retardée de plus de huit mois parce qu'il a interjeté appel à la suite de la décision du juge Bélanger qui déclarait qu'un document sur l'un des papiers déposés par le séminaire, et qui prétendait être le document du protonotaire de la cour, avait été falsifié.[168]

McLaren poursuivit en disant qu'il y avait eu non-lieu lors de l'appel, mais que l'avocat du séminaire allait tout probablement en déposer un autre. Il ajouta « [...] il est très difficile de progresser dans une cause compliquée comme celle-là quand le parti opposé a les moyens et le désir de la bloquer par des appels ».[169] Apparemment, le gouvernement n'appuyait pas l'idée d'une cause type et préférait plutôt faire avancer celle d'un déplacement. Le Département était d'avis que le peuple de Kanehsatà:ke et leurs sympathisants avaient eu plusieurs occasions de présenter une cause type devant les tribunaux et que, s'ils ne l'avaient pas déjà fait, c'était parce que « leur conseiller ne pense pas qu'une telle poursuite réussisse ».[170] L'agent indien, John McGirr, blama les membres de la Civil Rights Alliance pour le refus des Kanehsata'kehró:non des 20 000 $ offerts par le séminaire. « Il est assez évident que l'Alliance est résolue à garder les Indiens à Deux-Montagnes et à défendre leurs revendications territoriales, sauf [si] le séminaire leur offre un montant beaucoup plus important [...] ».[171]

Pendant ce temps, O'nahsakèn:rat, qui avait été envoyé à Kahnawà:ke par la mission méthodiste, reçut régulièrement des visites de N. O. Greene de la Civil Rights Alliance. Épuisé par les nombreux procès et isolé de son peuple, O'nahsakèn:rat signa finalement, avec deux autres chefs, un document rédigé par Greene, acceptant le déplacement.[172]

Le séminaire renouvela son interdiction de couper du bois et l'étendit encore davantage. Les Sulpiciens refusèrent de permettre au peuple de couper du bois, pour quelque raison que ce soit. Plusieurs Kanehsata'kehró:non demandèrent au gouvernement d'intervenir auprès du séminaire en leur faveur, mais le gouvernement s'y refusa. En octobre 1878, le séminaire commença à démolir des maisons construites avec du bois coupé sans sa permission.[173] Les Kanehsata'kehró:non étaient poussés à la limite de leur patience et de leur endurance. Ils avertirent McGirr que, si d'autres maisons étaient détruites, ils prendraient les armes.[174]

Le séminaire continua à aggraver les tensions dans la communauté. En novembre, il permit à l'un de ses employés, M. Fauteux, de couper des arbres et de construire une maison sur le terrain de Xavier Etienne.[175] John McGirr, l'agent indien, écrivit au supérieur du séminaire pour lui exprimer son désir qu'il y ait « le moins d'interférence possible avec les occupants indiens […] jusqu'à ce qu'une décision soit finalement prise […] concernant les droits respectifs des Indiens et du séminaire […] ».[176] Le séminaire ne tint pas compte de la requête de McGirr. Les Sulpiciens semblaient chercher la confrontation quand, en 1879, ils commencèrent à couper des arbres sur les terres où vivaient les Kanehsata'kehró:non. En février, le séminaire fit couper des arbres sur le terrain d'une femme Kanehsata'kehró:non[177] et, en avril, ils rasèrent toute l'érablière de Peter Decaire. En tout, 11 hectares d'érables disparurent. Decaire avait travaillé dans ce boisé pendant 28 ans et en tirait un bon revenu.[178] En décembre, le séminaire s'empara simplement du terrain de Simon Cook et y construisit une maison et une étable.[179] Les représentants du gouvernement, sur le point de préparer une cause type sur la question de titre de propriété, ne firent rien concernant ces trois incidents. De nombreuses années s'écoulèrent avant que cette cause passe par le système judiciaire canadien. Le gouvernement, dont l'unique solution au problème était d'exercer des pressions sur les Kanehsata'kehró:non pour qu'ils déménagent, espérait de toute évidence qu'une cause type ne soit pas nécessaire.

Des années de « persécution », comme Kanerahtáken:iate le décrivit, avaient brisé son esprit. Plusieurs autres Kanehsata'kehró:non étaient au bord du désespoir. En août 1881, comme le juge concluait les poursuites de l'incendie de l'église, le gouvernement fédéral agissait rapidement pour mettre les plans de déménagement en ordre. Trois mois plus tard, un groupe de familles emballaient leurs affaires et remontaient la rivière vers une autre terre où ils espéraient vivre une nouvelle vie exempte de harcèlement, d'arrestations, de controverse religieuse et d'insécurité financière. Une réserve que le peuple allait plus tard appeler « Wahta » avait été mise de côté pour eux à Muskoka, en Ontario. Le gouvernement assura au peuple de Kanehsatà:ke que, grâce à la Loi sur les Indiens qui les protégerait, alors qu'elle ne le pouvait pas auparavant, il pourrait mener une vie saine et productive à cet endroit.

Après presque 30 ans, le gouvernement avait finalement poussé quelques Kanehsata'kehró:non à déménager. La décision de partir mit un terme au long et tortueux processus sur le déplacement. Au cours de ce processus, les autorités britanniques et canadiennes avaient exploré pratiquement toutes les possibilités dans tout le pays pour inciter le peuple à quitter Kanehsatà:ke. La toute première suggestion avancée par le séminaire en 1781 pour que les Kanehsata'kehró:non déménagent à Saint-Régis avait été totalement rejetée par le peuple.[180] En 1840, une deuxième proposition soumise par les autorités britanniques pour déplacer le peuple à l'île Manitoulin mourut dans l'œuf avant même de démarrer. En 1853, Doncaster fut mis de côté pour le peuple. À la fin des années 1860, quand les Algonquins et les Népissingues partirent pour Maniwaki, quelques Kanehsata'kehró:non quittèrent la communauté pour s'installer à Hull,[181] mais le groupe en fut plus tard expulsé. En 1871, Georges-Étienne Cartier suggéra un déplacement dans les Territoires du Nord-Ouest.[182] En 1875, un territoire à Mattawan, en Ontario, fut considéré,[183] mais l'idée fut rapidement abandonnée. Une autre suggestion, un territoire au Québec sur la rivière Rouge, dans le comté de Montcalm, fut en même temps mise de l'avant.[184] En 1878, une proposition fut encore soumise pour un déplacement sur l'île de Manitoulin, mais cette idée fut abandonnée pour un déménagement à l'île Cockburn, à la frontière du Manitoba.[185] En 1879, une suggestion, un territoire entre le lac Kippewa et la rivière des Outaouais, fut présentée[186] et, en 1881, les gouvernements de l'Ontario et du Canada s'entendirent finalement sur un territoire à Muskoka.

À l'hiver 1721, le peuple de Kanehsatà:ke se tenait sur les rives du Lac des Deux-Montagnes pour accueillir les prêtres de Saint-Sulpice dans leur communauté et partager avec eux le territoire et toutes ses richesses. En octobre 1881, il se tenait au même endroit, contemplant son passé et son avenir. Pendant des milliers d'années, ce territoire, l'eau, le ciel et la montagne lui avaient donné la vie. Pour certains Kanehsata'kehró:non, tout cela était sur le point de prendre fin, mais pour d'autres, rien, ni le gouvernement ni le séminaire de Saint-Sulpice ne les sépareraient de l'attachement qui les liait à cette terre.

Origine du nom du village d'Oka

Chaque automne, les Kanehsata'kehró:non partaient pour la chasse, mais seulement après avoir récolté tout leur maïs. Ils le décortiquaient, en nattaient les extrémités, puis les attachaient ensemble et les suspendaient pour les faire sécher. Tout le village participait, après quoi les hommes partaient à la chasse au fin fond des bois. Ils chassaient tout l'hiver et revenaient au printemps. À cette époque, ils se déplaçaient en canot et rentraient quand il n'y avait plus de glace sur les rivières et les ruisseaux. Ils revenaient au Lac des Deux-Montagnes où nous vivons encore aujourd'hui, puis ils se nourrissaient du maïs qu'ils avaient récolté l'année précédente. C'est ce qu'ils faisaient chaque année.

Il y avait un Français qui suivait les Kanehsata'kehró:non et vivait parmi eux; il s'appelait Oka. Il était marié à une femme indienne qui, dit-on, était une des Ratirontaks (Algonquins). Le couple avait un jeune enfant. Cet homme, Oka, ne savait pas chasser, mais il suivait le peuple dans les territoires de chasse d'hiver. Arrivé au lieu de chasse, il se fit un abri comme les autres, mais son abri était assez éloigné d'eux. Oka ne réussissait pas à attraper quoi que ce soit à manger et, durant l'hiver, sa famille commença à avoir très faim. Il dit à sa femme : « Demain, si je n'attrape rien, nous mangerons notre enfant. » La femme lui répondit qu'elle ne lui permettrait pas de tuer leur fille pour qu'ils la mangent. Elle préférerait qu'ils meurent tous ensemble plutôt que de manger leur petite fille, mais il lui dit : « Non, c'est ce que nous ferons. »

Le jour suivant, il retourna chasser, mais n'attrapa toujours rien. Quand il revint, il envoya sa fille chercher de l'eau. Elle ne savait pas qu'à son retour, il allait la tuer. Quand la fillette revint avec l'eau, elle raconta à son père que quelque chose était pris à l'endroit où elle était allée chercher l'eau. Ne l'ayant pas crue, il lui commanda d'y retourner et d'aller chercher d'autre eau. Elle lui dit pour la troisième fois qu'un animal y était pris.

Le Français décida qu'il y avait assez d'eau et que le temps était venu de tuer sa fille. La mère s'enfuit car elle ne voulait pas voir ce qu'il allait faire à sa fille. Elle courut et courut même si elle était faible et affamée. Oka tua sa fille et la mangea. Après cela, il vit qu'un chevreuil était pris où ils puisaient leur eau. Mais il était trop tard : il avait déjà tué sa propre fille. Il alla donc à la recherche de sa femme.

Pendant ce temps, quelques chasseurs avaient trouvé la pauvre femme affamée. Comme elle était mourante, ils la ramenèrent au camp et la ranimèrent. Elle raconta aux chasseurs que son mari avait tué et mangé leur fille, et qu'elle avait refusé d'y participer. Plus tard, le mari arriva au camp et la trouva, mais elle refusa de retourner avec lui. Les autres virent que cet homme avait les yeux vitreux et la bouche tachée de sang qui ne partirait jamais.

Au printemps, les chasseurs retournèrent à Kanehsatà:ke, et quand les gens entendirent ce qu'Oka avait fait, ils furent vraiment étonnés. À partir de ce moment, le peuple appela le village Oka, parce que c'est l'endroit d'où venait cet homme et où il avait fait cette chose terrible. C'est ainsi que les événements se sont produits : il tua sa fille et la mangea.

Ma grand-mère a dit qu'elle a déjà vu cet homme. Il gardait un linge sur sa bouche pour cacher les taches de sang. Il avait honte de ce qu'il avait fait.[187] Ne croyez jamais qu'Oka était un Indien, il n'en était pas un.[188]

[1] Pétition des Iroquois du Lac des Deux-Montagnes à l'honorable vicomte Charles Stanley Monck, 8 août 1868, Centre national des arts, RG 10, vol. 2029, dossier 8946.

[2] J. A. Baile à l'honorable Hector Langevin, secrétaire d'État, 9 novembre 1869, RG 10, vol. 2029, dossier 8946.

[3] Ibid.

[4] Urgel Lafontaine p. s. s. cahier 11, p. 160, 161.

[5] J. A. Baile à l'honorable Joseph Howe, secrétaire d'État, 23 janvier 1871, RG 10, vol. 2029, dossier 8946.

[6] Ibid.

[7] John Borland à Lord Lisgar, gouverneur général du Canada, 3 novembre 1870, A. S. S. S., classeur 41, n° 127.

[8] John McGirr à l'honorable surintendant général des Affaires indiennes, 19 janvier 1878, RG 10, vol. 2033, dossier 8946-1, pt. 1.

[9] J. A. Baile à Hector Langevin, 9 novembre 1868, RG 10, vol. 2029, dossier 8946.

[10] Ibid.

[11] Pétition des Iroquois du Lac des Deux-Montagnes à l'honorable vicomte Charles Stanley, 8 août 1868, Centre national des arts, RG 10, vol. 2029, dossier 8946.

[12] Baile à Langevin, 9 novembre 1868, RG 10, vol. 2029, dossier 8946.

[13] Dictionnaire biographique du Canada, volume XI 1881-1890, Presses de l'université de Toronto, p. 655.

[14] Ibid.

[15] Ibid.

[16] Selon l'histoire orale de Kanehsatà:ke.

[17] Brian Young, p. 162.

[18] Beaucoup de personnes à Kanehsatà:ke soupçonnent qu'O'nahsakèn:rat ait été tué à cause de ses activités. Cependant, bien des gens ne savent peut-être pas qu'à au moins une autre occasion, O'nahsakèn:rat a tenté de se suicider. Il se peut qu'à cette occasion, vaincu par les circonstances, Joseph Swan se soit enlevé la vie. Pariseau p. 91.

[19] Pétition des Iroquois du Lac des Deux-Montagnes à l'honorable vicomte Charles Stanley Monck, 8 août 1868, Centre national des arts, RG 10, vol. 2029, dossier 8946.

[20] Claude Pariseau, *Les troubles de 1860-1880, choc de deux cultures*, thèse présentée au département d'histoire de l'Université McGill, p. 75.

[21] Urgel Lafontaine p. s. s., *Les Droits du Séminaire*, cahier 11, lettre de J. A. Baile à l'honorable H. Langevin, 7 septembre 1868, A. S. S. S., Université de Montréal.

[22] J. A. Baile à l'honorable Hector Langevin, 9 novembre 1868, Centre national des arts, RG 10, vol. 2029, dossier 8946.

[23] Charles J. Coursol à l'honorable Gédéon Ouimet, 15 octobre 1868, Centre national des arts, RG 10, vol. 2029, dossier 8946 (voir le glossaire pour la bonne épellation des noms Mohawk).

[24] Ibid.

[25] J. A. Baile à l'honorable Hector Langevin, 9 novembre 1868, RG 10, vol. 2029, dossier 8946.

[26] Charles J. Coursol à Gédéon Ouimet, 15 octobre 1868, RG 10, vol. 2029, dossier 8946.

[27] Hector Langevin à Ononkwatkó:wa, 20 octobre 1868, Centre national des arts, RG 10, vol. 2029, dossier 8946.

[28] Baile à Langevin, 9 novembre 1868, RG10, vol. 2029, dossier 8964.

[29] Hector Langevin à Atonsa Sakokeni, Atonsa Retsitonsenio, Ignace Toniontakoen, Michel Shakowenté:tha et d'autres, 9 décembre 1868, Centre national des arts, RG 10, vol. 2029, dossier 8946.

[30] À l'honorable Sir John A. Macdonald, mémorial des chefs indiens et des Iroquois du Lac des Deux-Montagnes, 10 décembre 1868, RG 10, vol. 2029, dossier 8946.

[31] À Sir John Young, gouverneur général, de Só:se O'nahsakén:rat, Louis Kanerahkén:iate et John Ohsennakén:rat, 8 février 1869, Centre national des arts, RG 10, vol. 2029, dossier 8946.

[32] Dictionnaire biographique du Canada, p. 655.

[33] Au gouverneur général de Joseph O'nahsakén:rat, Louis Kanerahkén:iate, Jean Ohsennakén:rat, 26 février 1869, RG 10, vol. 2029, dossier 8946.

[34] J. A. Baile à Tallet, 28 février 1869, cahier 11, p. 124,125, A. S. S. S. Université de Montréal.

[35] À Lord Lisgar, gouverneur général, de John Borland, 3 novembre 1870, papiers du séminaire n° 127.

[36] Procès verbal de l'entrevue de M. Tallet, p. s. s., directeur de la mission du Lac des Deux-Montagnes, avec les chefs Iroquois qui demandent le départ des missionnaires, 26 février 1869, A. S. S. S., classeur 41, n° 108.

[37] Urgel Lafontaine p. s. s., Procès des Indiens 1877, cahier 1, A. S. S. S., Université de Montréal.

[38] Claude Pariseau, p. 88.

[39] Ibid.

[40] Affidavit M. G. T. Delaronde, N. P., 18 mars 1869, D. Dewar, juge de paix, témoin, Centre national des arts, RG 10, vol. 2029, dossier 8946.

[41] E. Parent à Joseph O'nahsakèn:rat et à d'autres chefs, 15 mars 1869, Centre national des arts, RG 10, vol. 2029, dossier 8946.

[42] E. Parent aux Iroquois d'Oka, 26 février 1869, Centre national des arts, RG 10, vol. 2029, dossier 8946.

[43] M. G. T. Delaronde, 18 mars 1869, Centre national des arts, RG 10, vol. 2029, dossier 8946.

[44] Urgel Lafontaine p. s. s., *Les Droits du Séminaire*, cahier 11, lettre de M. Tallet à M. Arrand, 11 mars 1869, A. S. S. S., Université de Montréal.

[45] Claude Pariseau, p. 89.

[46] Claude Pariseau, p. 89.

[47] Ibid.

[48] Ibid.

[49] Baile à Tallet, 6 mai 1869, cahier 12, Urgel Lafontaine, A. S. S. S. Université de Montréal.

[50] Ibid.

[51] J. A. Baile à l'honorable Joseph Howe, 23 janvier 1871, RG 10, vol. 2029, dossier 8946.

[52] Claude Pariseau, p. 93, 94.

[53] Tallet à Baile, 25 mai 1869, cahier 12, Urgel Lafontaine, A. S. S. S. Université de Montréal.

[54] Claude Pariseau, p. 93.

[55] Claude Pariseau, p. 93.

[56] John McGirr au surintendant général des Affaires indiennes, 19 janvier 1878, RG 10, vol. 2033, dossier 8946-1, pt. 1.

[57] Ibid.

[58] Claude Pariseau, p. 95.

[59] John Borland à l'honorable Joseph Howe S. S., 13 mars 1871, Centre national des arts, RG 10, vol. 2029, dossier 8946.

[60] Ibid.

[61] Ibid.

[62] Claude Pariseau, p. 97.

[63] Ibid., p. 98.

[64] Hector Langevin à Charles Coursol, 8 septembre 1869, Centre national des arts, RG 10, vol. 2029, dossier 8946.

[65] Ibid.

[66] Coursol à Langevin, 18 septembre 1869, Centre national des arts, RG 10, vol. 2029, dossier 8946.

[67] Sessional Papers, volume VI, troisième session du premier parlement du Dominion du Canada, session 1870, Sessional Papers, nº 55, document nº 29, Coursol à Langevin, 27 octobre 1869.

[68] Sessional Papers, nº 55, document nº 31.

[69] À son excellence Sir John Young K. C. B., K. C. M. G., gouverneur général du Dominion du Canada, Lac des Deux-Montagnes, 7 février 1870, Centre national des arts, RG 10, vol. 2029, dossier 8946.

[70] Débats parlementaires du Dominion du Canada, troisième session, volume 1, 1870, p. 202, Ottawa, 1870 Ottawa Times Printing and Publishing Co.

[71] Ibid.

[72] Deux lettres de J. A. Baile à Joseph Howe et à George-Étienne Cartier, 25 et 26 février 1870, A. S. S. S., classeur 42, nº 118.

[73] Ibid.

[74] Baile à l'honorable Hector Langevin, 25 février 1870, A. S. S. S., classeur 42, nº 117.

[75] D. L. Dumouchel à M. Tallet, 7 mars 1870, A. S. S. S., Université de Montréal, classeur 42, nº 120.

[76] Débats parlementaires du Dominion du Canada, troisième session, volume 1, 1870, p. 203, Ottawa, 1870 Ottawa Times Printing and Publishing Co.

[77] Ibid.

[78] Pétition des Iroquois à Lord Lisgar, 31 décembre 1869.

[79] Beta, *Pour une meilleure compréhension de la question d'Oka et une aide en vue d'un arrangement équitable et rapide*, Montréal, 1879.

[80] Voir la constitution de la Civil Rights Alliance, Centre national des arts, RG 10, vol. 2029, dossier 8946.

[81] John Borland à l'honorable Joseph Howe, 17 février 1870, Centre national des arts, RG 10, vol. 2029, dossier 8946.

[82] Sessional Papers, volume VI, troisième session du premier parlement du Dominion du Canada, session 1870, Sessional Papers, n° 55, document n° 36, Joseph Howe S. S. à John Borland, 12 mars 1870.

[83] Ibid.

[84] John Borland à l'honorable Joseph Howe, 17 mars 1870, Centre national des arts, RG 10, vol. 2029, dossier 8946.

[85] Joseph Howe S. S. à John Borland, 26 mars 1870, Sessional Papers, n° 55, document n° 37.5.

[86] John Borland à l'honorable Joseph Howe, 13 mars 1871, Centre national des arts, RG 10, vol. 2029, dossier 8946.

[87] Permis d'occupation de terre pour les Indiens de la mission du Lac des Deux Montagnes (après 1867), aux alentours de 1870, A. S. S. S., Université de Montréal, classeur 42, n° 128.

[88] John Borland, Les suppositions du séminaire de Saint-Sulpice examinées et réfutées, exposées et dénoncées, The Gazette Printing House, Montréal, 1872, p. 27.

[89] John Borland, Les suppositions du séminaire de Saint-Sulpice, p. 28.

[90] Abraham Sickles à William Spragge esq, 16 janvier 1873, Centre national des arts, RG 10, vol. 2029, dossier 8946.

[91] Ibid.

[92] Ibid.

[93] John Borland, Les suppositions du séminaire de Saint-Sulpice, p. 29.

[94] John MacLean M. A., Ph. D., D. D., Vanguards du Canada, La société missionnaire de l'Église méthodiste, Le mouvement des jeunes pour l'avancement, Toronto, Copyright Canada, 1918, p. 175.

[95] Urgel Lafontaine, p. s. s., Procès des Indiens, 1877, cahier 1, A. S. S. S., Université de Montréal.

[96] Ibid.

[97] Ibid.

[98] Ibid.

[99] Ibid.

[100] Ibid.

[101] Ibid.

[102] Ibid.

[103] Conseiller d'Argenteuil, 4 février 1874.

[104] Ibid.

[105] William Spragge, 31 mars 1874, Centre national des arts, RG 10, vol. 1925, dossier 3114.

[106] Urgel Lafontaine p. s. s., Procès des Indiens, 1877, cahier 1, A. S. S. S., Université de Montréal.

[107] La Congregational Union envoya une pétition à la reine Victoria pour attirer son attention sur la condition des Indiens du Lac des Deux-Montagnes, Centre national des arts, RG 10, vol. 1993, dossier 6822. Le gouvernement reçut également des pétitions, entre autres des résidents de Huntingdon, d'Elgin, de Franklin et de Hitchinbrooke, Centre national des arts, RG 10, vol. 2050, dossier 9436. Les habitants du comté de Deux-Montagnes envoyèrent également une pétition de soixante signatures demandant au parlement de régler les difficultés entre le séminaire et les Indiens d'Oka, A. S. S. S., classeur 42, n° 133.

[108] Greene Papers, département des livres rares de la bibliothèque McGill.

[109] Une note historique sur les difficultés survenues entre le séminaire de Saint-Sulpice de Montréal et certains Indiens d'Oka, au Lac des Deux-Montagnes. Une simple question de droit de propriété, « En aucun cas, une question religieuse », deuxième édition, La Minerve Steam Printing Job Office, Montréal, 1876.

[110] E. Meredith à John Borland, 20 décembre 1875, RG 10, vol. 2033, dossier 8946-1, pt. 1.

[111] Les Indiens protestants d'Oka et le séminaire de Saint-Sulpice, appel au gouvernement, rencontre de masse, Montreal Herald, 12 décembre 1875.

[112] Note historique, Une simple question de droit de propriété, « En aucun cas, une question religieuse ».

[113] Note historique, Une simple question de droit de propriété, « En aucun cas, une question religieuse ».

[114] Claude Pariseau, p. 124.

[115] Beta, Pour une meilleure compréhension de la question d'Oka et une aide en vue d'un arrangement équitable et rapide, Montréal, 1879, page 59.

[116] Ibid.

[117] Claude Pariseau, p. 138.

[118] Ibid.

[119] Ibid.

[120] Ibid.

[121] Ibid.

[122] Ibid.

[123] Ibid.

[124] Ibid.

[125] Beta, p. 58.

[126] Interrogatoire des témoins au procès des Indiens d'Oka accusés d'avoir participé à l'incendie de l'église de leur village, A. S. S. S., Université de Montréal, classeur 42, n° 152.

[127] Autobiographie, *The life of Amand Parent*, p. 202.

[128] Ibid., p. 120.

[129] Ibid., p. 205.

[130] Civil Rights Alliance, conseil pour l'année 1877, RG 10, vol. 2033, dossier 8946-1, pt. 1.

[131] Constitution de la Civil Rights Alliance adoptée au conseil tenu au Mechanics Hall, Montréal, 27 mars 1877, RG 10, vol. 2033, dossier 8946-1, pt. 1.

[132] Beta, p. 60.

[133] The Oka Troubles, Montreal Daily Star, le jeudi 28 juin 1877.

[134] Claude Pariseau, p. 140.

[135] Interrogatoire des témoins au procès des Indiens d'Oka accusés d'avoir participé à l'incendie de l'église de leur village, A. S. S. S., Université de Montréal, classeur 42, n° 152.

[136] Ibid.

[137] Ibid.

[138] Ibid.

[139] Ibid.

[140] Ibid.

[141] Ibid.

[142] Ibid.

[143] Urgel Lafontaine p. s. s., Procès des Indiens, 1877, cahier 1, A. S. S. S., Université de Montréal.

[144] Ibid.

[145] Ibid.

[146] T. A. Baile au ministre de l'Intérieur, Montreal Telegraph, 15 juin 1877, Centre national des arts, RG 10, vol. 6607, dossier 4020RC, pt. 0.

[147] Amand Parent à l'honorable David Mills, Montreal Telegraph, 16 juin 1877, Centre national des arts, RG 10, vol. 6607, dossier 4020RC, pt. 0.

[148] Urgel Lafontaine, p. s. s., Procès des Indiens, cahier 1, A. S. S. S., Université de Montréal.

[149] The Oka Troubles, The Montreal Daily Star, 28 juin 1877.

[150] Urgel Lafontaine, p. s. s., Procès des Indiens, cahier 1, A. S. S. S., Université de Montréal.

[151] Autobiographie, *The life of Amand Parent*, p. 206.

[152] Urgel Lafontaine p. s. s., Procès des Indiens, cahier 1, A. S. S. S., Université de Montréal.

[153] A. N. McNeil à l'honorable David Mills, 27 juin 1877, Centre national des arts, RG 10, vol. 2020, dossier 8304.

[154] A. N. McNeil au département de l'Intérieur, 30 juin 1877, Centre national des arts, RG 10, vol. 2020, dossier 8304.

[155] Ibid.

[156] Ibid.

[157] Urgel Lafontaine, p. s. s., Procès des Indiens, 1877, cahier 1, A. S. S. S., Université de Montréal.

[158] J. A. Mousseau à A. R. Auger, 5 février 1878, A. S. S. S., classeur 42, n° 139, Université de Montréal.

[159] Ibid.

[160] Amand Parent, p. 140.

[161] Ibid., p. 141.

[162] Ibid., p. 143.

[163] John J. McLaren à L. O. Loranger, 22 juin 1881, A. S. S. S., classeur 42, n° 187, Université de Montréal.

[164] Voir Centre national des arts, RG 10, vol. 2033, dossier 8946-1, pt. 1.

[165] Suggestions en référence au traitement des Indiens dans l'éventualité où ils seraient déplacés d'Oka à un emplacement que le gouvernement leur fournirait, John Borland, octobre 1878, Centre national des arts, RG 10, vol 2033, dossier 8946-1. pt. 1.

[166] John McGirr, au surintendant général des Affaires indiennes, 10 janvier 1878, RG 10, vol. 2033, dossier 8946-1, pt. 1.

[167] John McGirr à l'honorable David Mills, ministre de l'Intérieur et surintendant général des Affaires indiennes, 9 mars 1878, Centre national des arts, RG 10, vol. 2033, dossier 8946-1, pt. 1.

[168] J. J. McLaren à L. Vankoughnet, 25 décembre 1879, Centre national des arts, RG 10, vol. 2033, dossier 8946-1, pt. 1.

[169] Ibid.

[170] Département de l'Intérieur à John McGirr esq., 23 mars 1878, Centre national des arts, RG 10, vol. 2033, dossier 8946-1, pt. 1.

[171] John McGirr au surintendant général des Affaires indiennes, 15 mars 1878, Centre national des arts, RG 10, vol. 2033, dossier 8946-1, pt. 1.

[172] Greene Papers, département des livres rares de la bibliothèque McGill, 10 août 1880.

[173] Claude Pariseau, p. 155, 156,

[174] Ibid.

[175] John McGirr au surintendant général des Affaires indiennes, 7 novembre 1877, Centre national des arts, RG 10, vol. 2071, dossier 10 629.

[176] Ibid.

[177] Ibid., vol. 2078, dossier 11 476.

[178] Claude Pariseau, p. 156.

[179] John McGirr à l'honorable ministre de l'Intérieur, 11 décembre 1879, Centre national des arts, RG 10, vol. 2100, dossier 17 468.

[180] Olivier Maurault, *Les vicissitudes d'une mission sauvage*, p. 131.

[181] Collette Michaud, *Une étude du campement des Indiens à Hull durant la deuxième moitié du dix-neuvième siècle*, préparée pour la Commission de la capitale nationale, avril 1987, p. 5, D. I. A. N. D. Centre de recherche historique, classeur 1-224.

[182] À titre d'information, George-Étienne Cartier occupa les fonctions d'avocat pour le séminaire et le Grand Trunk Railway en même temps qu'il était ministre dans le gouvernement, Brian Young, p. 123.

[183] À l'honorable secrétaire d'État, 18 décembre 1875, Centre national des arts, RG 10, vol. 2033, dossier 8946-1, pt. 1.

[184] À l'honorable L. Church, ministre de la Justice, 27 septembre 1875, Centre national des arts, RG 10, vol. 2033, dossier 8946-1, pt. 1.

[185] John McGirr à l'honorable David Mills, 9 mars 1878, Centre national des arts, RG 10, vol. 2033, dossier 8946-1, pt. 1.

[186] John McInnes à l'honorable ministre de l'Intérieur, Oka, 7 novembre 1879, Centre national des arts, RG 10, vol. 2033, dossier 8946-1, pt. 1.

[187] Selon l'histoire orale de Kanehsatà:ke.

[188] Selon Urgel Lafontaine, un homme appelé Paul Oka, qui a donné son nom au village, est mort le 25 juin 1882, à l'âge de 95 ans.

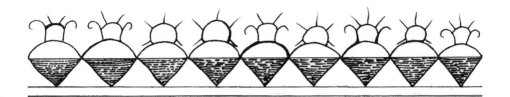

CHAPITRE 6

LE DÉPLACEMENT VERS GIBSON

UN TEMPS D'ÉPREUVES ET D'HISTOIRES TRISTES

D'où je me dresse, les eaux sont calmes et retiennent la lumière pour tout refléter. Un moment si tranquille, mais combien rempli de vie, comme si toute la création pense à la même chose.

Cette rivière a si souvent été un remède pour le peuple et, quoique turbulente par moments, elle était leur subsistance et leur voie de navigation.

Le cours de la rivière a ramené beaucoup de Kanehsata'kehró:non à la maison, mais par une froide journée d'automne, elle emportait au loin une famille après l'autre. Certains étaient soulagés d'échapper au pouvoir des Roti'kharahón:tsi (robes noires), mais tous avaient le cœur lourd. Ils disaient au revoir à leurs frères et sœurs, à la rivière et à la montagne parce que leur vie était devenue insupportable.

Je m'en souviens très bien. C'était un temps d'épreuves et d'histoires tristes. Ne pouvant obtenir aucune justice, partir semblait la seule issue aux nombreux mauvais traitements. Les Roti'kharahón:tsi menaçaient la survie même du peuple. Les hommes étaient traqués, tirés de leur sommeil durant la nuit, battus et envoyés derrière les barreaux. Les femmes devaient fuir et se cacher dans les bois avec de petits enfants effrayés. Leur seul tort était de couper du bois pour garder la famille au chaud ou pour réparer leur demeure.

Comme un manteau de neige, l'inquiétude et l'agitation couvraient Kanehsatà:ke. Lors des conseils, les chefs s'exprimaient, mais tous faisaient la sourde oreille : les Roti'kharahón:tsi n'écoutaient pas, personne n'écoutait.

Finalement, après de longues discussions, certains des Kanehsata'kehró:non ont cherché une vie meilleure ailleurs, même si cela leur coûtait très cher.

Ils ne reposeraient jamais près de leurs ancêtres, et Kanehsatà:ke ne serait plus le chez-soi de leurs enfants. À part les vêtements qu'ils avaient sur leur dos, ils emportaient peu de choses. Dans mon esprit, je les vois encore regroupés dans un bateau, les yeux fixés sur le rivage, sur le peuple et la terre qu'ils laissaient derrière eux. Oui, c'était vraiment une journée froide!

À LA RECHERCHE D'UNE SOLUTION

Les conditions à Kanehsatà:ke devenant de plus en plus intolérables, régler la situation devint urgent. Plusieurs groupes, comme la Civil Rights Alliance et la Protestant Defense Alliance, s'engagèrent à appuyer les Kanehsata'kehró:non. Alors que l'appui de ces groupes servait à attirer l'attention du public sur le problème, il contribuait également à embrouiller la situation qui se transforma en une revendication de droits protestants contre la domination catholique. Dans les débats publics qui s'ensuivirent dans la presse, la question des droits territoriaux de Kanehsatà:ke était souvent éclipsée par celle de la liberté religieuse. Le fait que les Kanehsata'kehró:non s'étaient tournés vers l'Église méthodiste pour se libérer des prêtres, et non en raison d'un attachement profond à cette religion, n'était pas pertinent. L'opinion publique accordait plus d'importance à libérer les Indiens « protestants » de la persécution qu'ils subissaient aux mains du séminaire. Protéger les droits territoriaux des Kanehsata'kehró:non était tout au plus de seconde importance. Supprimer la source et la cause du problème, en l'occurrence le séminaire, était hors de question. La Couronne, représentée par le Département indien, une fois de plus manqua de courage moral et de volonté politique pour rendre justice aux Kanehsata'kehró:non. Malgré leurs revendications répétées de leurs droits territoriaux et leur refus constant de s'installer ailleurs, leur déplacement complet était la seule solution activement recherchée par tous les partis concernés. Ces derniers considéraient favorablement le déplacement proposé, mais pas le peuple de Kanehsatà:ke. Le séminaire pouvait finalement se débarrasser des Kanien'kehà:ka encombrants, tout en gardant un petit nombre d'Indiens catholiques à la mission. Le gouvernement croyait qu'il était arrivé à une solution acceptable à une dispute de longue date.

Même les sympathisants des Kanehsata'kehró:non croyaient que le déplacement était la meilleure solution. Il semblait que tout le monde savait mieux que le peuple lui-même ce qui était mieux pour lui. Auparavant, il avait rejeté catégoriquement des propositions de déplacement, mais cette-fois-ci, c'était différent.

Après quelques acquittements et plusieurs jurys aux opinions partagées lors des procès successifs des hommes accusés d'avoir incendié l'église catholique, le séminaire intensifia sa campagne de harcèlement à l'endroit des Kanehsata'kehró:non. Une atmosphère de peur et d'incertitude régnait dans la communauté. De fréquentes descentes de nuit effectuées par la police provinciale et de violentes agressions commises par certains Canadiens français accentuaient les tensions et, dans certains cas, servaient à affaiblir la résolution du peuple de rester.

À l'été 1880, les Kanehsata'kehró:non montraient des signes qu'ils allaient craquer sous la pression. Le déplacement proposé créait de la dissension dans la communauté : ceux qui partaient et ceux qui restaient éprouvaient de la rancœur les uns envers les autres. Tandis que la grande majorité était toujours opposée au déplacement, certains croyaient que partir était leur seule chance de vivre dans la paix et la prospérité. Só:se O'nahsakèn:rat (Joseph Swan), qui avait été un dirigeant et un défenseur de poids de son peuple, avait apparemment été vaincu par la persécution acharnée du séminaire et du système judiciaire. Comme il vivait à Kahnawà:ke, séparé de son peuple, et qu'il devait subir un autre procès, Só:se abandonna sa position. Catégoriquement opposé au déplacement du peuple de Kanehsatà:ke au début, il manifestait maintenant un intérêt à cet égard. En août 1880, O'nahsakèn:rat désigna N. O. Greene, membre de la Civil Rights Alliance, comme agent pour son peuple.[1] À l'exception de quelques personnes, ce choix se fit vraisemblablement sans que les Kanehsata'kehró:non ne le sachent. Le peuple ne voulait pas être représenté par Greene et le communiqua au Département indien en octobre 1880.[2] Alors que Greene et d'autres, comme lui, prétendaient travailler dans l'intérêt des Kanehsata'kehró:non, le séminaire et le gouvernement leur versaient des compensations pour les problèmes que leurs efforts leur causaient. En réalité, ils ne travaillaient que dans le but de persuader le peuple de quitter Kanehsatà:ke.[3] Ils jouirent d'une réussite partielle. Greene, appuyé par O'nahsakèn:rat, continua à agir comme agent pour le peuple. En octobre, O'nahsakèn:rat envoya une lettre au Département, suggérant qu'une délégation se rende en Ontario pour choisir un site pour la nouvelle réserve.[4] En raison de la saison avancée et de l'imminence du début de l'hiver, ce voyage fut reporté.[5]

Les Kanehsata'kehró:non étaient déçus par leur chef après son changement d'opinion et les actions qui suivirent. Ils savaient qu'O'nahsakèn:rat avait écrit des lettres et pris des décisions concernant leur déplacement, sans qu'ils ne le sachent ni n'y consentent. Le 2 février 1881, le peuple tint un conseil et décida unanimement de le destituer.[6] Só:se O'nahsakèn:rat mourut cinq jours plus tard, à l'âge de 35 ans, dans des circonstances mystérieuses.[7] Les Kanehsata'kehró:non avaient perdu un chef de valeur et un porte-parole éloquent. On ne peut qu'imaginer les circonstances qui portèrent un homme si dédié à son peuple à abandonner totalement l'espoir d'une résolution juste du problème et à décider qu'il valait mieux que son peuple quitte sa terre natale pour toujours.

Plus tard, au cours du même mois, 39 familles exprimèrent leur désir de quitter Kanehsatà:ke.[8] Plusieurs des noms (des chefs de famille) qui se trouvaient sur la liste des personnes qui allaient être déplacées étaient ceux des hommes qui avaient plusieurs fois été accusés et traduits en justice pour l'incendie de l'église catholique.[9] En mars 1881, les Kanehsata'kehró:non qui voulaient quitter Kanehsatà:ke présentèrent une liste des conditions liées à leur déplacement.

Ces conditions étaient les suivantes :

1. Qu'une réserve d'une superficie de 25 000 hectares leur soit accordée dans la province de l'Ontario.

2. Que le gouvernement paie le coût du déplacement.

3. Que le gouvernement paie à chaque Indien la valeur de ses bâtiments et de son terrain à Oka, et lui fournisse l'outillage agricole sur la nouvelle réserve.

4. Que le gouvernement fournisse toutes les provisions et tous les vêtements nécessaires pour trois années, commençant la première année de l'installation, ainsi que des semences pour un an.

5. Que le gouvernement fournisse à chaque famille une vache et un cheval, ainsi qu'un taureau pour la bande avec le fourrage nécessaire pour une année.

6. Que le gouvernement construise et entretienne une école publique.

7. Que le gouvernement fournisse un médecin en cas de maladie.

8. Que le gouvernement construise une scierie et une meunerie s'il n'y en a pas déjà une près de la réserve.

9. Que le gouvernement paie le montant de… pour défricher la terre, et fournisse à chaque famille un poêle et des ustensiles.

10. Que le gouvernement ouvre une route de la réserve à la route publique la plus proche.

11. Que le gouvernement fournisse les petits articles nécessaires dans une ferme.

12. Que le gouvernement obtienne du séminaire la somme de dix mille dollars (10 000 $) en paiement pour les droits territoriaux que les Indiens revendiquent au Lac des Deux-Montagnes, que ledit montant soit placé à leur crédit entre les mains du gouvernement et que les intérêts accumulés soient remis deux fois par année à la bande.[10]

Il était clair que le peuple de Kanehsatà:ke ne désirait plus avoir affaire avec le séminaire de Saint-Sulpice. Il était également évident que même ceux qui voulaient partir soutenaient qu'ils possédaient des droits territoriaux à Kanehsatà:ke. En effet, ce qu'ils avaient proposé était un traité dans lequel ils abandonnaient leurs droits territoriaux en retour d'une compensation financière, une réserve en Ontario, ainsi que d'autres biens nécessaires à la survie et au bien-être futur de la communauté. Ces conditions ne furent pas acceptées par le gouvernement, et il n'y a aucune preuve qu'elles furent même sérieusement considérées. De plus, il n'y a aucune indication que les Kanehsata'kehró:non furent informés avant le déménagement que les conditions proposées n'étaient pas acceptées. En fait, il y a tout lieu de croire qu'ils furent délibérément trompés et maintenus dans l'ignorance relativement aux conditions de leur déplacement. Aussi tard qu'en 1883, ils ignoraient toujours les détails du plan du déplacement. Dans une lettre datée du 8 janvier envoyée au Département, les Rotiiá:nehr (chefs) de Kanehsatà:ke écrivirent :

> On nous demande d'aller sur des terres dont nous ne savons rien et qui ont été choisies sans que nous le voulions ni que nous donnions notre consentement. Nous sommes désolés de sembler opposés au gouvernement, mais il n'en est rien. Nous pensons que le gouvernement désire faire ce qui est juste et défendre nos intérêts. Cependant, nous ne pouvons cacher notre regret de constater que le gouvernement qui s'est entendu avec le séminaire pour nous envoyer à un endroit dont on ne nous a pas parlé jusqu'à ce que le marché soit conclu. C'est ainsi que la question se présente. Cette grave erreur doit d'une manière ou d'une autre être corrigée. Nous savons que nous sommes faibles, mais nous ne sommes pas aveugles et nous ne pouvons pas nous laisser mener comme si nous n'avions pas d'yeux et aucune perception de justice et de droits [...].[11]

Au début d'avril 1881, une délégation constituée de Louis Sanation, Angus Cooke, Peter Decaire et l'agent indien, John McGirr, se rendirent au comté de Gibson (Muskoka) pour inspecter le territoire qui avait été choisi pour leur nouvelle réserve.[12] Selon Charles A. Cooke, un garçon de sept ans à l'époque, voici ce qu'ils trouvèrent :

> [...] Le jour suivant, ils examinèrent le lac Black et le territoire en aval, jusqu'à Muskoka Mills, où ils constatèrent que les terres dans cette partie du comté étaient très pauvres sur le plan agricole.

> Le surlendemain, ils examinèrent les terres à l'extrémité nord du comté. Ils revinrent en faisant un détour par le camp Webster et, le jour suivant, ils retournèrent à Bala en traversant le bois près du site où se trouve l'autoroute actuelle entre Bala et la réserve.

> Dans l'ensemble, ils étaient satisfaits des vastes étendues de forêts de pins et de toutes sortes de bois dur; les rivières et les lacs regorgeaient de poissons, et le gibier, tel que le chevreuil, se trouvait en abondance, assez pour faire déborder de joie le cœur d'un chasseur indien [...].[13]

Sur le chemin du retour, la délégation s'arrêta à Ottawa où elle fit un rapport de ses conclusions au Département.[14] Le gouvernement et le séminaire ne perdirent pas une minute pour organiser le déplacement. Peu de temps après, apprenant par un article paru dans *The Witness* que le séminaire se mêlait du déplacement, les Kanehsata'kehró:non hésitèrent devant la possibilité que les Sulpiciens les suivent jusqu'à Muskoka. Le père Lacan, curé du séminaire, rapporta que le fait que le peuple soit au courant de leur participation présentait un obstacle au déplacement. Il recommanda que le séminaire fasse comme s'il était très peu engagé dans l'affaire et que le gouvernement paraisse s'occuper de tous les arrangements.[15]

En juin 1881, le gouvernement de l'Ontario vota un décret autorisant la vente de 10 353 hectares dans le comté de Gibson au gouvernement fédéral.[16] Le séminaire fournirait l'argent pour l'achat à raison de 20 cents l'hectare, soit un coût total de plus de 12 000 $. La campagne pour déplacer les Kanehsata'kehró:non était bien amorcée. Les partisans du plan restaient sûrs qu'un jour tout le peuple accepterait volontiers de partir. En octobre de la même année, *The Witness* rapporta que le gouvernement avait empêché l'ensemencement des terres au printemps et menaçait de retirer l'agent indien, ainsi que toute aide gouvernementale au peuple, dans le but de le convaincre de partir.[17] Subissant une persécution croissante de la part du séminaire et de ses acolytes, les Kanehsata'kehró:non risquaient de passer un long hiver sans nourriture, ainsi que de perdre toute aide extérieure.

Le 26 août 1881, le séminaire présenta sa propre liste, tenue secrète, de conditions pour le déplacement, qui s'intitulait « Projet de règlement dans l'affaire du déménagement des Indiens ».[18] Les obligations proposées du séminaire étaient les suivantes :

1. Payer les terres, 10 353 hectares à 20 cents l'hectare.

2. Payer au Département, selon les estimations, la valeur des bâtiments et des clôtures appartenant aux Indiens au Lac des Deux-Montagnes.

3. Payer le transport des Indiens du Lac au comté de Gibson.

Le gouvernement devra :

1. après trois ans, rembourser sans intérêts au séminaire les montants qu'il aura déboursés pour le territoire inoccupé par les Indiens d'Oka ou transférer la propriété au séminaire.

2. transférer au séminaire toute partie dudit territoire devenue vacante ou lui verser 20 cents par hectare.

3. veiller à ce que chaque famille indienne occupe un lot de 60 hectares et s'engage à suivre les conditions de vente imposées par l'Ontario.

4. empêcher toute possibilité de retour des Indiens au Lac. Si certains d'entre eux y revenaient quand même, ils ne seraient plus protégés par le gouvernement et ne feraient plus partie d'aucune bande.

5. déclarer qu'après trois ans, tous ceux qui n'ont pas profité de l'offre, l'ont refusée. De ce fait, ils cesseront d'être considérés comme une bande ou une tribu.[19]

Le séminaire était prêt à se donner beaucoup de mal pour se débarrasser des Kanehsata'kehró:non. Il semblait que les Sulpiciens ne seraient satisfaits qu'avec le déplacement complet des Kanehsata'kehró:non ou la fin de leur existence comme groupe distinct. En réalité, ils voulaient leur disparition. Le peuple de Kanehsatà:ke avait présenté une liste de conditions pour le déplacement (traité), mais les gouvernements de l'Ontario et du Canada avaient chacun passé un décret afférent au déplacement des Kanehsata'kehró:non à Gibson. Les Sulpiciens n'honoreraient que les conditions qu'ils avaient eux-mêmes formulées au début, c'est-à-dire seulement celles liées directement au déplacement du peuple de Kanehsatà:ke. En septembre 1881, le gouvernement du Canada promulgua un décret ouvrant la voie au déplacement. Les conditions du décret étaient considérablement différentes de celles proposées par le peuple, mais presque identiques aux propositions du séminaire. Le 17 octobre 1881, le gouvernement fédéral reçut du séminaire un chèque de 12 791 $ pour le territoire à Gibson.[20] Si les Kanehsata'kehró:non n'avaient aucun droit au territoire, pourquoi le séminaire était-il prêt à payer pour les déplacer ?

Tandis que le plan était de déplacer le peuple au printemps 1882, le premier groupe de Kanehsata'kehró:non partit pour Gibson cinq jours après la remise du chèque, soit le 22 octobre 1881.[21]

À ce moment-là, nul ne fit mention de l'époque, de la saison avancée ni du début imminent de l'hiver. Il ne semblait pas important que le peuple parte vers un environnement inconnu juste à l'approche de la saison la plus dure, et ce, avec très peu de provisions. Leur départ était la seule chose qui comptait.

Ceux qui passent inaperçus

Quand le temps tourne à l'orage et que le voyageur ressent chaque goutte de pluie comme un caillou à cause de la force du vent, il ne peut que baisser la tête et s'empresser de trouver un abri. En marchant, il ne remarquera pas ce qui l'entoure; dans sa précipitation pour se réchauffer, il peut même négliger un autre voyageur.

Autour de moi, des voix s'élèvent toutes en même temps, chacune essayant d'être la plus forte; elles ressemblent à ces gouttes de pluie. Étant tellement occupées à se faire entendre, elles n'écoutent pas et oublient ceux qu'elles défendent.

Les Kanehsata'kehró:non deviennent ceux qui passent inaperçus. Ils ne peuvent que regarder, alors que des voyageurs se hâtent pour trouver un abri et des vêtements secs.

Le débat

Pendant plusieurs années, avant et pendant la planification du déplacement proposé des Kanehsata'kehró:non, le débat sur le sujet faisait rage. Jusqu'à ce moment-là, leur situation n'avait pas beaucoup retenu l'attention du public. Toutes les discussions relatives à leurs droits territoriaux s'étaient tenues en privé. L'étendue des manipulations et des manœuvres du séminaire pour prendre le contrôle du territoire n'avait pas été révélée. Mais la question retenait maintenant l'attention de la presse, et plusieurs Montréalais importants entrèrent dans le débat. Plusieurs groupes participaient aux discussions : le gouvernement, le séminaire, l'Église méthodiste, la Civil Rights Alliance, la Protestant Defense Alliance, la Aborigines Protection Society, ainsi que des personnes intéressées à la question.

Même si, à de nombreuses occasions, les Kanehsata'kehró:non exprimèrent leurs opinions au gouvernement et aux membres de la Civil Rights Alliance, elles n'entraient jamais sérieusement dans le débat. Des critiques et des sympathisants du plan de déplacement soulevèrent des questions sur les revendications du séminaire, les droits des Kanehsata'kehró:non, l'inactivité du gouvernement, la domination de l'Église catholique et l'intolérance religieuse. Des pamphlets furent publiés sur le sujet, et de nombreux articles parurent dans les quotidiens. Tandis que de nombreux protestants étaient d'avis que le séminaire n'avait aucun droit de propriété au Lac des Deux-Montagnes, le séminaire puissant, ainsi que ses partisans, soutenait que ses droits à la seigneurie étaient absolus. Puisque le gouvernement manifestait beaucoup de réticence à s'engager, un critique, W. G. Beers, dentiste à Montréal et membre de la Protestant Defense Alliance, demanda : « Le gouvernement a-t-il peur de la question d'Oka? »[22] Le groupe s'engagea dans l'affaire à la suite de la persécution des Kanehsata'kehró:non; il devint plus tard la Civil Rights Alliance qui comptait dans ses rangs plusieurs Montréalais et des membres du clergé très en vue.

Beers, dont l'engagement découlait de son intérêt pour le jeu de lacrosse, commença en tant que fervent défenseur des droits des Kanehsata'kehró:non (bien qu'il ait plus tard recommandé leur déplacement). Il réfuta publiquement les revendications territoriales du séminaire et pressa le gouvernement à agir pour assurer et protéger les droits des Kanehsata'kehró:non. Voyant qu'aucune action n'était entreprise, Beers mit en doute les motifs de l'inaction du gouvernement.

La question qui s'impose aux citoyens de ce Dominion – car la question d'Oka est plus qu'une question locale – est celle-ci : « Le gouvernement a-t-il peur? » S'il n'a pas peur, pourquoi permet-il au séminaire, comme s'il anticipait un effondrement rapide suite à ses persécutions et à ses revendications absolues, de couper les chênes sur les seigneuries et d'en vendre le bois qui est, avec tout le minerai et les mines, la propriété exclusive du gouvernement? Le bois coupé et vendu par les Messieurs du séminaire est estimé à plus de 300 000 cordes pour un profit d'au moins 1000 $. Le gouvernement n'a-t-il pas même l'intention de veiller sur ses propres intérêts financiers à Oka? [...] Si les efforts du gouvernement pour rendre justice aux Indiens sont sincères, il doit obtenir cette justice positivement en leur accordant leurs droits aux seigneuries – non seulement à Oka, mais tous leurs droits dans les seigneuries entières. Les Indiens ne quitteront pas Oka. Pourquoi M. Mills ne propose-t-il pas au séminaire de quitter Oka?[23]

R. Laflamme, alors ministre de la Justice, a déclaré ce qui suit sur les intérêts du gouvernement dans le bois :

La réserve de chênes dans la concession ne diminue en rien le droit de propriété. Le gouvernement français avait fait la même réserve dans chaque titre de propriété concédant une seigneurie [...] Selon la loi seigneuriale de 1854, l'obligation seigneuriale de cette réserve a été abolie, et la propriété est devenue exempte de cette obligation, ainsi que celle des censitaires envers les seigneurs. De plus, supposant que les réserves existent encore, le gouvernement n'a pas plus le droit de l'enlever au séminaire qu'à toute autre terre seigneuriale dans la province de Québec.[24]

William Scott, pasteur anglican, défendit l'apathie du gouvernement en ces mots :

Le gouvernement est généralement responsable des Indiens et il est lui-même gouverné par la Loi sur les Indiens de 1880. Cette Loi concerne spécifiquement les Indiens avec qui le gouvernement a conclu des traités, qui possèdent donc des terres ou des réserves sous la direction du Département indien dans les intérêts de ces Indiens. Autant que possible, les Indiens d'Oka ont été compris dans l'application de cette Loi [...] Dans ce cas, comme dans beaucoup d'autres, le gouvernement ne peut aider que ceux qui sont disposés à s'aider eux-mêmes [...] Ayant montré la position particulière et douloureuse des Indiens d'Oka [...], il me semble que le public, au courant des faits, doit percevoir comme important et désirable de changer cette situation par tous les moyens convenables et légaux et de placer pleinement les Indiens d'Oka sous la Loi sur les Indiens.[25]

Scott était d'avis que le gouvernement avait fait tout en son pouvoir pour protéger les intérêts des Kanehsata'kehró:non, que l'influence du gouvernement était limitée par le fait qu'ils n'avaient pas de territoire qui leur appartienne et qu'ils n'étaient pas sous l'autorité de la Loi sur les Indiens. La solution naturelle était donc de les déplacer sur un territoire mis de côté pour eux, les plaçant ainsi sous la « protection » de la Loi sur les Indiens. Il ajouta :

J'ai également remarqué avec grand regret que tout ce qui est fait ou proposé par le gouvernement pour le bien des Indiens d'Oka a été plus ou moins dénaturé; les Indiens ont donc été menés à penser que le gouvernement est complètement indifférent à leur bien-être, tandis que la vérité est, à ma connaissance, que le département des Affaires indiennes a consacré plus de temps et de soin à l'égard de la condition des Indiens d'Oka et du règlement de questions à leur avantage que pour toute autre tribu ou bande au Canada.[26]

Selon Scott, le fait que les Kanehsata'kehró:non croient sincèrement que le territoire leur appartient ne faisait qu'ajouter à la difficulté auquel le gouvernement faisait face pour essayer de protéger leurs intérêts.

> […] une difficulté importante pour traiter avec les Indiens d'Oka vient du fait qu'ils ont été induits à accepter, au-delà de toute contradiction, ce que, dans le passé, Sir John Johnson et, plus récemment, M. Spragge, leur ont présumément déclaré : qu'ils étaient les propriétaires de la seigneurie du Lac des Deux-Montagnes.[27]

Un autre critique, écrivant sous le pseudonyme de Beta, avait ceci à dire :

> Le gouvernement du Dominion, sur qui repose spécifiquement le devoir de régler cette longue question fastidieuse, a depuis des années fui ses responsabilités et davantage cherché des excuses pour ne pas avoir essayé de la régler que de preuves de ce qui devrait être fait dans la cause.[28]

Dans son pamphlet intitulé, *Pour une bonne compréhension de la question d'Oka et une aide pour un règlement équitable et rapide*, Beta exposa en détail pour la toute première fois comment le séminaire en était arrivé à contrôler le territoire de Kanehsatà:ke et comment les gouvernements britannique et canadien avaient fermé les yeux sur ses activités. Il insinua que le gouvernement n'avait pas protégé les intérêts des « Indiens d'Oka » par crainte de contrarier le séminaire. Même si le gouvernement avait toujours persisté à dire que le séminaire n'avait aucun titre de propriété valide, la crainte de bouleversements politiques au Québec l'empêcha d'agir. De plus, le gouvernement avait récompensé le séminaire pour services rendus durant la rébellion de 1837 en lui accordant le titre de propriété, s'assurant ainsi sa loyauté.

Il faut signaler qu'une rébellion a éclaté au Canada en 1837 et qu'elle s'est poursuivie l'année suivante. À ce sujet, les chroniques font l'observation suivante : « Il était notoire que la région de Montréal, où les Sulpiciens sont établis, était la partie la plus instable de la province, et dans aucune autre région les rebelles se sont opposés aux forces de Sa Majesté. Presque tous les dirigeants francophones réputés de la rébellion avaient été instruits au collège des Sulpiciens à Montréal » […] Il avait été entendu qu'en raison de services importants rendus à la Couronne durant la rébellion, le séminaire serait récompensé par une confirmation de ses titres de propriété. De prime abord, le geste des Sulpiciens semble bien attiser une rébellion, puis, en trahissant leurs dupes au profit du gouvernement, ils vendaient leur peuple pour racheter un titre de propriété.

Quoi qu'il en soit, une chose est certaine : dès la fin de la rébellion, le gouvernement, pour des services soi-disant rendus par le séminaire durant cette dernière, a confirmé les titres de propriété au séminaire. Par conséquent, il l'a laissé tranquillement en possession de ces propriétés jusqu'à présent. Il est donc évident que la confirmation de ces terres servait à acheter le silence de ceux qui pouvaient, quand ils le voulaient, être des ennemis gênants et dangereux, mais qui, avec un certain traitement, devenaient des amis précieux et utiles.[29]

Selon Beta, non seulement le séminaire utilisa des moyens moins qu'honorables pour obtenir du gouvernement le titre de propriété du territoire de Kanehsatà:ke mais, ce faisant, il trahissait impitoyablement son propre peuple, les Canadiens français. Historiquement, pour appuyer sa position, le séminaire avait cité diverses lois desquelles découlaient leurs « droits absolus ». Ces lois étaient les concessions de 1717, 1718 et 1735, les articles de l'Acte de capitulation de 1763, la Loi de 1840 et la Loi seigneuriale de 1853. En 1881, Choquet, l'agent du séminaire, dit ce qui suit dans *The Globe* :

> De 1789 à 1840, le séminaire détenait un titre de propriété du territoire du Lac des Deux-Montagnes, mais le titre de ses autres propriétés était contesté par le gouvernement colonial. Cependant, au cours de la dernière année, les disputes ont été finalement réglées par une charte approuvée par la Reine, au chapitre 43 des Lois codifiées du Bas-Canada, en faveur du séminaire lui accordant une reconnaissance de toutes ses propriétés au Canada, y compris le territoire du Lac des Deux-Montagnes, et décrétant que les propriétés devaient être tenues dans les mêmes conditions que lorsqu'elles ont été originalement cédées par la couronne française.[30]

Beta soutenait que, depuis la défaite des Français aux mains des Britanniques, les droits du séminaire au Canada étaient déchus. Pour le prouver, il cita les opinions de plusieurs représentants juridiques de la Couronne, dont Sewell, ministre de la Justice du Bas-Canada, Sir Christopher Robinson, avocat, Sir Viedy Gibbs, ministre de la Justice et Plumer, adjoint du procureur général. « Leur rapport commun nous apprend que les Sulpiciens au Canada n'avaient aucun titre de propriété valide pour les territoires qui leur avaient été transférés par la communauté de Paris ».[31] Beta ajouta :

> Tout d'abord, selon Sewell « le motif pour lequel Paris donna l'île de Montréal au séminaire de Saint-Sulpice en 1663, par une association pour la conversion des Indiens sur cette île, a créé une fiducie qui ne s'est jamais réalisée, et le titre de propriété était mauvais pour le non-utilisateur.[32]

N'ayant pas satisfait ses obligations établies par la couronne française lors des concessions (par exemple, la construction d'un fort en pierre), le séminaire ne possédait donc pas de titre grâce à cette concession. De plus, il écrivit :

> Jusqu'à maintenant, la preuve claire et convaincante suit une conséquence naturelle que les propriétés en question reviennent à la Couronne par droit de conquête, comme la propriété d'une société étrangère domiciliée à Paris au moment de la conquête et de la cession de la colonie.[33]

Manifestement, jusqu'en 1840, selon le gouvernement et la loi, le séminaire n'avait aucun droit territorial dans le Bas-Canada.

> […] à plusieurs reprises, le gouvernement avait demandé au séminaire de céder les propriétés qu'il détenait. Et si le séminaire les détenait, c'était seulement parce que le gouvernement hésitait à prendre des mesures extrêmes pour les contraindre à renoncer à leurs propriétés. Le séminaire considérait évidemment cette hésitation du gouvernement comme le produit de la peur et savait qu'il n'osait pas agir selon ses menaces. Même si cela peut être vrai, il est on ne peut plus clair qu'à chaque occasion où la question lui a été présentée, le gouvernement a déclaré que le séminaire n'avait aucun titre de propriété valide.[34]

Malheureusement, les droits des Kanehsata'kehró:non et leur possibilité de posséder un territoire ne furent jamais reconnus par les gouvernements coloniaux français et britanniques. Les gouvernements canadiens qui se succédèrent perpétuèrent cette attitude colonialiste. Selon M. Laflamme, ministre de la Justice :

Il ne sera pas reconnu que, sous la souveraineté française ou anglaise, on ait déjà considéré que les Indiens puissent posséder ou acheter des terres, et on ne peut trouver aucune trace de concession de propriété seigneuriale ayant été faite à un Indien, ni à Deux-Montagnes ni ailleurs.[35]

Le pasteur William Scott, qui faisait office de représentant du gouvernement auprès des Kanehsata'kehró:non, déclara :

Il m'a souvent semblé qu'affirmer que les tribus autochtones d'Amérique étaient des « seigneurs de la terre », des propriétaires du territoire, et ainsi de suite était une absurdité totale. « À l'Éternel la terre et tout ce qu'elle renferme. Il l'a donnée à tous les fils des hommes. Il a déterminé les bornes de leur demeure. » [...] Nos amis autochtones semblent avoir confiné leur attention et leur entreprise sur les « poissons, les oiseaux, et toute chose vivante qui se meut sur la terre ». Remplir la terre et la dominer pour qu'elle porte du fruit au semeur et du pain pour qu'il mange sont des exigences au-delà de leurs aspirations. [...] Pendant ce temps, il y a des millions d'hectares de territoire non cultivés et des millions de personnes désireuses de remplir le décret original.

Découvrir ces étendues de terres immenses qui n'ont aucune valeur pour les autochtones, sauf pour la chasse, et qui sont requises par la nécessité des populations civilisées qui croissent, il est tout à fait naturel qu'il faille s'efforcer de coloniser les territoires inoccupés.[36]

W. Badgley, secrétaire d'État à l'époque, fit la déclaration suivante sur les droits des Kanehsata'kehró:non :

Il est clair que les Indiens d'Oka n'étaient pas des participants directs à la concession du Lac et rien de tel n'a été produit en leur faveur. En fait, l'histoire de la mission montre que, soit à la mission originale à Montréal ou à celle de Sault-au-Récollet ou finalement à celle du Lac, ils étaient simplement des orphelins et des vagabonds recueillis par la charité chrétienne des ecclésiastiques du séminaire de Montréal, et qu'ils n'ont jamais eu, ou prétendu avoir, un titre de propriété quelconque, soit pour la seigneurie de Montréal, leurs premier et deuxième emplacements, ou au Lac des Deux-Montagnes, où ils se sont établis en dernier.[37]

Sur ce point, l'opinion de George Beers divergeait de celle de Badgley. Selon lui, les « Indiens de la mission » ne furent jamais des « orphelins et des vagabonds ». Au contraire, ils constituaient un aspect important de la sécurité de la colonie naissante de la Nouvelle-France et, comme tel, jouissaient d'un pouvoir considérable. Ils ne seraient pas devenus subordonnés et serviteurs de ceux qui dépendaient d'eux pour survivre. Beers déclara :

Il est par ailleurs improbable que les Indiens, détenant l'équilibre des forces sur l'île, auraient déménagé au Lac sur un ordre péremptoire ou sous les conditions que le séminaire affirme avoir existé depuis le début. Il est peu probable qu'après avoir sauvé les Français et les Sulpiciens de l'anéantissement, ils auraient placé leur tête sous le pied de l'un ou de l'autre. Une telle suggestion de servitude ou de simple occupation sans titre était plus que le séminaire ou le roi de France n'ont osé offrir. Quelle aurait été la réponse donnée au séminaire si, en 1718, celui-ci avait dit aux Indiens d'Oka qu'il voulait qu'ils utilisent la seigneurie du Lac comme occupants sans titre, soumis à être éconduits, à se faire enlever leurs terres, et à être les simples instruments de son ambition?[38]

Badgley croyait que les Kanehsata'kehró:non avait un intérêt minime dans le territoire du Lac des Deux-Montagnes. Ils ne détenaient aucun titre de propriété, car ils n'occupaient le territoire que selon le bon plaisir du séminaire.

Il faut admettre que c'est seulement en tant que locataires et occupants du territoire sur la seigneurie du Lac que les colons ou les résidents indiens peuvent avoir un intérêt quelconque pour la propriété sur le territoire qui leur est, en fait, concédé au moyen d'un permis d'occupation, même si aucun contrat censitaire n'a été conclu […] Les Indiens d'Oka n'ont aucun droit de simple résidence sur la seigneurie du Lac des Deux-Montagnes, sauf les droits d'occupation continue des terres accordées par concession ou permis d'occupation par les seigneurs aux bénéficiaires des terres pour leur usage, celui de leurs enfants et de leurs descendants, et leur droit de vendre leur permis d'occupation dont il est question ci-dessus. Ces Indiens d'Oka, qui sont protestants, ne peuvent plus réclamer avoir de liens avec la mission ou ses missionnaires ni recevoir d'eux de l'aide spirituelle ou de l'instruction.[39]

À l'époque, Badgley émit ce qui paraît avoir été un argument irréfutable en faveur du séminaire. Néanmoins, il semble y avoir une certaine confusion dans son raisonnement. Par exemple, si les Kanehsata'kehró:non n'étaient que de simples locataires, comme l'affirmait Badgley, pourquoi n'étaient-ils pas obligés de payer un loyer, et comment se fait-il qu'« aucun contrat censitaire n'ait été établi »? Aussi, de son propre aveu, il disait que les Kanehsata'kehró:non avaient de véritables droits, de quelque manière qu'ils puissent avoir été décrits, au territoire du Lac des Deux-Montagnes tant qu'ils continuent de l'occuper. Il est donc compréhensible que le séminaire s'emploie avec autant de force à faire déplacer le peuple de leur territoire vers Muskoka. Les terres de Kanehsatà:ke étaient devenues extrêmement précieuses, et la présence des « Indiens » sur le territoire diminuait considérablement leur valeur. En tant que « propriétaire absolu » du territoire, le séminaire était prêt à récolter un profit immense en vendant des terres, si seulement ils pouvaient se débarrasser des Kanehsata'kehró:non. À cette époque, la question de l'existence d'un propriétaire fiduciaire fut également mise de l'avant. Certains pensaient que les Sulpiciens n'étaient que des administrateurs d'une fiducie caritative au nom des Kanehsata'kehró:non, tandis que d'autres croyaient qu'ils étaient les administrateurs de ces propriétés pour le gouvernement. D'autres encore affirmaient qu'aucune propriété fiduciaire n'existait. La fiducie, croyait-on, fut créée par la couronne française quand elle concéda le territoire au séminaire dans le but de christianiser les Indiens; elle continua à exister après la défaite des Français et fut confirmée par la Loi de 1840. En conséquence, cette fiducie accordait certains droits au peuple autochtone pour qui elle fut créée.

Sous l'administration de Lord Sydenham, une loi votée en 1841 confirmait le titre de ces propriétés au séminaire. Un effort avait précédemment été fait, sous l'administration de Lord Colborne, pour la réaliser au moyen d'un décret, mais en raison de sa rigidité, le décret fut rejeté par le gouvernement. Ayant échoué dans ce cas, les Sulpiciens étaient maintenant heureux de recevoir la confirmation de 1841, même si elle contenait des « termes, des clauses, des conditions et des restrictions » qui indiquaient suffisamment la détermination du gouvernement pour qu'ils se considèrent toujours comme les administrateurs des propriétés dont les titres leur étaient confirmés, et seulement comme tel […] Il est tout de même reconnu que, dans un sens, parce que la loi traite les Indiens comme des *mineurs*, leurs revendications territoriales sur la propriété de ladite seigneurie du territoire du Lac ne peuvent pas être vraiment considérées comme légitimes. Cependant, si le séminaire n'est que l'administrateur des propriétés qu'il détient par fiducie, il est alors clair que ces Indiens ont certainement plus qu'un droit immense et incontestable d'habiter et d'entretenir le territoire du Lac, mais aussi celui de l'île de Montréal (car celui-ci avait été accordé au séminaire pour la conversion des Indiens).[40]

W. Badgley rejeta ce point de vue affirmant qu'il n'y avait aucune fiducie et que, même s'il y en avait une, elle n'était pas exécutable en vertu de la loi.

Le devoir exigé de la mission se limite à l'*instruction et à l'aide spirituelle*, et n'inclut rien d'autre. Et tout autre droit réclamé par les Indiens, tel que les parcelles de terre qu'ils ont reçues des ecclésiastiques du séminaire, se trouve dans la catégorie des droits administrés en vertu de la loi provinciale, droits qui ne peuvent être appliqués qu'en recourant à cette loi ou grâce à l'accord des ecclésiastiques eux-mêmes. Le but de la mission n'est pas une fiducie au-delà du devoir explicite qu'elle doit remplir, et la fiducie anglaise en cause ne fait pas partie de la loi de la province.[41]

George Beers, commentant l'attitude des Kanehsata'kehró:non, déclara :

Du début à la fin, ces derniers ont été pour la plupart laissés dans l'ignorance quant à la véritable nature des contrats de concession, tout comme ils ont été ensuite, plus astucieusement, empêchés de connaître les réelles conditions de la Loi de 1840 qui confirmait le titre de propriété du séminaire. Toutefois, aucune tradition n'est plus clairement établie dans leur esprit que celle voulant que ces terres concédées aient été et sont toujours gardées en fiducie pour eux par le séminaire et qu'en aucun cas elles soient sa propriété absolue.[42]

Aussi :

Les Indiens d'Oka ne se sont pas engagés à demeurer fidèles aux personnes et aux croyances du séminaire quand ce dernier a été nommé administrateur de leur territoire. Le séminaire s'est lui-même chargé des conditions et des responsabilités – qu'il n'a pas remplies pour la plupart.[43]

D'autres, comme Scott, estimaient que le séminaire avait peut-être certaines obligations, mais qu'elles cessèrent quand les Kanehsata'kehró:non abandonnèrent l'Église catholique, puisque les obligations du séminaire consistaient à leur fournir instruction et aide spirituelle.

Les romanistes, qu'ils puissent être toute autre chose, ne sont pas des latitudinariens, et le séminaire n'a pas reçu de dotations pour poursuivre tout autre but que celui d'enseigner la doctrine de l'Église catholique romaine. En quittant le séminaire, les Indiens ont cessé de se soumettre à son instruction, et sont devenus semblables à des brebis sans berger.

[…] Cependant, on ne peut supposer un seul instant que le supérieur du séminaire soit dans l'obligation d'appuyer un pasteur méthodiste ni des enseignants protestants à Oka. Même si ces ecclésiastiques étaient les propriétaires de richesses considérables, je doute que ce soit dans leur pouvoir de les affecter à des usages protestants […].[44]

Toutefois, il était bien connu que le peuple de Kanehsatà:ke se tourna vers l'Église protestante en signe de protestation contre les traitements qu'ils subissaient aux mains du séminaire. Ce geste ne servait pas à dégager le séminaire de quelque obligation envers les « Indiens d'Oka ». Beta, au moins, reconnut que les droits des Kanehsata'kehró:non étaient considérés insignifiants comparativement à ceux du séminaire.

Il est important de se rappeler que la mission protestante à Oka remonte à cette époque et qu'elle résultait des traitements des prêtres envers les Indiens. Par conséquent, si quelqu'un devait s'en plaindre, le séminaire, et lui seul, est responsable de cette situation.

Mais le séminaire est une entité puissante; ce fait bien connu lui confère une grande influence, non seulement sur les membres de sa propre Église, mais aussi sur beaucoup d'autres qui, ayant de fortes craintes ou des aspirations politiques, n'auraient sous aucune considération monté cette communauté contre eux. En outre, les Indiens sont pauvres et impuissants; alors, à côté du séminaire, beaucoup les considèrent comme de simples *rien du tout*. Par conséquent, quand leurs revendications sont évaluées et ajustées, et qu'il est connu qu'elles entrent en conflit avec certaines demandes ou certaines prétentions du séminaire, il n'est pas difficile de comprendre qu'elles soient très désavantagées.

[...] Un effort a été fait pour montrer que, parce que les Indiens ont quitté l'Église catholique romaine, le séminaire est maintenant relevé de toute autre obligation ou responsabilité envers eux. Cela, comme tout ce qui a été écrit au détriment des Indiens, repose sur certaines suppositions non fondées qui sont trompeuses et vaines, dont celle voulant que les Indiens aient renoncé à l'Église catholique romaine sans raison valable. Mais ce n'est pas le cas. Les faits, qui sont nombreux, prouvent abondamment que les prêtres du séminaire les ont chassés de leur Église.[45]

Durant cette période pendant laquelle l'intérêt public était intense, la Aboriginal Protection Society basée à Londres fut informée de la situation à Kanehsatà:ke. La société écrivit au comte de Carnarvon, secrétaire d'État des colonies, pour lui demander de « presser le gouvernement à discerner et à protéger les droits des Indiens ». Elle le pressa également pour qu'une commission d'enquête soit instituée afin d'étudier la situation. Elle croyait que le peuple de Kanehsatà:ke devait détenir certains droits simplement en vertu d'avoir occupé le territoire pendant si longtemps.

[...] Les Indiens n'auraient pas pu jouir du privilège (si vraiment c'est le mot exact à employer) pendant cent ans sans avoir acquis certains droits concrets, et dont la nature et l'étendue doivent être assurées par le gouvernement pour que justice soit rendue. Le comité pense que c'est une question sur laquelle le gouvernement impérial, le protecteur naturel des sujets autochtones de la Couronne, a éminemment le droit d'user de son influence dans le but d'obtenir un arrangement juste et équitable pour résoudre un problème qui, s'il n'est pas réglé, peut mener à une effusion de sang.[46]

Il est sans doute vrai que les Kanehsata'kehró:non devaient avoir obtenu des droits dans la seigneurie, mais ils en furent empêchés à cause d'une manœuvre habile au moment de voter la Loi d'abolition des terres seigneuriales de 1853.

Pendant ce temps, l'Église méthodiste s'était engagée dans la lutte par les activités de ses missionnaires et de certains pasteurs qui ne mâchaient pas leurs mots. À cause de positions divergentes sur le sujet, il y eut une division importante au sein même de l'Église méthodiste. D'une part, il y avait ceux qui préconisaient que les Kanehsata'kehró:non n'avaient aucun droit territorial sur la seigneurie et favorisaient donc un déplacement. D'autre part, il y avait les membres qui, comme le pasteur John Borland, pensaient que le peuple avait des droits très concrets à Kanehsatà:ke et s'opposaient à son déplacement. Toutefois, les opinions de Borland n'étaient pas constantes. Il alternait entre son soutien et son opposition aux droits des Kanehsata'kehró:non. Ses activités lui valurent de vives critiques des autres membres du clergé. Un critique de Borland alla jusqu'à l'attaquer personnellement en disant :

Je suis convaincu qu'une hallucination et un engouement pénibles affectent l'intellect de M. Borland, et je suis persuadé que ses nouvelles tentatives d'agiter le public et l'Église méthodiste les convaincront profondément qu'il est indigne de confiance dans toutes les questions se rapportant aux Indiens d'Oka et à la conduite des Messieurs du séminaire [...] Sa façon de procéder depuis le début jusqu'à maintenant a été malicieuse et misérable. La malheureuse dispute entre les Indiens et le séminaire aurait depuis fort longtemps été amicalement réglée par le gouvernement n'eut été des conseils malveillants de M. Borland et de quelques autres.[47]

Apparemment, cette personne estimait que, sans l'influence perturbatrice de Borland et d'autres individus comme lui, les Kanehsata'kehró:non n'auraient jamais d'eux-mêmes pensé à revendiquer des droits sur leur propre territoire. Ils auraient probablement acquiescé en toute soumission aux désirs du séminaire et seraient partis joyeusement vers Muskoka sans du tout se préoccuper du territoire de leurs ancêtres ni de l'avenir de leurs enfants si Borland n'était pas intervenu. À un moment donné, Borland pensa que, depuis l'époque des concessions françaises originales jusqu'à la Loi de 1840, les droits du séminaire étaient intimement liés à ceux des Kanehsata'kehró:non. En fait, le séminaire obtint les concessions seulement en raison de son association avec les Indiens de la mission. Durant une période où il appuyait les droits des Kanehsata'kehró:non, Borland écrivit :

Le séminaire de Saint-Sulpice a fait une demande au roi de France, d'abord pour la seigneurie du Lac des Deux-Montagnes, puis pour celle qui y est adjacente. Mais au nom de qui et pour qui la demande a-t-elle été faite? Au nom des Indiens de cette mission. Aucun autre parti n'est cité par le séminaire et aucun autre objet n'est spécifié. Et pour rendre sa demande encore plus convaincante, il s'est obligé à certaines conditions et a offert certaines considérations, chacune d'entre elles faisant référence à ces Indiens, et à eux seuls.[48]

Il poursuivit en disant que la Loi, plutôt qu'éliminer les droits des Kanehsata'kehró:non, les confirmait, ainsi que ceux du séminaire.

Cette loi contient la déclaration de son but : confirmer les titres de propriété et les droits acquis par le séminaire, qui ont été soumis à l'influence de « doutes et de controverses ». Son objet n'était donc pas de trouver de nouveaux titres de propriété, mais de clarifier et de confirmer ceux qui existaient déjà. Quelle que soit la manière de l'exprimer, il ne faut jamais laisser supposer que les droits des partis, ceux des Indiens, par exemple, pas plus que ceux du séminaire, ne devraient être considérés comme rejetés ou annulés [...] Malgré l'effort évident de la part des auteurs de la Loi de 1840 de faire des Sulpiciens les « propriétaires absolus » de la seigneurie du Lac des Deux-Montagnes, deux choses doivent les faire échouer. Premièrement, la loi est faite pour *confirmer* un titre déjà existant, et elle ne *révoque* ni n'*annule,* explicitement ou implicitement, les clauses du titre, telles qu'elles étaient détaillées et comprises originalement. Deuxièmement, la mission envers les Indiens, l'une de ces clauses, est énoncée distinctement dans la loi comme dans les documents originaux [...].[49]

Par ailleurs, le pasteur William Scott pensait que les Kanehsata'kehró:non n'avaient d'autres droits que ceux accordés par le séminaire, sans que ce dernier n'ait l'obligation de les leur accorder. Il écrivit :

> [...] le séminaire adopte la même position que le gouvernement du Dominion envers les Indiens de Caughnawaga et d'autres tribus. Malheureusement, les Indiens d'Oka n'ont pas les mêmes droits et revendications que ceux de « Caughnawaga et d'autres tribus » [...] Depuis 1868 jusqu'à aujourd'hui, ils expriment les mêmes revendications et désirs [...] Sous trois administrations, la même réponse leur a été donnée. Ils ont par ailleurs été plusieurs fois informés essentiellement qu'ils occupent le territoire du Lac des Deux-Montagnes selon le bon plaisir du séminaire et les conditions qu'il désire exiger.[50]

Quant au déplacement comme tel, les divers groupes et individus avaient tous une opinion. Certains le considéraient même comme offensant, mais d'autres le voyaient comme la seule solution possible à une situation difficile. Certains critiques du plan de déplacement mettaient en doute la sagesse de déplacer le peuple vers la région éloignée de Muskoka alors que l'hiver approchait à grands pas. Un critique du plan affirma :

> Il est scandaleux de penser qu'on devrait demander aux pauvres Indiens d'Oka, qui sont là depuis 173 ans, de partir maintenant simplement pour plaire à des prêtres avides de s'emparer du territoire pour l'amour de leur influence politique. La possession constitue les neuf dixièmes de la loi, et cela les Indiens l'ont [...] Les Indiens ont autant le droit de penser par eux-mêmes que n'importe qui d'autre, et s'ils décidaient d'aller à Muskoka, je suppose que personne ne les empêcherait, mais les envoyer là simplement parce que le séminaire n'aime pas avoir des protestants près d'eux, c'est dérober d'honnêtes gens de leur droit pour plaire au diable et à ses agents, les Sulpiciens [...] Il est bien connu que le séminaire de Saint-Sulpice de Montréal est plus riche que la Banque de Montréal et qu'il est aussi avide d'acquérir quelques hectares de territoire occupés par quelques pauvres Indiens innocents que s'il mourait de faim. Il se vante de la supériorité du beurre fabriqué au monastère des Trappistes à Oka et il utilise toute son ingéniosité pour faire croire qu'Oka n'est pas une terre fertile et que la réserve de Gibson à Muskoka en est une où coulent le lait et le miel. Pourquoi les Sulpiciens n'y vont-ils pas si c'est si bon?[51]

William Scott favorisait bien sûr le déplacement et ne voyait aucun problème avec le plan :

> Le déplacement d'une bande d'Indiens d'un endroit à un autre n'est pas nouveau dans l'administration de leurs affaires. Au cours des 30 ou 40 dernières années, de tels changements de lieux se sont effectués avec le consentement des Indiens, selon des conditions équitables [...] Des difficultés peuvent surgir à l'égard de cette entreprise, mais elle est réalisable. Si les efforts du gouvernement et du séminaire sont appuyés par le zèle et la persévérance des Indiens, chaque difficulté ordinaire sera vaincue, et les Indiens pourront atteindre un bon niveau de confort et d'indépendance.[52]

Des correspondants de *The Gazette*, de *La Minerve*, ainsi que d'autres journaux locaux, avaient aussi leurs opinions sur le sujet :

> Le déplacement des Indiens, avec leur consentement, à un autre endroit qui offre des installations adéquates pour subvenir à leurs besoins est peut-être le meilleur moyen d'en venir à une entente et, si cette entente est réalisée, le déplacement mériterait de sincères félicitations. Mais même si c'était le cas, nous doutons sérieusement que la saison choisie pour le déplacement soit la meilleure. On dit que ceux qui ont consenti

à partir, et ils ne sont qu'une petite minorité, sont presque exclusivement des catholiques romains. Les Indiens, comme nous le comprenons, ont reçu la promesse des Messieurs du séminaire qu'ils leur accorderaient des provisions pour une quinzaine de jours après leur établissement dans leur nouvelle demeure. À première vue, cela peut sembler suffisamment généreux, mais la condition de ces Indiens, dans un lieu étranger, au début de l'hiver, peut difficilement être considérée comme enviable [...] Selon nous, ce n'est rien de moins qu'un acte de grande cruauté envers les Indiens, un acte dont ils n'ont pas demandé à être victimes.[53]

Et :

Quant à la sagesse de leur consentement au déplacement, il ne peut y avoir aucun doute. Chaque famille à Muskoka aura une ferme de quarante hectares qu'elle pourra cultiver au lieu du petit jardin qu'elle a présentement. Il y a de nombreuses possibilités d'emploi dans les camps de bûcheron et les scieries qui abondent dans la région de Muskoka. Il y a des avantages financiers à tirer de la pêche et de la chasse. En outre, toute question concernant les droits des Indiens au territoire qu'ils cultivent est écartée.[54]

Un correspondant de *The Gazette,* commentant un article qui parut dans un journal de la même époque, *The Witness,* réfutait certaines des déclarations faites par ce journal, l'accusant de déformer des faits.

Parmi les fausses déclarations les plus notables, en voici quelques-unes : « Ce printemps, le gouvernement a interdit à plusieurs familles d'ensemencer leurs terres, et ils se meurent de faim à cause de cette interdiction ». Aussi : « Les Indiens ont été informés que, s'ils ne partaient pas, des poursuites plus sévères que jamais seraient intentées contre eux, qu'ils perdraient leur agent du gouvernement et qu'ils seraient laissés sans défense contre leurs ennemis. Le Dominion peut-il faire endurer aux Indiens un déplacement par de tels moyens ? » Et encore : « L'agent indien a d'abord refusé avec persistance de reconnaître que les Indiens qui ne voulaient pas quitter leur maison étaient sous sa responsabilité. Il est l'agent de la petite minorité qui, ayant été persuadée d'accepter la proposition du déplacement, est maintenant obligée de partir par manque de nourriture ; il n'est pas l'agent des plus sages et des plus indépendants qui restent. » Il n'y a pas un mot de vrai dans chacune de ces déclarations.[55]

Les points de vue exprimés par les partis engagés dans le débat étaient nombreux et variés. Cependant, il y a une omission qui saute aux yeux dans les opinions publiées sur le sujet, à savoir les sentiments et les opinions des Kanehsata'kehró:non. Comme toujours, leurs déclarations concernant leurs droits territoriaux et leurs sentiments au sujet du déplacement n'étaient jamais considérés. Leurs droits en ayant occupé le territoire depuis des temps immémoriaux étaient ignorés en faveur de considérations de droits provenant de concessions octroyées à la mission. Le fait que les « Indiens de la mission » ne constituaient qu'une partie de la communauté de Kanehsatà:ke fut aussi ignoré lorsqu'on considérait leurs droits.

De plus, il est évident dans les opinions exprimées que, même si le concept des droits des autochtones était considéré, ces droits étaient insignifiants comparativement aux besoins toujours grandissants des colons blancs et des ambitions financières du séminaire. Même si plusieurs personnes émirent l'opinion que les diverses lois du gouvernement ayant trait au territoire du Lac des Deux-Montagnes confirmaient les droits des « Indiens », ainsi que ceux du séminaire, il y en avait beaucoup plus qui croyaient que ces lois abolissaient les droits territoriaux des Kanehsata'kehró:non. En fait, ce fut l'interprétation appliquée chaque fois que le peuple comparaissait devant les tribunaux canadiens pour défendre ses droits territoriaux.

Des allégations de fraude et d'abus furent lancées contre le séminaire et appuyées par des preuves très convaincantes. Beta, quant à lui, exposa avec des détails accablants les activités douteuses du séminaire. Cependant, le gouvernement ne fit rien à propos de ces allégations, donnant l'impression que, non seulement il ne condamnait pas les actions du séminaire, mais qu'il était aussi un partenaire consentant et actif dans le complot visant à dérober les Kanehsata'kehró:non de leur territoire, ce qui créait une occasion pour que les partenaires profitent de gains incalculables. L'engagement de groupes comme la Protestant Defense Alliance et la Civil Rights Alliance, ainsi que de personnes comme Norman Murray et le pasteur John Borland, détournait l'attention du public de la question des droits territoriaux des Kanehsata'kehró:non. Ils soulevèrent ou suscitèrent l'expression de certains sentiments fanatiques anticatholiques, et toute la question d'intolérance religieuse, bien qu'importante, n'était pas la question centrale dans la dispute. Elle contribua à empêcher toute résolution adéquate du problème et permit au gouvernement d'éviter de parler de la question des droits territoriaux d'une manière juste et vraiment équitable.

[1] Lettre signée par O'nahsakèn:rat, 10 août 1880, A. S. S. S., Université de Montréal, n° 157.

[2] Vankoughnet à N. O. Greene, 28 octobre 1880, Greene Papers, département des livres rares de l'Université McGill.

[3] N. O. Greene à Choquet, 19 janvier 1881, A. S. S. S., Université de Montréal, n° 172.

[4] O'nahsakèn:rat, 7 octobre 1880, Greene Papers, département des livres rares de l'Université McGill.

[5] Mémorandum, 26 septembre 1881, D. I. A. Ottawa, D. I. A. N. D. section des recherches historiques, classeur K-59.

[6] Pétition pour remplacer des chefs, Oka, 2 février 1881, Greene Papers, département des livres rares de l'Université McGill.

[7] Nécrologie, Joseph O'nahsakèn:rat, Dictionnaire biographique du Canada, vol. XI, 1881 à 1890, Université de Toronto, p. 655.

[8] John McGirr au surintendant général des Affaires indiennes, 21 février 1881, A. S. S. S., Université de Montréal, n° 177.

[9] Liste des familles indiennes qui ont quitté Oka, 1881, A. S. S. S., Université de Montréal, n° 214.

[10] Les chefs à John McGirr, 5 mars 1881, A. S. S. S., Université de Montréal, n° 177.

[11] Réponse aux chefs, Oka, Québec, Centre national des arts, RG 10, vol. 2034, dossier 8946-2.

[12] Charles A. Cooke, Rappel des moments de troubles à Oka, il y 13 ans, Ottawa Citizen, 6 juillet 1990.

[13] Ibid.

[14] Ibid.

[15] Lettre, J. Lacan, 18 avril 1881, A. S. S. S., Université de Montréal, n° 181.

[16] Décret en Ontario.

[17] The Montreal Gazette, 18 octobre 1881, en référence à l'article paru dans The Witness.

[18] Projet de règlement dans l'affaire du déménagement des Indiens, 26 août 1881, A. S. S. S., Université de Montréal, n° 192.

[19] Ibid.

[20] Vankoughnet à Choquet, 17 octobre 1881, A. S. S. S., Université de Montréal, n° 201.

[21] Charles A. Cooke, Rappel des moments de troubles à Oka, il y 13 ans, Ottawa Citizen, 6 juillet 1990.

[22] George Beers, Le gouvernement a-t-il peur de la question d'Oka? Broadside, Centre national des arts, C138881.

[23] Ibid.

[24] R. Laflamme, Le séminaire de Montréal, leurs droits et leurs titres de propriété, Saint-Hyacinthe, Courrier de Saint-Hyacinthe, 1880, p. 126, 127.

[25] William Scott, Rapport relatif aux affaires des Indiens d'Oka fait par le surintendant général des Affaires indiennes, imprimé par McLean, Roger & Co., janvier 1883, p. 36-38.

[26] Ibid.

[27] Ibid.

[28] Beta, Pour une meilleure compréhension de la question d'Oka et une aide en vue d'un arrangement équitable et rapide, Montréal, 1879, p. 72.

[29] Ibid., p. 30, 31.

[30] Choquet, The Globe, Toronto, lundi 10 octobre 1881.

[31] Beta. Pour une meilleure compréhension de la question d'Oka et une aide en vue d'un arrangement équitable et rapide, Montréal, 1879, p. 7.

[32] Ibid.

[33] Ibid., p. 12.

[34] Ibid., p. 22.

[35] R. Laflamme, Le séminaire de Montréal, leurs droits et leurs titres de propriété, Saint-Hyacinthe, Courrier de Saint-Hyacinthe, 1880, p. 110, 111.

[36] William Scott, Rapport relatif aux affaires des Indiens d'Oka fait par le surintendant général des Affaires indiennes, imprimé par McLean, Roger & Co., janvier 1883, p. 48, 49.

[37] L'honorable W. Badgley, Sur les questions de la seigneurie du Lac des Deux-Montagnes et de l'opinion des Indiens d'Oka, Montréal, 7 mai 1878, p. 12, 13.

[38] George Beers, Le spectateur canadien, Montréal, samedi 2 février 1878.

[39] L'honorable W. Badgley, Sur les questions de la seigneurie du Lac des Deux-Montagnes et de l'opinion des Indiens d'Oka, Montréal, 7 mai 1878, p. 13.

[40] Beta. Pour une meilleure compréhension de la question d'Oka et une aide en vue d'un arrangement équitable et rapide, Montréal, 1879, p. 13, 37, 38.

[41] Honorable W. Badgley, *Sur la question de la seigneurie du Lac des Deux-Montagnes et l'opinion des Indiens d'Oka*, Montréal, 7 mai 1878, p. 13.

[42] Beers, *Le spectateur canadien*, Montréal, samedi 2 février 1878, p. 41.

[43] Ibid.

[44] William Scott. Rapport relatif aux affaires des Indiens d'Oka fait par le surintendant général des Affaires indiennes, imprimé par McLean, Roger & Co., janvier 1883, p. 44, 45.

[45] Beta, *Pour une meilleure compréhension de la question d'Oka et une aide en vue d'un arrangement équitable et rapide*, Montréal, 1879.

[46] Chesson au comte de Carnarron de la Aboriginal Protection Society, 11 juillet 1877, Centre national des arts, RG 10, vol. 1967, dossier 5170.

[47] William Scott, *L'éviction d'Oka au président de la conférence de Montréal*, 1883, imprimerie de la *Gazette*.

[48] John Borland, *Les suppositions du séminaire de Saint-Sulpice d'être le propriétaire de la seigneurie du Lac des Deux-Montagnes et de celle qui y est adjacente examinées et réfutées et son traitement des Indiens du Lac des Deux-Montagnes exposé et dénoncé dans quatre lettres adressées à l'honorable Joseph Howe, secrétaire d'État du Département indien.* Surintendant des missions françaises et indiennes dans la province de Québec appartenant à l'Église méthodiste wesleyenne du Canada, Montréal, 1892, imprimerie de la *Gazette*, p. 9.

[49] Ibid., p. 10-16.

[50] William Scott, *Rapport relatif aux affaires des Indiens d'Oka fait par le surintendant général des Affaires indiennes*, imprimé par McLean, Roger & Co., janvier 1883, p. 24, 27.

[51] Norman Murray, *La question d'Oka contenant le titre de propriété original et un bref exposé du système féodal de la tenure seigneuriale au Canada et son abolition en 1854*, avec une révision générale de la question d'Oka en particulier et de l'agression romaine en général.

[52] William Scott, *Rapport relatif aux affaires des Indiens d'Oka fait par le surintendant général des Affaires indiennes*, imprimé par McLean, Roger & Co., janvier 1883, p. 52, 54.

[53] Coupure du journal *The Gazette*, mardi 8 octobre 1881, Montréal.

[54] Ibid., 11 octobre 1881, Montréal.

[55] Ibid.

CHAPITRE 7

DIRE AU REVOIR

Entre l'ombre et la lumière

Parce que la lumière produit un effet sur tout ce qu'elle touche, elle semble changer la forme et la couleur du monde en y créant des ombres. Les apparences ne sont pas toujours le reflet de la réalité.

C'est ce qui arriva quand un groupe de Kanehsata'kehró:non décida finalement de quitter le territoire. Des membres du peuple étaient fâchés que certains des leurs abandonnent la terre où l'on pouvait toujours ressentir l'esprit des ancêtres. Le désespoir et même la lâcheté étaient des raisons invoquées pour expliquer leur départ en terre lointaine. Ceux qui choisirent de rester se sentaient vraiment trahis parce que leur nombre diminuait. Ils seraient moins nombreux à s'accrocher au territoire et à résister aux Roti'kharahón:tsi (robes noires).

Tous les Kanehsata'kehró:non luttaient quotidiennement pour nourrir et vêtir leurs enfants. Souvent, leurs ventres étaient vides et leurs petits pieds nus, malgré le froid qui s'intensifiait. Ceux qui avaient ouvertement défié les Roti'kharahón:tsi étaient maltraités. Personne ne se sentait en sécurité. Les Roti'kharahón:tsi avaient tellement de pouvoir que beaucoup de Kanehsata'kehró:non vivaient constamment dans la peur de perdre leur liberté et leur terre et de voir leur famille mourir de faim. Vivre au jour le jour n'était pas facile pour des gens qui connaissaient bien la terre et qui savaient comment se conduire dans les conseils.

Ce beau village près du lac devenait lentement un véritable cauchemar pour la plupart des Kanehsata'kehró:non. D'un village honoré où l'on avait déjà tenu des conseils importants et dont le nom était mentionné dans les très anciennes cérémonies de condoléances des Rotinonhseshá:ka, il était devenu un endroit où la tristesse et la crainte l'emportaient sur les rires et la joie.

Même si certains ne pouvaient pas comprendre les événements, je pouvais voir deux choses émerger de tout cela : l'espoir pour ceux qui partaient et la continuation des conditions difficiles pour ceux qui restaient. Un but commun se mêlait aux ombres : l'importance des sept générations à venir, la responsabilité du peuple de bâtir quelque chose pour les enfants qui naîtraient.

Les Kanehsata'kehró:non qui avaient accepté de partir croyaient que leurs enfants et leurs petits-enfants auraient une vie meilleure ailleurs, loin des Roti'kharahón:tsi. C'est pourquoi, de la douleur de partir brillait la promesse de jours plus heureux pour leurs enfants.

Et ceux qui sont restés s'attachaient à la terre. Ils continuaient à enseigner à leurs enfants et à leurs petits-enfants ce que leurs ancêtres leur avaient enseigné : que Kanehsatà:ke était leur foyer et qu'ils devaient toujours en prendre soin.

Tous les sentiers deviennent clairs pour celui qui perçoit le jeu entre l'ombre et la lumière.

LE DÉBUT DU DÉPLACEMENT

Le plan du déplacement progressait. Malgré l'intérêt énorme du public et les intenses discussions sur la situation des Kanehsata'kehró:non, on restait sourd à leur voix, c'est-à-dire jusqu'à ce que certains d'entre eux disent : « Nous irons à Muskoka ». Les questions légales étant réglées et la nouvelle réserve étant payée, on fit rapidement des arrangements pour déplacer le peuple à Gibson. En ce matin du 22 octobre 1881, l'aube paraissait lumineuse et claire. Les cœurs étaient lourds, et plusieurs se sentaient trahis par ceux qui partaient. Trente-neuf familles avaient signé en faveur de leur déplacement; une grande foule était venue leur faire leurs adieux. C'était un jour mémorablement triste autant pour ceux qui partaient que pour ceux qui restaient. Charles A. Cooke, qui était du nombre de ceux qui partaient, raconta plus tard ses impressions de la journée :

> [...] Je me rappelle l'après-midi où nous avons dit adieu à notre maison dans le village. Un Canadien français, appelé La Baie, un bon voisin, est venu nous dire au revoir avec un panier de pommes rouges juste pour nous garder les mâchoires occupées sur la route vers Muskoka. Nous avions apporté nos effets personnels au village afin d'être prêts à les mettre dans le bateau à vapeur le jour suivant.
>
> Je me rappelle le matin du 22 octobre : nous avons quitté la maison de François Jacob où nous avions passé notre dernière nuit à Oka. Nous, les plus jeunes, avions dormi sur le plancher. Nous sommes allés à la hâte vers le bateau appelé *Dagmar* trois heures avant l'heure de départ prévue. Le quai était rempli de monde venu de partout pour voir le départ en masse de personnes décidées à quitter Oka pour de bon.
>
> Ce matin-là, les cinq routes menant à Oka étaient bondées de gens aux sentiments partagés. Certains étaient portés par la curiosité, tandis que d'autres avaient le cœur triste de dire adieu à leurs bien-aimés. D'autres encore, par leur visage malicieux, montraient qu'ils n'étaient pas tristes de voir ces voyageurs en route pour Muskoka secouer finalement la poussière d'Oka de leurs mocassins.
>
> Puis, on a entendu les trois coups de sifflet du bateau à vapeur, indiquant qu'il allait bientôt quitter le quai. Les salutations se mêlaient aux larmes et aux accolades. Sur le bateau, les chanteurs se sont réunis à l'avant du pont et ont commencé à entonner leur chant d'adieu en langue indienne – un chant spécialement composé pour l'occasion. Certains parmi eux ne pouvaient pas chanter tant la tristesse des mots étouffait leur voix.
>
> Je me souviens d'un « Ka rih wi yo », un violoneux gaucher, qui avait apporté son violon au quai et qui devait jouer quelques morceaux pour faire regretter aux voyageurs vers Muskoka leur départ d'Oka. Le chant était tellement touchant qu'il n'a pas pu jouer de son violon; tout ce qu'il pouvait faire était de s'essuyer les yeux et le nez.
>
> Je me rappelle aussi un jeune homme qui était monté à bord du bateau pour donner des poignées de main et dire au revoir à quelques-uns de ses amis partant pour Muskoka. Il était tellement occupé à les saluer qu'il n'a pas remarqué que le bateau avait quitté le quai. Il a été obligé de les accompagner jusqu'à Muskoka où il a vécu jsuqu'à sa mort des années plus tard.[1]

Départ pour Gibson
de Katsi'tsakwas

Le récit de cette journée ressemble aux histoires que les Kanehsata'kehró:non transmettent de génération en génération. La tradition orale rappelle aussi qu'un prêtre, qui se tenait sur le rivage pour regarder le peuple partir, pleurait à chaudes larmes. Une personne intriguée lui demanda s'il était triste de les voir partir. Le prêtre lui répondit : « Oui, je suis triste. Je suis triste parce qu'il y en a tant qui restent toujours ici ».[2]

Le voyage vers le comté de Gibson dura environ dix jours. Les déplacés remontèrent la rivière des Outaouais sur un cargo et, de Sainte-Anne, ils prirent un train pour Gravenhurst. En route, Mme Antoine Dewasha (Tewísha) accoucha d'une petite fille qu'elle nomma Watahí:ne.[3] Plusieurs familles s'arrêtèrent à Gravenhurst où ils passèrent l'hiver avant de se rendre jusqu'à Gibson. Le reste se rendit à Bala par bateau à vapeur. Comme aucune route n'atteignait la réserve, le groupe dû traverser des rapides en radeau jusqu'à leur destination finale. Le peuple avait peut-être de grands espoirs et de formidables attentes pour leur nouveau foyer, mais ce qu'ils rencontrèrent, en cette première année, fut des épreuves et une extrême pauvreté.

Selon les conditions du décret voté par le gouvernement canadien, le séminaire devait construire une grande maison de bois rond pour chaque famille. Dans sa précipitation à déplacer les gens à Gibson, le gouvernement n'avait chargé aucun représentant de s'assurer que cette exigence soit satisfaisante avant leur départ. À part les vêtements qu'ils portaient, ils arrivèrent à Gibson avec peu de choses, des tentes étaient leur seul abri. Le jour suivant, le 1er novembre, comme une neige abondante tombait, ils se précipitèrent pour installer des abris de fortune afin de se protéger du froid. Ils n'avaient pas de vêtements appropriés, et les femmes durent couper de vieilles couvertures en de longues lisières et en envelopper les pieds des enfants pour les réchauffer.[4] Les gens déplacés à Gibson s'étaient attendus à ce que le gouvernement leur fournisse des provisions et des vêtements adéquats pour une longue période, mais ils ne reçurent de la nourriture que pour deux semaines. En peu de temps, non seulement ils souffraient de froid et vivaient sans abri, mais ils se mouraient aussi de faim. Le 15 novembre, Louis Sanation écrivit à l'agent indien, John McGirr, au sujet de la promesse de provisions.

[…] l'information que vous m'avez transmise selon laquelle le gouvernement ne peut pas (ou ne veut pas) nous fournir des provisions pendant l'hiver comme nous nous y attendions est une grande surprise pour nous. Que pouvons-nous faire, nous sommes étrangers dans un nouvel environnement? Nos baraques ne sont pas en condition pour y entrer – nos provisions sont très maigres et environ deux tiers d'entre nous n'ont même pas assez d'argent pour acheter des provisions pour un jour […].[5]

Le gouvernement canadien avait promis de fournir des provisions au peuple pour aussi longtemps qu'il en aurait besoin; cela faisait partie de l'entente d'achat du territoire avec l'Ontario.[6] Le gouvernement ontarien ne voulait pas se retrouver responsable du bien-être des Indiens, mais il voulait s'assurer que les devoirs liés à l'installation soient exécutés. Le gouvernement canadien n'honora pas cet engagement et négligea de faire respecter les conditions imposées au séminaire. En général, il adoptait l'attitude « loin des yeux loin du cœur » relativement à la condition du peuple déplacé à Gibson. Le 19 novembre, Lawrence Vankoughnet, surintendant général adjoint des Affaires indiennes, pour la forme écrivit à A. Choquet, agent du séminaire, afin de s'informer des raisons pour lesquelles aucun bâtiment n'avait pas encore été construit.[7] Sa réponse fut assez simple. Puisqu'il n'existait aucune route de Bala à la réserve, il était impossible de transporter les matériaux nécessaires à la construction. De plus, les Indiens avaient choisi de s'installer au même endroit que les squatters.[8] En réalité, le séminaire, ayant payé le gouvernement pour les bâtiments laissés par les gens à Kanehsatà:ke, ne se sentait pas du tout obligé de construire de nouvelles maisons pour eux à Gibson.[9] Le gouvernement suivait le modèle du séminaire, qui consistait à accepter des obligations pour atteindre ses buts, puis à s'organiser pour s'en décharger.

En octobre 1882, le séminaire essaya de se dégager de l'engagement de construire des maisons pour le peuple de Gibson. Il invoqua les dépenses considérables déjà encourues par le déplacement afin de justifier son hésitation à honorer ses engagements.[10] Le fait que la majorité des Kanehsata'kehró:non demeuraient toujours au Lac des Deux-Montagnes et refusaient de partir suscita sûrement une hésitation à investir plus d'argent dans le projet. Trois ans après le premier déplacement, quelques maisons furent finalement construites, mais elles ne répondaient pas aux normes formulées dans le décret.[11] Elles n'étaient rien de plus que des baraques que les gens s'étaient construites à la hâte. Le séminaire, soutenu par l'apathie du gouvernement, réussit à éviter d'assumer cette obligation, malgré le fait qu'il était, ainsi que le gouvernement, lié par le décret.

Pendant ce temps, le peuple à Gibson continuait de lutter pour survivre. Au début de décembre 1881, trois baraques avaient été construites, mais la majorité des gens vivait toujours sous des tentes.[12] Ayant quitté Kanehsatà:ke pour avoir la paix à Gibson, ils y trouvèrent le froid, la faim et la maladie. Incroyablement, ils rencontrèrent une autre difficulté : les squatters canadiens-français. Se sentant inquiets, faute d'une entente avec le gouvernement, les squatters menacèrent d'user de violence envers les Kanien'kehà:ka.[13] Il semblait que, pour les Kanehsata'kehró:non, la paix était introuvable.

À la fin de décembre, les gens à Gibson étaient tous dans leurs baraques, mais n'avaient toujours reçu aucune provision. De ces familles qui avaient passé l'hiver à Gravenhurst, plusieurs souffraient de la typhoïde. Avant la fin de l'année, six enfants étaient décédés et une femme était au seuil de la mort.[14] Le séminaire commença à craindre que la nouvelle de ces difficultés atteigne Kanehsatà:ke et empêche d'autres personnes de déménager à Gibson. A. Choquet déclara dans une lettre à J. A. Mousseau, secrétaire d'État, qu'il avait rencontré mille misères pour convaincre le journal *The Witness* de ne pas publier de récits sur les privations endurées par le peuple à Muskoka. Il poursuivait en disant qu'il avait pressé le gouvernement d'envoyer des provisions, mais sans résultat.[15] Tandis que le gouvernement et le séminaire s'activaient à limiter les dégâts, aucun d'eux n'acceptait la responsabilité du problème. Le 5 novembre 1881, un article dans le *Globe and Mail* décrivait en termes élogieux la réserve à Gibson et les conditions qui y prévalaient :

> [...] il y avait un bâtiment de bois 30 m x 12 m, jadis utilisé par la compagnie forestière. Cette maison servira de demeure aux Indiens pendant l'hiver et offrira amplement de logement pour tous puisqu'elle est équipée de 70 lits arrangés côte à côte comme des couchettes dans un bateau à vapeur [...].

> Le gouvernement leur a donné suffisamment de provisions pour leur suffire tout l'hiver; et même s'ils n'avaient aucune provision, le gibier est abondant dans les environs [...] Il y a beaucoup de perdrix, et les lacs avoisinants abondent de poissons [...].

> On se sentait comme en été, et il faisait tellement doux et chaud que de nouvelles feuilles apparaissaient sur les buissons, certaines mesurant quatre centimètres [...].[16]

Les gens qui avaient été délogés de leurs maisons à Kanehsatà:ke étaient abandonnés aux dures réalités de la faim, du froid et de la maladie dans le comté de Gibson. Chaque jour, ils luttaient pour calmer les estomacs creux des enfants affamés et travaillaient dur rien que pour se protéger du froid. Le public canadien, dans une ignorance confortable, était amené à croire que tout allait très bien.

Même les feuilles donnent des avertissements

Quand on se promène sur la terre et qu'on en prend soin, plusieurs choses peuvent se révéler. En regardant au loin, je peux savoir si une tempête s'en vient d'après la manière dont coule la rivière. Je peux voir de très petits nuages et savoir ce qui arrivera. Les feuilles aussi avertissent de l'arrivée d'une tempête par la façon dont elles pendent aux branches.

Le monde naturel révèle toujours ces choses si on s'arrête pour l'écouter. Par ailleurs, il y a ceux qui ne peuvent voir plus loin que le soleil, la pluie et les nuages. Ils ne sauront jamais lire sans lettres ni écouter des voix silencieuses.

Premiers jours à Gibson
de la collection de photos de Roy Rennie

TERRE PROMISE DÉCEVANTE

Tandis que les voyageurs en direction de Muskoka remontaient la rivière vers leur nouvelle demeure, la persécution contre ceux qui restaient à Kanehsatà:ke se renouvelait vigoureusement. Quelques heures après leur départ, un groupe de la police du séminaire, que la presse de l'époque qualifiait de « fiers-à-bras », accompagné par environ « 40 Canadiens français attaquèrent une maison indienne, armés de bâtons et de haches ».[17] La maison avait été laissée par une famille déplacée à Gibson et reprise par des parents. Durant cette attaque, quatre femmes qui étaient à l'intérieur de la maison furent gravement battues, et leurs effets personnels endommagés et jetés dehors. Mme Pierre Beauvais, victime de l'attaque, raconta son expérience :

> J'étais assise dans la maison en train de coudre quand les hommes sont entrés. Fauteaux m'a attrapée par le bras; en me levant, il m'a poussée fort et je suis tombée sur le poêle, ce qui m'a causé des contusions. Je n'ai pas eu le temps de prendre ce que je cousais. Il m'a donné des coups de pied à la cuisse et aux côtes gauches. Fauteaux a pris un bâton pour me frapper. Chrétien lui a défendu de me frapper, puis, Fauteaux a couru après MaryAnne Petitcrit.[18]

Pierre Beauvais raconta plus tard que « sa femme était enceinte et risquait de mourir » à cause de l'attaque. Elle avait des côtes cassées et plusieurs échymoses.[19] Les chefs écrivirent au département des Affaires indiennes pour rapporter l'attaque brutale et solliciter sa protection. Ils demandèrent que les malfaiteurs soient accusés de voies de fait selon la loi.[20] Le Département envoya son représentant, William Scott, pour examiner cet incident, ainsi que d'autres qui s'étaient également produits. Pendant ce temps, Vankoughnet, surintendant général adjoint, leur donna l'ordre de « rester tranquilles et de ne pas enfreindre la loi ».[21] Scott passa plusieurs jours à Kanehsatà:ke pour s'entretenir avec des témoins. Pour sa part, le séminaire affirma qu'il avait été nécessaire d'user de force pour prendre possession de la maison, mais assura que personne n'avait été blessé pendant l'incident.[22] Après l'enquête, Scott rapporta ses conclusions au Département. Résultat? En décembre 1881, Vankoughnet écrivit au séminaire pour lui demander de cesser de persécuter les Indiens, car cela pouvait entraîner leur colère et leur refus de déménager à Gibson.[23] Cet incident n'était qu'un parmi beaucoup d'autres conçus pour forcer le peuple à suivre leur parenté à Gibson. Alors que des rapports négatifs sur les conditions à Gibson arrivaient peu à peu à Kanehsatà:ke, des efforts furent faits pour contrer leur effet. En juillet 1882, John McGirr, agent indien à Gibson, écrivit à Mitchel Frett, un des chefs de Kanehsatà:ke. Il rapporta la merveilleuse situation du peuple dans sa nouvelle réserve :

> [...] leurs récoltes paraissent remarquablement bonnes. Je n'en ai pas vues de meilleures entre Ottawa et la réserve. Certaines produisent 1 tonne de foin par hectare. Leurs pommes de terre, leur maïs, leur avoine, leurs pois et leur blé leur donneront aussi un bon rendement [...] Alors, vous voyez qu'ils sont dans une bien meilleure situation qu'à Oka [...] Ils sont très heureux de leur nouvelle réserve et disent qu'ils ne retourneraient à Oka pour rien au monde.[24]

Pendant que McGirr écrivait sa lettre, des gens quittaient Gibson pour d'autres endroits et certains retournaient même à Kanehsatà:ke. En août 1882, vingt-deux familles avaient déjà quitté Gibson pour aller ailleurs, comme à Saint-Régis, à Kahnawà:ke ou à Thyendinaga.[25] En décembre 1882, William Scott écrivit aux chefs de Kanehsatà:ke. Il leur affirma que le gouvernement avait seulement « leur prospérité et leur bonheur » à cœur.[26] Il les encouragea à profiter des arrangements en leur faveur. Son baratin comprenait une menace subtile selon laquelle ils ne trouveraient pas la paix aussi longtemps qu'ils demeureraient à Kanehsatà:ke.

Déterminés à rester, les Kanehsata'kehró:non envisagèrent une fois de plus la possibilité de présenter devant les tribunaux une cause type qui prouverait une fois pour toutes leurs droits territoriaux à Kanehsatà:ke. Scott fut envoyé pour les mettre au courant de la position du Département sur la question. Il leur dit qu'il était impossible de choisir une cause type appropriée.[27] De plus, tous les avis juridiques antérieurs avaient favorisé le séminaire. Les Kanehsata'kehró:non n'auraient alors aucun appui pour présenter leur cause devant les tribunaux.

Pendant ce temps, le peuple à Gibson affrontait son premier hiver. Les emplois promis aux déplacés ne se concrétisèrent pas la première année. Ils étaient arrivés trop tard dans la saison, et les compagnies forestières avaient déjà engagé tous les hommes dont elles avaient besoin. Les provisions étaient insuffisantes, et toute leur énergie était consacrée à construire des abris et à défricher la terre pour l'ensemencement du printemps prochain. En mars 1882, le surintendant général adjoint des Affaires indiennes écrivit à Louis Sanation pour l'informer que le gouvernement n'accorderait plus d'aide au peuple à Gibson.

> Veuillez informer votre communauté que le Département n'a plus l'intention de lui accorder d'autre aide alimentaire et qu'elle doit trouver un moyen de gagner sa propre subsistance et de devenir autonome dans l'avenir.[28]

Camp de bûcheron
de la collection de photos de Roy Rennie

En avril de cette année-là, l'agent indien John McGirr se rendit à Kanehsatà:ke pour évaluer les propriétés des habitants dans le but d'accélérer leur déplacement. Il les trouva peu disposés à discuter de la question du déplacement et fâchés qu'on arpente leurs terres.[29] Pendant ce temps à Gibson, les problèmes entre les Onkwehón:we et les squatters s'intensifiaient. Les Kanien'kehà:ka à Gibson vivaient sous la constante menace de violence de la part des squatters et, le 10 avril, ils reçurent des avis d'éviction d'Abraham Houle, l'un des squatters.[30] Louis Sanation écrivit au Département pour l'informer de la dernière action des squatters et pour demander son aide. Il dit : « […] nous avons quitté Oka pensant trouver la paix et la tranquillité, mais nous éprouvons encore les mêmes difficultés ».[31]

Le problème attira l'attention des plus hautes instances de gouvernement. Dans un rapport d'un comité du Conseil privé, on recommandait un règlement rapide au problème des squatters. Le rapport disait qu'« il était très souhaitable que tout motif de plainte possible des Indiens concernant ladite réserve où ils sont déménagés disparaisse ».[32] Le comité poursuivait en recommandant que le séminaire avance la somme de 5000 $ pour régler le problème avec les squatters. Le 13 juin 1882, le surintendant général adjoint écrivit à A. Choquet, agent du séminaire, pour se plaindre que le séminaire n'avait pas rempli ses obligations quant au logement à Gibson. Il indiquait son inquiétude que cela entraîne un retard dans le déplacement de ceux qui étaient toujours à Kanehsatà:ke.[33]

En réponse, le séminaire promit d'envoyer des charpentiers à Gibson pour construire des maisons. En septembre 1882, aucun charpentier n'était encore arrivé et, un an après le vote du décret et le déplacement, les prêtres commencèrent leur campagne pour se dégager de leurs obligations.[34] Ils proposèrent de donner 20 $ pour la construction de chaque maison si les hommes les construisaient eux-mêmes.[35] Cette proposition était inacceptable pour les gens, car ils avaient à peine le temps de chasser pour se nourrir et étaient occupés à défricher la terre. De plus, ils avaient estimé que pour se loger adéquatement il en coûterait environ 100 $ par maison. En août 1882, le chef Louis Sanation écrivit à John McGirr pour l'informer qu'un mois s'était déjà écoulé depuis que Choquet avait promis des charpentiers. Le temps froid arrivait et leurs baraques n'étaient pas convenables pour passer un autre hiver.[36] Le séminaire écrivit ensuite au Département pour lui demander d'être dégagé de toute autre responsabilité.[37]

Selon le décret, les Kanehsata'kehró:non avaient quatre ans pour profiter de la possibilité de partir pour Gibson. Toute une année s'était écoulée depuis le premier déplacement, et ils ne manifestaient toujours pas de désir de rejoindre les autres à Muskoka. Le gouvernement fit d'autres efforts pour les persuader de partir. William Scott se rendit plusieurs fois à Kanehsatà:ke pour rencontrer le peuple. En janvier 1883, il arriva au village pendant les cérémonies de la mi-hiver. Après avoir assisté aux cérémonies, puis entendu un sermon dominical, il rencontra les chefs et les principaux hommes de la communauté pour discuter d'une dépêche envoyée par le Département qui expliquait en détail le déplacement proposé. Simplement et éloquemment, ils parlèrent à tour de rôle de leurs sentiments concernant le déplacement. Une fois de plus, ils réitérèrent leurs objections et leur refus d'être déplacés. Ils ne voulaient pas quitter le lieu de repos de leurs ancêtres ni abandonner le droit de leurs enfants à la terre pour satisfaire l'avidité du séminaire. Un homme dit qu'il « ne partirait que lorsque Dieu prendrait son âme ».[38] Ils remercièrent Scott d'être venu pour transmettre leur réponse au gouvernement, mais le chargèrent de lui dire de ne plus leur proposer de telles offres parce qu'ils les trouvaient offensantes. Malgré cette réponse nettement négative, Scott rapporta qu'il pensait avoir obtenu quelques bons résultats durant cette rencontre.

Deux mois plus tard à Gibson, le peuple faisait face à une autre crise. Angus Cooke écrivit au Département pour demander de l'aide. Le sol dans les hauteurs était, semble-t-il, très pauvre, trop pauvre pour cultiver. En conséquence, la plupart des gens avaient semé dans les marais. Mais la compagnie forestière de Muskoka avait construit un barrage sur la rivière Black, inondant ainsi les basses terres de la réserve.[39] Les récoltes étaient perdues. Ce problème devint récurrent à Gibson, mais la solution était lente à arriver. L'agent indien rapporta la difficulté en disant que les plaintes des Indiens étaient exagérées, et le Département négligea d'agir sur-le-champ.[40] En 1883, les récoltes furent donc encore une fois perdues. Les responsables de leur bien-être manifestaient une indifférence froide et une apathie paralysante à l'égard des épreuves que subissait le peuple à Gibson. À Kanehsatà:ke, le gouvernement suivait le modèle établi depuis longtemps, celui d'envoyer des agents et des représentants pour rencontrer les Kanehsata'kehró:non sous prétexte de vouloir entendre leurs points de vue sur les sujets qui concernent leur vie. Pendant tout ce temps, le gouvernement s'employait à faire avancer impitoyablement et systématiquement son propre plan (c'est-à-dire celui du séminaire). On entendait la voix du peuple comme on entend le vent, mais on n'écoutait jamais leurs paroles ni n'en comprenait le sens.

Le 24 novembre 1882, William Scott rencontra de nouveau les Kanehsata'kehró:non. Encore une fois, on discuta du déplacement. Il rapporta que les gens à Gibson prospéraient, que le sol y était de bonne qualité et qu'il y avait une abondance de bois qu'ils pouvaient couper quand ils le voulaient.[41] Scott omit de mentionner que les compagnies forestières avaient déjà loué de grandes étendues de terres boisées pour leur propre usage et que tous les pins étaient réservés au gouvernement de l'Ontario. Même si les gens pouvaient couper du bois pour défricher la terre, selon les devoirs liés à leur installation, ils ne pouvaient pas le couper pour le vendre. Malgré tous les avantages que Scott présenta en faveur du déplacement, le peuple de Kanehsatà:ke ne changeait pas d'avis. Ce qui ne fut jamais compris ni considéré par les prêtres, le gouvernement ou les soi-disant sauveurs du peuple était le lien indissociable des Kanehsata'kehró:non avec leur mère, la terre d'où ils étaient sortis. Quand il était reconnu, ce lien était considéré comme quelque chose de négatif, une attitude qui présentait un obstacle à la civilisation et au progrès des « sauvages ». La terre faisait et fait partie intégrante de l'identité du peuple qu'elle soutient. Le gouvernement canadien et ses agents faisaient fi des rancœurs des Kanehsata'kehró:non envers ceux qui les avaient quittés. Tandis que le peuple à Gibson attendait impatiemment l'arrivée des autres Kanehsata'kehró:non, ces derniers ne voulaient pas aller vivre avec eux. En réponse à la présentation de Scott, ils lui dirent :

> Nous sommes heureux que les Indiens à Gibson aillent bien et aient de bonnes perspectives d'espoir. Nous sommes également heureux d'entendre que le sol est bon et qu'il y a du bois en abondance. Nous sommes satisfaits d'apprendre que la réserve est de bonne qualité, mais nos objections à y déménager sont aussi fortes qu'avant. Les préjugés que nous avons toujours ne sont pas contre le territoire, mais contre les gens qui ont brisé notre unité et qui, sans nous consulter ni avoir bien considéré nos droits, ont accepté de fausses promesses et compromis nos revendications.[42]

Il est clair que ces sentiments étaient profonds et constituaient un obstacle considérable au plan de déplacement. Ils ne furent pas pris au sérieux jusqu'au moment où, plusieurs années plus tard, des Montréalais commencèrent un mouvement pour trouver un autre lieu pour le déplacement. Pour sa part, Scott minimisait l'importance de ces réponses négatives en rapportant qu'elles n'étaient pas partagées par tous. Il tenta de circonvenir les chefs en rencontrant des personnes en privé et rapporta que certaines étaient très en faveur du déplacement.[43] De toutes façons, ce que les Kanehsata'kehró:non disaient sur ce qu'ils voulaient avait peu d'importance. Ils ne faisaient pas le poids contre la puissance et l'influence du séminaire ou du gouvernement qui semblait être son instrument. Tout ce que le peuple pouvait faire était de rester. Il pouvait être une source constante d'embarras et d'irritation pour le gouvernement et le séminaire, et il le serait.

En avril 1884, Scott recommanda qu'Angus Cooke se rende à Kanehsatà:ke pour rencontrer le peuple et lui faire part de tous les avantages de vivre dans le comté de Gibson. Scott pensait que Cooke «pouvait exercer une influence positive sur les chefs à Oka durant la présente crise»,[44] mais la visite de Cook n'eut pas l'effet désiré. La plupart des Kanehsata'kehró:non restaient opposés au plan de déplacement.

Il y eut toutefois deux personnes qui, à ce moment-là, décidèrent d'accepter l'offre de partir. En janvier 1884, Vankoughnet écrivit à M. Colin, supérieur du séminaire, pour l'informer que Peter White et Louis Laforce, récemment déménagés à Gibson, avaient besoin d'aide.[45] Selon le décret de 1881, les Kanehsata'kehró:non avaient quatre ans pour profiter de l'offre de déplacement, et il était raisonnable de présumer que les obligations du séminaire couvraient aussi cette période. Trois ans s'étaient écoulés depuis le déplacement original, et le séminaire cherchait à éviter d'assumer ses responsabilités quant à ces deux hommes. En décembre, ils n'avaient toujours pas reçu d'aide.[46] De plus, jusqu'en 1895, les gens de Gibson n'avaient toujours pas de logement adéquat.[47] Le séminaire maintenait qu'il n'avait jamais accepté cette partie du décret relative à la construction de maisons et qu'il n'y était pas lié. De plus, il s'était déchargé de toute obligation à cet égard en payant 20 $ pour la construction de chaque maison.[48] En ce qui concerne Louis Laforce, la maison qu'il avait laissée à Oka était depuis occupée par ses enfants. La propriété de la maison était disputée, et le séminaire ne pouvait pas « approuver de telles procédures ».[49] Peter

White vivait à Aylmer, au Québec, au moment du déplacement, et le séminaire estimait qu'il n'avait pas droit à l'offre.[50]

Au cours des années qui suivirent, plusieurs « amis » des Kanehsata'kehró:non firent des tentatives sporadiques pour les persuader de déménager à Gibson ou ailleurs. En juin 1887, Samuel Dawson proposa qu'ils déménagent sur un territoire de leur choix dans la province de l'Ontario ou du Manitoba parce qu'ils (les Kanehsata'kehró:non) estimaient que les terres à Gibson n'étaient pas bonnes.[51] Vankoughnet affirma que le gouvernement ne s'opposerait pas à ce plan, à condition que le séminaire assume l'achat des terres choisies.[52] En décembre 1889, Richard White, directeur du journal *The Montreal Gazette*, écrivit à E. Dewdney, alors secrétaire d'État, pour lui rapporter qu'il avait eu des discussions avec le séminaire par l'entremise de son supérieur, M. Colin, et avait constaté que le séminaire était en faveur du plan de Dawson et disposé à payer pour qu'il y ait des améliorations à Oka.[53]

Pendant ce temps, des « négociations » avaient lieu entre les Kanehsata'kehró:non et des individus, tels que George Beers, William B. Shaw et J. A. Mathewson.[54] En novembre 1889, Beers écrivit à Dewdney pour lui signifier qu'il « avait décidé de ne pas faire confiance aux chefs » et qu'il ferait imprimer la proposition en mohawk et en anglais pour en remettre une copie à chaque famille.[55] Il avait apparemment rencontré de l'opposition au déplacement.[56] En janvier 1890, en essayant de contourner la direction de Kanehsatà:ke, Beers envoya à la communauté la lettre promise dans laquelle il parlait du travail entrepris dans son intérêt par leurs « amis », de la bonne volonté du gouvernement, de l'opinion de l'Église méthodiste et de la générosité du séminaire. Il poursuivait en la pressant d'accepter l'offre :

> [...] c'est la dernière proposition que vous recevrez. Le séminaire semble prêt à l'accepter, mais si vous refusez cette bonne offre, vous devrez vous attendre à ce qu'il exerce les droits qu'il réclame. Qui vous défendra alors? Vous ne pourrez blâmer vos amis s'ils refusent de vous défendre.[57]

Malgré ces efforts pour les persuader de déménager et l'offre d'aller ailleurs qu'à Gibson, les Kanehsata'kehró:non refusaient toujours le déplacement. En 1890, ce refus leur avait coûté la perte de l'appui du public. En mars de cette année, Beers écrivit une lettre au journal *The Gazette* expliquant ses raisons en faveur du déplacement. Dans l'ensemble, elle disait ceci : Leur chef Joseph était mort, plusieurs de leurs sympathisants étaient morts ou avaient déménagé, J. J. Maclaren était maintenant juge en Ontario, le public était fatigué de toute l'affaire et « la question de titres de propriété était également morte à cause des opinons du gouvernement et de l'indifférence du public ».[58]

Ainsi se termina l'appui en faveur de « la situation désespérée des Indiens d'Oka ». Même si bien des gens avaient travaillé fort pour faire ce qu'ils considéraient être le mieux pour le peuple, leur attitude paternaliste empêcha la véritable résolution des problèmes. Les droits des Kanehsata'kehró:non n'avaient jamais été discutés de manière juste et équitable. Le peuple avait présenté toutes les questions de droits territoriaux devant les tribunaux coloniaux, mais l'objectif de toutes les décisions judiciaires était de valider les revendications du séminaire au territoire des Kanien'kehà:ha à Kanehsatà:ke. Sans aucun autre appui extérieur, les Kanehsata'kehró:non faisaient face à un adversaire complètement irrépressible. Le peuple à Gibson réussissait à vaincre de grandes difficultés en se créant une nouvelle vie, mais ce ne fut pas sans beaucoup de pertes et de sacrifices. Durant les premières années, des enfants et des femmes moururent à cause des conditions extrêmes auxquelles ils étaient exposés. Découragés par les épreuves, plusieurs quittèrent Gibson. Le travail n'était pas toujours facile à trouver, et une grande partie des terres n'était pas propice à l'agriculture. Les gens établis à Gibson étaient soumis à des restrictions sur la coupe du bois et à la « Loi sur le règlement territorial ». Selon cette dernière, ils avaient un délai pour défricher la terre qu'on leur accordait, sinon ils devaient l'abandonner. L'Ontario se servit plus tard de cette loi pour exproprier les Kanien'kehà:ka des terres qui leur étaient réservées à Gibson.

Pendant ce temps, le peuple de Kanehsatà:ke s'était résigné à parcourir une longue route. La persécution et l'oppression incessantes qui en avaient chassé plusieurs ne servirent qu'à fortifier ceux qui restaient. Sous les ordres du séminaire, ainsi que des autorités municipale et provinciale, la police provinciale continuait à utiliser la force contre eux. Tout cela se faisait sous les prétextes les plus transparents pour persuader le peuple de quitter ses terres ou d'abandonner pour toujours son droit acquis à la terre. Le gouvernement fédéral continuait à négliger ses responsabilités quant à la protection du territoire de Kanehsatà:ke contre les empiétements des colons blancs, tandis que les Kanehsata'kehró:non continuaient à affirmer leurs droits territoriaux malgré l'opposition insurmontable.

De la manière la plus malicieuse, sans même prétendre à la justice ou au franc-jeu, le gouvernement avait appliqué ses lois aux Kanehsata'kehró:non et s'attendait à ce qu'ils se soumettent fidèlement à l'« autorité de la loi ». Malgré ses revers et ses pertes, le peuple de Kanehsatà:ke manifestait une patience et une bonne volonté incroyables. Cependant, le moment viendrait où sa patience serait épuisée et tout le Canada ressentirait les effets des centaines d'années de persécution et d'oppression qu'il a supportées.

C'EST LA TERRE QUI DONNE LA VIE

Le peuple et moi avons vu plusieurs choses : des levers et des couchers de soleil, des journées hivernales froides et des vents chauds printaniers qui font fondre la glace. Plusieurs événements se sont déroulés devant nos yeux et sont gravés dans la mémoire et imprégnés dans l'âme du peuple, de la terre et de cette montagne.

La période qui suivit le départ du bateau à vapeur fut remplie d'épreuves pour les Kanehsata'kehró:non. Moins nombreux, ils n'avaient pas beaucoup de temps pour pleurer la perte subie à cause du déplacement à Muskoka. Ils devaient reprendre leurs forces pour affronter un adversaire encore plus fort et plus déterminé. Après la division du peuple, les Roti'kharahón:tsi campaient encore plus sur leurs positions. Ils se disaient que si quelques-uns déménageaient, les autres pourraient un jour être convaincus de partir si les conditions à Kanehsatà:ke étaient toujours difficiles. S'ils m'avaient écoutée, j'aurais pu leur dire que ceux qui étaient restés ne partiraient pas, qu'ils ne pouvaient pas partir.

Même l'air semblait retenir les sons et les sentiments des Kanehsata'kehró:non; ils continueraient à vivre ici et à élever leur famille, à grimper sur mon sommet pour se reposer et regarder la terre.

Ils participaient toujours aux conseils et écoutaient pendant que d'autres essayaient de leur faire croire qu'il n'y avait aucun avenir sur ces rives et que des temps durs ne cesseraient pas jusqu'à ce qu'ils abandonnent leur maison et leur terre et poursuivent leur chemin. Certains se demandaient s'ils n'étaient pas entêtés à rester, alors que partir soulagerait leur sort. Je dirais qu'ils s'accrochaient au premier commandement du Créateur :

soyez gardiens de la terre. C'est elle qui donne la vie et nourrit le peuple, c'est pourquoi il doit en prendre soin en retour. Au-delà des mots et de leur signification, obéir au commandement constituait l'essentiel de la lutte. Ce lien que le peuple ne pouvait pas rompre s'étendait au-delà de la perception des hommes, bien plus loin que l'horizon.

S'il n'en était pas ainsi, le chef Louis serait resté à Muskoka, entouré de sa famille et de ceux qui l'ont suivi vers de nouvelles terres. En prenant de l'âge, il désirait vivement revenir à ce qu'il avait connu, à ses points de repère familiers, aux visages de son enfance. Il vendit ce qu'il possédait et fit le voyage de retour pour passer le reste de sa vie comme Kanehsata'kehró:non.

Il ne pouvait pas rester éloigné plus que le tonnerre au printemps ou que l'esprit des anciens qui veille sans cesse sur nous.

[1] Charles A. Cooke, Recalling Troubled Times in Oka 13 Years Ago. *Ottawa Citizen*, 26 juillet 1990.

[2] Tradition orale de Kanehsatà:ke.

[3] Philip Laforce, *History of Gibson Reserve,* Bracebridge, Ontario, C. A. 950, Bracebridge Gazette Ltd. p. 3. Watahí:ne signifie en voyage.

[4] Ibid., p. 11

[5] Louis Sanation à John McGirr, 15 novembre 1881, Bala Muskoka, A. S. S. S., Université de Montréal, n° 203.

[6] Décret en Ontario.

[7] Vankoughnet à Choquet, 19 novembre 1881, A. S. S. S., Université de Montréal, n° 105.

[8] Choquet à Vankoughnet, 26 novembre 1881, A. S. S. S., Université de Montréal, n° 206.

[9] Choquet au surintendant général des Affaires indiennes, 18 septembre 1881, Centre national des arts, RG 10, vol. 2034, dossier 8946-2.

[10] Lettre signée LeClair, 16 octobre 1882, Centre national des arts, RG 10, vol. 2034, dossier 8946-2.

[11] Thos. Walton au surintendant général des Affaires indiennes, 2 septembre 1884, Centre national des arts, RG 10, vol. 2034, dossier 8946-2.

[12] Louis Sanation à John McGirr, Bala, 5 décembre 1881, A. S. S. S., Université de Montréal, n° 208.

[13] William O'Brien à S. G. du Département indien, The Woods, Shanty Bay, 14 mars 1882, Centre national des arts, RG 10, vol. 2164, dossier 34 151.

[14] Louis Sanation à N. O. Greene, 28 décembre 1881, A. S. S. S., Université de Montréal, n° 212.

[15] Choquet à J. A. Mousseau, 30 décembre 1881, A. S. S. S., Université de Montréal, n° 212.

[16] The Oka Indians, *The Toronto Globe*, 5 novembre 1881.

[17] Rapport de Scott à Vankoughnet, 28 octobre 1881, Centre national des arts, RG 10, vol. 2033, dossier 8946-1, p. 2.

[18] Ibid., p. 7.

[19] Ibid., p. 6.

[20] Les chefs Frett et Tewisha au surintendant général des Affaires indiennes, Centre national des arts, RG 10, vol. 2033, dossier 8946-1.

[21] Rapport de Scott à Vankoughnet, 28 octobre 1881, Centre national des arts, RG 10, vol. 2033, dossier 8946-1, p. 2.

[22] Ibid., p. 16.

[23] Vankoughnet à Choquet, 14 décembre 1881, A. S. S. S., Université de Montréal, n° 209.

[24] McGirr à Frett, 25 juillet 1882, Centre national des arts, RG 10, vol. 2104, dossier 34 151.

[25] Le chef Louis à John McGirr, 10 août 1882, Centre national des arts, RG 10, vol. 2034, dossier 32 475.

[26] Scott aux chefs d'Oka, 18 décembre 1882, Centre national des arts, RG 10, vol. 2034, dossier 8946-2.

[27] Lettre de Vankoughnet à John Tewisha, 8 avril 1882, Centre national des arts, RG 10, vol. 2034, dossier 8946-2, Scott à Vankoughnet, 15 mai 1882, Centre national des arts, RG 10, vol. 2034, dossier 8946-2.

[28] Lettre au chef Louis Sanation, 16 mars 1882. Centre national des arts, RG 10, vol. 2164, dossier 34 151.

[29] Lettre de McGirr au surintendant général des Affaires indiennes, 24 avril 1882, Centre national des arts, RG 10, vol. 2034, dossier 8946-2.

[30] Abraham Houle à Louis Sanation, 10 avril 1882, Centre national des arts, RG 10, vol. 2164, dossier 34 151.

[31] Sanation à Vankoughnet, 10 avril 1882, Centre national des arts, RG 10, vol. 2164, dossier 34 151.

[32] Rapport d'un comité du Conseil privé, 11 avril 1882, Centre national des arts, RG 10, vol. 2164, dossier 34 151.

[33] Vankoughnet à Choquet, 13 juin 1882, Centre national des arts, RG 10, vol. 2034, dossier 8946-2.

[34] Louis Sanation à John McGirr, août 1882, Centre national des arts, RG 10, vol. 2158, dossier 32 475.

[35] Memorandum, John A. MacDonald au département des Affaires indiennes, 26 septembre 1882, Centre national des arts, RG 10, vol. 2034, dossier 8946-2.

[36] Louis Sanation à McGirr, 10 août 1882, Centre national des arts, RG 10, vol. 2158, dossier 32 475.

[37] Lettre de LeClair, 16 octobre 1882, Centre national des arts, RG 10, vol. 2034, dossier 8946-2.

[38] Scott à Vankoughnet, 8 janvier 1883, Centre national des arts, RG 10, vol 2034, dossier 8946-2.

[39] Cooke à Vankoughnet, 27 mars 1883, Centre national des arts, RG 10, vol. 2034, dossier 8946-2.

[40] Walton à Vankoughnet, 15 avril 1883, Centre national des arts, RG 10, vol 2034, dossier 8946-2.

[41] Scott au surintendant général des Affaires indiennes, 24 novembre 1883, Centre national des arts, RG 10, vol. 2241, dossier 46 394.

[42] Ibid.

[43] Ibid.

[44] Scott au surintendant général des Affaires indiennes, 4 avril 1883, Centre national des arts, RG 10, vol. 2034, dossier 8946-2.

[45] Vankoughnet à M. Colin, 14 janvier 1884, A. S. S. S., Université de Montréal, n° 255.

[46] Sanation à Walton, 12 décembre 1884, Centre national des arts, RG1 0, vol. 2034, dossier 8946-2.

[47] Mémoire à Daly, 20 et 21 juin 1895, A. S. S. S., Université de Montréal, n° 291.

[48] L. Colin à J. A. MacDonald, 5 février 1885, A. S. S. S., Université de Montréal, n° 267.

[49] LeClair à Vankoughnet, 13 janvier 1884, Centre national des arts, RG 10, vol. 2034, dossier 8946-2.

[50] L. Colin à J. A. MacDonald, 5 février 1885, A. S. S. S., Université de Montréal, n° 267.

[51] S. Dawson à Colin, 30 juin 1887, A. S. S. S., Université de Montréal, n° 272.

[52] Vankoughnet à A. Desjardins, 4 juillet 1887, A. S. S. S., Université de Montréal, n° 273.

[53] White à Dewdney, 30 novembre 1889, A. S. S. S., Université de Montréal, n° 278.

[54] Mémoire, Shaw et Mathewson, 21 juillet 1887, A. S. S. S., Université de Montréal, n° 227.

[55] Beers à Dewdney, 30 novembre 1889, A. S. S. S., Université de Montréal, n° 278.

[56] Beers à Colin, janvier 1890, A. S. S. S., Université de Montréal, n° 281.

[57] Beers aux Indiens protestants d'Oka, janvier 1890, A. S. S. S., Université de Montréal, n° 281.

[58] Beers, The Oka Indians Case, *The Gazette,* 27 mars 1890, Montréal.

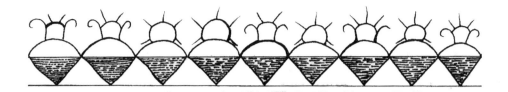

CHAPITRE 8

CEUX QUI RESTENT À OKA DOIVENT EN SUBIR LES CONSÉQUENCES

Le même voyage

Des nouvelles des déplacés arrivent petit à petit chez les Kanehsata'kehró:non. L'hiver a saisi ceux qui sont partis les doigts glacés. Les promesses reçues étaient des mots vides. Ils le ressentent bien, alors qu'ils enterrent leurs morts et retournent à leurs abris de fortune. Même s'ils sont habitués à la souffrance, rien ne les avait préparés à survivre, très loin du seul foyer qu'ils avaient connu sans toit ni nourriture.

N'eut été de leur détermination, ils seraient tous partis. Même si beaucoup ont quitté Gibson et sont retournés à Kanehsatà:ke, d'autres sont restés et ont travaillé très dur pour se créer un bon foyer.

Les Kanehsata'kehró:non ne sont pas étonnés de la tournure des événements, mais ils en sont attristés. Leur situation n'est guère meilleure. Les Roti'kharahón:tsi (robes noires), encouragés par le départ des déplacés, continuent de les harceler et de les maltraiter dans l'espoir qu'ils partent tous.

Les Kanehsata'kehró:non sont seuls, et leurs récoltes sont désastreuses. Les temps sont durs pour eux. Ils représentent donc une proie facile pour ceux qui se disent leurs gardiens. « Si vous partez, leur disaient-ils, vous recevrez toute l'aide que vous désirez. » Leurs requêtes répétées se transforment en menaces, mais c'est au tour du peuple de faire la sourde oreille.

Par ses propres idées et sa propre voix, chaque génération contribue à la lutte. Quelqu'un est toujours là pour prendre la place de ceux qui ne peuvent plus se battre. Les Kanehsata'kehró:non sont un rappel à tous que la terre est vivante.

Nous vous avions fourni une réserve à Gibson

Tandis que le peuple à Gibson luttait pour se faire une vie dans l'étendue désolée de Muskoka, les Kanehsata'kehró:non, ignorés et abandonnés, subissaient aux mains du séminaire de Saint-Sulpice une persécution permanente. Ils étaient seuls pour traiter du mieux qu'ils pouvaient avec l'hostilité des Canadiens français et les empiétements acharnés du séminaire sur leur territoire. À chaque occasion, leurs demandes d'aide étaient considérées avec indifférence et souvent avec mépris. Dans une lettre datée du 26 mai 1894, envoyée au chef John Tewisha, Hayter Reed, surintendant général des Affaires indiennes, écrivit :

Je dois spécifier que les diverses lois concernant les Indiens s'appliquent essentiellement aux Indiens qui vivent dans des réserves. Ceux qui vivent ailleurs sont à peu près pareils aux Blancs et ne peuvent pas avoir droit aux privilèges que la loi accorde à ceux qui vivent dans des réserves. Vous savez que nous vous avions fourni une réserve à Gibson pour que ceux qui désirent être complètement protégés par la Loi sur les Indiens le soient. S'ils préfèrent vivre à Oka, ils doivent en subir les conséquences. Le Département a tout fait en son pouvoir pour votre peuple et il s'est donné beaucoup de mal pour l'aider et veiller à son bien. Il semble impossible de faire plus que ce qui a déjà été fait.[1]

N'ayant pas encore abandonné l'espoir que les Kanehsata'kehró:non partent en masse pour Gibson, le gouvernement semblait refuser d'aider ceux qui restaient à Kanehsatà:ke. En 1885, seulement quatre ans après le déplacement à Gibson, le séminaire entreprit un processus pour expulser les Kanehsata'kehró:non de leurs terres afin de vendre ces dernières aux Canadiens français. Ils le firent en toute impunité, puisque le gouvernement fédéral refusait d'intervenir. Le département des Affaires indiennes prétendait qu'il ne pouvait pas intervenir, étant donné qu'il n'avait aucun pouvoir sur les terres à Oka.

En mai 1885, le séminaire expulsa la veuve Marie Katénie's de la terre sur laquelle elle habitait depuis plus de 22 ans et qui avait auparavant été occupée par sa famille pendant de nombreuses années.[2] Timothy Ahrírhon écrivit à John A. MacDonald pour demander que le Département intervienne afin que sa terre lui soit rendue, car c'était son seul moyen de subsistance.[3] L. Vankoughnet écrivit au séminaire pour lui faire part de la lettre qu'il avait reçue de Timothy Ahrírhon,[4] mais le Département ne fit rien pour défendre les intérêts de Marie Katénie's.

À l'automne 1886, une dispute s'éleva entre Simon Anaié:ha et un Canadien français au sujet d'une terre réclamée par les deux hommes. Anaié:ha avait été expulsé de force de sa terre et privé de sa récolte pour cette année-là.[5] À nouveau, Timothy Ahrírhon écrivit au Département pour lui demander d'intervenir.

> Mes deux lettres du 15 septembre et du 9 octobre derniers vous donnaient des explications au sujet du terrain en question. Depuis lors, nous attendons un mot de votre part pour connaître les mesures que vous comptez adopter. Je crois que le Département interviendra sûrement, sans délai, dans cette affaire d'empiétement flagrant et qu'il essaiera de rendre justice à ce pauvre homme. Ce dernier a besoin de protection maintenant que l'hiver est arrivé. Il est vraiment dommage que ce pauvre homme et sa famille soient laissés dans cette situation misérable pendant l'hiver, privés de leur récolte, etc. (sans céréales ni paille pour leur bétail).[6]

Une plainte avait également été déposée contre le shérif et les huissiers qui avaient, en état d'ébriété, expulsé et grandement maltraité Simon Anaié:ha.[7] Dans un rapport du 13 décembre 1886,[8] le shérif nia les allégations d'ivresse et de mauvais traitements. Il continua en disant qu'Anaié:ha n'avait pas été privé de ses récoltes, et que si ses céréales étaient perdues il était le seul à blâmer, puisqu'il avait eu la permission de les récolter même après son expulsion. En fait, Anaié:ha aurait pu récupérer ses céréales à condition d'abandonner toutes revendications de sa terre[9], ce qu'il n'était pas disposé à accepter. La réponse du Département disait simplement qu'il ne pouvait pas intervenir. En mai 1887, Vankoughnet écrivit à Timothy Ahrírhon:

> En réponse, je tiens à vous informer que la loi permet à un Indien d'intenter un procès pour toute injustice commise à son égard par un ou des partis et, par conséquent, Anaieta [Anaié:ha] a le pouvoir d'en appeler aux tribunaux pour corriger tout tort qu'il estime avoir subi.[10]

Cependant, le Département indien n'était pas disposé à assumer les coûts d'un tel procès, et Anaié:ha n'avait pas les moyens de l'intenter.[11] Plus tard au cours du mois, il fut appréhendé pour avoir démoli une clôture érigée sur la terre contestée.[12]

Durant la même période, le conseil municipal d'Oka, avec l'appui du séminaire, commença à essayer d'exproprier des Kanehsata'kehró:non du village sous prétexte de construire ou d'élargir des rues. Dans un de ces cas, le conseil municipal proposa de redresser la rue des Anges.[13] La nouvelle rue proposée traverserait cinq terrains occupés par les Kanehsata'kehró:non, les détruisant pratiquement.[14] Ceux-ci protestèrent énergiquement contre la proposition. Le séminaire déclara que les terres en question ne faisaient pas partie des terrains originaux occupés par les Kanehsata'kehró:non « qui les avaient progressivement pris sans que le séminaire ne conteste ».[15] Malgré cette déclaration, ce dernier promit de déplacer sur de nouveaux terrains ceux qui seraient touchés par les changements. Cependant, les Kanehsata'kehró:non refusèrent d'abandonner leur terre pour aller ailleurs. En mai 1894, les représentants McKenna et Campbell, envoyés par le Département pour s'informer du problème, dirent ce qui suit au sujet de leur attitude :

L'Indien principalement touché par les améliorations était assez disposé à laisser la rue traverser son terrain pourvu qu'il soit justement dédommagé, et il ne semblait pas y avoir d'objection. Les trois autres Indiens en question ont justifié leur refus en disant que l'argent qu'on leur verserait serait vite dépensé, tandis que la terre est une source permanente de subsistance, mais il était très évident que c'était simplement un prétexte.[16]

Les deux représentants poursuivirent en recommandant que le Département n'intervienne pas dans la dispute :

Tout considéré, nous sommes fortement enclins à conclure que la meilleure solution au problème serait de laisser les choses suivre leur cours et de faire comprendre aux Indiens que s'ils ne sont pas disposés à écouter la voix de la raison ils devront se battre seuls sans s'attendre à recevoir une aide quelconque du Département; et jusqu'à présent, dans la mesure où nous l'entendons, c'est le moyen qui devra être adopté, à moins que les Indiens ne soient vraiment persuadés de suivre ceux qui ont déjà déménagé à Gibson.[17]

Ils blâmèrent Timothy Ahrírhon pour l'attitude des gens, ainsi que pour leur détermination et leur désir persistant de demeurer sur leurs terres.

Dans cet homme, il semble y avoir toute l'obstination naturelle et démesurée de la race iroquoise à laquelle il appartient; on ne doit donc pas s'étonner de le voir s'acharner à contester le titre du territoire du Lac des Deux-Montagnes avec le séminaire, quand on se souvient combien certains milieux ont alimenté la croyance en la justice de sa revendication.[18]

En 1904, comme le redressement proposé de la rue ne se réalisa pas, le séminaire demanda au Département d'intervenir pour que la rue planifiée soit construite.[19] Le chef arpenteur, S. Bray, fut plus tard envoyé pour examiner le site et rencontrer les chefs et les propriétaires des cinq terrains en question. Il constata qu'ils étaient « absolument résolus » et qu'« ils ne permettraient pas l'ouverture de la rue ni ne consentiraient à l'élargissement de la rue existante pour l'améliorer ».[20] Il constata également qu'en réalité un seul homme insistait pour améliorer la rue et qu'il ne le faisait que pour contrarier les autres résidents. Plusieurs personnes se plaignaient qu'il était un « voisin des plus exécrables qui avait tiré sans raison sur trois de leurs chiens, un cochon et un chat, et qui est ordinairement désagréable ».[21] Bray rapporta également :

Il faut remarquer que, si nous construisons une nouvelle rue, nous devrons toujours garder l'ancienne, puisqu'il y a de nombreuses maisons construites sur le côté nord, ce qui nécessite l'utilisation de l'ancienne rue. De ce point de vue, il est absurde d'avoir deux rues parallèles à douze mètres seulement l'une de l'autre, comme mentionné ci-dessus.[22]

Grâce à leur détermination, les Kanehsata'kehró:non sortirent victorieux dans cette cause. Cependant, dans beaucoup d'autres cas, le contraire se produisit. Chaque famille à Kanehsatà:ke peut nommer un parent ou un ancêtre qui, pendant qu'il était parti à la chasse ou en quête de travail pour faire vivre sa famille, a perdu sa terre aux mains du séminaire, qui la vendait ensuite aux colons canadiens-français. Dans chaque cas, les Kanehsata'kehró:non contestaient les empiétements sur leurs terres et les violations de leurs droits. Pendant tout ce temps, le département des Affaires indiennes les gardait occupés à rédiger des lettres, mais restait là sans rien faire.

Très souvent, on récompensait ceux qui osaient protester en les envoyant en prison ou en saisissant leur propriété comme dans le cas de Timothy Ahrírhon. Au cours de l'été 1896, sa vache et ses céréales furent saisies pour non-paiement de dettes. Timothy Ahrírhon écrivit au gouverneur général pour lui demander son aide. Hayter Reed, surintendant général adjoint des Affaires indiennes lui répondit :

> Je crains que vous ne puissiez demander que votre vache et vos autres biens ne soient pas saisis. De telles exemptions s'appliquent seulement à un bien dans une réserve au sens de la Loi sur les Indiens. J'ajouterais qu'un des objectifs du Département en organisant le déplacement des Indiens d'Oka à Gibson était qu'ils puissent jouir de tous les privilèges appartenant aux Indiens qui vivent sur des réserves ordinaires. Aussi longtemps qu'ils continuent à vivre à Oka, il ne sera pas dans le pouvoir du Département de les protéger des conséquences qui résultent de leur situation anormale.[23]

C'était peut-être la position « officielle » du Département, mais une lettre envoyée par Reed à Scott révéla une tout autre raison à l'hésitation persistante du Département à s'engager. « […] vous verrez que si le gouvernement intervient dans le cas auquel le chef fait référence, la question surgirait probablement à savoir s'il y a ou non une réserve à Oka au sens de la Loi ».[24] Selon Reed, le gouvernement ne désirait pas du tout s'engager dans « des litiges lassants et coûteux »[25] avec le séminaire, dans lesquels le gouvernement « aurait à soutenir que le territoire occupé par les Indiens à Oka était une réserve ».[26] S'il intervenait pour empêcher la saisie, il devrait prouver que les terres à Kanehsatà:ke étaient vraiment des terres réservées pour les Indiens. Dans le meilleur des cas, cela aurait été une proposition compliquée que le Département n'avait aucun désir de défendre. Après avoir écrit au Département, au gouverneur général et au premier ministre du Canada, Timothy Ahrírhon reçut pour toute réponse que son seul recours était d'en appeler aux tribunaux qui lui étaient ouverts comme à tout autre sujet de Sa Majesté.[27] À ce point, bon nombre des Kanehsata'kehró:non en étaient arrivés à la conclusion qu'il n'y avait pas de justice pour les peuples autochtones dans les cours canadiennes. Timothy Ahrírhon estimait qu'en appeler devant les tribunaux n'était pas un plan d'action viable.

En plus des saisies et des expulsions, les Kanehsata'kehró:non devaient aussi subir de nombreuses et fréquentes arrestations pour coupe de bois. Le séminaire, avec l'aide du Département indien, commença à appliquer des mesures plus sévères concernant celle-ci. Il désigna une parcelle de terre boisée où les Kanehsata'kehró:non pouvaient couper du bois de chauffage. Il ne leur permettait pas de couper du bois à des fins de construction ni même de le vendre à d'autres parmi les leurs. De plus, il essaya parfois de les restreindre à ne ramasser que le bois mort au sol. Pendant ce temps, il permettait aux Canadiens français de couper librement du bois où ils voulaient. Quand les Kanehsata'kehró:non coupaient du bois à l'extérieur des limites prescrites, le séminaire les faisait arrêter avec la collaboration de l'agent indien. Par l'entremise de l'agent, le séminaire adressait d'abord une plainte au Département, après quoi des policiers de la GRC étaient envoyés pour exécuter les arrestations. Ce harcèlement constant empêchait les Kanehsata'kehró:non de gagner leur vie et de pourvoir aux besoins de base de leur famille. Le département des Affaires indiennes, aidé de la police, appuyait l'oppression du peuple par le séminaire. En octobre

1909, Angus Corinthe écrivit à Frank Pedley pour lui demander si le Département avait envoyé des policiers arrêter des siens. Ils étaient venus chez lui pour l'avertir que ceux qui étaient pris à couper du bois seraient arrêtés. Il écrivit :

> Depuis des temps immémoriaux, les Indiens d'Oka prennent leur bois à la Commune, sur des terrains vagues ou dans les montagnes environnantes. Si on les en empêche maintenant, où trouveront-ils leur bois ? Les Canadiens français haïssent les Indiens d'ici seulement parce qu'ils veulent posséder toutes leurs terres, et ils feront n'importe quoi pour les persécuter. Si le Département aide le séminaire à rendre les choses difficiles pour les Indiens, je ne sais pas où nous finirons.[28]

Même si une cause type était devant les tribunaux, le Département ne fit rien pour améliorer la situation, préférant apparemment patienter. En avril 1910, Mme Angus Jacobs écrivit à Frank Pedley pour l'informer que des policiers les harcelaient parce qu'ils avaient acheté du bois d'un autre Indien.[29] L'agent indien avait apparemment écrit au Département pour se plaindre que des Indiens coupaient et vendaient du bois. Les Jacob avaient besoin de bois pour construire leur maison et, à cause du harcèlement, il restait là à pourrir. Mme Jacobs poursuivit en disant que la police fouillait même les bagages des gens qui revenaient de Montréal et les traitait comme des voleurs.[30] La politique non officielle du Département de punir ceux qui n'étaient pas partis pour Gibson laissait les Kanehsata'kehró:non sans recours pour rétablir la situation. En juillet 1910, Angus Corinthe fut encore une fois accusé d'avoir illégalement coupé du bois.[31] À cette occasion, le séminaire se plaignit qu'il avait coupé du bois à l'extérieur des limites prescrites. J. D. McLean, sous-ministre adjoint et secrétaire, visita Kanehsatà:ke pour essayer de régler l'affaire à l'amiable. Il rapporta :

> Je peux dire que j'ai connu ma plus grande difficulté à mon arrivée au village. En fait, le chef maintenait durant tout l'entretien qu'il était dans son droit de couper des arbres et qu'il n'était pas lié par la décision des tribunaux ni par l'entente conclue entre le séminaire et les Indiens le 31 décembre dernier.[32]

Corinthe affirma plus tard qu'il avait coupé le bois dans les limites permises. En mars 1911, le Département écrivit au prêtre Lefebvre du séminaire pour le lui rapporter. Ce dernier répondit que Corinthe « vous a mal informé »[33] et suggéra qu'on se renseigne sur la situation. Après cette lettre, le Département envoya son inspecteur, S. Stewart, s'informer de la question. Il rencontra M. Lefebvre qui accepta la suggestion que Stewart aille lui-même voir où le bois avait été coupé. Il rapporta :

> Le chef Corinthe, deux autres Indiens et moi-même avons parcouru environ six kilomètres jusqu'à l'endroit où le bois avait été coupé. En chemin, on nous a montré une ligne jalonnée qui avait cependant été faite très récemment, et au-dessus de laquelle on pouvait lire « Interdiction aux Indiens de couper du bois ». Cependant, la coupe avait été faite environ 12 hectares au-delà de la ligne, et les souches, dont certaines avaient plus de 50 centimètres de diamètre, montraient que les meilleurs arbres avaient été pris. Les représentants du séminaire ont admis que la ligne avait été jalonnée après la coupe, mais ils ont affirmé que les Indiens connaissaient bien les limites où ils pouvaient couper […].[34]

Après avoir visité la parcelle boisée, Stewart fut témoin de la signature d'une entente entre le séminaire et les chefs. Était également présent, un avocat qui prétendait représenter Corinthe et qui lui conseilla de signer l'entente rédigée en français. On découvrit plus tard que cet homme, M. Fauteux, s'était présenté sous un faux jour, car il ne venait pas de la firme montréalaise qui représentait les Kanehsata'kehró:non, mais de

Saint-Scholastique. De plus, il fut révélé que Stewart avait été trompé quant à la nature exacte de l'entente. Il avait été manipulé pour aider le séminaire à conclure une entente avec les Kanehsata'kehró:non, entente nuisible à leurs intérêts. Il indiqua donc qu'il informerait le séminaire qu'il avait signé l'entente sans en connaître le contenu.[35]

Plusieurs années plus tard, en 1919, puis en 1925, les Kanehsata'kehró:non rapportèrent au Département que des Canadiens français empiétaient sur des terres qui leur étaient réservées et y prenaient le bois, les restreignant ainsi à un espace de plus en plus petit.[36] Plusieurs lettres circulèrent entre le Département, l'agent et le séminaire, mais rien ne fut fait pour empêcher ces empiétements. À la fin, le séminaire nia que des Blancs aient coupé du bois sur des terres indiennes, et la question fut abandonnée.[37] Mais ce n'était jamais le cas quand des Kanehsata'kehró:non étaient accusés de couper du bois sur les terres occupées par des Canadiens français, comme dans le cas de Thomas Martin. Ce dernier fut accusé de couper illégalement du bois sur la « ferme de Fauteux »[38], une ferme appartenant au séminaire qui voulait y construire une scierie. Un agent de la police provinciale de Saint-Jérôme fut envoyé pour arrêter Martin à la demande du séminaire. L'agent Daoust n'arrêta pas Martin, et l'incident fut grandement couvert par la presse. Dans un rapport au secrétaire des Affaires indiennes, l'agent Brisebois commenta l'incident :

> Étant effrayé par le nombre d'Indiens qui s'étaient réunis parce qu'il avait discuté trop longtemps avec Martin et sa bande, l'agent Daoust est retourné chez lui à Saint-Jérôme. Aujourd'hui, le 4 mai, l'agent est revenu avec trois autres personnes qui, m'a-t-on dit, étaient des agents de la police provinciale qui avaient pour mandat d'arrêter Martin, mais ses résultats ne furent pas meilleurs. Comme les Sulpiciens insistaient pour faire exécuter le mandat et que les agents de la police provinciale semblaient incapables de faire leur boulot, il est probable que vous recevrez une demande pour faire exécuter le mandat par la Police montée.[39]

Quand l'agent Daoust arriva pour procéder à l'arrestation, il fit face à plusieurs Roiiá:nehr qui l'informèrent qu'ils n'étaient pas assujettis aux lois de la province et du Canada, mais qu'ils étaient gouvernés par leurs propres lois. On lui dit qu'« il n'avait aucun droit de donner des ordres aux Indiens ni d'effectuer des arrestations ».[40] Le 7 mai 1934, les chefs tentèrent d'attirer l'attention du gouverneur général sur ces événements. Ils écrivirent :

> La province de Québec a dépassé sa juridiction en incitant ses agents à pénétrer sur notre territoire et à nous imposer la loi des Blancs. Ce faisant, elle annule les termes de nos ententes et de nos traités conclus avec le gouvernement de Sa Majesté.[41]

Manifestement, le département des Affaires indiennes joua un rôle actif dans les efforts du séminaire pour rendre la vie des Kanehsata'kehró:non difficile. Non seulement il ne fit rien pour les aider, mais il semblait chercher activement à augmenter l'affliction du peuple de Kanehsatà:ke. Le séminaire n'avait qu'à demander l'intervention de la GRC ou de la police provinciale, et le Département prenait des mesures pour leur fournir ses services. Historiquement, les forces de l'ordre furent utilisées pour asservir les Kanehsata'kehró:non, mais jamais pour protéger leur propriété ou leur personne. Cependant, quand une occasion se présentait pour atténuer le problème, le gouvernement n'agissait pas. En 1905, le séminaire proposa de vendre les terres non vendues au Département. Le gouvernement tarda à prendre une décision, et l'offre fut retirée par un nouveau supérieur qui invoqua des « raisons théologiques ».[42] Le séminaire vendit plus tard une grande partie du territoire revendiqué par les Kanehsata'kehró:non à une compagnie belge dirigée par le baron Empain. Cette compagnie prévoyait coloniser ces terres par des Belges. Cette vente engendra une toute nouvelle série de conflits territoriaux pour les Kanehsata'kehró:non. Un nouveau siècle débutait, mais ils avaient peu de raisons d'espérer que les choses s'améliorent.

NOUS NE LAISSERONS PAS LE CHEMIN DE FER TRAVERSER NOS TERRES

À l'automne 1911, les Kanehsata'kehró:non commencèrent à apercevoir des arpenteurs sur leurs terres. La présence d'arpenteurs en était venue à signifier la perte imminente de terres, et cela engendra beaucoup d'inquiétude chez le peuple. Des enquêtes révélèrent qu'une compagnie de chemin de fer planifiait de faire passer une voie ferrée à Kanehsatà:ke et d'y construire un hôtel. En novembre, Joseph K. Gabriel écrivit au ministre de l'Intérieur pour lui dire qu'ils ne laisseraient aucun chemin de fer traverser leur territoire parce qu'il était déjà trop petit.[43] La réponse du gouvernement arriva un mois plus tard:

Je dois dire que la compagnie a certainement le droit d'arpenter les terres mentionnées, mais ne peut y construire un chemin de fer jusqu'à ce qu'elle obtienne le droit de passage.[44]

Cette brève déclaration ne fit pas grand-chose pour apaiser les craintes du peuple qui prit alors des mesures pour empêcher les arpenteurs de poursuivre leur travail. En février 1912, la Central Railway Company écrivit au Département pour se plaindre que leurs ingénieurs avaient été menacés de coups de feu et qu'on les empêchait d'arpenter les terres revendiquées par les Indiens d'Oka.[45] La compagnie se disait inquiète que ce retard lui cause des problèmes et demanda au Département de « prendre tout de suite les mesures qui s'imposent pour assurer que nos ingénieurs ne se fassent pas agresser en exécutant leur travail selon les lois du pays ».[46] Notons que, même si les lois du pays étaient conçues pour empêcher les peuples autochtones de se faire harceler sur leurs propres terres, en général elles étaient rarement appliquées à cet effet.

En mars 1912, Joseph K. Gabriel écrivit à R. L. Borden, premier ministre du Canada, pour lui rappeler ces lois et lui expliquer qu'en protégeant leurs terres d'autres empiétements, les Indiens faisaient respecter les lois du pays.[47] Ils ne violaient pas la loi en empêchant la compagnie Central Railway Company de prendre les terres qui leur étaient réservées. Par la suite, il y eut une période d'inactivité relative qui dura environ 18 ans, pendant laquelle le peuple n'entendit pas ou très peu parler de la compagnie de chemin de fer et de ses plans.

En janvier 1930, on avisa plusieurs Kanehsata'kehró:non qu'ils étaient expropriés de leurs terres par la Canadian Northern Railways.[48] Le séminaire avait vendu le droit de passage sur ces terres, sachant très bien qu'elles étaient occupées par trois familles qui avaient des fermes productives dont elles tiraient leur revenu.

Les familles touchées étaient celles de Charles Murray, de Pierre Murray et d'Hyacinthe Vincent. Au début, le séminaire avait essayé d'expulser les Murray pour non-paiement de loyer d'après une entente qu'il affirmait avoir conclue avec eux plusieurs années auparavant. Selon le séminaire, ces familles ne possédaient pas la terre, mais la louaient. Par ailleurs, elles occupaient plus de terres que l'entente originale le spécifiait, terres qu'elles avaient acquises graduellement sans qu'on s'y oppose. Comme toujours, la version du séminaire différait de celle des Kanehsata'kehró:non.

Néanmoins, le séminaire conclut une entente avec la compagnie de chemin de fer pour dédommager les familles touchées par l'expropriation de leur terre. Étant donné sa perspective sur le sujet, il est peu probable que le séminaire avait l'intention de remplir son obligation de dédommager les Kanehsata'kehró:non touchés. Dans une lettre datée du 31 décembre 1930, Aimé Geoffrion, avocat du séminaire, révéla quelque peu les intentions de ce dernier :

En vertu d'un contrat daté du 18 mars 1910, les droits de Pierre Murray semblent lui donner un droit de jouissance de la terre à condition d'effectuer certains paiements. Quand tous les paiements sont effectués, il peut en jouir toute sa vie et la transférer à ses descendants algonquins grâce à une loi approuvée par M. Lefebvre. Murray perdra ses droits, ses actifs et leurs améliorations s'il omet de s'acquitter régulièrement des paiements. Nous nous demandons si un tel contrat est valide.[49]

À ce stade, le séminaire cherchait déjà des moyens d'éviter de remplir cette obligation. Les Murray et les Vincent reçurent une offre de 75 $ l'hectare, tandis qu'on offrait à leurs voisins blancs une compensation de 300 $ l'hectare. Les deux familles étaient constamment surveillées et harcelées par la police. Le 24 décembre 1930, Charles Murray écrivit au Département pour protester contre le traitement que Vincent et lui recevaient et pour demander de l'aide ou un conseil :

Pourquoi devrions-nous être tenus à la gorge avec une telle contestation, et même être surveillés par deux agents de la CNR qui se trouvent actuellement sur la propriété et qui nous suivent comme des criminels. Cependant, vous admettrez qu'après avoir vécu en paix pendant plus de trois quarts de siècle, il est plus qu'humiliant et déconcertant d'être maintenant sommés de partir. Je comprends qu'on nous accordera une compensation plus pour des préjudices moraux si on n'admet pas des dommages matériels. Cela est tout de même très décevant si l'on considère que j'avais réalisé tous mes rêves, mon verger, etc.[50]

La police empêcha aussi ces familles de couper du bois sur leur propriété de sorte qu'elles ne purent plus chauffer leur maison. Encore une fois, le gouvernement refusa de leur prêter assistance, affirmant n'avoir aucun pouvoir sur ces terres. Dans une lettre adressée à F. Harbour, agent indien, A. F. MacKenzie écrivit :

Puisque les terres en question sont reconnues comme étant la propriété du séminaire de Saint-Sulpice, le Département ne peut intervenir dans l'affaire présente. Cependant, je suggère que vous ayez un entretien avec les autorités du séminaire pour découvrir s'il y aurait d'autres sites où ces trois Indiens en particulier pourraient déménager.[51]

Pierre Murray écrivit également au Département pour demander de l'aide. « Ce que je possède pour y vivre m'est enlevé, et ils sont très vite en affaires. Je compte sur la bonté du Département qui devrait me protéger dans cette question. »[52] Les Murray attendirent la réponse du gouvernement pour savoir comment réagir à cette menace et promirent de suivre le conseil du Département.

En janvier 1931, McGookin, inspecteur du Département, se rendit à Kanehsatà:ke pour rencontrer Charles et Pierre Murray, Hyacinthe Vincent et deux représentants du séminaire. Il recommanda qu'ils acceptent l'offre de 75 $ l'hectare pour leur terre. Dans son rapport au Département, il écrivit :

Ces Indiens ne sont certainement pas ignorants des conditions sous lesquelles ils occupent ces terres. Ils savent que le titre de propriété est un droit acquis par le séminaire, mais ils réclament avoir droit à la même compensation que les fermiers blancs qui reçoivent 300 $ l'hectare. Le chef Charles Murray, qui agissait comme porte-parole, a manifesté une attitude défiante jusqu'à la fin et a refusé de discuter davantage de la question sur la base de l'offre. En quittant le bureau, il a déclaré : « Nous tiendrons une réunion, puis enverrons nos réclamations au département des Affaires indiennes si nous décidons de vendre. »[53]

Après que les Kanehsata'kehró:non eurent quitté la réunion, les représentants du séminaire informèrent McGookin que « si ces Indiens étaient expropriés sans un dollar de compensation, le séminaire ne leur devrait rien ».[54] Ils expliquèrent que chacun d'eux avait conclu une entente de location avec le séminaire, mais puisqu'ils avaient négligé d'effectuer leurs paiements, ils ne pouvaient pas revendiquer les terres qu'ils occupaient.

En 1938, la compagnie de chemin de fer réussit à obtenir la ferme d'Hyacinthe Vincent.[55] Les méthodes qu'elle utilisa pour arriver à ses fins étaient peut-être discutables. Hyacinthe Vincent, un homme âgé, avait transféré sa terre à son neveu, Johnny, à condition qu'il prenne soin de lui dans sa vieillesse. Hyacinthe vivait dans le village d'Oka quand la compagnie prit possession de sa terre. Puisque son neveu était absent à ce moment, la compagnie ne rencontra aucune résistance. L'agent indien fut alors informé que la compagnie en avait pris possession, mais elle n'avait pas encore réussi à prendre possession des terres des Murray. En novembre 1940, un avocat de la compagnie de chemin de fer écrivit au Département :

> On nous a laissé entendre que Charles et Pierre Murray tiennent toujours à occuper leur terre. Cela cause un problème à la CNR qui ne peut en prendre définitivement possession. La présente lettre vous est envoyée précisément pour vous demander de vérifier avec précaution si Charles et Pierre Murray renonceraient à leurs droits s'ils recevaient respectivement les montants mentionnés ci-dessus et étaient déchargés de toutes leurs dettes.[56]

Les Murray refusèrent l'offre et ne consentirent jamais à quitter leur terre. En 1951, la CNR leur fit l'offre suivante[57] : en échange d'une compensation financière, ils devaient abandonner tout droit à la propriété en question, mais ils avaient le droit de déménager leurs bâtiments. Repousser l'offre mènerait à leur expulsion en bonne et due forme des lieux. Refusant de se laisser intimider, les Murray demeurèrent fermement sur leurs terres. Plus tard, la compagnie de chemin de fer abandonna ses plans de prolonger la voie ferrée et de construire un hôtel.

Le début d'une nouvelle saison

Enfin, une nouvelle saison a commencé. Le tsiskó:ko (merle d'Amérique) est revenu. La rougeur de sa poitrine égaie le paysage et son chant remplit l'air de musique. De nouvelles pousses vertes apparaissaient partout. La vie jaillit de la terre. Je peux la ressentir tout autour de moi, mais quelque chose d'autre a changé. Il y a plus que la saison.

Les gens marchent maintenant en sautillant allègrement et avec un nouvel éclat dans leurs yeux. Il y a si longtemps que je ne les ai pas vus ainsi. L'espoir renaît et ils reprennent courage. Je revois les fins rubans de fumée qui transportent leurs prières et leurs paroles. Je peux maintenant entendre plus souvent le son des chants, des tambours et des hochets. Je sais que le peuple vit encore des temps durs; je le vois aussi. Il connaît encore beaucoup de luttes avec des malfaisants qui viennent faire beaucoup de bruit et effrayer les enfants la nuit. Les hommes sont traqués et incarcérés durant de longues périodes. Et même s'il ne reste pas beaucoup de terre à prendre, les O'serón:ni en veulent toujours plus. Leur avidité est dévorante, et ils ne se reposeront pas tant qu'ils n'auront pas chassé les Kanehsata'kehró:non de cet endroit.

Le peuple a entendu dire que les O'serón:ni construiraient un chemin de fer pour qu'un plus grand nombre d'entre eux viennent ici. Les Kanehsata'kehró:non ne le permettront pas; ils n'ont nulle part où aller, et même s'ils le pouvaient ils ne partiraient pas. Ils sont retournés à leurs anciennes traditions, pas toutes, mais suffisamment pour le moment. La puissance des cérémonies fortifie de nouveau leur esprit et ils sont prêts à affronter n'importe quoi.

JOSEPH KANÁ:TASE GABRIEL DIT KANEHWA'TÍ:RON

Au début du 20ᵉ siècle, un nouveau chef des Kanehsata'kehró:non se leva pour défendre leurs droits. Son nom était Joseph Kaná:tase Gabriel dit Kanawa'tiron. Orateur éloquent, il fut aussi un auteur prolifique de demandes juridiques. Durant toute sa vie, Joseph se battit inlassablement pour regagner et préserver la terre, la culture et les traditions des Kanehsata'kehró:non. Selon la tradition de son peuple, il avait recours à des moyens diplomatiques pour y parvenir. Il adressa de nombreuses demandes aux différents paliers gouvernementaux et se rendit même en Angleterre pour présenter sa cause au roi. Quand la diplomatie échoua, Joseph n'hésita pas à prendre les armes pour défendre la terre et le peuple. Ce fut le cas en 1911 quand la Central Railway Company essaya de faire passer la voie ferrée à travers Kanehsatà:ke. Kaná:tase mena environ quarante hommes armés pour empêcher l'arpentage de la voie ferrée,[58] mais pas un seul coup de feu ne fut tiré. La compagnie abandonna ses plans, et la question ne refit surface qu'environ vingt ans plus tard quand la Canadian Northern Railway Company obtint du séminaire le droit de passage à travers Kanehsatà:ke.

Kaná:tase s'opposa souvent au conseil de bande élu dirigé par son frère Angus Corinthe et préconisa la perpétuation du gouvernement traditionnel. Il raviva la tradition de la maison longue qui avait été contrainte à la clandestinité à Kanehsatà:ke et apporta un nouvel espoir à un peuple qui avait peu de raisons d'être optimiste. Pendant plusieurs années, les Kanehsata'kehró:non avaient dû dissimuler leurs cérémonies et leurs fêtes spirituelles à cause de l'intolérance religieuse et des pressions de la société dominante pour qu'ils adoptent une apparence de « civilisation ». Ils avaient été obligés de pratiquer leur spiritualité en privé et de s'adonner à leurs cérémonies en quasi-secret. Beaucoup avaient complètement abandonné leurs traditions pour faciliter leur acceptation dans la société canadienne. Ils retournaient maintenant vers la tradition pour y puiser la force et la consolation dans les moments difficiles. Menés par Joseph K. Gabriel, ils trouvèrent une nouvelle détermination à poursuivre la lutte.

Les traités que les couronnes britannique et française avaient conclus avec les Rotinonhseshá:ka, ainsi que les lois du parlement conçues pour protéger les terres indiennes, furent les outils qu'il utilisa pour défendre la cause de son peuple. Malheureusement, Kaná:tase rencontra une réticence tenace de la part des gouvernements britannique et canadien à honorer ces traités. Pour tous ses efforts, Joseph K. Gabriel fut étiqueté de fauteur de troubles par les autorités et traqué sans merci par la police. À maintes occasions, il fut traîné devant le système judiciaire canadien pour la moindre infraction. Souvent, en revenant de la cour à Saint-Scholastique, il était de nouveau appréhendé et ramené directement en prison, accusé d'avoir coupé illégalement du bois, d'une valeur de trois ou quatre dollars, pour chauffer sa maison. À un certain moment, il fut contraint de chercher refuge aux États-Unis durant sept ans.

Le gouvernement considérait les activités et les croyances traditionnelles de Kaná:tase comme une menace et encourageait implicitement les mesures employées par la police. On raflait souvent sa maison au beau milieu de la nuit pour l'arrêter en tirant des coups de feu et en terrorisant sa famille. En 1902, Kaná:tase, ainsi que Louis Beauvais, furent accusés d'avoir coupé du bois illégalement.[59] Un mandat d'arrêt fut émis contre lui, mais quand les agents de police se présentèrent chez lui, il n'y était pas.[60] Il était parti pour l'Angleterre en mars 1902 dans le but de solliciter une audience auprès du roi.[61] Même si son retour fut très annoncé, la police ne réussit pas à le dénicher. Ne pouvant pas l'appréhender, les autorités choisirent un autre plan d'action. On décida de saisir ses biens personnels et son équipement agricole pour payer le bois qu'il avait soi-disant volé,[62] tout cela, malgré le fait qu'il n'avait été ni appréhendé, ni accusé officiellement d'un délit, ni reconnu coupable d'aucun crime. À nouveau, les agents de la police provinciale se rendirent à Kanehsatà:ke, cette fois pour effectuer la saisie. Quand ils arrivèrent à la maison de Kaná:tase, tous ses effets avaient disparu. Son frère Angus Corinthe, qui avait été désigné comme administrateur de la propriété, fut plus tard arrêté et détenu pour entrave à la justice.[63]

Pendant ce temps, Joseph revint de Londres avec sa femme, car il n'avait pas réussi à obtenir une audience auprès du roi. Dans une interview tenue dans un endroit secret avec le journal *Star*, il exprima ses opinions sur la situation du peuple de Kanehsatà:ke. Il dit :

Je serais heureux de vous expliquer nos problèmes pour que le grand public ait une idée juste de notre situation. En quelques mots, la question se résume simplement à ceci : il y a des gens qui veulent que nous partions d'ici, l'endroit où nos pères ont vécu, et ils utiliseraient n'importe quel prétexte pour arriver à leurs fins […] Mais nous ne partirons d'ici que lorsque nous mourrons. Si ces persécutions se poursuivent, s'ils ne nous laissent pas tranquilles, si leurs agents de police et leurs détectives continuent de nous pourchasser et d'essayer de nous traîner en prison, alors il y aura la guerre. Ils n'en viendront pas à bout de mon vivant.[64]

Joseph poursuivit en parlant des afflictions et de la persécution que sa famille et son peuple avaient subies :

Je me rappelle la fois où mon père a été emprisonné pendant trois mois pour avoir coupé trois petites bûches dans la forêt parce qu'il voulait réparer sa maison. Je me rappelle aussi comment d'autres de mes relations, y compris le père de Beauvais, qui, en sortant pendant l'hiver pour couper du bois afin de garder leur femme et leurs enfants au chaud, ont été arrêtés dans le bois et emmenés en prison. Pendant ce temps, ne sachant pas ce qui causait l'absence prolongée de leur mari et de leur père, les femmes et les enfants tremblotants attendaient en vain le combustible pour réchauffer leur corps à demi gelé.[65]

Kaná:tase n'avait aucune intention de se rendre aux autorités puisqu'il était fermement convaincu qu'elles n'avaient aucun droit de l'appréhender n'ayant aucune juridiction à Kanehsatà:ke. Cette conviction était manifeste dans bon nombre des demandes qu'il adressa à divers représentants du gouvernement, y compris le gouverneur général et le roi d'Angleterre. Il y déclarait clairement que les tribunaux canadiens et les agents de police n'avaient aucune juridiction sur les affaires d'une autre nation et demandait que leurs interventions cessent. En juin 1902, la police provinciale n'avait toujours pas réussi à intercepter Kaná:tase qui s'était retiré dans les bois où il restait caché.[66] Pendant ce temps, les policiers se contentaient en harcelant et en terrorisant sa femme et sa famille. Un état de grande inquiétude régnait dans la communauté à cause des fréquentes visites de la police.

Des rumeurs d'émeute et de meurtres dans le village d'Oka circulaient dans la région, et des reportages à sensation ne servaient qu'à jeter de l'huile sur le feu. Le 19 juin, le *Montreal Daily Star* rapporta que les Indiens d'Oka avaient acheté tous les revolvers et les munitions disponibles à Saint-Placide, puis en avaient commandé d'autres.[67] Le département des Affaires indiennes avait immédiatement envoyé des hommes pour protéger les habitants du village d'Oka et des environs. Il semblait que les forces qui étaient à l'œuvre, et sur lesquelles le peuple n'avait aucun contrôle, ne faisaient qu'empirer une situation déjà tendue.

Pendant ce temps difficile, Kaná:tase jouissait du soutien massif de son peuple, et peu de gens toléraient une quelconque divergence d'opinion de celle qu'ils avaient adoptée. Au début de juin, les Kanehsata'kehró:non prirent des mesures pour destituer un chef qui avait agi contrairement à leurs désirs. Il s'était rendu à Como (Hudson) pour rencontrer un secrétaire du département des Affaires indiennes. Ensemble, ils avaient discuté d'un accord territorial possible pour Kanehsatà:ke et négocié une entente provisoire. Une partie de l'entente proposait la vente des terres à Doncaster pour acheter celles à Kanesatà:ke. Cependant, ce chef n'avait reçu aucun mandat pour négocier une telle entente, et le peuple ne voyait aucune raison de vendre une parcelle de leurs terres pour en acheter une autre qui leur appartenait déjà. Amable Roussin fut destitué.[68] Cependant, le gouvernement continua de reconnaître Roussin et d'autres qui étaient d'accord avec sa façon de penser comme la seule autorité légitime à Kanehsatà:ke, même s'ils ne jouissaient d'aucun appui populaire.

En mars 1918, Kaná:tase et les autres chefs traditionnels firent une demande au gouverneur général du Canada pour l'informer une fois de plus de leurs droits et pour décrier les empiétements de la Commune par les Canadiens français. Il écrivit :

Voici ce que nous avons vu; cependant, nous ne souhaitons jamais ne penser qu'au passé, mais nous faisons confiance au Grand Esprit qui nous a tous créés pour que justice soit faite et que l'avenir soit meilleur.

Frère : nous vous prions de considérer cette question et de faire pour nous ce que vous aimeriez qu'un frère fasse pour vous. Voici ce que nous désirons : que les droits de chaque frère soient respectés dans tout le continent et que tous soient d'un même esprit et vivent ensemble dans la paix et l'amour comme il convient à des frères; qu'entre vous et nous il y ait une chaîne d'amitié si forte qu'elle ne pourra être brisée et si polie et brillante qu'elle ne rouillera jamais. Voilà notre désir sincère.[69]

Kaná:tase faisait référence à la Chaîne d'alliance en argent, une entente d'amitié décrivant une relation politique entre deux nations souveraines et indépendantes : la Grande-Bretagne et les Rotinonhseshá:ka. Ce qu'il suggérait était un retour aux politiques et aux principes énoncés dans cette entente. Cependant, comme en témoigne l'imposition de ses lois sur le peuple de la maison longue et son hésitation à intervenir au nom des Kanehsata'kehró:non contre les colons blancs, le gouvernement du Canada a été, et est toujours, réticent à comprendre et à honorer cette entente, et il néglige de le faire.

En janvier 1923, Kaná:tase fut arrêté sous de fausses accusations d'agression contre un agent indien. Il semble que l'agent s'était rendu chez Gabriel sous prétexte de vérifier si les enfants fréquentaient ou non l'école. L'homme était provocant et insultait Kaná:tase et sa femme. Il revint plus tard l'arrêter, prétendant qu'il avait été agressé.[70] A. E. Harvey, avocat et ami de Kaná:tase, écrivit en sa faveur à Charles Stewart, ministre des Affaires indiennes à l'époque :

Le 13 janvier 1923, un agent a arrêté Gabriel pour agression et l'a fait sortir de chez lui pour l'emmener au village d'Oka devant le juge de paix Perillard, où on lui a fait verser une caution de 200 $ comptant. Le 21 janvier (huit jours plus tard), six hommes lourdement armés sont revenus chez lui et l'ont emmené devant un juge de paix où on lui a encore demandé une caution. Le samedi 27 janvier, ces agents sont revenus chez Gabriel et l'ont emmené à Montréal pour le déposer à la station de police n° 1 où il est resté jusqu'au lundi après-midi sans possibilité d'être remis en liberté conditionnelle. Le dimanche, des amis étaient venus pour le tirer d'affaire, mais la caution a été refusée. Ils sont revenus le lundi et Gabriel a été libéré sous caution. À cette occasion, il avait été détenu pendant deux jours et deux nuits sans aucune raison valable. Pour son procès, accompagné par sept témoins, le chef Gabriel a été obligé de se rendre quatre fois à Saint-Jérôme et à Saint-Scolastique où tous ont dû rester sept jours, chaque fois aux frais de Gabriel. Cela lui a occasionné de lourdes dépenses et une perte de temps qu'il n'avait pas les moyens de se payer. Après avoir gardé Gabriel sur une plaque chauffante, pour ainsi dire, pendant deux ans au cours desquels il a plusieurs fois été détenu comme prisonnier, incarcéré, souvent appelé à payer une caution, traîné devant les tribunaux à des kilomètres de chez lui, forcé à effectuer des dépenses qu'il ne pouvait assumer, harcelé et contrarié au-delà de toute endurance humaine, le jury a prononcé un verdict de « non-culpabilité ». Peu de temps après, sous une autre section du droit pénal, la même accusation pour la même prétendue offense a été portée contre lui. Et il a de nouveau été arrêté et soumis à la même procédure humiliante et aux mêmes dépenses exorbitantes durant une autre année jusqu'au 5 février 1926 où l'accusation a encore été rejetée.[71]

Harvey demanda au Département de rembourser Kaná:tase pour les dépenses encourues durant ses récentes difficultés juridiques, puisque les accusations ne furent jamais prouvées et que le traitement imposé à Kaná:tase était injustifié. Duncan C. Scott, surintendant adjoint des Affaires indiennes répondit :

En réponse, je dois dire que je n'ai rien à ajouter à la lettre qui vous a été adressée par le surintendant général à la deuxième occasion. Par ailleurs, les Indiens d'Oka ont toujours été traités très généreusement par le Département, et vous êtes tout à fait libre d'intenter, au nom de Gabriel, toute poursuite devant les tribunaux que vous jugerez nécessaire.[72]

Après avoir laissé les autorités provinciales persécuter Kaná:tase, le Département indien n'était pas prêt à couvrir ses dépenses. De plus, en le gardant occupé autrement, les autorités avaient réussi à détourner son attention de la question des droits territoriaux des Kanehsata'kehró:non. Depuis toujours, c'était la stratégie courante pour neutraliser les chefs « militants » des communautés autochtones. À chaque occasion où Kaná:tase prenait position contre la politique du gouvernement pour défendre l'intérêt de son peuple, il recevait pour toute récompense l'interruption de sa vie et l'intervention soutenue de la police. Chaque nouveau round de la lutte était immédiatement suivi par une période longue et pénible d'arrestations fréquentes et délibérées, d'emprisonnements et de batailles juridiques coûteuses. Par exemple, au début des années 1900, après avoir résisté activement à des empiétements sur la Commune, Kaná:tase lutta contre la compagnie de chemin de fer, puis connut d'autres difficultés avec le séminaire après le verdict du procès de Corinthe. Chaque fois, on essayait de le faire taire en l'immobilisant par le système judiciaire canadien.

En outre, Kaná:tase et plusieurs de ses partisans avaient pris la décision de ne pas laisser leurs enfants fréquenter les écoles dirigées par l'Église méthodiste et le département des Affaires indiennes pour préserver leur langue et leur culture, ainsi que pour protéger les enfants des maladies qui étaient endémiques dans les écoles. En avril 1921, Helen Earl, enseignante de l'école du village d'Oka, écrivit au Département demandant l'intervention de la GRC pour régler le problème d'absentéisme.[73] Selon Mlle Earl, une fois que la résistance de Joseph K. Gabriel serait vaincue, toute résistance serait éliminée.[74] À Kanehsatà:ke, nombreux sont ceux qui se rappellent les rafles de la police au petit matin, quand on arrêtait ou harcelait les parents pour avoir refusé d'envoyer leurs enfants à l'école. Pendant des années, plusieurs Kanehsata'kehró:non furent arrêtés pour cette raison et accusés en vertu de la loi canadienne. Une loi qui s'appliquait seulement aux peuples autochtones du pays.

Dans les années 1930, une nouvelle série de difficultés débuta avec la vente de la Commune à une compagnie belge. Celle-ci ne permettait pas aux Kanehsata'kehró:non de couper du bois ni de faire paître leur bétail sur la Commune, ce qu'ils avaient toujours fait.[75] Les Canadiens français avaient aussi commencé à y jouer au golf, chassant ainsi le bétail.[76] La menace contre la Commune touchait tous les Kanehsata'kehró:non. Beaucoup en dépendaient pour faire paître leur bétail, et cela était devenu encore plus important puisque de plus en plus de familles perdaient leurs terres au profit des colons blancs. Le 11 juillet 1933, les chefs traditionnels de Kanehsatà:ke écrivirent au gouverneur général :

Nous, les Indiens, qui vivons sur notre dite réserve, désirons vous informer des ennuis que nous éprouvons maintenant sur nos pâturages que nous appelons la Commune. Les Canadiens français qui se sont fait un terrain de golf, où notre bétail a déjà l'habitude de paître, causent des dommages à ce terrain commun. Ils ont installé des poteaux et utilisent des tondeuses pour couper l'herbe partout sur le terrain. Il n'en reste donc plus pour y faire paître nos vaches qui y vivent et qui se font chasser à coup de bâton de golf.[77]

Les chefs, qui avaient déjà parlé sans résultat au séminaire, estimèrent qu'il ne servirait à rien de contacter le Département parce qu'il ne ferait rien de toute façon.[78] Ils demandèrent alors au gouverneur général d'examiner la question et d'y mettre un terme. Si on compare les besoins de pâturage de quelques pauvres fermiers indiens aux besoins récréatifs des riches Canadiens français de la région, la décision était facile à prendre. Mais rien ne fut fait pour protéger la Commune des Kanehsata'kehró:non, et la vente de ces terres à une compagnie belge empira la situation. Dans ce cas, le peuple de Kanehsatà:ke avait décidé d'affirmer ses droits, et les arrestations reprirent de plus belle. En mars 1938, Royal Werry, avocat des Kanehsata'kehró:non, écrivit au ministère des Mines et des Ressources à propos de la friction entre la compagnie belge et le peuple de Kanehsatà:ke. Il lui rappela la dispute de longue date et l'informa des récents développements :

Au cours des dernières années, une certaine compagnie belge a acheté des Sulpiciens tous ses droits sur ce qui semble être une bonne partie de la réserve d'Oka. Peu à peu, elle applique ses droits au détriment des Indiens, ce que les frères sulpiciens ne désiraient pas faire. Les Indiens se trouvent maintenant dans une situation où ils commettent des crimes quand ils font ce que leurs ancêtres ont toujours fait au cours des 250 dernières années. Récemment, quelques policiers sont allés appréhender un certain Indien qui est censé avoir volé ou coupé du bois qui, semble-t-il, appartenait à la compagnie belge. La police l'a emmené dans une cabane pour discuter de certaines choses avec plusieurs Indiens, ils y sont restés environ une heure et demie. Alors que tout le monde parlait, le prisonnier, qui se tenait à environ un mètre et demi des policiers, est tout simplement sorti de la cabane et n'a pas été revu depuis ce jour. Pour se venger d'avoir été négligents au travail, les policiers ont arrêté quelques Indiens et possèdent des mandats d'arrêt pour quatre autres qui sont soupçonnés d'avoir aidé le prisonnier à s'échapper. Vu les circonstances, tout cela n'est que persécution et enfantillage.[79]

L'homme qui s'était échappé était Joseph K. Gabriel. Quatre autres Indiens furent ultérieurement appréhendés pour avoir aidé Kaná:tase à s'évader et pour avoir résisté à la police. Werry décrit la résistance alléguée :

Un des Indiens a été appréhendé pour avoir résisté à la police. Le policier est censé lui avoir demandé où se trouvait un autre Indien, et quand l'homme appréhendé a dit qu'il ne le savait pas, le policier a braqué son fusil sur lui pour le forcer à parler. L'Indien, qui n'a pas aimé voir le revolver, l'a saisi des mains du policier. C'est pourquoi il a été arrêté pour avoir résisté à un agent de police.[80]

Dans une lettre précédente, Werry avait critiqué l'inaction du gouvernement pour protéger les droits des Kanehsata'kehró:non:

Si ce pays était l'Éthiopie ou l'Espagne, je pourrais comprendre votre attitude par rapport au traitement de ces gens, mais dans un pays civilisé comme le Canada est censé l'être, je ne comprends pas votre manque absolu de considération et votre inaction à l'égard des droits et des sentiments d'êtres humains.[81]

L'incapacité de Werry à comprendre le traitement mesquin du gouvernement envers les Kanehsata'kehró:non est normal pour quelqu'un qui possède une conscience et fait preuve de compassion. Ce qui est encore plus difficile à comprendre, c'est que cette dispute qui débuta avec l'arrivée du séminaire de Saint-Sulpice à Kanehsatà:ke s'est poursuivie durant plus de 270 ans. Les Kanehsata'kehró:non supportèrent d'innombrables persécutions aux mains du séminaire et du gouvernement. Ils furent opprimés, culturellement étouffés, injustement accusés de crimes, emprisonnés sans raison, expropriés contre leur volonté et dépouillés de leurs enfants. Ils n'eurent pas droit aux nécessités de la vie et aux droits humains fondamentaux. Ils subirent des attaques contre leur langue, leur culture et leur spiritualité et furent l'objet de politiques d'assimilation paternalistes. Malgré le fait qu'ils n'eurent jamais droit à la justice, ils ne furent jamais vaincus. Des hommes comme Aughneeta, O'nahsakèn:rat, Kaná:tase, Simon K. Simon, James S. Montour, Martin Martin et plusieurs autres soutinrent le peuple dans des temps difficiles. Des hommes et des femmes de force et de caractère préservèrent la langue et la culture des Kanien'kehà:ka pour les générations futures. Grâce à leurs efforts, il y a des Kanien'kehà:ka à Kanehsatà:ke aujourd'hui qui continuent de lutter contre toute attente pour le territoire et l'avenir de leurs enfants.

À divers moments, diverses personnes, dont Joseph K. Gabriel et Angus Corinthe, utilisèrent différents moyens pour poursuivre le combat. Le gouvernement profitait souvent de ce fait pour diviser et affaiblir le peuple davantage. Un fait demeure: malgré l'ingérence et la manipulation extérieures, le peuple de Kanehsatà:ke resta toujours uni pour protéger son territoire. En 1945, le gouvernement fédéral acheta du séminaire les terres non cédées qui restaient.[82] Cette mesure, visant à résoudre le conflit pour de bon, était trop peu trop tard. La Commune avait été vendue à une compagnie belge et allait être revendue à la municipalité d'Oka (pour une explication détaillée, voir chapitre 10). Il ne restait aux Kanehsata'kehró:non que quelques petites fermes et de très petits lots dans le village. Dans les années 1960, malgré beaucoup de protestation, la municipalité engagea la construction d'un terrain de golf privé sur la Commune. Les Kanehsata'kehró:non contestèrent ce geste en envoyant des délégués à Ottawa pour tenter d'y mettre fin, mais ne réussirent pas, et la construction alla de l'avant sans incident. Mais ce ne fut pas le cas trente ans plus tard quand la municipalité annonça qu'elle planifiait agrandir le terrain de golf privé en prenant le reste des terres communes sans même consulter les Kanehsata'kehró:non. Après des siècles de sévices, ceux-ci n'étaient pas prêts à laisser des intérêts récréatifs avoir priorité sur leur droit à leur terre.

IL N'Y AURA PAS DE CAPITULATION

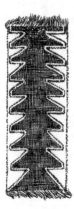

Il semble donc que les Kanehsata'kehró:non doivent subir encore plus d'épreuves. Ils ont parcouru trop de chemin pour abandonner, ils se sont battus trop longtemps pour capituler. Ils savent qu'ils doivent résister pour les sept générations futures, car s'ils ne le font pas, qui le fera? Le Créateur nous a tous donné des responsabilités, et les Kanehsata'kehró:non sont conscients que s'ils ne portent pas leur fardeau, ils ne pourront pas regarder leurs petits-enfants et dire : « J'ai fait tout ce que j'ai pu pour assurer ton avenir afin que tu deviennes aussi grand que le pin et que tu voies tes petits-enfants apprendre les traditions. » Je sais que ce sont ces pensées qui continuent de les motiver à lutter et à résister. Même s'ils sont épuisés, en regardant leur mère la terre, ils savent au fond de leur cœur qu'ils ne peuvent pas l'abandonner, car s'ils le faisaient ils deviendraient comme leur oppresseur. Ne comprenant plus le monde naturel, ils deviendraient confus et seraient perdus. Ils s'en iraient et ne me reconnaîtraient plus. La lutte qu'ils mènent aujourd'hui servira de leçon pour l'avenir, et leurs petits-enfants raconteront cette histoire pendant longtemps.

[1] Hayter Reed à John Tewisha, 26 mai 1894, Centre national des arts, RG 10, vol. 2757, dossier 149 498.

[2] Timothy Ahrírhon à Sir John A. MacDonald, 8 mai 1885, Centre national des arts, RG 10, vol. 2299, dossier 59 649.

[3] Ibid.

[4] Vankoughnet, 20 mai 1885, Centre national des arts, RG 10, vol. 2299, dossier 59 649.

[5] Timothy Ahrírhon à L. Vankoughnet, 4 décembre 1886, Centre national des arts, RG 10, vol. 2353, dossier 71 175.

[6] Ibid.

[7] À Powell, sous-secrétaire d'État, 15 novembre 1886, Centre national des arts, RG 10, vol. 2353, dossier 71 175.

[8] Bureau du shérif à Walter Smith, 13 décembre 1886, Centre national des arts, RG 10, vol. 2353, dossier 71 175.

[9] Timothy Ahrírhon à L. Vankoughnet, 8 mars 1887, Centre national des arts, RG 10, vol. 2353, dossier 71 175.

[10] L. Vankoughnet à Timothy Ahrírhon, 7 mai 1887, Centre national des arts, RG 10, vol. 2353, dossier 71 175.

[11] Ibid.

[12] Timothy Ahrírhon à L. Vankoughnet, 12 mai 1887, Centre national des arts, RG 10, vol. 2353, dossier 71 175.

[13] Procès verbal du conseil municipal, 11 octobre 1884, Centre national des arts, RG 10, vol. 7697, dossier 23 020 p. 1.

[14] James Campbell à Hayter Reed, 31 mai 1894, Centre national des arts, RG 10, vol. 7697, dossier 23 020 p. 1.

[15] Ibid.

[16] Ibid.

[17] Ibid.

[18] James Campbell à Hayter Reed, 31 mai 1894, Centre national des arts, RG 10, vol. 7697, dossier 23 020 pt. 1.

[19] Lecuoq à J. D. McLean, 30 septembre 1904, Centre national des arts, RG 10, vol.7697, dossier 23 020 pt. 1.

[20] S. Bray au surintendant général des Affaires indiennes, 21 octobre 1905, Centre national des arts, RG 10, vol. 7697, dossier 23 020 pt. 1.

[21] Ibid.

[22] Ibid.

[23] Hayter Reed à Timothy Ahrírhon, 30 juillet 1896, Centre national des arts, RG 10, vol. 2874, dossier 176 418.

[24] Hayter Reed à William Scott, 1er septembre 1896, Centre national des arts, RG 10, vol. 2874, dossier 176 418.

[25] Ibid.

[26] Ibid.

[27] Hayter Reed à Timothy Ahrírhon, 28 janvier 1897, Centre national des arts, RG 10, vol. 2874, dossier 176 418.

[28] Angus Corinthe à Frank Pedley, 22 octobre 1910, Centre national des arts, RG 10, vol. 11 203, dossier n° 2, 1902-1910.

[29] Mme Angus Jacobs à Frank Pedley, 27 avril 1910, Centre national des arts, RG 10, vol. 11203, dossier n° 2, 1902-1910.

[30] Ibid.

[31] Mémorandum, surintendant général adjoint, 14 juillet 1910, RG 10, vol. 7816, dossier 30 020.

[32] J. D. McLean à D. J. Lefebvre, 3 mars 1911, Centre national des arts, RG 10, vol. 7816, dossier 30 020.

[33] D. J. Lefebvre à J. D. McLean, 4 mars 1911, Centre national des arts, RG 10, vol. 7816, dossier 30 020.

[34] James Campbell à Hayter Reed, 31 mai 1894, Centre national des arts, RG 10, vol. 7697, dossier 23 020 pt. 1.

[35] Ibid.

[36] Secrétaire adjoint à C. F. Bertrand, 3 janvier 1919, Centre national des arts, RG 10, vol. 7816, dossier 30 020.

[37] J. Labelle à A. F. McKenzie, 12 janvier 1926, Centre national des arts, RG 10, vol. 7816, dossier 30 020.

[38] F. Brisebois au secrétaire du département des Affaires indiennes, 9 mai 1934, Centre national des arts, RG 10, vol. 7816, dossier 30 020.

[39] Ibid.

[40] Indian Woodsman Balks At Arrest, 4 mai 1934, Centre national des arts, RG,10, vol. 7816, dossier 30 020.

[41] Chefs de Kanehsatà:ke au gouverneur général du Canada, 7 mai 1934, Centre national des arts, RG 10, vol. 7816, dossier 30 020.

[42] W. Smith à E. L. NewComber, 20 mars 1908, Centre national des arts, RG 13, vol. 2437, dossier A500.

[43] Joseph K. Gabriel au ministre de l'Intérieur, 4 novembre 1911, Centre national des arts, RG 10, vol. 10 258, dossier 373 131-2-2-1.

[44] Secrétaire adjoint à Joseph K. Gabriel, 11 décembre 1911, Centre national des arts, RG 10, vol. 10 259, dossier 373 31-2-2-1.

[45] Vice-président de la Central Railway Co. au département des Affaires indiennes, 2 février 1912, Centre national des arts, RG 10, vol. 10 259, dossier 373 131-2-2-1.

[46] Ibid.

[47] Joseph K. Gabriel à R. L. Borden, 18 mars 1912, Centre national des arts, RG 10, vol. 10 259, dossier 373 131-2-2-1.

[48] Avis d'expropriation, J. A. G. Belisle, N. P., 20 décembre 1930, Centre national des arts, RG 10, vol. 10 259, dossier 373 131-2-2-1.

[49] Aimé Geoffrion à Donat Lalande, 31 décembre 1912, Centre national des arts, RG 10, vol. 10 259, dossier 373 131-2-2-1.

[50] Charles Murray au secrétaire du département des Affaires indiennes, 24 décembre 1930, Centre national des arts, RG 10, vol. 10 259, dossier 373 131-2-2-1.

[51] A. F. MacKenzie à F. Harbour, 25 décembre 1930, Centre national des arts, RG 10, vol. 10 259, dossier 373 131-2-201.

[52] Pierre Murray au secrétaire du département des Affaires indiennes, 10 janvier 1931, Centre national des arts, RG 10, vol. 10 259, dossier 373 131-2-2-1.

[53] McGookin au département des Affaires indiennes, 29 janvier 1931, Centre national des arts, RG 10, vol. 10 259, dossier 373 131-2-2-1.

[54] Ibid.

[55] Norman Saylor à S. C. Caldwell, 30 septembre 1938, Centre national des arts, RG 10, vol. 10 259, dossier 373 131-2-2-1.

[56] Cas. Aug. Bertrand à T. R. L. MacInnes, 15 novembre 1940, Centre national des arts, RG 10, vol. 10 259, dossier 373 131-2-2-1.

[57] F. Thomas à Pierre Murray, 19 juin 1951, Centre national des arts, RG 10, vol. 10 259, dossier 373 131-2-2-1.

[58] Indians threaten war against railroad men, Montreal Daily Star, 20 décembre 1911.

[59] Chief of tribe threatens war, Montreal Daily Star, 26 mai 1902.

[60] Chief Kaná:tase's home surrounded, but was not at home, Montreal Daily Star, 18 juin 1902.

[61] Oka Indians divided in opinion, Montreal Daily Star, 11 mai 1909.

[62] Ibid.

[63] Guarded against arrest "Kinatosse" talks to Star, Montreal Daily Star, 28 mai 1902.

[64] Ibid.

[65] Ibid.

[66] An attempt made to arrest chief, Montreal Daily Star, 11 juin 1902.

[67] Detectives hot on trail of chief Kaná:tase: Indians purchase arms, Montreal Daily Star, 19 juin 1902.

[68] Kaná:tase is still defiant, Montreal Daily Star, 5 juin 1902.

[69] Joseph K. Gabriel, Louis Rivers, Mitchel Martin à son Excellence le duc de Devonshire, gouverneur général du Canada, 12 mai 1918, Centre national des arts, RG 10, vol. 11 203, dossier n° 6.

[70] A. E. Harvey à l'honorable Charles Stewart, 19 février 1926, Papers of Joseph K. Gabriel.

[71] Ibid.

[72] Duncan C. Scott à A. E. Harvey, 19 mars 1926.

[73] Helen Earl au secrétaire du département des Affaires indiennes, 7 avril 1921, Centre national des arts, RG 10, vol. 6096, dossier 323-1 p. 1.

[74] Ibid.

[75] Simon K. Simon, Philip Angus et James Montour à Lord Tweedmeir, gouverneur général du Canada, 22 avril 1937, Centre national des arts RG10, vol. 11 203, dossier n° 7.

[76] Martin Anonhsawén:rate, Arakente Kareweyo et Martin Sawennakarathie à Lord Wessbourough, gouverneur général du Canada, 11 juillet 1933, Centre national des arts, RG 10, vol. 11 203, dossier n° 7.

[77] Ibid.

[78] Ibid.

[79] Royal Werry à W. J. F. Pratt, 16 mars 1938, Centre national des arts, RG 10, vol. 11 203, dossier n° 7.

[80] Royal Werry à R. B. Cochrane, 2 mars 1938, Centre national des arts, RG 10, vol. 11 203, dossier n° 7.

[81] Royal Werry au département des Affaires indiennes, 30 novembre 1937, Centre national des arts, RG 10, vol. 11 203, dossier n° 7.

[82] Entre Sa Majesté le roi et les prêtres de Saint-Sulpice, Centre national des arts, RG 10, vol. 11 203, dossier n° 7.

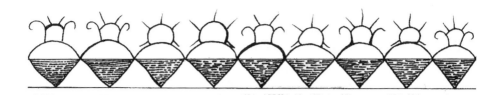

CHAPITRE 9

COUPER LES RACINES

LE SIFFLET DU TRAIN

Parfois, l'air peut porter les sons sur de grandes distances. C'est ainsi ce matin, et j'entends le sifflet du train. Je me demande s'il transporte des petits enfants.

De temps à autre, certains sont envoyés très loin à un endroit appelé « école ». Quand ils en reviennent, ils sont de jeunes hommes et de jeunes femmes. Personne ne les reconnaît, et eux-mêmes semblent perdus et confus. C'est vraiment une journée triste quand des familles envoient leurs petits au loin, mais en faisant ainsi ils croient que leurs enfants souffriront moins. On leur dit que ces derniers auront une vie meilleure, plus de nourriture, des chaussures et des vêtements chauds et qu'à leur retour, ils seront des gens instruits.

Les petits sont alors envoyés, et le son du sifflet ressemble à un cri lointain. Toutes leurs craintes et leur mal du pays restent en suspens comme de la fumée dans l'air.

L'ÉVOLUTION DU SYSTÈME DES PENSIONNATS

Des années 1890 jusque dans les années 1950, au moins 150 enfants de Kanehsatà:ke fréquentèrent les pensionnats.[1] La majorité fut envoyée dans des institutions créées spécialement pour les Onkwehón:we et la plupart, environ 120, allèrent à l'école Shingwauk, à Sault-Ste-Marie, en Ontario. Environ dix autres jeunes enfants fréquentèrent le pensionnat Chapleau, à Chapleau, en Ontario. Au moins un enfant fut envoyé à un pensionnat à Brandon, au Manitoba. Toutes ces écoles étaient administrées par les Églises catholique romaine et protestante et financées, en partie, par le département des Affaires indiennes. Ensemble, le Département et les Églises établirent les politiques éducationnelles des écoles.[2] Vingt autres enfants de Kanehsatà:ke fréquentèrent l'école protestante francophone de Pointe-aux-Trembles, au Québec. Cette école était gérée par l'Église méthodiste et recrutait des enfants blancs, aussi bien qu'autochtones. Elle ne faisait pas partie de ce qu'on appelle le système des pensionnats.[3]

Au début des années 1840, les représentants de la colonie britannique commencèrent à explorer l'idée de créer des pensionnats à caractère industriel et agricole pour les Onkwehón:we.[4] Le but, tel qu'affirmé par les représentants, était de mater les jeunes soi-disant indisciplinés en les séparant de leur communauté. En réalité, le but était de les assimiler. En éloignant les enfants de l'influence de leur famille, les écoles inculquaient vigoureusement les valeurs de la société canadienne. Les enfants étaient complètement coupés de leur monde pour être façonnés de manière à se conformer à des concepts étrangers hostiles. La bonté, l'amour et la famille élargie étaient remplacés par des règles, des codes et un dur endoctrinement. Les pensionnats visaient à enseigner à ces jeunes à devenir domestiques et journaliers. On leur enseignait aussi certaines matières scolaires, comme l'anglais ou le français. Cependant, beaucoup d'élèves faisaient davantage de durs travaux qu'ils ne recevaient de cours.

Avant la Confédération canadienne, presque toutes les écoles pour les Onkwehón:we étaient financées et gérées par des sociétés missionnaires ou des ordres religieux. Deux pensionnats pour des garçons de Kahnawake furent établis à Châteauguay et à Christieville. Le département des Affaires indiennes décrivit qu'elles étaient des « expériences intéressantes » où les enfants « recevaient une formation dans la classe et dans la ferme ».[5]

Dans les années 1930, le Département finança 80 pensionnats : 44 gérés par l'Église catholique romaine, 21 par l'Église anglicane, 13 par l'Église unie et 2 par l'Église presbytérienne. En 1921, environ 4360 enfants Onkwehón:we des communautés de tout le pays fréquentaient les pensionnats. En 1932, le nombre augmenta à 7400 enfants, et à plus de 8000 en 1936.[6] Le gouvernement commença à fermer ces écoles dans les années 1970 et 1980. La dernière ferma ses portes en 1988.

Seul un très petit nombre de pensionnats indiens étaient établis au Québec, et dans les années 1920 et 1930, aucun n'existait. Les enfants Onkwehón:we de la province étaient donc envoyés dans d'autres pensionnats, le plus souvent en Ontario. Même si les externats à Kanehsatà:ke étaient gérés par les Églises méthodiste et catholique, les enfants de la communauté étaient le plus souvent envoyés à l'école Shingwauk dirigée par l'Église anglicane.

L'école industrielle Shingwauk, à Sault Ste-Marie, fut fondée en 1871 par le missionnaire et enseignant britannique E. F. Wilson. Elle fut nommée en l'honneur du chef obijway Shingwauk. Le fondateur la quitta en 1893, et l'Église anglicane en reprit la gérance. L'école ferma ses portes en 1970. Un an plus tard, les bâtiments et le terrain furent repris par Algoma University College. En 1981, et en 1991, l'université parraina des réunions pour les anciens élèves de l'école Shingwauk. Plusieurs Kanehsata'kehró:non y participèrent.[7]

Les enfants de Kanehsatà:ke qui fréquentèrent l'école Shingwauk restaient souvent de 10 à 15 années loin de chez eux. En raison de la distance, ils ne retournaient presque jamais à la maison avant d'avoir terminé leur scolarité ou atteint l'âge de seize ans. Bon nombre d'entre eux retournèrent dans une communauté et une famille qu'ils ne reconnaissaient plus. Certains quittèrent définitivement Kanehsatà:ke, se refirent une nouvelle vie et fondèrent une famille ailleurs. D'autres durent lutter pour réintégrer leur communauté et faire de Kanehsatà:ke leur foyer.

Les pensionnats entraînèrent des sentiments de froideur et d'isolement chez beaucoup de leurs diplômés, rendant difficile pour certains d'appartenir à quelque endroit que ce soit.

Dans l'histoire du Canada, les enfants d'aucun autre peuple ne furent systématiquement retirés de leur famille et de leur communauté. En examinant nos ressources et notre bien-être spirituel, nous estimons que le système des pensionnats fut l'une des causes principales, sinon la principale, de beaucoup d'afflictions. La langue et l'histoire forment une partie du fondement sur lequel repose l'identité d'un peuple. À l'école Shingwauk, on interdisait aux enfants Onkwehón:we de parler leur langue maternelle et on ne leur enseignait pas l'histoire des autochtones. Ces restrictions et une négligence orchestrée sont considérées avec tristesse, regret et colère par ceux qui fréquentèrent l'école, et même par ceux qui valorisent l'instruction qu'ils y reçurent. La plupart des anciens élèves considèrent les mesures disciplinaires appliquées par les autorités scolaires comme extrêmes et inhumaines. Tous critères confondus, ces mesures étaient abusives.

Le premier enfant de Kanehsatà:ke envoyé à l'école Shingwauk fut probablement Charles White, âgé de neuf ans en 1895. Il fut rejoint par Thomas White, âgé de onze ans en 1899. Les deux garçons fréquentèrent l'école au moins jusqu'en 1906. Charles travaillait dans la buanderie et Thomas dans la ferme. John Angus, âgé de 19 ans, résida à l'école Shingwauk de 1896 à environ 1898. En 1903, Elias Martin, âgé de huit ans, y fit son entrée. Les enfants ayant un lien de parenté avec Kanehsatà:ke vécurent aussi à l'école Shingwauk. En 1901, Mary White de Gibson alla à cette école à l'âge de neuf ans et, en 1906, Gladys Jacobs et Mary Jane Jacobs de Saint-Régis y firent leur entrée.[8] Henry Etienne et Gordon Simon, tous deux de Kanehsatà:ke, y allèrent en 1919. Gordon Simon, qui avait alors trois ans, retourna chez lui à l'âge de 18 ans.

De loin, le plus grand nombre d'enfants de Kanehsatà:ke allèrent à l'école Shingwauk dans les années 1920, 1930 et 1940. Ils venaient des familles Beauvais, Bonspille, Cree, Gabriel, Martin, Nelson, Oke, Simon et Wilson. Souvent, plusieurs enfants de chaque famille fréquentaient cette école. Par ailleurs, des enfants de presque chaque groupe familial de la communauté y vécurent. Le nombre des enfants, environ 120, est très élevé par rapport à la population de Kanehsatà:ke. Ce système scolaire eut des répercussions considérables sur la communauté.

SOUVENIRS DE L'ÉCOLE SHINGWAUK

Les récits qui suivent sur la vie à l'école Shingwauk, à Sault Ste-Marie, sont tirés d'interviews réalisées auprès d'hommes et de femmes Kanehsata'kehró:non qui fréquentèrent l'institution dans leur jeunesse.

☐ « Eh bien, je pense que je suis arrivé à l'école Shingwauk vers 1939 après avoir terminé ma 7e année à Oka. C'était le plus loin qu'on pouvait aller. Je voulais aller à cette école parce que je savais que ma sœur y était et que c'était le seul moyen d'acquérir plus d'instruction. À Oka, il n'y avait pas d'école secondaire ni même de transport scolaire; ça n'existait pas à l'époque. Pour ce qui était de m'envoyer dans une autre ville comme pensionnaire, c'était hors de question; nous n'en avions tout simplement pas les moyens. »

☐ « Quand Gordon est parti, il avait des boucles, vous savez, des cheveux frisés et blonds, presque blancs. Quand il est arrivé à Sault Ste-Marie, il n'avait que trois ans. À l'âge de quatre ans, on lui a coupé les cheveux comme un garçon. Il couchait dans le dortoir des filles parce qu'il était trop petit pour se mêler aux autres garçons. On a gardé ses boucles quand on lui a coupé les cheveux et je les ai encore aujourd'hui; de longs cheveux avec un petit ruban bleu. Son père s'était noyé, c'est pourquoi il est allé à l'école Shingwauk. À son retour, il avait 18 ans et cinq mois. »

☐ « On m'a envoyée à l'école Shingwauk alors que je venais tout juste d'avoir six ans, avec ma sœur qui n'en avait que quatre. Pouvez-vous vous imaginer être séparée de votre mère à cet âge? Je n'ai pas revu ma mère avant d'avoir 19 ans. Je pense que c'était trop une grosse charge pour ma mère et mon père; ils avaient deux autres enfants. Nous étions si pauvres. »

☐ « J'y suis allée en train, en fait c'est le Dr Westlake qui m'y a amenée. Nous étions six en tout. Nous avons pris le train à Hudson, non je pense que c'était Como à cette époque, puis nous avons remonté la rivière jusqu'à Ottawa où nous avons dû nous arrêter et attendre le prochain train pour Sault Ste-Marie. Là, nous devions changer de train et nous y sommes restés durant quelques heures ou plus, parce que je me souviens que nous nous étions éparpillés dans toute la station. Nous avons eu beaucoup de plaisir. Puis, nous sommes arrivés à Sault Ste-Marie le soir du 26 janvier 1926. J'y suis restée 10 ans. »

☐ « Ça fait si longtemps, c'est embrouillé. Je me rappelle qu'on nous a tous acheté de nouveaux ensembles, de nouveaux vêtements et que nous dansions en rond, toutes belles, vous savez. C'était spécial. En fait, mon père a ramé pour nous faire traverser le lac et il nous a amenés à bord du train. Quelle expérience! J'avais entre cinq ans et demi et six ans. Je me rappelle que je ne savais pas que notre père nous disait au revoir. J'étais si contente d'avoir de nouveaux vêtements. Le train a commencé à bouger, puis mon père a sauté en bas et nous a dit: Bye! Bye! Comme ça. Je me suis assise dans le train et j'ai pleuré pendant deux jours. Le premier jour et la première nuit, je pense que j'ai pleuré presque tout le temps. Je me rappelle que quelqu'un est venu vers moi, une femme, et qu'elle a commencé à me bercer et à me prendre dans ses bras pour me calmer. C'est ainsi que s'est déroulé le voyage, et je suis arrivée à l'école. Je me suis enfuie de Shingwauk à l'âge de 17 ans. »

☐ « J'ai pleuré pendant tout le trajet, puis chaque soir à l'école Shingwauk. »

☐ « J'ai demandé à mon père de s'informer pour que j'aille à l'école Shingwauk et je pense... je pense que j'y suis allée en janvier. En tout cas, je sais que la guerre avait commencé et je me rappelle avoir vu tous les soldats à bord du train. Je crois que c'était l'hiver quand je suis arrivée, alors ça devait être en janvier. C'est Canon Minchin qui m'a rencontrée au train. À cette époque, j'avais les cheveux longs, assez longs. Il semblait que tous les enfants qui arrivaient tout juste des réserves devaient se faire couper les cheveux. Quand je suis arrivée, on ne m'a pas coupé les cheveux. J'étais probablement le premier enfant qui soit entré dans l'école sans avoir eu à se faire couper les cheveux. »

☐ « Ils savaient qui arrivait à l'école, et le directeur était là. Il avait une voiture scolaire pour nous y amener. Ce devait être l'hiver... Je me rappelle que c'était l'hiver. Nous ne parlions que la langue indienne. Alors, on a trouvé deux filles qui ont plus ou moins interprété pour nous ce qu'ils voulaient qu'on fasse. S'asseoir... rester tranquille... arrêter de pleurer et d'autres choses du genre. Nous ne connaissions pas un mot d'anglais, et c'était dur pour nous. Avec le temps, nous avons dû nous mêler au groupe et apprendre l'anglais en conversant avec les autres enfants. Nous parlions tous un mauvais anglais. »

☐ « J'y suis allée avant mon frère. Il est venu après moi; je me souviendrai toujours du jour de son arrivée. J'avais hâte de le voir. Je savais qu'on était allé le chercher; il était descendu du train et je savais qu'il était dans l'école, mais on m'a dit que je ne pouvais pas le voir avant le souper. C'était le règlement; je devais attendre. Nous devions tous les deux rester assis pendant le souper avant de pouvoir nous voir et parler ensemble. Après, tout ce qu'on pouvait faire était de pleurer. »

☐ « La surveillante arrivait tôt le matin, et tout le monde devait sortir de son lit. Chaque matin, nous récitions des prières dans la classe. Nous y allions et chantions un cantique et une prière. Quand on savait que c'était notre anniversaire de naissance, nous pouvions choisir le chant cette journée-là. Puis, nous allions déjeuner. De là, nous partions pour l'école secondaire; nous devions donc nous hâter et nous préparer. Une voiture nous y amenait. Pendant l'hiver, nous avions une petite charrette et une couverture de fourrure, et les deux chevaux galopaient jusque-là. Nous suivions un programme scolaire régulier. Tout le monde aidait, vous savez. »

« Les filles de l'école secondaire ne pouvaient faire aucun travail pendant l'année scolaire. Alors, nous devions servir le déjeuner, une fille d'un côté et une autre de l'autre côté, nous distribuions du gruau à tout le monde, tandis qu'une autre petite fille courait pour distribuer le sucre, et qu'une autre encore, avec un seau et une grande tasse, distribuait le lait. Dans la cuisine, deux filles coupaient tout le pain, puis on nous donnait du Crisco. C'était notre beurre. Juste avant de commencer à manger, la surveillante criait: « C'est l'heure des rôties! » Et tous les enfants se précipitaient à la cuisine. D'autres lundis, il y avait une équipe qui devait se lever plus tôt que les autres. Je pense que nous nous levions à 6 h 30, mais l'équipe avait une pause agréable vers 9 h. On leur donnait du thé et du pain avec de la confiture. »

☐ « Voici comment se déroulait notre emploi du temps. Le matin, dès notre lever, nous nous mettions à genoux à côté du lit et récitions une prière. Puis, nous nous lavions, nous habillions et montions à l'étage. Il y avait un très grand auditorium où nous devions tous écouter le directeur qui était prêtre. Il faisait une cérémonie, chantait quelques chants et priait. On nous enfonçait la religion dans la gorge peu importe si nous comprenions ou non. Ensuite, nous sortions et faisions nos corvées. Je devais traire les vaches. Après, nous revenions et nous lavions encore, puis nous allions déjeuner. »

☐ « Nous avions une journée de couture. Certains des élèves faisaient une demi-journée d'école et une demi-journée de travail. Un jour, nous faisions de la couture et l'autre jour, du repassage. Sur le gazon, il y avait des terrains de basket où nous avions l'habitude de jouer. Les enfants formaient leurs propres équipes. Nous marchions jusqu'à la barrière, puis revenions au point de départ et recommencions. Avec notre meilleure amie, nous marchions et discutions de toutes sortes de choses ou faisions ce que nous aimions. »

☐ « La plupart des jeunes enfants et des plus vieux avaient une demi-journée d'école et une demi-journée de travail. La moitié d'entre eux travaillait le matin et l'autre moitié, l'après-midi. On m'exemptait de beaucoup de choses parce que j'étais très petite. J'avais l'âge de les faire, mais à cause de ma taille, on ne voulait pas que je fasse les gros travaux. Le matin avant l'école, j'aidais à frotter les planchers. Nous lavions les fenêtres et des choses comme ça. J'étais même exemptée des travaux de cuisine. Ce n'est qu'une fois mariée que j'ai appris à faire bouillir de l'eau. J'étais si petite qu'on ne voulait pas que je fasse ce genre de travail. Je passais alors toute la journée en classe. J'étais chanceuse, vraiment chanceuse. »

☐ « Nous allions à l'école seulement la moitié de la journée. Certains cours se donnaient le matin, et d'autres l'après-midi. Pendant l'autre moitié de la journée, nous faisions des travaux dans l'école. Les filles nettoyaient et les garçons travaillaient dans la ferme. »

☐ « Le dîner consistait en deux tranches de pain avec un gros morceau de saindoux – toujours du saindoux, jamais de beurre ni de beurre d'arachide – et parfois un peu de confiture. C'était soit du ragoût de bœuf, soit des haricots ou quelque chose comme ça. Du lait écrémé, pas de café, ni de thé, ni de lait entier. Le souper était pratiquement pareil. Dans la ferme scolaire, nous avions environ 200 poules, peut-être plus, et toutes couvaient. Où allaient tous les œufs de ces poules? C'est une question que je me suis posée souvent durant toutes ces années parce qu'on nous en donnait rarement. De temps à autre, on faisait tuer quelques têtes de bétail, mais je vous dis que nous n'en mangions jamais. Parfois, nous avions un ragoût liquide avec des petits morceaux de viande.

« Quand je suis devenu un peu plus vieux, l'une de mes tâches consistait à m'asseoir à l'ancienne machine à beurre. Nous devions la tirer pour faire tourner le baril. Nous n'avions jamais de beurre sur un morceau de pain. Nous savions ce qu'était le beurre, nous en connaissions le goût. J'ai vu des enfants qui avaient les dents branlantes et qui saignaient des gencives. Ce n'est pas joli à voir.

« Je me rappelle que nous avions l'habitude d'attraper des lapins avec des frondes. J'étais un excellent tireur. J'ai attrapé quelques lapins et quelques perdrix. Les enfants tuaient les petits oiseaux comme des mésanges et des merles pour les faire cuire et les manger. Souvent, je vendais les lapins pour 15 cents. Dans ce temps-là, on allait loin avec 15 cents. On pouvait acheter un pain pour deux ou trois sous. »

❑ « Nous n'avions jamais de fruits. Ça ne faisait pas partie de notre alimentation habituelle. Le seul que nous mangions, c'était un peu de compote de fruits quand on nous en donnait le dimanche soir. Nous recevions une pomme et une orange une fois par année à Noël. Nous mangions les baies des roses sauvages qui bordaient la clôture devant l'école. Pour déjeuner, nous avions un bol de gruau et deux tranches de pain avec du Crisco. Pour dîner, je pense que nous avions un genre de hachis, probablement deux tranches de pain et peut-être un pouding ou quelque chose du genre. Puis, pour souper, nous avions parfois des haricots, d'autres fois, des crêpes ou du macaroni et encore deux tranches de pain. Nous mangions beaucoup de pain. »

❑ « Le soir avant Noël, on nous remettait à chacun des bas de Noël, et nous les suspendions à des bancs. Puis, on nous enfermait dans le dortoir; nous nous réveillions à toute heure. Nous voulions sortir en courant et voir ce que nos bas contenaient. Bien sûr, nous l'ouvrions et y trouvions de gros bonbons, une orange et des petites choses – une petite poupée en bois. Les plus vieux recevaient des billes ou un jeu. C'était très amusant. Puis, le jour de Noël, nous avions un repas spécial : une sorte de gruau différent. Nous recevions une orange ou une pomme. Il y avait aussi un concert. On nous enseignait toutes sortes de petits chants et nous montions sur l'estrade pour chanter. Nous jouions même dans une pièce de théâtre, puis invitions les gens de la ville à venir nous voir. Ils étaient tous bons envers nous. Certains ont eu la vie dure, mais pas moi; j'ai été très bénie. »

À l'école Shingwauk, le jour de Noël était plus agréable que les autres parce qu'on rendait les enfants heureux en leur donnant beaucoup de cadeaux dont plusieurs, bien sûr, spécialement conçus dans le but de « faire du bruit ». Le concert présenté dans la soirée, auquel assistaient un bon nombre d'amis de Sault Ste-Marie, était plaisant et intéressant. Les présentations et les chœurs faits des enfants montraient qu'ils avaient bien pratiqué, et les talents musicaux déployés par Agnes Jobson au piano et Beatrice Quatchigan au violon étaient complimentés. Le monologue d'Ada Bonspille démontrait un grand talent et était très divertissant. À la fin, le père Noël faisait son apparition et, malgré ses nombreuses visites ailleurs la veille de Noël, il avait toujours « à la fin d'une journée parfaite » un sac rempli de cadeaux pour les enfants indiens de l'école Shingwauk.[9]

PRIX SCOLAIRES ET REMISE DES DIPLÔMES

Les six paires de patins offertes généreusement en cadeau par M. Hayter Reed à l'école Shingwauk récompensaient la bonne conduite des garçons suivants : Charley Johnson (72), Solomon Masuk (28), Hymen Smith (30), Fred Fox (55), John Angus (75) Tommy Williams (7).[10]

Deux des filles de nos écoles indiennes à Sault Ste-Marie ont aussi entrepris leurs études secondaires : Barbara Michael a terminé sa troisième année et Flora Gilbert sa première année. Trois autres élèves de la même école se sont qualifiés pour entrer au secondaire : Mary Simon, Daniel Wandahbeesh et Philip Montour. Mary et Daniel ont réussi avec mention d'honneur. Félicitations à tous.[11]

Dorothy Bonspiel a lu l'adresse d'adieu [...] Mme W. L. Wright a présenté des prix à Sylvia Cree et à Andrew Martin, ces deux enfants ayant obtenu les meilleures notes en 8e année, et à Jeannette Pinnance et Maurice Bonspiel, les enfants qui ont fait le plus de progrès durant l'année.[12]

☐ « Benjamin Fuller était le directeur de l'école Shingwauk quand j'y suis arrivée. Il était dur avec les filles. Il utilisait la ceinture beaucoup trop souvent pour des choses sans importance. J'en ai reçu des coups assez souvent. Je n'étais pas l'une de ses élèves préférées. Sa fille avait l'habitude de nous donner des coups, pas avec une ceinture, mais avec une baguette longue et large comme ça. Je vous dis que lorsqu'elle nous frappait avec ça, on le savait. Ça chauffait.

« Un jour, après avoir utilisé sa baguette, elle l'a oubliée dans un des dortoirs, celui des plus vieilles. Quelqu'un l'a trouvée; j'ignore qui l'a prise. De toute façon, elles ont demandé : "Qu'est-ce qu'on va faire avec la baguette?" J'ai dit : "Donne-la-moi", puis je l'ai mise dans mes sous-vêtements, sur le côté, et je suis descendue dans la salle de jeux des filles où le poêle chauffait à plein régime. J'ai pris la baguette et l'ai jetée dans le poêle. Je l'ai brûlée. Après cela, Mlle Fuller n'a plus jamais frappé personne. Jamais. »

☐ « Eh bien oui, je me suis enfui de là. Nous avions coutume d'aller nager dans la rivière Sault Ste-Marie. Voici ce qui est arrivé. Nous étions tous à la rivière et la cloche a sonné, ce qui voulait dire que tout le monde devait rentrer. Le fils du directeur – son nom était Arthur, si je me souviens bien – et moi étions les derniers à sortir de l'eau. J'étais en train de me rhabiller – nous avions des tâches à faire, comme nourrir les animaux – quand il m'a dit que je devais rester. C'était le fils du directeur, vous savez, et nous devions lui montrer du respect, n'est-ce pas? Alors, je lui ai dit que je resterais, et il est allé faire un autre plongeon. Je lui ai dit : "Viens, je dois partir, je dois partir." Il est resté et, à cause de lui, je suis arrivé en retard. Les autres enfants étaient tous partis, et je devais m'assurer qu'il ne restait pas seul; il aurait pu se noyer. On nous avait toujours dit que c'était le gros bon sens.

« À mon arrivée, on m'a dit de monter me coucher; c'était une de leurs punitions. Je suis donc monté et j'étais assis en train de me déshabiller pour aller au lit quand ce gars, un professeur, est arrivé avec une lanière de cuir. Je jure qu'elle avait deux centimètres d'épaisseur, environ quatre centimètres de largeur et plus d'un demi-mètre de longueur Avec ses deux mains, il a balancé cette chose et m'a frappé le dos. J'en ai encore la marque. Puis, tout ce que j'ai vu est une explosion. Je ne peux même pas me rappeler, mais je sais que j'étais en train de courir partout dans le dortoir pour essayer d'ouvrir des fenêtres, mais elles étaient toutes verrouillées. J'ai essayé l'escalier de secours. J'allais sauter et me tuer. J'ai descendu l'escalier en courant. Le professeur criait aux autres garçons : "Attrapez-le! Attrapez-le! Attrapez-le!" Je courais comme un fou, mais on m'a rattrapé là-bas à la rivière. J'allais sauter dans l'eau et traverser la rivière à la nage. Et les garçons ont dit : " Reviens ou nous allons nous faire battre." Certains d'entre eux pleuraient déjà parce que s'ils ne réussissaient pas à me ramener, ils allaient aussi être frappés. Alors, je suis revenu avec eux. Vous savez… ce professeur… il ne m'a rien dit, rien. Il a agi comme s'il n'avait rien fait, mais il a dû se rendre compte qu'il avait fait quelque chose; battre un enfant comme ça, c'est insensé. J'aurais dû aller à la police, mais il n'y avait jamais d'agents aux alentours. De toute façon, ce n'était pas de leurs affaires, n'est-ce pas? Je suis resté à l'école pendant un certain temps, puis je me suis mis dans la tête que je ne pouvais pas rester dans cet endroit, et c'est ce que j'ai fait. »

☐ « Un jour, alors que je jouais à la "tag" dans la salle de jeu, je suis tombée sur le coude, qui s'est cassé. Il y avait quelque chose de brisé, mais on ne pouvait pas trouver ce que c'était. En tout cas, ma sœur m'a amenée directement chez l'infirmière au lieu d'aller voir la surveillante d'abord. À cause de cela, on n'allait rien faire pour m'aider. Jusqu'à aujourd'hui, mon bras n'a jamais vraiment guéri correctement. Il était enflé et je devais demander à une amie de m'aider à m'habiller parce que mon bras était gros comme ça.

« M. Fuller était un tyran. Dans la salle de jeu, il y avait un poêle à bois, une truie. Le directeur avait l'habitude de nous tenir la main au-dessus de cette chose pour nous la brûler lorsque nous avions volé ou commis une autre faute. M. Fuller faisait cela [...] tenir les mains des enfants au-dessus du poêle [...] jusqu'à ce que leur peau commence à brûler. »

SEPT GARÇONS S'ENFUIENT DE L'ÉCOLE SHINGWAUK

« Attrapés par les inspecteurs Quinton E. Wolf et Archie Duroe, dans une ferme à onze kilomètres de Michigan Soo, sept garçons indiens qui s'étaient échappés de l'école Shingwauk depuis quelques jours ont été remis au département de l'Immigration des États-Unis pour être déportés. Les garçons s'étaient enfuis de nuit de l'institution, juste à l'est du sault, en passant par la fenêtre du troisième étage à l'aide de cordes faites de draps. Ils avaient ensuite traversé la frontière par Sugar Island.

Les garçons sont tous nés au Canada. Deux d'entre eux sont Chippewas, deux Iroquois, deux Delawares et un Cree. L'un d'eux, Melvin Laforme, âgé de 16 ans, est considéré comme le chef des soulèvements indiens à l'école Shingwauk. C'est la troisième fois qu'il fugue et qu'il est capturé. Les autres sont Russel Oka, 13 ans, Iroquois; Norman Logan, 14 ans, Delaware; John Wesley, Iroquois; Huron Sturgeon, 15 ans, Chippewa; Earl Schrater, 15 ans, Delaware; et Vaugh Monagne, 16 ans, Chippewa.

Les garçons ont raconté à l'inspecteur Wolf, responsable de la patrouille de l'immigration américaine, qu'on ne leur donnait pas assez à manger et qu'ils étaient maltraités, mais l'inspecteur a déclaré qu'ils semblaient tous gras et en santé. »[13]

☐ « Je me suis enfui, mais je m'en suis tiré de justesse. Je me rappelle cet Indien à Garden River. Il savait que je n'étais pas de la région et il m'a dit : "Tu dois être de cette école." Je l'ai accompagné chez lui, où sa grand-mère a fait cuire du pain indien, du pain frit. Ils m'ont bien nourri. Ils parlaient dans leur langue, mais j'ai compris qu'ils allaient téléphoner à l'école. J'ai donc mangé très vite et, bien sûr, quand je suis sorti, la grand-mère a essayé de m'arrêter. En regardant par la porte, j'ai vu le fils du directeur. J'ai alors détalé en direction de la forêt. Je pouvais courir. Ensuite, j'ai rampé dans un étang et je me suis caché dans les buissons. Il a fait le tour d'un côté, puis de l'autre, et a continué son chemin. J'ai couru en direction opposée. Je l'ai échappé belle; ils ne m'ont jamais attrapé.

« Je suis revenu à pied à la maison, j'ai fait beaucoup d'auto-stop. J'avais une paire de chaussures que j'ai usée jusqu'au bout; il y avait un gros trou ici au talon. Je mettais toujours du papier goudronné ou autre chose pour boucher le trou et je suis arrivé chez moi. J'avais toujours faim. Un jour, je suis allé le long du chemin de fer. On y jetait des vidanges qui contenaient des pelures d'orange et du pain. J'avais tellement faim que j'ai mangé ces aliments. Pendant que je marchais sur la route, lorsque je voyais un morceau de pain, je le ramassais et le mangeais. Il m'a fallu deux semaines pour arriver chez moi. »

☐ « C'était triste pour nous tous quand nous avons quitté l'école parce que nous ne connaissions pas nos parents. Nous avons dû établir de nouveaux liens et réapprendre à nous connaître. Quand j'ai quitté l'école pour retourner à la maison, j'ai passé seulement un court laps de temps sur la réserve. Je devais sortir et trouver un emploi parce que je ne pouvais pas rester là et juste vivre aux crochets de mes parents. En fait, ils ne pouvaient pas prendre soin de moi. »

☐ « Gordon est arrivé chez lui à l'âge de 18 ans et cinq mois, et c'était la première fois qu'il voyait sa mère. Il s'est rendu premièrement à Montréal, car sa mère travaillait sur l'avenue Elm. Quand les policiers de Westmount – qui surveillaient les maisons vides des gens partis à Hudson pour l'été – l'ont vu, ils lui ont demandé son nom. Il leur a dit qu'il n'arrivait pas à trouver sa mère. Les policiers l'ont emmené à Hudson où il a trouvé sa mère. Ils ont téléphoné à cette dernière pour lui dire : "Il y a un garçon nommé Gordon Simon qui cherche sa mère; il est assis ici sur les marches". »

☐ « Quand j'ai pris le train pour retourner à la maison, les larmes coulaient sur mon visage. J'avais tellement de peine de partir… tellement de peine. Puis, quand je suis arrivée à la maison, ma famille n'était même pas au courant de mon arrivée. Mon père… personne n'était là pour m'accueillir. J'ai dû aller jusqu'au bout de la campagne où il vivait. »

☐ « Je suis arrivé à la maison après une si longue absence. J'ai frappé à la porte, ma mère a ouvert et m'a regardé; elle ne savait pas qui j'étais. N'est-ce pas insensé? Elle m'a regardé, et je ne pouvais pas converser avec elle parce qu'elle ne parlait que la langue indienne et le français. Je parlais seulement anglais. Devant moi se tenait une étrangère. Elle me regardait et me regardait toujours, et elle a commencé à fermer la porte. Imaginez! Alors, quelqu'un est arrivé, j'ignorais qui c'était, et a dit : "C'est ton fils!" Après toutes ces années, mon père pouvait à peine me reconnaître; il ne s'arrêtait pas de rire. C'est vraiment dommage!

« Nous n'étions que trois enfants quand je suis parti de la maison, mais à mon retour, il y avait sept petits enfants; nous étions dix en tout. Imaginez que vous arrivez chez vous dans une famille que vous ne connaissez même pas […] chez des parents que vous ne connaissez même pas. »

☐ « C'était étrange d'arriver à la maison parce que j'ai vu cette femme qu'on m'a dit être ma mère. La première fois que j'ai vu mon père – j'étais avec mon ami et nous sortions du traversier –, il était là debout, qui attendait… attendait, un homme trapu, et mon ami m'a dit : "C'est ton père!" Et je lui ai demandé : "C'est mon père? Je ne l'aurais pas reconnu. J'aurais marché droit devant lui." Il ne m'aurait pas reconnu non plus. »

☐ « Je suis allée au collège de Saut Ste-Marie. Je devais aller à l'école technique et apprendre le dactylo et la sténo pour devenir secrétaire, mais mon professeur à l'école Shingwauk, Mme Moran, a changé la direction de ma vie. Elle m'a dit d'aller au collège, qu'avec mon diplôme de secondaire, je pouvais faire tout ce que je voulais. Et elle avait raison, vous savez. Je suis partie pour le nord et j'ai enseigné l'école. J'ai étudié à North Bay Normal School, à North Bay, et je suis allée enseigner l'école d'été encore dans le nord. Puis, je suis retournée aux études pour devenir infirmière. Je me suis mariée, j'ai vécu en Australie pendant 12 mois, puis je me suis installée en Californie. J'ai élevé mes enfants, pour ensuite me spécialiser dans les soins intensifs. J'ai toujours voulu retourner aux études pour obtenir mon baccalauréat. »

☐ « Quand elle a quitté l'école, Mary a travaillé comme femme de ménage; elle était l'aînée de la famille. Eva est restée à Sault Ste-Marie, elle a épousé un Écossais et a eu huit enfants. Puis, Catherine est retournée à la maison, et j'étais la dernière qui est sortie de là. J'avais deux sœurs plus jeunes que moi et, quand elles ont été placées, une a été adoptée au village d'Oka, et nous ne l'avons revue qu'en 1970 parce qu'elle a vécu à New York et ailleurs. Et l'autre, Alma, a été envoyée au Manitoba, dans un autre pensionnat.

« Elle n'était pas très grande, et elle a été envoyée à un autre pensionnat à Brandon. Elle n'a jamais été heureuse là-bas, mais elle s'est mariée. Elle a eu deux enfants, mais n'en a qu'un maintenant, et elle vit toujours à Brandon. Ce n'est qu'en 1970 que nous ne l'avons revue quand elle est venue à Montréal. »

☐ Je pense qu'en allant là-bas, les avantages que j'ai eus plus tard prouvent que cela a valu la peine pour moi. Ma formation à l'école Shingwauk m'a préparée à une carrière dans le monde extérieur. Je suis allée à l'école technique de Sault Ste-Marie. Nous avons tous bien réussi, malgré le fait que nous n'avions qu'une demi-journée de grammaire à l'école. Durant ces années, nous avons établi beaucoup d'amitiés durables avec le personnel et les élèves. »

☐ « Je suis resté là-bas seulement un certain temps, puis mon père et moi sommes allés dans le bois à Petawawa. Nous avons coupé du bois et restions dans un camp de bûcheron. Je vous le dis que ce n'est pas une vie pour un enfant. Un jour, à mon retour, j'ai eu l'idée stupide de m'enrôler dans l'armée canadienne où je suis resté pendant un bout de temps. Quelle différence! Mais j'y suis resté seulement un an environ. Je suis sorti pour des raisons médicales : je ne vois rien la nuit, je suis aveugle comme une taupe. C'est un problème héréditaire.

« Je me suis pris en main et je suis retourné aux études. Pendant que j'étais dans cette école, jamais on ne nous a enseigné un métier. J'en ai appris un et j'ai trouvé un boulot. Je n'aimais pas cela […] J'en avais assez fait. Puis, j'ai commencé à travailler dans l'installation de poutres d'acier. J'ai ici un insigne pour avoir été 32 années dans un syndicat comme poseur de poutres. J'ai travaillé partout : à Détroit, à New York, à Long Island, à Greenland, à Philadelphie. Nommez-moi un endroit; j'y suis allé. »

☐ « Je ne pouvais pas quitter cet endroit assez vite. J'ai terminé ma 10ᵉ année, et tout ce que je voulais c'était de sortir de cette école pour enfin manger convenablement. Je me rappelle un jour de Noël où ma sœur et moi arrivions de Montréal. Nous rapportions une dinde et tous les accompagnements traditionnels à la maison, un cadeau pour maman et un pour papa. Nous étions alors adultes et nous avions un emploi. Nous sommes arrivés en autobus au village d'Oka, puis quelqu'un a offert de nous emmener en traîneau tiré par des chevaux. Nous sommes restés pris dans la neige, et ma sœur a perdu un de ses pendants d'oreilles, mais c'était un beau Noël. Nous avons vraiment aimé cela, mais c'est le seul Noël que je me rappelle avoir passé avec ma mère et mon père. »

☐ « J'ai quitté Oka en 1937, à l'âge de sept ans. Je ne parlais pas anglais. Je me rappelle avoir appris l'anglais aussi vite que j'ai perdu mon indien. Quand je suis revenue dans la réserve, j'ai rencontré ma cousine qui avait le même âge que moi. Mais voici la différence entre nous : ma mère m'a envoyée à l'école Shingwauk où j'ai appris l'anglais et reçu de l'instruction, alors que ma tante n'a envoyé ma cousine dans aucune école, ni ici ni ailleurs. Je peux lire et écrire mon nom, mais pas elle. Elle m'a dit : "J'aurais aimé que ma mère m'envoie au loin comme ta mère l'a fait." »

☐ « Eh bien, j'ai glané quelques mots et appris à compter avec mon père durant les quelques mois que j'ai passés à la maison en 1936. Et je n'ai pas entendu de mots indiens depuis ce temps-là, sauf les différentes langues, mais je ne les ai pas oubliés. Je me rappelle ces quelques mots. Je peux compter jusqu'à dix. Je peux dire *mère, père* et *fille* ».

☐ « J'ai appris la fierté d'être Indien par mon père. Il nous l'a inculquée quand nous étions jeunes. Alors, quand je suis allé à cette école, je la ressentais. Je pouvais parler un peu l'indien, mais je l'ai tout perdu. Je ne me rappelais pas grand-chose quand je suis parti de là et, bien sûr, je n'ai rien appris depuis. »

☐ « Vous perdez votre langue quand vous parlez seulement en anglais. Je ne peux pas parler ma langue, mais ma sœur aînée, elle, le peut. Quand elle est revenue de là-bas, elle a recommencé à parler sa langue maternelle. Je ne connaissais pas l'histoire des Indiens. Je ne sais rien d'eux, sauf ce que j'ai lu dans un livre. Mon père et ma mère ne nous ont rien enseigné sur la vie indienne. Je ne comprends pas ce que sont les mères de clans [...] Je ne comprends rien, sauf ce que j'ai lu. Je ne crois certainement pas à ça pour aujourd'hui. »

☐ « Savez-vous ce que les professeurs faisaient aux nouveaux enfants qui parlaient en langue indienne en arrivant à l'école? Tout de suite, ils les faisaient taire et leur lavaient la bouche avec du savon. "Vous ne devez plus parler la langue indienne, vous devez apprendre l'anglais. Si vous voulez vous adapter, vous devez apprendre l'anglais." Ça balaie tout votre héritage, vous savez. Ils voulaient que nous grandissions dans un monde blanc, et c'est pourquoi nous ne pouvions pas parler notre langue. À l'école Shingwauk, on nous a enseigné à survivre dans le monde blanc... à travailler dans un bureau... à recevoir une paie... à payer nos taxes et à éviter les ennuis, à se marier... à avoir une famille et à s'adapter. »

☐ « C'était tabou, nous ne pouvions même pas parler notre langue. Vous voyez mes mains, on m'a frappé tellement de fois que je ne serais pas étonné que ces jointures-là soient fracturées. Dès que nous parlions dans notre langue maternelle, le professeur nous donnait des coups de baguette ou de règle. J'en ai reçu si souvent. »

☐ « La première fois que j'ai su que j'étais Indien, c'était... laissez-moi voir, en 6ᵉ année. On nous disait : "Vous êtes Indiens, vous êtes des sauvages." Ils racontaient à quel point notre peuple était sanguinaire et guerrier, et tous ensemble ils disaient : "Vous êtes Indiens!" »

☐ « Je serai toujours reconnaissant envers les Minchins, des gens très très gentils. Mais en repensant au passé, si je peux le dire... la chose qui me dérange le plus et à laquelle je pense souvent est le fait que, pendant tout le temps que nous étions à l'école Shingwauk, personne n'a jamais mentionné quoi que ce soit sur le fait que nous étions autochtones ou que nous avions une quelconque culture. Ils n'ont jamais essayé de nous inculquer la fierté d'être Indien. Je pense que c'est très triste [...]

« En repensant au passé, je trouve ça épouvantable. Nous avons une histoire si riche, et on ne nous a rien dit sur les Indiens qui ont combattu pour notre pays aux côtés des Britanniques lors de la guerre de 1812. Même pas sur l'incident de Louis Riel, qui fut une grande lumière dans notre histoire. Je trouve que c'est déplorable. Ça m'attriste toujours de repenser à tout ça et au fait que nous n'ayons pas revu nos parents. Je crois que savoir que leurs enfants étaient là-bas a fait beaucoup de peine à mes parents. »

EXCUSES DE L'ÉGLISE ANGLICANE DU CANADA

En août 1993, lors de la deuxième assemblée nationale autochtone tenue à Minaki, en Ontario, l'archevêque Michael Peers, primat de l'Église anglicane du Canada, a présenté des excuses aux autochtones pour la participation de l'Église anglicane au système des pensionnats indiens. Vi Smith, une aînée haïda de Hazelton, en Colombie-Britannique a répondu aux excuses. Des extraits de chacun des textes sont reproduits ci-dessous.[14]

Frères et sœurs,

Ici, réuni avec vous, j'ai écouté pendant que vous racontiez vos histoires sur les pensionnats.

J'ai entendu les voix qui ont parlé de douleur et de blessures subies dans les écoles et des cicatrices qui durent jusqu'à ce jour.

J'ai ressenti de la honte et de l'humiliation en entendant les souffrances que mon peuple vous a infligées, et en pensant au rôle que notre Église a joué dans cette souffrance.

Je suis profondément conscient de la révérence des histoires que vous m'avez racontées et j'estime au plus haut point ceux qui les ont racontées.

J'ai entendu avec admiration les histoires de gens et de communautés qui ont travaillé à la guérison et je suis conscient qu'il y a encore un grand besoin de guérison.

Je sais aussi que j'ai besoin de guérison, que mon propre peuple a besoin de guérison et que notre Église a besoin de guérison…

J'accepte et je confesse, devant Dieu et devant vous, notre échec dans les pensionnats. C'est un échec envers vous, envers nous et envers Dieu.

Je suis désolé, plus que les mots ne peuvent le dire, que nous ayons fait partie d'un système qui vous ont arrachés, vous et vos enfants, de votre maison et de votre famille.

Je suis désolé, plus que les mots ne peuvent le dire, que nous ayons essayé de vous refaire à notre image, en vous enlevant votre langue et les signes de votre identité.

Je suis désolé, plus que les mots ne peuvent le dire, que dans nos écoles tant d'enfants aient été agressés physiquement, sexuellement, culturellement et émotionnellement.

Au nom de l'Église anglicane du Canada, je présente nos excuses.

Je les présente selon le désir des fidèles de l'Église, dont les membres du Conseil exécutif national, qui connaissent quelques-unes de vos histoires et qui m'ont demandé de le faire.

Je le fais au nom de beaucoup de gens qui ignorent ces histoires.

Et je le fais, même s'il y a des fidèles dans l'Église qui n'acceptent pas que ces gestes aient été posés en notre nom […]

Je sais que vous avez souvent entendu des paroles qui étaient vides parce qu'elles n'étaient pas accompagnées par des actions. Je m'engage envers vous, en mon nom et au nom de notre Église à l'échelle nationale, à faire de mon mieux pour marcher avec vous le long du chemin de la guérison de Dieu […]

Michael Peers

LA RÉPONSE

De la part de cette assemblée, nous reconnaissons et acceptons les excuses du primat offertes de la part de l'Église anglicane du Canada. Il les a offertes de son cœur avec sincérité, sensibilité, compassion et humilité. Nous les acceptons de la même manière. Nous louons et remercions notre Créateur pour son courage [...]

Vi Smith

PROMESSE D'UN AVENIR MEILLEUR

Beaucoup des Kanehsata'kehró:non qui ont fréquenté l'école Shingwauk voient leur enfance comme une période de solitude et de crainte. Même si le but déclaré était l'éducation, le progrès et la religion, l'objectif ultime était l'assimilation par une acculturation forcée. La première étape de ce plan était de déraciner les enfants et de les isoler de leur environnement et de leur famille. Ils étaient ceux qui pouvaient être facilement contrôlés et manipulés. Ainsi, les pensionnats ont laissé des cicatrices et des blessures durables qui ont toujours besoin d'être guéries.

Les excuses de l'Église anglicane doivent offrir plus que des mots. Nous espérons qu'elles marqueront le début d'un changement d'attitude envers les Onkwehón:we. Ces excuses sont peut-être importantes par le simple fait qu'elles reconnaissent la participation de l'Église dans un système brutal de répression contre les peuples autochtones.

Le système des pensionnats indiens n'est qu'un élément du long registre historique déplorable des politiques du gouvernement canadien envers les Onkwehón:we. Si certaines écoles furent meilleures que d'autres, toutes étaient dédiées au même idéal : l'extinction ultime d'un groupe distinct d'individus. Le gouvernement canadien doit toujours offrir ses excuses pour le rôle qu'il a joué dans l'implantation et le soutien de ce système.[15]

Aujourd'hui, comme adultes, les survivants des pensionnats croient que leur peuple ne doit plus jamais se voir refuser sa langue, son histoire, sa culture et sa famille. Leur perte a contribué à ce que les Kanehsata'kehró:non s'efforcent à enseigner la langue, l'histoire et la culture Kanien'keha aux enfants, ainsi qu'aux adultes. Le peuple de Kanehsatà:ke refuse de nier son héritage pour avoir accès à l'instruction. Par le passé, la société blanche croyait qu'elle avait quelque chose à nous enseigner, et elle l'a fait. Nous avons appris à la dure que le pouvoir de décision n'appartient qu'à nous. Nous ne nous soumettrons plus pendant que les autres prennent des décisions pour nos enfants, notre vie et notre avenir.

LES PETITS APPRENNENT EN ÉCOUTANT, EN OBSERVANT ET EN PRATIQUANT

 Auparavant, les enfants avaient l'habitude d'apprendre ce qu'ils avaient besoin de savoir en regardant faire les aînés. Les leçons étaient enseignées par l'exemple et les petits apprenaient en écoutant, en observant et en pratiquant. Chaque aspect de leur vie comportait un enseignement. En réalité, on apprenait en vivant. Tout le monde avait quelque chose à enseigner et quelque chose à apprendre. Cela se faisait en partageant, en se côtoyant dans la vie de tous les jours.

Les femmes enseignaient aux filles à prendre soin d'une famille pour que chaque membre grandisse et devienne fort et attentionné. Les filles apprenaient à semer, à récolter et à entreposer la nourriture. Elles apprenaient au sujet de la beauté, de la joie et, parfois, de la tristesse qui sont associées à leur identité féminine. Elles apprenaient sur le pouvoir des femmes qui donnent la vie et assurent l'équilibre entre les sexes. En grandissant, elles apprenaient à connaître leurs responsabilités et recevaient la force, la connaissance et l'assurance nécessaires pour les assumer.

Les jeunes garçons apprenaient des hommes à devenir de bons chasseurs afin que le peuple n'ait pas faim. Les garçons apprenaient à protéger le peuple pour que tous soient en sécurité et dorment l'esprit tranquille. Ils apprenaient aussi l'équilibre qui existe en eux et dans leur monde. Ils apprenaient que, peu importe leur âge, il y avait toujours quelqu'un qui les considérait comme un enseignant ou un guide. Ils apprenaient à agir en conséquence. Ils apprenaient leurs responsabilités de futurs hommes et recevaient les outils pour les assumer.

Nous savons que beaucoup de temps a passé et que bien des choses ont changé. Il est difficile de s'occuper des récoltes quand il y a moins d'espace pour cultiver. On ne peut pas apprendre à chasser quand il n'y a pas de gibier. Le peuple doit apprendre les connaissances et les aptitudes des arrivants. C'est pourquoi ils envoient leurs enfants dans un endroit appelé « école ». L'espoir des Kanehsata'kehró:non est que leurs enfants soient mieux équipés pour comprendre tous les changements afin qu'ils survivent pour garder l'esprit Onkwehón:we vivant.

Allons. Regardons les petits enfants. Certains d'entre eux sourient et, d'autres, non. Regardez de très près maintenant, et peut-être que vous aurez un reflet des ancêtres qui vous regardent à travers les yeux des enfants.

Le village et les écoles de campagne

Collection de Frances Oke

Collection de Roy Rennie

Collection de Gordie Oke

Collection de Gordie Oke

Collection d'Eleanor Montour

Collection d'Eleanor Montour

Collection d'Helen Beauvais

Collection de Frank Nelson

Collection de Gordie Oke

Collection de Gordie Oke

Collection de Gordie Oke

Collection de Gordie Oke

Collection de Frank Nelson

Collection de Ruby Bonspille

Collection de Raymond Kanatase Gabriel

Collection d'Eleanor Montour

Collection de Jessie Nelson

Collection de Jessie Nelson

Collection de Jessie Nelson

Collection de Susan Oke

Collection de Susan Oke

Collection de Susan Oke

Collection de Susan Oke

Collection de Susan Oke

Collection de Susan Oke

Collection de Susan Oke

Collection de Susan Oke

[1] Les registres des naissances, des confirmations, des mariages et des décès pour la chapelle et le cimetière Bishop Fauquier Memorial sont maintenant conservés aux bureaux du synode du diocèse anglican d'Algoma, à Sault Ste-Marie, en Ontario. Une liste des monuments du cimetière a été compilée en 1985 par le district de Sault Ste-Marie de la Société généalogique de l'Ontario. Une copie est gardée à la Bibliothèque nationale du Canada, à Ottawa. Plusieurs listes d'enfants Onkwehón:we décédés à Shinwauk sont également gardées aux bureaux du synode, mais celles-ci sont probablement incomplètes. Le nombre exact d'enfants Onkwehón:we enterrés au cimetière Bishop Fauquier est donc inconnu puisque la plupart des pierres tombales ne sont pas gravées.

Quatre enfants Kanehsata'kehró:non sont décédés à l'école Shingwauk. Ils sont enterrés dans des tombes non gravées au cimetière Bishop Fauquier Memorial. Peter Beauvais, 20 novembre 1929; Mary Martin, 16 décembre 1937; Lily Nicholas, dans les années 1940; Doreen Wilson, 8 septembre 1942.

En 1981, le personnel de l'époque et d'anciens élèves ont érigé un monticule de pierres en l'honneur de ceux qui sont enterrés dans le cimetière.

[2] Pour des discussions sur le système des pensionnats indiens au Canada, voyez J. R. Miller, Reserves, residential schools, and the threat of assimilation, dans *Skyscrapers Hide the Heavens: A History of Indian-White Relations in Canada*, édition révisée, Toronto, les Presses de l'Université de Toronto, 1991, 99-115, ainsi que J. R. Miller, Owen Glendower, Hotspur, and Canadian Indian Policy, dans J. R. Miller, éd. *Sweet Promises: A Reader on Indian-White Relations in Canada*, Toronto, les Presses de l'Université de Toronto, 1991, 323-352.

[3] Le nombre exact d'enfants Kanehsata'kehró:non qui ont fréquenté les pensionnats indiens est inconnu. Les renseignements sur les enfants qui sont allés à l'école Shingwauk proviennent de plusieurs sources, dont les registres de la chapelle et du cimetière Bishop Fauquier Memorial; les premiers registres de l'école gardés à la bibliothèque de Bishophurst, la résidence de l'évêque d'Algoma, à Sault Ste-Marie; les registres et les photographies gardées au projet Shingwauk, à l'université Algoma, à Sault Ste-Marie; les rapports annuels des écoles Shinwauk et Wawanosh et les publications du diocèse d'Algoma *Algoma Missionary News*, qui sont gardés à la bibliothèque de l'université d'Algoma. Les archives du ministère des Affaires indiennes, RG 10, gardées dans les Archives nationales du Canada, à Ottawa, contiennent plusieurs dossiers sur Shingwauk. Toutefois, ces dossiers sont malheureusement incomplets en ce qui a trait aux inscriptions des élèves. Des renseignements sur les enfants de Kanehsatà:ke qui ont fréquenté l'école protestante francophone à Pointe-aux-Trembles, au Québec, est contenu dans les registres de la Conférence de Montréal de l'Église unie du Canada gardés à la bibliothèque de l'université Bishop, à Lennoxville, au Québec.

[4] *Rapport sur les affaires des Indiens du Canada*, 1847, Montréal : imprimé par Rollo Campbell, James Hughes, surintendant du département des Affaires indiennes, Suggestions privilégiées par le surintendant du département des Affaires indiennes pour l'amélioration de la condition de la jeunesse indienne, appendice T, 24 juin 1843.

[5] Dominion du Canada, Rapport annuel du département des Affaires indiennes, Ottawa : F.A. Acland; 1932 et 1936, sections sur les pensionnats indiens.

[6] Ibid.

[7] Pour une brève histoire de l'école Shingwauk, Le projet Shingwauk, *From Teaching Wigwam to Shingwauk University: Algoma University College Founders'Day 1992*.

[8] Les renseignements au sujet de ces enfants proviennent des rapports annuels des écoles Shingwauk et Wawanosh de 1895 à 1906.

[9] *The Algoma Missionary News*, 1929.

[10] Hayter Reed, surintendant adjoint des Affaires indiennes, *The Algoma Missionary News*, février 1896.

[11] *The Algoma Missionary News*, juillet 1922.

[12] Ibid., 1945.

[13] *The Sault Star*, 31 mars 1928.

[14] Michael Peers, Texte d'excuses, et Vi Smith, Réponse des autochtones, *Anglican Journal*, septembre 1993, p. 6. L'Église unie du Canada, l'Église presbytérienne du Canada et l'Église romaine catholique ont offert des excuses semblables aux autochtones du Canada.

[15] Depuis la parution de la version originale du présent livre, soit le 15 mai 2008, le gouvernement canadien a offert ses excuses officielles aux anciens élèves des pensionnats indiens, ces institutions d'enseignement subventionnées par le fédéral et conçues pour assimiler les autochtones.

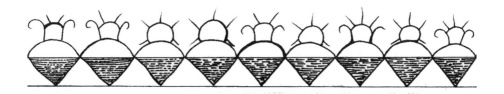

Chapitre 10

Corinthe et autres contre le séminaire de Saint-Sulpice

Bien que nous reconnaissions que le gouvernement et les tribunaux canadiens croient en leur autorité et en leur capacité d'abolir nos droits, nous ne reconnaissons pas celles-ci. Même s'ils ont agi comme s'ils avaient autorité sur nos terres, nous ne leur reconnaissons pas ce droit. Encore une fois, nous réitérons que nos droits sur ce territoire ne viennent ni de la couronne française ou britannique ni du gouvernement canadien. Nos droits à ce territoire ne nous ont pas été conférés par la Loi sur les Indiens ou le système judiciaire canadien. Nos droits territoriaux découlent du fait que cette terre est notre terre. Notre Créateur nous y a placés et nous a confié la responsabilité d'en prendre soin et de la protéger. Personne ne peut nous l'enlever.

NÉGOCIATIONS PRÉLIMINAIRES AU PROCÈS

Le matin du 10 février 1909, Joseph Denny, un aîné de Kanehsatake, fut appelé à la barre de la Cour suprême, dans le district de Montréal, pour témoigner sous serment devant le juge Hutchison sur la question de titre de propriété à Kanehsatà:ke. Joseph Denny avait 81 ans, et ses souvenirs remontaient à plus de soixante-dix années. Il décrivit clairement divers événements qui avaient eu lieu depuis son enfance. Il répondit à diverses questions sur la relation entre les Kanehsata'kehró:non et le séminaire de Saint-Sulpice et énonça exactement comment le peuple de Kanehsatà:ke percevait cette relation, ainsi que leur relation avec la terre. Il parla en Kanien'kéha, la langue de son peuple, et William Reeb lui servit d'interprète.[1]

Le procès le plus décisif de l'histoire sur la question territoriale à Kanehsatà:ke commença par le témoignage de Joseph Denny. L'après-midi du 10 février 1909, le chef Angus Corinthe fut appelé à la barre après Joseph Denny. Corinthe parla posément en rappelant comment et pourquoi les Kanehsata'kehró:non avaient quitté l'Église catholique romaine et quelles en furent les répercussions.[2]

Les questions soulevées étaient si complexes et explosives qu'il fallut six ans avant que le procès soit présenté devant les tribunaux. Les préoccupations concernant l'explosivité du procès ne découlaient pas d'inquiétudes sur la réaction des Kanehsata'kehró:non si l'issue leur était défavorable. Bon nombre d'entre eux avaient exercé des pressions sur le gouvernement fédéral pour que les tribunaux tranchent la question territoriale, mais au cours des années de discussions, de négociations et de décisions menant aux poursuites, ils avaient manifesté une grande retenue. À ce moment-là, la principale préoccupation du gouvernement était la manière dont l'issue du procès serait perçue par les partis concernés au Québec et en Ontario.

Les représentants du gouvernement reconnurent qu'il fallait prendre toutes les précautions nécessaires pour s'assurer qu'un semblant de justice minimale soit maintenu. Même les Sulpiciens se rendirent compte que leurs actions pouvaient créer une agitation généralisée. Le séminaire n'allait concéder aucun droit territorial aux Kanehsata'kehró:non, mais les Sulpiciens se hâtèrent d'assurer aux représentants qu'aucune des terres sur lesquelles le peuple vivait et qu'il cultivait ne serait prise ni vendue par le séminaire.[3]

La situation était si embarrassante et le procès si important pour la crédibilité du gouvernement du Canada que le premier ministre lui-même, Sir Wilfrid Laurier, intervint directement pour le présenter devant les tribunaux. Il sembla s'intéresser personnellement à la situation, mais son intérêt ne relevait pas d'une préoccupation du bien-être des Kanehsata'kehró:non. Comme il le disait : « Je suis grandement obligé envers le supérieur des Sulpiciens, le père Colin ».[4] De toutes façons, Sir Wilfrid rencontra les représentants des Kanehsata'kehró:non à plusieurs occasions. Il correspondait également avec l'avocat du séminaire, Aimé Geoffrion, ainsi qu'avec les avocats des Kanehsata'kehró:non, R. C. Smith, de Montréal, et N. W. Rowell, de Toronto, et les rencontrait.

Après avoir consciemment permis que le problème des empiétements et des expropriations de terres se poursuive pendant des années, au point où il ne restait que très peu de terres au peuple, le gouvernement se décidait maintenant à agir en ce qui concerne la question de titre de propriété. Cependant, c'était le département de la Justice qui prendrait la décision définitive quant à la forme et à la date d'un éventuel procès. À un moment où plusieurs nations autochtones du Canada cherchaient à résoudre des questions de droits territoriaux devant les tribunaux, le département de la Justice n'était pas très désireux de créer des précédents favorables envers les autochtones. Les négociations se poursuivirent et le ministre de la Justice accepta finalement un procès beaucoup plus modéré, fondé sur la loi coloniale canadienne et britannique, pour traiter des questions très strictes de titre de propriété.

Enfin, au moins quelques Kanehsata'kehró:non croyaient avoir percé les murs de l'indifférence et de l'apathie dans les milieux gouvernementaux et pensaient que justice serait faite. Ils ne se doutaient nullement que leurs problèmes étaient loin d'être terminés.

Cette dispute, amorcée environ 200 ans plus tôt à l'arrivée du séminaire de Saint-Sulpice à Kanehsatà:ke, avait à plusieurs occasions risqué de se terminer par une explosion de violence.[5] Depuis les années 1870, elle avait périodiquement capté l'attention du public et l'intérêt réticent du gouvernement. En 1903, le gouvernement fédéral recommença à chercher une solution définitive à la dispute de longue date entre le séminaire de Saint-Sulpice et les Kanehsata'kehró:non. Il espérait résoudre le problème une fois pour toutes de manière à satisfaire le public canadien qui désirait que justice soit rendue. Cette fois-ci, il crut qu'il était plus prudent d'inclure le peuple de Kanehsatà:ke dans le processus. Comme d'habitude, le gouvernement n'était pas motivé par la compassion, l'amour ou l'impartialité, mais par la crainte. Dans tout le Québec et l'Ontario, on faisait campagne pour que le problème soit résolu. Des contestations en Ontario menées par le juge John J. MacLaren, ancien allié des Kanehsata'kehró:non, étaient particulièrement fortes. Des gens de tous horizons se mêlaient à la question. La situation aurait pu facilement déraper.

Une fois de plus, pour beaucoup de gens, la situation se définissait ainsi : les pauvres Indiens protestants contre la puissance du séminaire catholique. La question des droits territoriaux était confondue avec celle de l'intolérance religieuse. Le public ne pouvait pas voir sous la surface jusqu'à la racine profonde du problème qui commença à l'arrivée du séminaire de Saint-Sulpice en 1721. Peu importe la religion que les Kanehsata'kehró:non disaient pratiquer, un fait demeurait : le séminaire avait à tort pris leurs terres avec l'approbation complice du gouvernement.

Dirigé par Sir Wilfrid Laurier, le gouvernement procéda lentement en prenant bien soin de s'assurer que l'issue du procès satisfasse le public. De concert avec les avocats du séminaire et des Kanehsata'kehró:non, il planifia, organisa et orchestra l'issue du procès dans l'espoir que cette vieille histoire en vienne à une conclusion définitive. À de nombreux égards, le plan réussit très bien. Il mit fin, pour très longtemps, à tous recours « légaux » des Kanehsata'kehró:non pour défendre leurs droits à la terre.[6]

En 1903, toute la question du déplacement refit surface quand une confrontation entre le séminaire et le peuple de Kanehsatà:ke au sujet de la coupe de bois atteignit de nouveaux sommets. Frank Pedley, surintendant adjoint des Affaires indiennes, élabora et suggéra un plan d'action au gouvernement pour l'aider à régler la question pour de bon. Il exprima ainsi son avis :

Il est pratiquement admis que ce serait presque impossible de faire partir les Indiens d'Oka de leur propre gré. Ils s'accrochent tenacement à cet endroit sur la base d'associations et en raison de certaines manières de vivre qu'ils ont adoptées. Ils croient que leur droit d'occuper cette terre est primordial.[7]

Seth P. Leet, un avocat de Toronto, était d'accord jusqu'à un certain point avec Pedley. De la part des Kanehsata'kehró:non, il écrivit au Département pour dire qu'il « était inutile de suggérer aux Okas de déménager à Doncaster, puisque l'expérience de Muskoka les avait rebutés à toute idée de déplacement ».[8] À ce moment-là, plusieurs de ceux qui avaient été déplacés à Gibson étaient revenus à Kanehsatà:ke, et personne n'était prêt à songer à déménager où que ce soit.

Pedley ne proposa qu'une solution : « Pour régler la question, j'ai suggéré qu'on confirme le patrimoine actuel des Indiens d'Oka en leur donnant un titre de propriété absolu aux terres pour qu'elles forment une réserve selon la Loi sur les Indiens ».[9] Pedley savait que la question était délicate et, pour assurer la réussite de la proposition, il suggéra que le département des Affaires indiennes évite les négociateurs. Dans une lettre confidentielle à Leet, Pedley écrivit : « Il faudra faire preuve de beaucoup de prudence lors de la discussion sur divers points pendant que vous essayez d'en arriver à une résolution. Je suggère aussi qu'il serait bien de garder le Département à l'écart des négociations jusqu'à ce que vous déterminiez si les Indiens sont disposés à accepter la proposition ».[10]

À cause de ce qu'il appelait leurs « idées exagérées sur leurs droits à la terre », Leet crut qu'il serait improbable que les Kanehsata'kehró:non acceptent une telle proposition et suggéra qu'ils seraient satisfaits si une cause type était menée à bien au Conseil privé. Il ajouta qu'« ils aimeraient mieux que tout leur soit ainsi enlevé plutôt que d'abandonner volontairement leurs droits ».[11] C'est alors que commença un processus qui ramènerait une idée avancée par John Borland 30 ans plus tôt. Des « amis » des Kanehsata'kehró:non avaient mis de l'avant depuis de nombreuses années la proposition de confirmer leurs droits devant les tribunaux, mais d'autres, comme Kaná:tase, préféraient une façon plus directe pour les affirmer.

En juin 1909, alors que le procès commençait, Kaná:tase conduisit environ trente hommes à reprendre possession de la terre d'une des fermes du séminaire.[12] Le séminaire avait empiété sur cette terre originalement occupée par un Kanehsata'kehró:non. Kaná:tase et les autres hommes en clôturèrent environ 24 hectares pour la séparer de la ferme du séminaire. L'agent indien et l'avocat du séminaire écrivirent au gouvernement pour lui demander son aide.

Le séminaire m'a donné la consigne de demander au gouvernement de prendre les mesures nécessaires pour ramener les Indiens à l'ordre et au bon sens. Si je me souviens bien, c'est Sir Wilfrid Laurier qui avait fait la promesse que les Indiens seraient gardés à l'ordre pendant que le procès est en instance.[13]

En peu de temps, deux agents de police arrivèrent au village pour rétablir l'ordre. L'agent indien déclara que les Indiens, sous l'influence de l'alcool, étaient dangereux.[14] Il fut plus tard rapporté par Baptiste Gaspé que c'était un Canadien français à la solde du séminaire qui y était allé ivre et y avait proféré des menaces.[15] Même l'agent qui s'y rendit pour rétablir l'ordre rapporta plus tard que, même s'ils allaient et venaient, les Indiens ne semblaient pas dangereux.[16]

En mars 1903, Leet reçut la visite d'Angus Corinthe, qui remplaçait Joseph K. Gabriel comme chef pendant que ce dernier était à l'extérieur du pays. (À ce moment-là, Kaná:tase qui était fugitif, vivait en exil politique aux États-Unis.) Selon Leet, Corinthe pensait que la plupart des Kanehsata'kehró:non préféraient une cause type. « Ils sont si impressionnés à l'idée que tout le territoire leur appartienne et que le séminaire n'en soit que le fiduciaire, qu'il est difficile de discuter de toute autre proposition avec eux. »[17]

Une réunion fut organisée entre Sir Wilfrid Laurier et les chefs de Kanehsatà:ke pour le 8 mai. Leet essaya de s'y faire inviter, mais sans succès. Il écrivit à Frank Pedley que « le gouvernement ne devrait pas nous inviter parce que les Indiens y verraient une tentative pour les influencer. Le gouvernement devrait plutôt dire aux chefs que s'ils veulent que leur avocat vienne avec eux, le Département ne s'y opposerait pas. Nous pourrions ainsi les influencer ».[18] Avec des amis comme Leet, les Kanehsata'kehró:non n'avaient nul besoin d'ennemis. À la réunion du 8 mai, il fut entendu entre Sir Wilfrid Laurier et les chefs qu'une cause serait entendue devant les tribunaux. Frank Pedley écrivit à Leet pour lui expliquer que « les Indiens n'auront pas voix au chapitre, sinon le choix exclusif de leur avocat […] vous conviendrez que ces disputes de longue date en viendront probablement à une conclusion satisfaisante si l'Indien a pratiquement ce qu'il veut quant aux moyens à adopter ».[19] Les Kanehsata'kehró:non ne choisirent pas Leet pour les représenter, et celui-ci crut que c'était principalement parce qu'il n'était pas méthodiste.[20] Cependant, il est plus probable qu'ils n'avaient simplement pas l'impression de pouvoir lui faire confiance.

Plus d'une année s'est écoulée avant que des discussions au sujet d'un procès commencent à prendre forme en septembre 1904. Même en cette date précoce, R. C. Smith, avocat du peuple, avait des doutes concernant leurs chances de gagner le procès. Dans une lettre, il écrivit : « Nous ne devrions rien négliger pour présenter leur cause le plus clairement possible. »[21] Smith doutait également de pouvoir élaborer une cause type. « Il faudrait énormément de documents, dit-il, et accorder beaucoup de considération aux plaidoiries présentées » en faveur des Kanehsata'kehró:non.[22] Rien n'indique que Smith partagea ses appréhensions avec les Kanehsata'kehró:non.

À ce moment-là, le séminaire s'opposa à ce qu'une cause type soit présentée parce qu'il croyait que cela créerait de la rancœur entre les Sulpiciens et les Kanehsata'kehró:non, mais qu'un renvoi à la Cour suprême n'en créerait aucune. Selon lui, une cause type entre les partis en serait une de confrontation qui pourrait engendrer beaucoup d'animosité, tandis qu'un renvoi à la Cour suprême impliquerait simplement les deux partis et demanderait à la cour de déterminer certaines questions.[23] Représentés par Corinthe, les Kanehsata'kehró:non avaient apparemment accepté d'être liés par la décision de la cour.[24] À un certain moment, Sir Wilfrid Laurier écrivit à Aimé Geoffrion, avocat du séminaire, pour lui dire de ne pas s'inquiéter. Les Kanehsata'kehró:non ne pourraient jamais obtenir le titre du territoire du Lac des Deux-Montagnes car, d'après la loi, ils étaient mineurs et ne pouvaient donc pas posséder de terres.[25]

Néanmoins, les coûts d'un tel procès seraient considérables, plus que ce que le séminaire acceptait de payer. Ce dernier proposa plutôt que le gouvernement achète d'eux pour les Kanehsata'kehró:non les terres non cédées dans la seigneurie, pour un total d'environ 1620 hectares, y compris la Commune.[26] Sir Wilfrid Laurier écrivit à Geoffrion pour lui dire que même s'il n'avait pas l'autorité pour prendre la décision définitive, il recommanderait au gouvernement d'accepter l'offre.[27] Des négociations se poursuivirent pendant un certain temps, elles menèrent presque à une entente. Cependant, Laurier écrivit encore une fois à Geoffrion pour lui communiquer qu'il avait reçu la visite des trois chefs d'Oka l'informant de leur intention de soumettre une cause au Conseil privé. Il poursuivit en disant que, si le séminaire refusait d'aller en cour pour ce procès, il serait aux prises avec une série interminable de procès avec les Indiens « qui penseront être les propriétaires absolus de la seigneurie ».[28] Peu de temps après, l'offre du séminaire de vendre les terres au gouvernement pour les Kanehsata'kehró:non fut abandonnée pour des « raisons théologiques ».[29]

Les Sulpiciens adoptèrent alors une autre position : ils n'accepteraient d'aller en cour que si le gouvernement du Canada consentait à régler leurs frais, comme il avait consenti à défrayer les Kanehsata'kehró:non. Les Sulpiciens prétendaient que le séminaire n'avait tout simplement pas les moyens de payer les frais des procédures judiciaires. Irrité par cette condition, Sir Wilfrid Laurier fit parvenir une lettre aux propos crus à Aimé Geoffrion. « Aucune raison ne justifie que le gouvernement doive payer pour les deux partis, et je dois vous dire franchement que si le séminaire ne veut pas payer ses dépenses et accepter l'offre que nous lui avons proposée, la situation qui dure depuis si longtemps continuera d'exister ».[30]

Puis, en 1905, les négociations pour le procès vinrent tout près d'échouer quand le séminaire énonça une autre condition. Avec un peu de gêne, Aimé Geoffrion écrivit à Laurier pour lui dire que le séminaire voulait que le procès soit présenté devant un tribunal régulier plutôt que devant la cour supérieure du Québec. Geoffrion exprima son « infini » regret à Laurier pour les ennuis que cette « affaire lui avait causés ».[31]

Le séminaire continua de refuser d'aller en cour à moins que le gouvernement accepte de payer ses dépenses, comme il le faisait pour les Kanehsata'kehró:non. En mai 1907, Frank Pedley écrivit à Aimé Geoffrion pour l'informer que le gouvernement acceptait maintenant de défrayer les deux partis.[32] Geoffrion répliqua que le séminaire accepterait de participer aux conditions suivantes : que le séminaire choisisse son propre avocat, que le procès soit préparé conjointement avec les avocats du séminaire et ceux des Kanehsata'kehró:non et que le gouvernement paie leurs dépenses jusqu'au Conseil privé, au besoin.[33] Ces conditions furent apparemment acceptées, et les négociations entre les avocats et le gouvernement pour déterminer les questions à soumettre à la cour suprême débutèrent aussitôt. Cependant, il semble que le séminaire décidait du plan d'action et qu'en réalité la contribution du peuple de Kanehsatà:ke était bien petite.

En octobre 1907, les avocats étaient presque venus à une entente sur les trois questions suivantes :

1. Quels sont les droits du séminaire dans et sur la seigneurie?

2. Quels sont les droits des Indiens dans et sur la seigneurie?

3. Quels devoirs, le cas échéant, le séminaire a-t-il envers les Indiens?[34]

R. C. Smith, avocat des Kanehsata'kehró:non, doutait que le titre des Indiens pouvait être défendu par les lois,[35] c'est-à-dire, bien sûr, la loi pour incorporer le séminaire et confirmer ses titres (1840), ainsi que les lois seigneuriales de 1853 à 1859. Ces lois accordaient au séminaire un titre « légal » qu'il n'avait pas auparavant.

Cependant, Frank Pedley croyait que « quelque chose qui ferait référence au titre indien, tel que réclamé par les occupants autochtones, pourrait être incorporé dans la liste de questions ».[36] Les avocats des deux partis en discutèrent et soulevèrent trois nouvelles questions.

1. L'occupation ancestrale du territoire dont fait partie le Lac des Deux-Montagnes par les Indiens leur en a-t-elle donné le titre de propriété?

2. Si oui, les descendants directs de ces Indiens, le cas échéant, hériteraient-ils du titre?

3. Si oui, le titre est-il touché par la découverte et l'occupation du territoire par la France, ou par des lois exécutives ou législatives subséquentes, ou par tout autre fait indiqué sur le registre?[37]

Les trois autres questions demeurèrent fondamentalement les mêmes. Le séminaire refusait d'admettre qu'il y ait eu une quelconque occupation autochtone, que des descendants des occupants originaux habitaient la seigneurie, ou même que les Indiens présents étaient des descendants des bénéficiaires originaux. Pendant ce temps, Rowell, avocat de Toronto, suggéra une septième question : « Quel est l'effet, s'il y a lieu, des lois 3 et 4, Vict, chapitre 30 et de la loi seigneuriale de 1859 sur les droits, les obligations et les titres respectifs du séminaire et des Indiens? »[38] Il y eut plus de négociations concernant les trois premières questions, mais celles-ci furent remaniées pour satisfaire Geoffrion et le séminaire.

Quand les sept questions furent soumises à E. L. Newcombe, ministre de la Justice, il s'objecta aux trois premières questions, celles qui traitent du titre ancestral, en disant qu'elles présentaient un « état de fait présumé et des questions générales ou abstraites ». Il déclara : « C'est la première fois, autant que je sache, qu'il a été proposé de demander à la cour de trancher des questions de titre, d'après un état de fait présumé sujet à des réserves, qui dans certains cas pourraient rendre le jugement de la cour inefficace […]. »[39] Il pensait improbable que la cour supérieure considère ces questions et il conclut ainsi : « Par conséquent, considérant l'improbabilité d'obtenir une résolution satisfaisante par les procédures proposées, et tenant compte des dépenses, le ministre ne peut pas recommander de recourir à cette procédure. »[40] Les déclarations de Newcombe reflétaient les attitudes de la société et des tribunaux selon lesquelles le titre ancestral était plus ou moins fictif; il n'avait jamais existé. Selon lui, une cause type entre les partis obtiendrait plus de succès. Après toutes les négociations, les sept questions furent rejetées et les avocats devaient présenter une nouvelle cause.

Smith écrivit à Newcombe pour lui dire :

Puisque la question du titre a provoqué des animosités au Québec et en Ontario, le gouvernement pense qu'il vaut mieux la retirer. Le premier ministre veut que la question soit réglée une fois pour toutes par une décision qui ne sera pas exposée à la critique des gens qui ont manifesté un très grand intérêt pour les Indiens.[41]

Tandis que toutes ces négociations se poursuivaient, le conseil municipal d'Oka annonça son intention d'ériger des clôtures sur la Commune. En réalité, les clôtures proposées diviseraient la Commune en trois parties, laissant les animaux paître dans certains endroits sans avoir accès à de l'eau. Le problème commença en 1905 quand la commission d'hygiène d'Oka se plaignit au conseil municipal au sujet des animaux qui erraient dans le village, souillant les routes publiques, menaçant la santé publique et étant généralement une nuisance au village.[42] La commission d'hygiène se plaignit que le séminaire ne faisait rien pour régler le problème, qu'il « se vantait publiquement devant votre honorable conseil de jeter vos règlements dans la poubelle » et qu'il s'opposait à toutes règles de la municipalité.[43] Le conseil déclara : « Une société ne peut plus tolérer une telle négligence criminelle de la part d'une corporation privée, aussi puissante puisse-t-elle être. »[44]

Quelques années plus tôt, le séminaire de Saint-Sulpice avait vendu à la municipalité d'Oka une grande partie des terres du village et des alentours, y compris des terres sur lesquelles vivaient des Kanehsata'kehró:non. Le conseil municipal obtint donc le droit d'administrer et de contrôler ces terres et, au cours de l'été 1906, le conseil adopta une motion pour clôturer la Commune afin d'empêcher le bétail d'errer dans le village.[45] Cette décision suivait une nouvelle loi provinciale sur la santé publique, exigeant que les municipalités améliorent leur hygiène. Le village d'Oka grandissait, et la croissance augmentait le risque de propager des maladies. Selon le conseil municipal, les vaches dans les rues du village représentaient un risque pour la santé. Le conseil aurait pu simplement séparer le village des pâturages de la Commune par une clôture, mais il décida plutôt d'entourer la Commune d'une clôture. En 1906, deux routes avaient été tracées dans les pâturages et, pour rendre les clôtures utiles, chaque section fut clôturée. On installa des barrières où les clôtures traversaient les deux routes.

Les Kanehsata'kehró:non faisaient paître leur bétail librement sur la Commune depuis aussi longtemps qu'on puisse s'en souvenir. Le matin, on sortait le bétail, puis on le laissait brouter et errer jusqu'au lac pour s'abreuver quand les ruisseaux séchaient au plus fort de l'été.[46] Au moment où le conseil municipal prit cette décision, les Kanehsata'kehró:non avaient déjà érigé une clôture autour de la Commune. Elle avait toujours été entretenue par le peuple, en particulier par les hommes de la communauté. En 1876, le séminaire avait essayé d'ériger une clôture, mais le peuple de Kanehsatà:ke l'avait immédiatement démolie : les Sulpiciens n'avaient aucun droit de clôturer les terres.[47]

La clôture érigée par les Kanehsata'kehró:non convenait à leurs besoins et suffisait à empêcher trop d'animaux d'errer dans le village. En désaccord, le conseil du village d'Oka fit dresser une nouvelle clôture. Le chef Angus Corinthe expliqua exactement comment la clôture mettait en péril la subsistance de son peuple. Il raconta au juge Hutchison une conversation qu'il avait eue avec le supérieur du séminaire de Saint-Sulpice en 1907 :

> Je lui ai expliqué comment était la clôture et comment elle divisait la Commune en trois parties : il y avait une clôture le long de la route et en certains endroits de la Commune, vers le mois de juillet – en période de temps sec – il n'y a pas d'eau. Je lui ai dit que le bétail ne pouvait pas rester là sans eau. J'ai parlé de cela au supérieur du séminaire et lui ai dit que ce n'était pas acceptable, que mon peuple n'aimait pas cela et qu'il n'était pas du tout d'accord […] Bien sûr, nous n'avons pas le temps d'abreuver le bétail chaque jour; nous avons d'autres travaux à faire. Si je laisse mon bétail paître chaque matin, je ne le surveille pas durant le jour et je ne devrais pas avoir à lui faire traverser les barrières pour qu'il aille s'abreuver. Généralement, la Commune sert au bétail qui devrait pouvoir aller à la rivière pour boire quand il le veut.[48]

Selon les Kanehsata'kehró:non, la Commune leur appartenait et le conseil du village n'avait aucun droit de la clôturer. Ils se sont immédiatement préparés à l'abattre comme ils avaient abattu la clôture du séminaire en 1876.[49] Ils demandèrent au Département d'intervenir pour empêcher une confrontation.[50] Celui-ci leur répondit de ne rien faire qui contreviendrait à la loi.[51] En juillet, le conseil municipal écrivit à Frank Pedley pour lui dire que permettre aux animaux qui paissent dans la Commune d'errer dans le village contrevenait aux lois et aux règlements municipaux, et que le procès à l'égard du titre de propriété des terres ne pouvait aucunement modifier ni avoir des répercussions sur le code municipal. Le conseil municipal affirma que le travail qui devait être fait l'était dans l'intérêt du public, qu'il y avait de l'eau dans chaque section de la Commune et qu'aucun animal n'en manquerait.[52] Le Département ne voulut pas se mêler de la question, sauf pour dire aux chefs de ne rien faire, puisque leur procès serait bientôt présenté devant les tribunaux et que la question serait alors résolue.[53]

Les Kanehsata'kehró:non attendirent plus d'un an pendant que leurs avocats, l'avocat du séminaire et le gouvernement fédéral se concentraient sur les points à présenter devant les tribunaux. Quand 1909 arriva, ayant peu d'espoir que le procès ait lieu, le chef Angus Corinthe présenta clairement son point de vue et celui de son peuple. Les Kanehsata'kehró:non ne pouvaient pas passer une autre année avec la Commune divisée en trois parties par des clôtures. Le séminaire adopta alors une attitude passive, préférant laisser les Kanehsata'kehró:non se débattre avec la municipalité. Dans un mémorandum adressé au surintendant, le conseil municipal demanda une force policière suffisante pour intimider les Indiens durant l'érection des clôtures. Il demanda également l'avis du Département en lui signalant qu'avant d'agir il pouvait attendre le verdict au procès cité.[54]

Nous ignorons quel avis le Département donna au conseil municipal, mais nous savons que le conseil alla de l'avant avec l'érection d'une clôture avant qu'un procès soit présenté devant les tribunaux. Le conseil disposait de nombreux policiers pour l'aider à ériger la clôture, et l'idée d'un exposé de cause ou d'un renvoi à la Cour suprême fut abandonnée.[55] Cette cause, qui commença par une dispute entre le séminaire et le conseil municipal, fut plutôt choisie comme cause type entre le séminaire et les Kanehsata'kehró:non.

À LA COUR SUPRÊME

Le 20 mars 1908, une plainte au nom d'Angus Corinthe, Peter Gaspé et Amable Roussin fut déposée à Saint-Scholastique contre le séminaire de Saint-Sulpice. Elle était très différente de la cause présentée à la cour supérieure. Les avocats des deux partis s'entendirent pour omettre toute véritable question de titre ancestral, à condition que l'avocat du séminaire admette que la plupart des Indiens au Lac des Deux-Montagnes étaient les descendants directs de ceux mentionnés dans les concessions.[56] Il fut convenu que les Kanehsata'kehró:non ne pouvaient pas gagner un tel procès sans cette admission parce qu'ils ne pouvaient prouver leur descendance directe ni leur titre ancestral. Ils n'avaient aucun registre écrit, seulement leur tradition orale. Geoffrion accepta la question de prescription parce qu'elle ne serait liée qu'aux statuts de 1839 à 1841 et aux lois seigneuriales de 1853 à 1859. Il fut convenu que M. Rowell, avocat de Toronto, serait présent lors du procès, puisque l'objet principal du procès était de satisfaire les Ontariens,[57] alors qu'il aurait dû être d'obtenir justice.

En mars 1908, R. C. Smith, avocat pour les Kanehsata'kehró:non, écrivit à E. L. Newcombe pour lui dire qu'il ne croyait pas que le procès devant les tribunaux entraînerait une définition des droits des Kanehsata'kehró:non. Si le procès devait échouer, la cour ne se donnerait pas la peine de définir quels droits, le cas échéant, les Indiens possédaient. Si on lui demandait de les définir, cela prendrait plus de temps et coûterait plus cher. Il croyait qu'il valait mieux chercher à savoir si le séminaire reconsidérait vendre des terres au gouvernement en faveur des Indiens.[58] À ce moment-là, le séminaire n'était pas prêt à recevoir une telle proposition. En fait, ni le département de la Justice ni le département des Affaires indiennes ne souhaitaient déterminer les droits du peuple ni aborder le sujet. Il semblait également qu'aucune des agences gouvernementales ne s'intéressait à résoudre le problème. Elles désiraient simplement apaiser l'électorat par un simulacre de justice.

Le procès débuta le 9 février 1909 devant la cour supérieure du Québec, à Montréal. Onze personnes témoignèrent comme demandeurs et six comme défendeurs.[59] Le procès ne se préoccuperait que du titre de la Commune, tandis que les demandeurs, Corinthe et les autres, revendiquaient tous les droits collectifs de propriété dans la Commune des Kanehsata'kehró:non. Ils affirmèrent qu'ils en faisaient usage depuis des temps immémoriaux, qu'ils en avaient le titre ancestral, que le séminaire n'avait aucun droit de vendre ou d'aliéner une quelconque partie des terres et qu'il n'en était que le fiduciaire. Ils demandèrent qu'on oblige le séminaire à leur remettre la seigneurie. Le séminaire nia l'existence de toute occupation ancestrale, ainsi que l'existence de tout droit d'occupation originale. Même si un tel droit existait, il avait été aboli par la découverte de l'Amérique. Parce que le séminaire refusa d'admettre une occupation autochtone, le titre ancestral fut réduit aux quelconques droits que les Kanehsata'kehró:non auraient pu obtenir des concessions, et les temps immémoriaux furent limités à la période qui débuta en 1721, l'année de la première concession.[60]

Le cabinet d'avocats représentant les Kanehsata'kehró:non avait envoyé un délégué en Europe pour rechercher des documents pertinents au procès. Les avocats avaient découvert l'existence de documents très importants, documents qu'on ne pouvait trouver nulle part au Canada. La recherche des archives de Paris révéla quelque 40 documents, dont 25 furent fournies comme preuve, qui confirmaient solidement la position des Kanehsata'kehró:non, à l'effet que les terres furent concédées au séminaire pour raisons de commodité seulement et que les concessions leur furent accordées pour le bénéfice des Kanehsata'kehró:non.[61]

À la cour supérieure du Québec, le juge Hutchinson décréta que le séminaire était le propriétaire légitime de la seigneurie en vertu des statuts consolidés du Bas-Canada, qui lui en confirmaient le titre.[62] Il était d'accord avec les toutes premières opinions émises par Sewell et Stewart, à savoir que le séminaire de Montréal n'avait aucune capacité légale de recevoir des terres du séminaire de Paris et que leurs droits furent créés en 1840. Il décréta que les droits garantis aux Indiens en vertu de l'article 40 de l'Acte de capitulation étaient ignorés par les diverses lois relatives au territoire et qu'ils étaient sans effet. Cependant, il croyait que l'ordonnance de 1840 créait une obligation au séminaire, celle de poursuivre sa mission, ce qui accordait certains droits aux Indiens.[63] Le juge Hutchinson décréta également que les Kanehsata'kehró:non n'avaient acquis aucun droit par prescription parce qu'ils n'avaient jamais été propriétaires des terres qu'ils occupent. Les demandeurs et les défendeurs en appelèrent de la décision, et le procès fut référé à la Cour suprême.

Les quatre juges, Messieurs Lavergne, Trenholme, Cross et Carrol, rejetèrent les deux appels. Le juge Carrol écrivit dans ses notes :

D'ailleurs, il est bien douteux que l'article 40 de l'Acte de capitulation ait eu pour but de protéger les Indiens sur les terres qu'ils occupaient et qui, plus tard, ont été nommés « réserves indiennes » par les autorités. Ni le roi de France ni le roi d'Angleterre n'ont entendu confirmer des droits de propriété aux Indiens. Ils les traitaient avec tolérance et bienveillance pour des raisons politiques et humanitaires, mais personne n'aurait songé à donner des titres de propriété à ces enfants des bois qui, dans leur propre intérêt, sont tenus en tutelle.[64]

Le juge Cross était du même avis que la cour inférieure : il croyait que le peuple de Kanehsatà:ke avait certains droits, mais pas ceux qu'ils revendiquaient devant les tribunaux. Il poursuit en décrivant quelle était, selon lui, la nature de ces droits.

Les défendeurs ont donc l'obligation légale de maintenir cette mission et cette œuvre pour les buts désignés. Cette obligation ne s'applique pas aux terres, dans le sens où elle donnerait au bénéficiaire une propriété. Elle repose plutôt sur une obligation contractuelle que le parlement, agissant pour les deux groupes intéressés, a créée. Celle-ci peut être exécutée, à la demande de celui pour qui l'obligation a été établie, au moyen d'une action appropriée.[65]

Cependant, tout comme Smith l'avait prédit, le procès entrepris ne mena pas à une définition des droits ni à une mise en application de ceux-ci. Le juge Cross déclara : « Le but principal du demandeur dans le présent procès est de solliciter des terres ou d'avoir un intérêt dans des terres, et non de réclamer l'exécution de l'obligation de la charte à laquelle on vient de faire référence [...] »[66] Il croyait toutefois que les Kanehsata'kehró:non avaient une bonne capacité juridique pour faire respecter leurs droits et que le séminaire n'avait pas honoré ses obligations. Au sujet du contre-appel du séminaire, le juge Cross déclara :

De plus, il a été discuté à l'appui du contre-appel des défendeurs que, même s'ils avaient été soumis à une obligation de maintenir la mission, cette obligation a été abolie par la réalisation de son objet, puisque depuis plusieurs années, il n'y a plus d'Indiens païens [...] Non seulement les défendeurs sont responsables des besoins spirituels des Indiens, mais ils sont également sous l'obligation de les instruire [...] Des onze Indiens adultes qui ont comparu et qui ont donné leur témoignage dans ce procès, dix étaient incapables de parler suffisamment l'anglais ou le français pour témoigner dans l'une de ces langues [...] À cet égard qui est des plus importants, c'est-à-dire l'instruction élémentaire, le travail des défendeurs, plutôt que d'être terminé, ne semble pas avoir été efficacement commencé.[67]

Inutile de mentionner que ni le séminaire ni l'avocat des chefs n'étaient satisfaits de cette décision. Une fois de plus, les deux partis interjetèrent appel, et le procès fut soumis au Conseil privé. Cela s'était passé exactement comme Sir Wilfrid Laurier l'avait prévu. Aucun tribunal ne reconnaissait le droit des Kanehsata'kehró:non de posséder des terres parce qu'aux yeux de la loi, ils étaient considérés comme mineurs. La décision reflétait l'attitude d'une société qui, un jour, dépendit des Kanehsata'kehró:non pour survivre et qui, maintenant, les considérait comme inutiles et dérangeants. Les juges ne pouvaient pas croire que leurs ancêtres avaient vraiment l'intention de protéger les droits territoriaux des Onkwehón:we quand la société, en 1912, n'était pas prête à reconnaître l'existence de quelque droit que ce soit. Peu de temps après le procès Corinthe, en 1912 ou en 1913, la Loi sur les Indiens fut amendée, rendant presque illégale pour les nations autochtones d'adresser des revendications territoriales devant les tribunaux. Cette interdiction dura jusqu'en 1951.

AU CONSEIL PRIVÉ

Le comité judiciaire du Conseil privé confirma les décisions des cours inférieures et rejeta les deux appels. Il alla jusqu'à dire :

Les juges pensent que l'effet de cette loi était de rendre incontestable le titre des défendeurs à la seigneurie et de rendre impossible pour les demandeurs d'établir un titre de possession indépendant et de contrôler l'administration de ladite seigneurie. Ils sont d'accord pour dire avec les savants juges spécialisés des cours inférieures que, ni par titre ancestral, ni par prescription, ni sur la base qu'ils sont bénéficiaires de fiducie de la corporation, les demandeurs ne peuvent revendiquer devant les tribunaux aucun titre tel que celui que cet appel a soulevé.[68]

Cette décision reflétait la croyance que les droits des autochtones furent concédés par la Couronne et qu'ils étaient soumis à des changements selon son bon vouloir. « Elle présumait que l'usage du titre ancestral était limité parce qu'il appartenait à la Couronne et qu'il stipulait que le chef de l'État pouvait enlever ce qu'elle avait gracieusement concédé (selon la bonne volonté du souverain) ».[69] Cependant, les juges du comité judiciaire poursuivirent en disant que la loi de 1840 créait aussi une fiducie caritative que le gouvernement pouvait peut-être faire respecter au moyen d'un autre procès ou par des mesures législatives. Le gouvernement n'avait aucune intention de faire une telle chose.

En fait, le procès de Corinthe et autres avait réalisé le désir du gouvernement en permettant aux Kanehsata'kehró:non de présenter leur cause jusqu'au Conseil privé. Le public canadien était satisfait de ce que le peuple de Kanehsatà:ke avait finalement obtenu justice. Qu'il ait perdu importait peu, tout ce qui était possible de faire avait été fait. Non seulement justice avait été rendue, mais elle donnait l'apparence d'avoir été rendue. La question était réglée et elle ne pouvait être « mise en doute par ceux qui aimaient profondément les Indiens ». Une seule chose faisait défaut : la course avait été arrangée depuis le début. Tout se passa comme Sir Wilfrid Laurier, ce grand « bienfaiteur » des Kanehsata'kehró:non, l'avait dit, à savoir qu'aux yeux de la société et de la loi, ils étaient mineurs et ne pouvaient donc pas posséder de terres. Les faits mêmes sur lesquels ils avaient compté pour protéger et confirmer leurs droits avaient été utilisés pour les dépouiller de ces mêmes droits. Ils avaient commis une erreur fatale.

Les Kanehsata'kehró:non avaient fait confiance à un système qui les considérait comme des êtres de moindre importance avec des droits de seconde classe. Ils avaient cru en une société qui les voyait comme inutiles et dérangeants. Ils crurent, et plusieurs le croient toujours, que les articles de l'Acte de capitulation et de la Proclamation royale de 1763 protégeaient leurs droits. En réalité, la proclamation fut utilisée dans tout le Canada pour abolir les droits des autochtones et aliéner le titre ancestral. Elle servit d'outil pour conclure des traités menant à l'abandon de leurs terres (voir Boyce Richardson).

La loi canadienne décida de l'issue du procès en utilisant des lois qui avaient été créées spécifiquement pour priver les Kanehsata'kehró:non de leurs droits et les conférer au séminaire. Leurs droits territoriaux ne découlent pas d'une proclamation royale ni de toute autre décision exécutive ou tout autre instrument juridique français, britannique ou canadien, mais viennent de l'occupation ancestrale du territoire par les Kanehsata'kehró:non depuis des temps immémoriaux. Ces droits ne furent pas créés par le Canada et ne peuvent être abolis par le Canada sans le consentement des Kanehsata'kehró:non, consentement qu'il ne lui a jamais été accordé. En 1910, le peuple ne pouvait pas prouver l'occupation ancestrale à la satisfaction de la cour et, même s'il le pouvait, l'attitude de la société était telle que tout droit provenant de l'occupation ancestrale était considéré comme purement imaginaire.

Ces lois qui auraient dû protéger les droits du peuple de Kanehsatà:ke furent ignorées et écartées. Le Canada est un pays dont les lois furent créées pour des raisons de commodité et soutenues ou ignorées également pour des raisons de commodité. C'est un pays qui choisit les lois auxquelles il obéira, tout en insistant pour que les peuples autochtones, ceux qui viennent d'ici, soient soumis à l'autorité absolue de leurs lois, des lois étrangères. C'est un pays qui continue à insister pour que les peuples autochtones d'ici prouvent qu'ils y vivaient avant l'arrivée des Blancs. En 1763, les Britanniques entreprirent de se protéger contre leur propre désir d'acquérir les terres non cédées et occupées par les peuples autochtones de ce pays. Ils reconnurent qu'ils ne pouvaient pas faire confiance à leur peuple pour traiter équitablement et honnêtement avec la population autochtone relativement aux terres et à toute autre chose d'ailleurs. En 1763, le roi émit une proclamation pour empêcher que les « énormes fraudes et abus » survenus dans le passé se reproduisent. Cela ne fit rien, ou très peu de choses, pour garder le peuple sur ses terres. En peu de temps, les arrivants prouvèrent que, malgré leurs lois, leurs traités et leur civilisation, ils n'étaient pas dignes de confiance. En 1910, les représentants du gouvernement s'étaient convaincus que leurs ancêtres n'avaient jamais eu l'intention de reconnaître ni de protéger les droits ou les titres ancestraux; ils disaient que ces droits n'avaient jamais existé. Ils justifièrent ainsi leur mépris absolu des lois et des ententes conclues par leurs prédécesseurs.

Avec la décision du Conseil privé, une autre porte avait solidement été fermée au nez des Kanehsata'kehró:non. Angus Corinthe et son groupe avaient peut-être eu de grands espoirs que le peuple obtienne finalement justice, mais cela ne se produisit jamais. Une décision prise en 1912 serait utilisée pour matraquer les Kanehsata'kehró:non chaque fois qu'ils exprimeraient leurs préoccupations au sujet des empiétements constants sur les terres qu'ils continuent de revendiquer comme leurs.

LA SUITE

Après la décision du Conseil privé, la situation à Kanehsatà:ke retourna vite à la normale, c'est-à-dire que le séminaire recommença à vendre les terres qui restaient, tout en continuant à harceler et à persécuter les Kanehsata'kehró:non. Il devint de plus en plus difficile pour eux de gagner leur vie à Kanehsatà:ke. Le gouvernement n'y fit absolument rien. Quelques jours après la décision, la société missionnaire de l'Église méthodiste pressa le gouvernement « de prendre immédiatement les mesures nécessaires pour protéger les droits des Indiens sur leurs terres ».[70] Malheureusement, la décision du comité judiciaire ne fut pas assez énergique pour contraindre le gouvernement ou le séminaire à agir. Il y eut un débat sur la nature des fiducies caritatives en général et de la fiducie du séminaire en particulier. Il y eut beaucoup de discussions entre les divers Départements du gouvernement pour choisir quelle action entreprendre, s'il y avait lieu. Absolument rien ne fut fait.

Dans une certaine mesure, la Cour supérieure, la Cour d'appel et le Conseil privé avaient déclaré que les Kanehsata'kehró:non possédaient de véritables droits, bien que limités, sur les terres de Kanehsatà:ke. Chaque cour avait aussi recommandé que des mesures soient prises pour déterminer la nature et l'étendue de ces droits. Le gouvernement négligea leurs recommandations. Même si plusieurs des juges avaient exprimé leurs opinions quant à la nature de ces droits, aucune de ces opinions n'avait la force d'une décision judiciaire parce qu'aucune cour n'avait été mandatée pour statuer sur cette question. En raison des décisions prises par le Conseil privé et du fait que les cours inférieures n'avaient pas défini les droits des Kanehsata'kehró:non, ces droits étaient considérés comme inapplicables. Une note de service du département de la Justice disait :

> Au Québec, aucune cour représentant le public n'a l'autorité d'étendre, de modifier ou de faire respecter une fiducie relative aux fiducies caritatives sous le système juridique anglais au moyen d'un projet. Le seul moyen d'étendre ou de modifier les pouvoirs des fiduciaires en général, dans l'intérêt du *cestuis que trustent*, consiste à recourir à la législature par un projet de loi privé [...] Dans cette cause, la concession de la seigneurie ne constitue pas une fiducie, mais un « don à titre onéreux », et l'exécution des conditions imposées peut être exigée par tous les partis directement intéressés et rigoureusement appliquée – s'il y a lieu – par la Cour supérieure.[71]

Alors qu'il y avait beaucoup d'ambiguïté quant aux droits « juridiques » des Kanehsata'kehró:non, le gouvernement aurait pu prendre des mesures claires pour garantir et protéger ces droits et pour préserver les terres qui restaient pour leur usage. En novembre 1912, William Smith, avocat des Kanehsata'kehró:non, écrivit à E. L. Newcombe pour suggérer que le gouvernement prenne des mesures pour garantir un règlement. La majorité du peuple n'acceptait pas la décision du Conseil privé, et le séminaire continuait à vendre des parcelles de terrain à 240 $ l'hectare.[72] Rien ne fut fait à ce moment-là.

Trois ans plus tard, N. W. Rowell écrivit à Duncan C. Scott, alors surintendant général des Affaires indiennes, pour lui proposer un règlement qui garantirait suffisamment de terrain aux Kanehsata'kehró:non :

> [...] d'après le Conseil privé, il est clair que le séminaire détient cette propriété en fiducie au bénéfice des Indiens et que, si cela n'est pas appliqué, et à défaut d'en arriver à un règlement satisfaisant, une action judiciaire ou législative devrait être prise pour garantir aux Indiens leurs droits.[73]

Selon Rowell, « [...] la fiducie pour les Indiens implique le droit de résidence sur la seigneurie dans des conditions qui leur permettent de subvenir à leurs besoins ». Et aussi : « [...] le séminaire possède toujours suffisamment de propriétés pour fournir aux Indiens les terres qu'ils demandent et qu'ils sont prêts à accepter ».[74] Malheureusement, c'était au gouvernement d'agir en faveur des Kanehsata'kehró:non pour contraindre le séminaire à remplir les devoirs que la fiducie lui impose. Précisément, la décision semblait être restée entre les mains d'un haut fonctionnaire du département de la Justice : E. L. Newcombe, l'homme qui avait décidé que la Cour supérieure ne considérerait pas les questions de titre ancestral. Sa réponse fut simple. Ce que Rowell proposa pour les Kanehsata'kehró:non était exactement ce que le Conseil Privé avait décidé : ils n'avaient pas de droit de posséder de terres. Newcombe semblait déterminé à ignorer la suggestion du Conseil privé, à savoir que le gouvernement prenne des mesures pour déterminer et garantir les droits du peuple. Il déclara :

[…] selon moi, l'affirmation de M. Rowell n'a aucun fondement juridique. Les ordonnances, dont vous m'avez envoyé un extrait, semblent garantir la terre au séminaire « pour les buts, les objectifs et les plans (parmi d'autres) de la mission du Lac des Deux-Montagnes, pour l'instruction et les besoins spirituels des Indiens algonquins et iroquois et pour aucun autre but, objectif ou plan ». Je ne comprends pas que l'instruction et les besoins spirituels de ces Indiens imposent nécessairement l'obligation au séminaire de leur fournir des terres agricoles pour leur subsistance.[75]

La décision de Newcombe allait nettement à l'encontre des avis des juges du Comité judiciaire du Conseil privé. Cependant, personne ne s'opposa à un fonctionnaire qui ne tenait pas compte de la décision de l'autorité juridique la plus importante au pays. Par ailleurs, Newcombe n'était pas opposé à un règlement. « Cependant, si le séminaire pouvait être persuadé d'accepter la proposition de M. Rowell au moyen d'un règlement, je présume qu'il n'y aurait aucun problème à obtenir la législation nécessaire pour le légaliser ».[76] Toutefois, le département de la Justice ne prendrait aucune mesure pour encourager le séminaire à accepter une proposition de règlement. À la suite de ses victoires juridiques, le séminaire ne se sentit aucunement contraint de le faire. Les avocats des Kanehsata'kehró:non furent laissés à eux-mêmes pour discuter d'un règlement. Sans le soutien du gouvernement, le peuple de Kanehsatà:ke manquait de ressources financières pour faire aboutir le règlement de la question. Ce n'est que 30 ans après la décision du Conseil privé de 1912 que le gouvernement prit des mesures pour leur garantir un territoire. À ce moment-là, le séminaire avait déjà vendu toutes les terres, sauf les petits terrains où vivait le peuple. L'intervention du gouvernement était trop peu trop tard. Elle survint, non pour satisfaire les besoins du peuple, mais en réponse à une demande d'un séminaire aux prises avec des soucis financiers.

L'ACHAT DE 1945

En juin 1941, Bernard Bourdon, avocat des fiduciaires des propriétés commerciales de Saint-Sulpice, communiqua avec le gouvernement pour lui proposer d'acheter les terres occupées par le peuple de Kanehsatà:ke. Plusieurs années auparavant, le séminaire avait vendu à un consortium belge de grandes étendues de terrain, y compris la Commune. Le gouvernement provincial avait assumé le contrôle de la majeure partie des terres appartenant toujours au séminaire.

[…] quand les Sulpiciens furent incapables de repayer les 1 025 000 $ qu'ils avaient empruntés de la province de Québec en 1933, l'ordre remit 100 terrains à la province qui, beaucoup plus tard, en transféra quelques-uns à la municipalité d'Oka pour un dollar.[77]

Dans une lettre, le séminaire déclara plus tard que « le problème des Indiens d'Oka était devenu de plus en plus difficile pour les prêtres de Saint-Sulpice […] par exemple, les taxes se révèlent maintenant un lourd fardeau ».[78] N'étant pas naturellement sympathique aux problèmes du séminaire, le gouvernement manifesta un intérêt soudain dans les droits des Kanehsata'kehró:non. T. A. Crerar, ministre des Mines et des Ressources, répondit :

[…] il est regrettable qu'aucune mesure n'ait été prise puisque le jugement a été rendu pour établir, soit devant les tribunaux ou par médiation, d'une part leurs droits et, d'autre part, les obligations imposées aux ecclésiastiques du séminaire sous la loi de 1841.[79]

Le ministre continua à discuter longuement des avis des divers juges de paix des cours du Québec qui avaient statué sur la cause et déclara :

La situation est que les deux cours du Québec ont décidé que les Indiens possèdent certains droits sur les terres de la seigneurie et que le séminaire a une obligation légale qui peut être appliquée [...] par conséquent, comme ministre du Département, qui contrôle et gère les terres et la propriété des Indiens, et gardien de leurs droits, je ne peux, vu les faits soulignés ci-dessus, recevoir aucune proposition d'achat de terres pour les Indiens, dont le titre légal est au nom du séminaire, mais qui est soumis aux droits et devoirs mentionnés [...].[80]

Puis, il informa les fiduciaires que le gouvernement s'attendait à ce que le séminaire assume ses obligations envers le peuple de Kanehsatà:ke, sans quoi il était disposé à entreprendre des procédures légales contre le séminaire.

Il devint vite apparent que les paroles dures du ministre des Mines et des Ressources équivalaient à rien de plus qu'à de la démagogie. Le gouvernement frappa fort par une faible tentative d'intimider le séminaire pour qu'il révèle ses véritables états financiers. En fait, il ne montra aucune disposition à forcer le séminaire à respecter ses obligations ni aucun désir de protéger les droits des Kanehsata'kehró:non. En juin 1942, Charles Camsell, ministre des Mines et des Ressources, écrivit au ministère de la Justice pour lui suggérer que, « puisque M. Crerar n'a reçu aucune réponse à sa lettre, il faudrait maintenant considérer s'il serait recommandable d'adopter des procédures en faveur des Indiens [...] ».[81] Ce qui suivit fut une discussion au sein du ministère de la Justice où il fut décidé que les Kanehsata'kehró:non n'avaient aucun droit exécutoire. Même si le Conseil privé avait recommandé que des mesures soient prises pour déterminer et garantir les droits du peuple de Kanehsatà:ke, en 1942, le gouvernement n'était toujours pas disposé à appliquer ces mesures. Une note de service interne du ministère de la Justice disait : « Dans l'ensemble, M. Lafleur pense que les droits des Indiens dépassent la juridiction des cours du Québec et qu'ils sont propres à la négociation ou à la législation de redressement ».[82] Un règlement serait négocié entre le gouvernement et le séminaire; en réalité il mettait fin aux droits « juridiques » que le peuple avait contre le séminaire. Les Kanehsata'kehró:non ne furent jamais consultés et ne participèrent aucunement au processus.

Pendant ce temps, l'association Belgo Canadian, qui avait acheté du séminaire une grande partie de la Commune, ainsi que plusieurs autres parcelles de terrain, se trouva entraînée dans un conflit avec les Kanehsata'kehró:non. Cette compagnie avait en toute bonne foi acheté les terres du séminaire, ignorant apparemment la dispute au sujet du titre. Elle se rendait maintenant compte qu'elle avait acheté beaucoup plus que des terres. En juillet 1942, un représentant de la compagnie belge écrivit au Ministère pour lui demander d'intervenir afin de rétablir la paix dans la région. Il décrivit certains incidents qui s'étaient produits et informa le Ministère que la police avait été appelée. Cependant, la compagnie était disposée à se retirer du territoire si le gouvernement lui fournissait les documents démontrant que les Kanehsata'kehró:non avaient des droits sur celui-ci.

[...] s'il est vrai que des documents récemment découverts prouveraient que les Indiens possèdent certains droits aux terres et aux boisés à des fins de pâturage, nous aimerions recevoir l'information nécessaire pour engager des poursuites contre le séminaire de Saint-Sulpice qui, comme nous l'avons déjà dit, nous a vendu les terres alléguant qu'il en détenait le titre officiel.[83]

Le gouvernement n'était pas disposé à poursuivre le séminaire et s'assura que personne d'autre ne le fasse. Il n'envoya aucun renseignement à la compagnie belge et ne l'avisa pas non plus de l'existence d'une telle information. Le gouvernement répondit ainsi à la demande de la compagnie : « C'est à vous que revient la responsabilité de régler la question relative à votre titre de propriété auprès de l'ordre des Sulpiciens de qui vous l'avez acheté ».[84]

En août de cette année-là, les fiduciaires des propriétés commerciales de Saint-Sulpice soumirent de nouveau leur proposition. Celle-ci comprenait une garantie selon laquelle le gouvernement protégerait le séminaire « contre toute réclamation qui pourrait être faite par ou pour lesdits Indiens ».[85] Si le gouvernement acceptait la proposition des fiduciaires, les Kanehsata'kehró:non seraient dans l'impossibilité d'en appeler devant les tribunaux pour que le séminaire répare ses torts ou d'intenter un procès dans lequel le séminaire pouvait être cité. Il annulerait par le fait même les droits, bien qu'imprécis, que les cours avaient reconnus au peuple. Le gouvernement accepterait la proposition sans que les Kanehsata'kehró:non ne le sachent ni ne donnent leur consentement. Une autre note de service du ministère de la Justice cita plus tard les opinions de plusieurs juges dans le procès Corinthe et disait : « Dans ces circonstances, il ne semble pas que les Indiens aient des droits légaux à l'égard des terres. »[86] Même si au ministère de la Justice on connaissait très bien l'existence de ces droits ainsi que celle d'une fiducie caritative, on se souciait peu de les faire respecter et on éprouvait peu de scrupules à les abolir. La principale préoccupation était de vérifier si le séminaire pouvait ou non respecter ses obligations.

La dernière proposition de quelques fiduciaires de la propriété commerciale est de la transférer à Sa Majesté pour les Indiens à condition que la Couronne décharge les fiduciaires de la responsabilité des arrérages de taxes qui s'élèvent à environ 7000 $.

J'ai discuté avec l'agent des Mines et des Ressources qui traite de cette affaire. Il a affirmé que les terres qui restent, et qui doivent être transférées, sont tout à fait insuffisantes pour pourvoir au bois et au pâturage des Indiens et qu'en fait il ne reste rien, sauf les terrains sur lesquels ils vivent. Il ne veut prendre aucune mesure qui soulagerait l'ordre des obligations revendiquées par les Indiens. En réalité, il affirme qu'il doit intenter une poursuite contre l'ordre à moins qu'il soit satisfait en apprenant que l'ordre est insolvable et incapable de faire respecter une décision.[87]

À ce moment-là, il est évident que, par ses activités, le séminaire n'avait presque rien laissé aux Kanehsata'kehró:non. Comme il était soi-disant le « gardien des Indiens », le gouvernement aurait dû intervenir pour obliger le séminaire, soit à rendre les terres au peuple, soit à les compenser. Il ne fit ni l'un ni l'autre. Même s'il pouvait négocier avec la compagnie belge pour qu'elle rende les terres qu'elle avait achetées, le gouvernement ne le fit pas non plus. Il alla plutôt de l'avant et mit en œuvre le plan pour assumer la gestion des terres occupées par les Kanehsata'kehró:non, même si tous savaient que ce plan ne satisferait aucun d'entre eux et qu'il serait loin de répondre aux besoins de la communauté. Le ministère des Mines et des Ressources envoya un inspecteur à qui « on demanda particulièrement de s'informer de la déclaration des fiduciaires selon laquelle les terres sont abondantes à tous égards pour fournir le pâturage et le bois aux résidents indiens ».[88] Les affirmations du séminaire se révélèrent totalement fausses.

Son rapport indique que, dans seulement cinq ou six cas, les Indiens ont suffisamment de bois sur leur propriété pour subvenir à leurs besoins personnels. Dans ces cas particuliers, les Indiens occupent maintenant de plus grandes superficies à l'extérieur du village, alors que ceux qui vivent dans le village n'ont aucune source de bois garantie ni des pâturages en commun.[89]

Malgré ces faits, le ministère des Mines et des Ressources acceptait de considérer l'offre si le ministre délégué pouvait « être convaincu hors de tout doute que les terres à transférer à la Couronne constituent tout ce qui reste des propriétés de l'ordre »,[90] et aussi « s'il n'y a aucun droit juridique pour imposer une revendication contre les propriétés commerciales ou religieuses ».[91] En fait, presque rien n'indique qu'il y eut enquête sur la possibilité d'acquérir les propriétés religieuses ou commerciales du séminaire. Par ailleurs, le gouvernement ne considéra pas sérieusement acheter les terres de la compagnie belge, même s'il fit une offre.[92] Plus tard cette année-là, des négociations débutèrent pour en venir à un règlement.

Le gouvernement savait très bien que ce règlement ne ferait pas grand-chose pour résoudre les griefs historiques de la communauté et satisferait peu de gens. Il préféra minimiser l'opposition, prétendant qu'elle représentait une minorité de partisans de la ligne dure qui ne seraient satisfaits de rien. Dans une lettre au ministre de la Justice, T. A. Crerar, ministre des Mines et des Ressources, déclara : « Il y aura bien sûr quelques Indiens qui contesteront vigoureusement tout jugement négocié. Ce sont ces Indiens qui refusent toujours d'accepter ou de reconnaître la décision du Conseil privé ».[93] Encore une fois, il y eut des discussions concernant les droits du peuple de Kanehsatà:ke. Le consensus général semblait être le suivant : « Il semble n'y avoir aucun doute que l'ordre se trouve dans une très mauvaise situation financière, et que les droits que les tribunaux peuvent concéder aux Indiens s'avéreront inutiles ».[94] Si leurs droits ne serviraient vraiment à rien, alors il serait inutile d'essayer de les faire respecter par les tribunaux. À ce point, le problème auquel le ministère des Mines et des Ressources faisait face était que le jugement tel que proposé aurait certainement l'effet d'abolir des droits des autochtones. Le ministre des Mines et des Ressources, T. A. Crerar, craignait que la participation du parlement soit nécessaire. Une note de service du ministère de la Justice révèle l'attitude adoptée à l'égard de cette préoccupation :

> En bref, nous pourrions répondre au ministère des Mines et des Ressources que les soi-disant droits des Indiens auxquels les décisions du Conseil privé font référence sont inexécutables ou que la question est suffisamment douteuse pour recommander un règlement. Notre réponse peut aussi faire référence à la situation financière de l'ordre qui est telle que toute exécution des droits que les Indiens pourraient avoir au détriment de l'ordre se révélerait inutile. En conclusion, nous pourrions dire que, dans les circonstances, l'approbation du parlement n'est pas nécessaire.[95]

Le ministère de la Justice avait apparemment évolué au point où il était parfaitement satisfait de prétendre que les Kanehsata'kehró:non n'avait aucun droit. En conséquence, les ignorer ou aviser le ministère des Mines et des Ressources, le soi-disant « gardien des Indiens », de faire de même ne lui posait aucun problème. Au cours de l'année suivante, le règlement sur le transfert des terres fut finalisé et certains détails furent négociés. En avril 1945, le Conseil privé approuva la recommandation du ministre des Mines et des Ressources pour que l'offre des fiduciaires des propriétés commerciales soit acceptée.[96] La proposition était la suivante :

a. une entente pour déterminer les obligations des pères de Saint-Sulpice envers les Indiens, à part les besoins spirituels de ceux qui sont de foi catholique;

b. l'abandon de toute revendication que le gouvernement ou les Indiens peuvent avoir contre les pères;

c. le paiement de tous les arrérages de taxes qui selon un accord peuvent être établis sur la base de 40 % des taxes évaluées pour les terres concernées et présentement dues.[97]

On prépara un contrat de vente et on donna autorité à l'agent indien Brisebois de signer au nom de la Couronne.[98] En plus des conditions soulignées dans le règlement, la Couronne paya la somme d'un dollar pour les terres reçues du séminaire. Finalement, ce dernier était complètement relevé de ses obligations envers les Kanehsata'kehró:non et avait réussi à vendre chaque petit lopin de terre sans jamais avoir à les dédommager. Le gouvernement s'en était bien assuré. Il avait promis au séminaire qu'il serait protégé contre toute revendication que les Kanehsata'kehró:non pourraient faire. De plus, la Couronne et le séminaire continuèrent à nier que le peuple de Kanehsatà:ke avait des droits à ces terres.

Il est bien clair que rien dans ce règlement ne sera interprété comme une reconnaissance par Sa Majesté le roi que les personnes qui occupent actuellement une partie de la propriété en question, quelle qu'elle soit, sont des Indiens ayant droit d'occuper ladite partie ou toute partie de la propriété. En outre, rien n'imputera aucune responsabilité à Sa Majesté le roi pour les actions ou les omissions passées desdits prêtres de Saint-Sulpice envers lesdits Indiens algonquins et iroquois.

Par ailleurs, rien dans le présent règlement ne devra être interprété comme une reconnaissance, implicite ou expresse, que les prêtres de Saint-Sulpice aient accepté dans le passé, soit par acte ou omission, une quelconque responsabilité envers les Indiens algonquins et iroquois.[99]

Ils avaient aboli les obligations du séminaire même si personne n'admettait leur existence. Ils avaient aussi aboli certains droits du peuple sans le consulter. Sachant que l'entente ne résoudrait pas les difficultés qu'éprouvaient les Kanehsata'kehró:non, le gouvernement alla de l'avant et la décréta quand même. Le peuple ne fut pas consulté parce qu'il n'aurait jamais été d'accord. Il n'est pas étonnant que, non seulement les problèmes ne disparurent pas, mais les tensions qui en découlaient s'intensifièrent aussi.

À L'USAGE ET AU BÉNÉFICE DES GOLFEURS

À la fin des années 1950, la municipalité d'Oka décida de construire un club de golf privé dans la pinède de Kanehsatà:ke, sur des terres antérieurement appelées la Commune. Même si ces terres n'étaient plus utilisées comme pâturage, le peuple de Kanehsatà:ke s'en servaient toujours pour une multitude d'activités. Les plans de la municipalité allaient réserver une grande partie de la Commune à l'usage et au bénéfice exclusifs des membres du club de golf d'Oka.

En 1959, la municipalité obtint un projet de loi émanant d'un député dans la législature du Québec qui lui permettait de commencer la construction. Cela se fit facilement parce que le projet de loi fut déposé par le premier ministre, Paul Sauvé. « La capacité d'Oka d'obtenir la législation spéciale s'expliquait peut-être par le fait que la municipalité et l'étendue de terre en question se trouvaient dans la circonscription électorale du premier ministre ».[100] Le peuple de Kanehsatà:ke ne fut pas avisé du projet de loi et n'eut aucune chance de s'y opposer. Légalement, le projet de loi aurait pu être rejeté en moins d'un an par le gouvernement fédéral. Émile Colas, avocat des Kanehsata'kehró:non, déclara ce qui suit au comité mixte du Sénat et de la Chambre des communes sur les affaires indiennes :

> Le 1er juin 1960, nous avons écrit au ministre de la Citoyenneté et de l'Immigration à propos de cette question. Nous avons fourni au gouvernement fédéral tout le raison-nement juridique qui lui permettrait de rejeter le projet de loi. À ce moment-là, on nous a dit : "Ce n'est plus le ministère des Affaires indiennes, mais le ministère de la Justice qui s'en occupe." Et quelques jours avant que le ministre de la Justice quitte le conseil, il nous a donné une réponse d'une page où il disait : "Nous ne croyons pas que c'est le rôle du ministère de la Justice de rejeter ce projet de loi en particulier."[101]

Les Kanehsata'kehró:non n'eurent d'autre choix que d'écrire à un ministère après l'autre dans l'espoir de trouver une façon de faire avorter le projet du club de golf. Chaque fois qu'ils écrivaient à une nouvelle personne, on les recommandait à quelqu'un d'autre. Sans qu'ils ne s'en rendent compte, une année s'était écoulée, et le gouvernement fédéral avait refusé de rejeter le projet de loi. En mars 1961, une délégation de Kanehsatà:ke comparut devant le comité mixte pour exposer sa cause.

> Nous, Mohawks des six nations de Kanehsatà:ke, du Lac des Deux-Montagnes, tenons le gouvernement canadien responsable de notre détresse actuelle [...] En restant criminellement silencieux devant l'injustice, le gouvernement est aussi léga-lement et moralement coupable que ceux qui ont commis l'injustice, même s'il n'a pas lui-même pris part aux procédures [...] Depuis plus d'un siècle, la controverse sur cette terre est débattue à notre détriment. Nous nous sommes opposés à une organisation beaucoup plus riche et beaucoup plus influente que nous. Chaque fois, nos appels ont été étouffés et contrecarrés et nos droits ignorés. Cette fois, renversons l'ordre habituel et laissons la justice prévaloir.

> Chef James, Sakokate Montour

> et Samuel Sohenrese Nicholas

La plupart des membres du comité furent sympathiques, mais ils ne firent rien pour arrêter le projet du club de golf ni pour aider de quelque façon le peuple de Kanehsatà:ke. En ce qui concerne la demande de James Montour et de Samuel Nicholas, à savoir que justice soit faite, les Kanehsata'kehró:non attendent toujours.

Hommes dans un camp de bûcheron
Collection de Gordie Oke

La Commune
Collection de René Marinier

Conseil des tribus
Collection d'Helen Simon

La Commune – L'Annonciation
Collection de René Marinier

Collection de Gary Carbonnell

À Doncaster
Collection de Raymond Gabriel

[1] Interrogatoire des témoins, le 9 mai 1909, Centre national des arts, RG 10, vol. 2030, dossier 8946 pt. 4.

[2] Ibid.

[3] Maître Geoffrion au surintendant général des Affaires indiennes, 20 octobre 1907, Centre national des arts, RG 10, vol. 2030, dossier 8946 pt. 4.

[4] Native Studies Review p. 33 ou Centre national des arts, MG 26, Papers of Sir Wilfrid Laurier, vol. 791G, dossier 225747, (copie) W. Laurier à Clifford Sifton, 17 novembre 1902.

[5] Même si, depuis l'arrivée des prêtres en 1721, les Kanehsata'kehró:non ont souvent été victimes de plusieurs types de violence, particulièrement après 1840, ils ont rarement agi de manière violente envers leur entourage qui est venu et a dérobé leurs terres.

[6] Ce n'est qu'en 1973 que le gouvernement a introduit une nouvelle politique de revendications territoriales. Kanehsatà:ke, Kahnawake et Akwesasne soumirent une revendication complète basée sur l'occupation ancestrale.

[7] Mémorandum de Pedley à M. Sifton, 19 février 1903, Centre national des arts, RG 10, vol. 2031, dossier 8946X-1.

[8] Leet à Pedley, 25 mars 1903, Centre national des arts, RG 10, vol. 2031, dossier 8946X-1.

[9] Mémorandum de Pedley à M. Sifton, 19 février 1903, Centre national des arts, RG 10, vol. 2031, dossier 8946X-1.

[10] Pedley à Leet, correspondance confidentielle, 24 février 1903, Centre national des arts, RG 10, vol. 2031, dossier 8946X-1.

[11] Leet à Pedley, 25 mars 1903, Centre national des arts, RG 10, vol. 2031, dossier 8946x-1.

[12] Jos. Perillard au secrétaire du département des Affaires indiennes, 3 juin 1909, Centre national des arts, RG 10, vol. 2037, dossier 8946-7.

[13] Geoffrion à F. Pedley, 4 juin 1909, Centre national des arts, RG 10, vol. 2037, dossier 8946-7.

[14] Jos. Perillard au département des Affaires indiennes, 3 juin 1909, Centre national des arts, RG 10, vol. 2037, dossier 8946-7.

[15] Chef Baptiste Gaspé à Frank Pedley, 11 juin 1909, Centre national des arts, RG 10, vol. 2037, dossier 8946-7.

[16] H. Giroux au lieutenant-colonel A. P. Sherwood, C.M.G., 18 juin 1909, Centre national des arts, RG 10, vol. 2037, dossier 8946-7.

[17] Leet à Pedley, 30 mars 1903, Centre national des arts, RG 10, vol. 2031, dossier 8946X-1.

[18] Leet à Pedley, 24 avril 1903, Centre national des arts, RG 10, vol. 2031, dossier 8946X-1.

[19] Pedley à Leet, 19 mai 1903, Centre national des arts, RG 10, vol. 2031, dossier 8946X-1.

[20] Leet à Pedley, 16 mai 1903, Centre national des arts, RG 10, vol. 2031, dossier 8946X-1, 1903-1908.

[21] Lettre de Smith, 7 octobre 1904, Centre national des arts, RG 10, vol. 2031, dossier 8946X-1.

[22] Ibid.

[23] Smith à Rowell, 30 septembre 1904, Centre national des arts, RG 10, vol. 2031, dossier 8946X-1.

[24] Ibid.

[25] Sir Wilfrid Laurier au séminaire, Centre national des arts. M1650, Urgel Lafontaine, cahier 21, p. 231-244.

[26] Aimé Geoffrion à Sir Wilfrid Laurier, 27 juin 1905, Centre national des arts, RG 10, vol. 2031, dossier 8946x pt. 1.

[27] Maître Geoffrion à M. Lecoq, supérieur du séminaire, 3 juillet 1905, A. S. S. Montréal, n° 297.

[28] Laurier à Geoffrion, 7 décembre 1905, A. S. S. S., Montréeal, n° 299.

[29] R. C. Smith à E. L. Newcombe, 20 mars 1908, RG 13, vol. 2432, dossier A500.

[30] S. W. Laurier à Geoffrion, Ottawa, 6 juin 1905, Centre national des arts, C823, vol. 368, p. 98 186.

[31] Geoffrion à S. W. Laurier, 22 octobre 1905, Centre national des arts, C827, vol. 384, p. 10 2310.

[32] Pedley à Geoffrion, 6 mai 1907, Centre national des arts, RG 10, vol. 2031, dossier 8946x pt. 1.

[33] Geoffrion à Pedley, 29 mai 1907, Centre national des arts, RG 10, vol. 2031, dossier 8946x pt. 1.

[34] Smith à Pedley, 7 octobre 1907, Centre national des arts, RG 10, vol. 2031, dossier 8946x pt. 1.

[35] Ibid.

[36] Pedley à Smith, 9 octobre 1907, Centre national des arts, RG 10, vol. 2031, dossier 8946x pt.1.

[37] R. C. Smith à Frank Pedley Esq., 10 octobre 1907, Centre national des arts, RG 10, vol. 2031, dossier 8946x pt.1.

[38] Rowell à Geoffrion, 30 octobre 1907, Centre national des arts, RG 10, vol. 2031, dossier 8946x pt.1.

[39] E. L. Newcombe à Frank Pedley, 7 janvier 1908, Centre national des arts, RG 10, vol. 2031, dossier 8946x pt.1.

[40] Ibid.

[41] R. C. Smith à E. L. Newcombe, 26 novembre 1907, Centre national des arts, RG 13, vol. 2432, dossier A500.

[42] Du conseil de la santé de la paroisse de l'Annonciation, village d'Oka, au maire et au conseil de la paroisse de l'Annonciation, 30 juillet 1905, Centre national des arts, RG 10, vol. 3097, dossier 297070.

[43] Ibid.

[44] Ibid.

[45] Maire Léon Clermont et le conseil à l'Honorable M. Pedley, 9 juillet 1906, Centre national des arts, RG 10, vol. 3097, dossier 297070.

[46] Déposition d'Angus Corinthe, Centre national des arts, RG 10, vol. 2030, dossier 8946 pt. 4.

[47] Traduction, Oka, 29 mai 1876, Centre national des arts, RG 10, vol. 1988, dossier 6492.

[48] Déposition d'Angus Corinthe, Centre national des arts, RG 10, vol. 2030, dossier 8946 pt. 4, p. 39-42.

[49] Ibid., p. 38.

[50] Ibid., p. 35.

[51] J. D. McLean à Jos. Perillard, 27 avril, Centre national des arts, RG 10, vol. 3097, dossier 297070.

[52] Conseil municipal à Frank Pedley, 9 juillet 1906, Centre national des arts, RG 10, vol. 3097, dossier 297070.

[53] Déposition d'Angus Corinthe, Centre national des arts, RG 10, vol. 2030, dossier 8946 pt. 4, p. 35.

[54] Mémorandum au surintendant général, 27 mars 1907, Centre national des arts, RG 10, vol. 3097, dossier 297070.

[55] Constable A. Marcoux au commissaire de police du Dominion, 5 juillet 1907, Centre national des arts, RG 10, vol. 3097, dossier 297070.

[56] Déclaration du plaignant, province de Québec, district de Terrebonne, 20 mars 1908, Centre national des arts, RG 10, vol. 2031, dossier 8946x pt. 1.

[57] Note aux Indiens d'Oka de E. L. Newcombe, 4 février 1908, Centre national des arts, RG 13, vol. 2432, dossier A 500.

[58] R. C. Smith à E. L. Newcombe, 20 mars 1908, Centre national des arts, RG 13, vol. 2432, dossier A500.

[59] Dépositions des témoins, Centre national des arts, RG 10, vol. 2030, dossier 8946 pt. 4.

[60] Justice A-500, dossier RG 13, vol. 2432, registre des procédures, vol. 1, p. 7-9.

[61] N. W. Rowell à E. L. Newcombe, 20 avril 1912, Centre national des arts, RG 13, vol. 2409, dossier 115711916.

[62] À la Cour supérieure, le juge de paix Hutchinson présente le jugement n° 2001, Centre national des arts, RG 13, vol. 2432, dossier A500.

[63] Ibid.

[64] Notes du juge Carrol, 29 décembre 1911, Centre national des arts, RG 13, vol. 2432, dossier A500, Trans, B. G.

[65] Notes du juge de paix Cross, 5 janvier 1912, RG 13, vol. 2342, dossier A500.

[66] Ibid.

[67] Ibid.

[68] Jugement des juges du comité judiciaire du Conseil privé sur l'appel d'Angus Corinthe et autres contre les ecclésiastiques du séminaire de Saint-Sulpice de Montréal, de la Cour suprême de la province de Québec (appel), livré le 19 juillet 1912, Centre national des arts, RG 13, vol. 2437, dossier A500.

[69] J. R. Miller, *Great White Father Knows Best: Oka and the Land Claims Process, Native Studies Review*, vol. 7, 1er novembre 1991, p. 35.

[70] J. D. McLean au ministre de la Justice, 5 novembre 1912, Centre national des arts, RG 13, vol. 2342, dossier A500.

[71] Mémorandum pour M. Gisborne, 8 novembre 1912, Centre national des arts, RG 13, vol. 2432, dossier A500.

[72] W. Smith à E. L. Newcombe, 19 novembre 1912, Centre national des arts, RG 13, vol. 2432, dossier A500.

[73] N. W. Rowell à Duncan Campbell Scott (copie non datée), Centre national des arts, RG 13, vol. 2409, dossier 115711916.

[74] Ibid.

[75] E. L. Newcombe à Duncan C. Scott, 29 mars 1915, Centre national des arts, RG 13, vol. 2409, dossier 115711916.

[76] Ibid.

[77] J. R. Miller, *Great White Father Knows Best: Oka and the Land Claims Process, Native Studies Review*, vol. 7, n° 1, p. 36.

[78] Bernard Bourdon à T. A. Crerar, 2 janvier 1942, Centre national des arts, RG 13, vol. 2437, dossier A500.

[79] T. A. Crerar aux fiduciaires des propriétés commerciales de Saint-Sulpice, 10 décembre 1941, Centre national des arts, RG 13, vol. 2432, dossier A500.

[80] Ibid.

[81] Charles Camsell au ministre de la Justice, 12 juin 1942, Centre national des arts, RG 13, vol. 2437, dossier A500.

[82] Mémorandum pour le ministre de la Justice, 12 août 1942, Centre national des arts, RG 13, vol. 2342, dossier A500.

[83] Compagnie immobilière pour favoriser l'agriculture au directeur du ministère des Affaires indiennes et du ministère des Mines et des Ressources, Oka, 3 juillet 1942, Centre national des arts, RG 13, vol. 2342, dossier A500.

[84] C. W. Jackson à Pierre Roche Esq., 24 juillet 1942, Centre national des arts, RG 13, vol. 2342, dossier A500.

[85] Bernard Bourden à l'Honorable T. A. Crerar, 3 août 1942, Centre national des arts, RG 13, vol. 2342, dossier A500.

[86] Mémorandum : A500, 16 octobre 1942, Centre national des arts, RG 13, vol. 2342, dossier A500.

[87] Ibid.

[88] Charles Camsell à F. P. Varcoe, Esq., 7 décembre 1942, Centre national des arts, RG 13, vol. 2342, dossier A500.

[89] Ibid.

[90] Mémorandum pour le ministre, 5 janvier 1943, Centre national des arts, RG 13, vol. 2342, dossier A500.

[91] Ibid.

[92] T. A. Crerar à l'Honorable L. S. Saint-Laurent K. C., ministre de la Justice, 28 septembre 1943, Centre national des arts, RG 13, vol. 2342, dossier A500.

[93] Ibid.

[94] Mémorandum pour le ministre, 7 octobre 1943, Centre national des arts, RG 13, vol. 2342, dossier A500.

[95] Ibid.

[96] Exemplaire authentique du procès verbal d'une réunion du comité du Conseil privé, approuvé par son Excellence le gouverneur général, le 2 avril 1945, RG 13, vol. 2342, dossier A500.

[97] Ibid.

[98] Victor Morin à E. Miall, 15 mai 1945, Centre national des arts, RG 13, vol. 2347, dossier A500.

[99] P.C.2124(a) entre Sa Majesté le roi et les prêtres de Saint-Sulpice, Centre national des arts, RG 13, vol. 2342, dossier A500.

[100] J. R. Miller, *Great White Father Knows Best: Oka And The Land Claims Process, Native Studies Review.* 7 novembre 1991, p. 37.

[101] Comité mixte du Sénat et de la Chambre des communes sur les affaires indiennes, 1960-1961, p. 8, D. I. A. N. D., section de recherche historique, classeur Oka.

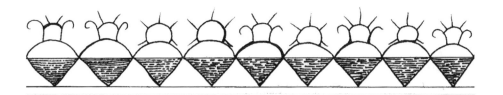

CHAPITRE 11

INCIDENTS À LA PINÈDE

LE RETOUR DES AIGLES

Il y a bien longtemps, beaucoup d'aigles vivaient sur mon sommet, mais ils ont tranquillement quitté le territoire. J'ignore où ils sont allés. Cependant, un jour, ils sont revenus et ont peu à peu reconstruit leurs nids. Les premiers Kanehsata'kehró:non qui les ont vus se sont réjouis de leur retour. Mais ceux qui connaissaient les traditions se rappelaient que c'est l'aigle qui les avertit de dangers imminents. C'est pourquoi beaucoup de Kanehsata'kehró:non attendaient et se préparaient; ils ne prenaient pas ces avertissements à la légère.

En effet, la terre appelait à l'aide, et le peuple a entendu et s'est levé pour défendre leur mère la terre. Le sol sur lequel ils marchaient, les arbres qui les entouraient, les cours d'eau, les animaux, les oiseaux, toute la force de la vie du monde naturel leur donnait la vision et la solution dont ils avaient besoin. Ils allaient la défendre ou tomber. Néanmoins, ils honoreraient leurs ancêtres et resteraient comme le Créateur les avait faits, des Onkwehón:we, les gardiens de la terre.

Beaucoup de choses sont arrivées. Les yeux des petits enfants étaient remplis de consternation et de crainte. Même aujourd'hui, ils poussent des cris dans leur sommeil, ils tremblent toujours nerveusement.

Mes paroles ne sont que des paroles, mais si vous les écoutez avec votre cœur, vous ressentirez les émotions que le peuple a ressenties. Vous humerez l'odeur du pin en voyageant avec eux. Vous connaîtrez la peur et peut-être que vous découvrirez quelque vérité pour vous aider à être une meilleure personne.

Mon temps pour raconter des histoires est maintenant terminé. Je m'installe encore une fois pour veiller sur le peuple. Voici venir leurs voix. Elles font partie du cycle de sept générations et sont le pont entre les ancêtres et les enfants à naître. Écoutez une fois de plus le son du hochet et celui du tambour d'eau, alors que beaucoup de cœurs battent en harmonie.

THÓ NIKAWÉN:NAKE

ET ÇA RECOMMENCE

En 1989, le peuple de Kanehsatà:ke apprit que la municipalité d'Oka prévoyait agrandir son terrain de golf privé de neuf trous à dix-huit trous. Elle n'avisa pas officiellement les Kanehsata'kehró:non ni ne les consulta d'aucune façon, malgré le fait qu'elle comptait réaliser l'agrandissement sur leur cimetière, une terre qu'ils avaient à maintes reprises revendiquée depuis des siècles. Elle ne sentit aucune obligation de le faire puisqu'elle ne leur reconnaissait aucun droit ancestral à la terre. Cette manifestation d'arrogance était simplement le dernier exemple de la manière tyrannique dont les intérêts des Kanehsata'kehró:non avaient été ignorés.

Le peuple organisa plusieurs marches de protestation pacifiques, mais n'obtint aucun engagement de la part du gouvernement pour régler la question.[1] Mis au pied du mur, les Kanehsata'kehró:non décidèrent, au cours de l'hiver 1990, de protéger leur ancien cimetière et la forêt de pins de la Commune. En mars 1990, plusieurs personnes commencèrent à occuper la pinède et à bloquer un chemin de terre y donnant accès. La municipalité d'Oka fit une demande d'injonction contre les manifestants et l'obtint.

À ce moment-là, il y avait beaucoup de discussions au sein de la communauté pour décider du type et de l'étendue de la mesure à prendre. Cependant, une chose était certaine : il n'y aurait pas de terrain de golf construit sur le cimetière. La municipalité ne prendrait plus de terre à la communauté.

À mesure que les événements se déroulaient, on faisait grand état des divisions au sein de la communauté pour essayer d'augmenter le clivage de ses membres. Le gouvernement et les médias prétendaient qu'il était inhabituel pour des membres d'un même groupe d'avoir des opinions différentes sur certaines questions. Comme s'ils pouvaient affirmer que dans la société des Blancs tout le monde était toujours d'accord sur tout. (Si c'était le cas, on n'aurait pas besoin de tous ces partis politiques, Églises, syndicats, groupes d'intérêts particuliers, etc.).

Au printemps, l'occupation de la pinède fut une longue et solitaire manifestation pour ceux qui y prirent part. Même si la majorité du peuple les appuyait, plusieurs étaient physiquement incapables de participer à l'occupation. D'autres appuyèrent les occupants en leur donnant de la nourriture ou en passant les voir avec du café et des mots d'encouragement. Certains se tinrent à l'écart parce que les médias rapportaient la présence d'armes dans la pinède. Les docteurs Dubé et Imbeau, résidents du village et membres fondateurs du Regroupement des citoyens d'Oka (RCO)[2], avaient allégué que des hommes armés dans la pinède les avaient menacés, et ces allégations furent rapportées comme si elles étaient des faits.

En réalité, ces rapports furent publiés longtemps avant qu'il y ait des armes dans la pinède. Après réflexion, ils semblent avoir été conçus pour empêcher tout soutien au mouvement.[3] Cette stratégie réussit pour un temps, comme toutes les stratégies ultérieures, à miner la solidarité des Kanehsata'kehró:non.

Durant tout le printemps, les occupants de la pinède firent de nombreux efforts pour initier un processus de négociation en vue de régler le conflit. Une fois de plus, leurs efforts échouèrent. En juin 1990, la municipalité d'Oka reçut une deuxième injonction contre les manifestants dans la pinède. En juillet, le maire d'Oka demanda à la Sûreté du Québec de faire respecter l'injonction et de disperser les occupants de la pinède pour que la construction du terrain de golf puisse débuter. Le 11 juillet, deux jours après l'expiration de l'injonction, la Sûreté du Québec attaqua la petite barricade érigée sur le chemin de terre accédant à la route 344 à Kanehsatà:ke.[4]

Aucun effort ne fut fait pour disperser pacifiquement les gens assemblés dans la pinède. La police utilisa plutôt des gaz lacrymogènes, des grenades à concussion et, finalement, ouvrit le feu sur les occupants. En quelques minutes, presque tout le monde de Kanehsatà:ke se rassembla dans la pinède. Le peuple de Kahnawà:ke bloqua le pont Mercier en signe de solidarité avec les Kanehsata'kehró:non. Un échange de coups de feu survint entre la Sûreté du Québec et les occupants. Durant l'échange, le caporal Marcel Lemay de la Sûreté du Québec fut atteint d'une balle et mourut. La Sûreté du Québec battit rapidement en retraite, laissant derrière un chargeur sur roues et plusieurs véhicules de la police.

Les Kanehsata'kehró:non agirent rapidement pour fortifier leur position et se défendre contre une autre attaque. Quelques heures après le raid matinal, environ 2500 agents de police convergèrent vers les territoires Kanien'kehà:ka de Kanehsatà:ke et de Kahnawà:ke. Akwesasne avait déjà été occupé par trois différentes forces de police pendant plusieurs mois. Avant la fin de l'été, 4000 soldats des Forces armées du Canada avaient été envoyés dans la région. La saison qui allait plus tard être décrite comme un « été indien » chaud et long avait commencé.

Pour beaucoup de Canadiens, les événements de l'été 1990 semblaient sans précédent dans l'histoire du pays. En fait, tout ce qui arriva cet été-là trouve des parallèles dans l'histoire de Kanehsatà:ke et dans celle des peuples autochtones dans tout le Canada. L'attitude qui prévalait au sein des divers paliers de gouvernement, de la police et des forces armées relativement aux questions soulevées était simplement la continuation d'un modèle historique : l'évitement. Ils avaient régulièrement évité de traiter honnêtement des questions tout en détournant l'attention du public en manipulant l'information et en propageant la méfiance et la peur.

Durant la crise de 1990, le gouvernement fédéral tenta de présenter un grief historique légitime comme une activité terroriste et criminelle. Dans une conférence de presse tenue le 23 juillet 1990, Harry Swain, ministre des Affaires indiennes, essaya de dépeindre les « Warriors » comme une organisation criminelle qui avait pris en otage les communautés de Kahnawà:ke et de Kanehsatà:ke. Il décrit la crise comme une insurrection par un groupe armé.[5]

Au moyen d'une campagne de relations publiques de plusieurs millions de dollars, le gouvernement fédéral essaya de transformer la question de droits territoriaux en une menace de contrebande de cigarettes et de jeu illégal. Il fut plus tard rapporté qu'il avait dépensé, relativement à la crise, plus de huit millions de dollars en relations publiques. Le gouvernement réussit dans une certaine mesure à déshumaniser les Kanehsata'kehró:non en les dépeignant comme des voyous, des criminels et des terroristes et, ridiculement, comme des immigrants illégaux. Le premier ministre Brian Mulroney, qui resta ostensiblement indifférent à la situation, émergea assez longtemps pour accuser les Kanien'kehà:ka, dont plusieurs n'étaient même pas Canadiens, d'être des criminels et des terroristes,.[6]

Tandis que les politiciens du Québec présentaient les Kanien'kehà:ka comme une menace à la souveraineté, des représentants des médias québécois incitaient activement la population à la haine et au racisme contre eux. Gilles Proulx, commentateur à la station radiophonique CJMS, exprima souvent en onde des sentiments racistes anti-Mohawks, suscitant la peur et la haine parmi les auditeurs francophones. Beaucoup croient que ses excitations furent directement responsables du lancement des pierres, à Lasalle, sur le convoi des Kanien'kehà:ka qui quittait Kahnawà:ke. Tandis que la police freinait le convoi sur le pont Mercier, Proulx entraînait ses auditeurs dans une frénésie. Au moment où la police permit au convoi de passer, une grande foule en colère qui s'était assemblée lança des pierres sur les gens dans les voitures qui circulaient. Plusieurs furent blessés et un homme âgé mourut deux jours plus tard.

Proulx ne fut pas le seul à rapporter les événements de manière irresponsable et provocatrice. Plusieurs journaux montréalais présentèrent aussi les gens et les événements sous un faux jour pour faire un reportage à sensation et discréditer le peuple qui luttait pour leur terre. Un éditorial publié dans *The Montreal Gazette*, le 17 juillet 1990, décrivait les Warriors comme des « mafioso » qui tenaient les trois communautés Kanien'kehà:ka « sous la menace d'une arme pour extorquer ce qu'ils veulent ». On y lisait : « Ils ont le plus souvent utilisé leur puissance armée pour obtenir un empire sordide d'activités illégales : le jeu (par des casinos à Akwesasne et le bingo à Kahnawà:ke) et la vente de cigarettes de contrebande hors-taxe ».[7] De tels éditoriaux, basés évidemment que sur une connaissance superficielle des faits, donnaient délibérément une fausse image du peuple impliqué dans la crise afin de le discréditer et détournaient l'attention du public de la question des droits territoriaux.

On refusa au peuple de Kanehsatà:ke, de Kahnawà:ke et d'Akwesasne l'accès à la nourriture, à des soins médicaux et à des conseillers juridiques et spirituels. Plusieurs furent arrêtés sans raison légitime, retenus sans accusations et violentés pendant qu'ils étaient détenus. Du 12 au 25 juillet 1990, la Commission des droits de la personne du Québec répondit à plus de cinquante appels de personnes affirmant que leurs droits avaient été violés.[8] La Commission trouva que ces allégations étaient suffisamment sérieuses pour dépêcher des représentants à Kanehsatà:ke afin qu'ils se penchent sur la question. Pendant plusieurs jours, la Sûreté du Québec les empêcha d'entrer à Kanehsatà:ke, mais quand on le leur permit finalement, ils constatèrent que les Mohawks étaient les seuls qui n'avaient pas accès à la nourriture et aux médicaments. À la fin de juillet, John Ciacca déclara : « Il n'a jamais été question de les priver de nourriture ».[9] Seulement quelques jours plus tôt, soit le 21 juillet, Claude Ryan disait que la décision d'empêcher la nourriture d'entrer dans les communautés était une politique gouvernementale officielle et non un acte de vengeance de la part de la police.[10] Ainsi, pendant que les gouvernements canadien et québécois démentaient ces faits devant la communauté internationale et leurs propres citoyens, les Kanien'kehà:ka étaient privés de leurs droits fondamentaux.

Plusieurs hommes, y compris Angus Jacobs et Daniel Nicholas, reçurent des menaces et furent battus par la police pendant leur détention. On leur interdit de communiquer avec leur famille et leur avocat et on les força à signer des feuilles de papier vierges sans leur dire pourquoi ils étaient détenus. Aux postes de contrôle de la police, on retenait les Kanien'kehà:ka plus longtemps que les Blancs, souvent en pointant des fusils sur leur tête pendant qu'on fouillait et refouillait leur véhicule. Certains furent fouillés à nu en pleine rue, à la vue des curieux. Les mesures que les Kanien'kehà:ka prirent pour protéger la terre à Kanehsatà:ke furent criminalisées et plusieurs furent obligés de comparaître devant les tribunaux canadiens. Tandis qu'un bon nombre furent acquittés de toutes accusations, d'autres servirent d'exemples.

Cinq ans plus tard, le peuple n'avait toujours pas obtenu justice, et la question territoriale à Kanehsatà:ke n'était pas réglée.

Pendant les 78 jours de siège, des milliers d'autochtones de partout sur l'île de la Tortue (Amérique du Nord) vinrent à Kanehsatà:ke et à Kahnawà:ke dans les camps de la paix et les bunkers pour exprimer leur appui. Beaucoup d'autres tinrent des manifestations et bloquèrent des routes dans leur propre communauté en solidarité avec les Kanehsata'kehró:non.

Même si les événements de 1990 furent rapportés et enregistrés de diverses manières, peu fut raconté sur la vie quotidienne des gens qui vécurent ces événements. À mesure que la situation évoluait d'une manière souvent surréelle et choquante, les Kanehsata'kehró:non n'eurent d'autre choix que de réagir, parfois par la colère ou la peur, avec prudence, et souvent avec humour. Ils furent forcés de faire des choix difficiles pour eux-mêmes et leur famille. Pour certains, cela signifiait rester jusqu'à la fin quelle qu'elle soit. D'autres, confrontés à la menace d'une intervention militaire à grande échelle, n'eurent d'autre choix que de partir. Tout le peuple de Kanehsatà:ke (Kahnawà:ke et Akwesasne) perdit ses droits humains et vit sa survie menacée. Il fut forcé de traiter quotidiennement avec le racisme, la propagande haineuse, la brutalité policière et fut privé de nourriture et de soins médicaux. Chaque acteur de la crise doit être reconnu, quel que fût son rôle. Voici quelques-uns de leurs témoignages.

Témoignages du peuple

☐ « Tout ce qui est arrivé nous a forcés à défendre ce en quoi nous croyons. C'était à peu près temps. La chose la plus choquante a été le raid de la police. Nous avons essayé d'empêcher le camion de monter la colline, mais les policiers nous ont dit qu'ils allaient nous arrêter. Ils sont montés et nous avons entendu des coups de feu. Nous sommes morts cette journée-là.

« Nous avions toujours peur. Quand les médias parlaient du Treatment Center (Centre de réadaptation), nous étions inquiets. Même aujourd'hui, je ressens la même chose envers la Sureté du Québec, mais je suis fier que le peuple se soit levé. Si cela devait se reproduire, je me joindrais à eux, mais cette fois nous sommes restés pour nous assurer de tout voir. Nous faisions notre possible pour aider au cas où un problème arriverait. Quand les gens sont sortis de la pinède, c'était à la fois un jour de fierté et de tristesse. Ils étaient toujours fiers de ce qu'ils avaient fait, mais également tristes à cause de la façon dont ils ont été traités. Même aujourd'hui, les larmes me montent aux yeux quand j'y repense. »

☐ « La pire chose pour moi a été l'écrasante présence de la Sûreté du Québec et de l'armée. Même aujourd'hui, quand je passe près du traversier, je peux encore voir les agents de la SQ avec leurs fusils. Rien ne pouvait être pire que ça. À mon avis, ils ont joué un rôle important et très redoutable. J'étais tellement inquiet. On ne savait pas ce qu'ils allaient faire : tirer ou quoi? Allaient-ils envahir nos maisons? Ou faire autre chose? »

☐ « J'étais prise à Montréal. Je ne pouvais pas revenir à la maison et voir ma mère. C'était dur de suivre les événements à la télé; c'était toujours dramatique. Ma mère me rassurait tout le temps. À mon travail, la fille du propriétaire était mariée à un agent de la SQ. Avant la crise, elle avait toujours été aimable, mais maintenant elle me faisait payer la facture. Elle blâmait "les sauvages" pour tout. Ça me ramenait 25 ans en arrière, je subissais de la haine et du racisme.

« La chose la plus difficile a été de perdre ma mère. Si ce n'était pas de la crise, elle vivrait probablement aujourd'hui. Elle ne voulait pas partir, mais quand l'armée est arrivée, elle est allée vivre à Ottawa. Et quand elle a téléphoné chez elle, c'est un militaire qui a répondu au téléphone. Elle en a été très bouleversée, et après cela son état de santé s'est détérioré. Elle n'a plus jamais été la même. »

☐ « Je me souviens des fusils de la police et du harcèlement. J'avais de la difficulté à dormir; on ne savait jamais si on allait se réveiller. On se sentait comme des proies. On est partis durant les deux dernières semaines. On pensait bien avoir la paix, mais non. La police savait où chacun se trouvait, et elle nous surveillait toujours beaucoup et nous harcelait. On recevait des contraventions pour la moindre chose. Si une personne était de la mauvaise couleur ou portait trop de colliers, on l'arrêtait. Si j'avais su que mon père et mon frère allaient bien, je me serais mieux senti. Je me faisais du souci pour eux plus que toute autre chose. »

☐ « Quand je songe à cette période-là, je me rappelle que les barbelés en ont fait une réalité bien difficile. J'ai réalisé que l'armée nous tenait vraiment en otage. Je m'inquiétais des gens d'ici. Je n'avais pas le droit de rendre visite à ma tante. Cela me dérangeait beaucoup.

« Les gens ne me voyaient pas comme une autochtone. Une fois, alors que j'étais chez Zellers, il y a eu une panne électrique. Une femme m'a regardée et a dit que c'était probablement à cause "des sauvages". Après cela, je n'ai plus jamais été la même. Je voyais la police et les autorités sous un autre jour. »

☐ « J'ai eu mon premier choc quand le caporal Lemay a été tué. Ma préoccupation immédiate a été : "Ils vont nous massacrer." Je n'étais pas dans les environs et pas vraiment au courant de ce qui se passait. »

☐ « Ce qui m'a vraiment frappé a été le nombre de personnes qui sont parties plutôt que de rester sur place et de faire front commun. Personne ne voulait que les arbres soient coupés ni que le terrain de golf soit agrandi. Cependant, je n'ai rien contre eux parce la peur est si différente pour chacun. J'étais surtout étonné. Je suis allé voir qui restait à Kanehsatà:ke, et quand j'ai vu, je ne pouvais pas en croire mes yeux. C'était comme un village fantôme. C'était incroyable […]. »

☐ « Nous avons quitté la communauté parce que nous pensions qu'on nous avait oubliés. Tout semblait changer, dont la raison pour laquelle nous étions là. Nous entendions parler de tous les événements par les médias, mais nous ne savions pas vraiment ce qui se passait. Nous avons cru qu'il n'y avait aucune raison de rester. »

☐ « À l'intérieur des barricades, il y avait un vrai bel esprit communautaire qui facilitait les négociations avec l'armée et la SQ. Les gens qui sont restés devaient appuyer la lutte. Nous avions l'impression que, si nous partions, la SQ et l'armée auraient la liberté de faire comme bon leur semble. Nous étions des intermédiaires pour protéger le territoire. Ce qui m'a vraiment frappé a été la cupidité des diverses factions politiques dans la poursuite de leur propre programme. »

☐ « J'ai vu beaucoup de bonnes choses. À ce moment-là, les gens se sont unis pour défendre une cause commune : la terre. Les gens respectaient la terre, le Créateur et eux-mêmes. Ils sont devenus plus conscients de ce qui se passait. Avant cela, ils étaient dans une sorte de limbes, mais ils ont commencé à prendre conscience de leur identité et à être fiers d'eux. Ce qui était difficile à voir est jusqu'à quel point le gouvernement est allé pour diviser le peuple. »

☐ « L'aspect positif dont je me souviens est les gens qui sont restés jusqu'à la fin. Il faut leur tirer notre chapeau. D'autres avaient leur raison de partir, mais c'est grâce à ceux qui sont restés que nous avons été victorieux. Les traditionalistes ont vraiment changé ma façon de penser.

« Ce qui m'écœure vraiment, c'est toutes les conneries qui ont suivi. Le peuple doit apprendre à rester uni et à travailler ensemble. »

☐ « Ce que je retiens le plus dans tout ça, c'est ma part en tant que femme mohawk. Donner, partager, être présente dans la communauté, rester jusqu'à la fin est devenu ma responsabilité. La crise m'a vraiment frappée en pleine figure, brassé la cage. On ne peut pas se promener et dire qu'on est Mohawk sans en prendre la responsabilité […]. Il y avait aussi la tranquillité à l'intérieur des barricades. J'ai parfois une forte envie d'éprouver ce sentiment parce que je sais qu'il est toujours là parmi nous. »

☐ « Je suis partie pour l'école le 8 juillet, et le mercredi 11 juillet est arrivé. J'étais dans ma classe quand j'ai reçu un message me disant de téléphoner à la maison. La première chose que j'ai vue à la télé a été les coups de feu. On n'avait pas encore annoncé que quelqu'un avait été tué. J'ai rappelé à la maison, mais personne n'y était. J'ai téléphoné à ma mère, et elle m'a dit que la SQ avait attaqué le peuple. La seule chose qui m'a aidée à garder mon calme était la présence des gens avec qui j'étais; j'étais entourée de conseillers. Je voulais seulement sortir de là. J'ai passé toute la journée rien qu'à essayer de garder mon équilibre mental.

« Je n'avais pas eu de nouvelles de ma famille ni de personne dans la pinède. Plus tard, on me répétait tout le temps que tout allait bien, mais je ne pouvais pas les voir ni les entendre. Je me serais mieux sentie si j'avais été là. Quand j'ai finalement réussi à parler à quelqu'un, on m'a dit qu'ils étaient contents que toute la communauté se soit pointée. Cela voulait dire beaucoup pour eux.

« Je ne peux pas décrire mes sentiments parce que j'étais à l'extérieur. C'est comme si j'avais été jetée dans un puits profond. Je ne voyais aucun moyen d'en sortir, je n'apercevais pas le bord du puits. Il m'a fallu environ trois jours pour me remettre du choc. »

☐ « Quand la crise est survenue, je travaillais à Ottawa. Une de mes collègues est venue vers moi et m'a demandé ce qui se passait à Oka. Elle avait entendu dire que quelqu'un avait été tué. J'ai téléphoné à ma mère, et elle m'a raconté ce qui était arrivé, que la SQ avait essayé de démanteler les barricades. Mes parents étaient très nerveux. Ma superviseure m'a dit que je pouvais partir si je le voulais. Le même jour, je suis partie avec mon frère.

« C'est la première journée que je me rappelle le plus. J'étais inquiète de ma famille et de mes amis. Je ne savais pas à quoi m'attendre. »

☐ « Je sais que j'éprouvais beaucoup de colère. J'étais écœuré de la police. Ils nous retenaient toujours aux postes de contrôle, pour toutes sortes de raisons. Ils fouillaient et refouillaient la voiture. Au début, je sentais que tout le peuple était d'un même esprit; on mettait nos différences de côté. Pour une fois, Kanehsatà:ke était uni. Le premier jour, tout le monde avait peur, les sentiments étaient mitigés. On ne savait pas s'ils allaient revenir. »

☐ « Ce que je retiens le plus, c'est qu'un membre du groupe d'intervention m'a lancé une grenade à concussion juste avant qu'il entre dans la pinède. Je me rappelle avoir été étouffé par les gaz lacrymogènes et qu'on m'ait tiré dessus. Je me souviens que l'armée a tiré dans ma direction le 1er septembre.

« Mais tout n'était pas mauvais. La plupart du temps, c'était paisible derrière les barricades. Après le départ de la majorité des gens la communauté, on pouvait parler avec beaucoup de personnes à qui on n'avait jamais vraiment parlé auparavant. Je me suis fait beaucoup d'amis de partout. C'était vraiment agréable de faire partie d'un événement comme ça. Je ne regrette rien. »

☐ « Le jour où les policiers ont voulu évacuer toutes les vaches, nous avons ri et blagué, mais c'était vraiment sérieux. Ils nous avaient presque fait croire qu'ils allaient nous lancer du napalm ou quelque chose du genre. Ils voulaient protéger les vaches, mais pas les Indiens. Ils l'ont vraiment fait; ils ont évacué les vaches. »

☐ « Le jour où la Croix-Rouge a apporté toutes les civières, je me suis rendu compte que quelque chose pouvait vraiment se passer. On nous a montré comment trier les blessés et les classer à l'aide d'étiquettes de couleur qu'on attache au gros orteil. Orange, rouge… et noir pour les morts. C'était pas mal dur. »

☐ « Chez ceux d'entre nous qui sont restés, il y avait un sens réel de la communauté. Les gens n'avaient pas peur de montrer qu'ils s'aimaient. Nous avions besoin les uns des autres, et il y avait un véritable sentiment d'appartenance. Je sais que cela nous a aidés, parce que la tension était toujours forte malgré l'humour occasionnel qui nous soulageait. Je pense que, pour ceux d'entre nous qui sont restés à Kanehsatà:ke, il y avait toujours l'impression sous-jacente que nous pourrions ne pas voir le lendemain. C'est pourquoi nous résistions avec tant d'acharnement, pour que les enfants et leurs enfants n'aient pas à connaître cela.

« Il y a eu un moment où j'ai eu à considérer la possibilité de mourir pour cette terre et ces gens. J'imagine que nous avons tous pensé à cela. Ça été un moment très personnel pour moi, mais une fois que j'avais pris ma décision, je me suis senti très libre et en paix. Ça ne me dérangeait pas qu'il y ait des milliers de policiers et de soldats juste à l'extérieur des barbelés. Mon esprit était libre, et ils ne pouvaient pas changer cela. »

☐ « Nous discutons souvent de la question de la société blanche qui nous dit toujours que nous devons guérir pour être heureux et rester amis. C'est de la foutaise! Ça ne veut rien dire pour moi. La guérison, c'est de savoir qui est l'ennemi. La guérison, c'est un processus de toute une vie, ce n'est pas un projet du gouvernement.

« Nous devons expliquer et réexpliquer cela à nos enfants, à notre peuple. La guérison doit se faire à notre façon, selon notre définition de ce qu'est la guérison. Il semble qu'elle veule dire d'oublier ce qui est arrivé, et ce sera deux fois plus difficile pour nos enfants. Quand nous parlons de nos affaires, nous sommes perçus comme des radicaux. Si la guérison veut dire oublier ce que la SQ a fait, tirer 2000 coups de feu dans ma direction…, oubliez ça. Je ne guérirai jamais. Je vais transmettre ça à mes enfants pour qu'ils sachent ce qui s'est vraiment passé.

« L'attitude de con que nous pouvons avoir envers la SQ, le gouvernement et les policiers, c'est de les regarder comme un sous-groupe. »

☐ « Je me suis senti très coupable de ne pas avoir été là jusqu'à la fin parce que je prenais soin de mon grand-père. C'était difficile rien qu'à regarder tout ça à la télé. Le 11 juillet, j'ai essayé d'y aller en voiture, mais la police ne me laissait pas passer. Ma grand-mère a essayé de m'en empêcher, mais j'y suis allé quand même. Je savais que j'avais quelque chose à faire, mais je ne savais pas à quoi m'attendre. C'était un soulagement total quand j'y suis arrivé, d'avoir réussi. Je ne me souciais pas de rentrer à la maison; je suis resté là toute la journée. Le soir, je pouvais dire que j'ai appris comment travaille la SQ. Les policiers se fichaient complètement de tout le monde là-bas.

« Je les ai regardés dans les yeux parce qu'on était très près d'eux. Je me rappelle en avoir vu un et lui avoir dit : "J'espère que tu as embrassé ta femme avant de partir ». Plus tard, je me suis senti mal quand j'ai su que c'était Lemay. Puis, je me suis senti coupable pendant un certain temps. Finalement, j'ai dit : "Je m'en fiche". Se sentaient-ils coupables de tirer sur les enfants?

« C'était un jour où tout le peuple, toutes les factions, était uni. Ce jour a été le plus terrifiant de ma vie. Je ne peux pas prétendre comprendre tous ceux qui sont derrière les barricades, mais j'essaie. Je ne sais pas si j'aurais pu survivre tout l'été là-bas. Mais à bien y penser, si j'ai survécu au 11 juillet, j'aurais pu réussir.

« Il n'y avait aucune sécurité dans le village. Une fois, alors que j'avais commandé un cornet de crème glacée, j'ai soudainement éprouvé une sensation vraiment désagréable.

Les policiers nous ont arrêtés et demandé nos papiers d'identité. Je leur ai demandé pourquoi nous devions les leur montrer juste pour manger de la crème glacée. Je suppose que j'étais un peu sarcastique. Ils nous ont fait monter dans leur voiture. Je n'avais peur de personne, sauf d'eux. Je n'avais pas peur de me battre avec qui que ce soit parce que c'est notre terre. C'est dans des situations pareilles que vous apprenez qui sont vos vrais amis.

« Ce n'est qu'en 1990 que j'ai vraiment su qui j'étais. Je l'apprends maintenant et je l'enseigne à mon fils. Je vais m'assurer qu'il sait qui il est. Il y a maintenant beaucoup de gens qui vont à la maison longue, qui retournent aux traditions et qui, en se regardant dans le miroir, disent : "C'est ce que je suis".

« Le 11 juillet, quand on m'a tiré dessus, je ne savais pas si j'allais revoir ma famille. À un moment donné, j'étais dans la tente bleu et jaune, en train de pleurer à cause des gaz lacrymogènes. Puis, je suis retourné en courant et j'ai sauté sur quelqu'un pour le protéger. J'ai pensé que, si je mourais, au moins j'aurais sauvé quelqu'un. »

☐ « Pendant l'été 1990, je me suis senti coupé des autres ; j'étais dans le village. On n'aurait pas dit que ça se passait à quelques mètres plus loin. Je me sentais impuissant ; je n'avais aucun pouvoir sur les événements. Je ne pouvais pas aider les gens derrière les barricades ni m'aider moi-même.

« À ma grande surprise, peut-être que j'étais naïf, mais je ne savais pas qu'il y avait tant de gens racistes. J'étais consterné. Ce n'est pas il y a des centaines d'années ; les gens qui avaient l'habitude de me parler ne me parlaient plus.

« Ce n'est pas facile de dire exactement ce que j'ai appris de ça. Tant de choses ont changé. J'ai appris à apprécier davantage ce que nous avons ici, comme la pinède. Dans un sens, c'était un rappel à la réalité, qu'on ne peut pas nous faire cela. À l'école, je n'étais pas très bavard. C'était plus facile ainsi.

« C'était difficile d'utiliser le téléphone parce que la police écoutait toujours. Ça m'embêtait vraiment. Ils peuvent faire ça ? Rien que parce que je suis Indien ? Ils écoutent encore parfois ; on le sait. C'est choquant comme si quelqu'un entrait dans votre maison sans rien prendre, mais qu'il reste là.

« Pour moi, la réalité a pris forme l'été suivant quand j'ai vu un film des événements. J'ai pensé que j'aurais dû être là comme pour le mariage d'amis. Ça m'a vraiment dérangé de voir ce film. Je n'ai pas réalisé tout ce qui était arrivé, mais on ne peut pas croire les médias. C'est comme pour la police : quand on est jeunes on nous apprend à leur faire confiance. Après ce qui s'est passé, pas question. Qu'est-ce qu'on va montrer à nos enfants ? »

☐ « Aux alentours, il y avait beaucoup plus de racisme qu'on le pensait ; il est soudainement sorti de partout. Pendant la crise, j'étais à Montréal, mais je ne voulais pas y rester ; je voulais être ici avec tout le monde. Ça me faisait sentir davantage comme si je faisais partie de la nation ; tout le monde était d'un même esprit. La crise a fait sortir le racisme que j'avais envers les autres peuples, et j'éprouvais toujours cette haine. Ça m'a fait prendre davantage conscience de notre culture et du fait que nous existons toujours. J'étais le seul dans ma famille qui savait depuis sa naissance que nous étions autochtones. Nos parents ne nous l'avaient pas dit jusqu'à ce qu'on retourne là-bas. Nous allons enseigner à notre fille ce que tout cela veut dire. »

☐ « Nous avons déménagé le bureau et continué à travailler. Nous avons essayé de négocier avec le gouvernement pour évacuer les gens ; nous sommes chanceux qu'aucun des nôtres ne soit mort. De toute façon, je ne pense pas qu'ils aient fait quoi que soit de mal; ils ne faisaient que protéger la terre. C'est le maire Ouellet qui a tout commencé, et il a encaissé beaucoup d'argent. »

☐ « La chose que je suis vraiment contente d'avoir vécue à l'intérieur des barricades quand beaucoup de gens ont été évacués, c'est un sentiment qu'il fallait vivre, un sentiment de bien-être vraiment difficile à décrire. C'est ce que je me rappelle. C'est aussi le premier été où j'ai conduit une moto; c'était une sensation si agréable : aucun policier, rien que des gens que je connaissais.

« Le côté négatif est que ça n'aurait pas dû arriver. Je ne suis pas entièrement d'accord avec la manière dont les médias ont dépeint la situation. Je voyais des choses à la télé sur des gens que je connaissais et, après leur avoir parlé, je découvrais que ce n'était pas vrai. Le mois dernier (septembre), j'ai essayé de retourner à l'école, mais je ne pouvais pas à cause de ce que j'ai vu. À Montréal, je me sentais exclue, comme si les gens ici n'étaient pas mon peuple. Nous étions assiégés, et ces gens continuaient leur train-train quotidien comme si de rien n'était. J'étais fâchée parce qu'ils n'essayaient même pas de comprendre.

« Les Québécois nous percevaient comme des terroristes. Toute la situation les irritait et les dérangeait. Ils ne comprenaient pas et ne comprennent toujours pas.

« Quant aux communautés autochtones, la crise en a peut-être réveillé plusieurs, sauf la nôtre on dirait.

« En ce qui nous concerne, c'est bien que quelques-uns aient voulu être évacués, mais nous aurions pu être une communauté unie. Il y a encore une différence entre ceux qui sont restés et ceux qui sont partis.

« La crise a permis aux gens de montrer leurs vraies couleurs, de savoir qui était leur ami et qui ne l'était pas. Dans un sens, ça facilite les choses.

« Une fois, alors que je m'étais faufilée dans le bois, on m'a fait le message d'appeler mon père. Il voulait me parler; j'ai donc dû retourner au village. Juste en sortant du bois, une voiture de la SQ a surgi. Les policiers m'ont arrêtée et posé des questions sur ce que je faisais, puis l'un d'eux a fouillé mes affaires. Il a ouvert mon sac à dos, et la première chose qu'il a sortie était mon soutien-gorge. Il l'a envoyé dans les airs. Bon sang! Comme c'était drôle!

« J'ai perdu mon emploi à cause de la crise. J'ai choisi de rester et d'aider; puis, il y a eu un malentendu et on m'a congédiée. On a finalement blanchi mon nom, mais ça n'aurait pas dû arriver. »

☐ « D'une façon, je pense que la crise a eu du bon. C'était bon parce que, pendant un certain temps, elle nous a réunis. Auparavant, Kanehsatà:ke n'était pas grand-chose, mais grâce à la crise nous avons été reconnus par le monde entier.

« Je ne regrette rien, sauf pour les maisons qui ont été vandalisées. J'ai de la sympathie pour ces gens. Même si rien n'a été réglé, c'est une bonne chose que la crise soit arrivée. J'avais seize ans à l'époque et ça m'a fait mûrir bien vite. Les enfants autour d'ici ne sont pas comme tous les enfants; ils ne savent pas comment jouer. J'ai de la peine pour eux. Tout le monde a peur; j'ai peur de laisser mon fils sortir dehors.

« Une de mes principales préoccupations est de défendre et d'aider mon peuple parce que la lutte va durer longtemps. Longtemps après que je ne serai plus là, ça va toujours continuer. Nos enfants vont poursuivre la lutte. Beaucoup de gens pensent que, si cela ne touche pas directement leur famille, ce n'est pas grave, mais mon peuple, c'est mon peuple. Je sens que c'est mon devoir d'être là pour eux. Je serai là pour ceux qui n'y sont pas. »

☐ « Tout ce que nous avons subi a eu un côté positif. Le gouvernement sait qu'il ne va pas nous bousculer. Le côté négatif, c'est qu'il y a des gens qui pensent qu'ils peuvent faire tout ce qu'ils veulent. Nous avons toujours notre pinède, il n'y a pas de golf 18 trous.

« Tout ça m'a fait prendre conscience que je ne pouvais plus être un enfant. Ça m'a donné une perspective différente. Les gens qui étaient là-bas devaient avoir un point de vue différent sur tout. Maintenant, quand quelque chose arrive, certains réagissent de façon excessive. Mais ceux qui étaient là voient les choses d'une manière différente.

« Je suis le héros de mon jeune frère; il m'admire. Je crois que beaucoup d'entre nous doivent être des modèles pour les jeunes. Nous devons donner un bon exemple de ce qu'il faut être, montrer que ce n'est pas bon de toujours être fâché et de devenir violent. Souvent, les jeunes enfants viennent à nous et nous posent des questions; ils veulent des conseils. Nous n'y pensons peut-être pas toujours, mais ils regardent ce que nous faisons. »

☐ « Ça été une nuit terrible quand les policiers ont sorti les vaches. On ne pouvait pas s'imaginer ce qu'ils allaient nous faire. De toutes les choses qu'ils ont faites pour déclencher la panique dans la communauté, c'était la meilleure. Quand l'histoire s'est répandue, la panique était plus grande que lorsque l'armée est entrée plus tard. Beaucoup de gens sont alors partis. Les vaches de Dagenais ne sont pas restées loin bien longtemps. Elles ont cessé de donner du lait, alors il les a ramenées. J'imagine qu'elles ne voulaient pas partir non plus.

« Une fois, je suis allé me promener avec le reporter Baxendale. Je n'avais pas vu beaucoup de personnes de la communauté en dehors de la banque alimentaire. Je ne m'étais pas rendu compte à quel point la communauté était vide. J'avais l'impression que seulement quelques-uns avaient été abandonnés ici. Puis, j'ai vu toutes les armes que l'armée possédait. Pourquoi en avait-elle besoin autant? Qu'est-ce qu'elle prévoyait nous faire? Il y avait un char de combat dont le fusil était pointé en direction de ma maison. Je me demandais à quel point le gouvernement et la police étaient stupides pour nous faire ça. Toute l'affaire était ridicule. La situation dans laquelle le gouvernement nous avait mis était ridicule.

« Je me rappelle la première fois que les employés de la Croix-Rouge sont arrivés. J'imagine qu'ils pensaient que nous faisions partie du tiers-monde. Ils ont préparé des sachets de nourriture : deux tranches de fromage et de pain pour chaque personne. C'était toujours une lutte pour faire entrer de la nourriture. Les promesses que le gouvernement et la police faisaient n'étaient jamais tenues.

« Par ailleurs, il y avait un bel esprit communautaire dans notre milieu; tout le monde s'entraidait. C'était tellement beau, une sensation si agréable. Quand on circulait en voiture, tout le monde se saluait et souriait. Si quelqu'un avait un problème, tout le monde voulait l'aider. Malgré tout, nous avons eu du plaisir. Il y avait beaucoup d'humour pour nous aider à traverser la crise, comme la fois où la SQ paradait devant la banque alimentaire. Il y avait environ vingt voitures remplies, et les policiers essayaient de nous intimider. Nous avons suspendu une pancarte Dunkin Donuts à l'extérieur.

« Une fois, lorsque nous avons apporté de la nourriture au centre de réhabilitation, il nous a fallu quatre heures pour parcourir la distance, d'environ 3 km, qui le sépare de la banque alimentaire. Un des enfants avait mis une poignée de pissenlits dans les boîtes de nourriture. Quand nous sommes arrivés au premier poste de contrôle, un sergent ou quelque chose du genre les a pris et jetés par terre. Il a dit qu'on ne pouvait pas les apporter là-bas. J'imagine qu'il pensait que nous avions caché des messages secrets à l'intérieur. Un autre soldat, un caporal, les a ramassés et les a remis dans la boîte. Ho! Il venait de s'attirer des ennuis! Plus tard, un des soldats avait des larmes aux yeux. Il a ouvert une des boîtes, et il y avait des couches à l'intérieur. Je me suis dit que certains d'entre eux étaient humains après tout.

« Pour ma part, je n'ai aucun regret. J'ai fait ce que j'ai pu pour aider et je ne pense pas que j'aurais pu en faire davantage. S'il y a une chose que je regrette, c'est de ne pas avoir pris de notes sur les événements qui se déroulaient. Durant la crise, nous n'avions aucune notion du temps. C'est difficile maintenant de se rappeler exactement quand les choses sont arrivées et dans quel ordre.

« Après la crise, nous nous sentions tellement mal d'aller où que ce soit. On ne voulait pas quitter la communauté. Quand j'allais au centre commercial, j'étais tellement mal à l'aise; j'avais hâte de revenir. Je me sens encore comme ça quand je sors. Ce sentiment est toujours en moi, et je cherche des excuses pour ne pas sortir. Je pense que les choses se seraient déroulées différemment si plus de gens étaient restés. »

☐ « Le racisme a toujours existé là-bas; il était simplement caché, mais il est soudain devenu très évident, très flagrant. Je n'étais pas vraiment présent parce que j'ai continué à travailler; je n'ai donc pas beaucoup pris part aux activités. Je me sens maintenant coupable de ne pas y avoir davantage participé, de ne pas m'être davantage engagé.

« Le 11 juillet, quand quelqu'un a téléphoné à la maison pour dire que les policiers attaquaient notre peuple, je trouvais cela tellement irréel. Je ne pouvais pas croire que, dans un pays comme le Canada, on pouvait attaquer ainsi les autochtones. Mon incrédulité s'est transformée en colère et en dégoût. Je ne pense pas que qui que ce soit s'attendait vraiment à ce que ça se passe ainsi. Ceux qui discutaient avec les policiers ce matin-là s'attendaient peut-être à cela dans une certaine mesure, mais pas comme c'est survenu. Ils croyaient qu'ils se feraient arrêter, mais pas qu'on leur tirerait dessus ou qu'ils seraient battus comme c'est arrivé plus tard.

« Ce que j'ai appris de toute la crise est que, pour que quelque chose réussisse, il faut que tout le monde travaille ensemble. Durant les deux ou trois premières semaines, la faction ou la famille à laquelle nous appartenions n'avait aucune d'importance; tout le monde avait le même but. Puis, différents groupes ont commencé à promouvoir leur propre programme. Des gens sont sortis de nulle part et ont essayé de prendre les choses en main. Les médias ont manipulé certaines personnes, et parfois il était difficile de dire si c'était les événements qui façonnaient les médias ou le contraire.

« J'ai découvert que notre liberté est vraiment limitée. Le droit à l'information est limité par la censure et la manipulation des médias. La liberté est une comédie ici; les choses que nous croyons vraies ne le sont pas réellement. Mon sentiment d'impuissance m'a vraiment troublé. Je n'avais pas le temps de me poser des questions ou de philosopher. La crise n'est pas devenue une expérience spirituelle pour moi comme ça été le cas pour beaucoup d'autres personnes. Parce que j'ai continué à travailler, je n'étais pas confiné comme les autres et je n'ai pas réfléchi à la situation. C'est seulement lorsque l'armée est arrivée et que je ne pouvais plus aller travailler que je suis resté ici avec mon peuple. Puisque je ne pouvais rien faire pour régler le problème, je me suis donc contenté de harceler les policiers. J'ai fait tout ce que je pouvais pour rendre leur séjour ici aussi misérable que possible.

« Une autre chose qui m'a vraiment choqué a été le moment où Spudwrench a été battu. J'étais avec ma copine quand j'ai entendu la nouvelle dans les médias. On disait qu'il avait reçu cinquante coups sur la tête. J'étais absolument révolté et écœuré qu'une chose pareille puisse arriver. Puis, il y a les mensonges qui sont plus tard sortis; on disait qu'il avait attaqué quatre soldats. De l'intérieur, nous avions la vraie version de l'histoire; les mensonges et la manière absurde que les médias rapportaient les faits étaient de la merde. Ils ont essayé de le faire passer pour un criminel.

« Le rôle de l'armée était absurde. Au début, ils étaient censés servir d'intermédiaires entre la SQ et les Warriors : les policiers seraient de ce côté-là, les Warriors de l'autre côté et l'armée serait au milieu pour garder la paix. Je pense que beaucoup de gens étaient soulagés quand on a annoncé que l'armée arrivait, moi y compris. Mais la première chose qu'on a constatée, c'est qu'ils sont assis là à manger des beignes avec la SQ et qu'ils jouent le rôle de policiers.

« La crise, c'était un véritable moment de fierté mohawk. Les autres nations nous regardaient pour trouver en nous direction et leadership. Je pense que ce qui est arrivé a été une inspiration pour les autochtones de partout, que cela a façonné la suite des choses. Ça a eu un effet bénéfique sur les autochtones. C'est dommage ce qui arrive ici maintenant. »

☐ « Beaucoup de gens se sont sentis exploités physiquement et mentalement. Bien des fois, ils repensaient à toutes les choses qui sont arrivées il y a de bien des années. Quelqu'un m'a dit que, lorsqu'il y a une guerre, beaucoup de gens sont blessés, physiquement, émotionnellement ou spirituellement. Ce qu'ils voient peut les blesser.

« Bien des gens là-bas étaient révoltés et fâchés de voir qu'on acceptait d'aller jusqu'à leur faire mal. Ce qui m'a le plus étonné a été que seulement une poignée de personnes a tenu tête aux Canadiens. J'ai été étonné de voir que le gouvernement canadien aille jusqu'à attaquer un si petit groupe. L'esprit du peuple était fort et sa foi était là. De nombreuses personnes, même si elles n'étaient pas là physiquement, y étaient en esprit. Leur cœur était là, et toutes les cérémonies se poursuivaient pour s'assurer que les choses n'empirent pas.

« Le matin où c'est arrivé, je passais par là. Les gens n'étaient ni affolés ni confus. Ils étaient calmes, se demandaient ce qui allait arriver. De l'autre côté, on ne s'attendait pas à ce qu'un si petit groupe de personnes défende ses droits.

« J'ai aussi vu et entendu des gens dire que le peuple est fort quand tout le monde est uni. Toutes les nations Onkwehón:we sont venues unies pour nous appuyer; il y avait de la force dans cette unité. Le gouvernement n'a pas aimé ça. S'il avait pu se cacher, il l'aurait fait, mais il a été forcé de s'occuper de la situation. »

☐ « Le matin où c'est arrivé, je m'en allais travailler. Il y avait un barrage routier, et on tirait des coups de feu. Pendant un moment, on éprouve une sensation terrible et on se demande ce qui se passe.

« Il y a eu beaucoup de moments terribles, comme lorsque ma mère a dû renouveler une ordonnance et que la police nous a causé beaucoup de problèmes. Les policiers s'en fichaient. On était en 1990, mais on avait l'impression d'être dans un autre monde.

« Tout le harcèlement que les enfants ont subi à être pris en grippe sans raison, à être humiliés, à se faire demander s'ils avaient tué Lemay.

« Durant toute la crise, je suis resté parce que je le voulais bien. Ma mère a refusé de partir; elle ne voulait pas quitter sa maison.

« Il y a eu beaucoup de moments paisibles, comme quand je marchais le soir dans la pinède avec mes sœurs. Ceux qui sont restés se sentaient unis. Après cela, le sentiment persistait et les gens voulaient effectuer des changements. Les jeunes veulent maintenant que leur ami de cœur soit Onkwehón:we d'ici, de Kahnawà:ke ou d'Akwesasne. Il y a plus de solidarité.

« Nous vivons à l'ère moderne, mais le gouvernement n'a pas changé; il n'a aucun respect pour nous. C'est une lutte de longue date et ce n'est pas fini. J'ai appris que nous pouvons être unis; des gens de partout se sont rassemblés pour nous aider. Mais c'est triste qu'aujourd'hui les enfants aient des sentiments forts, comme l'animosité envers la SQ, et rien n'est fait pour les aider.

« Une chose est certaine, les gens ici n'abandonneront jamais la pinède. Une autre chose que nous avons apprise est que les médias disent des demi-vérités, ils ne rapportent pas bien les faits. Les gens ne savent pas vraiment ce qui se passe. Certains venaient à moi et m'accusaient de choses qu'ils voyaient à la télé, et je leur disais que ce n'était pas vrai. Ils me répondaient qu'ils les avaient vues à la télé, et je leur répliquais : "Écoute, j'arrive de là, et ce n'est pas ce qui est arrivé". Les médias nous montraient comme des gens très violents.

« À la fin d'août, on nous a dit que si nous partions nous ne pourrions pas revenir, mais je suis quand même parti. Après avoir stationné ma voiture dans le village, j'ai commencé à traverser le bois. Une voiture me suivait, et le gars qui était à l'intérieur avait une radio. J'avais tellement peur parce que je me disais : *Oh non, il va appeler l'armée et on va me descendre*. C'est la course la plus rapide que j'aie faite à travers le terrain de golf.

« Ce jour-là dans la pinède, quand tout le monde était là, nous nous sommes tenus par la main. J'ai vu là des gens qui se détestaient se tenir la main pour défendre la terre. »

☐ « Eh bien, je suis fatigué des gens qui me disent qu'on ne devrait pas aller ici et là parce que c'est ce qu'ils nous ont fait. J'étais là et j'ai vu qui faisait quoi. Je peux penser par moi-même et prendre mes propres décisions.

« Les sentiments que j'éprouvais étaient la haine, l'incrédulité et la méfiance. J'ai encore de la haine et de la méfiance. Même envers les gens de mon propre peuple, j'ai une certaine méfiance.

« J'ai appris beaucoup de choses que je ne connaissais pas auparavant. J'ai aussi appris que je ne devrais pas haïr. Pendant cette courte période de temps, il y avait une unité dans la communauté, mais une fois que tout a été terminé, tout est revenu comme avant. Quand je suis retourné au travail, je me sentais exclu par mes collègues. Dans le village, nous devions traiter avec la SQ, la GRC et les mouchards. Nous ne pouvions pas y échapper. C'était différent d'ici, mais là-bas nous n'étions pas en sécurité.

« À quelques reprises, on m'a demandé d'aller chercher des médicaments pour les gens qui ne pouvaient pas partir, et j'y suis allé. Je ressentais de l'excitation, mais aussi de la peur. La peur parce qu'il y avait toujours des gens qui me surveillaient. Je conduisais et soudain la SQ était derrière moi. On ne pouvait aller nulle part; il fallait se faufiler. Je voulais rester au village pour voir ce qui se passait.

« Au milieu de tout ça, nous nous sommes rapprochés, et il y avait aussi des Blancs parmi nous. Ils n'étaient pas tous contre nous.

« Disons que c'était bien pendant ces deux mois, mais maintenant nous sommes de retour à la case départ. C'était encourageant de recevoir beaucoup d'appui. Des gens sont venus de partout pour nous aider. Ferions-nous la même chose pour les autres? Combien de gens seraient prêts à plier bagage et à quitter leur emploi pour aller aider des frères quelque part comme ça? Pas beaucoup selon moi.

« Je regrette qu'à cause de certaines choses qui se passent ici, je ne sais pas si mon cœur veut vraiment être autochtone. Parfois, je veux tout simplement ne rien être. D'après ce que je vois, comme ce qui s'est passé récemment, je serai l'un des premiers à partir s'ils veulent recréer la crise. »

☐ « J'étais confus à ce moment-là. Sur le plan émotionnel, je traversais une période difficile. Le matin où la crise est survenue, j'ai vu l'hélicoptère alors que j'étais dans le verger derrière ma maison. Le soleil venait de se lever, l'appareil est passé droit devant nous à la hauteur des arbres. Il était proche. Puis, en entendant beaucoup de voitures sur l'autoroute, nous savions que quelque chose se passait. Nous avons donc essayé de nous rendre à la pinède par le rang de l'Annonciation, mais il y avait des agents secrets stationnés là; nous pensions qu'ils étaient des nôtres. D'un bond, ils sont sortis et ont pointé leurs fusils vers nous; le franc-tireur a pointé le sien sur notre tête. Quel choc! Nous avons dû rebrousser chemin. Nous avons essayé de monter la rue Saint-Michel, mais en vain. Alors nous avons communiqué par radio aux gars là-bas pour leur dire qu'il y avait beaucoup de policiers qui entraient.

« La prochaine fois, je vais m'assurer d'y arriver. Je m'inquiétais de mes amis. Ici, les policiers nous harcelaient tout le temps. Ils ont essayé de me tendre un piège. Ils m'ont arrêté et fait sortir de ma voiture. Un policier a laissé son fusil de calibre 12 sur le capot devant moi. Ils voulaient que j'y touche pour qu'ils puissent me sauter dessus. Ils étaient trois qui me surveillaient. Finalement, une policière, qui a vu le scénario, a pris le fusil et leur a lancé un regard désapprobateur.

« C'est tout ce que j'ai à dire, je ne pense pas que c'est fini. Je peux ajouter que la crise a uni les gens, et c'est une bonne chose. »

☐ « La crise a uni beaucoup de nations indiennes pour un combat commun : la question territoriale. Vous avez vu combien les femmes étaient fortes spirituellement et physiquement. Ça nous a fait retourner à nos racines. Autrefois, les femmes jouaient plusieurs rôles : elles s'occupaient de la maison longue, elles prenaient soin de notre mère la terre, elles éduquaient leurs enfants. Leur lien avec la terre a été renouvelé.

« Elles ont maintenu la paix et l'unité derrière les barricades. Certains des gars étaient très impatients et, si ce n'avait pas été des femmes, quelques-uns d'entre eux auraient pu s'attirer bien des ennuis.

« Je demande au Créateur de bénir toutes les femmes de la terre. »

☐ « J'ai quitté mon emploi aux États-Unis et je suis revenu ici parce que j'étais inquiet de ma famille. Quand je suis revenu, à 2 h du matin, il y avait ce gros projecteur qui nous éblouissait. Nous sommes allés à la barricade. Les policiers avaient tous des fusils et, à cause du projecteur, nous ne pouvions pas voir leur visage. Je conduisais; j'ai descendu ma fenêtre et le policier m'a demandé mes pièces d'identité. Nous étions tous d'ici, et j'ai dit : "Excusez-moi, suis-je arrivé dans un pays communiste? C'est notre terre, et nous ne devrions pas être soumis à ça." Ils nous ont causé des ennuis parce que mon neveu n'avait pas de pièces d'identité. Après une longue discussion, ils nous ont laissés entrer.

« Le jour suivant quand nous sommes partis, ils ont fouillé la voiture de fond en comble. Ils ont vu des bottes de cow-boy et le policier nous a demandé : "À qui sont ces bottes et qu'est-ce qu'elles font dans la voiture?" C'était tellement irréel; ils ont même fouillé notre nourriture. C'est tellement dur à expliquer. C'était si bouleversant d'être traités comme des moins que rien.

« Quand je suis arrivé aux États-Unis, j'ai lu dans un journal local la citation des paroles de quelqu'un de Kanehsatà:ke. J'ai téléphoné là-bas pour en vérifier l'authenticité, et tout était faux. J'ai téléphoné au journal, et ils ont présenté leurs excuses. Ils m'ont dit qu'ils avaient reçu la nouvelle d'un service d'information et qu'ils l'avaient publiée. Après leur avoir expliqué la situation, le journal a publié un désaveu. Même là-bas, on publiait des faussetés. »

☐ « Il ne fait aucun doute que quelque chose dominait mes pensées. Voici ce que c'était exactement. Même si j'étais à plus de 320 kilomètres au moment où la crise a éclaté, elle m'a totalement saisi pendant deux semaines. Je ne pouvais pas me concentrer sur mes études. Assez souvent, en pensée, je retournais à Kanehsatà:ke et je voyais des scènes de combat. C'était incontrôlable. J'en suis arrivé au point où les professeurs ont remarqué mon problème, et l'un d'eux m'a demandé s'il pouvait faire quelque chose pour m'aider. Je lui ai dit que j'étais indécis à savoir si je devais aller à Kanehsatà:ke puisque tout le monde avec qui j'avais grandi était là. Il m'a aidé à voir à long terme. J'ai finalement décidé de rester et de poursuivre mes études, même si chez moi mes frères et sœurs étaient assiégés.

« La crise m'a motivé à vouloir en savoir plus sur les traditions, et j'ai appris à quel lieu j'appartenais vraiment. J'ai aussi appris ou découvert quelles étaient les vraies couleurs des gens, à savoir la société québécoise, j'ai vu ce qu'elle avait au fond du cœur.

« Parce que j'étais à l'extérieur des barricades, certaines personnes ont essayé de m'imposer leurs croyances. C'était difficile même si je n'étais pas à l'intérieur. J'y suis allé une fois à l'occasion de la première grande manifestation dans le parc. Après cela, j'ai traversé la pinède pour livrer une lettre. En revenant, je suis sorti près d'un poste de contrôle de la police. Ils m'ont demandé mes pièces d'identité. J'ai commencé à parler avec eux et ils ont commencé à me poser des questions sur les raisons pour lesquelles nous faisions cela. En tout cas, j'ai répondu et peu à peu plus de policiers sont arrivés. Ils écoutaient, puis posaient plus de questions comme : "Les autres minorités obéissent aux lois, pourquoi pas vous?" Un autre policier s'est arrêté et est sorti de son véhicule. Il était vraiment grand, et il a demandé aux autres si je leur donnais du fil à retordre, comme s'il allait s'en occuper. Je lui ai dit : "Eh! merci. C'est un compliment de penser que je cause des problèmes à...", puis je me suis arrêté de compter... "à 12 gars de la police". Cette interruption les a déconcentrés, et ils sont retournés à leur voiture. Puis, j'ai marché jusque chez ma mère. »

☐ « J'ai appris qu'on ne peut pas faire confiance aux politiciens, qu'on doit tout le temps être sur nos gardes. Pour eux, c'était un jeu. Nous étions sérieux, mais eux non. Ils voulaient régler la situation à Oka, mais sans toucher aux questions de droits territoriaux. Aussi, la SQ avait la main haute; c'est comme un État policier; personne ne peut la contrôler. Il faut écouter les politiciens sinon ils envoient leur gars après vous, et il n'y a rien pour les maîtriser. Au début, quand tout a commencé, il y avait des marches de protestation et autres choses du genre, et certains des gars m'ont dit que je devais y être. Je leur ai répondu que si ça devenait risqué, je serais là et j'ai tenu ma parole. Ma principale constatation est que ce n'est pas réglé. Beaucoup de Blancs pensent le contraire, mais c'est faux. Il faudrait demander à l'Église de nous dédommager; c'est à cause d'elle que tous ces problèmes de territoire sont arrivés.

« Beaucoup de jeunes enfants ne comprennent pas ce qui se passe, et quand ils voient les plus vieux adopter un mauvais comportement, se saouler et tirer des coups de feu, ça ne fait qu'ajouter au problème. C'est vraiment difficile pour ces enfants. Les ados ressentent peut-être qu'ils n'ont pas profité de la crise. Dans les années 1990, ils ont eu peur de la prison et, maintenant, ils essaient de la recréer parce qu'ils se sentent coupables. Mais ça ne marchera pas. »

ÉPILOGUE

Les souvenirs de l'été 1990 resteront gravés dans la mémoire de nombreux Onkwehón:we dans toute l'île de la Tortue, ils les transmettront aux générations futures. Ces souvenirs grossiront les rangs de la tradition orale telle que racontée par les aînés aux petits enfants. Espérons qu'ils parleront des années 1990 en gardant l'essentiel intact, qu'elles représenteront la lutte de tous les peuples autochtones pour leur territoire, leur langue et leur culture, qu'elles évoqueront le refus des gouvernements de trouver des solutions justes et équitables concernant les droits et la liberté de notre peuple. Des décisions unilatérales et des politiques génocidaires ont guidé la volonté politique depuis trop longtemps. Le 11 juillet 1990 est une date qui marque les injustices infligées aux autochtones depuis les 500 dernières années.

Même si, en 1990, beaucoup de pays ont été inspirés par le peuple de Kanehsatà:ke et ont appuyé les efforts, celui-ci ne s'en est jamais tout à fait remis. Cinq ans plus tard, le temps n'a pas encore cicatrisé les blessures éprouvées par le peuple. Beaucoup de jeunes et de vieux portent leur colère comme un bouclier. Si beaucoup ont vu leur conscience spirituelle et politique se réveiller, celle-ci a souvent été éclipsée par la haine et les actes de violence de soi-disant voisins blancs. La douleur que la communauté s'infligeait était pire encore que les années de souffrance et de colère soigneusement emmagasinées depuis des générations lui ont apportées. Si l'année 1990 a été un catalyseur, elle a été implosive.

Malgré le traumatisme, la communauté a agi conformément à une promesse non exprimée qui semble être le soutien d'efforts inouïs pour préserver sa langue et sa culture. C'est une période de croissance et d'attitudes nouvelles pour Kanehsatà:ke. Et si parfois la communauté ne semble pas en bon état, c'est parce que la stabilité peut être difficile à maintenir au cours des étapes qui jalonnent son développement. L'équilibre sera atteint si nous sommes patients et persévérants. Même si Kanehsatà:ke a beaucoup de défis à relever, il demeure une communauté où vivent des gens qui se soucient des autres et où la famille élargie n'est pas un concept obscur, mais une réalité.

Après tout ce qui a été écrit et lu, il faut se rappeler que ce n'est qu'une partie de notre histoire collective. Chaque famille qui vit à Kanehsatà:ke a sa propre histoire de violation de droits, de saisies illégales de terrains par les soi-disant autorités et d'emprisonnements injustifiés. En étudiant notre passé, nous ne pouvons qu'être étonnés par nos aptitudes de survie. En regardant vers l'avenir, engageons-nous à nous rappeler l'essentiel des paroles qui viennent en premier, à l'orée des bois, pour que nous puissions terminer notre voyage en toute sécurité.

Collection de Brian Beaver

Collection de Brian Beaver

Collection de Brian Beaver

Collection de Brian Beaver

Collection de Brian Beaver

Collection de Brian Beaver

Collection de Brian Beaver

[1] Au moins deux marches pacifiques ont eu lieu en 1989 pour protester contre l'agrandissement du terrain de golf proposé. La première s'est tenue en avril et la deuxième en octobre.

[2] Le Regroupement des citoyens d'Oka (RCO) est une organisation composée de résidents d'Oka. Il a été créé en 1986 pour s'opposer à l'ouverture du centre de réhabilitation pour autochtones à Kanehsatà:ke. Des membres du RCO prétendaient que le centre de réhabilitation proposé ferait diminuer la valeur des propriétés et menacerait la sécurité du voisinage. Ce qui est intéressant est qu'aucun d'eux de s'est opposé à l'ouverture de la Maisonnée d'Oka, un centre de réhabilitation pour non-autochtones situé en face du site proposé pour autochtones. Ils n'ont pas réussi à empêcher l'ouverture du centre (maintenant appelé Onen'to:kon), mais ils ont empêché que le terrain sur lequel il est situé soit transféré aux Kanien'kehà:ka.

En 1990, ce regroupement a été réactivé par un groupe d'autodéfense qui s'est engagé à « utiliser toute la force nécessaire pour démanteler les barricades ». Ce groupe a été celui qui s'est fait le plus entendre dans son opposition à la manifestation dans la pinède. Les membres du RCO prétendaient que les Kanehsata'kehró:non utilisaient l'agrandissement du terrain de golf comme prétexte pour attirer l'attention sur leur revendication territoriale. Durant la crise de 1990, ils ont tenu des manifestations anti-Mohawks et harcelé les non-autochtones du village qui appuyaient les Kanehsata'kehró:non.

[3] Le *Journal de Montréal*, le 4 mai 1990.

[4] La deuxième injonction de la cour contre la manifestation dans la pinède est entrée en vigueur le 30 juin et a pris fin le 9 juillet 1990.

[5] Geoffrey York et Loreen Pindera, *People of the Pines,* Little Brown & Company (Canada) Ltd., Boston, London, Toronto, 1991, p. 219.

[6] Alanis Obomsawin, *Kanehsatà:ke 270 années de résistance,* 1992

[7] *The Montreal Gazette*, 17 juillet 1990, éditorial

[8] Le choc collectif est un rapport de la Commission des droits de la personne du Québec, préparé par Monique Rochon et Pierre Lepage, avril 1991, p. 18. « La mesure de similarité et de crédibilité des nombreuses déclarations faites le 19 et le 21 juillet aux représentants de la Commission les a portés à croire que les pouvoirs exercés par certains membres de la Sûreté du Québec pourraient constituée une violation de certains droits de citoyens dans la région cernée, tels que des droits fondamentaux (sécurité, inviolabilité, assistance, liberté d'expression, réputation, libre disposition de propriété [...]), le droit de ne pas être soumis à la discrimination ou au harcèlement, les droits juridiques (protection contre les fouilles et les saisies déraisonnables, droit d'être informé des motifs d'arrestation, d'être traité avec le respect dû à la personne dans des cas d'arrestation ou de détention, d'aviser immédiatement un membre de la famille et de chercher des conseils juridiques [...]. » p. 19

[9] *People of the Pines*, York et Pindera, p. 211

[10] Ibid.

GLOSSAIRE

A

Ahentaríhtha : [nom] il cuit le champ [ou] réchauffe le champ {chef Ahentaríhtha}

Ahrírhon : [nom] aucune signification connue de ce nom {Timothy Ahrírhon}

Ahsennénhson : centre

Aionwatha : [nom] aucune signification connue de ce nom

Akwirá:'es : [nom] petite branche qui bat {Matthias Akwirá:'es}

Akwirén:te : [nom] petite branche qui pend {Lazare Akwirén:te}

Anaié:ha : [nom] lui, le fier {Simon Anaié:ha}

Anenhrén:te : [nom] petites branches qui pendent {François Anenhrén:te}

Anonhsawén:rate : [nom] par-dessus la maison {Martin Anonhsawén:rate}

Aronhiá:ke : [nom] où est le ciel (chef Warraghiyagey)

Aronhiaké:te : [nom] il porte le ciel {Antoine Aronhiaké:te}

Arrière-fief : fief relevant d'un autre fief

C

Cens et rentes : redevance à payer pour loyer

Censitaire : colon sous le régime féodal

Censive : terres devant payer des cens

D

Des lettres de terrier : titres de propriété

Droit de banalité : droit d'imposer des devoirs à des vassaux

Droit de quint : droit au cinquième

Droit de retrait : droit de rachat

E

En roture : titulaire d'une terre par service

F

Franc alleu roturier : bail gratuit à un serviteur

I

Iako'tarakéhte : mère de clan

Ioti'tarakéhte : mères de clan

K

Kahnawà:ke : sur les rapides {Kahnawake}

Kahnawa'kehró:non : peuple de Kahnawà:ke

Kaianere'kó:wa : Grande Loi de la paix

Kaién:kwire : [nom] flèche {Nicholas Kaièn:kwire}

Kaionkeháka : peuple de la grande pipe {Cayugas}

Kaná:tase : [nom] nouveau village {Joseph Kaná:tase Gabriel}

Kanehsatà:ke : sur les dunes sablonneuses {Kanesatake}

Kanehsata'kehró:non : peuple de Kanehsatà:ke

Kanerahtakén:iate : [nom] terminaison d'une feuille

Kanién:keh : territoire Mohawk

Kanien'keha : langue parlée par les Kanien'kehà:ka

Kanien'kehà:ka : peuple du silex {Mohawks}

Karenhatá:se : [nom] vigne entrelacée {Gabriel Karenhatá:se}

Karihwí:ios : [nom] bonne nouvelle {Xavier Karihwí:ios}

Kastho'serí:io : [nom] belle plume

Katénie's : [nom] elle change les choses {Marie Katénie's}

Katsi'tsakwas : [nom] elle cueille des fleurs

Kó:wa : [nom] gros {Thomas Kó:wa}

L

Lods et vents : dettes et ventes

M

Mouvance : dépendance d'un tarif sur un autre bail

O

Oheróskon : [nom] rempli d'épis de maïs {Pierre Dicker}

Ohsennakén:rat : [nom] nom blanc ou pâle, aussi nom rare {chef Ohsennakén:rat}

Oien'kwa'on:we : tabac original

Onkwehón:we : Indiens

Ononhkwatkó:wa : [nom] grande médecine {Joseph Ononhkwatkó:wa}

Ononta'keháka : peuple de la colline {Onondagas}

O'nahsakèn:rat : [nom] cygne blanc ou pâle, aussi cygne rare {chef O'nahsakèn:rat}

O'nientehá:ka : peuple de la pierre debout {Oneidas}

O'serón:ni : les Français, les Européens

P

Procès verbaux : déposition de témoins

R

Ratirontaks : Algonquins, mangeurs d'écorce

Rateriiosserakwe'ní:io : chef de guerre

Ratihnará:ken : les Blancs, peau pâle

Ratitsihenhstá:tsi : ministres, pasteurs, prêtres

Ratiwè:ras : tonnerres

Rawè:ras : tonnerre

Roiiá:nehr : chef traditionnel

Rononhkwíhseres : [nom] cheveux longs, celui qui a les cheveux longs

Ronteriiohersakwe'ní:io : chefs de guerre

Rotiiá:nehr : plusieurs chefs traditionnels

Rotinonhseshá:ka : peuple de la maison longue

Rotisken'raké:ta : guerriers, hommes

Roti'kharahón:tsi : robes noires, prêtres

Ro'kharahón:tsi : robe noire, prêtre

S

Shakokéhte : [nom] il les porte {chef James Montour}

Shakotewenté:tha : [nom] il les quitte

Sha'teionkwá:wen : la Commune, les terres que nous partageons

Sha'tewa'skó:wa : [nom] même grande taille

Shenekeháka : peuple de la grande montagne {Sénécas}

Sho'èn:rise : [nom] lui, la longue clôture {Samuel Nicholas}

Skénn:en : paix

Sóse : [nom] le nom Joseph transformé dans le dialecte mohawk

Só:se Tiaokáthe : [nom] celui qui sépare le grain {Joseph Denys}

T

Thó nikawén:nake : c'est tout ce qu'il y a à dire

Teharihó:ren : [nom] nouvelles fractionnées {Michel Teharihó:ren}

Tekanató:ken : [nom] carrefour {Napoleon Commandant}

Tekaniehtón:tens : neige collante

Tekaniéhtatens : neige épaisse, neige soufflée par le vent

Terra-Nullius : terre inhabitée (concept juridique européen)

Thaientané:ken : [nom] bois un à côté de l'autre

Thanonhianíhtha : [nom] il exagère {Matthias Thanonhianíhtha}

Tharonhianá:non : [nom] il est plein de ciel {Moses Tharonhianá:non}

Tharonhiawá:kon : [nom] il tient le ciel

Tiekonhsá:se : [nom] nouveau visage

Tiohtià:ke : où le groupe se sépare, Montréal

Tiononte'kó:wa : grosse montagne

Tio'rhen'shá:ka : les Anglais

Tsiskó:ko : merle d'Amérique

W

Wathahí:ne : [nom] elle parcourt le chemin, fait le voyage {Wathahí:ni Tewíshia}

BIBLIOGRAPHIE

ABLER, Thomas S. *Longhouse and Palisades: Northeast Iroquoian Villages of the Seventeenth Century*, Ontario History, vol. 62, 1970.

ALLEN, Robert S., Gerry T. ALTOFF et Calvin ENDERS. *The Michigan Historical Review*, vol. 14, n° 2, automne 1988.

ALLEN, Robert S. *His Majesty's Indian Allies, British Indian Policy in The Defence of Canada, 1774-1815*, Toronto et Oxford, Dundurn Press, 1992.

An Overview of the Oka Issue, Indian and Northern Affairs, juillet 1990.

Appel d'une ordonnance pour incorporer les ecclésiastiques du séminaire de Saint-Sulpice de Montréal pour confirmer leur titre au fief et à la seigneurie du Lac des Deux-Montagnes et du fief et de la seigneurie de Saint-Sulpice dans cette province : à la province pour l'extinction graduelle des droits et des dûs seigneuriaux, dans les limites seigneuriales des dits fiefs et seigneuries et pour d'autres usages, Montréal, A. H. Armour et H. Ramsay, 1839.

ARDEN, Harvey. *The Fire That Never Dies*, National Geographic, octobre 1991.

BARREIRO, José. *Indian Roots of American Democracy*, Ithaca, New York, Presses Akwe:kon, Université Cornell, 1992.

BAUCH, Herbert. *Quebec's Memory*, la Gazette de Montréal, samedi 25 mars 1995.

BEAUBIEN, Charles. *Le Sault-au-Récollet : ses rapports avec les premiers temps de la colonie*, Montréal, C. O. Beauchemin & Fils, Librairies Imprimeurs, Mission-Paroisse, 1898.

BEAUCHAMP, William M. *Aboriginal Place Names of New York*, Albany, 1907, département de l'Éducation de l'État de New York, Detroit, 1971, réédité par Grand River Books.

BEERS, W. George. *The Story of the Oka Indians*, Canadian Spectator.

BEERS, W. George. *Is the Government Afraid of the Oka Question?*, Broadside, Nation archives C138881.

BEGIN, Patricia, Wendy MOSS et Peter NIEMCZAK. *The Land Claim Dispute at Oka*, Ottawa, Département de la recherche, bibliothèque du parlement, 1990.

BÉLISLE, Maître Guy et Hélène THIBAULT. *Oka au sortir de la crise amérindienne*, rapport final présenté à monsieur Benoît Bouchard, ministre de la Santé et du Bien-être social, ministre responsable du développement économique régional du Québec, Montréal, 26 avril 1991.

BENSON, Adolph B. *Peter Kalm's Travels In North America*, The English Version of 1770, vol. II, New York, Wilson-Erickson, 1937.

BETA, *A Contribution to a Proper Understanding of the Oka Question and a Help to its Equitable and Speedy Settlement*, Montréal, Witness Printing House, 1979.

BIGGAR, H. P. et B. LITT. (Oxon). *The Voyages of Jacques Cartier*, Ottawa, F. A. Acland, imprimeur de Sa très Excellence sa Majesté le Roi, 1924.

BIGSBY, John J., md. *The shoe and canoe, or pictures of travels in the Canadas*, vol. 1, London, Chapman et Hall, 1850.

BLANCHARD, David S. *Kahnawake. A Historical Sketch,* Kahnawake, Presses Kanien'kehaka Raotitiohkwa, 1980.

BLANCHARD, David S. *Seven Generations: A History of the Kanienkehaka*, Kahnawake, 1980, publié par le Center for Curriculum Development, imprimé par Church, Baines, Montréal.

BOILEAU, Gilles. *Les Silence des Messieurs : Oka, terre indienne*, Montréal, Méridien, édition du Méridien, 1991.

BOILEAU, Gilles. *Almanach historique de Deux-Montagnes*, Saint-Eustache, 1981.

BORLAND, John. *Un appel à la conférence de Montréal et à l'Église méthodiste, généralement à la suite d'une accusation par le révérend William Scott où il montre que son accusation est invalide et que sa défense du séminaire de Saint-Sulpice contre les Indiens d'Oka est sans fondement, un fait prouvée à laquelle il a largement contribué*, Montréal, Witness Printing House, 1883.

BORLAND, John. *Les prétentions du séminaire de Saint-Sulpice d'être les propriétaires de la seigneurie du Lac des Deux-Montagnes et de celle qui y est attenante, examinées et réfutées, exposées et dénoncées dans quatre lettres adressées à l'honorable Joseph Howe, secrétaire d'État pour le département Indien*, Montréal, 1872, The Gazette Printing House.

BOUCHETTE, Joseph. *Description topographique de la province du Bas-Canada*, Londres, 1815.

BOURGEOIS, Donald J. *Rapport de recherche sur la revendication territoriale des Mohawks de Gibson*, Ottawa, 1982.

BRUCHACT, Joseph. *Otstungo: Mohawk Village in 1491*, National Geographic, septembre 1987.

Bulletin de recherches historiques, juillet 1990.

CHAGNY, André. *François Picquet, le Canadien,1708-1781, Un défenseur de la Nouvelle-France*, Montréal, librairie Beauchemin, 1913.

CHAMBRE DES COMMUNES. *L'été 1990: cinquième rapport sur comité permanent sur les affaires aborigènes Fifth*, Ken Hughes, M. P. Chair, mai 1991

CHAMPLAIN, Samuel De. *The Publications Of The Champlain Society, The Works of Samuel De Champlain*, vol. 1-IV, Toronto, The Champlain Society.

CHRISTIE, Robert. *A History of the Late Province of Lower Canada*, vol. VI, Montréal, 1866, Richard Worthington.

CLERMONT, Norman et Claude CHAPDELAINE. *Pointe-Du-Buisson 4: quarante siècles d'archives oubliées*, Montréal, recherches Amérindiennes au Québec, 1982.

COLDEN, Cadwallader Hon. *The History of the Five Nations of Canada*, vol. II, Toronto, George N. Morang & Company Ltd., 1902.

COLIN, L. (Louis). *Réponse de M. Vankoughnet à deux lettres adressées au supérieur du séminaire de Saint-Sulpice, respectivement du 12 septembre 1884 et du 13 janvier 1885, ainsi qu'un extrait d'une lettre de M. T. Walton, surintendant des Affaires indiennes à Parry Sound, du 2 septembre 1884*, Montréal, 1885.

COLWELL, Eleanor J. *The Oka Land Question*, Montréal, octobre 1968.

COMITÉ MISTE DU SÉNAT ET DE LA CHAMBRE DES COMMUNES SUR LES AFFAIRES INDIENNES. procès-verbal de la réunion et évidence, n° 1, mercredi 1er mars 1961, mardi 14 mars 1961, Ottawa, 1961, Roger Duhamel, Fr. S. C., imprimeur de la reine.

COMMISSION BAGOT. *Rapport des Affaires indiennes du Canada déposé devant l'assemblée législative*, Sessional papers 1844-1845, Ottawa, 20 mars 1845.

COOKE, Charles Angus. *Recalling Troubled Times at Oka, 13 Years Ago*, The Ottawa Citizen, 8 juillet 1970.

COOKE, Charles Angus. *Dear Friends of Gibson Reserve: Recalling Troubled Times in Oka 113 Years Ago*, Ottawa Citizen, 16 juillet 1990.

CORNELIUS J. *Historical Background of Kanesatake (Oka)*, Ottawa, 1990.

CORNPLANTER, J. J. *Iroquois Reprints, Legends of the Longhouse*, Philadelphie, édité originalement en 1938 par J. B. Lippincott et réédité en 1966 par Mme Jese Cornplanter, publié par arrangement avec Harper & Rowe Publishers Inc., Ontario, Ohsweken, 1966, réédité par Iroqrafts Ltd.

COURVILLE, Louis-Leonard Aumasson. *Mémoires sur les affaires du Canada*, de 1749 à 1760.

COURVILLE, Serge. *Origine et évolution des campagnes dans le comté de Deux-Montagnes 1755-1971*, Montréal, 1793, thèse de maîtrise, Département de géographie, Université de Montréal.

COURVILLE, Serge. *Les caractères originaux de la conquête du sol dans les seigneuries de la Rivière-Du-Chêne et du lac Des Deux-Montagnes*, Québec, manuscrit déposé le 16 septembre 1974.

CUOQ, André. *Notes pour servir à l'histoire de la mission du Lac-des-Deux-Montagnes*, Montréal, 1898.

DAWSON, Samuel Edward. *The Saint Lawrence, Its Basin and Border-Lands*, New York, Federick A. Stokes Company, 1905.

D'CALLAGHAN, E. B. *The Documentary History of the State of New York*, arrangé sous la direction de l'Honorable Christopher Morgan, secrétaire d'État, vol. 1, Wied, Parsons & Co, Public Printers, Albany 1849.

DESROSIERS, Léo-Paul. *Iroquoisie, tome 1(1534-1646)*, Les études de l'institut d'histoire de l'Amérique française.

DESSUREALT, Christian. *La seigneurie du Lac-des-Deux Montagnes de 1780 à 1825*, Montréal, thèse de maîtrise, Département d'histoire, Université de Montréal, 1979.

Dictionnaire biographique canadien, vol. XI, 1881-1890, Presses de l'Université de Toronto.

DICKASON, Olive Patricia, *Canada's First Nations*.

DOMINION DU CANADA. Débats parlementaires, troisième session, vol. 1, comprenant la période entre le 15 février 1870 et le 12 mai 1870, Ottawa, 1870, Ottawa Times Printing & Publishing Co.

DOMINION DU CANADA. *Rapport annuel du département des Affaires indiennes*, 1932 et 1936, Ottawa F. A. Acland.

DUBOIS, Abbé Émile. *Le feu de la Rivière-du-Chêne, étude historique sur le mouvement insurrectionnel de 1837 au Nord de Montréal*, Montréal, 16 avril 1937, Ém. A. Deschamps, V. G. Évêque de Thennesis, auxiliaire de Montréal.

DUNN, Guillaume. *Les Forts de l'Outaouais*, Montréal, Éditions du jour, 1975.

DUPIN, André-Marie-Jean-Jacques. *Opinion de M. Dupin, avocat de la cour royale de Paris sur le droit du séminaire de Montréal au Canada*, 18 août 1819, Paris, 1826, réédité à Montréal, John Lovell, 1840.

DUVERNET, Sylvia. *An Indian Odyssey, Tribulations, Trials and Triumphs of Gibson Band of the Mohawk Tribe of the Iroquois Confederacy*, Islington, Ontario, Muskoka Publications, 1986.

EASTBURN, Robert. *Un récit fidèle des innombrables dangers et souffrances, ainsi qu'une merveilleuse et étonnante délivrance de Robert Eastburn durant sa captivité parmi les Indiens*, Philadelphie, imprimé à Boston, 1758, réimprimé et vendu par Green & Russell.

ECCLES, W. J. *Frontenac the Courtier Governor*, Toronto, McClelland and Stewart, 1959.

ECKERT, Allan W. *Wilderness Empire, A Narrative*, Little Brown and Company, Boston, Toronto.

EDWARDS, Ann. *Cahiers d'histoire des Deux-Montagnes*, vol. 6, n° 2, décembre 1983.

Exposé sur la situation à Oka, Kanesatake et Kahnawake, Ottawa, ministère de la Défense nationale, 1990.

FENTON et TOOKER. *Handbook Of The North American Indian*, vol. 5.

FENTON, William N. *Structure, Continuity and Change in the Process of Iroquois Treaty making, The History and Culture of Iroquois Diplomacy*.

FINLEY, Gerald E. *George HERIOT, série éditée par Dennis Reid, curateur de l'art post-confédération*, La galerie nationale du Canada, Ottawa, Musée national du Canada, 1979.

FIRST INDIAN RESERVES IN CANADA. *Revue d'histoire de l'Amérique française*, vol. 4, n° 2, septembre 1950.

FLENLEY, Ralph. *A History of Montreal 1640-1672*, London & Toronto, J. M. Dent et Sons Ltd., New York, E. P. Dutton, 1928.

FORAN, J. K. *Chroniques d'Oka, le Canada, A Garland, Lectures and poems*, Montréal, 1918, Gazette Printing Co.

FRANCIS, Daniel. *A History of the Native Peoples of Quebec 1760-1867*, décembre 1983.

FRANQUET, Louis. *Voyages et mémoires sur le Canada (1752-1753)*, Montréal, Élysée, 1974.

GAUTHIER, Jean-Marie. *Les troubles de 1860-1880 à Oka : choc de deux cultures.*

Gazette de Montréal, *The Oka'Question*, mai 1878.

2 GEORGE, V. A. *Handbook of Indians of Canada*, appendice au dixième rapport du Conseil géographique du Canada, Conseil géographique, Canada, 1912, Ottawa, C. H. Parmelee, imprimeur de Sa très Excellence sa Majesté le Roi, 1913.

GIRARD, Michel F. *Étude historique sur la forêt du village d'Oka*, travail réalisé pour la direction de la conservation et du patrimoine écologique, mai 1990, ministère de l'Environnement du Québec.

GREENE, N. O. *The Greene Papers*, bibliothèque McGill, département des livres rares.

GOUVERNEMENT DU QUÉBEC. *Opinions et attitudes envers les peuples autochtones : un sondage auprès des Québécois*, secrétariat aux Affaires autochtones, automne 1991.

GOUVERNEMENT DU QUÉBEC. *Orientations et projets du gouvernement en matière d'aménagement du territoire ; municipalité régionale de comté de Deux-Montagnes*, 1985.

GOUVERNEMENT DU QUÉBEC. *Relations entre les peuples aborigènes et non-aborigènes du Québec : points de vue respectifs*, secrétariat aux Affaires autochtones, automne 1991.

GRAND SÉMINAIRE DE SAINT-SULPICE. *Le séminaire de Montréal, leurs droits et titres*, Saint-Hyacinthe, Courrier de Saint-Hyacinthe, Presses Power, 1880.

GRAYMONT, Barbara. *The Great Peace*, éd. Terrance Dolan, Karen Hammonds, États-Unis, Chelsea House Publishers, 1988.

GRAYMONT, Barbara. *The Iroquois, Indians of North America*, Frank W. Porter III, éd. général, États-Unis, Chelsea House Publications, 1988.

GREY, Charles. *Crisis in the Canada, 1839: The Grey Journals and Letters*, éd. William Ormsby, Toronto, Macmillan of Canada, 1964.

GUILLET, Edwin C. *Who fired Oka Seminary? A Study of the Evidence in the Five Trials of the Oka Indians*, 1877-1880, Toronto, 1944.

HALE, Duane Kendall. *Tribal Histories Researching and Writing*, Grand Rapids, Michigan, publié par The Michigan Indian Press, Grand Rapids Inter Tribal Council, 1991.

HARRIS, Richard Colebrook. *The Seigneurial System in Early Canada: A Geographical study*, The University of Wisconsin Press, Les Presses de l'Université Laval, Quebec, 1966.

HOCKETT, Homer C. *Political and Social Growth of the American People, vol. 1, 1492-1865*, New York, The Macmillan Company, septembre 1940.

HODGSON, Roderick. *Historic Hudson, Part II*, Hudson, publié par la Société historique d'Hudson, imprimé par les Éditions Vaudreuil, 1991.

HOOK, Richard et Michael G. JOHNSON. *American Woodland Indians*, Men-At-Arms Series, éd. Martin Windrow, London, Ospry Publishing, 1990.

HOPGOOD, Victor G (éd.). *David Thompson, Travel in Western North America 1784-1812*, Toronto, 1971.

HORNUNG, Rick. *One Nation Under the Gun: Inside the Mohawk Civil War*, Toronto, Stoddard Publishing Co., 1991.

Indian Corn of the Americas, Gift to the World, Northeast Indian Quaterly, printemps-été 1987.

JAENEN, Cornelius J. *The French Relationship with the Amerindians*, Messina, Université Messina, 25 mars 1981.

JAENEN, Cornelius J. *Amerindian Responses to French Missionary Intrusion,1611-1760: A Categorization*, Ottawa, Association for Canadian Studies, 1985.

JAMIESON, Milvill Allan. *Medals Awarded to North American Indian Chiefs, 1714-1922*, London, S. W. I. Spink & Son, 1936.

JENNINGS, Francis, William N. FENTON, Mary A. DRUKE et David R. MILLER. *The History and Culture of Iroquois Diplomacy. An Interdisciplinary Guide to the Treaties of the Six Nations and Their League*, Syracuse, New York, Syracuse University Press, 1985.

JENNINGS, Francis. *The Amibiguous Iroquois Empire*, W. W. Norton and Company, New York, London, 1984.

JOHNSON, Sir William. *The Papers of Sir William Johnson*, 14 vol., Albany, James Sullivan et autres, Université de l'État de New York, 1921-1965.

KENTON, Edna. *The Indians of North America*, vol. 1, New York, Harcourt, Brace & Company.

LACAN, Jean. *Mémoire sur les difficultés survenues entre Messieurs les ecclésiastiques du séminaire de Saint-Sulpice de Montréal et certains Indiens de la mission d'Oka, lac des Deux-Montagnes : un simple cas de droit de propriété,* Montréal, La Minerve, 1876.

LACOSTE, Alexander Sir. *The Seminary of Montreal their rights and titles*, Saint-Hyacinthe, 1880, Presses Power, Courier de Saint-Hyacinthe.

LAFITAU, père Joseph François. *Mœurs des sauvages américains, comparées aux mœurs des premiers temps*, édité et traduit par Willia, N. Fenton; Elizabeth L. Moore, vol. 1, Toronto, 1974, The Champlain Society.

LAFLAMME, R. *Le séminaire de Montréal, ses droits et ses titres*, Saint-Hyacinthe, Courier de Saint-Hyacinthe, 1880.

LAFLEUR, Eugène. *Opinion au sujet des droits des Indiens iroquois et algonquins d'Oka dans la seigneurie du Lac des deux-Montagnes*, Ottawa, 1916.

LAFORCE, Phillip. *History of the Gibson Reserve*, imprimé par Bracebridge Gazette Scribe : n. d. vers 1952.

LALANDE, Germain P. S. S. *Une Histoire de bornage qui dure près d'un siècle,* vol. 3, n° 4, août 1980, cahier d'histoire de Deux-Montagnes.

LAMARCHE, Jacques A. *L'été des Mohawks : bilan des 78 jours*, Montréal, Stanke, 1990.

Legends of Our Nations, North American Indian Travelling College, R. R. n° 3, Cornwall Island, Ontario.

LEGGET, Robert. *Ottawa River Canals and the Defence of British North America*, Toronto, Buffalo, London, Presse de l'Université de Toronto.

Le message des Haudenosaunee au monde occidental, Genève, Suisse, automne 1977.

Le procès des Mohawks, non coupable, édité par le CIDMAA, Montréal, Regroupement de solidarité avec les autochtones, 1992.

Les Prêtres de Saint-Sulpice, 1982.

LÉTOURNEAU-SICOTTE, Lorraine. *Kanesatake-Oka*, cahiers d'histoire de Deux-Montagnes, 1978.

LONG, John. *Voyages and Travels of an Indian Interpreter and Trader*, London, imprimé par l'auteur et vendu par Robson, Bond-Street, Debrett, Picadilly, T. & J. Egerton, Charing-Cross, White & Son, Fleet-Street, Sewell, Cornhill, Edwards, Pall Mall, Messrs. Taylors, Holborn, London, Fletcher, Oxford, & Bull, Bath M,DDD,XCI.

LORNA. *700 Year old farming implement uncovered on Quarry Point*, Hudson, 11 août 1987, Gazette d'Hudson.

MACLAINE, Craig et Michael BAXENDALE. *This Land is Our Land: The Mohawk Revolt at Oka*, Montréal, Optimum Publishing International, 1990.

MACLEAN, John. *Vanguards of Canada, The Missionary Society of the Methodist Church, The Young People's Forward Movement*, Toronto, Copyright Canada, 1918.

MARINIER, René. *Histoire d'Oka: la mission du Lac des Deux-Montagnes*, fondée en 1721, Cahiers d'histoire de Deux-Montagnes, 1980.

MATHESON, G. M. *The Seminary of Montreal Their Rights and Titles*, Saint-Hyacinthe, Courrier de Saint-Hyacinthe, Presses Power, 1880.

MATHESON, G. M. *Blue Book*, Ottawa.

MAURAULTt, Olivier. Revue *Trimestrielle Canadienne, Les vicissitudes d'une mission sauvage*, Montréal, juin 1930, Le Devoir.

MCLEAN, John. *The Publications Of The Champlain Society*, notes de John McLean sur vingt-cinq ans de service sur le territoire de la Baie d'Hudson, Toronto, The Champlain Society.

MERRELL, James H. et Daniel K. RITCHER. *Beyond the Covenant Chain: The Iroquois and their Neighbors in Indian North American 1600-1800*, préface de Wilcomb E. Washburn, Syracuse, New York, Syracuse University Press, 1987.

MICHAUD, Collette. *A Study of the Indian Encampment in Hull During the Second Half of the Nineteenth Century*, préparé pour la Commission nationale Capitol, D.I.A.N.D., recherche historique, avril 1987.

MILLET, J. R. *Great White Father Knows Best: Oka and The Land Claims Process*, vol. 7, n° 1, 1991, Native Studies Review.

MILLER, J. R. Reserves, *Residential Schools and the Threat of Assimilation; Skyscrapers Hide the Heavens; A History of Indians - White Relations In Canada*, édition révisée, Toronto, University of Toronto Press, 1991.

MILLER, J. R. éd. *Sweet Promises: A Reader on Indian - White Relations in Canada*, Toronto, University of Toronto Press, 1991.

MITCHELL, Elaine Allan. *Fort Timiskaming and The Fur Trade*, Toronto et Buffalo, University of Toronto Press.

MONROE, William B. *Documents relating to the Seigniorial Tenure in Canada*, Toronto 1908.

MURRAY, Norman. *The Oka question: containing the original title, and a brief account of the feudal system of seigniorial tenure in Canada and its abolition in 1854: with a general review of the Oka question in particular and roman aggression in general*, Québec, imprimé par E. Fréchette, 1852.

Northeast Indian Quarterly, printemps, vol. VII, n° 1, Cornell, American Indian Program, Cornell University, 1990.

O'NEIL, Jean. *Oka*, Montréal, édition du Ginkgo, 1987.

Opinion des douze avocats les plus éminents de Paris sur le droit du séminaire de Montréal au Canada à certaines propriétés, 18 août 1819, Montréal, John Lovell, 1840.

ORMSBY, William (éd.). *Crisis in the Canadas: 1839 The Grey*. Jourals and Letters, Toronto 1964, Macmillan of Canada.

PARENT, Rév. Amand. *The Life of Rev. Amand Parent: Eight Years Among the Oka Indians*, Toronto, William Briggs, Wesley Buildings, n. d. vers 1887.

PARKMAN, Francis. *The Old Regime in Canada*, 1893.

PARISEAU, Claude L. *Les Troubles de 1860-1880 à Oka : choc de deux cultures*, Montréal, thèse de maîtrise, département d'histoire, Université McGill, 1975.

PARKER, Arthur C. *Parker on the Iroquois, Iroquois Uses the Maize and Other Food Plants, The Code of Handsome Lake, The Seneca Prophet, The Constitution of the Five Nations*, édité avec une introduction de William N. Fenton, Syracuse, New York, 1968, Syracuse University Press.

PENDERGAST, James F. *The St. Lawrence Iroquoians: Their Past, Present, and Immediate Future*, printemps 1991, n° 102.

PINDERA, Loreen. *The Making of a Warrior*, Saturday Night, avril 1991, vol. 106, n° 3, p. 30-39.

PINDERA, Loreen et Geoffrey YORK. *People of the Pines*, 1991.

PORTER, John et Jean TRUDEL. *Le Calvaire d'Oka*, Ottawa, Galerie nationale du Canada, 1974.

PRITCHARD, J. S. *For the Glory of God: The Quinté Mission (1669-1680)*, Ontario Historical Society, 1973.

Procès verbal de la réunion et évidence du comité permanent sur les affaires aborigènes; conformément à son ordre de dates de référence du 22 octobre 1990, en considération des évènements à Kanesatake et à Kahnawake durant l'été 1990, n° 46-55, Ottawa, Groupe de communication canadien, Publishing, Supply and Services Canada, Ottawa, 1991.

Protestant Defence Alliance, *The Indians of the Lake of Two Mountains and the Seminary of St-Sulpice*, Montréal, Witness Printing House, n. d. vers 1875.

Provincial Statutes of Canada, Enacted by Her Most Excellent Majesty, Our Sovereign Lady Victoria, by the Grace of God, of the United Kingdom of Great Britain and Ireland, Queen, Defender of the Faith, & c., by and with the Advice and Consent of the Legislative Council and Assembly of the Said Province Constituted and Assembled by Virtue of and Under the Authority of an Act of the Fourth Years of Her Majesty's Reign, Intituled, *An Act to Re-Unite The Provinces of Upper and Lower Canada, and for the Government of Canada*, Toronto. 1851, Stewart Derbishire et Georges Desbarats.

Publication éditée par la Bibliothèque nationale du Québec, Montréal, Bibliothèque Nationale du Québec, 1992.

QUAIFFE, Milo Milton. *John Long's Voyages and Travels in the Years 1768-1788*, Chicago, The Lakeside Press, R. R. Donnelley & Sons Company, Christmas, 1922.

QUEVILLON, Sylvain. *La mission du Lac des Deux-Montagnes : première époque 1717-1750*, vol. 7, n° 1, décembre 1985, cahiers d'histoire de Deux-Montagnes.

Rapports annuels des écoles Shingwauk et Wawanosh, 1895-1906, Publications du diocèse d'Algoma, bibliothèque de l'Université d'Algoma.

Rapports de l'archiviste de la Province de Québec, 1928.

Rapport sur les affaires des Indiens au Canada, déposé devant l'assemblée législative, 20 mars 1895, département des Affaires indiennes.

Rapport des commissions spéciales nommées le 8 septembre 1856 pour examiner les affaires indiennes au Canada, Toronto, imprimé par Stewart Rerbishim et George Resbarats, 1858, département des Archives ayant trait aux affaires indiennes.

Réfutation des représentants de la couronne sur le droit du séminaire de Montréal à la propriété en sa possession, Montréal, C. P. Leprohon, n. d. vers 1840.

Revue d'histoire de l'Amérique française, vol. 4, n° 2, septembre 1950.

RICHARDSON, Boyce. *People of Terra Nullius, Betrayal and Rebirth in Aboriginal Canada*, Vancouver, 1993, Douglas & McIntyre Ltd.

RITCHER, Laurette B. *L'Église paroissiale d'Oka*, Montréal, L. B. Richer, 1980.

ROBINSON, Michael. *Touching the Serpent's Tail*, Ontario, Martin House Publishing, 1992.

ROCHON, Monique et Pierre LEPAGE (éd.). *Oka-Kanesatake – Été 1990: Le choc collectif. Rapport de la Commission des Droits de la Personne du Québec*, Montréal, avril 1991, Commission des Droits de la Personne du Québec.

RUMILLY. *Histoire de Montréal*, Montréal, Fides, 1970-1974.

SCHAFF, Gregory. *Wampum Belts, and Peace Trees, George Morgan Native Americans and Revolutionary Diplomacy*, Golden Colorado, 1990, Fulcrum Publishing.

SCHULL, Joseph. Rebellion, *The Rising in French Canada*, Toronto, Macmillan of Canada, 1837.

SCOTT, Duncan C. *Traditional History of the Confederacy of the Six Nations*, préparé par un comité des chefs.

SCOTT, Rév. William. *The Oka Eviction to the President of the Montreal Conference*, The Gazette Printing House, 1883.

SCOTT, Rév. William. *Rapport relatifs aux affaires des Indiens d'Oka préparé pour le surintendant général des Affaires indiennes*, Ottawa, imprimé par MacLean, Roger & Co. Wellington Street, janvier 1883.

Sessional Papers, vol. 6, troisième session du premier parlement du Dominion du Canada, session 1870, n° 55.

Seven Generations, éd. Gary O'Brien, Kahnawake Survival School, Center for Curriculum Development, 1980.

SHEA, Gilmary John. *History of the Catholic Missions Among the Indian Tribes of the United States, 1529-1854*, New York, P. J. Kennedy, publié pour the Holy See, Excelsior Catholic Publishing House, 1899.

Statement of the Affairs of the Corporation of the Ecclesiastics of the Seminary of St-Sulpice, Montréal, Québec, R. Campbell, imprimé par ordre de l'assemblée législative, 1853.

ST. LOUIS, A. E. *Ancient Hunting Grounds of the Algonquin and Nipissing Indians Comprising the Watershed of the Ottawa and Madawaska Rivers*, Ottawa, 1951.

STONE William L. *The Life and Times of Sir William Johnson, Bart.*, vol. II, Albany, J. Munsell, 1865.

The Durham Papers, Journal gardé par le défunt Amury Girod, traduit de l'allemand et de l'italien, vol. 1, 1924, Public Archives Sessional Papers, n° 23.

The Historical Background of Indian Reserves and Settlements in the Province of Quebec, juillet 1973, Thunderbird, préparé pour les Indiens de l'Association du Québec.

The Oka Troubles, The Montreal Daily Star, jeudi 18 juin 1877.

The Oka Indians, The Toronto Globe, 5 novembre 1881.

The Oka question, Montreal Gazette, mai 1878.

The Shingwauk project, from teaching Wigwam to Shingwauk University, Algoma University College Founder's Day, 1982.

The Valley of the Six Nations, édité avec une introduction de Charles M. Johnston, The Champlain Society for the Government of Ontario, University of Toronto Press, 1864.

THOMAS, Earle. *Sir John Johnson: Loyalist Baronet*, Toronto, Dundurn Press, 1986.

THOMPSON, Edward H. *The Life of Jean-Jacques Olier, Founder of the Seminary of St-Sulpice*, London, Burns et Oates, 1885.

Traditional Teachings, North American Indian Travelling College, R. R. 3 Cornwall Island, Ontario.

TREMBLAY, Louise. *La politique missionnaire des Sulpiciens au XVIIe et au début du XVIIIe siècle, 1668-1735*, Montréal, thèse de maîtrise, département d'histoire, Université de Montréal, 1981.

TRIGGER, Bruce G., (éd.). *Handbook of North American Indians*, vol. 15, Northeast Indian Quarterly, Washington, D. C. Smithsonian Institution, 1978.

TUGWELL, Maurice et John THOMPSON. *The Legacy of Oka*, Toronto, Mackenzie, 1991.

TUPPER, Charles A. *Two Centuries in Oka*, Ottawa, avril 1936, Canadian Geographical Society, vol. XII, n° 4.

VILLENEUVE, Larry. *Historique des réserves et villages indiens du Québec*, révisé et mis à jour par Daniel Francis, Département de recherche des Indiens et des affaires du nord du Canada, 1984.

VOOHIS, Ernest. *Historic Forts and Trading Posts of the French Regime and of the English Fur Trading Companies*, Ottawa, département de l'Intérieur, 1930.

WALDMAN, Carl. *Atlas of the North American Indian*, New York, Facts on File Publications, 1985.

WEBSTER, Clarence J. *The Journal of Jeffrey Amherst*, Toronto, Canada, The Ryerson Press, Chicago, University of Chicago Press.

WESTAWAY, Jennifer. *Oka: Are Mohawks Criminals?*, Ottawa, Bowdens, 1990.

WHITE, Richard, *The Middle Ground*.

WILLIAMS, Marianne. *Kanian'kéha Okara'shon'a, Mohawk Stories*, Albany, New York, The University of the State of New York, 1976.

WRAXALL, Peter. *An Abridgment of the Indian Affairs*, London, Oxford University Press, 1915

WRIGHT, J. V. *Ontario Prehistory, An Eleven-Thousand-Year Archaeological Outline*, Ottawa, 1972, Musée national du Canada.

WRIGHT, J. V. *Quebec Prehistory*, Toronto, Van Nostrand Reinhold, 1979.

WRIGHT, Ronald. *Stolen Continents: The World Through Indian Eyes*.

YOUNG, Brian. *In it's Corporate Capacity: The Seminary of Montreal as a Business Institution, 1816-1817*, McGill – Queen's Press, Kingston et Montreal.

YORK, Geoffrey. *The Dispossessed: Life and Death in Native Canada*, Vintage UK, Copyright Geoffey York, 1990.

LISTE DES ARCHIVES

Archives de la Baie d'Hudson.

Archives photographiques Notman. Archives du musée McCord.

Archives de la Société Historique de Deux-Montagnes.

Archives de la Société historique Hudson.

Archives de la Société historique d'Argenteuil.

Archives de The Montreal, The Montreal Witness, The Montreal Gazette, Nouveau Monde, etc.

Archives du ministère des Affaires indiennes.

Archives du séminaire de Saint-Sulpice, MG17A, 7-1,7-2. Archives nationales du Canada.

Archives du département des Affaires indiennes, RG10. Archives nationales du Canada.

Archives du ministère de la Justice, RG13. Archives nationales du Canada.

Archives du Conseil privé, RG2. Archives nationales du Canada.

Archives du gouverneur général, RG7. Archives nationales du Canada.

Archives du premier ministre, Sir John A. Macdonald, Sir Wilfrid Laurier. Archives nationales du Canada.

Archives de la société missionnaire méthodiste, MG17C. Archives nationales du Canada.

Archives nationales du Québec.

Collection Shingwauk de la Bibliothèque Arthur A. Wishart, Université d'Algoma.

Dictionaire biographique national.

Discours du chef Agneetha, CO42/66. Archives nationales du Canada.

Guerre de 1812. Archives du musée McCord.

Papers of Sir John Johnson. Archives nationales du Canada.

Papers of Sir William Johnson, MG19. Archives nationales du Canada.

Papers of Sir John Johnson. Archives nationales du Canada.

Papers of Sydney Bellingham, MG24, B25. Archives nationales du Canada.

McKay Papers. Archives du musée McCord.

Ministère des Affaires culturelles du Québec (Archélogie).

Rapports du département des Affaires indiennes (1823), bibliothèque du département des Affaires indiennes.

Registres militaires, guerre de 1812. Archives nationales du Canada.

Société pour la protection des aborigènes, MG40, Q31. Archives nationales du Canada.